SELECTED PAPERS OF

WILL CLAYTON

SELECTED PAPERS OF

WILL CLAYTON

EDITED BY

FREDRICK J. DOBNEY

THE JOHNS HOPKINS PRESS

Baltimore and London

For My Mother and Stepfather
Flossie and Bill Shofner

Contents

FOREWORD

ACKNOWLEDGMENTS   xi

STATEMENT OF EDITORIAL METHOD   xiii

GUIDE TO EDITORIAL APPARATUS   xvi

INTRODUCTION   1

I CAPITALIST IN THE DEPRESSION ERA

A STATEMENT ON THE PROBLEMS OF THE
COTTON FARMER   21

A STATEMENT ON WAR DEBTS AND TARIFFS   26

TO JOUETT SHOUSE   32

TO HON. CHESTER DAVIS   33

A SPEECH ON CAPITALISM   36

TO LEON O. WOLCOTT   43

TO SIR OWEN CHALKLEY   45

TO HON. ALBEN W. BARKLEY   47

A SPEECH ON THE WORLD COTTON SITUATION   48

TO HON. HENRY A. WALLACE   55

II GOVERNMENT SERVICE IN WARTIME, 1940–1944

MEMORANDUM ON SYNTHETIC RUBBER   59

viii

MEMORANDUM ON THE STRAIN OF OVERSEAS SHIPPING 60

TO HON. JESSE JONES 61

MEMORANDUM OF CONVERSATION WITH
   MR. MILO PERKINS 62

TO J. C. NICHOLS 64

TO HON. JESSE JONES 64

A STATEMENT ON PRECLUSIVE AND
   STRATEGIC PURCHASES 66

TO PAUL G. HOFFMAN 71

A SPEECH ON WORLD TRADE 74

TO DR. CALVIN HOOVER 78

TO HON. JESSE JONES 79

A SPEECH ON THE ECONOMIC REQUIREMENTS OF PEACE 81

TO HON. JAMES F. BYRNES 85

TO *LIFE* MAGAZINE 87

A CAMPAIGN SPEECH FOR RE-ELECTION OF ROOSEVELT 88

A STATEMENT ON POST-WAR ECONOMIC POLICY AND
   PLANNING 92

COMMENT ON DEAN HOOVER'S STUDY OF
   INTERNATIONAL TRADE AND DOMESTIC EMPLOYMENT 96

III ASSISTANT SECRETARY OF STATE, 1944–1946

A STATEMENT ON HIS NOMINATION AS
   ASSISTANT SECRETARY OF STATE 105

TO HON. EDWARD R. STETTINIUS, JR. 109

A STATEMENT ON THE PROBLEMS OF WAR AND PEACE 111

A STATEMENT ON THE CHAPULTEPEC CONFERENCE 120

A STATEMENT ON THE RECIPROCAL TRADE
   AGREEMENTS ACT 122

TO RICHARD G. HEWLETT 128

A SPEECH ON FOREIGN ECONOMIC POLICY 129

TO HON. JAMES F. BYRNES 136

A STATEMENT ON THE POTSDAM CONFERENCE 138

A STATEMENT ON UNRRA 140

Contents

A Statement on the British Loan and Lord Keynes   145
To Hon. Fred Vinson   147
To Hon. James Byrnes   150
A Speech on the Anglo-American Agreement   153
Memorandum for Bernard Baruch   161
To Hon. Kenneth McKellar   164
A Speech on U.S. Foreign Economic Policy and Goals   168
To the Editor of the *WASHINGTON POST*   172

IV UNDERSECRETARY OF STATE, 1946–1947

To Bernard Baruch   179
A Statement on Post-UNRRA Relief   181
To Hon. James F. Byrnes   185
A Statement on the Economic Situation in Greece   190
A Speech on the Economic Commission for Europe   195
Memorandum on the Creation of a
    National Council of Defense   198
Memorandum on the European Crisis   201
A Statement on the Geneva ITO Conference   204
A Statement on the Marshall Plan   206
A Statement on Negotiations with France   207
To Herbert Elliston   208
An Article on GATT, the Marshall Plan, and
    OECD   211
To Hon. Harry S Truman   218
Memorandum on the Marshall Plan   219
To Norman Armour   222
A Speech on the Marshall Plan   224

V THE CONTINUING FIGHT FOR FREE TRADE

A Speech on the ITO Charter   233
A Statement on the Geneva Agreement on Tariffs
    and Trade   238

x

To Hon. Alben W. Barkley   242

To Lamar Fleming, Jr.   244

To John Kenneth Galbraith   245

A Speech on the Havana Conference   247

To W. H. Harrison   254

Memorandum on United World Federalists' Policy   256

To John S. Knight   258

A Statement on Government Agricultural Policy   262

A Statement on Foreign Economic Policy   269

Memorandum on the Middle East Resolution   279

To Hon. J. William Fulbright   281

To Ellen Garwood   282

To Hon. J. William Fulbright   283

Memorandum on U.S.-China Relations   284

To Hon. J. William Fulbright   286

A Statement on Latin America   287

To R. F. Moody   291

Index   293

ACKNOWLEDGMENTS

This edition of Will Clayton's papers was made possible by the generosity of Clayton's eldest daughter, Ellen Clayton Garwood. In addition to a financial grant, she also furnished a wealth of information about her father and provided access to several significant documents in her possession. Without her aid, this project could not have reached fruition.

I am especially indebted to Dr. Frank E. Vandiver, who was responsible both for bringing the Clayton papers to Rice University and for assigning me the task of editing them, and to Dr. Allen J. Matusow, who forced me to ask the right questions about Clayton's career. Each in his own way played an important role in the completion of this volume. Others who have provided thoughtful criticisms and helpful suggestions are Michael A. Reese, Patrick G. McLeod, Jim McIntosh, and Gene Riddle.

In the process of collecting documents, a number of people were most helpful. I am indebted to the following: Kenneth A. Lohf of the Columbia University Libraries, C. Moffett Moore of the Cossitt Library of the Memphis Public Libraries, Lewis Douglas, William Y. Elliott, Senator J. William Fulbright, Dwight M. Miller of the Herbert Hoover Library, Arthur Krock, Walden Moore, Y. Noda, Alexander P. Clark of the Princeton University Library, H. G. Dulaney of the Sam Rayburn Library, Governor Nelson A. Rockefeller, Elmo Roper, Elizabeth B. Drewry of the Franklin D. Roosevelt Library, Walt W. Rostow, William M. Franklin and Arthur G. Kogan of the State Department, Marjan Stopar-Babsek of the United Nations Library, Senator Ralph Yarborough, and the staff of the Library of Congress. Providing the greatest help of all were Philip C. Brooks and Philip D. Lagerquist of the Harry S Truman Library and the staff of the National Archives, including Jeanne McDonald, Joseph Howerton, Kathleen Riley, Helen Finneran, Jane Smith, Norwood Biggs, Charles Neal, Albert Blair, Edward Flatequal, John F. Simmons, and Richard Maxwell.

Access to Clayton's personal files at Anderson, Clayton and Company was expedited by S. M. McAshan, J. M. Johnson, Martha Mattox, and Sylvia Porter, to all of whom I am grateful.

Finally, in the preparation of the manuscript, I was aided immeasurably by Linda Pike Alexander, Suzanne Saunders, and particularly Linda Williams. One last debt must be noted: to my wife Elaine, who tolerated me and helped me from beginning to end.

Statement of Editorial Method

When I first examined the bulk of Will Clayton's correspondence, my initial reaction was one of disappointment that his papers contained so little in the way of significant new factual material. Surprisingly, there were few letters showing Clayton in action during his government years. There seem to be two reasons for this state of affairs. Part of the problem is that much of Clayton's correspondence during his State Department years remains in the closed or restricted files of the Department and is therefore not available for publication. A second factor is that bane of the recent historian, the telephone. His correspondence indicates that Clayton conducted much of his government business either in person or by telephone, thus depriving the student of a written record of numerous important interchanges. For these reasons, Clayton's available writings for the government years consist primarily of routine correspondence and formal statements of various kinds—not exactly the sort of treasure trove historians dream about. Furthermore, Clayton's papers for the period prior to 1930 (the years of Anderson, Clayton and Company's early development and vigorous overseas expansion) were destroyed some years ago, and extensive searching has failed to turn up much for that period. Yet the Clayton papers have a definite value. His writings for the period 1930 to 1966 are virtually complete, with the exception of those in the State Department files. These documents enable the reader to trace the development of an economic ideologue who exercised great influence on both the domestic economy, as a businessman, and on foreign economic affairs, as a policy-maker. This edition should provide significant insights into the theory and practice of an economic ideology.

Clayton was an exceptionally prolific writer. Eleven filing cabinets, covering most of the last forty years of his life, remain at Anderson, Clayton and Company's general offices in Houston, Texas, and another large collection of forty-four boxes is on deposit at the Truman Library. In addition, much of his official correspondence is scattered throughout a number of record groups in the National Archives. Other significant holdings of Clayton material are deposited at Rice University and at the Cossitt Library in Memphis, Tennessee. Although there are numerous manuscript collections in various repositories which contain Clayton correspondence, they generally duplicate material available in Clayton's own files. The most extensive and valuable holdings consulted included the following: Herbert H. Lehmann papers and Board of Economic Warfare papers, Columbia University; Jesse Jones papers, Tom Connally papers, and Cordell Hull papers, Library of Congress; Bernard Baruch papers and James Forrestal papers, Princeton University; Franklin D. Roosevelt papers and Harry Hopkins papers, Franklin D. Roosevelt Library; United Nations Relief and Rehabilitation Administration papers, United Nations Archives; Alben Barkley papers, University of Kentucky; William Y. Elliott papers, Harvard University.

Given the quantity of material available, it has been necessary to be highly selective in choosing documents. Every effort has been made to include the most important papers. As I have mentioned, a large part of Clayton's official correspondence is still in the restricted files or the closed files of the State Department, but much of it will be made available to the public shortly in the Department's official *Foreign Relations of the United States* series. As of this writing, all volumes for 1945 and volumes II–VII and XI for 1946 have been published. With the exception of these restricted papers, the editor has examined all extant Clayton documents, foraging through an estimated half a million pages over a period of three years. Mass mailings to Clayton's former colleagues, scholarly journals, and libraries were utilized to insure that no document was overlooked.

It was decided at the outset to use photocopies of the documents in the editorial process. Photocopies not only provided flexibility in working with the documents themselves, but also afforded a certain leisure in examining the documents which is generally not possible when working in repositories. Upon acquisition, each photocopy was catalogued and cross-indexed in master files according to author, recipient, date, and location of document. The entire file of photocopies, together with a number of original documents, accumulated notes and indexes, and other data, has been deposited in the Fondren Library at Rice University, where it will be made available to scholars.

The documents in this volume are arranged topically within a broad chronological framework. Reminiscences appear in the time span to which they refer along with other papers of that period. A standard pattern has been followed in footnoting the documents. In every case the first footnote will provide the physical description and location of the document. This footnote will appear in abbreviated form, as indicated in the Guide to Editorial Apparatus which follows. Thus the designation "LS, DNA, RG 16" denotes a letter, signed by the author, which is in the National Archives, Record Group 16, and "*ACCO Press*, June 1931, pp. 4–5" indicates a periodical or pamphlet printed by Anderson, Clayton & Co. Press. Where necessary, the editor will provide additional footnotes identifying persons and events. Such identification, as a rule, will be brief, furnishing only that information which is essential to an understanding of the significance of the document. If further amplification of the document's significance is deemed necessary, an editorial introduction will precede the particular paper or group of papers. Clayton's peculiarities of punctuation and capitalization have not been altered unless the meaning of the document is unclear. When corrections are necessary, they will be made silently.

A final word of caution is perhaps in order with regard to the whole of this work. Limiting Clayton's writings over a forty-year period to one volume inevitably means elimination of some documents which the editor would like to include. In order to avoid redundancy it is often the case that an illustration of consistency of thought is not possible. Where appropriate, the editor will indicate such consistency in the editorial introductions to documents. Similarly, change in outlook or attitude will be noted.

L	Unsigned carbon copy of letter
LS	Typed letter signed by the author
ALS	Handwritten letter signed by the author
T	Telegram
Memo	Memorandum
CP	Clayton Papers
ACCO	Anderson, Clayton & Co.
DNA	National Archives
RG	Record Group
Rice	Fondren Library, Rice University
TL	Truman Library

SELECTED PAPERS OF

WILL CLAYTON

INTRODUCTION

The extent to which ideology is a motivating factor in both individual and governmental decisions has long been a perplexing problem for historians.[1] Generally, the role of ideology in decision-making has been so nebulous as to be quite difficult to assess. But such is not the case with William Lockhart Clayton; seldom has any individual been so dominated by ideological considerations, both in theory and in practice. Will Clayton was an economic ideologue of the first order. He was also one of the most successful businessmen and one of the truly important government policy-makers in twentieth-century America. The documents in this volume illuminate his economic ideology and illustrate how that ideology guided his attempts to influence the business community and the federal government in the formulation of economic attitudes and policies. This introductory essay will provide a context within which to analyze and evaluate Clayton's writings.

Will Clayton was a product of the nineteenth century and perhaps the greatest example in the twentieth century of the "southern gentleman." An imposing figure physically, he always conducted himself with the greatest dignity, modesty and courtesy. He was unfailingly polite, even in the bitterest of debates and negotiations, and he was never in his eighty-six years known to precede anyone through a door. Such exceptional behavior would bear comment even in an antebellum southern planter, but this subscription to the code of the

---

[1] An ideology is defined here as a pattern of beliefs centering on a single theory or idea which, if consistently applied in all situations, will according to its proponents provide the best possible society. For a detailed treatment of the various connotations assigned to the term "ideology," see Julius Gould and William L. Kolb, eds., *A Dictionary of the Social Sciences* (New York: The Free Press, 1964), pp. 315–17.

1

cavalier in the son of an unsuccessful cotton farmer and bankrupted railroad contractor was especially noteworthy.

Born February 7, 1880, on a cotton farm near Tupelo, Mississippi, Clayton was the eldest son of James Monroe and Fletcher Burdine Clayton. His father's inability to provide the family with more than the bare necessities of life profoundly affected the young lad. He became determined that his family would never know want. Upon completion of the seventh grade in 1893, Will quit school to become an assistant to the clerk of the chancery court of Madison County, Tennessee, at a salary of ten dollars a month, four dollars of which he invested in shorthand lessons. So dedicated was he to self-improvement that he even practiced his shorthand at the dinner table: he would use his finger or his fork to trace on the tablecloth a transcript of dinner conversation. When objection was made to this habit, he began writing instead on his trouser leg. As a result of his diligence, a year later at the age of fourteen he was performing the duties of deputy clerk.

His proficiency in typing and shorthand enabled him to obtain extra work at night in the local hotel, typing for transient businessmen and dignitaries in need of a secretary. A speech that he typed for William Jennings Bryan blaming all of the ills of the South on the tariff made a lasting impression on Clayton. Clayton pondered Bryan's viewpoint, adopted it, modified it, and spent a large part of the rest of his life propagating it. At this hotel Clayton also met Jerome Hill, a Saint Louis cotton merchant, who offered Clayton a position as his private secretary in Saint Louis. At the age of fifteen Clayton moved to Saint Louis, and a year later he followed Hill to New York, where through diligent application Clayton rose rapidly in the American Cotton Company. In June of 1902 he was named secretary-treasurer of the Texas Cotton Products Company—a corporation formed with one million dollars capital to take over the American Cotton Company's Texas business. On August 14 of the same year he married Sue Vaughan, a popular Kentucky girl who numbered among her suitors Alben Barkley. By 1904, when Clayton terminated his association with the American Cotton Company, he was assistant general manager of the company, and he was drawing a salary between $3,000 and $3,600 a year.[2]

[2] On Clayton's early life, see Ellen Clayton Garwood, *Will Clayton: A Short Biography* (Austin, Texas: University of Texas Press, 1958), pp. 43–76; Ross Pritchard, "Will Clayton: A Study of Business-Statesmanship" (unpublished Ph.D. dissertation, Fletcher School of Law and Diplomacy, 1955), pp. 4–10; "The Reminiscences of William Lockhart Clayton" (unpublished oral history, Oral History Research Office, Columbia University, 1962), pp. 1–22; Clayton interviews with Ellen Clayton Garwood, 1936 and 1956, CP, Rice University; "William L. Clayton," *Current Biography*, 1944, pp. 95–96.

Now Clayton was ready for bigger things. He struck out on his own when his brother-in-law, Frank Anderson, proposed starting a new cotton firm in Oklahoma City. Clayton agreed to Anderson's proposal, and, with Frank's brother, Monroe, opened the firm of Anderson, Clayton and Company (ACCO). Each of the three partners supplied $3,000 capital; in the first year they cleared a $10,000 profit, and the following two years netted a total of $100,000. Meanwhile, in 1905, Will's brother Ben joined the firm as a full partner. Anderson, Clayton and Company prospered as a result of the contacts Clayton had made while working for the American Cotton Company. When that company failed shortly after Clayton left it, the availability of American's physical facilities proved invaluable to the growing young firm. During this period of his life Clayton worked from early in the morning until midnight every day. The oldest of his four daughters, Ellen Garwood, has said that he was under considerable strain in a business that required snap decisions and quick action to insure success. In banking circles Anderson, Clayton and Company was known as a one-man firm, as evidenced by the fact that Clayton's life was insured for two million dollars "in order to offset any credit slump that might result from his death." By 1939 he was the sole active partner: Frank Anderson had died in 1924, Ben Clayton retired in 1929 because of ill health, and Monroe Anderson died in 1939.

Since a port location would afford the most economical line of transit from producer to consumer, the firm moved into Houston, Texas, in 1915 and established headquarters there the following year. World War I marked a turning point in ACCO's economic development. In spite of the fact that Clayton spent a year in wartime Washington as a member of the Cotton Distribution Committee of Bernard Baruch's War Industries Board, it was during this period that Clayton laid the foundations for Anderson, Clayton and Company's future financial greatness. As a result of the shift in the U.S. financial position from that of a debtor to a creditor nation, the banking center of the world moved from London to New York. This in turn meant that more risk capital was available for investment, and ACCO was one of the first American firms to capitalize on that situation. Several innovations were accomplished by the aggressive young firm, the most important being the building of its own warehouses and the opening of European offices. By taking advantage of the financial distress of European cotton merchants resulting from the war, ACCO was able to break the colonial pattern of European cotton marketing and gain a greater share in the distribution of cotton to European markets. ACCO opened offices in France and Italy during the war and in Germany and England shortly thereafter. On the basis of capital accumulated and offices opened, ACCO had established a firm economic advantage over its competitors during the war which it exploited fully during the succeeding ten years— years which saw Anderson, Clayton and Company become the world's greatest cotton factor.[3]

Although the interwar period was a time of great economic growth for ACCO, it was also a period of unhappy national exposure and investigation. In 1928, 1929, 1930, and 1936 "Cotton Ed" Smith's subcommittee of the Senate Committee on Agriculture and Forestry investigated ACCO. The ostensible purpose of these investigatory hearings was to discover the reason for the decline in cotton prices in 1926 and again in 1935. But apparently the investigations were aimed at Clayton himself. This desire to blame Clayton for the price drops stemmed from Clayton's fight for Southern Delivery.

Southern Delivery meant simply that cotton sold on futures contracts could be delivered to southern ports such as Houston and New Orleans instead of New York. Futures contracts at the time stipulated that the cotton had to be delivered to New York upon demand of the buyer; and such delivery was exorbitantly expensive since New York was not in the normal line of commercial transit for cotton. If the seller refused to pay the high freight costs necessary to get the cotton to New York, he had to buy the cotton back at whatever inflated price the buyer set on that month's futures contracts. "Thus the New York manipulator was able to operate a 'squeeze' on the merchant, forcing him to buy in at an unnaturally high figure . . . . Naturally under such conditions, the New York futures contract was a very unreliable device for the hedging of merchants' risks."[4] Clayton campaigned against this system to no avail, so he fought back by playing the speculators' own game. "His method was to do his own squeezing, but to do it so often, so fast and so hard, that cotton men would rise in arms, forcing the Exchange to modify the rule. His operations are still referred to by those who got burned as nothing less than 'fiendish.' "[5] Some small merchants were incidental victims of Clayton's squeezes, and consequently he gained immediate unpopularity in some cotton circles.

Although the long-term effect of the adoption of Southern Delivery by the New York Cotton Exchange on February 27, 1930,

[3] On the early history of Anderson, Clayton and Company, see Garwood, *Will Clayton*, pp. 77–94; Pritchard, "Will Clayton," pp. 10–15; Oral History, pp. 22–46; "Will Clayton's Cotton," *Fortune*, 32 (November 1945): 146, 231–34.

[4] Garwood, *Will Clayton*, p. 98.

[5] "Cotton and King," *Time*, August 17, 1936, p. 58.

was to reduce speculation and stabilize the cotton market, Clayton's crusade had made him numerous enemies on the Exchange, enemies who "had the ear" of "Cotton Ed" Smith. Hence the investigations. However, the most serious charge that Smith was able to prove was that Clayton "dominated" the cotton market.[6] Although the investigations were arduous, embarrassing, and often insulting, Clayton did not regret participating in them. In each case he appeared before the subcommittee voluntarily. He later pointed out that without these investigations, it could have taken "10, 15, maybe 20 years longer getting Southern Delivery."[7]

At the same time that Clayton was defending himself and his company from congressional attacks, he was attacking Franklin D. Roosevelt's farm policies. He objected strenuously to the New Deal's efforts to make a supported market pay the farmer, contending that if subsidies were necessary they should be paid directly to the farmer. Just as he rejected artificial price-fixing in agriculture, he rebelled against the maintenance of artificial price levels through the erection of tariff barriers. He firmly believed that tariffs, by forcing the farmer to sell in a free market and buy in a protected market, had relegated the South in general and the Southern farmer in particular to an exploited colonial status. Clayton's concern for the South and the farmer were genuine. He opposed government farm policies even though his firm had profited from them. In the five seasons preceding 1935 ACCO made at least half of its profits as a result of government policies which allowed the sale of cotton at subsidized prices.[8]

In 1934 Clayton's opposition to New Deal farm policies took the form of membership in the American Liberty League, an organization of anti-Roosevelt businessmen, conservative lawyers, and disgruntled Democratic politicians. Clayton explained to his wife that he had joined at the request of his friend, John W. Davis. Clayton saw the League as a means of fighting New Deal agricultural policies by turning Roosevelt out of office. But in 1935 he resigned from the League "because of certain League actions which he did not approve."[9] Clayton's discontent with the League derived in part from its failure to accept his plan for a Texas organization to disseminate League philosophy. On several subsequent occasions Clay-

---

[6] "Conversations about Cotton," *Time*, April 20, 1936, p. 82.

[7] Oral History, p. 54.

[8] U.S. Congress, Senate, Committee on Agriculture and Forestry, *Hearings to Investigate the Causes of the Decline of Cotton Prices*, 74th Cong., 2d sess., 1936, p. 419.

[9] Garwood, *Will Clayton*, p. 103.

ton would again dissociate himself from organizations which were not operating in what he considered to be an efficient or economical manner.

Also responsible for his defection from the Liberty League was Cordell Hull's enunciation of a philosophy of liberal international trade in the Reciprocal Trade Agreements program. If the Democratic administration would back free trade, Clayton would support it. In 1936 he created a minor sensation by announcing that he intended to vote for Roosevelt contrary to his earlier announcement that he would ignore the election altogether. In explaining this change of heart Clayton told newsmen, "A vote for President Roosevelt is a vote to keep Secretary Hull in office, where his work, just beginning to bear fruit, may go forward with infinite benefit to the nation and to the world."[10]

From this time forward Clayton was to spend much of his time and energy in propagating the idea of free trade, or at least liberalized trade policies. His southern agricultural background told him that the South and the farmer would benefit from such a policy because they could buy in an unprotected market as well as sell in one. He pointed out time and again that the United States owed its great economic preeminence to the absence of tariff barriers between the states. On this basis he generalized that the entire world would benefit from a broad reduction or abolition of tariff barriers. Free trade was to be the panacea of modern man.

By 1936 Clayton was no longer only a businessman. He was now concerning himself with national economic policy, and although free trade would benefit his firm ultimately by increasing the market for cotton exports, he was concerned with the benefits it would bring to mankind rather than just the financial benefit which might accrue to Anderson, Clayton. Clayton's assumptions about the American political economy belonged to a democratic-capitalist tradition whose most brilliant spokesman was Woodrow Wilson.[11] Clayton believed in American exceptionalism—the idea that the United States differed from all other nations in the purity and benevolence of its motivation and goals—and regarded the United States as uniquely fitted to lead all nations to a rational world society based on an efficient economy. The United States would lead the crusade against trade barriers, and the destruction of these barriers would result in a beneficent world economic order in which the United States could sell its

[10] *The New York Times,* October 20, 1936, p. 20.

[11] For a discussion of Woodrow Wilson's theories of capitalism and exceptionalism, see N. Gordon Levin, *Woodrow Wilson and World Politics* (New York: Oxford University Press, 1968).

surpluses abroad, permitting other countries to obtain needed goods while allowing the American economy to produce at peak efficiency. The first step toward this world economy was extensive adoption of Hull's Reciprocal Trade Agreements program. It is important to remember that, although Clayton's economic philosophy became more sophisticated with the passing of the years, it was always predicated on the assumption of the ultimate desirability of free trade.

In 1940 Clayton was invited to come to Washington as an official of the Reconstruction Finance Corporation by Jesse Jones, the Federal Loan Administrator and head of the RFC. In deference to his wife's wish that he not undertake such responsibilities at the age of sixty, he initially refused, but a personal call from President Roosevelt won Mrs. Clayton over, and Clayton went to Washington. After helping Nelson Rockefeller set up the Office of Inter-American Affairs, Clayton was appointed Deputy Federal Loan Administrator and Vice-President of the Export-Import Bank. He also held positions at the policy-making level in a number of RFC subsidiaries, in which he was responsible for overseas purchases of strategic and critical materials for stock-piling purposes.

When Roosevelt abolished the Federal Loan Administration and shifted its responsibilities to the Secretary of Commerce, Clayton was named Assistant Secretary of Commerce. Given additional duties as President of the War Damage Corporation and Chairman of the Board of the U.S. Commercial Company, he was now also charged with preclusive buying of strategic materials. His most spectacular wartime work was in the field of monopolizing strategic materials in order to prevent their acquisition by the Axis powers, and his agents were involved in considerable international intrigue. But in 1943, by executive fiat, Clayton's duties were transferred to the Board of Economic Warfare under Vice-President Henry Wallace.

His responsibilities reduced from the policy-making to the administrative level, Clayton decided that his services were no longer required in Washington and resigned from the Commerce Department in January 1944. A month later, at the behest of Bernard Baruch,[12] Clayton was appointed Surplus War Property Administrator. His tenure was short and stormy. In June his name was linked with a movement in Texas to deny electoral votes to Roosevelt unless certain Southern demands were met. Although Lamar Fleming, President of ACCO, and another high ACCO official were prominent in the movement, Clayton, despite the allegations of the *Wash-*

[12] Oral History, p. 103.

ington Post, was not in any way involved.[13] In July James Patton of the National Farmers Union accused him of secretly assigning the disposal of surplus farm lands to an inappropriate agency—the RFC.[14] The *Nation* and *The New Republic* were outraged at this disclosure, and Clayton endured severe censure.[15] Clayton had assigned disposal of the lands to the RFC, and, even though his motives were honorable, he had to quiet the furor by issuing a reassuring statement that the farm lands would be sold in family-size lots.[16] Moreover throughout 1944 Clayton was dueling with Congress over the form that the surplus war property bill was to take. He was convinced that a single administrator would be far more efficient than the Senate's proposed three-man board. When Congress passed the bill establishing this three-man administrative board, Clayton pronounced it unworkable and resigned effective December 1, 1944. His judgment was vindicated a year later when the board was scrapped and a single administrator appointed.

Clayton was packing his bags to leave Washington when he was contacted by James F. Byrnes, Director of the Office of War Mobilization, who asked Clayton to serve as his deputy. Clayton accepted, but as he prepared to join Byrnes he was approached by Secretary of State Edward Stettinius, who offered him the position of Assistant Secretary of State for Economic Affairs. After several days of haggling with Byrnes and the President, Stettinius won Clayton's services.[17] His nomination was approved by the Senate on December 12, 1944, by a vote of fifty-two to nineteen. *PM*, a left-wing New York daily, strongly opposed Clayton's nomination charging that he was "an intellectual . . . as articulate and intelligent a spokesman for capitalist conservatism as Henry Wallace is of capitalist liberalism."[18] Yet Clayton never considered himself an intellectual and was in fact sometimes guilty of anti-intellectual bias. Nor would he have classified himself as a spokesman for capitalist conservatism. In later years he described himself as a "liberal capitalist" who believed that "it is necessary for government to put on the brakes occasionally, and to lay down rules which people should follow."[19]

[13] Will Clayton to Wayne Coy, June 27, 1944, RG 250, DNA; Will Clayton to Eugene Meyer, June 29, 1944, Baruch Papers, Princeton University.
[14] *The New York Times*, July 10, 1944, p. 12.
[15] "The War Surplus Bill," *Nation*, August 26, 1944, p. 228; "Clayton and the NAM," *The New Republic*, August 7, 1944, p. 160.
[16] "Surplus Disposal Plans Set," *Business Week*, July 29, 1944, p. 17.
[17] Clayton interview with Ellen Clayton Garwood, December 1947, CP, Rice University.
[18] Quoted in *Current Biography*, 1944, p. 98.
[19] Oral History, p. 69.

Confirmation of Clayton's appointment set the course for State Department economic policies in the postwar years. Clayton was to become one of the two most influential men in the State Department (along with Dean Acheson), and his influence was exercised with unfaltering zeal in behalf of liberal economic policies. Although Clayton's significance for American history is larger than just his State Department career, one of the themes of this volume is the extent to which Clayton's ideas and philosophy shaped national economic policy in the crucial period 1945–1948. In his roles as Assistant Secretary and Undersecretary of State for Economic Affairs Clayton was instrumental in preserving the capitalistic basis of the Western European economy and thus denying a foothold to communism and revolution. An examination of the documents which follow will provide useful insights into the liberal-capitalist mentality that shaped the American response to Soviet imperialism in the early Cold War.[20]

Clayton's first important assignment as Assistant Secretary of State for Economic Affairs was to head the economics section of the U.S. delegation to the Chapultepec Conference in Mexico City. There Clayton assured the Latin Americans of American intentions to help the Latin economies make the transition from war to peace, but he hastened to add that the United States (through the Export-Import Bank) would not make loans "for the establishment of enterprises which can only make their way through government subsidies or excessive tariffs."[21] Thus Clayton asserted his dedication (and, by implication, that of the State Department) to the destruction of trade barriers. This statement provided the theme for Clayton's State Department career: trade as free as possible between economies as efficient as possible.

Following the end of the war in the European theater, the great Allied powers convened in Potsdam, Germany, to settle a number of

[20] Our knowledge of events and attitudes in the State Department during this period has been increased immeasurably by the recent publication by three department members of their reminiscences: George Kennan's *Memoirs 1925–1950* (Boston: Little, Brown, 1967), Dean Acheson's *Present at the Creation* (New York: Norton, 1969), Charles Bohlen's *The Transformation of American Foreign Policy* (New York: Norton, 1969). Although these works provide valuable insights into the nature of policy formulation, they are to some extent misleading. All three give the impression that policy-makers were concerned only with political matters, such as national security and its military corollaries, when in fact there was a large and clearly stated economic component in official policy. The latter is readily traceable in Clayton's papers, so this volume should provide a needed corrective to a somewhat one-sided picture of the factors influencing policy decisions.

[21] "A Statement on the Problems of War and Peace," Department of State *Bulletin*, March 4, 1945, p. 338.

policy questions, most notably Russia's insistence upon the Oder-Neisse line as the western boundary of Poland and Russia's demand for ten billion dollars in reparations from Germany. As chairman of the American economic delegation, Clayton addressed himself to the latter problem. He worked out a compromise with Amazasp Arutyunyan, the Russian representative, whereby Russia received 25 percent (15 percent free, 10 percent in exchange for goods) of German industrial plants designated for dismantling by the Reparations Commission. Although in later years Clayton felt Stalin's decisions at Potsdam had generally been "pretty fair," he found Russian reparation demands unreasonable. Clayton left the conference "with the hope that we might be able to get along with the Russians."[22]

Clayton early recognized the necessity of extensive postwar aid to Europe if European economies were to return to viability. Consequently in 1945 and 1946 he strongly advocated United Nations Relief and Rehabilitation Administration aid to Europe and a large loan to Britain. In July 1945, President Truman appointed Clayton U.S. member of the United Nations Relief and Rehabilitation Council. Although he had assigned Colonel Tyler Wood the responsibility for State Department relations with UNRRA, Clayton served as liaison between UNRRA and Congress and in fact was the moving force in obtaining approval of UNRRA funds from a reluctant Congress in 1946. This approval was purchased at a dear price: Clayton promised that no more UNRRA funds would be requested. But he had done all that he felt was possible to extend the life of this international relief organization.

Clayton's role in securing adoption of the British loan was also influential. He had early perceived the necessity of post-war aid to the British economy and had strongly but unsuccessfully opposed the abrupt termination of Lend-Lease to the British in 1945. Clayton was in London at the time the decision was made, and when he heard of it immediately placed a call to Secretary Byrnes. As Roy Harrod phrased it, "On Monday morning Mr. Clayton took up the transatlantic telephone and vented the vials of his wrath."[23] As Clayton later related the event to his daughter, "I called Byrnes from London and just told him it was shocking, it was going to floor the British; they were bowled off their feet by it. I said everything possible should be done to restore Lend-Lease."[24] Unable to reverse the de-

[22] Oral History, p. 156.
[23] Roy Harrod, *The Life of John Maynard Keynes* (London: Macmillan and Company Ltd., 1951), p. 596.
[24] Clayton interview with Ellen Clayton Garwood, 1958, CP, Rice University.

cision, he was able to soften the blow. Clayton was certain that further aid would be required, and he immediately began to lay the groundwork for the British loan. Emilio Collado called Clayton "the great architect of the British-American financial agreement in 1945,"[25] and all available evidence seems to justify that assessment.

Negotiations were conducted by Lords Halifax, Keynes, and Brand on the British side and Secretary of the Treasury Fred Vinson and Clayton on the American side. In addition to the actual work of negotiating, Clayton found himself serving as referee and pacificator between Vinson and Keynes, who had formed an immediate dislike for one another, and not the least of his accomplishments was keeping these two from each other's throats. The British wanted a six billion dollar grant-in-aid, finally compromising on a three and three-quarter billion dollar loan; they also wanted an interest-free loan but had to compromise at 2 percent interest.[26] These compromises were reached not on the basis of what the United States could do but rather on the basis of Clayton's knowledge of what the American people and Congress would be willing to accept.

As the price for the British loan, Clayton exacted from the British acceptance of State Department trade principles, especially the elimination of British preferences in return for reduction of American tariffs. These principles, embodied in the "Proposals for Consideration by an International Conference on Trade and Employment," were considered by a large segment of British leadership to be contrary to British interests because such policies would aggravate the balance of payments problem and weaken essential economic ties with the commonwealth nations. The "Proposals" were released to the public by the United States concurrently with the text of the financial agreement "so that the American Government could claim the 'Proposals' as one of the benefits received in return for the loan to Britain and the writing off of Lend-Lease." Because of domestic politics, the British government was unwilling to cosponsor the "Proposals," but as a result of American insistence it did state its concurrence with the sense of the document.[27] The Anglo-American Financial Agreement itself contained no commitments concerning the imperial preference system, a system of preferential trade practices among members of the British Empire, but Clayton believed that the loan was necessary to create the economic climate which would per-

[25] Emilio Collado, director of the Office for Financial and Development Policy of the Department of State (1945–1946), interview with Ellen Clayton Garwood, November 6, 1958, CP, Rice University.

[26] Richard Gardner, *Sterling Dollar Diplomacy* (Oxford: Clarendon Press, 1956), pp. 188–207.

[27] *Ibid.*, p. 146.

mit elimination of the preference system. Clayton felt that Britain had committed herself to eventual elimination of preferences in Article Seven of the Mutual Aid Agreement of 1942, and he fully expected that elimination to occur in the negotiations which Britain had agreed to in the "Proposals."[28] Article Seven stated that the two countries would work toward "the elimination of all forms of discriminatory treatment in international commerce, and . . . the reduction of tariffs and other trade barriers."[29] That the British had no intention of eliminating preferences in exchange for anything less than across-the-board American tariff reductions is now clear, but Clayton foresaw no such intransigence on the part of British leaders. In a letter to General R. E. Wood of Sears, Roebuck and Company, Clayton asserted that the financial agreement would enable the British people "to open up their commerce to the United States and all other countries instead of confining it to the British Empire as they would largely be compelled to do if they were not able to obtain the necessary assistance to get their trade back on a multilateral basis."[30]

After the agreement was signed, Clayton undertook the most difficult part of the process—winning congressional approval of the agreement. Here Clayton was invaluable. He stressed the benefits to be had by elimination of the preference system and the sterling dollar pool, he argued that the United States had a moral obligation to the British for carrying the brunt of the battle against fascism, and he pointed out the possible deleterious consequences of failure to ratify the agreement. Among the opponents of the bill whom he was able to convert was Representative Hatton Summers of Texas, a man of considerable influence and prestige whose support was crucial in the House. Clayton also helped "educate" the public and mobilize public opinion behind the loan through a number of speeches early in 1946, emphasizing the trade benefits which would accrue to the United States as a result of the loan.[31] In a speech before the National Farm Institute on February 13, 1946, Clayton said, "Britain is enabled by this credit to join with the United States in full partnership in supporting our Proposals . . . . We have discussed and considered these proposals with the British in great detail and our two countries are in substantial agreement."[32] A large part of Clayton's success in obtaining eventual approval of the financial agreement was this

---

28 *Ibid.*, pp. 152–53.
29 Leland Goodrich, ed., *Documents on American Foreign Relations* (Boston: World Peace Foundation, 1942), vol. 4, p. 237.
30 Will Clayton to R. E. Wood, November 17, 1945, CP, TL.
31 Pritchard, "Will Clayton," pp. 234–53.
32 Speech before the National Farm Institute, Des Moines, Iowa, February 15, 1946, CP, ACCO.

conception of the loan as a means of eliminating the British Empire preference system.[33] Time and again he assured the Congress that the financial agreement was more than just a loan, and that the United States stood to benefit as much as Great Britain ultimately through the expanded trade which it would promote. By picturing the agreement in terms which redounded to America's economic advantage, he gained much-needed support for passage of the act.

It was in 1947, however, that Clayton's pursuit of multilateralism brought its most memorable result. On May 19, 1947, Clayton finished a memorandum, which Dean Acheson called "the concrete outline for the Marshall Plan."[34] Although Clayton later modestly disclaimed the title of "father of the Marshall Plan,"[35] his influence was profound not only in its conception and proclamation but also in its application. On March 5, 1947, while en route by plane to Tucson, Arizona, for a convalescing vacation, he recorded his preliminary reflections on the European crisis.[36] Although his memorandum was never handed to Secretary Marshall—Marshall left on March 5 for the Moscow Foreign Ministers Conference—it reflects Clayton's early preoccupation with the necessity for further aid to Europe. This memo was undoubtedly prompted by the research Clayton had been doing for the Truman Doctrine. In studying Greece and Turkey (he was "in the center" of that research, according to Acheson)[37] he delved into the situation of the rest of Europe and was deeply disturbed at what he saw there.

Clayton became even more distressed after spending a month in Europe in the spring of 1947. He arrived in Geneva on April 15 to assume his role as head of the U.S. delegation to the International Trade and Employment Conference, at which the General Agreement on Tariffs and Trade (GATT) was negotiated. According to Clayton the purpose of the Geneva meeting was twofold: "to negotiate reciprocal reductions in tariffs, multilaterally, and to discuss the charter for an international trade organization."[38] While engaged in these negotiations, Clayton relayed to the State Department a depressing portrait of European economic conditions. According to Dean Acheson, "messages from Clayton showed that statistics were lagging behind facts, said facts were worse than statistics showed." When Clay-

[33] Gardner, *Sterling Dollar Diplomacy*, p. 160; Garwood, *Will Clayton*, p. 26; *Foreign Relations of the United States, 1945*, vol. 6, pp. 54–56.

[34] Acheson, *Present at the Creation*, p. 228.

[35] Oral History, p. 213.

[36] Will Clayton, memorandum, March 5, 1947, CP, Rice University.

[37] Acheson interview with Ellen Clayton Garwood, November 2, 1958, CP, Rice University.

[38] Oral History, p. 180.

ton found it necessary to return to Washington to fight a wool tariff bill that threatened to wreck GATT negotiations, he once again wrote out his thoughts on European recovery. Although he was ill at the time he arrived in Washington on May 19, he had the memorandum in circulation before May 27. It "made a profound impression on the State Department. . . . It was a dark frightening picture [Clayton] gave."[39] This memorandum (supplemented by George Kennan's policy planning staff memorandum) served as the basis for Secretary Marshall's Harvard speech on June 5, which announced to the world the intention of the United States to aid Western European economic recovery.

Two weeks later Clayton was winging his way back to Europe. He had a victory on the wool tariff measure, but, more important, he had instructions to stop in London to begin negotiations for the enactment of the Marshall Plan. For the duration of the summer Clayton divided his time between negotiations at the Geneva conference and consultations on the Marshall Plan in Paris. He worked closely with Ambassador to Great Britain Lewis Douglas and Ambassador to France Jefferson Caffery in conferring with European representatives to the Marshall Plan discussions on the final form of the European organization to administer Marshall Plan aid. Clayton helped create the Committee for European Economic Cooperation, the forerunner of the Organisation for Economic Cooperation and Development. He enjoyed further success by the end of the summer: in Geneva the twenty-three participating nations completed 122 agreements for mutual tariff reductions, and in Paris sixteen countries agreed to American stipulations attached to granting of Marshall Plan aid.[40]

Clayton's concern for long-term economic goals was at no time more evident than during the Marshall Plan discussions in the summer of 1947. That this emphasis on long-term goals was somewhat unique in the State Department is indicated by an unsigned memorandum dated August 22, 1947, concerning a meeting in the Department attended by Charles Bohlen, George Kennan, Charles Kindleberger, and others.[41] They agreed that Clayton departed from departmental thinking rather abruptly in his emphasis on the development of a European customs union and his advocacy of financial and multilateral trade agreements among European countries.

[39] Acheson interview with Ellen Clayton Garwood, November 2, 1958, CP, Rice University.

[40] Will Clayton, "GATT, The Marshall Plan, and OECD," *Political Science Quarterly*, 78 (December 1963): 493–503.

[41] Memorandum, August 22, 1947, Marshall Plan files, State Department.

Clayton, on the other hand, believed that the European crisis was the ideal catalyst for promoting free trade in Western Europe, and he encouraged liberalized trade and financial agreements as the cure for European economic problems. Four days after the departmental policy meeting Kennan arrived in Paris to consult with Clayton and bring his thinking into agreement with that of the rest of the department. Kennan's success was reflected in a *New York Times* story on August 31: "The United States has given its blessing to the customs union idea, but recognized it was a long-range possibility, and the United States diplomats did not press for it today."[42]

Much has been written of Clayton's role in the development of the Marshall Plan, but generally the plan has been treated as an end in itself, a stopgap measure conceived in reaction to an emergency situation. However, a true appreciation of Clayton's conception of the Marshall Plan cannot be attained unless it is recognized that in Clayton's economic philosophy the plan was but one step in an economic progression, a progression which required restoration of a healthy European economy to achieve success. Clayton's entire State Department career can be seen in terms of this progression—the renewal of the Reciprocal Trade Agreements Act, the Chapultepec Conference, the British loan, the Marshall Plan, the General Agreement on Tariffs and Trade, the International Trade Organization— all of these were steps toward Clayton's ultimate goal, the propagation of free trade principles throughout the world.

The most advanced step in the progression was the International Trade Organization, for which Clayton was largely responsible. Clayton headed the U.S. delegation to the final world trade conference in Havana, Cuba, in November 1947, in his role as Special Advisor to the Secretary of State. As the direct result of an ultimatum from his wife, Clayton had officially resigned from his post in the State Department on October 15, 1947, at the same time refusing the proffered post of European Recovery Plan Administrator,[43] but he did agree to handle occasional special assignments such as the ITO conference. Fifty-seven nations attended the Havana conference to consider approval of the proposed ITO charter and, after considerable haggling, the charter was approved and signed by fifty-four of the fifty-seven participating nations. The ITO had as its goal the development of liberal commercial policies rooted in multilateralism. However, the charter was diverted so far from its original free trade goals by compromises and concessions necessary to achieve agreement on its final form that many who had supported it in its original

---

[42] *The New York Times*, August 31, 1947, p. 25.
[43] Will Clayton to Alfred Clason, November 16, 1953, CP, ACCO.

conception now turned a deaf ear to Clayton's plea that it was the best document possible under the circumstances and was better than no charter at all. All of Clayton's work in behalf of ITO came to naught, for it soon became apparent that Congress had no intention of accepting the charter, primarily because of the opposition of big business, generally staunch supporters of freer trade policies. Big business opposition to the charter was primarily a reaction to the extraordinary concessions made by the State Department to U.S. agricultural interests, concessions necessary to meet the objections of the Agriculture Department; these concessions necessitated further concessions to special interests in other countries and thus destroyed the free trade character of ITO and cost the proposal crucial support.[44] The charter never reached the floor of Congress, and Clayton suffered the bitterest disappointment of his government career.

After the Havana conference Clayton reluctantly returned to Houston in November 1948. As he told Paul Nitze shortly before he left, "I guess I'll go back to Anderson, Clayton and Company. . . . Lamar Fleming has been running the firm with great success. . . . When I go back to Houston they'll give me a great big office and give me respect, but there won't be a thing for me to do." And as he spoke, "tears came into his eyes."[45] But Clayton was to do an admirable job of keeping himself occupied for the last seventeen years of his life, devoting his not inconsiderable energies to the doctrines of economic internationalism for which he had labored throughout his State Department career. The agency for his most fervent efforts was the Atlantic Union Committee, an organization of idealistic internationalists who envisioned a political, military, and economic union of the free nations of the world (for "free" read "non-Communist"), beginning with Western Europe, the United States, and Canada.

The political goals of Atlantic Union seemed somewhat visionary to Clayton, but he used its forum to spread the gospel of economic liberalism to all who would listen. A trademark of Clayton's Atlantic Union statements was his emphasis on the economic struggle with Communism, a struggle which held the key to the future of the free world. He scorned the notion that Russia would physically attack the free world, contending instead that without at least an Atlantic economic union the Communists would conquer the free world by "boring from within."[46] Even during his term in the State Depart-

[44] Allen J. Matusow, *Farm Policies and Politics in the Truman Years* (Cambridge, Mass.: Harvard University Press, 1967), pp. 79–109.

[45] Nitze interview with Ellen Clayton Garwood, November 4, 1958, CP, Rice University.

[46] Will Clayton to John S. Knight, July 30, 1949, CP, ACCO.

ment Clayton had scoffed at the possibility of Russian military at-tack.[47] Yet the vehemence of his anti-Communist rhetoric escalated as he convinced himself of the imminence of Communist economic victory.

Clayton's exertions on behalf of Atlantic Union spanned the period from 1949 until shortly before his death in 1966. At that time, as in the case of the American Liberty League and the Surplus War Property Administration, he once again demonstrated by his resignation his unwillingness to remain affiliated with an organization which he felt operated inefficiently or uneconomically. Like the good businessman that he was, Clayton insisted until the end that even the most idealistic goals be pursued in a rational, businesslike manner. A month later, on February 8, 1966, Will Clayton died in Houston, Texas, bringing to an end a career of unqualified business success and unblemished ideological consistency.

[47] Will Clayton, memorandum, March 5, 1947, CP, Rice University.

I

CAPITALIST IN

THE DEPRESSION ERA

§ By 1930, Will Clayton's antitariff bias had evolved into a mature philosophy of free trade, which would later guide him during his years in the State Department. For Clayton, liberal trade policies provided the answer to the problems of world economic depression. The following documents illustrate his basic attitudes toward international trade.

A STATEMENT ON THE PROBLEMS
OF THE COTTON FARMER

---

*   *   *

Our exports of raw cotton have several times since the World War exceeded in value one billion dollars annually.[1]

The Nation cannot be indifferent to any development which seriously threatens the life of this vast international trade, woven as it is into the very fabric of our national economic structure.

Nevertheless, every student of the subject has recognized that foreign growths of cotton have for several years been gaining steadily on our own.

*   *   *

American domination in cotton for the past century has rested upon a foundation, the component parts of which presented a varied assortment of conditions favorable to such domination.

*   *   *

American supremacy in cotton has rested also on the exploitation of rich virgin soil requiring little or no fertilization and relative

[1] This statement appeared in pamphlet form under the title "What Congress Can Do for the Cotton Farmer: A Sequel to: *What Price Cotton?*" April 15, 1930 (Anderson, Clayton & Co., Houston, Texas), pp. 2, 4–10, 14.

freedom from insect pests. Thirty years ago average yields of 200 to 250 pounds of lint cotton to the acre were fairly common. For the 10 years since the World War the yield of lint cotton has averaged only 156 pounds to the acre, due principally to the boll weevil and to impoverishment of the soil.

Coincident with this serious decline in yield has been an equally serious deterioration in quality due to the same causes and to new strains of early maturing seed.

Throughout the nineteenth century the South had no labor problem. At first there were the African slaves, and after that the freed negroes, living in rural isolation, knowing nothing of urban industries and unattracted by them. Meantime, there was a large and steady influx of cheap foreign labor to supply the ever growing needs of the factories, so that industry had no necessity to recruit its labor from agricultural districts.

About 15 years ago we substantially closed our doors to immigration; the War came on, drawing men out of the country into munitions works and other War industries where they got wages such as they never dreamed of before. Furthermore, in the past quarter of a century the South has greatly increased its manufacturing industries, especially in textiles, the labor for which was drawn from the country. During the same period we have developed the automobile, good roads, rural free delivery, the telephone and the radio, so that there is no longer any such thing as rural isolation. The cities have drawn heavily on the country for labor.

The cost of producing a pound of cotton in the past 20 years has certainly more than doubled.

And during the past 20 years the list of manufactured articles unprotected by tariff has grown much smaller, whereas the rate of protection has grown greater.

More than 100 years ago Thomas Jefferson said, "The way to encourage purchasers is to multiply their means of payment." Our tariff policy as it affects our great export commodities, like cotton, is the reverse of this.

During the past 15 years, our foreign purchaser's means of payment has been artificially maintained by liberal American credits and loans. Dr. Anderson, the economist of the Chase National Bank,[2] recently said that our excess of exports over imports for that period has amounted to twenty-five billion dollars, and that this was just about the sum of our own securities repurchased. In other words, we sold the goods largely on credit and the bill is still unpaid.

[2] Benjamin M. Anderson, Jr., economist of Chase National Bank (1920–39).

No nation, however rich it may be, can go on indefinitely selling its goods on credit and never collecting the bills. This has finally been realized, and we have practically ceased adding to these loans. So now the foreign purchaser, instead of buying on credit, not only must pay cash for his current purchases but also must pay the interest on the accumulated debts of the last 15 years.

He is thus in this situation: either he must buy less from us for lack of cash to pay with, or else he must sell us something in exchange for our goods.

Congress answers him on this point with a tariff bill which raises barriers against the goods that he might sell us so high as virtually to say, "Thou shalt not pay."

So, instead of multiplying our foreign purchaser's means of payment, we are fast destroying it; and, as a consequence, our export trade dwindles month by month and there are upwards of four millions of people walking our streets unable to find work.

Is there any wonder that England, France, Germany, Italy and Japan turn for their raw cotton to those countries which are willing to receive payment in their manufactured goods? When will we learn that trade is a reciprocal thing, and consists both of buying and selling?

In analyzing the factors contributing to our success as the world's chief supplier of raw cotton up to the beginning of this century, and contemplating the enormous changes which have taken place in the past quarter century, affecting this situation, the wonder is that we have not lost far more ground than we have.

What can be done about the matter? It is quite clear, if we continue in the direction in which we are moving, that it is only a question of another generation or so until we shall have lost to other countries substantially all of our export trade in raw cotton. Meantime, must our cotton farmers be ground down to an even lower standard of living, and only learn through the painful process of attrition that they are waging an impossible fight? There are over two million of them, making, with their families, ten million people; and then there are other millions in the towns and cities of the South whose economic existence is tightly bound up with that of the cotton farmer.

Can we do nothing about the matter except to advise reduction of acreage? We tell all farmers to cut acreage. When a farmer reduces his acreage in one crop, he generally substitutes another. Hence, cutting acreage just carries us around in a circle. There are in the United States so many hundreds of millions of acres of agricultural lands devoted to such staple crops as cotton, wheat, corn, oats, rye, tobacco, etc., and there are so many millions of people who are earning their living, such as it is, by the tilling of this land. If we cut the total acreage 10 percent, we are going to have a good many idle people in the country as well as in the city.

Mr. Legge[3] and others have told the wheat farmer that he would be far better off if he reduced his output to a point where it would barely cover domestic requirements, in order that he might then benefit from the tariff on wheat. Is the cotton farmer to be told the same thing? If so, it introduces the highly interesting problem of finding some other use for twenty-five million acres of land and some other means of earning a livelihood for about five million people.

It ought to be apparent to every thinking person that the productive capacity of the United States, both in agriculture and in manufactures, is far in excess of domestic requirements, and that our national policy of raising higher and higher the tariff is doing these two things: elevating our costs of production and depriving our foreign customers of the ability to pay.

It is impossible for the cotton producers of the United States, operating behind this high wall of protection, to continue to lift over that wall and into the channels of international trade their present percentage of 40 bales out of every 100 which are consumed outside of the United States. We have lost a very substantial share of the world trade in raw cotton in the past quarter century, and we must continue year after year, a little at a time, to relinquish that which is left, unless the cotton producer can get some relief from the unjust burdens which his Government has permitted the urban and industrial population to place upon him.

The Agricultural Marketing Act is entitled "An Act for the Purpose of Placing Agriculture on an Equality with Other Industries."

Most of the gentlemen who assisted in the framing and passage of this legislation knew perfectly well that it never could do any such thing; hence it was conceived in deceit.

Unless the Federal Farm Board, acting under the present Farm Relief Act, can devise some means of curtailing agricultural production (as suggested by Mr. Legge for wheat) to the point where there will be no surplus for export, and unless they can at the same time find some other employment for about 1,500,000 farmers, totalling with their families, about 7,500,000 people, they will never place agriculture on an economic equality with industry.

[3] Alexander Legge, Chairman of the Federal Farm Board (1929–31).

Will any one deny that the highest obligation of Government is the preservation of equality of opportunity to all the people?

Under existing conditions, equality of opportunity to the cotton farmer in the United States has been absolutely destroyed.

Equality, under a protective tariff, is a contradiction in terms. Somebody must be left to pay the bill. Equal protection to all is the equivalent of free trade.

The only way to get equality for agriculture without abolishing all protection is to give to agriculture the same measure of protection that is afforded other industries.

The farmer spends the proceeds of his unprotected labor for the products of protected industry. Year by year, his unprotected proceeds command less of these protected products.

This is the major farm problem.

It will only be settled when we either protect the farmer's labor or "unprotect" the things he must buy. He cannot continue to buy in a protected market and sell in a free one.

Where is the boasted American standard of living if ten millions of our people on cotton farms are known to have a lower standard than the farmers of any country in Europe except Russia and possibly the Balkans?

The cotton producer is not asking for protection against foreign competition, but he should demand and receive protection against his exploitation by the capital and labor of other American industries.

The right way, of course, and the one which will prevail in the end, is the abolition of protective tariffs, so that all exchanges of goods and services will be made on the basis of real values, as opposed to fictitious or "protected" values. Only in this way can the world's fast growing population maintain itself.

The needs of the cotton-growing industry, however, are pressing; they cannot await so remote a relief. Something must be done for them quickly, not alone on the producer's account, but for the preservation of this vast international trade, which affects in one way or another our entire population.

Since Congress is just now engaged in raising instead of lowering tariff walls, what can be done to restore to the cotton farmer a measure of equality of opportunity in this country?

The most practicable plan by which Congress can grant the cotton farmer the relief to which he is entitled, is through an export bounty or debenture on cotton. An export bounty of two cents per pound on cotton would not equalize costs of production with foreign producers, nor would it entirely relieve the cotton farmer of the full measure of the unjust burdens which he suffers by the operation of our high tariff, but such a bounty would go far toward enabling him to compete for his share of the world's cotton trade, and to continue to produce from 40 to 50 per cent of the cotton consumed by the world outside of the United States.

* * *

Only two courses are open to the cotton farmer: Either, he must get some relief from the inequalities which have been imposed upon him by his Government, or, failing this, he must substantially change his occupation.

If the Congress of the United States is unwilling to grant relief to the cotton farmers from the inequalities which Congress itself has imposed upon them, then in common honesty Congress should say to the cotton farmers that no relief is to be expected, and that the only course open to them is gradually to abandon, through a systematic reduction in acreage, the export trade in raw cotton, and seek some other means of earning a livelihood.

A Statement on War Debts and Tariffs

Remedies wide in range and limitless in number are being offered for the relief of cotton.[4] Destroy part of the surplus; restrict acreage by legislation; let the government buy the surplus on condition that the farmer refrain from planting, etc., etc.

Prosperity to be restored through a sort of injunction against the fructifying processes of nature!

A world, sick unto death from an overdose of artificiality, is asked to swallow more of the same as the only means of relief.

How long will we go on with a patch here and one there trying to cure that which only a major operation can reach?

To say that our troubles are due to overproduction is too easy.

[4] This statement (which was entitled "How Long?") appeared in the *ACCO Press*, October 1931, pp. 4–6.

One suffering from arthritis is not benefitted by the mere knowledge of the technical name of his malady. He wants to know how to get rid of it, but first he must know what causes it.

In spite of a surplus of all commodities, producers are no longer able to effect exchanges among themselves on a fair basis. Stocks pile up and everybody cries: "Overproduction"—"cut down production to fit consumption, etc."

Before condemning the farmer for producing too much and seeking means of forcing him to curtail, let us carefully examine the highways of international trade to see if the trouble may not be due to obstacles there in the way of a free exchange of goods.

Instead of serving an injunction on nature to "cease and desist" from bringing forth her bounties, is it not wiser to seek the reason for inability to keep commodities moving in the customary processes of exchange. Why should there be great unmarketable surpluses of wheat and cotton, etc., when many millions of the world's population are cold and hungry?

What are the facts surrounding the so-called overproduction of cotton?

Cotton is now selling on the farm at one-half the average price obtained by the farmer for ten years prior to the war. Other farm products show approximately the same price comparison. Practically every product of the farm is selling far below the cost of production.

For every five bales of American cotton sold to mills in this country, six to seven bales must be sold abroad; hence the price of cotton depends more upon foreign than upon domestic buying power.

One of the consequences of the war was a quick reversal of the international financial position of the United States from that of a debtor nation to a creditor nation.

During the first decade following the war, citizens of the United States made enormous investments in foreign countries. The proceeds of these investments were, for the most part, spent in the United States for raw materials, manufactured goods, machinery, etc., to repair and renew the wastage of war.

By the end of 1928, the United States was the world's greatest creditor nation and had reached a position of apparent prosperity unequalled in the history of the world.

We now see that our house was built on a foundation of sand.

We were lending our customers the money with which to buy our goods and then lending them more money with which to pay the interest on the loans.

Obviously a halt had to come to this process.

When it came in 1928–29, the highly artificial foundation on which our exports had been built, crumbled with the stock market.

It took England centuries to win the position of chief banker to the world.

Along with the laborious process incident thereto, she also gained an understanding of the significance of her position and the ability to carry its vast responsibilities.

The displacement of England by the United States as the world's chief banker came almost overnight through a quick turn of the wheel of fortune. But those cultural processes represented by experience, understanding and the ability to accept heavy responsibilities do not lie on any wheel of fortune.

It can hardly be questioned that an examination of our stewardship as chief banker to the world for the past ten years will convict us of gross and stupid incompetence.

We should have recognized that our new responsibilities placed us in the position of requiring payment from the rest of the world, not only for the goods which we were still expecting them to buy from us—cotton, wheat, automobiles, radios, etc., etc., but in addition that we should have to receive heavy annual payments as interest and amortization on the vast sums of money which we had loaned abroad. We should have known that these payments could only be made in goods; that any requirement of payment in gold if persisted in would undoubtedly crack the economic foundations of the world.

Heedless of the insistent warnings of international bankers and economists, we proceeded to raise our tariff barriers to a higher level than ever before. We practically put the rest of the world on notice that they need not expect to sell to us any commodity which we could manufacture or grow in the United States; that they must pay their debts to us in gold and pay for our cotton, wheat, etc., in gold.

The debts due us by foreign countries had their origin *not* in the loan of gold but in the loan of goods, the value of which was expressed in gold when gold's purchasing power was very low. Now we decline to accept payment in goods even though due to a great increase in the value of gold, we can get three or four times the weight of goods that we loaned.

Thus, the war debts and the protective tariff have operated to siphon into the United States over one-half of all the monetary gold in the world; 40 percent of the remaining supply is held by France; hence these two countries, with about 12 percent of the population of the world, now hold approximately 70 percent of the world's stock of monetary gold.

As one economist has aptly put it, *the United States and France are running a gigantic corner on gold.*

While the corner is in process, the price of gold rises and rises, which is another way of saying the price of everything else, expressed in gold, goes down and down. This is one reason why cotton sells on the farm at 5 cents a pound and wheat at 25 cents a bushel.

Two years ago, when the cornering process had just commenced to tighten the screws on its victims, five pounds of cotton or three-fourths of a bushel of wheat on the farm would buy a dollar in gold. Today on the farm it takes twenty-pounds of cotton or four bushels of wheat to buy a dollar in gold.

The larger our pile of gold grows, the scarcer it becomes in other countries of the world and the greater the difficulty experienced by our foreign customers to pay the interest on their debts, and to buy our products like wheat and cotton and copper. Like King Midas, everything we touch turns to gold.

Fortunately, there is a safety valve, otherwise the top of the world would be blown off under the pressure. The first operation of the safety valve came with England's announcement that she could no longer pay in gold. Other distressed countries will almost certainly follow suit.

One of the "shorts"[5] has thus announced to the world its inability to make further deliveries of the cornered article. With pressure released, the price of gold ceases to rise and the price of commodities remains steady or advances.

England is to be commended for taking this courageous step. It is a constructive development, not only for England but for the whole world.

History will also convict us of another stupid thing. Not content with arranging matters so that our debtors and our customers would have to pay in gold, we thought of another cunning device by which (as we believed) the amount of gold which they would have to send us in exchange for our commodities would be greatly increased. It was so easy! So we drank deep of the poisonous nostrum of government stabilization of commodity prices.

Not content with cornering gold, *we* would also corner wheat and cotton! Why not? Were we not the richest nation in the world? If $500,000,000 were not enough to do it, wouldn't Congress give the all powerful Farm Board another $500,000,000 and another and another? Of course they would! We had their (F. B.) word for it.

[5] A term used in commodity and security markets to indicate one who has sold goods or property which he does not possess but expects to acquire later for future delivery.

So our Uncle Sam started in just before planting time in 1930 when the farmer had sold 95 percent of his previous crop and proceeded to corner May and July cotton. There was no reason for doing so, because the farmer had practically no cotton left for sale; on the contrary there were weighty reasons against it, as, for instance, the serious effect which such artificial action would have on the consumption of our cotton as well as the importance of avoiding any move which would give the farmer false hopes as to prices for the next crop, thus preventing a natural reduction in acreage so much to be desired. But what has reason to do with $500,000,000 appropriated by Congress to "stabilize" the prices of commodities and to "minimize speculation!"

So away we went. And how Uncle Sam did make the shorts dance! They were wicked fellows who had had the audacity to buy the farmers' cotton at a time when no mill wanted it and to hedge it by the sale of futures so that they would be in position to borrow from banks without jeopardizing the money entrusted to the banks by their depositors! Uncle Sam actually made some of them bring their cotton back from foreign lands where it had been shipped in the hope of finding a buyer. We would show them what the United States government could do with the price of cotton!

What was the result? The story is too long to tell here in its entirety: in good time it will all come out, but this is open to anyone to see: Cotton acreage in 1930 was reduced only 4 percent whereas if the market had been left to itself, we would have had a much heavier reduction. *Consumption of American cotton in season 1929–30 declined 2,200,000 bales, whereas consumption of foreign grown cotton increased 1,100,000 bales. In the following season 1930–31, consumption of American cotton declined another 2,000,000 bales, whereas consumption of foreign grown cotton remained stationary. During the past season, for the first time since the invention of the cotton gin (except for the civil war period), the consumption of foreign grown cotton has exceeded that of American cotton and by the substantial total of 566,000 bales (11,134,000 American vs. 11,700,000 foreign) and in spite of the depression, the consumption of foreign cotton (11,700,000 bales) was the highest figure ever known.* In 1926–27 consumption of American exceeded that of foreign grown cotton by 6,000,000 bales; 1927–28 by 5,700,000 bales; 1928–29 by 4,600,000 bales.

There is now held by or under the control of the Federal Farm Board a market interest in excess of 3,000,000 bales of cotton. Every cotton mill, every cotton speculator, every large distributor of cotton goods, every cotton merchant in the whole world knows of this huge stock of cotton held under government control and they are all asking themselves the question: "When will it be sold?" Someone has said "when the government goes into business, the wise man goes out." Our government invaded the cotton business only to find that the enemy—the wicked cotton speculator—had evacuated, leaving the government to hold the position in undisputed ruin. One of the stated objects of the Federal Agricultural Marketing Act was to "minimize speculation." In this it has succeeded far beyond the dreams of its authors. It has destroyed speculation.

This is another reason why cotton sells at 5 cents per pound on the farm.

The Federal Agricultural Marketing Act, conceived in deceit, and administered in ignorance (destroy every third row; corner May, July, etc., etc.), lives as a towering monument to our economic folly.

The losses to farmers, to merchants, to mills and to taxpayers in this grandiose scheme to set aside natural law will never be fully known, but it is a staggering total.

And then there's the question of union wages which the government has attempted to hold at the inflated levels established during and after the war, where as the cotton farmer and wheat farmer (agricultural laborers) *have had their wages cut to one fourth* of such levels. How can the agricultural laborer go on buying the products of *industrial* labor on any such inequitable basis? Factories will continue to close, railroads will continue to lay off men until this condition is changed.

Most thoughtful men will agree that labor should and will in future receive a larger share of each dollar of production than in the past, but quite apart from the question of equity, it is impossible for the agricultural population, with its income cut 75 percent in the past three years, to go on supporting the urban population at the old rates of pay just as if nothing had happened.

How long will we go on depending on artificiality? How long will it take us to recognize the wisdom of Macauley, the great historian of a hundred years ago who is so widely quoted today:

> It is not by the intermeddling of the omniscient and omnipotent state, but by the prudence and energy of the people, that England has hitherto been carried forward in civilization; and it is to the same prudence and the same energy that we now look with comfort and good hope.
>
> Our rulers will best promote the improvement of the people by strictly confining themselves to their own legitimate duties, by leaving capital to find its most lucrative course, commodities their fair price, industry and intelligence their natural reward, idleness and

folly their natural punishment—by maintaining peace, by defending property, by diminishing the price of law, and by observing strict economy in every department of the state.

Let the government do this—the people will assuredly do the rest.

How long will it take our government to rise to its responsibilities and call an international conference to substantially reduce war debts and tariffs, and thereby cut the Gordian Knot which now binds the nations of the earth in economic helplessness?

What are we waiting for?

Will we act in time?

§ *The government agricultural policies occasioned by the Depression were, as the previous documents indicate, offensive to Clayton's philosophy of free trade. Increased governmental interference in the cotton business eventually drove him, along with many other opponents of the New Deal, into the American Liberty League. His membership on the Executive Committee of the League dated from September 8, 1934, to June 6, 1935, during which time he labored diligently at increasing the League's membership.*

To Jouett Shouse

Houston, Texas
November 12, 1934

Dear Mr. Shouse:

I am putting the following postscript on every letter I write:

"I am on the Executive Committee of the American Liberty League and am taking a great deal of interest in the affairs of the League. I enclose a little pamphlet stating the principles and purposes of the League. If you approve of same, as I am sure you will, perhaps you may want to fill in the membership blank on the back page and send it in to Washington."[6]

Sincerely yours,

W. L. Clayton

§ *Although the modification of government cotton policies, dissatisfaction with the leadership of the American Liberty League, and enunciation of Cordell Hull's Reciprocal Trade Agreements program allowed Clayton to return to the Democratic Party in 1936, he was still critical of national agricultural policies. Anderson, Clayton and Company, for instance, found in the thirties that it was facing increasingly heavy competition from cotton cooperatives. Government policies favorable to the cooperatives were a source of considerable concern to cotton merchants, and ACCO was no exception. In the following letter Clayton expresses his anxiety that further government favors to the cooperatives might result in the substantial destruction of privately owned cotton firms.*

To Hon. Chester Davis

Houston, Texas
September 14, 1935

My dear Mr. Davis:

Having been abroad at the time the new cotton policy was decided upon, this is the first opportunity I have had of congratulating you[7] and the Administration on the wisdom of dropping the loan value to 10 cents, compensating the farmer by a bounty, or subsidy.

---

[6] An unsigned carbon copy of this letter to Jouett Shouse, president of the American Liberty League (1934–40), may be found in CP, ACCO.

[7] Letter to the Administrator of the Agricultural Adjustment Administration (1933–36), LS, RG 145, DNA.

I think the new plan is a great improvement over the old and I am very hopeful that it will enable the United States to export considerably more cotton during the present cotton season than in the season just finished.

You and Secretary Wallace[8] and your associates are entitled to great credit for your courageous action in this matter!

May I, however, call your attention to another very serious matter, of which I have just become aware, in connection with the marketing of the present crop?

I am informed that the Cotton Cooperatives will probably be accorded the right to act as Agents of the A.A.A. in adjusting and paying to their members the bounty due the producer under the new plan.

If this action should be taken, it would be almost equivalent to giving the Cooperatives a monopoly for the purchasing of the cotton produced by their members.

What is, perhaps, of greater significance, a principle would have been established, the logical extension of which would, in time, destroy what is left of the private cotton trade in this country.

I am familiar with the statute authorizing the Secretary of Agriculture to confer this favor on the Cooperatives. The last sentence in subsection (b) (1) of Section 10 of the Agricultural Adjustment Act, as amended, reads as follows:

> The Secretary, in the administration of this title, shall accord such recognition and encouragement to producer-owned and producer-controlled cooperative associations as will be in harmony with the policy toward cooperative associations set forth in existing Acts of Congress, *and as will tend to promote efficient methods of marketing and distribution.*

The [italics are] mine.

I do not think the Cooperatives, themselves, would deny that substantial destruction of the private cotton trade in this country, placing the distribution of the crop almost entirely in the hands of the Cooperatives would certainly not "tend to promote efficient methods of marketing and distribution," but that it would have the opposite effect.

This is not to be construed as a statement that the Cotton Cooperatives are inefficient in their business methods.

I merely want to say that such efficiency as the Cotton Cooperatives have achieved (and they have achieved much) is due largely

[8] Secretary of Agriculture Henry A. Wallace (1933–40).

to the influence upon them of the highly competitive struggle which is constantly going on between the Cotton Cooperatives and the private cotton trade.

Bring the struggle to an end by destroying the private cotton trade and the Cooperatives will inevitably drop into wasteful and inefficient methods.

You are familiar with the problems involved in distributing crops like cotton and wheat and I am sure you will agree that the highly efficient methods which have been developed and the very small toll which such service commands is due to the highly competitive nature of the business and once the competitive element is removed, even though the commodity should then be handled by a Government or by a Cooperative, the costs of distribution would certainly increase greatly.

I am sure it is unnecessary to remind you that the ranks of the cotton trade have been greatly thinned in the past three years. The fittest only have survived and in some cases even the fittest have felt compelled to give up the struggle rather than sit by and watch their capital dwindle away.

This last step, if it should be taken, of making the Cooperatives practically the exclusive Agents of the Government to distribute to Cooperative members Governmental favors, or benefit payments, will, in my opinion, so demoralize what is left of the private cotton trade that many of them will give up without a further struggle.

I beg of you to consider carefully the grave consequences which the proposed action would have.

Please believe me when I tell you that I am trying to look at this question from the standpoint of the best interests of the South as a whole. Somehow I cannot get very excited as to the consequences to my own firm by the proposed action, but I do feel that the interests of the cotton producers, the cotton trade, including my firm, and even the Cooperatives, themselves, will be best served by keeping cotton merchandising activities on the present highly competitive basis, where success or failure, whether to a private firm or to a Cooperative, is dependent wholly upon quality of service.

Of course, you are familiar with the fact that, with one or two exceptions, the membership lists of the Cotton Cooperatives signify merely that the people named on that list have, from time to time, sold some of their cotton to the Cooperatives. Our original conception of a member of a Cooperative as a man who assumed an obligation to market all of his cotton through the Association, usually by placing the cotton in a marketing pool, no longer holds good. The typical member today sells to and not through the Association and he sells to us and to other people when in his interest to do so. In other words, he now is completely a "free lance," with one or two exceptions, and the Cooperatives and the A.C.C.A. have become merchants rather than Cooperatives in the old time sense of the word. I think it is fair to the Cooperatives to say, in this connection, that the one element of their original nature which still remains, is the fact, as I understand it, that if they make profits, these profits are distributed on a patronage basis to those from whom they have purchased their cotton.

I want you to know that I am sending a copy of this letter to my good friend, Mr. E. F. Creekmore, Vice-President of the American Cotton Cooperative Association, for whom I have the greatest respect and admiration, as I would not want to write you on a subject of this kind without sending a copy to him.

> Sincerely yours,
>
> W. L. Clayton

§ *In a speech before the Harvard Business School on September 16, 1936, Clayton expounded his theory of capitalism.*

A SPEECH ON CAPITALISM

Recent world social and political trends arouse much speculation regarding the future of capitalism.[9] Even in this country one is often met with the statement that capitalism is on trial, or that capitalism has broken down. European happenings, of course, are common knowledge. But it may be seriously doubted if many of the persons who discuss the subject have thought very deeply concerning the elementary principles of capitalism. Even if the restatement of

[9] The speech, "A Business Man Looks at Capitalism," was delivered before the Harvard Business School at its Tercentenary Meetings, September 16, 1936, and printed in the *Bulletin* of the Harvard Business School Alumni Association, November 1936, pp. 51–56.

these principles should appear trite, it seems necessary to direct attention to some of them.

Capitalism in its broadest aspects is merely an economic instrument for salvaging from present enjoyment a part of the fruits of production for use in promoting human progress.

No modern nation can function without some form of capitalism.

All cultural and religious institutions, every means of transportation, communication and production are the product of capitalism.

Objection is often made that the profits which a capitalistic society takes from production lower correspondingly the standard of living of the workers.

Had man literally followed the slogan of this philosophy "Production for use," which is the antithesis of capitalism, he would still be living in caves, eating the uncooked flesh of wild animals and using their skins for clothing. Those who parade under this slogan may think they are loyal disciples of Lenin and Stalin, but they are mistaken. Russia is relentlessly capitalistic. The small group of overlords who direct the destinies of the Russian state see to it that a generous share of the production of Russian hands and of Russian machines goes into capital goods for such use as the masters of the Russian people may decree. Indeed, it is probably true that Russia, under state capitalism, has diverted a larger share of her production to capital growth than has been possible in countries of private capitalism. If economic systems were to be judged solely by the degree of abstinence and frugality which they compel, important as that is, there can be little question that the Russian system would take first place. Under that system, the masters of the people can and do determine how much of the fruits of production may be consumed and how much shall be used by the state for purposes of capital. Resisters pay with their liberty or their life.

In countries of private capitalism, annual additions to capital come wholly from private savings.

Mr. Carl Snyder, of the New York Federal Reserve Bank, in an article entitled "Capital Supply and National Well-being," in the June *American Economic Review*,[10] shows that the development of the United States from a group of straggling colonies, without capital resources, into the world's greatest industrial nation, with the highest real wages and the highest standard of living of any of the larger countries, has been due to a steady annual supply of new capital, coming very largely from industry itself and from the owners of industry. He further shows that there has been a constantly increasing

[10] Carl Snyder, "The Capital Supply and National Well-being," *American Economic Review*, June 1936, pp. 195–224.

product per capita, due principally to increase and improvement in mechanical equipment, for which an adequate supply of capital was indispensable; that constant industrial expansion has necessarily required a considerable body of workers, chiefly employed in the construction of new plant, new machinery, the development of new industries, new processes and the like. It naturally follows that when there is depression and an arrest in the capital supply, there is unemployment, falling most heavily on workers in the capital goods industries. Since the publication of Mr. Snyder's paper, Federal Reserve statistics have been issued showing that although industrial production in the United States is now running 108 per cent of the period 1923–25, the sixth year of the present depression in this country finds construction contracts running only 58 per cent of that period. Other authorities conservatively estimate unemployment in the United States in July, 1926 at nine million persons.

It may be reasonably questioned whether the United States can show any net capital accretion in the past six years. The supply of sterile gold is larger, but real wealth as measured in goods, buildings and implements of production, transportation, and communication, considering obsolescence and depreciation, is probably less.

It seems abundantly clear that full employment in this country depends upon an amply annual supply of new capital invested in new buildings, new machinery, new plants, new processes, etc.

If, therefore, it be true that the cultural and material progress of society rests primarily upon man's willingness to submit to some method of lessening present enjoyment in order to provide the means of such progress, it remains only to be determined what form of capitalism is best suited to this purpose.

Two forms which our own times make familiar and which are separated by the widest extremes of technique, are state capitalism as practiced in Russia and private capitalism as practiced, notably, in the United States and Great Britain. Between these two extremes are to be found sundry capitalistic systems, most of them embodying some of the characteristics both of state and of private capitalism.

The principles underlying Russian state capitalism are well known. In the beginning private businesses of all kinds were prohibited and the workers were paid in food, clothing and shelter instead of money. Today workers are paid in money and much of the retail distribution of goods is in private hands. The ownership and exploitation of all minerals, the ownership and operation of all means of transportation and practically of all manufacturing are in the hands of giant trusts owned and operated by the state. With all competition eliminated, it is a simple matter to so adjust prices as to insure large profits for use in the augmentation of productive facilities and for other capital purposes.

Under private capitalism, as has been shown, the necessary additions to capital are derived largely in the same way as under state capitalism, from the profits of industry. The difference is that under private capitalism such profits belong to and are reinvested by individuals and the corporations which they own.

The important point to bear in mind is that in both cases, the profit system supplies the means of compelling a degree of abstinence and frugality without which there would be no such thing as capitalism and consequently no such thing as progress.

Under private capitalism, the profits available for reinvestment are necessarily diminished to the extent of the personal expenditures of the capitalist. This, and not the profit itself, is the toll which society pays for administration of its productive and capital-gathering agencies. While in the aggregate this toll is perhaps not disproportionate to the service rendered, nevertheless, it is unfortunately true that in many individual cases it is exorbitant. The wasteful vanity-inspired expenditures of some rich people constitute a grave indictment of our system of private capitalism. A reasonable relationship between personal expenditures and large incomes is proper, nevertheless there is a limit beyond which luxurious gratification merely becomes vulgar and wilful waste, influencing the cost of living and exciting envy and resentment.

Under pure state capitalism there is no competition, and political and economic management proceed from a central brain. The foundations of such a system must rest on the complete surrender of individual liberty.

Under private capitalism, there is decentralization of decisions, and keen competition in every department of life, the theory being that the competitive process fits men and capital into those places where they serve best. In practice the system by no means operates perfectly but, unless too much interfered with, its failures are usually self-regulated before they have gone too far. Under private capitalism, commerce has a way of automatically purging itself of its own ills, if not too much bound and fettered by man's attempt to outwit natural laws.

Liberty of person, of speech and of press are possible only under a system of private capitalism. Swings to the left may be steps away from liberty. When statutory equality comes through one door, liberty goes out another. As some one has said, "Equality and Liberty can never be companions, for liberty accelerates differentiation." History abounds in examples of the complete obliteration of the shadowy line which separates political liberalism from political despotism.

In a material sense, state capitalism can never match private capitalism because of the inefficiency inherent in the centralization of power and decision.

It has been well said that nature failed to endow any man or group of men with sufficient wisdom to manage the economy of a large nation as well as it can be managed by the individuals themselves, and even if she had done so, the system would not breed their successors.

State capitalism smothers individualism, without which there can be no spiritual and little cultural progress. On this point Mr. John Maynard Keynes, the English economist, says: "But, above all, individualism, if it can be purged of its defects and abuses, is the best safeguard of personal liberty, in the sense that, compared with any other system, it greatly widens the field for the exercise of personal choice. It is also the best safeguard of the variety of life, which emerges precisely from this extended field of personal choice, and the loss of which is the greatest of all losses of the homogeneous or totalitarian state. For this variety preserves the traditions which embody the most secure and successful choices of former generations; it colors the present with the diversification of its fancy; and being the handmaid of experiment as well as of tradition and of fancy, it is the most powerful instrument to better the future." But it is not sufficient for preservation of private capitalism that it be merely the best system. Every nation has the right to select the economic system under which it will live. Because of ignorance, or abuse, or both, the best system may not be the one in which the majority of a people believe, and may have to give way to something else.

Throughout the world private capitalism is today undoubtedly on the defensive.

Looking for the causes of this development we shall probably find one of the prime reasons to be deep resentment at the swollen profits arising out of the war. Even had the recipients of such profits conserved and wisely invested them, abstaining from an undue amount of personal consumption, which unfortunately was not generally the case, society should and doubtless will take measures to prevent profit from war. Capitalists will be wise to recognize and assist this movement. The next step should logically be a realistic study of the underlying causes of war and the prevention of war.

The present world depression and unemployment are popularly laid at the door of private capitalism. This could provoke endless discussion. If any two words in the English language tell the major cause of the depression they probably are: credit abuse. Its hand-maiden, unbridled speculation, follows closely as a matter of course. Statutory measures have been taken calculated to prevent a recurrence of the latter, but if one wishes to avoid a shock it is not well to look too closely into credit trends during the depression. It is within the power of the state to regulate both credit and speculation.

It seems unquestionably indicated that a highly industrialized society, used to amortization of machinery and plant, must now make provision for human obsolescence and for recurring periods of unemployment. It does not seem too much to hope that when this responsibility has been placed jointly upon capital and labor some means will be found of lessening the frequency and shortening the duration of periods of unemployment.

It is said that the wastes of competition condemn the system of private capitalism. Where the individual enjoys complete or almost complete liberty of choice, there will always be some obvious material waste. Where there is no liberty of choice, there is little obvious waste, but the material and spiritual waste hidden in the centralization of power and decision is infinitely greater. If man's course is to continue upward, he must retain his liberty of choice and its consequent burden of responsibility. To surrender these to an overlord is to halt human progress.

It is said that the power of large capital is used improperly to influence government. Too often this has been true. Tariff lobbies have written our tariff laws. Human nature remaining unchanged, they will probably continue to do so until the tariff is taken out of politics. When that is done, the way to peace, the world's most pressing problem, should appear less difficult. Meantime, let not our condemnation of business lobbies blind our eyes to the presence of numerous other minority pressure groups just as demoralizing and dangerous.

It is charged that the power of large capital is used to crush competition, and to exploit labor and the consumer.

Unfortunately, at a former time, this charge had some basis, but if applied to the past quarter century little substance can be found in it. Today the larger the corporation, the more pitilessly does the searchlight of public opinion play upon it. There was a time when managers of large enterprises thought almost exclusively of the interests of stockholders, but the modern business administrator has a keen sense of responsibility toward competitors, labor and the public.

The possibilities of further improving the relations between capital and labor by stock ownership, profit sharing, decentralization of plant, closer contact, etc. are certain to be further explored by enlightened capital.

Agreements between competitors to curtail production or to fix prices, with or without government sanction, are to be condemned on economic grounds. What the world needs is more production at lower prices, bringing ever higher standards of living. Faulty distribution, due to clogged trade channels, arising from government tinkering throughout the world, and not overproduction is the thing that plagues us.

The private ownership of property is a permissive, not an inherent right. The right to bequeath property at death is of the same nature but hangs by a more slender thread. Both rights have been greatly abridged in the past few years.

If Congress should pass a valid law taxing all incomes and inheritances, above nominal amounts, at a rate of 100 per cent, the right of private property would be substantially at an end in this country. State capitalism would then take the place of private capitalism and the state would henceforth be under the compulsion of providing the indispensable supplies of new capital, without which progress would cease and the nation surely drift backward. It is well to recognize that we have already gone some distance on this road. There is no intent here to do more than call attention to the implications involved in this method of taxation.

The income tax is a fruitful and politically popular source of revenue, but its effect is to diminish the supply of new capital. It could probably be so constituted as to penalize waste and encourage capital accumulation and investment by an upward gradation of rates related to a scale of the taxpayer's personal expenditures beyond a certain level. If a man with an income of one million dollars can be induced by preferential tax rates to hold his personal expenditures below $100,000, society benefits from the reinvestment of the remaining $900,000. There is no danger that capital will accumulate too rapidly. Additions to capital provide new and improved means of production, reducing costs and raising the standard of living. A rich man's income, usefully reinvested year by year, constitutes not a charge on society, but a service to it. The nominal owner is in fact only a managing trustee. His continuance as administrator of the trust depends upon the quality of his services. The system automatically eliminates the great majority of unworthy or incompetent trustees.

Estate and inheritance taxes as now treated also draw heavily on capital supply. This can and should be corrected by excluding all such taxes from normal government revenues, and using them only for retirement of the public debt.

Ignorance lies at the bottom of most of the attacks on the American economic system. Two things are essential to its preservation: the great majority of the American people must be made to understand the system, and its abuses must be recognized and substantially corrected.

This accomplished, there is no doubt that our capitalism of the future will be of a nature to preserve and develop further that individual initiative, courage, and instinct for cultural and material progress which have made our country great.

§ *Clayton was critical of U.S. economic policies throughout the interwar period. In the following letter he scores American economic nationalism, charging it with responsibility for the rise of dictatorships in Europe.*

To Leon O. Wolcott

Houston, Texas
October 26, 1939

Dear Mr. Wolcott:

Thank you very much for your letter of the 23rd inst. enclosing copy of a speech which Secretary Wallace is to make before the Commonwealth Club in San Francisco on Friday, October 27th.[11]

I have read this speech very carefully.

You ask for my comments and I am going to give them to you frankly.

I think the Secretary is a little hard on the Old World and a little easy on the United States.

[11] Letter to the Assistant (1939–40) to Secretary of Agriculture Henry A. Wallace, LS, RG 16, DNA.

He says—"The rise of dictatorship is the result of Europe's failure to make its economic imperialism bring abundance to its masses, and order and stability to its trade."

In my opinion, the absence of abundance to the masses of Europe and the lack of order and stability in Europe's trade are due to a world-wide revolt against the free market and a world-wide embrace of the destructive principle of autarchie.

Unfortunately the United States has had a prominent place in this movement, if it has not actually lead it.

Our unique position in the world clothed us with enormous postwar responsibility.

Enlightened selfishness dictated that we should mobilize our great influence and our vast resources in an attempt to help the postwar world rehabilitate itself on the basis of economic sanity.

Instead we led the way in the direction of economic nationalism.

Dictatorship in Europe was an inevitable consequence.

The Secretary hit some good licks for soil conservation. I agree with him 100 per cent but I think we have to be careful not to confuse soil conservation and price fixing.

The Secretary apparently sees international trade in terms of imports which do not compete with things grown or manufactured in this country.

I disagree with this conception of international trade. I think it inevitably leads to a breakdown of the Democratic system of Government.

Please be assured that what I have said is with great respect and esteem for the Secretary and his opinions and is only offered because you have been good enough to invite my comments.

Sincerely yours,

W. L. Clayton

§ *Clayton's belief that a free Western Europe was crucial to a rational world economy was to be a touchstone for the economic philosophy which would guide his actions during his State Department career. He was among the first to advocate American involvement in Europe in order to prevent a totalitarian triumph there. On May 27, 1940, Clayton was one of fifty Houston business and pro-*

fessional men who sent to various members of Congress a telegram which called for amendment of the Neutrality Act "to permit the granting of credits by our Government to the Allies for the purchase of agricultural, mineral and industrial products of the United States."[12] In July 1940 he became associated with the Century Group, an informal organization of twenty-eight citizens dedicated to convincing the American people of the necessity of American intervention in Europe.[13] The two letters which follow indicate that while Clayton felt the best interests of the United States to be so threatened by Germany that he refused to trade with the Axis powers of Europe, he did not feel the same concern about Japan in Asia. In his only pre-Pearl Harbor reference to Japanese-American tensions he gave no indication that he expected conflict in the Far East.

To Sir Owen Chalkley

Houston, Texas
December 21, 1939

My dear Sir Owen:

Relying upon the friendly and cooperative spirit evidenced at the recent conference of Cotton Shippers with you and your associates, Messrs. Helm, Foster and others, I take the liberty of informing you of certain incidents which have apparently aroused in the minds of the Ministry of Economic Warfare in London some suspicion that my firm has been trading with Germany since the beginning of the present war.[14]

* * *

My partners and I had to make a decision immediately on the outbreak of the war on September 3rd as to our policy regarding any further business with Germany, because we found ourselves promptly in receipt of definite proposals for the sale of substantial quantities of cotton to Germany through intermediaries in neutral countries.

[12] Will Clayton to Jesse Jones, May 27, 1940, L, CP, Rice.
[13] Mark Lincoln Chadwin, *The Hawks of World War II* (Chapel Hill: University of North Carolina Press, 1968), pp. 44–45.
[14] An unsigned carbon copy of this letter to Sir Owen Chalkley, Commercial Counsellor of the British Embassy in Washington, D.C., may be found in CP, Cossitt Library (Memphis, Tennessee).

We had no hesitancy whatever in deciding for ourselves and all of our subsidiaries in South America and other countries that for the duration of the war we would, directly or indirectly, sell no more cotton to Germany. This meant that we would not knowingly sell cotton for shipment to any neutral country, the ultimate destination of which was Germany.

This decision has been scrupulously observed throughout.

We had some cotton in Germany at the outbreak of the war and we had some 2000 bales in Poland. In addition, some shipments of our cotton which sailed before the outbreak of war arrived in Germany. The largest shipment of this kind was about 3000 bales on the German Steamer Welheim which sailed from the United States on August 26th *for Liverpool*. This ship was not heard of for several weeks but eventually, some time in October, arrived in Bremen. The cotton was taken over by the German Government and since it was our property they are paying us for same.

From time to time we have discussed these various matters with the British Consul in Houston, Mr. Slaymaker, to whom we have given a copy of this letter, and have offered to him and to the M.E.W. in London to show our books and records at any time this may be desired. I now wish to renew this offer to you. I do this because we know that War is War and that precautions have to be taken which would not be justified in normal times.

Nevertheless, I do feel that the standing of my firm in this country, coupled with the fact that we are by far the largest single suppliers of raw cotton to Great Britain and France; that we have for twenty years been members of an old and highly respected English firm; that we maintain branch offices in France, in Egypt and in Paris, together with the fact that the distribution in Europe of the products of our extensive cottonseed oil milling interests is in the hands of Messrs. Henry Kendall & Sons of London, ought to go a long way in satisfying the M.E.W. of the good faith of our assurances.

Aside from our feelings about the war itself, we would be very shortsighted businessmen if we allowed for a moment the lure of some temporary profit in German business to cause us to jeopardize all these things.

Nevertheless, I must point out again, as I did in the Washington conference, that, in my opinion, adequate control of shipments of cotton to European neutrals can only be had in the countries of destination and not in the countries of origin.

I have presented this matter to you for the reason that I want you to have the facts in case any of these situations should come to your notice and for whatever use you may wish to make of the information and also because I feel that the purposes of your Government, insofar as they touch any business of our firm, will be better served if we clearly understand what your Government wants and if your Government clearly understands who we are, what we are doing, what our policies are, and to what degree the good faith of our policies may be relied on.

Apologizing for the necessary length of this letter and with every good wish, I remain,

Sincerely yours,

W. L. Clayton

To Hon. Alben W. Barkley

Houston, Texas
February 23, 1940

Dear Senator Barkley:

Permit me to say that I feel decidedly that the situation arising from the abrogation of the Commercial Treaty between Japan and the United States should be dealt with through our State Department and not by legislation.[15]

I am sure it is unnecessary to point out to you that American cotton would be the greatest sufferer from any serious interruption of trade between this country and Japan.

Sincerely yours,

W. L. Clayton

[15] An unsigned carbon copy of this letter to Alben W. Barkley, U.S. Senator from Kentucky (1927–49), may be found in CP, ACCO.

§ *On the eve of his entry into government service, Clayton was already considering the effects of World War II on post-war international trade. The following documents indicate the policy he advocated to strengthen American international relations.*

A SPEECH ON THE WORLD COTTON SITUATION

Throughout the world, catastrophic events have taken possession of men's minds.[16]

The awful drama of total war, snuffing out empires and human life and human liberty on a brutal and colossal scale, dominates the daily thoughts and lives of people everywhere. With a kind of fascinated horror, they read and listen and wonder.

It seems petty to talk about the world cotton situation when the world itself has exploded and is on fire.

It is more appropriate tonight to talk about the world revolution, its meaning to the United States, and, incidentally, its effect on cotton.

Please, therefore, do not be surprised if I exercise generously the license usually permitted a speaker.

Anything which must be discussed in terms of world trade is obviously just now in an extremely difficult, even almost tragic, position.

The naked truth is that world trade, in any normal sense, lies prostrate.

Cotton, as the fibre from which about three-fourths of the world's clothing is made, is peculiarly an article of international trade.

In consequence, the cotton producer and every part of the great raw cotton industry, wherever located, faces a dark and uncertain future.

The situation must, nevertheless, be studied in terms of today and tomorrow.

* * *

[16] The speech, "The World Cotton Situation," was delivered before the Cotton Research Congress at Waco, Texas, on June 27, 1940, and printed in the *ACCO Press*, July 1940, pp. 1–4.

This much seems certain: If the dictators win this war, the United States must embark on a preparedness program of colossal proportions.

That means, among other things, an economic, and to some extent, a political revolution in the United States.

The awful shriek of the dive bomber, and the relentless march of the armored tank across Flanders and France brought to an end in the United States the so-called good old days when we became great and rich and complacent and a little soft.

The dictators built thousands of these instruments of destruction. We shall probably build them by the tens of thousands, bigger and still more destructive. And a two-ocean navy.

A new order which we hate, but a new order just the same. How many of us now realize what this means to our way of life? We hear much about the fifth column and the Trojan horse. These are not first problems. We shall know how to deal with these things. Our first problem is to decide what our international policy is to be.

As to the Western Hemisphere, the decision is apparently already made that the Monroe Doctrine is to be literally and rigorously enforced.

Anything less than that would probably mean that before many years we would meet the same fate which has recently befallen half a dozen other democracies.

But to a layman the enforcement of the Monroe Doctrine throughout the Western Hemisphere, with Europe in the hands of the dictators, looks like much the biggest order we have ever undertaken.

It probably means military preparation sufficient to meet and overcome the combined offensive military resources of any three dictators in the world.

Our second problem is to obtain from competent authorities blueprints and specification of an integrated defense program.

Our third problem is to organize the job itself, and, what is of enormous importance, to study and plan the necessary re-adjustments in our domestic economy, and to some extent, of our political philosophy. Without such re-adjustment it will be impossible to carry out this gigantic enterprise.

It would be fatal for the American people to underestimate the sacrifices involved.

It has been said that Germany's preparation for war cost forty billion dollars.

If that is correct, the cost to us will be much more. Call it sixty billions of dollars, to be spent at the rate of 15 billions of dollars annually for four years.

This is a lot of money, but we have become used to billions in spending Government money.

The man in the street probably will say, "Well, it's a big price to pay, but I guess it's worth it, so let's get on with the job."

But does he realize that it is impossible to put any such sum of money into the building of such a colossal military machine without automatically and drastically lowering the standard of living for every one now enjoying a standard above the very minimum?

The labor, the materials, the shop room, the capital required in this huge undertaking cannot also be used to supply us with the luxuries to which we have become accustomed in recent years.

Fifteen billions of dollars exceeds all the wages and all the salaries paid out by all the manufacturing plants in the whole United States in any year of our history. It is twice the value of our entire agricultural production, employing about one-third of our population.

Taxes must be drastically increased not only for raising the money to pay the bill, but to forcibly take buying power away from the middle and upper income groups, so that they will be compelled to substantially lessen their demands on productive capacity, freeing it for use in the vital preparedness program.

We cannot pass on much of the cost of this program to our children and grandchildren because we have already asked them to assume twenty-five billion dollars of new debt contracted during the past eight years. Modern children have a way of becoming disobedient when pressed too hard.

Public control needs to be exercised over new construction of all kinds so that no unessential demands will be made on the economy which may slow down or impede the preparedness program.

Labor must make its contribution in longer hours; the job cannot be done on a forty hour week. Strikes, either of capital or labor, cannot be tolerated.

Drastic economies must be effected in the administration of all non-military departments of the Government. Relief appropriations must be scaled down and finally discontinued; political distribution of P.W.A. and W.P.A. projects must cease, in fact these agencies must disappear entirely when the preparedness program gets under way.

There will be work for every one who can work, and local communities must take care of those who cannot.

In short, under the new order, legislation for and by minority pressure groups, thinking only of their own selfish interests, must cease if we do not want to go the way of the other democracies.

The emphasis for National endeavor must be taken off reform and placed on production.

Leon Blum[17] concentrated on reform and social progress in France to the point where he almost caused the ruin of his country long before the German army set foot on French soil; meantime, in Germany they were tightening their belts, working sixty hours a week and building the most colossal fighting machine the world has ever known. Hitler's victories were won in preparation for the battle, long before a gun was fired.

Do I hear someone say that's all very well, but this is the United States and we are not going to turn the clock back in this country in any such way as that? All right, but if the people of this country fail to realize, and quickly, that the old order has perished; that playtime is over; that we must work and economize as our forefathers did, then they are not worthy of the pioneers who subdued the savages, cleared the wilderness, and laid the foundations of our glorious country.

I do not mean to speak disparagingly of any group of men. Some of the finest patriots in this country are in Washington working fifteen to eighteen hours a day, but isn't it clear that the necessary decisions in this crisis cannot be made in time by a body of men, many of whom have their eyes and ears glued to the next election?

If we go on as we are now going, won't we repeat the tragic experience of France and England, finding ourselves pitfully unprepared and at a time when it is too late?

The only safe course is to recognize that although we are still at peace, the future is so menacing that we must act as if we're already at war.

Our slow-acting democratic system of checks and balances is the best in the world for conditions of peace, but it cannot cope with the problems of modern warfare.

We would be much wiser to recognize now, rather than later, that we must make a temporary surrender of some of our cherished institutions if we wish to preserve any of them for future generations.

Now, turning from war to peace, such as it will be, let me give you a picture, as I see it, of the world trade situation if the dictators win this war, or even if it ends in a kind of stalemate.

Here it is:

A bankrupt totalitarian Europe, returning to peacetime industrial production at starvation wages and long hours, requiring vast quantities of foodstuffs, fibres and other raw materials.

[17] President of the Socialist Party of France; French Prime Minister and Finance Minister (March–April 1938).

Latin America, Africa, and Asia, warehouses bulging with raw materials, the sale of which was interrupted by war, requiring manufactured goods of all kinds.

The United States with practically all the gold in the world, a huge industrial plant, working at high wages and short hours, large stocks of cotton, wheat, and corn, and other raw materials, and a high protective tariff.

This picture may be over-simplified but it certainly suggests that South America, Africa, and Asia will swap their raw materials to Europe for cheap manufactured goods, and that the United States will be left holding its surpluses both of agricultural and industrial products.

This has for us both economic and political implications.

Not only are there strong ties of race, culture and language between South America and the old world, but the economy of the two areas is much more complementary than that of the United States and South America.

Europe needs all South American products; we need only a few.

Indeed, South America and the United States are competitors in the production for export of numerous commodities, principally cotton and grain.

Closer economic relations between Europe and South America will almost certainly be accompanied by closer political contact which will render more difficult our enforcement of the Monroe Doctrine.

On the other hand if South America, Africa and Asia preempt the European cotton market, for example, what are we going to do with our cotton surpluses?

These momentous questions are a ringing challenge to our realism, our vision and our ingenuity.

Nobody knows the answers, but the direction in which we should seek a solution of these problems may be suggested.

First, as to Latin America:

It is vital to the successful enforcement of the Monroe Doctrine that everything possible be done to draw closer the ties of trade and amity which already exist between Latin America and the United States.

There must be no waving of the big stick. We must play the commercial game fairly. We must stop subsidizing our trade where it comes into competition with theirs.

We should study the development of resources and commercial possibilities in Latin America with the view of bringing their economy into a more complementary relationship to ours, and we must be prepared to invest large sums of capital there to that end.

We must find ways and means of buying more Latin American goods, or risk redoubled totalitarian penetration there of an extremely dangerous character.

Now, as to our trade with Europe.

For years we have sold much more to Europe than we have bought from her.

When the war ends this trade unbalance will certainly be corrected. If this correction is accomplished by the simple process of shifting European purchases of raw materials from the United States to those countries willing to accept payment in goods, it will be a heavy blow to our entire domestic economy.

American cotton would naturally be the chief sufferer.

We cannot afford to surrender our European markets for cotton and other raw materials without exerting the utmost endeavors to hold them.

The only apparent way to hold these markets is to be realistic about the matter and be prepared to trade our goods for theirs, scrapping the tariff in the process. With so much of our industrial plant and labor diverted to military production, this suggestion may not to be so difficult or radical as it may at first appear.

Bi-lateral, or barter, systems of international trade are cumbersome and destructive of trade itself. If any substantial part of world trade has to be done on that system, it will result in a serious contraction of world trade and a regrettable lowering in the standard of living. A lowering in the world standard of living is inevitable in any case, but it could be relatively short-lived with international trade conducted on a multi-lateral or free exchange—gold settlement basis.

With an Allied victory, international trade could be re-established at the end of the war, on a free exchange—gold settlement basis, using a portion of the huge gold holdings of the United States to get the system working.

A victory by the dictators appears definitely to bar any such solution, nevertheless it should not be excluded as one of the possibilities.

The United States has consistently stood for the principle of multi-lateral trade as opposed to the so-called barter system, but if the rest of the world adopts totalitarian methods of trade, we will be compelled to conform if we wish to sell our surpluses. Barter means the swapping of goods for goods. Obviously, that can only be done in our case by setting aside the tariff in many particulars.

The alternative to this course is to so re-adjust our economy as to become almost entirely self-contained. This would involve such far-reaching and radical changes, accompanied by so severe a reduction in our standard of living that it is very doubtful if democracy would survive the shock. Just as one example, there would be the problem of the two million farm families in the United States whose production is normally required for export, not to mention the more direct and immediate effect on the South of the loss of our cotton exports.

Rather than undertake any such radical readjustment, would it not be much wiser to trade with the rest of the world in whatever way may be open to us, meanwhile working with every means in our power to restore international sanity as quickly as possible?

Fateful days lie ahead.

Days which will test our patriotism, our mettle, our ability to make sacrifices.

Every one of us, each according to his circumstances, will now have to make a contribution to the preservation of our way of life.

History must not say of us, "Too bad, but they couldn't take it!"

When the situation becomes somewhat clearer, doubtless the President of the United States will tell us what we face and will give us a kind of blueprint of what we must do to stop this juggernaut of destruction before it reaches the western world.

The American people are entitled to the whole story, bad as it may be. That they can chin whatever program has to be followed, when they understand it, let no man for one moment doubt.

To Hon. Henry A. Wallace

Houston, Texas
August 1, 1940

My dear Mr. Secretary:

I do not think our ideas are as far apart on the Latin-American situation as our too brief discussion the other day may have seemed to indicate.[18]

I favor giving Export-Import Bank[19] money and power to:

1) Make loans on commodities at conservative values, treating each country and each proposal on its own merits. This relationship may incidentally give us some voice in the disposition of such commodities, but to attempt to make this a condition of the loan would be resented.

Opportunities may even occur to cartelize the production and disposition of specific commodities. This can only be determined after very careful study and negotiation.

2) Make loans for the development of Latin-American resources and opportunities. The aim should be as far as possible to develop activities which will contribute to inter-American trade, communication and travel, particularly between the United States and Latin America. Much of the necessary capital can and should be furnished in Latin America, particularly that portion expended for local materials and labor.

I believe the above corresponds to the economic accord reached at Havana.[20] I am convinced that this program can be carried out on a sound and cooperative basis. I would like to stress that it cannot be sound unless cooperative in the sense that the country which we are attempting to assist does its full part according to its circumstances.

In addition to the above, much can and should be done on the

[18] Letter to the Secretary of Agriculture (1933–40), LS, CP, Rice.

[19] Established by the United States on February 2, 1934, to encourage foreign trade by financing exchange of goods through short- and long-term credits and loans.

[20] A series of economic agreements were reached in July 1940 by the twenty-one republics of the Pan-American Union meeting in Havana. These agreements provided for the unification of the American nations against totalitarian political or economic penetration of the Western Hemisphere.

cultural side, such as an exchange of professors and students, the establishment of travel bureaus for stimulating inter-American travel, etc. Much can and should be done in the readjustment of tariffs to maintain or increase inter-American trade. Sugar and flaxseed are the first commodities which occur to me.

Possibly on my next trip to Washington you may be able to give me a little time to go into some of these matters with you.

Very sincerely yours,

Will Clayton

II

GOVERNMENT SERVICE IN WARTIME

1940–1944

§ On October 15, 1940, Clayton accepted appointment as Deputy Federal Loan Administrator, a position which entailed responsibility for numerous Reconstruction Finance Corporation subsidiaries. With the abolition of the Federal Loan Administration, he assumed the post of Assistant Secretary of Commerce, but the job remained the same. Clayton's policy-making duties were much more limited and specific than was to be the case in the State Department; yet even in the Commerce Department Clayton's concern for the international economy would leave its mark on RFC policies. The documents which follow are representative of the type of policy formulation in which Clayton was involved during his years under Jesse Jones.

Memorandum on Synthetic Rubber

Washington, D.C.
February 21, 1941

Referring to another memorandum which I am handing you today on the rubber situation:[1]

Feeling confident that our existing supplies of new and "scrap" rubber now in the United States or on the way here are sufficient to carry us for two and a half to three years under war conditions even if our source of supply were cut off at once, I see no justification for our Government putting out money to experiment on the manufacture of synthetic rubber.

Synthetic rubber is still in the experimental stage in the United States except for a special product called "neoprene," now being manufactured by Dupont. "Neoprene" is at present too valuable a

[1] This memo is in RG 234, DNA.

59

product to be used for tires. If we should get into war, however, we could build plants for a modified type of "neoprene" suitable for tires, and these plants could be constructed in time to take care of us before our existing supplies of rubber were exhausted.

The principal rubber companies—Goodyear, Firestone, Goodrich and U.S. Rubber—are all experimenting on the production of synthetic rubber and will continue to do so.

I am continuing to explore the matter—talking with the principal rubber executives—learning all I can. It may be that we would be justified in building one small plant, say of 5,000 tons capacity or of putting up a few hundred thousand dollars to accelerate experimental operations with the view of greatly expanding production as soon as we know we are on safe ground, but I do not believe more than this is justified on any consideration.

W. L. Clayton

MEMORANDUM ON THE STRAIN ON OVERSEAS SHIPPING

Washington, D.C.
April 24, 1941

The attached memorandum shows 1941 estimated over-seas imports for Government and commercial purposes of the principal strategic materials.[2] Only those materials which run into large tonnages have been listed.

Not only are our estimated 1941 requirements almost double our normal imports; but most of these materials must be transported over great distances—the Far East, Africa, Australia, South America, etc.

Obviously, the strain on ocean shipping is very great.

We should now squarely face the question of priorities in shipping in order to stop the over-seas transportation of non-essentials.

[2] This memo is in RG 234, DNA.

A very important economy in shipping can be effected by compelling all ships from Australia, the Dutch East Indies, Straits Settlements, Philippines, China and Japan to load and unload at Pacific Coast ports instead of going through the Panama Canal to Gulf and Atlantic ports as most of them now do.

Another very important saving can be made by a discontinuance of inter-coastal ocean transportation.

A rough calculation indicates that if these two things are done, ships totaling about 1,000,000 dead weight tons could be released.

This would obviously throw a burden on rail transportation. About 600,000 carloads are involved, but most of this tonnage already involves a rail movement to the ports.

Measures to effect economies in the civilian consumption of these materials should also be undertaken.

W. L. Clayton

To Hon. Jesse Jones

Washington, D.C.
February 24, 1942

More and more, certain South American countries are increasing their *dollar balances* in the United States.[3] This is due to the fact that they are expanding production of strategic and critical materials which we are buying at high prices, and at the same time they are unable to spend their dollars here because of inability to secure the goods.

It is inevitable, I think, that this trend will continue while the war lasts.

I heard some time ago from a cotton man in Peru that they had been unable recently to sell dollars forward, say for April–May delivery. There were no buyers. Ordinarily, the Central Bank there affords a market for such transactions, but evidently is unable or

[3] This memo is in RG 234, DNA.

unwilling to do so any longer, due to the fact that they have too many dollars.

One aspect of this situation is that these Latin American countries will have a very large buying power in the United States at the end of the war.

Another aspect of it may be that as time goes on and they are unable to spend the dollars here, they may commence to hold back on the sale of the things that we are buying.

W. L. Clayton

§ *In 1942 President Roosevelt bestowed on the Board of Economic Warfare, headed by Vice-President Henry Wallace, the responsibility for acquiring and stockpiling strategic and critical materials, formerly a responsibility of the Reconstruction Finance Corporation. The RFC, however, was still paying for the purchases, with the result that ever-increasing friction between Wallace and Jesse Jones culminated in open feuding. Exasperated by this internal bickering, Roosevelt stripped both agencies of their authority in the field of strategic and critical materials and called on Leo Crowley to take charge of the disputed duties. The following documents relate to this interagency strife.*

MEMORANDUM OF CONVERSATION
WITH MR. MILO PERKINS

Washington, D.C.
April 20, 1942

Mr. Perkins[4] gave the following outline of his interpretation of the recent Executive Order:[5]

He stated that he construed the Order as giving BEW administrative control over purchases abroad of strategic and critical ma-

[4] Milo Perkins was executive director of the Board of Economic Warfare (1942–43). This memo is in CP, Rice.

[5] Executive Order 9128, April 14, 1942, shifted control of stockpiling and acquisition of strategic and critical materials from the RFC to the BEW.

terials, as well as all arrangements for increasing the production of same: That it is impossible to make any realistic separation between policy and operation.

To this end, Mr. Perkins made it clear that BEW wanted their people working alongside ours on all negotiations; that they wanted to do this on a partnership basis; that they would see to it that they assigned to us men who would be cooperative and do their best to help in negotiations.

I pointed out to Mr. Perkins that the business transacted by Metals Reserve, Rubber Reserve, and Defense Supplies Corporation[6] is now of great volume; that numerous contracts of one kind or another are being negotiated all the time; that these negotiations are by conferences, correspondence, and telephone; that in order to keep current on all such negotiations, it would be necessary for BEW to have one of their representatives working almost constantly with each man in our three companies charged with the responsibility of conducting negotiations.

I further pointed out to Mr. Perkins that after the high points in any contract are agreed upon, a memorandum covering such points goes to the lawyers who draw the legal contracts and that these lawyers themselves often negotiate points not covered in the original negotiation, and even sometimes negotiate changes in the original negotiations. Mr. Perkins stated that he felt BEW should also have their lawyers working alongside ours in order for the two agencies to come to an agreement on all such points.

Mr. Perkins stated that it was not their intention to form any new corporations under the Executive Order unless the existing corporations were not doing an adequate job.

Mr. Perkins stated that it was intended to have weekly meetings of the BEW.

I said to Mr. Perkins that I was only expressing my own personal view, but that my opinion is that following and checking the details of all our work here, as indicated by him would very substantially slow the work down. He indicated that if this should prove to be the case it would then be necessary for them to take over completely.

W. L. Clayton

[6] Subsidiary corporations of the Reconstruction Finance Corporation.

64

To J. C. Nichols

Washington, D.C.
July 21, 1943

Dear Clyde:

I have your letter of the 17th and want to assure you[7] how very much I appreciate your interest in the recent controversy here.[8]

No doubt the war will end some day but the battle of Washington perhaps never. As you know, I came without any political ambitions and having acquired none during my three years stay, I can look all these fellows in the eye and tell them where to go.

Hoping you keep well and that everything is going as well with you as could be expected in these difficult times, I remain

Sincerely yours,
W. L. Clayton

To Hon. Jesse Jones

Washington, D.C.
July 24, 1943

Dear Mr. Jones:

During the three years I have been associated with you here, first as Deputy Federal Loan Administrator and then as Assistant Secretary of Commerce, my duties have been related principally to the importation of strategic and critical materials for the war.[9]

[7] President of Clyde Nichols Investment Company of Kansas City, Missouri. An unsigned carbon copy of this letter is in CP, TL.

[8] J. C. Nichols to Will Clayton, July 17, 1943, LS, CP, TL. Nichols commends Clayton for his part in the RFC–BEW controversy.

[9] Letter to Jesse Jones, LS, CP, Rice.

Since, by the President's order, this work has now been completely transferred to another government agency, I see no need to remain longer.

Please, therefore, accept my resignation as Assistant Secretary of Commerce, Chairman of the United States Commercial Company and the Rubber Development Corporation, President of War Damage Corporation, Vice President and Trustee of the Export-Import Bank of Washington and Director of Defense Supplies Corporation.

If you or Mr. Crowley wish me to do so, I shall of course be glad to remain for a reasonable time to help work out the new arrangement relating to the importation of materials for the war.

I am deeply grateful for the opportunity you have given me of performing some slight service in the war and for the unfailing courtesy and consideration you and your associates in the Department of Commerce and the RFC and its subsidiaries have always shown me.

I leave with the greatest admiration for you and the RFC family. Under your direction the RFC has demonstrated how efficiently a government agency can be operated.

With much appreciation and every good wish, I remain

Sincerely your friend,
Will Clayton

§ In December 1947 Clayton was interviewed by his daughter Ellen concerning his government work. The following excerpt from that interview records Clayton's recollections of his years in the RFC.

A STATEMENT ON PRECLUSIVE
AND STRATEGIC PURCHASES

You can't make hard steel without tungsten.[10] The only place Germany could get it was in Portugal and Spain and the War and State Departments thought it was important to keep the Germans from getting it. We bid tungsten in Portugal up $20,000 a ton so as to make it so high the Germans couldn't afford it. In Portugal we bought all the sardines they could pack just to keep Germans from buying them.

There were only 3 places where Germany could buy tungsten. They were Portugal, Spain, and Turkey. It was only in those places that we ran the price up high.

In the summer of 1940 when France fell Congress passed a law enlarging the powers of the RFC, authorizing it to act as purchasing agent for critical and strategical materials for defense. Under it were organized the Metal Reserves Corp., the Rubber Reserve Corp., Defense Supplies Corp. to buy everything the Metal and Rubber corporations didn't buy. I was in charge of the foreign operations of these corporations in their buying.

Then the BEW was organized with Henry Wallace at the head of it and we had an awful mess. BEW claimed Mr. Jones and I were too interested in making good trades and that we tried to buy too cheap, and the BEW didn't care what it paid. Then the BEW was authorized to do all the buying but it didn't have any money so we had to sign the contracts they negotiated. It was terrible!

The BEW was organized in 1943 partly for political reasons, in order to throw a sop to leftwingers by letting them use buying or purchases abroad for social and economic ideas they wanted to spread. Also Roosevelt hated to fire anybody so he put one agency over another to regulate it; he—instead of firing—just kicked 'em

[10] This interview with Ellen Clayton Garwood took place in December 1947.

upstairs and gave them a bigger title. Roosevelt stepped on Hull's toes with Wallace in the BEW and Hull read the riot act and then Roosevelt had the BEW modified so that Wallace would not take over the duties of Secretary of State. If Jesse Jones had acted forthrightly he could have got the thing adjusted—the difficulties between BEW and Department of Commerce—at the time.

One quarrel was because the BEW raised a big hullabaloo because we didn't act promptly and carry out its crazy ideas about making rubber from cryptosecia plantations in Haiti. It's true the cryptosecia is a rubber bearing plant, but it never gave a ton of rubber so far as I know, for it didn't do well in Haiti.

Before we got into the war I was buying, in August, 1941, all sorts of stuff from the Philippines, Malay Straits, Dutch East Indies, Australia, North Caledonia. We couldn't get enough ships and the stuff was piling up out there. Rubber and tin were two very critical things—coming over the Pacific, going thru Panama Canal, going up East Coast by ship. A . . . man (Harvard professor William Elliot)[11] at the War Production Board was working on me in August to get all this stuff in. We were sure to get into war with Japan any time and we had to get all this material in before. To do this we decided to have them unload the ships on the Pacific Coast which would save a 30 day trip but cost more. We then had to ship the West Coast by rail—rubber to Akron, tin to Pittsburgh. Then those West coast ports got blocked with these things, because the railroads couldn't take them away fast enough. The next 6 months this transportation cost 30 to 50 million dollars extra. You see I had to change the routing of all those ships to get them to unload at Pacific ports. But we got these things into the U.S., and when war broke out we were caught up on practically everything from those sections.

Anything that was susceptible to handling by the couriers of the Underground in Switzerland, France, and Portugal we got out that way. For instance—those little jewelled watch movements from Switzerland during the war—they came by Underground, and we had a time with those; we did it through the Treasury.

The BEW made a contract with Sengier—the head of the Belgian "Minerva" living in N.Y. who was running the Belgian Congo Co., a monopoly in copper—to increase his production by 20,000 tons a year. Sengier had been selling all his copper to England. Mr. Bridgman,[12] a mining engineer working with me in the Commerce

[11] William Y. Elliot, Harvard professor of government, served in the Office of Production Management in 1941.

[12] G. Temple Bridgman, executive vice-president of the Metals Reserve Company (1941–44) and deputy Surplus War Property Administrator (1944).

Department (when I was Assistant Sec. of Commerce then) said, "We can't sign that contract. I'm convinced we could make a better deal, because this will cost the government millions of dollars."

So I asked the BEW if they would mind if I tried to get Sengier to make a better deal. Sengier came over—the toughest fellow to get hold of in negotiation: he talked and talked. He came into my office and said, "Just what do you want, Mr. Clayton?" I started to tell him and he started to get up and he said, "You're wasting your time and mine, too."

"Evidently," I said. "I thought we could help your country and give it back its freedom. We need copper desperately. You won't lose anything and you might make some money."

He sat down again and I got him to make a deal which saved our government 2 or 3 million dollars. I went to New York later and saw him. His company had 5000 tons of copper stored at Lobito for the French Government, on its way to France from Chile when France fell to the Germans. Thinking the British would seize this copper, the French ship put the copper in a warehouse at Lobito. We tried to buy the copper from Vichy, but they wouldn't sell. We said, "You can't use it. We'll pay you the present market price." But they refused. "Let us have it and we'll try to replace it at the end of the war when you can use it." But they said they were going to keep it in the warehouse at Lobito.

Well, some of our smart boys got next to the warehouseman at Lobito, bought 5000 tons of zinc ores to be loaded at Lobito, and when the ship came they loaded her with the 5000 tons of copper instead. I didn't know it until a week before the ship was due to arrive in N.Y. These men then told me and said "We want you to break the news to Sengier, because he'll set up an awful howl and discharge his man. Tell him to take it philosophically and we'll give the copper back at the end of the war, or give them the price copper is selling for at the end of the war." I looked Sengier in the eye and told him. He didn't change his expression or bat an eye. "You stole it," he said.

We had to get graphite and mica in early 1941, to be ready in case of war. Mica is necessary to make radios, and they had to have so many of them, you know, on every plane—millions of them. And graphite is also a catalyst. Mica is found in India and Brazil, but graphite comes chiefly from Madagascar, which was ruled by the French.

At this time France was under the Petain[13] government, and the British—in the summer of 1941—had Madagascar under a tight

[13] Marshal Henri Petain, Premier of Unoccupied France (1940–44).

blockade. There were half a dozen importers in N.Y. who had contracts for the purchase of mica and graphite from Madagascar, but because of the British blockade, they could not get the stuff. So these importers turned their contracts over to the government. The suppliers in Madagascar were willing. Then we, the government, got in touch with the British.

I remember so well I had a bunch of men from the British Embassy in Washington for lunch at the Carlton Hotel and I told them the story of how we wanted to get out this graphite and mica from Madagascar. I asked them if they wouldn't let an American ship go in there and bring it out, and you know these fellows wouldn't say a word whether they would or wouldn't. They were mum. Stupid! Well, anyway they wouldn't talk. So I just said:

"All right, we're going to run a ship in there with the American flag and if you fire on us there's going to be war!"

You know what they did? They just smiled!

We had a time getting a ship—thought we were never going to get one. Finally we got a ship in N.Y. called "The Lone Star," a slow ship—10 knots. And we sent it in. But by the time she was loading in Madagascar, our government was having serious trouble with Vichy. Vichy was doing everything the Germans told them, you know. So in the midst of this loading, I had a call from Secretary Hull. He told me, "You'd better get that ship out of port. It looks like we might have war with Vichy!"

That put me on the spot in 2 ways—the ship was only half loaded and we didn't know how to get a message to her. If we sent it thru regular channels we were afraid it would be intercepted and the government in Madagascar wouldn't allow the ship to leave. So we went to the Navy and got them to send the message for us. It went from ship to ship. When the Captain of the Lone Star received it, he pulled out without any formalities, any notice; just took up his anchor and slipped out, and three Americans were left ashore.

Well, after that our relations with Vichy were smoothed out somehow and we were told we could send in another ship to load. Again we had a hard time getting one, but we finally got a ship, an old one, called the Western Something, and she went in to load the rest of the graphite and mica. She also picked up the 3 American sailors that had been left behind. Oh yes there was a soldier of fortune there at the time, a kind of roustabout, a ne'er-do-well. He was a writer. At least he had been there writing but he'd about had enough and he wanted like everything to come home. He begged the Captain to take him, but the Captain told him it was impossible, he wouldn't know what to charge him for his passage, besides he didn't know when they'd get to N.Y.—it might take 90 days, they might not get there at all. But the fellow kept begging him. He said he'd pay a dollar a day, so the ship got along, going 10 knots, and finally one engine gave out so she had to put into Capetown for repairs. While she was there, we got into the war!

We had a terrible time with that ship. The army was clamoring for the graphite and mica, had to have it right away, but the ship couldn't proceed by herself because the waters around there were infested with German submarines. We went to the Navy and asked them for a convoy—two destroyers, or whatever they could give us even two destroyers for that slow a ship. So finally we got 3 other ships—15 knot jobs—to go to the Western ——— and take off the cargo and bring it in. That's the way it finally got here!

§ Clayton foresaw that the end of the war would provide a great opportunity for liberalization of American trade policies, provided the American public could be properly educated. Consequently, in 1943 he turned his attentions to preparation for post-war economic policy planning, writing on July 26 that "the disastrous results of the policy we followed after the first world war are so fresh in the minds of people that I cannot help feeling we will avoid most of those mistakes, although doubtless making others."[14] Clayton hoped to minimize the "other" mistakes by mature consideration of post-war economic alternatives before the war ended. He believed that international economic and financial relations were the key to America's post-war economy. Especially significant to revisionist historians is Clayton's repeated emphasis on the need for foreign markets to absorb American surpluses.

To Paul G. Hoffman

Washington, D.C.
May 14, 1943

Dear Paul:

I am so engrossed in numerous meetings, preparation of papers, etc. in connection with the Food Conference which convenes at Hot Springs on Tuesday, that I regret to say that it will be impossible for me to attend the CED meeting in New York tomorrow and Sunday. I appreciate very much the special invitation you were good enough to extend to me.[15]

The more I think of the matter we discussed in New York, the more I feel convinced that the CED is making a mistake to relegate the question of post-war international economic and financial relations to a position of comparative unimportance.

---

[14] Will Clayton to Lamar Fleming, July 26, 1943, L, CP, TL.

[15] An unsigned carbon copy of this letter to the President of the Studebaker Company of South Bend, Indiana, and Chairman of the Committee for Economic Development may be found in CP, TL. Clayton was the U.S. delegate to the United Nations Conference on Food and Agriculture at Hot Springs, Virginia, in May 1943.

In my opinion, post-war employment by private enterprise depends upon the adoption of adequate measures at the peace conference to provide for peace and for an expanding world economy.

So far as the United States is concerned, and the same of course applies to England, we are much more dependent than ever upon world markets.

In a recent speech you said that private enterprise must employ 56,000,000 people in the post-war period and produce 135 billion dollars worth of goods and services.[16]

I agree with this statement.

It will be impossible to put so many people to work and produce such a huge volume of goods and services unless we employ substantially our total productive capacity.

This means that we will produce much more of many things than we can possibly consume.

At the end of this year we will be producing:

100,000 airplanes annually against 6,000 pre-war,
600,000,000 pounds of magnesium against 6,000,000 pre-war,
2,000,000,000 pounds of aluminum against 325,000,000 pre-war,

and many other things in the same or greater proportion.

We are all familiar with the fact that thousands of war plants will have to be converted to civilian production. Many of these plants are entirely new; some of them employ many thousands of people, for whom entire cities have been built, with homes, schools, churches, streets, sewerage, water, etc. Some way must be found to shift these plants to civilian production, otherwise they must be abandoned and their employees resettled elsewhere.

All of this means that we must find great new markets here and abroad to absorb our post-war production.

When peace comes, vast areas abroad must be reconstructed. ... others should be developed in order to raise the standard of living, which in itself creates new markets.

There will be many opportunities abroad for the investment of American capital. This capital will almost surely be in the form of goods, not money. Hence, every dollar of such capital will help put our people to work on peace time goods.

But the investment of American capital abroad would be wholly inconsistent with a policy of shutting out imports at home. If we

[16] Speech before the Chamber of Commerce of the State of New York on March 4, 1943.

are to invest and sell abroad, we must be prepared to buy abroad. Trade is a two way street, wherever you find it.

If approximately full employment can be maintained at good wages, our standard of living will certainly show a gratifying advance, particularly in the middle and lower brackets where most needed. In consequence, we should be able to absorb larger imports without serious injury to any single American industry and with great benefit to our economy as a whole. Such increased imports will contribute to a higher standard of living here and will establish the means of payment for the exportation of our own surplus production.

My conclusion is that the most careful and intelligent plans on a community or industry basis can easily prove to be of little if any help in providing a satisfactory level of employment if we make a mess of our international economic and financial relationships as we did in the last peace conference and during the interwar period.

At the last meeting in New York you spoke of the fact that it would take a long time to make the necessary investigation of this subject and would cost more money than the CED had to spend on it.

I don't think it would take very long and I don't think it would cost very much to make the necessary study; in fact, most of the work has already been done and the results are available.

I have had to dictate this in a great hurry in order to get it in Carroll Wilson's[17] hands before he leaves in the next two hours.

I am not at all satisfied with it but was anxious to send you something.

With best wishes for a good meeting,

Sincerely yours,
W. L. Clayton

[17] Secretary of the Committee for Economic Development.

A SPEECH ON WORLD TRADE

It may be interesting to speculate for a moment on what history will say about our part in this war.[18]

Judging by the familiar criticisms which we hear on all sides, one might expect that much attention will be given to the mistakes, the extravagance, and the confusion here at home.

But since history has a way of measuring great events by objectives and results, it is probably safe to predict that these delinquencies, typical of every war, will play a very minor role in the story of this one.

Instead, heavy emphasis is almost certain to be laid on the wise timing of those early critical decisions which placed us in a position of semibelligerency; on the bold conception of the magnitude of our war production job, once we were in the war; and on our immense output of the implements of war.

Failure in any one of these crucial steps could have lost the war for us.

The production of goods and services in the United States promises to reach an annual rate of $200,000,000,000 by the end of this year. This is double the 1940 production.

Stated differently, we are now expending more energy exclusively in the prosecution of the war than was put forth 4 years ago to keep the entire peacetime economy of the country going.

Our war production is already 50 percent greater than that of all the Axis countries combined, despite their many years of preparation.

This huge production, added to that of our allies, guarantees that the fighting forces of the United Nations will, in due course, completely overwhelm our enemies everywhere and dictate the terms of peace.

The conclusion of peace will find the United States in a world position of vast prestige and power, the full significance of which is perhaps better understood abroad than it is here.

[18] This speech, entitled "America's Stake in World Trade," was delivered before the Thirtieth National Foreign Trade Convention in New York, October 25, 1943, and printed in the *Congressional Record*, vol. 89, 78th Cong., 1st sess. (1943), pp. A4620–A4621.

One wonders what history will say of our part in the peace.

Will we be big enough to meet heavy responsibilities which only we can shoulder?

Impelled by the events of the last 4 years, a revolution has taken place in the thinking and understanding of the American people regarding the physical position of the United States in this shrinking world.

Most of us now recognize that the two oceans which have served as a basis for so much of our complacency no longer afford adequate protection in the modern world.

Popular polls show that we are now prepared to collaborate with neighbors who share our ideas regarding peace and the rights of others.

It is perhaps natural that the popular conception of this collaboration centers in political and military arrangements.

But it is quite impossible to obtain collective security through military arrangements if economic warfare as it was waged throughout the world in the inter-war period is to continue.

As someone has well said: "The greater the economic significance of political frontiers, the greater the danger of war; and the greater the facility with which all nations may secure through commerce the basic necessities of national life, the greater the prospects of peace."

This expression finds full recognition in the declarations of the Atlantic Charter and the lend-lease agreements.

These documents unequivocally declare that the trade and raw materials of the world shall be accessible on equal terms to all states, great or small, victor or vanquished; that all forms of discriminatory treatment in international commerce shall be eliminated; and that tariffs and other trade barriers shall be reduced, to the end that improved labor standards, economic advancement, and social security may be had for all.

That this platform is essential to world peace and a rising standard of living no one can successfully deny; that it will be vigorously opposed by selfish minority pressure groups here and elsewhere is unfortunately certain.

The great danger to democracy now, as in the past, is in the pressures of organized minorities.

To understand the broad over-all economic problem which will face the world at the end of this war it is necessary to examine the present situation.

The world today is passing through the greatest economic expansion of all times.

With the possible exception of certain Asiatic areas, employment and production are everywhere at an all-time high.

Throughout the British Empire everyone is working.

In Germany ten or twelve million foreign workers have been brought in.

The occupied countries in Europe must be working to capacity.

In Mexico, Central and South America, Africa, and the Middle East—areas which supply a great part of the exportable minerals and raw materials of the world—production and employment are at peak level.

In the United States we will soon have about 65,000,000 people employed, including the armed forces. This is 20,000,000 more than we employed in 1940.

Throughout the world millions of women are now working for the first time in factories and offices.

And still shortage of manpower is almost universal.

The output of the world's mines, factories and farms was never greater.

War devours all and calls for more.

In war only military frontiers obstruct the free movement of goods; mere political frontiers have little or no significance.

Will the coming of peace re-endow political frontiers with the same economic significance they held in 1939?

If the answer is "Yes," it probably means another war in the next generation; it certainly means that the world must expect, after a period of reconstruction and reconversion, a great shrinkage in economic activity, back to or below the 1939 levels.

In terms of our domestic economy this would give us an unemployment problem more serious than that of 10 years ago.

As has been pointed out by Paul Hoffman, chairman of the Committee for Economic Development, if we are to avoid serious unemployment in the post-war period, we must plan for a production of goods and services of at least $135,000,000,000, or, say 35 percent, over the 1940 rate.

To do this, we must operate our productive facilities at or near capacity. This will inevitably mean that we will produce a great deal more of some things than we can consume and a great deal less of other things than we require.

To dispose of this surplus production, great new markets must be developed abroad. To receive payment for our goods, we must import more than ever before, and must invest abroad more than ever before.

There is already a revival of the talk so prevalent at the end of the last war of the competition of foreign labor, working at starvation wages, and of the necessity of protecting our high standard of living.

Neither real wages nor the standard of living is raised by keeping goods out; both are improved by letting goods in as payment for other goods which labor and capital produce in surplus.

If a substantial part of the world's millions of new workers can be kept employed producing and distributing peacetime goods, a rising standard of living in the post-war period becomes automatic.

This is an attainable end to which all nations must work.

There will be much that must be done.

Great areas must be reconstructed. Other areas must be developed, opening up resources, raising living standards, and providing new markets.

This will call for substantial capital exports by the richer countries.

Unless we are prepared to take our proper part in this program, our own domestic employment problem will become acute.

No amount of post-war planning on a national level will provide productive employment in private undertakings for our millions of new workers if the rules surrounding the international exchange of goods continue so restrictive as to deny buyers the means of payment across political frontiers.

The world has now shrunk to a point where we can no longer sit in a small corner of it hugging our insularity and our riches to ourselves, unobserved and unmolested.

We have to decide now whether we will take our proper place in the world, politically and economically. The alternative is to turn our country into an armed camp, police the seven seas, tighten our belts, and live by ration books for the next century or so.

This is no preachment of imperialism; no one thinks any longer in terms of territorial aggrandizement.

It is simply a choice we cannot avoid—a choice made inevitable by the world revolution through which we are passing.

America's stake in world trade means much more for us than a great expansion in peacetime production and employment; it represents a great new hope of peace for America and the world.

To Dr. Calvin Hoover

Washington, D.C.
November 27, 1943

Dear Dr. Hoover:

I am glad to see that you are undertaking for the Committee for Economic Development, of which I am a Trustee, a study of the importance of foreign trade in our post war employment problem.[19]

I have made the point at meetings of the Trustees of the Committee that the best laid plans for employment on an industry, community and national basis may prove futile if the post war policies of the United Nations are such as to restrict or discourage the international exchange of goods.

Our own tariff-free domestic market is so large that we produce certain commodities on a scale which cannot be approached in any other part of the world. We have developed a peculiar genius for combining capital, management and labor in the mass production of goods. As a result, in spite of extremely high wages, we can produce many manufactured articles cheaper and better than anywhere else in the world.

It would be very short-sighted to narrow and limit our export opportunities in these industries by a policy which withholds from our prospective customers the opportunity to pay us for the products which they eagerly wish to purchase from us.

Nearly 20 billions of dollars have been put into Government war plants, most of which can be converted to peace time production. I have seen some of these plants and they are magnificent—a great improvement over factory construction of 15 to 20 years ago.

If we take full advantage of our opportunity for the mass production of goods in the post war period, it inevitably means that we will turn out a great deal more of some things than our people can possibly buy or consume. For markets for such surplus production we will have to look abroad. The markets are certainly there if we have the intelligence to develop them.

If we are to find work for some 56 or 57 million people in the

---

[19] An unsigned carbon copy of this letter to Calvin Hoover, Professor of Economics and Dean of the Graduate School of Arts and Sciences at Duke University (1938–48), may be found in CP, TL.

post war period, we must export more, import more and invest more abroad than ever before in our history.

Within two or three years after the war we should be exporting and importing 15 to 20 billion dollars worth of goods. Even the imports give substantial employment to our people because more than fifty cents out of each dollar paid by the consumer for imported goods is spent in this country—dock labor, transportation, handling, overhead, rents, etc.

I take the liberty of presenting these random thoughts to you for whatever they may be worth.

Sincerely yours,
W. L. Clayton

§ On February 19, 1944, the Surplus War Property Administration was established under the jurisdiction of the Office of War Mobilization; from February 21, 1944, to December 20, 1944, Will Clayton served as administrator of the new agency. "The primary purpose of the Clayton appointment was to have him set up a policy making organization which would coordinate and direct other agencies in the disposal problem."[20] *Once his wife had agreed to stay on in Washington, Clayton turned his attention to organizing the SWPA.*

To Hon. Jesse Jones

Washington, D.C.
January 22, 1944

Dear Mr. Jones:

Justice Byrnes called me over to his office Thursday and told me that he did not want me to leave government service but was very anxious to have me take over the job of disposal of surplus

[20] Ross Pritchard, "Will Clayton: A Study of Business-Statesmanship" (unpublished Ph.D. dissertation, Fletcher School of Law and Diplomacy, 1955), p. 177.

government property, that he had discussed the matter with the President that morning who was also very anxious to have me do this, etc.[21]

I told Justice Byrnes that I had promised my wife to go back home and that the matter would have to lie between the President and my wife. When I got home that night, Sue had received a very nice note from the President saying that he wanted to draft me, etc., as a result of which I appear to be drafted.

Justice Byrnes thinks we over here ought to have the job of disposing of government plants, equipment, machine tools, raw materials, etc., and he thinks that this should be done by a new corporation having only that specific job to do. He understands that we cannot organize any new corporations but thought that we could properly change the name, purposes, etc. of an existing corporation, and I confirmed to him that this could be done.

Justice Byrnes made the point that this country was caught unprepared for war and that we should not be caught unprepared for peace, with which I fully agree. This means that we ought to start organizing things in order to be ready as there is a lot of preparatory work to be done especially with the plants, equipment and machine tools.

My idea is that we should have two executive vice presidents of the corporation, one in charge of plants, equipment and machine tools, and the other in charge of everything else.

I have in mind Tom McCabe[22] as the best man for the first job and Temple Bridgman[23] for the second job. I have already discussed the matter with Temple who is agreeable.

If you agree, I will get Tom down here and see if I can sell him the idea of coming in with us and handling the plants, equipment and machine tools.

I think we ought to have Hans Klagsbrunn[24] as vice president and general counsel for the corporation. He strikes me as a very able man and of course is more familiar with the plants, equipment and machine tools than anyone else.

Sincerely yours,
W. L. Clayton

[21] Letter to Jesse Jones, LS, CP, Rice.
[22] President of Scott Paper Company of Chester, Pennsylvania.
[23] Executive vice-president of Metals Reserve Company (1941–44).
[24] Executive vice-president and general counsel of the Defense Plant Corporation (1940–45); assistant general counsel of the Reconstruction Finance Corporation (1933–45).

§ *In his capacity as Surplus War Property Administrator, Clayton became more convinced than ever of the necessity for disposing of American surpluses by rationalization of the world economy through liberalized trade—a prerequisite, Clayton argued, for world peace.*

A SPEECH ON THE ECONOMIC REQUIREMENTS OF PEACE

It has been well said that we can't win the war on the assembly line, but that we could lose it there.[25]

This is just another way of saying that modern wars are fought with machines.

Other things being equal, the nation which can out-produce its enemy will be victorious. We knew this in the tragic days of 1940 when France fell, and when everybody wondered how long England could stand alone against the Germans with their highly mechanized divisions.

At last, Pearl Harbor shocked us into a full realization of the grave peril which we faced, both from the East and from the West. We then determined that our war production plans would be pitched on a scale so vast that history could never accuse us of "too little too late."

The result is nothing less than a miracle of production.

The fighting men who will win this war for us will be fully supplied with everything needed to do the job.

There are so many imponderables in war that if there is to be enough of everything at the time and place needed, there will inevitably be a great deal too much of some things. In the end, there will be too much of everything.

Surpluses had already commenced to appear in some volume several months ago; so much so that it was deemed wise to set up some machinery for dealing with the entire surplus problem.

[25] This speech was delivered before a meeting of Freedom House, April 30, 1944, in New York City, and a copy may be found in Baruch Papers, Princeton University. Freedom House, founded in 1942, was an anti-Axis rallying point and information center in New York City.

Accordingly, on February 19, the President issued an Executive Order establishing the Surplus War Property Administration, and providing for a Surplus War Property Policy Board to assist and advise the Administrator.

This new agency has the responsibility of the general direction and supervision over the handling and disposition of surplus war property.

It will not actually sell anything.

The Executive Order names the Reconstruction Finance Corporation as the disposal agency for capital goods, Procurement Division of the Treasury for consumers' goods, except food, the War Food Administration for food, and the Maritime Commission for ships and maritime property.

It will be the function of the Surplus War Property Administration to sit between the owning agencies on the one hand—principally the War and Navy Departments—and the disposal agencies on the other hand; to see that they work effectively together, and to fix the policies for the disposal of surplus war property.

A very intensive study was made of this whole problem by Mr. Bernard M. Baruch[26] and Mr. John M. Hancock[27] whose findings are set out in the Baruch-Hancock report.[28]

The Executive Order establishing the Surplus War Property Administration was a consequence of that report.

For sound economics, realistic social philosophy, and good politics, the Baruch-Hancock report is considered by many to be the best manual on post-war planning which has yet appeared. We intend to use it as a guide in the disposal of surplus war property.

Following its recommendations, we shall press for the declaration and disposal of surpluses while the war is on; we shall use the regular channels of trade as far as practicable, avoiding sales to speculators and promoters; we shall see that all businesses, great and small, have equal access to surpluses; and we shall avoid actions which will encourage the growth or maintenance of monopolies.

The general problem of surplus disposal separates itself, rather naturally, into two phases—the war period and the post-war period.

During the war, the markets are hungry for most kinds of goods and prompt disposal should not be difficult.

The avalanche of surpluses will come with peace.

[26] Advisor to the War Mobilization Director (1943–45).

[27] Member of the advisory unit, Office of War Mobilization for War and Post-War Adjustment Policies.

[28] The Baruch-Hancock Report to the Office of War Mobilization contained extensive and detailed plans designed to expedite the transition of the nation's economy from wartime to peacetime.

Our current problems are very simple by comparison with the questions we must then face and the decisions we must then make.

The country's main post-war concern will be to find jobs in private activities for some 57 million workers, or about 12 million more than were employed in 1939.

Jobs depend upon markets for goods.

At present values and with present labor efficiency, 57 million workers should turn out 150 to 160 billion dollars worth of goods and services or, say, 50 to 60 percent more than the dollar volume of the production of 1939.

Where will we find markets in peacetime for this huge volume of production?

But that is not the whole problem.

Although these surpluses about which we have been speaking are the product of past labor, we must also find markets for these goods, and without serious disruption to trade and employment.

Over 15 billion dollars have been invested by the Government in plants and equipment for this war. Other billions are invested in goods and materials of all kinds.

Certain of these facilities and materials will be retained as a post-war standby, but most of this huge inventory should eventually be declared as surplus, for disposal.

In many cases, prompt disposal of plants and materials will create new jobs, in others, forced sales might so seriously disrupt industry as to cause unemployment. The Government's interest in getting its money out of surplus property is certainly secondary to that of promoting and maintaining a sound domestic economy.

In considering the possibilities of marketing these surpluses in the post-war period, consistent with the re-establishment and maintenance of normal trade and employment, one is struck with the fact that our domestic markets cannot absorb the whole of them.

The world is a big place, but any careful reflection on world markets and the exchangeability of goods and services therein is bound to give one the impression that man's commercial genius must have worked principally in the field of production.

Apparently, the theory was, if you produce a useful thing, distribution will be automatic, because man will always want to exchange one useful thing of which he has a surplus, for another useful thing, of which he has a need.

Indeed, this theory was sound and worked for awhile. Eventually, as production spread over the world, and competition commenced to pinch, man sought to divide the commercial world into water-tight compartments, so to speak, to prevent or restrict the flow of goods and services from one compartment or area to another.

In the past quarter century, man's genius operated so effectively in this field of restriction, freezing in each area the surplus goods produced therein, that the world's greatest depression found warehouses everywhere bulging with useful but unsaleable merchandise.

Will war uproot the foundations of this anomaly and give us a fresh start on the road to sanity?

Or will the peace be such that peoples will again, instinctively, withdraw behind national boundaries, absorbed in problems of their own economic and military security?

That kind of world is a world of fear, of restriction, of isolationism, of low living standards, and in the end, of war and destruction; in such atmosphere, markets wither and die.

It may be possible to gear our production pattern to our domestic markets and come out with full employment, but not under a democratic system of government.

If we are to preserve our democratic institutions, the post-war world must be organized to afford reasonable promise of freedom from attack, and economic barriers must be lowered so that all peoples may regard the world as their market.

Only in such a world can the genius of America in combining labor, capital, and management in the efficient mass production of goods find its full opportunity.

In a world so organized, there will be work for all, rising living standards for all, and freedom for all who have the desire to achieve it and the will to maintain it.

That kind of world is a big world, a rich world, but still a world of limitless needs, and in it that portion of our surplus property adaptable to civilian requirements should find a ready market.

§ *The Surplus Property Act of 1944 was conceived as a means for disposing of surplus property which had resulted from reconversion to a peacetime economy. On June 16, 1944, Clayton told a joint hearing of four Congressional committees that "legislation of this character must be administratively workable, and we are convinced that this can only be achieved by vesting in the Administrator a very large area of discretion.*"[29] *When it became apparent that Congress had other intentions, he wrote the following letters, and then submitted his resignation on October 3, 1944, "effective at the time the majority of the new Board take office."*[30]

TO HON. JAMES F. BYRNES

Washington, D.C.
September 14, 1944

Dear Justice Byrnes:

I have seen a copy of the Surplus Property Act of 1944 (H.R. 5125) which I understand the conference committee has tentatively agreed to report.[31] However, I am also informed that at a meeting which the committee will hold tomorrow morning, the conferees will still be free to make changes in the bill.

Whatever form the bill may finally take, I have come to the conclusion after mature consideration that I cannot accept appointment under it should such appointment be tendered me.

I hope, therefore, that the conferees, each of whom will receive a copy of this letter, will accept the views herein expressed as being completely disinterested.

My attempts at assisting in writing surplus property legislation were made at the urgent request of Congress. My only concern has been to get workable legislation drawn in the national interest.

My decision not to accept appointment under the bill springs from the conviction growing out of the Senate hearings and debates on the bill that the surplus property disposal program is no longer to be conducted in a businesslike manner. Under these circumstances, since all my experience has been in business, the responsibility for administering whatever bill may finally be passed belongs in other hands than mine.

[29] Statement regarding the Surplus Property Act of 1944, June 16, 1944, RG 250, DNA.

[30] Will Clayton to James Byrnes, October 3, 1944, LS, RG 250, DNA.

[31] Letter to James F. Byrnes, LS, RG 250, DNA. The Surplus Property Act of 1944 was signed into law on October 3, 1944. The final form of the bill provided for a three-man Surplus Property Board in the Office of War Mobilization.

The latest draft of the bill provides for a four man board and an administrator with no clear definition of their respective jurisdictions and with tie votes of the board decided by the Director of War Mobilization.

No agency of this type with diffused responsibility among a number of appointees with equal authority working through an Administrator with conflicting powers could ever get the job done. It would be better to omit altogether any statutory provision for an administrator than to adopt this unworkable compromise.

Unless the bill is changed in this respect it not only will not work but its impracticability will be so obvious on its face that the task of getting good men to accept appointment under it may be impossible.

I have never advocated the granting of unfettered discretion to one man.

I myself suggested to the conferees that all regulations and all single sales of any property which cost the Government one million dollars or more should be subject to the approval of the Policy Board (consisting of government officials like the present Board functioning under Executive Order 9425).

One man rule is thus not the issue.

The issue is administrative workability.

There are so many other unworkable provisions in the bill which appear to me to be contrary to the national interest that I will not attempt to comment on them.

My views on all such questions have been stated over and over in many hearings before committees of Congress, and are incorporated in the bill as it passed the House.

I only want to add that whatever the final form of the bill, the administrative agency for which it provides should be set up and begin to function without delay. Momentous decisions may have to be made at any time.

If desired, I shall of course be glad to help out unofficially in every way that I can until the new administration is functioning.

Sincerely yours,
W. L. Clayton

To *LIFE* Magazine

Washington, D.C.
September 16, 1944

Sirs:

Robert Coughlan's "Reconversion" is an excellent and succinct summary.[32] I was of course particularly interested in his treatment of the surplus disposal problem. Especially apt is his statement in connection with the pending legislation that the Left favored the Senate committee's eight-man board because it would be sure to have representation on it and could hope to dominate it, while the Right, seeking to attain sound national prosperity, saw a steadying influence in having a single administrator.

Though the issue is now decided, it is a significant sidelight on this question that the "Left" was enthusiastically joined by the United States Chamber of Commerce and the National Association of Manufacturers, though presumably the end objectives of these particular "Leftists" would not be the same as that of their associates in this enterprise. Surplus property makes strange, though successful, bedfellows.

I submit that Mr. Coughlan has correctly stated the true interest of the Right, but that in this instance their most vocal representatives let them down.

Sincerely yours,
W. L. Clayton

§ *Clayton believed that "nearly all great wars have an economic origin" and that permanent world peace would become a reality only when all nations enjoyed equality of economic opportunity through the destruction of trade barriers.*[33] *In 1944, as in 1936, Clayton again*

[32] Robert Coughlan, "Reconversion to What?" *Life*, August 28, 1944, p. 28. An unsigned carbon copy of this letter may be found in Baruch Papers, Princeton University.

[33] Will Clayton to Ralph Flanders, December 12, 1944, L, CP, TL.

*supported President Roosevelt and the Democratic Party because he
felt that they offered the best opportunity for liberalized international
trade policies, a point he makes clear in the following speech.*

A CAMPAIGN SPEECH FOR RE-ELECTION OF ROOSEVELT

The war drags on, with unbelievable destruction.[34]

Goebbels[35] was almost right when he boasted that the Germans
would conquer the world *or*, if they failed, they would slam the door
so hard, as they went out, that it would jar the universe.

Is there anyone, anywhere, who does not begin to feel that jar?

Does anything matter much in the world today except bringing
these mad-men to bay as quickly as possible, and then taking
measures which will give us some reason to hope that they cannot
get loose again?

If the answer is that nothing else does matter much, *then* we
should not change Commanders while these vital life and death issues
are still undecided.

At the end of this war the United States will be faced with
responsibilities and opportunities so great as to challenge the best
there is in us of vision, of courage, and of leadership.

We must not fail this time as we did before.

I am supporting President Roosevelt because I believe that he
and his party are better equipped than Governor Dewey[36] and his
party to lead us to victory in war and in peace.

While both candidates and both parties have expressed themselves in favor of a world organization for future peace and security,
I think it is proper to examine the question as to which candidate and
which party is the more competent to lead us in this field.

The maintenance of world peace is not merely a question of
armies and navies and guns and of rules for their use.

Unless our day to day relations with our neighbors in this fast-
shrinking world are such as to establish a climate friendly to world

[34] This speech was delivered before the Women's National Democratic
Club, Washington, D.C., October 18, 1944. A copy may be found in CP, TL.

[35] Joseph P. Goebbels, German Minister for Propaganda (1933–45).

[36] Governor Thomas E. Dewey of New York, Republican candidate for
president in 1944.

peace, the most elaborate military establishment will soon disintegrate.

While Governor Dewey and the Republican Party have spoken in favor of measures to establish military security, the record proves, I think, that they are unprepared, as they were at the end of the last war, to alter certain of their traditional policies to the extent necessary to establish those conditions of world economic peace, on which physical peace must rest.

Secretary Hull[37] in a forthright letter dated September 2, 1938, to Mr. John Hamilton, then Chairman of the Republican National Committee,[38] replying to Mr. Hamilton's blast against the Hull trade agreements program, asserted:

"That economic armaments result in a lowering of living standards throughout the entire world; foment internal strife; and offer constant temptation to use force, or threat of force, as a means of obtaining from other nations what could have been procured through the normal processes of trade.

"That the great fundamental approach to the problem of peace is the ordering of the economic life of the civilized world in a manner which will enable the masses of the people to work and live in reasonable comfort.

"That nations cannot produce on a level to sustain their populations in comfort and well-being unless there are reasonable opportunities to trade one with another.

"That this cannot happen in a world of extreme economic barriers and military hostility."

The Republican Party's position on extreme economic barriers for the past hundred years is well-known. . . .

* * *

It is true that one of the first statements made by Governor Dewey after his nomination at Chicago was that he believed in Secretary Hull's Reciprocal Trade Program and thought it should be continued.

But what does the Republican platform say on this subject? Here it is:

"We will always bear in mind that the domestic market is America's greatest market and that tariffs which protect it against foreign competition should be modified only by reciprocal bi-lateral trade agreements approved by Congress."

[37] Secretary of State Cordell Hull (1933–44).
[38] John D. M. Hamilton, Chairman of the Republican National Committee (1936–40).

Now this statement embodies two principles which would utterly destroy the Hull Reciprocal Trade Agreements program, i.e., that the agreements should be bi-lateral and that they should be approved by Congress.

Bi-lateral agreements were the favorite trade mechanism of Nazi Germany; they separate the world into water-tight trade compartments, lower the standard of living, breed international bitterness and foment internal and external strife.

Congressional approval simply means that the agreements would be subjected to the same disgraceful log-rolling tactics which have characterized the passage of every tariff bill for the last hundred years and which have usually resulted in every selfish group getting the protection it wanted.

If Governor Dewey favors the Hull Reciprocal Trade program why didn't he see to it that the Republican platform was drafted accordingly?

The answer is that the real rulers of the Republican Party wrote that platform; Governor Dewey was powerless to change it then and he will be powerless to change it in future.

The Republican Party has always despised the Hull Reciprocal Trade Agreements program, and has done what it could to destroy it.

The Republican Party has always stood for economic nationalism, a philosophy which leads inevitably to international strife.

The reason the Republican old guard hated Wendell Wilkie is that he tried so hard to breathe a little of the spirit of economic liberalism into the party.

They now give lip service to his philosophy in order to ensnare liberal votes, but they do not intend to follow any such philosophy.

Perhaps the greatest fraud ever perpetrated upon the American people is the age-old Republican doctrine that tariff protection is responsible for our high standard of living. Any undue restriction upon trade cannot possibly fail to reduce the amount and variety of goods available to the people, and thus reduce the standard of living.

Next to the question of future peace and security our most important problem in the postwar period is the question of employment.

We now have employed, including the Armed Services, about 65 million people, which is almost 20 million more than were employed before the war.

Unless we can keep at least half of these additional 20 million people employed, postwar, we will face a very grave unemployment problem with all its social and economic consequences.

Our industrial plant has been greatly expanded during the past three or four years of war. The only way we can hope to keep 55 or 56 million people employed is to make use of this expanded industrial capacity.

To do this means inevitably that we will produce a great deal more of some things than our domestic population can possibly consume.

Therefore, foreign markets for our surplus production are absolutely essential if we are to have a satisfactory condition of employment.

Foreign markets will exist in unprecedented volume but the difficulty will be for foreign buyers to find the necessary dollars with which to make payment. In the end, these dollars can only be made available through our purchase of their goods and services.

For many years, we tried to make a one-way street out of international trade. Unless the declarations of the Atlantic Charter and of the Lend-Lease Agreements are but empty generalities, we must now act.

Barriers which serve to keep the goods of other countries *out*, serve just as effectively to keep our goods *in*, or to let them out only at unremunerative prices to our producers.

Following the last war, the Republican Party, as has been seen, erected barriers which made it impossible for foreigners to pay back the money we loaned them or to pay for the products of our farms, mines and factories which they wished to buy.

Who will say that they will not do the same thing at the end of this war, and thus help plant the seeds of another world war?

The world has now shrunk to a point where we can no longer sit in a small corner of it, hugging our riches and our insularity to ourselves, unobserved and unmolested.

We must now take our proper place in the world, meeting courageously the responsibilities of leadership and helping chart the course of future peace, or we will find ourselves in due course fighting another world war with who knows what coalition of nations arrayed against us.

In taking our proper place, as I believe we shall, our interests will be much better served in the capable hands of President Roosevelt and Secretary Hull than if transferred at this critical time to the hands of Governor Dewey, inexperienced as he is in international affairs.

§ The following statement represents possibly the most succinct explication of Clayton's vision of a post-war world, the economic prosperity of which would be expanded through an increased flow of international trade resulting from reduced barriers to exchange of goods.

A STATEMENT ON POST-WAR ECONOMIC POLICY AND PLANNING

I think that it is not only desirable that we increase our foreign trade post-war as compared to pre-war, but I think that it is absolutely essential that we do so if we are to achieve anything like a satisfactory state of employment in the post-war period.[39]

When war started in Europe in 1939 we had about forty-six and one-half million people employed in the United States.

We now have a total of approximately 65,000,000 workers, including the men and women in the armed services.

It has been estimated by the Committee for Economic Development, I believe, that if we could keep employed post war one-half of those 20,000,000 additional workers over the prewar period, in other words, if we could have about 57,000,000 people employed post-war, that would be a satisfactory state of employment, any substantial number less than that of post-war workers would be an unsatisfactory state of employment.

Now, I think that to employ any such number of people post-war we would all agree it is necessary that we greatly expand our production post-war. If we do that it is going to be necessary to use a great many of the facilities we have created for war purposes.

As you know, during the war, there has been relatively little new private construction in industry but we have had about fifteen billion dollars worth of construction of plants and facilities by the Government during the war.

---

[39] Printed in *Post-War Economic Policy and Planning*, Hearings before the House Subcommittee on Foreign Trade and Shipping, Special Committee on Post-War Economic Policy and Planning, 78th Cong., 2d sess., and 79th Cong., 1st sess. (1944–45), pp. 1029–33. The statement was made October 27, 1944.

Many of these plants and facilities can easily be converted to peacetime production, and, as I said a moment ago, I think it will be necessary to use those facilities if we are to employ 57,000,000 people after the war.

Now, if we use these facilities largely, we will inevitably produce a great deal more of some things than our domestic population can possibly use or consume; the result being that we will have to find markets abroad.

If we are to find markets abroad for the sale of these products we must buy more foreign goods as well, because in the end the only way these goods of ours can be paid for is by dollars which will be created by the sale to us of foreign goods and services; or as the gentleman who just preceded me said, by the expenditures of American tourists abroad.

How soon this tourist trade can be resumed, none of us know. It is admitted that in due time it will be a substantial sum.

But by and large the only way that foreigners can pay us is to sell goods to us. In other words, an exchange of goods.

I think what is necessary to be done to bring about an expanded foreign trade is fairly simple.

In the beginning until foreign countries can reconstruct and reconvert and get into position to produce and sell us a surplus of goods, it is going to be necessary to extend some credits.

As you know, at Bretton Woods a tentative agreement was reached between some 40 nations for the setting up of an international investment bank with a capital of about ten billion dollars, and that bank would be in a position to extend very substantial credit abroad for reconstruction and development.

Obviously, whatever credits are extended will provide a buying power for our goods and for the goods of other industrial countries like Great Britain who are in a position to furnish goods.

It will most of it be capital goods, machinery, and equipment and things of that sort.

But, in my opinion, such loans would be very unwise—as loans made following the first war turned out to be extremely unwise—if our set-up is not such that in due time, as these countries get into production and increase their wealth and productivity and their exportable surpluses, we are in position to participate in the purchase of those goods and thereby create the dollars which will be used to amortize and retire these debts and to buy our goods.

Now, aside from the necessity of loans which I think is there in the post-war period, in order to create a condition precedent to a sound operation, I think it is going to be necessary to reduce our tariff to some extent.

As the gentleman who just preceded me said, our high standard of living is due largely to our technological progress and our mass production and our ability to combine men and capital and experience into the production of goods in mass quantities at low unit cost, and, stated in a little more general terms, as I think the economists all agree, it is due largely to the high proportion of land and capital to population that we have in this country.

All countries that have a large proportion of capital and land and wealth to the population have a higher standard of living, obviously, than the countries that have a small proportion of capital and land to population.

So I think that while we would have to be careful in tariff revision to see that we did not take steps which would be so drastic as to greatly undermine any particular industries, with a careful study of the situation, we can find many instances in which substantial reductions can be made in order to greatly increase the flow of goods between our country and foreign countries.

I think the experience of the Hull trade agreements program has proven that, and I believe that same principle could be carried on in the post-war period so that we would have reciprocal reductions in tariffs and trade barriers between countries which would greatly enlarge our trade and help to enlarge the trade of the world, with a resultant increased standard of living in our country and elsewhere.

Following the war there is going to be a simply enormous demand for all kinds of goods which we produce, all over the world, principally capital goods, in order to reconstruct and develop backward countries and help repair the damage and destruction of war; and we can sell almost any amount that we can make if some way can be found for the buyers to pay for it; and, as I say, for a few years they will not be able to pay by shipment of their own goods, because they will not be able to get into production quick enough. Of course, a good many of them have gold and foreign exchange. There are many countries that have very large balances in this country, and they will be in position to buy immediately; and a good many countries have gold which, if they care to part with that, will provide a buying power in the United States.

But if we want to build the foundations for a permanent expansion for our foreign trade, which I think is highly essential if we are to maintain a satisfactory condition of employment in this country, it will be necessary to effect some further reduction in our protective tariff, which is still very high even after the Hull trade agreement programs have brought it down about 25 percent.

I think, following the war, we ought to have, and we will have in all probability, investment of very large sums of American capital by American businesses, American corporations, abroad, in the construction of branch factories, branch offices, or branch businesses of one kind or another.

I think that is a very sound development and of itself will provide a certain amount of dollars for the purchase of our surplus production. And then—that takes in about the three principal categories of lending, say, of investing abroad—the investing by our private corporations in the way of building branch factories, and so on; investment by private capitalists in this country guaranteed by the United Nations Investment Bank; and the investments by that bank in the securities of governments abroad.

In those three ways we should reach a pretty high volume within 5 years after the war of foreign investment by this country, by citizens of this country and the two banks, which ought to give us the foundation for very good export trade.

But I want to reemphasize that all of this will be extremely unsound unless our whole international economy picture is put on a basis where those people will in due course be able to repay us what they have borrowed. The United States industries, which have planted their branches abroad, will be able to receive dividends from the work of those industries—which also depends upon our willingness to buy foreign products.

§ In November 1944, Clayton attended a meeting of the Research Advisory Committee of the Committee for Economic Development at which one of the primary topics of discussion was a study of international trade and domestic employment prepared by Dean Calvin Hoover of Duke University.[40] *In the following memorandum, Clayton takes issue with that study.*

Comment on Dean Hoover's Study of International Trade and Domestic Employment

---

Washington, D.C.
November 18, 1944

Dean Hoover's study, on the whole, is so good, that I reluctantly take issue with him on one important point.[41]

Disagreeing strongly, however, with one of his conclusions, I respectfully ask careful consideration of the following:

Throughout Dr. Hoover's two papers, there runs a strong implication that the level of foreign trade has little or nothing to do with the level of employment.

One can even imagine that Dean Hoover believes that contraction in our foreign trade would add to domestic employment.

In speaking of the "catastrophic unemployment of the great depression," he says:

> For, however unfortunate the effects of the import-export controls upon international trade, they did achieve a considerable degree of success in relieving domestic employment.

* * *

To the degree that the lowering of our protective tariff was effective in increasing purchasing power for American goods in foreign markets, employment in industries producing for export would be increased. This might not, however, offset immediately

---

[40] Will Clayton to James Byrnes, November 18, 1944, L, CP, TL.
[41] This memo is in RG 250, DNA.

the loss of employment in industries less sheltered under the tariff than before.

* * *

If strong measures are taken by our national Government whenever necessary to maintain domestic employment, *foreign trade need not be feared as a cause of unemployment.* On the other hand, expanding our foreign trade should not normally be considered a means of increasing domestic employment.

* * *

The fundamental reason for the existence of international trade is not to increase employment but to increase national income and standards of living.

Although Dr. Hoover probably agrees with the CED statement in its Second Annual Report, that "a mere reconversion of industry to the level of activity which prevailed in 1940 would be disastrous, to the point of causing unemployment for perhaps as many as 15 million Americans," he apparently takes the view that this applies exclusively to industries engaged in domestic trade. Does he face with equanimity the possibility of a reconversion in our export industries from the present level of 15 billion dollars annually to the pre-war level of 3 billion dollars?

Dr. Hoover states that a high level of international trade adds to national income, raises the standard of living, "would be a major step toward the maintenance of a peaceful post-war world" and "would manifestly provide a most favorable climate for all forms of peaceful international collaboration;" but in some strange way this is accomplished without adding to employment; indeed, employment might even be reduced.

The weight of distinguished academic opinion at the Chicago meeting supported this view:

China, in the days of the Great Wall, had, or could have had, full employment;
[5¢ a day and a bowl of rice!]
The United States could abolish all foreign trade and in fifty years could readjust its economy to a condition of full employment;
[Is CED overlooking a formula for achieving full employment?]
Germany reduced unemployment by restricting imports.
[Slave labor, preparing feverishly for war, in a completely regimented economy, with a constant shrinkage in the standard of living.]

Russia achieved full employment with almost no foreign trade. [Do we want to adopt the Russian system?]

* * *

Query No. 1: Will not an increase in national income, a rise in living standards, the promotion of a peaceful post-war world, inevitably result from, be accompanied by, or result in an expansion in productive employment?

Query No. 2: Is CED's objective merely employment, or is it employment at satisfactory wages in a free economy?

These two questions seem to answer themselves but to make sure, let us ask and try to answer another:

Query No. 3: If the present level of exports of 15 billion dollars annually can be substantially maintained, post-war, instead of dropping back to the pre-war level of 3 billions, will that contribute to the maintenance of post-war domestic employment at satisfactory wages in a free economy?

If I correctly understand Dean Hoover's position and the weight of academic opinion at Chicago, it is to the effect that since the only sound way we can be paid for these exports is by importing an equivalent value in goods and services, domestic employment is merely balanced in the process, with the probability that the imports may cause more unemployment than the exports provide.

I respectfully submit that this is a very superficial and inaccurate analysis of the subject.

If we are to achieve, post-war, a gross national product of goods and services of 150 billion dollars, employing about 56 million workers, we can probably only do so by making substantial use of the entire productive facilities of the country.

This will mean inevitably that we will produce a great deal more of some things than our domestic economy can absorb. Markets for these surpluses must be found abroad, if we are to avoid serious unemployment.

The world, post-war, will need enormous quantities of capital and producers' goods, machinery, equipment of all kinds, technical "know how," as well as durable and non-durable consumers' goods.

Except for non-durable consumers' goods, the United States will for several years be almost the only market which can supply these things in large quantities. It will be practically the only market in position to sell on credit.

In the beginning, due to the great shortage of goods abroad and the disorganization of productive facilities, payment for the most part can be made only in two ways:

By gold and the use of existing dollar balances;

By credits.

Credits will undoubtedly be available in very substantial amounts by some instrumentality of the United States Government, or of the United Nations, or both.

When the debtor countries have reorganized their production, they will have a surplus of goods and services with which to pay the interest on these loans and amortize the principal, although it is doubted if, on balance, the creditors (principally the United States) will wish to receive the principal. If we follow the policy pursued by England, after the Napoleonic Wars, we will add to rather than subtract from our investments abroad.

If, however, these credits are to be sound, and if our exports are to continue, we must be prepared to accept payment in goods and services, which means a reduction in our tariffs, abolition of import embargoes, quotas, etc.

But the question here arises:

Will this not cancel out all the employment benefits derived from the exports? The answer is definitely no, for the following reasons:

A. Payment to the extent of quite a few billions will, undoubtedly, be effected by means of U.S. investments abroad of a permanent nature.

B. Imports themselves provide much employment (in some cases more than exports). The American Manufacturers Export Association found from a study of a large variety of imported manufactured articles that on the average, out of each dollar paid by the U.S. consumer of such articles only 30 cents went abroad, the remaining 70 cents having been spent in the United States for labor, rent, taxes and profits, in handling, transportation, and distribution within the United States.

C. Many of the imports would not compete with U.S. production, such as luxury goods, specialities of one kind and another, and goods not produced in the United States.

D. In a radio address made by Secretary Hull March 23, 1935, he said:

A study made of 36 typical industries which are on an export basis or not aided by the tariff, and 36 industries whose products are highly protected, shows that in 1929 the average annual remuneration of wage earners in the unprotected industries was $1,704, while that in the highly protected industries was $1,109.

If in expanding pre-war exports we add a half million or so workers to the pay rolls of unprotected industries paying an annual wage rate of $1,704, we should not feel too badly if some of these workers come from highly protected industries with a wage rate of only $1,109.

E. With an expanded economy, an increased national income, and a higher standard of living, post-war, Americans will, within a very few years after the war, probably spend two or three times as much on foreign travel, as before the war.

F. Post-war remittances by foreign-born American citizens and residents to relatives abroad, will probably be considerably greater than pre-war.

If the 10 or 15 billion dollars worth of goods which we can annually export, post-war, are not exported, these goods will for the most part not be produced. What then will we do with the displaced labor?

Theoretically we could, as has been suggested, reconstruct and readjust our economy to a much more simple way of life and take care of all of these people.

They could return to the farm, dig their food out of the ground, spin and weave their own clothing and walk to Church on Sunday. They certainly could not return to the farm on a wage basis, because agriculture is being mechanized so fast that we are now producing record crops with the smallest number of farm workers in history. It is believed that this trend will go forward rapidly, post-war.

Is it not clear that unless private industry can provide employment for people in pretty much the same kind of environment in which they have been living and working, the workers will look to the Government to do so?

Is it not also clear that if industry is to do this job, it needs to mobilize markets for every possible dollar's worth of goods wherever those markets may be found?

Cannot industry face the future with much greater assurance of uninterrupted operation and full employment if it can look to the whole world as its market instead of merely the United States?

* * *

I have confined this discussion to the employment aspect of international trade.

I cannot, however, resist the temptation to add the following:

A great world creditor nation, as the United States is destined to be, must act like a creditor; otherwise, no Bretton Woods Monetary Fund[42] will long prevent exchange control, import quotas, embargoes and other similar devices for regulating the balance of payment between nations, with inevitable resurgence of international strife and bitterness such as grew out of our economic policies following the first World War.

The most elaborate military establishment for the preservation of physical peace will soon disintegrate in an atmosphere of bitterness created by international economic warfare.

As the greatest military, economic, and financial power in the world, the United States faces colossal responsibilities and opportunities in an atmosphere of economic isolationism such as that created by our economic policies following the first World War, culminating in the Smoot–Hawley Tariff Bill which practically destroyed our international trade and provoked retaliatory measures on the part of 31 nations.

Free enterprise will not survive another World War.

All of which has at least something to do with full employment at satisfactory wages, in a free economy.

> Respectfully,
> W. L. Clayton

[42] The Bretton Woods Conference, attended by forty-four nations in July, 1944, established an International Monetary Fund (capitalized at $8.8 billion) to stabilize national currencies and promote world trade.

III

ASSISTANT

SECRETARY OF STATE

1944–1946

§ From December 20, 1944, to August 18, 1946, Clayton served as Assistant Secretary of State for Economic Affairs. In his testimony before the Senate Foreign Relations Committee on December 12, 1944, he gave the following summary of his career and philosophy as a statement of his qualifications for the office of Assistant Secretary.

A STATEMENT ON HIS NOMINATION AS ASSISTANT SECRETARY OF STATE

In appearing before the Senate Committee on Foreign Relations for examination regarding my fitness to serve as Assistant Secretary of State for economic affairs, I wish to make a brief preliminary statement which may clear up some questions at once and save the committee's time.[1]

I was one of the organizers of the cotton merchant firm of Anderson, Clayton & Co. in 1904 and, with the exception of a short period in the First World War, was continuously in that business until August 1940. At that time I resigned as chairman of the board of Anderson, Clayton & Co. to enter Government service, first with Nelson Rockefeller, Coordinator of Inter-American Affairs, then as Deputy Federal Loan Administrator, then as Assistant Secretary of Commerce, to which position I was appointed by the President and confirmed by the Senate.

I resigned as Assistant Secretary of Commerce in February 1944 to become Surplus War Property Administrator, under Executive Order 9425.

On October 3, 1944, I resigned as Surplus War Property Administrator, effective when the new Surplus Property Board takes office.

[1] Printed in *Nominations—Department of State,* Hearings before the Senate Committee on Foreign Relations, 78th Cong., 2d sess. (1944), pp. 35–38. The statement was delivered on December 12, 1944.

It has been suggested by some persons that I am a believer in cartels.

Nothing could be further from the truth.

My commercial experience has been confined to the cotton business. The merchandising of raw cotton is known to be one of the most highly competitive businesses in the world.

Webster definies a cartel as "a combination of separate firms to maintain prices above a competitive figure."

The nature of the cotton merchandising business excludes any such arrangements.

Numerous investigations by the Committee on Agriculture of the Senate and the Federal Trade Commission have failed to disclose collusive practices in the cotton-merchandising business.

That there are no such practices is further evidenced by the fact that net profits in the business over a long period of years have been only 1 to 1½ percent of the dollar volume.

Having been brought up in this school of hard, keen competition, and liking it, I early formed a strong antipathy, in principle, to cartels.

I quote as follows from a speech I delivered at the Harvard Tercentenary Celebration in 1936:

Agreements between competitors to curtail production or fix prices, with or without Government sanction, are to be condemned on economic grounds.

There is a good deal of confusion in our thinking in this country on the subject of cartels.

We are inclined to denounce cartels on what we buy and favor them, although under a different name, on what we sell.

A cartel smells the same to me by whatever name it may be called or for whatever commercial purpose it may be organized.

If international agreements are entered into between governments in respect of some commodities in which burdensome surpluses have resulted from the war and other causes, the consuming countries should participate in the formation and administration of such agreements, the agreements should be temporary in character and should contemplate as their principal objective the shifting from inefficient to efficient production.

The committee may wish to know my views on other international economic questions.

For many years, I have been an ardent, outspoken, and consistent advocate of Cordell Hull's philosophy regarding international economic matters.

May I quote two paragraphs from a speech which Secretary Hull delivered on April 9, 1944:[2]

Along with arrangements by which nations may be secure and free must go arrangements by which men and women who compose those nations may live and have the opportunity through their efforts to improve their material condition. We will fail indeed if we win a victory only to let the free peoples of this world, through any absence of action on our part, sink into weakness and despair.

The heart of the matter lies in action which will stimulate and expand production in industry and agriculture and free international commerce from excessive and unreasonable restrictions. These are the essential prerequisites to maintaining and improving the standard of living in our own and in all countries. Production cannot go forward without arrangements to provide investment capital. Trade cannot be conducted without stable currencies in which payments can be promised and made. Trade cannot develop unless excessive barriers in the form of tariffs, preferences, quotas, exchange controls, monopolies, and subsidies, and others, are reduced or eliminated. It needs also agreed arrangements under which communication systems between nations and transport by air and sea can develop. And much of all this will miss its mark of satisfying human needs unless we take agreed action for the improvement of labor standards and standards of health and nutrition.

I unreservedly subscribe to this thesis.

Now, may I say a word regarding the operations of Anderson, Clayton & Co. which have been mentioned in some quarters in connection with my nomination to be Assistant Secretary of State.

The capital, surplus, and undivided profits of Anderson, Clayton & Co. is now a little over $50,000,000, of which members of my family and I own approximately 40 percent.

My only connection with the company is as stockholder. I have not attended a stockholders meeting since resigning as chairman of the board in August 1940; in fact, have not been back to my home in Houston, Tex., since March 1941.

Anderson, Clayton & Co. has offices throughout the Cotton Belt and cotton-consuming centers of the United States, and maintains branch offices or agencies in the principal cotton-consuming countries of the world.

The company also operates, through subsidiaries, in the following foreign cotton-producing countries: Mexico, Peru, Argentina,

[2] Speech on American foreign policy delivered by Secretary of State Cordell Hull on April 9, 1944, over the facilities of the Columbia Broadcasting System.

Paraguay, Brazil, and Egypt. The present book value of the company's fixed assets in these countries is about $10,000,000.

Anderson, Clayton & Co. have never owned any fixed assets or investments of any kind in Japan or Germany, although for many years prior to the war the company maintained sales agencies in both countries. The company also for many years did a very large business with Russia; was one of the first American firms to establish business relations with the Soviet Government after the revolution, long before recognition of that Government by the United States Government, and one of the few firms in the world to extend them substantial credits in those early days.

At the outbreak of the war between Germany, France and England, about September 3, 1939, Anderson, Clayton & Co. discontinued business with Germany and so instructed all its foreign subsidiaries.

The company and its subsidiaries made no sales to Japan for some time prior to Pearl Harbor.

Some persons apparently fear that my business interests abroad may influence my opinions and actions in the economic affairs of the United States Government.

The only answer I know how to make to this is to say that if any Senator believes that my own foreign interests would prevent me from taking an objective and patriotic position with reference to the interests of my country, I would expect him to vote against my confirmation.

I merely want to add that I am glad this hearing is an open one and that I freely invite any question regarding my private or public acts which may have any bearing, even though remote, on my fitness to serve in the position to which I have been nominated by the President.

§ Secretary of the Treasury Henry Morgenthau wrote to President Roosevelt on January 1, 1945, suggesting that the United States extend comprehensive aid to Russia "during her reconstruction period."[3] Such aid would be tendered under the provisions of Section 3(c) of the Lend-Lease Act which allowed the completion of aid agreements made before July 1, 1946.[4] Upon receiving a copy of Morgenthau's

[3] Foreign Relations of the United States, 1945, vol. 5, pp. 937–38.
[4] This section was amended on March 13, 1945. See Nineteenth Report to Congress on Lend-Lease Operations (Washington: U.S. Government Printing Office, 1945), pp. 60–61.

letter to the President, Secretary of State Edward Stettinius asked Clayton to "recommend to me the position which I should take on behalf of the Department on this matter."[5]

To Hon. Edward R. Stettinius, Jr.

January 20, 1945
Washington, D.C.

Mr. Secretary:

I feel that it would be helpful, in connection with any discussions you may have with the President or Secretary Morgenthau, to have the following comments on the proposals recently made by Mr. Morgenthau in regard to postwar trade with the Soviet Union:[6] Proposal 3(c) supplementary agreement to the Master Lend-Lease Agreement.

1. In regard to the Treasury proposal that we should now offer the Soviet Government the proposed 3(c) agreement without interest charges, it is felt that, if at this time we should change our ground, it, in all probability, would cause definite repercussions in other political or economic negotiations we may have with the Soviet Government. In this connection, we told the Soviet negotiators, in full good faith and with definite Treasury concurrence, that the last 3(c) proposals we made to them were our final offer, and that because of legal and other grounds, we could not grant them any better terms. If we should now make the same proposals except for the exclusion of interest charges we could not help but give the impression to the Soviet authorities that what we said last summer was not true, and thus we might unwittingly kindle the fire of suspicion which they have had in the past as to our good faith. Moreover, by making this new proposal, we would definitely give the impression that we were most anxious, almost on any terms, to make available postwar goods to the Soviet Union. While we are naturally desirous to increase our trade with the Soviet Union to the maximum, and it is in our interest to do so, it would be tactically harmful to deepen the

---

[5] *Foreign Relations of the United States, 1945*, vol. 5, p. 937n.
[6] Letter to the Secretary of State (1944–45), printed in *Foreign Relations of the United States, 1945*, vol. 5, pp. 964–66.

impression they already have that no matter what happens we are going to have to sell goods to the Soviet Union in order to keep our own economy going.

2. Apparently one of the reasons motivating the Treasury suggestion that the 3(c) agreement should bear no interest rate is tied with certain suggested proposals which may be made to the British and French providing for delivery of certain types of goods on a deferred-payment basis with no interest charges. I understand that in the case of the British these proposals only involve food stuffs which may be in the "pipeline" after the termination of hostilities and therefore would not amount to a great deal, and that the deferred payments, in all probability, would cover a comparatively short period. Moreover, the British are paying for all capital goods now delivered under Lend-Lease including many items offered to the Soviet Government in Schedule 1 of the 3(c) agreement (locomotives, freight cars, machine tools, etc.). In regard to the French negotiations, it is understood that Mr. Monnet has suggested arrangements by which they would obligate themselves on a deferred-payment basis to compensate the United States for all capital goods furnished during hostilities as well as subsequently. It will be seen, therefore, that the propositions which may be suggested to the British and French are not comparable to the proposals made under the Soviet 3(c) agreement. In view of this, the French and British proposals would not appear to be precedents for the Soviet case.

For the above reasons, it is felt that we should accept Ambassador Harriman's suggestions that the Soviet government be informed again that the proposals made in our 3(c) agreement are final.

Postwar Credits.

In regard to Secretary Morgenthau's proposal to offer the Soviet Government at the present time ten billion dollars at two percent interest coupled with an option to the United States to receive in repayment strategic raw materials, it is believed that the following factors make it impossible at this moment to accept the suggestions:

1. Because of legislative restrictions, it is impossible to offer postwar credit to the Soviet Union until these restrictions have been lifted by Congress.

2. From a tactical point of view, it would seem harmful for us to offer such a large credit at this time and thus lose what appears to be the only concrete bargaining lever for use in connection with the many other political and economic problems which will arise between our two countries. Ambassador Harriman concurs in this opinion.

3. The Soviet Government itself has only proposed a credit of six billion dollars, and there is some question as to their ability to

pay interest and amortization charges on a ten billion dollar loan as well as finance future trade after the initial purchases are made. Moreover, there is also some question as to the amount of surplus strategic materials which the Soviet Union will have available for sale abroad, and whether they would be willing to bind themselves categorically to furnish these strategic materials over a long period. Before making any proposals of this kind, careful studies must be made to ascertain the probable amounts of such strategic materials as might be available.

W[illiam] L. C[layton]

§ *From February 21, 1945, to March 8, 1945, the Inter-American Conference on War and Peace met in Mexico City to cement inter-American solidarity in the post-war world. As Ambassador to Mexico George Messersmith stated that one of the primary goals of the conference was "to consolidate the unity of the twenty Republics in the political and economic field."[7] Political unity was achieved through the adoption of the Act of Chapultepec, which provided for reciprocal defense assistance among the American nations. Leading the struggle for economic unity was Will Clayton, head of the Economics Section of the U.S. delegation and "the most important man at the conference."[8] In the following speech, he outlines the economic policies and goals which would guide American decision-making in the post-war years.*

A STATEMENT ON THE PROBLEMS OF WAR AND PEACE

MR. CHAIRMAN: I am grateful for this opportunity to address the two economic committees of this conference, meeting in joint session.[9]

[7] Quoted by Gabriel Kolko, *The Politics of War; the World and United States Foreign Policy, 1943–1945* (New York: Random House, 1968), p. 460.
[8] *Ibid.*, p. 460.
[9] This speech was delivered before a joint session of the economic committees of the Inter-American Conference on Problems of War and Peace in Mexico City, and printed in U.S. Department of State, *Bulletin*, 12 (March 4, 1945): 334–38.

On behalf of the United States Delegation, I wish to discuss with you some of the economic problems which are of great concern to the other American republics as well as to the Government and people of the United States.

As you will recall, the program of the United States Government for the procurement of strategic and critical materials, first for defense and later for war, was begun in the summer and fall of 1940.

As Deputy Federal Loan Administrator, I was then and for some time thereafter in charge of the foreign procurement programs of the Metals Reserve Company, the Defense Supplies Corporation, and the Rubber Reserve Company. I have a keen recollection of the negotiations and contracts which were entered into with the producers and the governments of the other American nations. These contracts involved a great variety of strategic and critical materials essential to the defense of my country and later to the prosecution of the war into which we were plunged by the Axis powers, intent upon world domination.

Looking back upon the negotiation of those early contracts, involving hundreds of millions of dollars, I take great pride and pleasure in saying that they were made without undue bargaining; that the prices were fair and equitable; that the contracts were on the whole performed with complete honesty and integrity; that every effort was made to extend production to meet our needs; and that the spirit throughout, in the negotiation and in the performance, was on the whole very fine and very cooperative. I am reliably informed that the same may also be said regarding later contracts and performance under them.

In the four and one-half years which have elapsed since those first contracts were made, the United States has by private and Government purchase bought more than five billion dollars worth of goods from the other American republics.

This is a very large sum, and there are people in my country who take a very narrow and one-sided view of these transactions. They say: "Just look at the billions that we have poured out to these people! They should be extremely grateful to us for supplying so lucrative a market for their production." And you probably have people in your country who say: "The United States might have lost the war if we had not supplied them with millions of tons of essential materials, and for this they are certainly under everlasting obligation to us."

Taken separately these views present a very distorted picture of the situation; taken together they merely state the facts which are that you and we have engaged in enormous transactions having a high degree of mutuality of interest and benefit.

It should further be said that these transactions have been abnormal both in size and in character; that they were entered into with the purpose of defeating a powerful and ruthless enemy, intent upon the destruction of your liberty and ours; that wars always come to an end, and that when this one finally drags its bloody and destructive course to a conclusion it will open up to all of us an untried and an unknown road on which we must travel, in converting from a war economy to a peace economy. Despite the hardships, the risks, and the dangers which this journey may involve, there is no way to avoid traveling that road. Every consideration of enlightened self-interest, every circumstance and condition which have brought and held us together throughout this war dictate that you and we should travel that road together.

Now what are these grave post-war problems which you and we must face?

We understand that one of your first concerns is that the ending of the war will bring a sudden termination to these huge procurement contracts about which we have been talking and that the resulting shock may, before peacetime markets are restored, precipitate economic and social disturbances of a very grave character.

You realize, I am sure, that we in the United States have that problem also and in a highly magnified form.

But we will talk about your problem first.

Let us not forget in doing so that it is the unknown which frightens us and that horrible imaginings are seldom realized.

Let us go back again to the summer of 1940.

France had fallen; Italy had entered the war; practically the entire continent of Europe, always a major market for your products, was cut off. If your recollection of those dark days is as keen as mine, and I am sure it is, you will recall the deep concern which all of us felt for the effect which this situation might have on the economic and social structure of your countries.

It was agreed that something had to be done.

In September 1940 the capital of the Export-Import Bank was increased by 500 million dollars "to assist in the development of the resources, the stabilization of the economies, and the orderly marketing of the products of the countries of the Western Hemisphere."

Relatively little of this money was ever called for by you to assist in the orderly marketing of your products.

You didn't call for it because you didn't need it for the purpose.

The United Nations took what you had for sale and called for more and more.

Almost five years have passed since those anxious days in 1940, and you and we are again deeply concerned regarding markets for your products, when war, like a huge maw, no longer feeds upon them.

That adjustments must then be made is obvious.

That there will be a breathing spell, within which peacetime demands will develop, as war requirements lessen, is probable.

No responsible person would be so rash as to predict when this war will end, but that it will end in Europe before it does in the Pacific seems highly probable. The transition period will begin with the end of the European war, but in all probability may not be marked by any large cut in war procurement.

We will continue as in the past to give appropriate notice of the curtailment or termination of procurement contracts. We will confer freely with you regarding such reductions and the necessary adjustments which they will involve. We will consider and cooperate with you in measures designed to effect these adjustments with the least possible shock to your economy. We recognize our responsibility in this field, and we propose to meet it, consistent with our laws, our public opinion and a due regard for your own economy.

There is some doubt whether we can legally stockpile materials which have no relation to our requirements for war.

Encouragement of production through stockpiling of materials for which there is no current or early prospective market is in any case a very dangerous procedure for the producers of such materials.

I am sure you will recognize that this statement is supported by the very considerable experience which the United States and other countries have had in connection with such stockpiles during the period between the two wars.

Markets are extremely sensitive to the existence of large surpluses and until such surpluses are absorbed their presence inevitably acts as a depressing influence on prices, on initiative, and on enterprise.

In due course we expect that there will be legislation in the United States authorizing a post-war stockpile of strategic and critical materials to provide for our military security and for our contribution to the maintenance of security in the Western Hemisphere and in the world. It is impossible to predict at this time what these stockpiles will consist of, but in any case they will probably be frozen for security purposes. It is expected that these stockpiles will be constructed partly out of stocks in the hands of the United States

Army and Navy and other Government agencies at the end of this war. To the extent that such stocks are so used they will not compete with new production in satisfying peacetime demands.

Now, when will these peacetime demands appear and in what volume?

With the war over in Europe, reconstruction and rehabilitation of the liberated areas will set in promptly. Orders for goods will commence to flow. Europe is starved for goods of all kinds.

But how can Europe pay before her productive capacity is restored?

Europe will pay in two ways.

In the first place, the gold and dollar reserves of the world outside of the United States are about 20 billions of dollars, or roughly four times what they were at the end of the first World War. In the second place, credits will be available.

About two weeks ago the President of the United States sent a message to Congress requesting approval of the Bretton Woods proposal for the establishment of an International Monetary Fund and an International Bank for Reconstruction and Development. The former will have funds totaling about 9 billion dollars for the stabilization of the exchanges of the United Nations, and the latter will have a capital of about 9 billions for reconstruction and development loans. Of these sums the United States will furnish a total of nearly 6 billion dollars, assuming that the proposal is approved by the Congress, which is confidently expected. In addition, the Congress is being asked to provide for an increase in the capital of the Export-Import Bank, which will enable the Bank to continue its operations as in the past, but on a much larger scale.

Besides these means of payment, UNRRA has, as you know, funds immediately available for rehabilitation and relief.

There is, then, no cause for pessimism regarding the urgent and, in many cases, desperate postwar need for useful goods of all kinds, or of the ability to provide the means of payment. Indeed, it is the expectation that within a few years after the end of the war the volume of international trade will expand to considerably higher than pre-war levels.

Your second serious concern, as you have expressed it to us, relates to the conservation and use of the very substantial dollar balances which you have accumulated during the period of the war by reason of the fact that you have sold considerably more goods during this period than you have been able to procure.

This problem has two aspects.

You have the very laudable ambition, as we understand it, to make use of these balances for the permanent improvement and development of your economies to the end that the levels of living in your respective countries may be substantially raised.

To this end you wish to prevent the draining off of these balances at the first opportunity through the purchase abroad of luxury goods.

Another aspect of this problem is your concern that the transitional and post-war demands upon the productive facilities of the United States for capital goods, tools, machinery and equipment, and technical knowledge will be so great as to make it difficult, if not impossible, for you to satisfy your requirements in this field.

We in the United States recognize that both aspects of this problem are difficult, and we are prepared to work actively with you to accomplish your objective.

We further recognize that our war-procurement transactions with you cannot really be considered completed until you have received from us or others an equivalent in goods and services, and that the dollars which lie at your credit in our country are of little use to you until they can be employed for that purpose.

It is obviously in our interest to furnish these goods and services at the earliest possible time.

It is also in our interest that you should, as you desire, use a very substantial portion of these dollars for the sound development of your industrial, agricultural, and mineral resources because in so doing you will raise the level of living of your peoples and thus furnish to us an enlarged market for our own production.

As you know, it is one of the principles of the post-war commercial policy of my country to avoid exchange controls. Indeed the International Monetary Fund about which we have already spoken is being set up for that purpose among others. It is recognized, however, that some reasonable controls may be unavoidable in the transition period, and this is provided for in the Bretton Woods proposal. We are prepared to consider with you the extent and manner to which such controls may be necessary to accomplish the purpose you have in mind. Exchange or similar controls should not be used for other motives such as the imposition of hidden tariffs, quotas, etc., for the protection of domestic industries.

With reference to the availability in the United States of the capital goods, tools, machinery, and equipment which you require in implementing your post-war policy of economic development, it must be admitted right off that we face here an extremely difficult problem.

For five years now the insatiable demands of war have made it impossible for you to satisfy your requirements for goods of this kind, for keeping your industries and transportation systems in working order, and for new developments, so greatly needed.

Whereas before the war the markets of several great industrial nations were open to you for supplying such goods, you have had to rely principally upon the United States for the past five years.

We realize that our performance has fallen far short of meeting your needs, but the record is better than most people know. Here it is:

For the past five years, 1940 to 1944, inclusive, our total exports to the other American republics have exceeded 4 billion dollars in value. For the year 1944 they exceeded 1 billion dollars in value as against 800 million in 1943, 700 million in 1942, and 500 million in a typical pre-war year. While there has been some increase in prices, pre-war volume has been well maintained.

These goods have been furnished at a time when we were fighting all over the world the greatest war in history, and at a time when we were furnishing our Allies with 35 billion dollars' worth of war materials and other vital goods for the prosecution of the war.

May I add that we in the United States have also had to do without equipment, tools, and machinery unless their need or use were directly related to the war. In consequence many of our plants which have been operating 24 hours daily are badly in need of repairs and new equipment. For some years now new construction of all kinds has been denied unless it had to do with the war.

As has been said, the demand for goods of all kinds in the postwar period is certain to be extremely heavy and particularly in the field of capital equipment for reconstruction, reconversion, and rehabilitation.

At the same time the productive facilities for goods of this character will have been substantially destroyed throughout the world except in two or three countries. In consequence, the load which will be placed on these two or three countries will be a very heavy one.

As you know, our facilities in the United States for the production of capital goods have been greatly expanded and in some cases enormously expanded. For example, we have facilities for manufacturing twelve to fifteen times as many machine tools as in the pre-war period.

So long as the existing controls which have been set up in the United States continue, we have the means at hand for an equitable allocation of our production, and it is the intention to continue to make use of such means to see that you obtain a fair share of such production. Meantime, we will carefully investigate other methods of assuring you of a fair proportion of our capital goods when our present governmental controls expire. I have tried to tell fairly the story of the relations between the United States and the other American republics in respect of our procurement from you of strategic and critical materials for the war and in respect of your procurement from us of the goods required by you.

I would like now to mention briefly the relations between your countries and mine in another field.

I have already spoken of the Export-Import Bank and of the authority which was given to the Bank by Congress "to assist in the development of the resources, the stabilization of the economies, and the orderly marketing of the products of the countries of the Western Hemisphere."

When in September 1940 the capital of the Bank was increased by 500 million dollars for these purposes, there were cynics in the United States and elsewhere who predicted that this money would be quickly borrowed, that additional sums would be requested and granted, and that the bulk of it would be wasted and never repaid.

Now, what are the facts?

Since its creation in 1934 the Export-Import Bank has made commitments to other American countries in excess of 800 million dollars but the borrowers have so far used only 263 million dollars or about one third of this commitment. Of this latter sum approximately one half has been repaid by the borrowers in accordance with the terms of the loan agreements so that at this time there are outstanding on the books of the Bank loans to other American countries of only 131 million dollars. No loan made by the Bank to countries of the Western Hemisphere is in default. All payments have been made as due.

This is a record of which you and the bank may be justly proud.

The Bank is ready now and later in the post-war period to consider applications for development loans of a sound nature.

The policy of the Bank does not permit it to make loans for the establishment of enterprises which can only make their way through government subsidies or excessive tariffs. I am sure you will recognize the correctness of this policy.

Now, may I also say a word regarding the post-war economic policy of the United States. The Secretary of State in the second plenary session of this conference expressed our basic objectives in this field and it has been our privilege to propose to the conference an economic charter of the Americas which sets forth the policies we believe to be necessary for the realization of these objectives.

The United States Government is definitely committed to a post-war policy looking to a substantial expansion in world economy. We recognize the interdependence of nations in the political, military, and economic fields for the preservation of peace in the world and for the creation of those conditions which will promote higher levels of living through an expansion in production, distribution, and consumption of goods and services and through international cooperation in fostering the betterment of labor standards and health and social conditions in general. To this end it is our intention to work actively for international agreements to remove all discriminations in trade, to reduce tariffs and other barriers to trade, and for the approval of the Bretton Woods proposal and the adoption of every other sound measure which will quicken and expand production and the international exchange of goods and services.

We recognize that international commodity agreements may be necessary in exceptional cases of important primary commodities in which burdensome surpluses have developed or threaten to develop. Both consuming and producing countries should have representation in such agreements, which should look to the expansion of consumption and the readjustment of production, with due regard to the requirements of an expanding world economy.

We do not believe that we can have a high level of employment and prosperity in our country if a substantial part of the world is suffering from depression, and we are quite sure that a satisfactory condition of employment and prosperity in the United States is a highly important factor in contributing to a like condition in other countries.

The United States is determined to remain strong economically and financially. Unless she does so, there is little chance that the rest of the world can prosper.

We recognize that the most elaborate arrangements for the preservation of peace will not long endure if economic warfare is to continue throughout the world in the way in which it was waged between the two world wars.

The United States Delegation, recognizing its responsibility to work for hemispheric and world security, peace, and progress, assures its American neighbors that it favors:

1. The promotion of equal and reciprocal opportunity for the nationals and goods of all the Americas in all markets.

120

2. Freedom, through adherence to principles of fair trade, from discrimination against smaller nations by stronger nations in hemispheric or world organization.

3. Establishment of such necessary hemispheric practices and agencies, consistent with the principles of the charter of the United Nations, when created, as will have the tendency and responsibility to foster the development of competitive enterprise, expansion of economic activity, and promotion of economic peace.

We are dedicated to the ways of economic peace in the world, in order that there may be created a favorable climate for the preservation of physical peace, and in order that the peoples of the world may be better fed, better clothed, and better housed.

As our President has said more than once, this generation has a rendezvous with destiny.

A STATEMENT ON THE CHAPULTEPEC CONFERENCE

I was head of the Economics Section of the U.S. Delegation to this conference.[10] Padilla[11] was Foreign Minister of Mexico at the time and was the outstanding character at Chapultepec. He had lifted the delegates out of their chairs by his oratory at Rio de Janeiro in 1943, when he appealed to them for a patriotic cooperation between all the American countries for defense and development. He came and spoke for 45 minutes in the Chamber of Deputies in Mexico City, spoke without notes, was not flamboyant but was restrained, made a remarkable oration.

At the Chapultepec Conference the Latin American countries were worried about what would happen to their economies at the end of the war—one reason for calling the conference. They were

[10] This statement is from an interview with Ellen Clayton Garwood in December 1947.

[11] Ezequiel Padilla, Foreign Minister of Mexico (1940–45).

afraid they would lose out on the sale of their raw materials and were afraid that their large dollar balances would be dissipated on non-essentials (automobiles especially) and they were anxious to import capital goods—machinery and tools to develop their industries. Many of these countries needed repair parts for their utilities and for railroads which had been built there by foreigners on whom they were dependent for spare parts. They were also afraid that their copper, tungsten, lead, zinc and coffee would stock up on them; and they wanted to be sure that when the war ended the U.S. would give them a fair share of capital goods.

Ed Stettinius[12] headed the conference.

I had charge of the Economic part of the Conference and that was a big part. We said we would, on the question of the sale of their raw materials, be prepared to study the situation with them and make further loans through the Export-Import Bank to tide them over and that their sales probably would not drop off suddenly but would taper off, for the European war would probably end first, and the Pacific War later, and our drop in orders from them would be gradual. We said we'd give them a fair share of our peace time production of capital goods, and would set up effective control machinery for that purpose. Chile and Bolivia were chiefly worried— Mexico and Peru too—about their people wanting to buy mostly luxury; they took a good deal of our capital goods which we made available for them—by loosening our control of exports—but they let their people spend too much for luxury even though they wanted to prevent this.

§ The Reciprocal Trade Agreements Act, first passed by Congress in 1934, granted to the executive branch the right to revise tariffs up to fifty per cent through the negotiation of bilateral, most-favored-nation agreements. Clayton early recognized this program as a step toward economic internationalism and supported the Act each time it came up for renewal. In 1940 he told the Senate Finance Committee that the principle of international division of labor was the best hope for the next world peace, and that "the trade-agreement pro-

[12] Edward Stettinius, Secretary of State (1944–45).

gram is a modest effort to keep alive that principle."[13] *In 1945 he gave the following statement to the House Ways and Means Committee.*

A STATEMENT ON THE RECIPROCAL TRADE AGREEMENTS ACT

The bill which is before this committee would accomplish the renewal and strengthening of an act of Congress which is now 11 years old.[14]

The reciprocal trade-agreements program has become a part of the economic history of the United States.

Over the past decade there has grown up around this program a record of legislative debate, newspaper comment, books, pamphlets, magazine articles which must run into millions of words.

The administration of the Trade Agreements Act has been subjected to the most searching scrutiny; on the three previous occasions when this act came before the Congress for renewal, friends and foes alike have had a full opportunity to make their views known. As a result, the American people are remarkably well informed on the terms, purposes, and achievement of this act, and their views, pro or con, are largely crystallized. Most people, by now, know where they stand on the reciprocal-trade agreements question.

I wish that this were not so. I say this despite the belief, which I think is borne out by the record that the great majority of the American people are favorably inclined toward the trade-agreements program.

I believe that all of us would profit from an effort to look at this bill, not in terms of what we thought about reciprocal trade agreements in 1934, 1937, 1940, and 1943 but as a new instrument for use in the world of tomorrow. For it is, in fact, a new instrument—made so not by new language but by a new world. Those who judge the trade-agreements program solely in the context of its pre-war operation are likely to miss the new and portentous mean-

---

[13] *Extension of Reciprocal Trade Agreements Act,* Hearings before the Senate Committee on Finance, 76th Cong., 3d sess. (1940), pp. 347–50.

[14] This statement was delivered before the House Ways and Means Committee, April 18, 1945, and printed in U.S. Department of State, *Bulletin,* 12 (April 22, 1945): 752–57.

ing of this idea. Actually, the trade-agreements plan was born, in 1934, into a world that was even then headed toward war. The Japanese had struck at China three years before, and Hitler was firmly in power. Economic warfare had already turned the world economy into a jungle of excessive tariffs, quotas, embargoes, subsidies, licenses, exchange controls, clearing-agreements, barter deals, preferences and discriminations of all kinds.

The Reciprocal Trade Agreements Act was a bold and far-sighted effort to stem the tide of economic nationalism. Under the wise and patient leadership of Secretary Hull we were able, by using the bargaining authority granted in the act, to moderate many of the more extreme practices of trade restrictionism and to provide a strong stimulus to the growth of our foreign trade.

The record of achievements under the act was carefully studied by this Committee two years ago and is generally well known. Trade agreements have been negotiated with 28 countries, and hundreds of concessions have been obtained and given. Over 65 percent of our normal foreign trade is carried on with trade-agreement countries. These countries have made concessions on 73 percent of their agricultural imports from us and on 48 percent of their non-agricultural imports from us. Between the years 1934–35 and 1938–39 our exports to non-trade-agreement countries rose by only 32 percent, while our exports to trade-agreement countries rose by 63 percent. Likewise, our imports from non-agreement countries rose by only 13 percent, while our imports from trade-agreement countries rose by 22 percent.

This is a remarkable record, but it is all the more remarkable in that it was accomplished in an era of world economic disintegration. It is a tribute to the trade-agreements program and to the men in the various departments of the Government who guided it that these impressive achievements were realized against such great adversity.

Thus in the years before the war the trade-agreements program was an instrument for defense against an epidemic of destructive and demoralizing trade warfare. Today, with the end of the great holocaust finally within sight, this same instrument is transformed into a powerful device for shaping a better world. This I believe is the new meaning of the trade-agreements program as it comes before the Congress for its fourth renewal.

The terrible events of the last six years have worked profound changes in the minds and spirits of people in every corner of the world. The people are sick of war and sick of the narrow economic practices which undermine material well-being, generate international friction, and set the stage for war. Minds are being cleared of old prejudices and old suspicions; everywhere there is a yearning for a new age of peace and prosperity rooted in international friendship and cooperation. Perhaps never again in our lifetimes will there be a time so auspicious as now for helping to build a world in which men may have the opportunity to live out their lives, free from fear and free from want.

All eyes look to the United States for leadership in this task of world reconstruction. At this juncture in world history we find ourselves in a unique role which entails grave responsibilities. We have become so important to the world, both politically and economically, that no plan for the future is more than an architect's dream without the approval of the United States.

After the war we shall have over half of the world's industrial capacity; we shall be the greatest creditor nation; and the world will look to us for the capital goods necessary to repair the devastation of the war. We own the greater part of the world's stock of gold. We are the greatest producer and the greatest consumer. We are the world's largest exporter, and we are the source of much of the world's technological progress. Certainly there have been few turning points in history at which a nation has been so well-equipped for leadership as we are today.

Destiny has placed us in a position to lead, and we must know where we want to go. The United Nations Conference on International Organization, which will convene in San Francisco this month, is the culmination of several years of planning for a house of nations to safeguard the peace. Secretary Stettinius, in his speech in Chicago earlier this month, filled in the framework of our plan to erect a firm economic foundation for the maintenance of peace. The need for dealing with trade barriers stands in the very center of that plan, for the creation of a healthy world economy cannot succeed in an atmosphere of exaggerated and repressive barriers to international trade.

Our purpose in the commercial-policy sphere is to move toward the goal of expanding world trade open to private enterprise, on a competitive and non-discriminatory basis.

We know of no better way than this to serve the economic interests of all peoples and to create the economic conditions which are conducive to the preservation of peace. The task will not be easy. The economic destruction and dislocation of war have raised new and serious economic problems and have put many barriers in the way of the general acceptance of the liberal trade principles we advocate. But the worst mistake of all would be to underestimate the great force of our moral leadership and to sell short the influence of the United States in world affairs.

* * *

The Trade Agreements Act must be strengthened if this Government is to be empowered to work for the liberalization of world trade. The proposal for increased authority, which would permit this country to reduce its *existing* tariffs, in exchange for reductions in the *existing* trade barriers of other countries, is merely another way of proposing that the program and policy of negotiating reciprocal trade agreements be continued. Simple renewal of the act, without the increased authority, would mean in effect that no important trade agreements of substantial benefit to this country could be negotiated with those foreign countries which are the principal outlets for American exports.

* * *

The conclusion is clear, and is particularly unsatisfactory to me as a business man: Under the act as it stands today, we are unable to negotiate to the extent required new and mutually advantageous business with our best customers. As a public servant, I would consider the failure to remedy such a situation unwise in the extreme. Only by relating the Trade Agreements Act to our present situation can we make it a fully effective device for the expansion of world trade.

* * *

The authority of the Trade Agreements Act, related as it was to the nearly impassable trade barriers of 1934, was, as we have seen, not sufficient to do more than ameliorate some of the excesses of the most virulent case of trade restrictionism the world has ever experienced. As a defensive weapon, the Trade Agreements Act did its job well; but our pride in our past accomplishments should not be allowed to obscure the fact that the existing network of barriers to world commerce is still so formidable as to be utterly inconsistent with the achievement of those high levels of production and consumption to which we are all devoting our best energies.

If we were living in a stationary world, if the underlying factors affecting each nation's foreign trade remained stable, it might be possible, even without pressing forward with our trade-agreements program, to hold the gains we have already made. The post-war world, however, will not be at rest. Entirely apart from the legacy of trade restrictions which we inherit from the pre-war period, there are new and critical trade problems which have arisen as a by-product of the war and which must be resolved in one way or another.

Many nations, surveying their post-war trade prospects, anticipate serious deficits in their international balance of payments. Such
deficits are remedied either by increasing exports or reducing imports.
If we stand still, these countries cannot. If we fail to take strong
action to make possible a solution by expansion, we shall force them
to choose a solution by contraction. If these countries have no choice
but to curtail their imports, the reduction of their orders from us
will be felt in fields and factories in every corner of America.

That is why our existing trade agreements are in danger, and
why increased authority under the Trade Agreements Act is necessary
to preserve through the further relaxation of trade barriers, the nations may be forced by the pressure of their economic circumstances
to free themselves from trade-agreements obligations in order to take
the actions they deem necessary to protect their economies.

What we have achieved in our existing trade agreements is a
kind of truce, between this country and individual foreign countries,
that in respect of the products covered by the agreements, neither of
us will resort to the extreme trade measures which, before 1934, we
employed in a futile effort to better ourselves at each other's expense.

If these agreements should be terminated, as almost all of them
can be on short notice, this truce would be broken, and these excessive restrictions would, of course, automatically come back into
operation.

There is now grave danger that this truce may be broken. Unless
the United States is prepared to assume the responsibility for world
leadership commensurate with its power and influence in world
economic affairs, our existing trade-agreements structure may give
way under the stress and strain of war's aftermath. If this should
happen we may witness a resurgence of trade restrictions and international economic warfare far surpassing anything in our previous
experience.

* * *

We are very fortunate to have at hand, at a time when we are
uniquely endowed with all the power and influence necessary to lead
the world toward economic reconstruction, an instrument which has
been tested and improved over the years, and in which the American
people have great confidence. It has been used with caution and with
wisdom, and it will continue to be used that way. It is a powerful
instrument, for behind it lies the richest market in the world and an
incomparable productive machine. The business men of other countries want the products of that economic machine, and they will buy
them just as fast as they are permitted to earn the dollars to pay for
them.

If we allow them to earn the dollars, we shall be backing up with the strongest kind of positive action our allegiance to the principles of economic liberalism and private enterprise. These principles are in the balance today, and words alone will not save them. They will survive so long as they are able to satisfy the honest aspirations of the people of the world for economic well-being. Expanding world trade is capable of bringing a greater volume and a greater variety of goods to the people of all countries. Our way of bringing about an expansion of trade is the way of economic liberalism and private enterprise, both of which principles are embodied in the trade-agreements idea.

If this way fails—and it cannot succeed without the vigorous participation of the United States—there are other ways. There is the way of economic blocs, in which a group of nations which cannot solve their problems by letting the rest of the world in, try to solve them by shutting the rest of the world out. There is also the way of governmental barter, in which governments take over the foreign-trade function and reduce it to the most primitive terms of direct two-way exchange of goods for goods. These are two of the ways most likely to be chosen to handle international trade if the liberal, free-enterprise system fails. Both tend in the long run to contract and restrict rather than expand international trade, and both are contrary to our deepest convictions about the kind of economic order which is most conducive to the preservation of peace.

The extension and strengthening of the Reciprocal Trade Agreements Act would, I believe, give confidence and courage to our friends throughout the world who share our economic creed. It would be a signal for all to hear that the United States is not only the greatest advocate of expanding world trade based on free enterprise, fair competition, and non-discriminatory treatment, but is also determined to take the steps necessary to make such a system work.

§ *At the request of Secretary of War Henry Stimson, President Truman appointed an interim committee in 1945 to consider the plethora of military, social, and political problems attaching themselves to the development and use of atomic weapons. Clayton was among the members of that committee, as he recalls in a letter to Richard Hewlett. Subsequent correspondence with his daughter indicated his faith in the efficacy of the nuclear deterrent,*[15] *but in 1963 he wrote a letter to Senator John Tower of Texas calling for ratification of the nuclear test ban treaty as the only alternative to an armaments race which would result in either war or "galloping inflation."*[16]

To Richard G. Hewlett

December 16, 1958

Dear Mr. Hewlett:

I am glad to give you such information as I can, as requested in your letter of December 9.[17]

So far as I can remember, the question as to whether the Atomic Bomb should be dropped on the Japanese was never voted on or seriously discussed by the Interim Committee, in any meeting of the Committee that I attended. The Bomb was developed as an instrument of war. I think it was just accepted as settled policy that it would be dropped on the Japanese. Whether this came to the Committee as a decision already made, I do not recall. I do recall that there were discussions by the Committee to the effect that the Bomb should be dropped at some place in Japan which represented a maximum possibility of destruction of military installations, such as ordnance depots, airplane factories, etc., and with a minimum loss of life or injury to the civilian population.

You say that a number of writers suggest that the target of the Bomb was not so much Japan as Russia. I know of no basis for this suggestion. There certainly was none in any discussions of the Committee at any meetings that I attended so far as I can recall.

Please bear in mind, however, that my official duties took me out of Washington a good deal and especially at the time of the dropping of the Bomb in New Mexico and on Japan. I left Washington about July 8, 1945, for Potsdam to attend the Potsdam Conference, which lasted about three weeks. The President and Secretary Byrnes were, of course, there also. I left Potsdam in the early days

---

[15] Will Clayton to Ellen Clayton Garwood, November 10, 1959, L, CP, TL.
[16] Will Clayton to John Tower, September 4, 1963, L, CP, ACCO.
[17] An unsigned carbon copy of this letter to the historian of the U.S. Atomic Energy Commission may be found in CP, ACCO.

of August and flew to London where I was kept on official business until around the 15th or 20th of August, 1945. It was while we were in Potsdam that the test bomb was dropped in New Mexico. The dropping of the Bomb on Hiroshima and on Nagasaki occurred while I was in London.

As I recall it, most of our discussions in the Interim Committee related to the dropping of the experimental bomb in New Mexico and the text of a statement that the President of the United States would make when this happened as well as the text of statements he would make when the Bomb was dropped on Japan. There was considerable fear that the dropping of the bomb in New Mexico might cause civilian damage, possibly loss of life, despite the fact that it was being dropped in a location twenty-five miles away from the nearest town.

If there are any other points which you would like to develop, please let me know and I will do the best I can.

Sincerely yours,

W. L. Clayton

§ *In a speech before the Economic Club of Detroit, Michigan, Clayton gave the following summary of State Department motives and goals in formulating foreign economic policy.*

A Speech on Foreign Economic Policy

The tragic drama now gripping the world is more than a World War, it is a world revolution.[18]

There is at issue something far more elemental than any mere political, social or economic problem could ever be.

[18] This speech, entitled "The Foregn Economic Policy of the State Department," was delivered before the Economic Club of Detroit, Michigan, May 21, 1945. A copy may be found in CP, ACCO.

130

That issue is simply this:

Nations must learn to live together cooperatively for their mutual security and prosperity; otherwise, civilization will be utterly destroyed and man will return to the dark ages.

This is the law of the machine.

Man created the machine to lessen his burden in supplying the necessities of life.

In doing this, the machine has enormously multiplied man's wants.

These ever-increasing wants make man more and more dependent upon other men, and nations more and more dependent upon all other nations.

One machine calls for another machine and another, and so it will be until the end of time.

Under the impact of the machine, the world continues to shrink rapidly; there is no such thing as isolation, and man now easily destroys in a few days what it took him centuries to build. What new hellish instrument of destruction tomorrow may bring forth no man knows.

The machine can set us free; or, uncontrolled, it can and will destroy us.

To control the machine, we must first learn to control ourselves.

Man lived in isolation and independence over such great reaches of time that it is with the greatest difficulty that his mental and spiritual concepts are adjusted to the condition of dependence which the machine and modern civilization impose.

Out in San Francisco, we are trying to set up the framework of an Organization[19] within which rules may be written to guide men in their cooperative efforts to build a new world on the foundations of peace and prosperity.

The delegates there and the peoples for whom they speak know that victory in this war will not bring enduring peace but only the opportunity to work for enduring peace. They know, too, as their predecessors of twenty-five years ago failed to realize, that the most elaborate arrangements for the maintenance of political and military peace will soon disintegrate if the world again engages in the type of economic warfare it waged between the two World Wars.

Nations which act as enemies in the marketplace cannot long be friends at the council table.

The peace structure has to be seen as a great arch supported by two strong columns, one political and the other economic.

[19] The United Nations.

If either column gives way, the whole structure falls.

While the delegates of 49 countries at San Francisco work to set up this organization, a struggle is going on in Washington to prevent our own country from re-tracking the same tragic path of economic nationalism which we followed after the first World War with such disastrous results.

There are two, and only two, roads open to us in shaping our economic policies in the post-war world.

We can follow the path of economic liberalism, in keeping with our democratic principles and traditions, and without which no peace structure will long stand, or we can take that same road we followed in the 1920's—the road to economic nationalism, restrictionism and regimentation, leading inevitably to international irritations and retaliation, and the creation of an atmosphere in which the seeds of conflict are sown.

It is impossible to stand still, even if we wished: the world is moving much too fast for that now.

In the State Department, we have planted our feet firmly on the road of economic liberalism and that's the road we propose to follow.

Our foreign economic policy revolves around the conception of an expanded world economy—free and equal access for all nations to the trade and raw materials of the world, increased production, much greater exchange of goods and services between nations, increased consumption and higher levels of living for all peoples everywhere.

Now, there is not one single element of the "Santa Claus" philosophy in this policy.

On the contrary, quite aside from the question of future peace, the United States will be one of its principal beneficiaries.

Next to this problem of future peace and security, the post-war problem which concerns the greatest number of people in the United States is the problem of employment.

As you know so well here in this great industrial City of Detroit, we have enormously increased our productive capacity during the war, especially in capital and producers' goods—machinery, equipment, tools and technical knowledge. This productive capacity is now far beyond our domestic requirements.

If we are to reach a satisfactory level of post-war employment, we must find markets abroad for this surplus production.

The markets are there all right in almost unlimited volume.

Many nations require enormous quantities of goods of this character in order to repair their war devastated areas.

Other nations require the same type of goods in order to develop their resources.

It is definitely in our interest to assist these countries to reconstruct and develop because we cannot long expect to have a high level of employment and prosperity in our own country if the rest of the world is in the throes of unemployment and depression.

Moreover, we should not forget that our best markets are in the industrially developed countries of the world because it is in such countries that we find the highest standard of living and the greatest buying power.

To sum up: we have the goods for sale, and there are buyers who must have these goods, the problem is to find the dollars with which to make payment.

In the final analysis, our customers must pay in their own goods and services but this will not be possible for several years for the obvious reason that they will first have to restore and develop their productive facilities before they can produce a surplus over and beyond their own requirements.

One means of payment will be provided through the facilities of the International Bank for Reconstruction and Development. I would like to tell you something about this institution and the International Monetary Fund.

A Bill is now before the Congress to authorize our Government to join in the formation of these two institutions.

As you know, proposals for the Bank and the Fund were agreed upon at Bretton Woods last summer by delegates from all of the forty-four United and Associated Nations.

The International Monetary Fund is designed to prevent a recurrence of one of the worst forms of international economic warfare so generally practiced in the period between the two world wars.

I refer to the manipulation of currencies, exchange discriminations and restrictions and competitive devaluation of exchanges in an effort to gain an unfair advantage in international trade.

The International Monetary Fund is designed to prevent this type of economic warfare.

Members of the Fund agree to define their money in terms of gold, and to keep their money within one percent of its defined value. They also agree to avoid exchange restrictions and to consult with the Fund whenever they consider a change in the value of their currency necessary.

This agreement forms the basic elements of stability and provides the rules of the game. Countries which join the Fund agree that they will abide by the rules and will act together for the common good.

The agreement provides that each member shall pay into the Fund a certain amount of its own currency and a smaller amount of gold. A member of the Fund is enabled to purchase from the Fund with its own currency the currency of another member.

In essence, the Fund is a common effort by the nations which subscribe to it to put aside practices which are destructive of others and of the common good of all, and to provide the means which make that possible. No nation has more to gain from such a result than our own.

The International Monetary Fund promotes collective security because it seeks to establish order in the financial and economic fields, and order in those fields cannot be divorced from order elsewhere.

The second institution proposed at Bretton Woods is the International Bank for Reconstruction and Development. The Bank will facilitate investments and productive enterprises where they are needed. This does not mean that the Bank will supersede private lending.

In the normal case, a country will borrow from private bankers, but where private banks, because of the risk, cannot make the loan upon terms which are possible for the borrower, both borrower and lender may need the assistance of the International Bank.

The Bank's function will be to investigate the soundness of the projects for which capital is desired and, provided they are sound, it will guarantee the loans made by private banks. It will also require the Government of the country in which the money is to be used to guarantee the loan.

There are other means, such as the Export-Import Bank, of financing our excess of exports over imports which it is estimated may reach very large totals in the first five or six years after the war.

In all probability our total investments abroad, Government and private, may easily reach 15 to 20 billions of dollars in the first few years after the war, assuming always that we are successful in building an organization for the preservation of peace which will give us reasonable hope to expect that the peace of the world will not again be broken, at least for many years to come.

In order to make it possible for the debtor countries to pay the interest and dividends on so large a sum, it is absolutely essential that trade discriminations be eliminated and excessive barriers to the international movement of goods such as tariffs, quotas, etc. be substantially lowered.

Indeed the Bretton Woods proposals make no sense unless this necessary action is taken so that our foreign debtors will be allowed to service their obligations to us.

Surely, we do not wish to repeat the course we followed after the first World War. We had somewhat the same problem then that we have now. The way we met that problem was to provide lavishly the necessary credits which foreign countries needed for buying our goods but we accompanied that with three separate advances in the tariff just to make sure that our foreign debtors would be unable to pay us no matter how much they wished to do so. Everybody remembers the tragic consequences of that policy. We not only lost our money but we created much international bad feeling as well. Thirty-two nations promptly retaliated by erecting all kinds of barriers against our trade, and from that time until the passage of the Hull Reciprocal Trade Agreements Act in 1934, there ensued a mad race between Nations to see which could do the most to destroy international trade. The resulting damage was so great that it could not quickly be repaired.

Through the authority given in the Hull Reciprocal Trade Agreements Act, the Government is authorized to make agreement with foreign countries whereby concessions in our import duties on goods we purchase from them are traded for reductions in their duties on goods they buy from us.

This Act has been in effect for eleven years with highly beneficial results and there is now pending before the Congress a bill to extend the Act for another three years and to give to the Government additional bargaining powers under the Act.

As you know, this bill made its first hurdle a few days ago when the House Ways and Means Committee approved it by a vote of 14 to 11. But it is being bitterly fought and the battle is not yet won.

Governments are not alone in setting up barriers to an expanding world trade. Private cartels have developed enormously in the last 25 years and through the control of production, prices and markets also act to restrict the international exchange of goods. We in the State Department are opposed to such arrangements.

The whole basis of the Bretton Woods proposals and of the Trade Agreements Act and of our anti-cartels program is the promotion of an expanding economy and collective security through common action.

As has already been announced by the Secretary of State, an International Conference to consider questions of trade and employment will probably be called in the next nine or ten months.

Unless we achieve a great expansion in world economy and an increase in the levels of living of all peoples, a solution of the vast problems before all the nations may well be rendered impossible.

Most wars originate in economic causes.

The bounties of nature are distributed unequally over the earth.

Some countries are rich in one resource and some in another; still others possess almost no sub-soil resources.

Hence equality of opportunity for development in the modern world is only possible if all nations have free and equal access to the trade and raw materials of the world.

The belief entertained by many that our high wages and high standard of living are the product of a high tariff is of course an economic fallacy of the first order.

Wages and living standards are high in those countries where the proportion of land and productive facilities is high to that of the population and low in countries where the opposite is true.

Before the first World War the country in Western Europe enjoying the highest standard of living had the lowest tariff and the country in Western Europe with the lowest standard of living had the highest tariff.

A few years ago Mr. Hull had a survey made which showed that 34 tariff protected industries in this country paid its workers an average wage of about $1100 a year whereas 34 industries having little or no tariff protection and requiring none, paid its workers an average of about $1800 a year.

The United States has the most efficient industrial plant in the world and there are very few industries in this country which cannot hold their own in the world market in competition with the industries of other countries.

We lead the world in the art of combining capital, management and labor in the mass production of goods.

Lying about equally between Europe and Asia, with thousands of miles of seacoast on the Atlantic, the Gulf and the Pacific, with the best systems of transportation and communication in the world, with great natural resources and a great reservoir of capital, we are in an incomparable position to take advantage of the unprecedented opportunities which lie ahead of us.

What are we afraid of?

The only thing we should be afraid of is another World War.

Let us never forget that world peace will always be gravely jeopardized by the kind of international economic warfare which was so bitterly waged between the two World Wars.

Democracy and free enterprise will not survive another World War.

For the second time in this generation, our country is faced with the responsibilities and opportunities of participation in world leadership.

At the end of the first World War, we stepped aside and the mantle fell to the ground. This time, the mantle is already around our shoulders, and a devastated and terrified world is hopefully looking to us to help them back to peace and life.

We can do this, but only if our wisdom and vision are equal to our power and influence.

§ *Churchill, Truman, and Stalin met at Potsdam, Germany, between July 17 and August 2, 1945, to discuss implementation of the Yalta agreements and to settle a number of European problems, such as German reparations and the drafting of peace treaties. Clayton was in charge of the Reparations Committee of the American delegation at Potsdam.*

To Hon. James F. Byrnes

July 29, 1945
Babelsberg, Germany

This memorandum is in confirmation of my statement to you this morning on reparations and is written merely for the purpose of placing my views on record and not for the purpose of prolonging the discussion.[20]

1. I think enough has been said at Yalta and at Moscow to justify the Russians in feeling that they have a right to 50 percent of whatever reparations in kind can be got out of Germany.

[20] Printed in *Foreign Relations of the United States, 1945*, vol. 2: *Conference of Berlin (Potsdam)*, pp. 900–901.

2. The only practicable method of apportionment between the different claimant countries is on a zonal basis so far as Russia is concerned.

3. If the Russian zone contained 50 percent of the movable industrial capital equipment of Germany of the kind which the Russians seek, the problem would be simple.

4. The most reliable information we have is that the Russian Zone contains only 40 percent of the movable industrial capital equipment of Germany and that this equipment consists predominantly of the light industries (textiles, printing, apparel, saw mills, etc.) and contains relatively little of the heavy industrial type which the Russians want.

5. I suggest, therefore, that we should be prepared to trade with the Russians on the following basis:

(a) Reparations claims of Russia and Poland to be satisfied from the Russian Zone plus 25 percent of such industrial capital equipment as we decide should be removed from the Ruhr (estimated roughly at ½ of such equipment) on condition that an additional like amount of such equipment would be exchanged for an equivalent value in food, coal, zinc, potash, timber and oil to be made available to us by the Russians from their zone.

(b) All other claimants for reparations (U.S., U.K., France, *et al.*) to be satisfied out of the Western Zone.

6. German merchant fleet not considered in the above but to be covered by a separate arrangement.

7. United Nations property in Germany and satellite countries, if taken for reparations, to be safeguarded or compensated for in accordance with memoranda of the U.S. Delegation of July 25.

Since the Russians must bow to the U.K. and U.S. decision regarding their right to receive reparations from the Western Zone, I feel that any decision to exclude them from any participation in the distribution of the heavy equipment in the Ruhr as reparation, would be considered by the Russians as a reversal of the Yalta and Moscow position, since no Allied understanding would be necessary to enable them to get reparations from their own zone. Furthermore, we are committed to the substantial de-industrialization of the Ruhr, and it is doubtful if other claimant nations for reparations will be able to use all the equipment which will be removed from that area. In other words, to give a reasonable percentage of such equipment to the Russians will cost nothing.

W L C[layton]

A Statement on the Potsdam Conference

Most of the trouble there was of two natures: Russia's insistence on putting the Western Boundary of Poland on the Oder–Neisse line, west of the pre-war boundary, and Russia's demand for $10,000,000,000 reparations from Germany.[21]

I worked on the second problem. At Yalta Roosevelt had agreed the Soviet Union could have 50 percent of whatever reparations should be exacted from Germany. The Russians, at Potsdam, stressed a claim for $10 billion and wanted to take it in factories and other goods. I was on the Commission which decided which plants should be dismantled. The Soviet was to have 25 percent, 15 percent free, 10 percent to be compensated for by shipment of raw materials—food, coal—from their zone to West Germany.

I had to talk to Vishinsky[22] and Maisky,[23] who had been Soviet Ambassador to England for 11 years. The interpreter for Vishinsky showed him to be a very aggressive, disagreeable kind of fellow. We were going over the memorandum which we had drawn up, which said the factories should be dismantled and furnished within a period of two years, and that, in the case of the 10 percent that were to be compensated for by the Soviet sending in raw materials from their zone, these factories were to be furnished to the Soviets "as soon as possible." I agreed to put that in. Then in the same period the raw materials came in. Vishinsky asked that we add here the words "to be furnished as soon as possible." I agreed to put that in. Then he saw on the 2nd page something he wanted me to change. I said he'd have to agree to the 2nd page as it was if he wanted me to add on the 1st page "as soon as possible." He swore and sputtered, then finally said, "Well, strike out 'as soon as possible,' then!"

One day Vishinsky was late at a meeting where I was Chairman. He always talked like a blue streak, and that day he came in talking and kept on talking as he sat down. I said "Mr. Vishinsky, before you came in we were discussing a suggestion by the British member.

[21] This statement is from an interview with Ellen Clayton Garwood in December 1947.

[22] Andrey Y. Vyshinsky, Deputy Minister of Foreign Affairs (1940–49), chief Russian delegate to the United Nations (1946–49).

[23] Ivan Maisky, former Ambassador of the U.S.S.R. in Great Britain (1932–43).

If you like, we can explain it to you." He kept talking. I repeated. Then he said, "We aren't children. We don't need so much talking to explain!" That's the way we parted.

We had had a big argument with the Russians for a week. They wanted reparations to be the first charge on exports out of Germany. We said, "No. We have to bring much into Germany—food, raw materials—to get factories going again for peacetime production and we must get paid for this before anything goes for reparations." They said, "We can never get the Russian people who have sacrificed so much to understand why the Wall Street bankers have to be paid before they are!" I tried to explain to them. "This is like the receivership of a big corporation. If a railroad company can't pay its debts, the receiver keeps that road going, issues receivers' certificates which take precedent over all creditors, for otherwise the creditors would get nothing." This was about 2 A.M. I was arguing with Dr. Arutyunyan,[24] a little shrewd Armenian Russian professor, with beady, cold, black eyes. "Now, Dr. Arutyunyan for the 10th time I tell you we won't do it." He said, "You did it in the First World War." "Yes," I said, "and that was a mistake and we'll never do it again." We could never agree on reparations!

Stalin is broad gauged, dignified, knows how to give in when it suits him; speaks clearly, briefly without notes, well-ordered mind—things stored there in proper sequence and order. He always spoke with no show of feeling. In one meeting Churchill spoke for 20 minutes, telling how badly the British Ambassador to Yugoslavia had been treated, how he had been shadowed and followed by the Soviet police, etc. Finally Stalin said, "Daydreams, daydreams all." Stalin is smaller than Truman and is pasty looking.

One day we came out of the Cecilienhof Palace late, about 1:45 P.M. and we saw in the palace park 3 autos, creeping one behind the other, with men walking in front. We started to pass. As we got up to them we saw Molotov and friends walking, and on both sides the woods were full of Soviet soldiers sticking bayonets in bushes, looking behind every bush and tree.

---

[24] Amazasp A. Arutyunyan, head of the Economic Department of the Russian Ministry of Foreign Affairs (1944–54).

§ As the U.S. delegate to the United Nations Relief and Rehabilitation Council, Clayton was in charge of UNRRA affairs for the State Department. Recognizing that reconstruction of foreign economies had to proceed promptly if the world economy were to lend itself to the liberal trade policies which he sought, Clayton was a consistent defender of UNRRA in its early days. He made the following statement on UNRRA before the House Foreign Affairs Committee.

A Statement on UNRRA

The commencement of these hearings on a new authorization by Congress for United States participation in the work of UNRRA is a reminder to me of the support and cooperation which we have received from this Committee in attempting to solve this whole vast problem of relief and rehabilitation in the war-devastated areas.[25] I was very gratified when the Chairman informed me last July that your Subcommittee would participate in the UNRRA Council deliberations. While the members of this group were in London during August I think they were able to gain for themselves some impression of the magnitude of the problems facing the national delegations to the Third Council Session, and the UNRRA Administration itself. Other members of this Committee had an opportunity during the summer to see UNRRA at work in the field as an international relief operation. Therefore, most of us are approaching these deliberations with a sense of the urgency and the importance of the continuance of this country's support for UNRRA.

My own introduction to UNRRA and its problems really occurred in the course of the Council meeting in London. I had been asked by the President to assume the Council membership in June because my responsibilities in the Department for economic affairs made it logical for me to replace Mr. Acheson.[26] Preparation for, and

[25] This statement was delivered before the House Foreign Affairs Committee, November 14, 1945, and printed in U.S. Department of State, *Bulletin*, 13 (November 18, 1945): 809–12.

[26] Dean G. Acheson, Undersecretary of State (1945–47) and Secretary of State (1949–53).

attendance at the Potsdam conference, made it practically impossible for me to familiarize myself in any detail with the UNRRA organization, its past progress, or its future plans until I arrived in London late in July. I then had an opportunity to survey all of the operations of UNRRA up to that time and to form an independent judgment of its significance, its performance, and its future.

UNRRA had been subject to considerable criticism for delay and administrative bungling in getting started. It had been competing unsuccessfully with military operations and other wartime activities for competent personnel and for the supplies and facilities which were necessary to do its job effectively. So long as total war continued in the Pacific, I knew UNRRA would have to face a continuation of these difficulties. These obstacles, however, were largely removed by the surrender of Japan which occurred in the course of the Council's deliberations.

The end of hostilities in Europe three months prior to the Council meeting had already burdened UNRRA with many other problems of relief and rehabilitation. Our armies and those of our Allies, which had been carrying the major burden of civilian supply to western Europe and the Mediterranean countries, were quite rightfully eager to shift that responsibility as soon as possible. A similar situation developed in eastern Europe where all supply and transport were necessarily under the control of the Soviet military command until victory over Germany was achieved. Then and then only could civilian governments and agencies begin to undertake their share of the work. We therefore realized that UNRRA, in the course of the summer, was entering upon the period of full-scale operations. It was the only functioning relief organization able to take over from the military and the only instrument through which all the European countries, as well as the other United Nations, could concert their common interests in helping to restore some semblance of economic order to that continent.

The urgency of the relief and rehabilitation problem in the Far East was equally apparent. The abrupt end of the war with Japan posed the immediate problem of relief for occupied China, a world responsibility for which no agency was sufficiently prepared except UNRRA. Although UNRRA of course had not anticipated beginning notice, it had established many months previously a mission in China which was working closely with the Chinese National Relief and Rehabilitation Agency. Not only had the plans for relief distribution been tentatively agreed upon but also preliminary screening of a target program for China had been completed and was before the Council for consideration. The fact that UNRRA's plans and personnel were so well prepared to assume immediate operating responsibilities made it easy for the Council to agree provisionally on the scope of UNRRA activities and expenditures in China, pending a further review when the mission on the spot could make reports of actual conditions.

The United States Delegation to the Council meeting, on which I was fortunate in having broad and competent representation from all the interested agencies of this Government, as well as from the Congress, reached early agreement on several objectives. We decided that the needs of all the liberated areas which were not to be under the continuing control of the military and which had insufficient foreign-exchange resources to purchase essential relief supplies abroad could best be met through a single channel. The use of any agency other than UNRRA for these new responsibilities would have meant creating a competing unilateral relief organization, which would have immediately indicated to the world that we doubted the feasibility of international cooperation. We therefore agreed to seek extension of UNRRA operations to Italy and Austria in Europe, and to Korea and Formosa in the Far East.

I would also like to mention in this connection the limited program of relief and rehabilitation assistance through UNRRA to the two Soviet republics of the Ukraine and White Russia. Any invaded country is entitled to seek UNRRA assistance provided that the established procedures and policies for such assistance, as agreed upon among the member nations and embodied in the UNRRA resolutions, are observed. The Soviet Union had made an application for UNRRA aid shortly in advance of the Council meeting in the amount of $700,000,000, which was only enough to cover a part of the minimum supplies essential to relieve their civilian population on terms similar to those of adjacent areas.

In the course of discussing this application with the Soviet Delegation, I emphasized that I did not see how such a program could be included in the UNRRA budget without serious penalty to other receiving countries. I also felt the people of America, as well as those of other contributing countries, would not sympathize with relief assistance of this magnitude to a country which had some foreign-exchange resources at the expense of countries which had none, though admittedly the Russian resources were inadequate to meet the necessary rehabilitation and reconstruction supplies which the U.S.S.R. would have to secure from abroad. The Soviet Delegation ultimately accepted our point of view and agreed to substitute for their original application one for $250,000,000, to be used exclusively for food and certain other relief articles in White Russia and the

Ukraine, the two most devastated Soviet areas. It was understood that UNRRA operations should be carried forward in these two republics just as in any other country receiving UNRRA assistance, with an UNRRA mission establishing the validity of requirements on the spot and observing distribution. This application for limited relief and rehabilitation assistance has already been reviewed under the regular UNRRA procedure for certification of ability to pay, and the two Russian republics have been determined by five UNRRA member governments, including the United States, to require the limited assistance requested.

The Delegation was also aware of the concern in many quarters that UNRRA might be undertaking rehabilitation responsibilities for a longer term than that originally envisaged. We concluded that if a cut-off date for UNRRA operations were established, the receiving countries would have a greater incentive to maximize their indigenous production of relief supplies. The Delegation therefore agreed to recommend a stoppage of UNRRA shipments to Europe not later than the end of 1946, and a similar stoppage of shipments to the Far East not later than three months thereafter.

In reviewing the criticisms which had been leveled at UNRRA in the past and the corrective measures that might be taken to improve participation in UNRRA activities by member nations, the United States Delegation felt that the governments concerned should take a more active interest in furnishing supplies, services, and competent personnel to UNRRA. We also decided that it would be desirable for the Director General to have the assistance and advice of the Council, through the Central Committee, in determining equitable distribution of UNRRA's resources among the various receiving countries.

Lastly, my advisers were aware that there remained many unsettled policy questions with regard to UNRRA displaced-persons operations. We knew that several Council members did not feel UNRRA should give any assistance to displaced persons without the consent of the government of origin. Such a restriction would not be acceptable to the American public, and UNRRA would face an impossible task administratively if it could not undertake the care of all categories of displaced persons for which it was responsible without reference to repatriability, or to race, creed, and political belief. Also, in scaling UNRRA demands down to a minimum, we recognized that the administration should not have to advance the cost of supplies needed for the care of displaced persons in enemy territory when such charges were ultimately to be borne by the enemy country itself. The Delegation therefore determined to recommend that the occupying authorities should furnish these supplies and be responsible for recovering their cost later from enemy assets.

As the record will show, and as most of you are aware, we succeeded in attaining all of our objectives at the Council meeting in London. In many instances, agreement was not reached with the member nations without considerable debate and in some instances only after major differences of opinion had been resolved. Nevertheless, agreement was reached on a basis which I believe was in the interests of the United States and also in the interests of UNRRA and all member nations. The very fact that such a meeting of the minds was achieved is a most encouraging sign that international cooperation on matters of common concern is possible.

I feel that the recommendations of the London Council meeting, which are financially embodied in the new legislation being considered by this Committee, represent a program which is in our best interests. I believe this Committee's examination of the problem before us will justify my sincere conviction that we are asking Congress to do what is right and necessary as our share of world relief and rehabilitation.

This Committee must reach conclusions on the two major aspects of the relief and rehabilitation problems which the world now faces—the need and the method. I have no doubt of your conclusion as to the need on the basis of the facts which are available and which will be laid before you. Nor have I any doubt as to your acceptance of the urgency and the necessity that this Government take the promptest possible action to announce to the world by legislative action our willingness to play our part in this great task. I hope also that this Committee will reaffirm that in UNRRA we have the proper method of furnishing relief and rehabilitation assistance.

I have recently heard criticisms to the effect that UNRRA is a cumbersome and ineffective mechanism, and that we should substitute for it a national relief agency. I am convinced that such ideas are held by relatively few of our citizens and arise chiefly from a failure to consider all aspects of the problem.

We, as a nation, have committed ourselves to international cooperation and collaboration. UNRRA is the first operating experiment in the implementation of this policy. I have recognized difficulties and weaknesses in the UNRRA administration, which are also recognized by the Director General, Governor Lehman,[27] and I will do all in my power as this Government's representative on the Council to

[27] Herbert Lehman, Director-General of the United Nations Relief and Rehabilitation Administration (1943–46).

help overcome or correct them. Any alternative method for giving relief and rehabilitation assistance to countries without sufficient foreign-exchange and credit resources to meet the problem themselves is, to my mind, unthinkable and impractical.

§ The following documents illustrate Clayton's early advocacy of post-war aid to Great Britain and indicate the importance he attached to commercial policy concessions from the British in return for such aid.

A Statement on the British Loan and Lord Keynes[28]

Early in the War Keynes,[29] Lionel Robbins,[30] and Lord Brand[31] and other British economists came over here. At one of the international conferences they were discussing how to weather inflation. They thought they could do it by manipulating money—they once had a scheme to stabilize commodities. Keynes thought the Allies should stabilize commodities, not from point of view of deflation—he would let prices fluctuate—but within a wider range. When product got so low that the owner would have to sacrifice it or have to sell it to stay solvent at that point you would freeze the price—at the extinguishing point. I went to bat with them on that one and they finally dropped it. I asked them how you ever determined the "extinguishing point." The answer is you can't.

I told them "We had a depression in this country from 1929 until World War II. In that time cotton sold for 25¢ a pound and the Farm Credit Board made a law it shouldn't go below 16¢ a

---

[28] This statement is from an interview with Ellen Clayton Garwood in 1958.

[29] Lord John Maynard Keynes, English economist and author.

[30] Lionel Robbins, English economist and Director of the Economics Section of Offices of the War Cabinet (1941–45).

[31] Lord Robert Brand, head of the British Food Mission to the United States (1941–44); representative to the United States for the British Treasury (1944–46).

pound and they put up $500,000,000 to help the cooperatives. Finally they just gave them 16¢ a pound for their cotton and then it fell to 5¢. Now, I asked, at what point in that fall from 25¢ to 5¢ would you have put a floor under the price and they couldn't answer."

Later at the FAO Conference at Hot Springs right after the war—one of the first international conferences—Sir John Orr,[32] a Scotchman—such a nice fellow—brought up the idea again of stabilizing commodities. I went to bat again with them and they dropped it.

Keynes thought you could spend away during depressions and in prosperous times pay back the debt. The trouble is the debt always gets bigger, for you never pay it back. We're prosperous now but not paying off our debt. The National Credit is beginning to be strained. Soon it will be hard to sell people government bonds. That means the government will sell to the banks more. When a bank buys $1,000,000 worth of bonds the government spends the money and someone who is paid it puts the paper money in the bank which creates more money, more inflation.

I was very impressed by what some economist once wrote. He wrote that the extravagance of the rich creates a rise of prices for the poor. A rich man, say, spends $100,000 to buy luxuries for his family; this, in turn, causes the man on a small income to have to pay more for things. I believe we should have consumption taxes instead of production taxes.

Lord Catto,[33] Director of the Bank of England, told me once that Keynes came into him one day (you know Keynes had been a Governor of the Bank of England for years) with some brilliant scheme he was sure would solve all the problems of the day at once.

Catto said, "But Maynard, you came in last week with a scheme just the opposite to this."

Keynes said, "Yes I know, but that was last week."

* * *

I felt that the British had not gone about the convertibility clause of the loan with a great deal of care or intelligence. As a result of the war the British owed about 4 billion pounds to India, Egypt and other parts of the British Empire which had delivered goods to them that they couldn't pay for; they had been dependent on these goods for all their factories were busy producing war ma-

[32] Sir John Orr, Professor of Agriculture at the University of Aberdeen (1942–45) and author; Director-General of the United Nations Food and Agricultural Organization (1946–47).

[33] Lord Thomas Catto, financial adviser to the British Treasury (1940–44).

terials. But the British had troops stationed in India and Egypt for which India and Egypt had charged them; I insisted much of their debt to those countries should be written off and that what was left should be at an extremely low rate of interest. We tried to provide in the British Loan Agreement that during the pendence of the Loan the British be limited as to how much they should pay on their old debts.

When the British did open up the doors of the Bank of London to free convertibility of the pound, a great deal of these old war debts pounds were cashed. I think at the time a lot of these countries got these old war debts paid off instead of just current transactions. If the banks had only cashed current transactions they could have weathered it better.

For the first six months this year the British exports have exceeded imports without counting shipping services and tourists, for the first time in this century. It's remarkable!

To Hon. Fred Vinson

Washington, D.C.
June 25, 1945

The British financial problem is admittedly the greatest present barrier to rapid progress towards free multilateral payments and relaxation of barriers to trade.[34] It threatens not only delay but, indeed, the ultimate success of our economic foreign program. It is, therefore, definitely to our interest to give Britain the financial help required to bridge the transition to peacetime equilibrium.

It would be quite unwise, however, to consider making Britain an outright gift of the required several billion dollars, as has been recently suggested by certain critics of Bretton Woods. It would be unwise even to supply the funds as a credit without laying down

[34] This memorandum to the director of the Office of War Mobilization and Reconversion (1945) is printed in *Foreign Relations of the United States, 1945*, vol. 6, pp. 54–56.

conditions that would insure a sound advance towards our post-war objectives.

On the other hand, it will be difficult to persuade the British to accept dollar credits rather than work out their financial problems within the Sterling Area by the devices of blocked balances, exchange control, exchange pooling, bilateral clearing arrangements and forced exports in liquidation of sterling balances. Hence the terms of the credit we offer Britain and the conditions we lay down for granting it must be devised very carefully, with a view to Britain's position as well as to ours.

I believe we should offer Britain a dollar credit of as much as $2 or $3 billion as required, repayable over 30 years, but with an option on the part of the British to make prepayments at earlier dates. The amount granted must be sufficient to meet Britain's adverse dollar balance under multilateral current payments, as laid out in the section on conditions below.

In view of British reluctance to borrow, and the fact that they are able to finance themselves to a very substantial extent by blocked sterling at a fraction of 1 percent, we must be prepared to grant them credit at the lowest possible rates. A rate of 2⅜ percent, such as we have used on 3c Agreements under Lend-Lease would, in my judgment, be high enough, and possibly we should go as low as 2 percent. The British will want even lower rates. Interest charges would, of course, apply only on balances actually outstanding.

British reluctance to incur dollar indebtedness could be appreciably reduced, and possible stifling effects of service and repayment at later times be avoided, by provisions that if, because of a slump in world demand, Britain's balance of payments became unfavorable, Britain would not be considered in default. The possibility of the U.S. accepting limited amounts of sterling as repayments under certain circumstances might be considered.

I would propose the following conditions for the granting of the above financial aid:

1. Upon the granting of the credit, the Sterling Area dollar pool arrangement is to be terminated and sterling proceeds thereafter acquired on current overseas account by non-residents of the United Kingdom are to be made convertible into dollars, at the option of the holder, for current transactions.

2. A substantial funding of the abnormal sterling balances which have arisen from the war should be required. In the case of India, Egypt and certain other areas, substantial writing down of these balances is justified and to the best interest of all concerned. European and Latin American balances should, on the other hand be

funded, and Britain might be left free to repay agreed portions thereof by exports during the transition years, so long as sterling proceeds of current trade are kept convertible into dollars.

3. Elimination of Empire preferences, probably as one term in a new reciprocal trade agreement reached under the strengthened act or as part of a multilateral trade convention. The British will resist this most strenuously. Perhaps a substantial reduction of preference is all we can hope.

4. Britain must continue domestic import controls over non-essentials to reduce the transitional strain upon her balance of payments and hence the amount of financial aid required. She will undoubtedly wish to do this in any case.

5. Canada, and perhaps other countries whose international financial position will be strong at the end of the war, should also grant transitional financial aid to Britain. India, for example, might be asked to make her contribution in the form of sharp reduction of her sterling balances.

The above proposals will be recognized as a compromise between full-fledged freedom of payments and the strict wartime controls. Aside from the elimination of Empire preferences, their main effect would be to secure substantial compliance with conditions laid down in the Bretton Woods Agreements very shortly after the war rather than at the end of a transition period of five years or more. It is nevertheless of the utmost importance to accelerate Britain's reconversion to multilateralism in this way, both because of the danger that bi-lateralism and restrictionism might otherwise become firmly imbedded in British policy during the transition, and because the American business public will demand early evidence that Britain is going to go along with us in our post-war trade policy if they are to continue to support it.

W. L. Clayton

TO HON. JAMES F. BYRNES

London, England
August 18, 1945

8390. For the Secretary and Acheson from Clayton.[35] I have now had a number of talks which I have separately reported with British officials both before and after the fall of Japan regarding immediate transitional and long-range financial and trade policies and programs and the wind-up and settlement of lend-lease.

The British position is undoubtedly very serious and the moving forward of V-J means that the British will have accomplished much less reconversion for import than they had hoped and planned. The same situation, of course, applies in some measure in the U.S. Keynes and the other British officials find it difficult to discuss financial and trade policy because the new Cabinet until Wednesday was entirely occupied with the preparation of the King's speech on the opening of the Houses of Parliament. Keynes hopes that in a few weeks he will be able to get sufficient clearance for further discussions with us but insists that if as a result of our pressure he urges early decisions they are likely to be the wrong decisions.

In this situation Keynes, Eady[36] and the other officials urge a breathing spell continuation of nonmunitions lend-lease as I have reported elsewhere; broad discussions in Washington early in September on the whole range of lend-lease wind-up, clean-up, and settlement supplemented by at least fairly concrete immediate financial discussions relating to the deficits anticipated by the British balance of payments during the next 3 years. The British recognize that we will insist on discussion of commercial, cartel and commodity policy in connection with such financial discussions but are trying to maneuver us into discussing finance without requiring full trade discussions at the same time. Keynes would probably readily agree that problems of exchange convertibility and the sterling dollar pool would have to be discussed at once but Empire preferences, reduction of tariffs and

[35] This memorandum is printed in *Foreign Relations of the United States, 1945*, vol. 6, pp. 103–5. Cables were sent over the name of the ambassador; the author's name was indicated in brackets at the end of the text.

[36] Sir Wilfrid Eady, Joint Second Secretary of the British Treasury (1945).

other trade barriers, cartel policy and commodity policy he would like to put off into next year as much as possible.

I have indicated that it is essential that we discuss both finance and trade simultaneously; that it will be necessary for us to come to a broad understanding as to postwar trading methods and policy before we can ask the Congress for any large scale financial aid to British. I have also pointed out that the clean-up and settlement of lend-lease which Keynes so strongly urges must be associated with article VII arrangements. It was finally left that I without waiting to return home and report more fully to you and the President would take up with you steps for further discussion.

I have been informed that you will probably not arrive in London for the Council of Foreign Ministers[37] before September 10. My recommendations as to further procedure with respect to more formal discussions of the British problem are based on the assumption that you will be in London for some period following September 10 but would return to Washington before any conversations with a British delegation would be nearing their conclusion. On these assumptions I would recommend the following course:

(1) That I return to Washington 2 or 3 days after the conclusion of the UNRRA council meeting after an appointment which I have tentatively planned with the Chancellor of the Exchequer and certain aviation discussions which the British have requested. I should arrive in Washington if the UNRRA meeting goes well by the 27th. This would give me a full 2 weeks in which to report in detail to you and go over with you and other appropriate officials the main lines of policy which we would take in discussions with Keynes and his British colleagues.

(2) That without awaiting my oral report you consider requesting the President to agree to the British sending the sort of delegates which Keynes has suggested for discussions beginning early in September.

(3) That after full discussion with you prior to your departure for London we with the collaboration of the various agencies involved lay the groundwork with the British for final discussions after your return hearing the British presentation of the detailed facts of their position and in particular attempting to work out with FEA details of lend-lease wind-up and clean-up.

(4) That we attempt to arrive at basic understandings with the British on Lend-Lease, financial assistance, and trade policy in October after you have returned.

[37] First session of the Council of Foreign Minsters, September 11–October 2, 1945.

If you approve and the President so decides I should like to inform the British when I have my meeting with Dalton[38] that we agree to their coming to Washington early in September. This will give the British some time in which to go into these matters adequately with Ministers and to formulate their own views.

In connection with my talk with Dalton I should greatly appreciate an indication of the decisions which have been taken on the lend-lease issues to which I referred in my earlier telegrams and if possible a specific statement of policy from you which I might transmit to Dalton.

In reviewing my communications to you I am a little afraid that I may have sounded too discouraged about the British attitude. I am not. I believe that the discussions ahead will be difficult but I am certain that we can and will get forward with them. [Clayton]

WINANT[39]

§ *On July 14, 1946, President Truman signed the Anglo-American Financial Agreement into law. As one of the principal negotiators of the agreement, Clayton was largely responsible for its final form. He felt that the agreement offered an excellent opportunity to force British postwar economic policy into liberal channels. On November 17, 1945, he wrote to General R. E. Wood, "If we make the loan, one of the principal purposes will be to enable the British people to open up their commerce to the United States and all other countries instead of confining it to the British Empire as they would largely be compelled to do if they were not able to obtain the necessary assistance to get their trade back on a multilateral basis."[40] Without the loan, Britain would be "driven to the only alternative which she has, i.e., further strengthening of the Empire Preference system."[41] In the following documents Clayton stresses the benefits which would accrue to the United States if the agreement were to be adopted.*

[38] Hugh Dalton, Chancellor of the Exchequer (1945–47).
[39] John Winant, Ambassador to Great Britain (1941–46).
[40] Will Clayton to General R. E. Wood, November 17, 1945, L, CP, TL.
[41] Will Clayton to Alben Barkley, January 28, 1946, L, CP, ACCO.

A SPEECH ON THE ANGLO–AMERICAN AGREEMENT

I am very grateful to the National Farm Institute for this opportunity to discuss with you the Anglo-American Agreement which was recently negotiated, involving, among other things, the extension by the United States Government of a 4 billion, 400 million dollar credit to Great Britain.[42] 650 million dollars of this amount covers Lend-Lease and surplus property which we are transferring to Britain and the remaining 3¾ billion dollars is new money.

Time does not permit of a discussion of the detailed terms of the credit such as the rate of interest, the maturity, and other similar conditions. I doubt if you would be particularly interested in such details. The terms of the credit were agreed upon after long and careful negotiation and, despite the feeling of some of our British friends that we drove too hard a bargain with them, I believe that these terms are fair to both countries.

The question is asked by many people as to why Britain needs this money and what she will do with it.

That is a proper question and deserves a proper answer.

Perhaps we might start by naming some of the things for which Britain will *not* use this money. She will not use it for nationalizing British industries and she will use very little of it for physical reconstruction, reconversion and modernization of her industries. It should be obvious to anyone that Britain requires no dollars for socializing British industries. She bought the Bank of England with sterling bonds. Sterling will buy anything in Britain. It is only for purchases abroad that some other kind of money is necessary.

In order to be able to understand the British economic and financial position, two important points must be kept constantly in mind. The first is that Britain lives by imports, which is just another way of saying that she lives by exports, because, obviously, her imports have to be paid for by exports.

The second point to keep in mind is that Britain mobilized for this war both in material and human resources to a considerably greater degree than we did in the United States. That she should mobilize to the limit was obviously in our interest.

[42] This speech was delivered before the National Farm Institute, Des Moines, Iowa, February 15, 1946; a copy may be found in CP, ACCO.

In doing so, she sacrificed substantially her export trade. That also was in our interest because it meant the maximum use of her resources and her productive capacity for fighting the war. At the end of the war, Britain was exporting only 30 percent of her prewar volume.

During the war, the United States and Canada supplied British import requirements through Lend-Lease, but this arrangement ended with the close of the war.

The 3¾ billions of dollars of new money which the proposed agreement would make available to the British is, therefore, for the purpose of enabling her to pay for a part of her necessary imports of food and raw materials until her industries can be reconverted to peacetime production and her export trade restored.

The British estimate that not until 1949 will their exports of goods and services be sufficient to cover their essential imports, even though such imports are on a considerably reduced volume as compared with prewar. Meantime, she faces an inevitable deficit in her accounts with the United States and the rest of the world of something like 5 billions of dollars. This proposed U.S. credit, plus other credits that Britain expects to obtain from Canada and elsewhere, will be used to meet that deficit.

The next question which arises in most peoples' minds is "Why should the United States lend this money to Britain and what advantage or benefit will we receive from so doing?"

That also is a proper question and deserves a proper reply. All of this money will be spent directly or indirectly in the United States. Our farmers, our industries and our workers will obviously benefit from that, but that alone, important as it is, is not sufficient consideration to us to make this loan.

I believe we can get a better understanding of the benefits which the United States will derive from this credit by considering, for a moment, what Britain's course will be if the Congress should refuse to ratify this agreement. In that event, Britain would be compelled to find some other means of paying for her essential imports during her period of reconversion. Britain does have an alternative course, a course which was strongly urged by a very powerful and vocal minority group in Britain which vigorously opposed the approval of this agreement in the British Parliament.

Lacking dollars with which to buy in the United States, Britain would be compelled to tighten her belt still further and to secure her major import requirements of food; cotton, and other raw materials in countries willing to take payment in sterling and wait until such time as Britain would be prepared to pay in British manufactures. This would mean that Britain would, of necessity, have to confine most of her trade to British Empire countries and other countries willing to enter into trade agreements of this character.

Stated differently, Britain would be compelled further to tighten and cement the economic ties which bind the British Empire; she would strengthen the sterling area dollar pool arrangements; she would extend and expand the Empire Preference System which grew out of our high tariff policy following the first World War; she would be compelled to continue in force those import and exchange controls which discriminate against U.S. goods; she would, of necessity, confine the bulk of her purchases to those countries agreeing to take payment in British goods.

If Congress should fail to approve this credit, Britain could, in the alternative course indicated, provide for her necessary imports during the reconversion period. At the end of that three or four-year period you may be sure that this whole, vast complicated system of government-controlled trade would have fastened itself so firmly on the British economy, that it would be practically impossible to change it. Moreover, the many countries whose trade is linked closely with that of Britain would almost certainly follow Britain in this direction.

Under such a system, one can no longer buy in the cheapest market and sell in the dearest; he buys and sells where governments direct, regardless of prices or other commercial considerations.

Under such a system, the total of international trade is materially reduced, production and consumption are curtailed and the standard of living declines.

Under such a system, economic power, in time, becomes linked to political power, and economic blocs become political blocs, to disturb the peace of the world.

The British know the harmful effects of this bilateral barter system of trade as well as we do. The British Empire was built on a multilateral system of world trade in which every country was free to trade with every other country on equal terms. Now that the war is over, Britain would like to return to that system. Unfortunately, her economy has been so greatly weakened by six years of total warfare that she will be unable to do so unless she can obtain a loan of the necessary dollars to enable her to shift back to normal peacetime methods.

With the aid of this credit, Britain agrees to abolish the sterling area dollar pool arrangement within one year from the effective date of the agreement. She further agrees that within one year whatever sterling is earned in Britain by anyone, anywhere in the world, will no longer be treated as frozen balance to be paid only with British or sterling area goods, but will be convertible into dollars or any other currency for buying in any part of the world. When you remember that Britain has always been our best customer, you can get some idea of the value of this pledge to us.

Of even greater long-term importance is the fact that Britain is enabled by this credit to join with the United States in full partnership in supporting our Proposals for the Expansion of World Trade and in our Government since the spring of 1943. They have now been delivered to the other countries of the world. They are to be considered in the World Trade Conference that we expect will be called by the United Nations Organization for the latter part of 1946. We have discussed and considered these proposals with the British in great detail and our two countries are in substantial agreement on them. These proposals deal with tariffs, preferences, cartels, quota arrangements, discriminations, etc. If we can achieve the objectives outlined therein, we will pull the world out of the nationalistic form of trade which has developed so insidiously and extensively during the last 30 years and get it back on a multilateral trade system such as existed prior to the first World War wherein every country is free to trade with every other country on equal terms. This would open the markets of the world to the United States. This is of enormous importance to all of us, and particularly, it seems to me, to agriculture.

Let us see what it means to our agricultural interests to have British markets open to us, not to speak of world markets. In normal times, we sell more farm products to Britain than to any other country. More than a third of our total agricultural exports went to Britain in 1938, the last prewar year. Our exports of agricultural products to Britain averaged around a quarter of a billion dollars annually in the years before the war. Prior to the first World War, the volume of these exports was still larger. If we should suffer the permanent loss of this business, it would hurt.

In the last year before the war, Britain bought 18 percent of our raw cotton exports; 21 percent of our corn exports; 31 percent of our wheat exports; 62 percent of our lard exports; 72 percent of our tobacco exports; 84 percent of our exports of canned fruits; and 85 percent of our exports of hams and shoulders.

This is the story of our agricultural exports to Britain in the recent past. But if world trade is freed of the unreasonable restrictions and impediments which now plague it, we have reason to believe that Britain will become an even better customer for our farm products in the future.

Just before the war, we negotiated a reciprocal trade agreement with Britain in which we obtained many concessions of direct benefit to American farmers. We secured the removal of the British import duties on non-Empire wheat and lard, and an increase in the quota for U.S. hams. In addition, we obtained duty reductions on rice, many fresh, dried and canned fruits, and canned vegetables. Altogether, we obtained import duty concessions from the British (including guarantees that certain duties would not be increased) on farm products which constituted about five-sixths of Britain's total agricultural imports from us.

These reductions in duty took effect too soon before the outbreak of war to have much effect on our prewar exports of farm products to Britain. How much effect they will have on our exports to Britain in the years ahead will depend very largely on whether Britain has the dollars to pay for an increased volume of agricultural imports from us. That, in turn, depends very largely on whether world trade is conducted on an open or a closed basis.

Demand for farm products is now at a high level, and many agricultural commodities are in short supply. It would be foolhardy, however, to conclude that the problem of farm surpluses has been permanently solved, and that foreign markets are no longer important to us. I remember, and many of you remember, what happened after the first World War: The value of our agricultural exports fell by nearly 50 percent from 1919 to 1921, and our cash income from the sale of farms products fell by more than 40 percent over the same two-year period. The collapse of the foreign market was unquestionably one of the main causes of the sharp decline in our farm income.

The British need our agricultural products, and need them desperately. Other countries need them, too. Before many months have passed, we will again need the British market as our chief foreign outlet for the products of our farms. We want to sell the goods that Britain wants to buy; but because of the financial dislocations resulting from the war, the British temporarily lack the means of payment. The proposed loan to Britain is a businesslike solution of this problem. Under the loan, we would carry our best customer on credit, thereby maintaining an outlet for our goods, until he is able to reestablish his earning power and pay his own way.

Without the loan, it is perfectly clear what path Britain would take, and how our farmers would be affected. The British would have to conserve their dollar resources very carefully, and spend them only for essential products which cannot be produced in Britain or bought elsewhere in the world. They would have to subsidize even further the expansion of inefficient British agriculture. They would have to obtain more and more of their agricultural imports from the countries of the sterling area, with whom they have special trading relationships. They would have to resort to primitive barter arrangements, obtaining agricultural products from countries which would be willing to accept an equal value of British goods in return. All of these things would tend to freeze the American farmer out of the British market, to pile up farm surpluses in the United States, and to depress the prices of our farm products.

It is said that Britain defaulted on her first World War debt and that this credit will suffer a similar fate. I do not agree.

The first World War debt was incurred for things which Britain had to have in order to fight the war—her war and our war. This time we knew better. Tanks were furnished Britain on Lend-Lease. Last time we insisted on payment for these things plus a high rate of interest; this time we do not propose to charge for food which was consumed, or ammunition which was shot away at the enemy, or airplanes which were used to bomb his war plants—all in a common effort to preserve the liberties of the English-speaking peoples and of our allies.

To keep the record straight, we should remember that Britain did pay over two billion dollars of the first World War debt, 1½ billion of which was for interest alone. For each four dollars she paid, only one dollar went for reduction of principal. She even made token payments after the moratorium of 1931. This is hardly a record of intentional default. Another important aspect of this matter is the fact that following the first World War we raised our tariffs three different times and made it impossible for Britain to sell us sufficient goods to earn the dollars with which to pay her debt to us. This time we don't propose to raise tariffs.

It is also urged by some that the British credit will add to the dangers of inflation.

Inflation is undoubtedly a serious threat to our domestic economy. It is very unlikely, however, that the granting of this credit would aggravate the danger of inflation, for the following reasons:

The British line of credit will be available over a period of five years and will undoubtedly be spent gradually.

Only a portion of it will be spent directly by Britain in the United States. That portion will be used largely for the purchase of food and raw materials, some of which we already have in surplus as, for example, cotton and tobacco. Wheat and corn may also be in surplus after the next crop or so. Our capacity to produce all of these things and many others besides is far greater than domestic requirements. If we can again open up the markets of the world to our products, the problem of surpluses will lose its threat.

The remaining part of the credit will be spent by Britain in South America and other parts of the world for the purchase of raw materials which she cannot obtain to advantage in the United States. Such other countries will, in turn, spend these dollars in the United States for the most part for capital goods, equipment, machinery, engineering services, etc. for the development of their resources and their economy. The United States has a great surplus capacity, created during the war, for the production of such things and we should welcome orders to keep these plants running. A prosperous manufacturing industry moreover will afford a better domestic market for the products of American agriculture.

It is also urged that the credit to Britain will serve as a pattern for other large loans and for that reason should not be made.

Upon examination, it will be seen that this is not an impressive objection.

The British agreement is unique. The commitments undertaken by Britain are of a character which no other country can match.

The British Empire accounts for one-third of the international trade of the world. Due to the elimination of Germany and Japan, in the world market, it is more likely that three-fourths of the international trade of the world will, in the next few years, be transacted in dollars and pounds sterling. Under these circumstances, Britain's partnership with us in putting world trade on the right track and keeping it there is of the highest importance. There is no other country whose support is so essential for the success of our world trade program.

Due to the unique character of the British Agreement, the commitments which it contains, and the size of the credit which it involves it is necessary to refer the matter to Congress for approval. The credit is not for reconstruction or reconversion but is for working capital until Britain can sufficiently recover her export trade to pay her own way.

The International Bank, to be organized under the Bretton Woods Agreements, should be ready for business within a year. This Bank is being organized for the purpose of making loans for reconstruction and development. This is the institution that will care for long-run credit needs of this character. Meantime, the Export–Import Bank has made some loans of this character and doubtless will give consideration to other applications to take care of essential needs pending the time when the International Bank will be ready.

Now that World War II is over, there are only two economic courses open to the countries of the world. They can continue on a nationalistic bilateral barter system, patterned along the lines developed so intensively by Nazi-Germany, or they can go back to the multilateral basis where every country is free to trade with every other country with a minimum of restrictions and discriminations. The former system gives rise to the formation of economic blocs. Under it we would certainly start out in the postwar world with three powerful economic blocs—a sterling bloc, a dollar bloc and a Russian or rouble bloc. There would be pulling and hauling between these blocs in their struggles for more power and more trade territory.

An economic bloc means the regimentation of international commerce. Lincoln said, "This Nation cannot exist half slave and half free." This applies to commerce as well as to human beings. If we have regimentation in our foreign trade, how long do you think free enterprise can continue in our domestic commerce?

No doubt you will agree that peace is hardly possible in the world without the collaboration and cooperation of the United States, the Soviet Union and Great Britain. I leave you to judge as to whether these countries would be likely long to continue to work together harmoniously for the preservation of peace in the world if they were at the same time carrying on the bitterest kind of economic warfare.

World wars contribute greatly to economic nationalism. Nations at war find it necessary or expedient to put themselves in an economic straight jacket. Such artificial and unnatural trading systems throttle competition and force trade into the narrow, restricted channels dictated by governments. Moreover, they build up vested interests which find protection and profit in their continuance.

On the other hand, the multilateral system of trade opens up the markets of the world to all countries on equal terms; economic blocs become impossible; the trade of the world develops and expands under a system of natural competition; production and consumption expand and the standard of living rises for all peoples everywhere. Surely it must be evident that this is the system best calculated to promote peace and plenty in the world.

The main prize of the victory of the United Nations in this war is a limited and temporary power to establish the kind of world we want to live in. I want to emphasize that this power is both limited and temporary.

The fundamental choice is whether countries will struggle against each other for wealth and power or work together for security and mutual advantage. That choice was made in principle at San

Francisco and has since been ratified by the overwhelming majority of the Governments concerned. The question now is whether we in the United States will seize this present opportunity to give leadership to the high enterprise of starting the postwar world off on the right track economically, or whether we will stand aside and let the world drift with the tide into dangerous waters of nationalism and restrictionism of all kinds.

Britain can only join with us in this high enterprise if she obtains the necessary assistance to enable her to make a revolutionary shift herself from the closed to the open multilateral system of world trade. With the help of Britain, leader of the greatest international trading area in the world, there is strong reason to believe that we can be successful in charting the right course—without her help we can hardly hope to succeed. We must choose now!

MEMORANDUM FOR BERNARD BARUCH

Washington, D.C.
April 26, 1946

Dear Mr. Baruch:

Please excuse me for delay in replying to your memorandum of the 17th.[43] I have been going at a pretty hard clip lately.

We always knew that the British would nationalize banking, railroads, aviation and coal. As a matter of fact, aviation was nationalized before the war and railroads partially so. The laws regarding the employment of labor in the coal mines practically nationalized coal before the war.

There was always some doubt about steel, but now the British have nationalized that, as you say.

[43] Bernard Baruch to Will Clayton, April 17, 1946, Baruch Papers, Princeton, in which Baruch expressed concern over the course of socialization in Britain. An unsigned carbon copy of Clayton's reply may be found in CP, ACCO.

Bulk buying of cotton and other raw materials is one of the unfortunate legacies of the war, not only in England but in France and other countries. We are continuing quite a bit of bulk buying by the Government in this country. Copper is one example.

We don't like bulk buying, and we are doing everything we can to discourage it, but we recognize that it cannot be abolished overnight. In some countries, five or six years of war has destroyed merchandising machinery so that government is compelled to do the buying for some time, in any case.

Bulk buying by foreign countries does not mean that we must have one seller of the commodity in the United States. We had bulk buying by the Russians for a number of years before the war in cotton and everything else.

Our agreement with the British, if ratified by Congress, will help to slow up or prevent further nationalization of industry and commerce by Britain. If Britain doesn't get the loan from us, she will be compelled to adopt all sorts of restrictive measures in order to make "buckle and tongue" meet, and complete nationalization of her foreign trade will be inevitable. Under our agreement this will be avoided, because Britain will go on a multilateral basis. Under the agreement, Britain also agrees that any bulk buying will be done on an economic, non-discriminatory, and not a political, basis.

Equal access to raw materials means, I think, that all countries may purchase such materials on equal terms. It certainly does not mean that each country gets raw materials according to its needs.

Equal access has certainly not been the rule in the past. Colonial powers have often so arranged matters that they had a preferred position. The cinchona bark of Java is one example that comes to my mind. Java, before the war, was almost the only producer of this commodity, and the Dutch so arranged matters that they had a quinine monopoly, because they didn't let anybody else buy the bark. This persisted up to and, indeed, into the war in spite of American Government efforts to the contrary.

There are many other examples. I will write you further on this subject in the next few days.

Moreover, if a country possessing large deposits of essential raw materials pushes its import tariffs so high that the ability of other countries to acquire and pay for such materials is greatly restricted, this may be equivalent to denial of equal access. This point is not generally understood, but I am sure it will be clear to you on a moment's thought.

Our task in restoring the world to a multilateral trade basis is an extremely difficult one, and we don't expect immediate success, but we are convinced that we must succeed if UNO is to have a fair chance of preserving the peace.

Suppose Massachusetts should say to Texas: "We buy 15 million dollars of cotton from you a year, but you buy your shoes in St. Louis instead of in Boston. Now, we will continue to buy cotton from you to this amount provided you buy our product—shoes. In other words, you must take your payment in shoes." And suppose other states in the Union should take the same position and all our trade was, in this way, converted to a bilateral basis. Of course the supposition is a ridiculous one, but it is a fair way to illustrate just what is taking place between nations when they conduct their trade on a bilateral basis.

The only way Britain can convert her foreign trade to a multilateral basis is through the assistance that she will get in this financial agreement in order to help her over the next three or four years of reconversion from war to peace.

You may be interested in the enclosed clipping from this morning's *New York Times* on "World Trade Aims Encounter Snags."[44]

Sincerely yours,

W. L. Clayton

[44] Michael L. Hoffman, "World Trade Aims Encounter Snags," *The New York Times*, April 26, 1946, p. 6.

§ The following discussion of UNRRA aid reflects Clayton's pre–Cold-War desire for Soviet-American cooperation in rehabilitating the world economy.

To Hon. Kenneth McKellar

Washington, D.C.
July 3, 1946

My Dear Senator McKellar:

Since the fundamental objective of our foreign policy is to create conditions in the world under which we can live in friendship and peace with all nations, I am gravely concerned about the action recently taken in the House of Representatives in adopting the so-called Dirksen Amendment to the Third Deficiency Appropriation Bill.[45]

This Amendment, as you know, would deny use of the U.S. contribution to UNRRA for aid to any country which refused to agree not to censor the reports of American press representatives concerning the distribution and use of UNRRA supplies. As the record of the debate in the House of Representatives will show, this Amendment was directed at the Soviet Union. This action was taken in consequence of a reply received from the Soviet Government, in answer to a request by the President that that Government undertake to permit reporting, with respect to UNRRA operations, free of the censorship rules which have been established in Soviet territories. The President made his request pursuant to the direction of Congress as expressed in Public Laws 259 and 262, 79th Congress.

I should like to take this opportunity to give you my views on this matter. At the outset let me say that I believe no one is more firmly convinced than the Secretary and I that the free interchange of information between the peoples and countries of the world is essential to the creation of a secure peace. We in the Department of

---

[45] This letter to U.S. Senator Kenneth McKellar of Tennessee (1917–53) is printed in Department of State, *Bulletin,* 15 (July 7, 1946): 35–37. The Dirksen Amendment was rewritten in the Senate to meet Clayton's objections on July 12, 1946.

State are constantly seeking to achieve this objective. My concern about the Dirksen Amendment therefore is not because I do not seek the freedom of information which I feel certain the House had in mind when it approved this Amendment, but because I feel that its passage would achieve precisely the opposite result.

The facts are these: While Russia, in its reply to the President's request, has not agreed to remove established general rules of censorship with respect to despatches from our correspondents on the use of UNRRA supplies, we have abundant evidence that no attempt has in fact been made to restrain the free flow of information regarding the distribution of UNRRA supplies.

Recently a group of correspondents, including representatives of the New York *Times*, *Newsweek* and the Associated Press have made an extensive tour of the Ukraine and White Russia—the Soviet Republics in which UNRRA is furnishing relief—and have been permitted to report freely and fully on the use which is being made of UNRRA supplies. In addition, UNRRA itself has missions in each of these two areas, both headed by Americans of unquestioned courage, integrity and high standing, and these missions have had complete freedom to travel about the country, to observe anything they wished to see and to report without interference of any sort. Both the UNRRA missions and our news correspondents report that these areas of Russia have suffered destruction greater than we had imagined, that the conditions are pitiful and the need most urgent, and finally that UNRRA supplies are being distributed with scrupulous attention to the principles which guide UNRRA's operations in all areas. In addition, there are reliable reports that the common people of these areas are not only fully aware that the supplies are coming from UNRRA, but are inclined to give the whole credit for UNRRA's activities to the United States. As a result, the good will being created for our country by the UNRRA programs is so great as to astonish the Americans who are there with the UNRRA missions.

One of the reasons why we are so concerned to promote the free interchange of information between countries is that only by such a process will the common people of all countries come to know and appreciate the achievements and points of view of each other. I believe from all I can discover that the UNRRA program in the two Soviet Republics is serving most effectively to promote the accomplishment of these objectives.

I am convinced that the adoption of the Dirksen Amendment would set us back immeasurably in this respect. I think I can indicate why I feel this way by examining the effect its adoption would have upon the Russian people. Undoubtedly, the Soviet Government and the people who are in such dire need and who are now receiving some relief through the UNRRA program would say, and I fear, with considerable justification, "We are scrupulously living up to the UNRRA principles of distribution; there has never been any attempt here to cover up what is being done with these supplies which are being sent in; there has, in fact, been complete freedom to American press representatives and to the Americans on the UNRRA missions to report anything they wish to report. What, then, is the reason the relief has stopped? Even if we should agree under pressure that we will never apply our rules of censorship to reports about UNRRA, it would not change the situation at all because we have never applied that censorship and we don't intend to. However, we are not going to have anyone dictate to us. We would rather suffer without help than bow to a threat of this kind."

I am sure you will agree with me that any proud people would react this way. As a result, we shall, if we insist on this point, merely give those who may be working against friendship and free interchange of information, a real basis for making the charge that we are using relief for political purposes and that we are making threats to achieve our objectives. We may very well, by such action, wipe out the gains we have already made toward this friendship and interchange of information through the activities of UNRRA in these areas.

This whole issue, of course, has a far wider significance than its effect on the UNRRA program. I feel sure that adoption of the Amendment would seriously complicate all our relations with the Soviet Union and would, without achieving any tangible benefit for us, make far more difficult negotiations on many other issues.

I should like to assure you that if there were not in fact freedom of observation for the UNRRA missions and for our correspondents to report on the use of UNRRA supplies in these two Soviet Republics, I should strongly advocate that the furnishing of supplies cease. In such a case there would be a real matter of principle involved, for we and other contributing nations to have the right to full information concerning the use of UNRRA supplies. Director General LaGuardia[46] feels just as strongly on this point as we do.

I would like to point out further, that all of the members of UNRRA, in approving the UNRRA agreement, subscribed to the policies and regulations governing its operations which had been set up by mutual agreement. If each of the contributing members should now by its own unilateral action attempt to establish new and special

[46] Fiorello LaGuardia, Director-General of the United Nations Relief and Rehabilitation Administration (April-December, 1946).

conditions, the operation of UNRRA would become impossible. There is no question but that the UNRRA Council and the UNRRA Administration have taken steps to assure adequate observation and complete reporting without censorship by UNRRA missions and by press representatives with respect to all matters of concern to UNRRA in the two Soviet Republics.

There is one other point which seems to me of great significance. One of our important concerns today is to demonstrate that international organizations can succeed in dealing with matters which affect the interests of all nations. This is not an easy task, as recent experience clearly proves, and we have made less progress at it than we had hoped for. Every success we do have, however, by showing that success can be achieved, tends to develop confidence in international organizations generally, and thus promotes success in other cases. Conversely every failure has the opposite effect. With all the difficulties which have beset UNRRA and with all the differences of opinion that have developed from time to time, nevertheless it cannot be denied that it is one of the international organizations that has succeeded, on the whole, in accomplishing the objectives for which it was designed. It has effectively brought relief to millions of people in the war-devastated areas, it has produced vast good will for this country and for the other contributing countries, it has increased contacts between citizens of all nations and promoted knowledge and understanding of each other among peoples throughout the world. It has demonstrated the fact that men of many different nations can work together successfully to solve a world-wide problem. It would be a tragic thing, in this critical period in international affairs, with UNRRA so close to the end of its period of operations, to destroy in large part the effect which UNRRA has had in promoting confidence and understanding between nations and to turn its success as an operating international organization into failure during the last months of its existence. I should very much regret to see such an outcome of an international effort which, otherwise, has such bright prospects of confounding those who doubt that any attempt at cooperation by nations in a common cause is possible.

I apologize for having burdened you with such a long discussion of this subject, but it is, in my opinion, of such vital importance in the whole field of our foreign relations that I must put before you fully the considerations which I believe would make the adoption of the Dirksen Amendment a very grave mistake.

Sincerely yours,

W. L. Clayton
Assistant Secretary

§ *On July 29, 1946, delegates from twenty-one nations convened for the Paris Peace Conference. Clayton accompanied Secretary of State Byrnes as his aide and, on August 3, made the following radio broadcast from Paris to the American people.*

A SPEECH ON U.S. FOREIGN ECONOMIC POLICY
AND GOALS

Paris, France
August 3, 1946

Here we are in Paris where for the second time in one generation a delegation from the United States is meeting with delegations from other countries to try to make peace after a great world war.[47] Altogether there are 21 nations represented here—countries which fought the war together against Axis aggression in Europe.

We have got so used to the radio in the last few years that some of my listeners may have forgotten that it was not possible during the drafting of the Versailles Treaty some 27 years ago to talk from Paris to the United States as I am now doing.

In the speech of Secretary Byrnes at the opening of the Paris Peace Conference, we find words which I want to use as my text this evening.

He said: "We want to plant the seeds of future peace and not the seeds of future wars."

The Department of State, where I work, has the responsibility, in conjunction with the President and the Congress of fixing the foreign policy of the United States Government. My own responsibility relates to the economic aspects of such policy.

The foreign economic policy of the United States is simple. Here it is:

The United States is committed to the support of all sound measures which will contribute to an increase in the production and consumption of goods throughout the world to the end that people

---

[47] This speech was delivered over the facilities of the National Broadcasting Company, August 3, 1946; a copy may be found in CP, ACCO.

everywhere will have more to eat, more to wear, and better homes in which to live.

We do not contend that higher living standards will of itself guarantee the peace but we do believe that it will create a climate conducive to the preservation of peace in the world.

In order to achieve our objective of a rising standard of living throughout the world, we are committed to the reduction of barriers to the international movement of goods and to the elimination of discriminatory practices in international trade. Such barriers and discriminations sprang up rapidly following the first world war.

The United States Congress has given the President ample authority to deal with these matters through the extension and enlargement of the Hull Reciprocal Trade Agreements Act.

Not only must barriers be lowered and discriminations eliminated if trade is to revive and flourish, but positive action must also be taken for the reconstruction of devastated areas and for the further development of the world's resources.

The Congress of the United States has also acted promptly and adequately in this field through a substantial increase in the lending power of the Export–Import Bank, by ratification of the Bretton Woods agreements, by a contribution of $2,700,000,000 to UNRRA for relief and rehabilitation purposes and by ratification of the credit to Britain. Add to this the foreign credits extended for the purpose of taking over Lend-Lease inventories and pipe lines, and sales made or to be made to foreign countries on credit of surplus property and we reach a grand total of nearly 20 billions of dollars invested by the United States Government since the ending of the war in its effort to assist in the restoration of economic life abroad.

All of which should be sufficient proof of our deep and substantial interest in the economic aspects of the peace treaties now being written here in Paris.

In the economic field, these peace treaties must provide workable settlements of the issues arising out of the war. They must likewise lay a basis for the resumption of normal economic relations between the former enemy states and the United Nations. But many of these problems give rise to conflicting views and interest.

Take, for example, the question of reparations. It is natural that the countries which suffered from aggression should demand reparations from the aggressor but we must take into account the aggressor's ability to pay. It would do much more harm than good to exact so much of the former enemy that his economic and social structure would be so seriously weakened, as to endanger not only his own stability but that of his neighbors as well. We must not repeat the mistakes of the Versailles Treaty.

The peace treaties must deal with a variety of other complicated economic subjects. The most obvious are the claims arising out of the war. In modern warfare all the numerous and complicated relations existing between warring nations in finance, trade, transport, and other fields of economic activity are severed. These relations must be reestablished. The legal position of business enterprises affected by the disruption of relations must be defined. Methods must be provided for the settlement of disputes regarding property relations, patents, shipping and many other items.

The United States wishes to see these and other war problems settled fairly and promptly. International business relations cannot be restored if there is to be a long period of uncertainty and if assets are to be tied up in protracted litigation for claims procedures. It took many years after the last war to settle many of these problems. The present treaties should provide for speedy settlements so that the former enemy states may promptly resume normal economic relations with the United Nations.

The draft treaties also include provisions of a temporary character governing trade and other economic relations between the former enemies and the United Nations. These provisions, which would assure non-discriminatory treatment, are designed to bridge the gap until new economic agreements can be concluded between the former enemy states and the United Nations. Unlike the provisions of the 1919 treaties on these subjects, which imposed unilateral obligations on the enemy states, the clauses proposed by the council of Foreign Ministers are reciprocal. The Allies will be entitled under these proposals to fair treatment of their trade and business enterprises only if they in turn grant similar treatment to the enemy states. Agreement on any other basis could not long endure.

Indeed there are many differences between the 1919 treaties and the drafts which are now being considered at this peace conference. We have really learned something from experience. One striking difference is in the length of the treaty provisions. In the first world war treaties the economic clauses contain a vast amount of detail and added together make up a book of substantial size. The drafts prepared by the Council of Foreign Ministers are short in comparison. Principles are laid down within the framework of which details can be worked out with the enemy states on a fair basis.

In attempting to deal with future economic relations, the clauses are brief and directed only toward the problems of the first year or so in the post-war period. Many of the rather lengthy and complicated provisions regarding trade, transport and other matters found in the 1919 treaties are avoided. After the present treaties are concluded, the enemy states will be eligible to apply for admission into the United Nations and into the various international organizations which the United Nations have already created in the economic fields, such as the International Bank, the monetary fund, food and agricultural organization and numerous others.

There are certain economic questions on which the Council of Foreign Ministers did not reach agreement or which the Council felt could be settled only after study and recommendations by the peace conference. These questions include certain aspects of the reparation problem, the status of regarding property relations. Some involve issues of principle. Others involve problems primarily of a technical character. The appropriate commissions of the conference will doubtless discuss these matters fully and will make recommendations which will facilitate the task of the Council of Foreign Ministers in drawing up the final treaty texts.

The economic provisions of the Versailles peace treaties were full of faults; the economic policies of the nations of the world, ours included, following the first world war were tragically wrong; we broke just about all the rules. No one can say with certainty just how much all of this contributed to the second world war. We do know that it was a powerful factor in the creation of conditions making for war.

In drafting the present treaties we have constantly striven to avoid the mistakes of the past, in the hope that wise economic provisions might help plant the seeds of future peace and not the seeds of future wars.

§ *In 1946 Clayton was vigorously attacked on the editorial page of the* Washington Post. *In the following letter to the editor he defends his conception of UNRRA as a temporary emergency relief organization.*

To the Editor of the *WASHINGTON POST*

Washington, D.C.
August 15, 1946

Dear Sir:

On my return from Europe, my attention has been called to your August 1st. editorial entitled "Gravy Train."[48] In that editorial you say that my use of the expression "gravy train" in connection with UNRRA was exceedingly inept; you criticize my promise to Congress that the State Department would not ask for a third contribution to UNRRA and you say that there will still be need for relief in 1947 and that UNRRA is the logical organization through which to extend such relief.

1. Your authority for asserting that I used the expression "gravy train" in connection with UNRRA may derive from an article by James Reston in the New York Times of July 27 in which he says: " 'The gravy train is going round for the last time,' Assistant Secretary of State W. L. Clayton told representatives of several other nations at the State Department this week."[49]

The meeting to which Mr. Reston refers was a small, informal off-the-record meeting to discuss the future of UNRRA. Only six people were present besides myself. Three of the six are now abroad and cannot be conveniently consulted. I have conferred with the other three, two of whom say categorically that I made no such statement at the meeting, the third says that he has no recollection that I made any such statement. I myself do not recall making this statement; if I had made it, I think I would remember it.

---

[48] An unsigned carbon copy of this letter may be found in CP, TL.
[49] James Reston, "End of UNRRA Is Sought by Agency's Big Backers," *The New York Times*, July 27, 1946, 1:4.

As your attribution of this statement to me is without any quali-
fication whatever, perhaps you will be good enough to give me your
source of information.

2. Now, as to your criticism of my promise to Congress that the
State Department would not request a third contribution to UNRRA
in addition to the total of $2,700,000,000 appropriated by the Con-
gress to UNRRA in the first and second installments, I have this to
say:

This promise was made when I appeared before the Congress in
support of our request for a second authorization for appropriations
of $1,350,000,000 to UNRRA.

I made the promise for these two reasons:

First, I felt strongly that UNRRA, organized as it was to do an
emergency job, would have finished that job by December 31, 1946,
and should come to an end at that time, in accordance with a resolution previously adopted at the UNRRA Council meeting in London
in August 1945. Second, the request for the second authorization of
$1,350,000,000 encountered such vigorous opposition that I believed
it was necessary to make the promise in order to obtain favorable
action.

3. As to your statement that there will still be need for relief
in 1947 and that UNRRA is the logical organization through which
to extend such relief, I have the following to say:

UNRRA was created as an emergency organization to do two
things in particular for the liberated countries:

First: to supply foreign exchange to furnish supplies to those countries which themselves lacked the means to pay for needed supplies.
Second: to provide an organization to procure, to ship and to deliver such supplies.

It is now quite evident that with one or two possible exceptions
all the liberated countries are in a position to perform for themselves the service of procurement, shipping and delivery of supplies.
No doubt you will agree that the sooner they take over the complete
responsibility for their own buying and shipping, the better it will be
for them and for everybody concerned. When a country can do these
things for itself, it can usually do them much better and much more
cheaply than any international organization which may be set up for
that purpose. To insist on continuing to do for them what they can
do for themselves is to treat them like public charges.

Thus, the problem becomes one exclusively of the mean of payment; in other words, it is no longer an emergency relief problem,

brought about by the breakdown of administrative and transportation machinery. It is a balance of payments problem. UNRRA was not organized to meet the general balance of payments problems of countries. You do not need a great expensive international relief organization employing thousands of people to meet this problem. Other institutions were created to assist in the solution of that problem.

Moreover, a moment's reflection should convince anyone that there has also been a vast improvement in the foreign exchange position of the liberated countries. Most of these countries are gradually regaining their export trade. It is true that so far the export of their goods is of modest proportions as compared with prewar levels, but it is confidently expected that the volume of such exports will increase rapidly since there is and will be for some time a great unsatisfied demand for all sorts of goods all over the world.

In addition to this normal method of providing foreign exchange, the United States and other countries have, by loans and otherwise, added enormously to the foreign exchange resources of the world.

The United States Government alone has supplied foreign exchange in the following important particulars: Three billions of dollars through loans by the Export–Import Bank, 3¾ billions of dollars credit to the British Government which will be spent all over the world, 6 billions of dollars as the United States contribution to the International Bank for Reconstruction and Development[50] and to the International Monetary Fund, several billions of dollars credit for financing lend lease inventories and pipelines and the sale abroad of surplus property on credit. Thus, including contributions to UNRRA, the United States Government has made available a total of nearly 20 billions of dollars to assist in restoring and stabilizing the economies of other countries.

Many other countries have contributed to the capital of the International Bank for Reconstruction and Development and to the International Monetary Fund. Indeed, these two institutions will have at their disposal some 15 billions of dollars with which to give assistance to United Nations countries having need of such assistance for reconstruction, development and the stabilization of their currencies. These two international financial institutions have now been organized and will soon be ready for operation. The International Bank has already made a call on the member countries for the first contributions to its capital and is now receiving applications for loans.

It will thus be seen that measures have been definitely taken

[50] Established at the Bretton Woods Conference in July, 1944, to extend loans to nations requiring economic rehabilitation.

for the provision of a total of nearly 30 billion dollars of foreign exchange to countries which need it.

It is not contended that the availability of this enormous amount of foreign exchange will be equally distributed over the world. But the point is that the buying power which these vast funds will generate will circulate around the world and will be a very great contribution to economic recovery everywhere. I would remind you, however, in any case, that nearly all the United Nations either are, or have a right to be, members of the International Bank for Reconstruction and Development and the International Monetary Fund. To the extent that these or other institutions such as the Export–Import Bank meet the reconstruction or other needs of countries having difficulties with the balance of payments problem, the other normal foreign exchange resources of such countries arising from their exports or otherwise are released for the purchase of food.

For example, the Export–Import Bank has recently made available to Poland a credit of 40 million dollars which will be used largely in the purchase of railway equipment for the movement of coal. Poland is now exporting about 120 million dollars worth of coal a year, half to Russia and the other half to Western Europe, and I was told last week by responsible Polish officials that this would increase to 260 million dollars as soon as the new equipment can be received and put into use.

Isn't it clear, therefore, that this 40 million dollar loan not only relieves the Polish Government from the necessity of using any of their foreign exchange for the purchase of essential railway equipment, thus freeing such exchange for the purchase of food, etc., but that it makes possible, soon, a great addition to such foreign exchange resources?

On numerous occasions I have fought UNRRA's battle before Congressional committees and elsewhere.

Looking back upon the original idea of the creation of a great international organization for emergency relief and rehabilitation, I have the highest admiration and praise for the man who first conceived it and whose leadership and energies brought it into being. It was an act of real statesmanship. The work of UNRRA will certainly go down in history as the greatest organized humanitarian achievement of all times.

But UNRRA's job was of a temporary and emergency character. The original UNRRA agreement and many of its resolutions amply attest to this. Indeed, in the beginning it was confidently believed that 1 percent contribution of national income of all the contributing countries would produce enough money to complete the job. This was implied in the hearings before our Congress on the bills to appropriate this 1 percent. The original 1 percent was expected to yield nearly 2 billion dollars and it was felt then that this huge sum would be sufficient to cover the emergency needs of the liberated countries until these countries were able to provide for themselves or until other means could be devised.

But it was quite evident at the London Council meeting a year ago that the job could not be done on 1 percent and it was decided to call for another 1 percent. The United States delegation, of which I was the head, took the lead in sponsoring this action. At the same meeting it was agreed that UNRRA would complete its programs for Europe by the end of this year and for the Far East by the end of the first quarter of 1947.

It is easy to start a great organization like UNRRA with billions to spend but it is not easy to stop it. The receiving countries would naturally like to continue it because they have found it easy to obtain very substantial assistance in this way. There are numerous receiving countries, each of which has a vote in the distribution of relief. Three countries furnish about 93 percent of the funds and each has one vote. The United States furnishes 72 percent of the funds and has one vote.

The United States is not a limitless reservoir of wealth and goods. We have some serious problems of our own. It cost us the blood and lives of hundreds of thousands of our boys and over 400 billion dollars to win the war. Our national debt is nearly 300 billion dollars and is difficult to manage from the point of view of the control of inflationary trends.

We don't want to see the people of any country suffer for the lack of food and have never turned a deaf ear to such people and I don't think we ever will. At the same time, now that the great emergency needs of other countries have either been provided for or institutions have been created for the purpose of providing for them, we must keep a careful watch over our own resources and our own liabilities.

Perhaps the most important economic consideration in the world today is that the United States should not repeat the experience of the '20's and early '30's—an experience of "boom and bust"— because if that should happen to us again the consequences would be disastrous, not alone to us but to the rest of the world as well.

Sincerely yours,
W. L. Clayton

IV

UNDERSECRETARY

OF STATE

1946–1947

§ During World War I, Will Clayton was a member of the Cotton Distribution Committee of Bernard Baruch's War Industries Board. In the course of their sporadic correspondence after that relationship, Clayton was generally deferential to Baruch's opinions. They found themselves in complete disagreement, however, on the desirability of the British Loan.

To Bernard Baruch

Washington, D.C.
December 16, 1946

My dear Mr. Baruch:

Please excuse me for delay in replying to your letter of November 23rd.[1] The UN, the CFM[2] and various international conferences have played havoc with our staff here.

I did say to you that I thought the British would socialize only three industries—coal, transportation and steel—.

Up to date, I believe they have socialized only coal. Transportation is now under consideration for socialization. So far as I know, the idea of socializing steel has been shelved for the present.

The Cotton Board was set up to handle importations of raw cotton. The British Government has announced that it will not socialize the cotton textile industry.

I do not consider such things as banking, insurance, cotton merchandizing as industries in the sense in which I discussed this matter with you. I think I told you at the time that it was the inten-

[1] This letter is in Baruch Papers, Princeton University.
[2] The Council of Foreign Ministers met in London (September 11-October 2, 1945), Paris (April 25-May 15; June 15-July 12, 1946), and New York (November 4-December 11, 1946).

tion of the British to continue government bulk buying of cotton which was established during the war.

The United States Government still retains the import monopoly on numerous commodities, for example, tin, rubber, quinine, antimony, etc. The United States Government continues to contract for the Cuban sugar crop and monopolizes the importation of same into the United States.

I believe the British will eventually turn back to private people the importation of cotton and other commodities.

Meantime, we have an understanding with the British that these governmental bulk purchasing programs shall be conducted on an absolutely non-discriminatory basis. On that understanding, the cotton South is no worse off with respect to the sale of American cotton to Britain than it was under the old system.

We loaded the British loan negotiations with all the conditions that the traffic would bear.

I don't know of anything that we could or should do to prevent England or other countries from socializing certain of their industries if that is the policy they wish to follow. To attempt to force such countries to adopt policies with respect to their domestic economies contrary to their wishes would, in my opinion, be an unwarranted interference in their domestic affairs.

Your statement that the policy of trying to lend other people money to buy things in short supply here is the height of absurdity is quite another matter. So far as I am concerned we are not *trying* to lend money to anybody.

You and I have differed about the British Loan. I respect your views. But I will stick to mine!

With kindest regards and every good wish, I remain,

Sincerely yours,

W. L. Clayton

§ *Clayton's advocacy of liberal trade policies was premised on a healthy European economy. When it became apparent that UNRRA aid would not restore European countries to an acceptable level of economic prosperity, Clayton made the following statement in support of President Truman's request for $350 million relief for Europe and China.*

A STATEMENT ON POST–UNRRA RELIEF

The purpose of the Resolution now under consideration by this Committee is to provide relief to millions of persons in war devastated countries who are still dependent upon outside assistance for food and other essentials of life.[3]

Through UNRRA and the military programs several billions of dollars have been made available to the peoples of the liberated areas for food, clothing, medicine and other essential supplies. Great progress has been made in these countries in their struggle to return to a normal life. The United States can be justly proud of the part it has played in helping these millions of unfortunate people to get back on their feet. Yet the task is not quite finished. The assistance still required is small relative to that already given, but without it many of these people will perish by starvation and millions will be seriously undernourished. We cannot hope to achieve permanent security and prosperity in a world where such conditions exist. Even with the minimum of assistance which has been planned, the peoples involved will still have barely enough to eat.

The UNRRA pipelines soon will run dry. The great bulk of UNRRA supplies will have been shipped to Europe by the end of March and shipments will practically cease during April.

The Committee is, I am sure, aware of the position taken by the Department of State and the President regarding post–UNRRA relief. It has not seemed wise or proper to meet the remaining needs through an international agency. Instead it is believed that the prob-

[3] This statement was delivered before the Foreign Affairs Committee of the House of Representatives, February 25, 1947; a copy may be found in CP, ACCO.

lem which remains can best be handled directly between the individual contributing countries and the recipient countries. The Secretariat of the United Nations will be useful as a clearing point for the exchange of relevant information.

One of the major arguments advanced by the United States representatives in making clear this position regarding relief in 1947 was that the problem, although of utmost urgency and seriousness, was not of the magnitude of past years and could be handled more efficiently and expeditiously without the cumbersome mechanism of an international relief agency.

That argument is still valid. Some of the UNRRA countries no longer require free assistance; others, not as fortunate, need relatively small amounts of additional assistance to carry them through another year. Thereafter, it is expected that they will be able to stand on their own feet. In addition we feel that we can more effectively adapt our program to meet changing needs and can maintain better supervision over the use of our funds and supplies by dealing directly with the countries needing assistance.

The State Department estimates that the minimum relief requirements for the calendar year 1947 of needy countries amount to about $610 million exclusive of remaining UNRRA shipments. The following European countries appear to have need of outside assistance: Austria, Greece, Hungary, Italy and Poland. It is anticipated also that China may have emergency needs for food imports to prevent suffering and starvation in certain areas and that some financial assistance may be required for this purpose.

*　*　*

The need for assistance in food imports is particularly acute, in most of the areas involved, during the Spring and early Summer months prior to the harvests, and suffering and a serious economic setback will occur if help is delayed. On the other hand if sufficient assistance is provided promptly there is every reason for anticipating that, with the possible exception of Austria, these countries will not need further free relief after 1947. In the case of Austria some further help, although on a reduced scale, will probably be needed during the calendar year 1948.

The President has recommended that the Congress appropriate $350 million as the United States contribution to help meet these needs. This sum represents in our opinion, our fair share of the total requirement, bearing in mind our capacity in relation to that of other supplying countries. It is 57 percent of the estimated need, compared with our UNRRA proportion of 72 percent. The British Government has already announced a program for assistance to Austria, amounting to $40 million and is currently considering what assistance can be rendered to other countries. Other governments are likewise studying the matter at this time. We are hopeful that through the efforts of all governments which are in a position to help, the minimum needs will be met.

I should like to emphasize at this point what we consider to be a fundamental principle—that is, that the total amount we would allocate to any country not be determined finally at this time. We should avoid a situation where any country might assume that it had a vested interest or right to a particular amount of money. We found in the case of UNRRA that whenever an amount was allocated even on a tentative basis to a recipient country, any attempt to reduce it in order to take account of changing needs caused resentment and consequent embarrassment. In making estimates of relief requirements we must necessarily make assumptions regarding future crop and weather conditions, export possibilities, the probability of credits and loans from private or public banking institutions and many other factors which are not susceptible of definite determination at this time. Emergencies may arise requiring an increase in present estimates for some countries whereas in others recovery may occur at a more rapid rate than we now anticipate. Furthermore, the assistance which will be provided to each of the countries by other contributors must be considered in determining how our funds should be allocated. We are not now fully informed in regard to this matter and should be in a position to adjust our program in collaboration with other contributors to prevent duplication of effort.

The Resolution under consideration provides that the control of the program remain firmly in American hands and that this control be exercised to the end that supplies be shipped where they are needed and that they are used within the receiving countries in a manner consistent with the purposes of the Resolution. We would also take steps to assure that the people of the countries receiving our help would be fully informed as to our interest in their welfare and the extent and nature of our contribution. It is our intention to limit the items which would be procured with our funds to a few basic essentials, primarily food, medical supplies, seeds and fertilizers. We might also find it necessary in some cases to include such things as clothing or raw materials for the production of clothing, fuel and similar basic supplies. We would not attempt to provide machinery and equipment for rehabilitation purposes. UNRRA has already imported those items of this nature which were needed for resumption of basic economic activities after the dislocation and destruction caused by the war. Further reconstruction and development of the productive and transport facilities of these countries should be provided through loans from the International Bank and other sources.

* * *

I have already pointed out that the immediate problem is to maintain the flow of relief supplies. To stop that flow would be disastrous; to interrupt it would be almost equally disastrous. If we fail to provide the relief now when it is needed, much of the humanitarian work heretofore done by our Government and others will be undermined, much suffering and economic deterioration will undoubtedly occur, with political and economic consequences to the rest of the world, ourselves included, not pleasant to contemplate. The President stated the problem clearly, when he said in transmitting this request to the Congress—

> The United States, in keeping with our traditions of immediate and whole-hearted response to human need, has stood in the forefront of those who have checked the forces of starvation, disease, suffering and chaos which threatened to engulf the world in the wake of the war. The task is nearly finished. I urge the Congress to act promptly to insure that we do not stop short of the goal; that we do not endanger the permanence of the gains we have so largely helped to achieve.

§ *On February 24, 1947, the British Ambassador in Washington informed the United States government that Great Britain could no longer protect the eastern Mediterranean area against Communist expansion, and would, in fact, soon withdraw from Greece completely. This communication provoked the enunciation of the Truman Doctrine, but long before Britain's announcement Clayton and other statesmen had seen Greece and Turkey as potential crisis areas.*

To Hon. James F. Byrnes

Washington, D.C.
September 12, 1946

My Dear Mr. Secretary:

* * *

That problem [which we face] is whether in view of the policy which the Soviet Union appears to be pursuing of endeavoring to undermine the stability and to obtain control of the countries in the Near and Middle East such as Greece, Turkey and Iran, we should make certain changes in our general policies, including those relating to the sale of combat equipment, to an extent which might enable us to strengthen the will and ability of the various Near and Middle Eastern countries under Soviet pressure to resist that pressure.[4]

You will recall that on February 5, 1946, the Staff Committee recommended that certain restrictions be imposed upon the sale of military-type surplus equipment to foreign countries. A copy of the Summary of Action of the Committee on that date is attached hereto for your convenience (Enclosure 2). You will observe that this recommendation excludes the sale of such equipment to any countries of the Near and Middle East. Insofar as can be ascertained, no formal blanket decision at a high level has been made with regard to the sale abroad of military-type equipment other than surplus equip-

[4] This letter is printed in *Foreign Relations of the United States, 1946*, vol. 7, pp. 209–13.

ment, and the Department has consequently pursued no fixed policy regarding the matter, but has handled each request on an ad hoc basis. Sales to the Near and Middle East by private American suppliers have been limited to commercial aircraft, sporting equipment or small arms for personal protection.

You will also recall that on February 5, 1946 Mr. Acheson, in testifying before the Mead Committee,[5] explained why the Department had decided to sell certain quantities of military-type surplus equipment to a number of selected countries and that the members of that Committee were inclined to be critical of our action in that respect. Although Mr. Acheson made no pledges to the Committee with regard to the future policies of the Department of State with respect to the sale to foreign countries of military-type surplus equipment, he made it clear that we had no intention of selling this type of equipment to countries other than those contained in the list, which did not include any Near or Middle Eastern countries. Mr. Acheson did not discuss with the Mead Committee what our policies might be with regard to new non-surplus military-type equipment. The Mead Committee has no jurisdiction over transactions involving sale of equipment which is not Government-owned. Shortly after the hearings in which Mr. Acheson participated, a sale of surplus airplanes was made inadvertently to Sweden by an FLC Representative and the matter was explained to the Mead Committee. The members of that Committee, while accepting the explanation, indicated that they reserved the right to criticize the transaction.

Mr. Acheson, however, did not consider that his action in offering an explanation of the Swedish sale to the Mead Committee established a precedent which would require consultation with the Committee on each subsequent proposal to sell military equipment. His explanation was given for the purpose of making it clear to the Mead Committee that he had acted in good faith in explaining our policy to that Committee on February 5 and that he did not know at that time that a sale to Sweden was under contemplation.

On March 21 the State-War-Navy Coordinating Committee made a decision (SWNCC 202/2) in which it was suggested that "In accordance with the United States' firm political policy of aiding the countries of the Near and Middle East to maintain their independence and develop sufficient strength to preserve law and order within their boundaries, it is consistent with United States policy to make available additional military supplies, in reasonable quantities, to

[5] The Special Committee to Investigate the National Defense Program, of which the chairman was U.S. Senator James Mead of New York (1938–47).

those countries." This decision also applied only to surplus and Lend-Lease equipment. It will be noted that it is not on all fours with the State Department Staff recommendations. At least one of these documents, therefore, must be changed.

During the period of more than six months which has elapsed since the formulation of the policies outlined above, there have been certain profound changes in the world situation. The Soviet Union has shown itself determined to continue to adhere to, and to pursue unswervingly, its policies of endeavoring to create instability in certain of the Near and Middle East countries contiguous to it or to its satellites and to endeavor to obtain hegemony over these countries.

In northern Iran the Soviet Union has equipped and trained a puppet Azerbaijan army said to number more than 20,000 men and is continuing to endeavor through this army and by other means to weaken and eventually gain control of the Central Iranian Government. It has made formal demands upon Turkey which, if accepted by the Turkish Government, would inevitably result in Turkey becoming a Soviet puppet.

It has aided its satellites, Bulgaria, Yugoslavia and Albania, in creating strong armed forces and is using these forces as a means of pressure upon Greece. Soviet agents are undoubtedly responsible for the smuggling of arms to, and for the strengthening of, groups in Greece which are endeavoring by force to set up in Greece a government which would be subservient to the Soviet Union.

This Government, as you are aware, has already decided that the establishment of a Soviet puppet government in Turkey would constitute a serious threat to the security of the United States and that we should endeavor to strengthen the will and ability of Turkey to defend Turkish independence and territorial integrity.

On a number of occasions we have informed both Greece and Iran of our deep interest in the maintenance of Greek and Iranian independence.

The Central Government of Iran has sent to the United States a Military Purchasing Commission to buy certain military-type equipment for the purpose of improving the quality of the Iranian army and strengthening the ability of the Iranian Government to maintain its authority throughout the whole country.

The Turkish Government has already indicated its desire to buy certain military-type equipment from us in order to strengthen its defenses.

Although Greece apparently has not approached us with a request to buy military-type equipment it is reasonable to expect, in view of the situation in which that country finds itself, that the

Greek Government will eventually seek to make some military purchases in this country.

If we should categorically refuse to sell to these countries any military-type equipment, even though it be clearly demonstrated that such equipment is urgently needed in order to preserve internal order or to protect frontiers, the governments and people of these countries may well obtain the impression that our interest in the maintenance of their independence is not deep and they cannot expect any concrete support from us in their efforts to preserve their independence. If such an impression should be created there is a danger that the governments and people of these countries will gradually become discouraged and that their will to resist Soviet pressure will be greatly weakened.

All of us working on the problem, including General Hilldring,[6] believe, in the light of the Dardanelles decision[7] (See Department's telegram to Paris 4122 of August 15.) that the time has now come for us to review existing policies with regard to the sale abroad of military-type equipment, both surplus and non-surplus. We believe it is clear that this review will demonstrate the necessity that changes be made in the recommendations of the Staff Committee of February 5, 1946 (SC/R-184). These changes could be effected in one of two ways. You may issue a statement of policy which would supplant the Staff Committee policy (SC/R-184) or, if you wish, the Staff Committee could issue a new statement in accordance with suggestions made by you. The advantage of the changes being effected by you personally would be that they would be known to a smaller circle in the Department and that the danger of a leak would be correspondingly reduced. It seems to us that in any event the new statement of policy should be broader than that set forth in SC/R-184, which covers only surplus property. It should cover the transfer or sale of all military-type equipment of United States origin, regardless of whether Government-owned or privately owned.

We are preparing a draft of a statement of a type which in our opinion will enable us to meet the situation which has developed since last spring and we are planning to send it to you under cover of another letter. We are couching this statement in most general terms in order that it will permit of a considerable degree of flexibility in application.

[6] Major General John Hilldring, Assistant Secretary of State for Occupied Areas (1946–47).

[7] A statement from the State Department expressing opposition to any Russian bases in the Dardanelles because "the primary objective of the Soviet Union is to obtain control of Turkey." See *Foreign Relations of the United States, 1946*, vol. 7, pp. 840–42.

You will, of course, understand that it is not our idea that we should begin to sell military-type equipment immediately in large quantities to various countries subject to external pressure. We feel, however, that the new policy should enable us, with the discretion and restraint required by the circumstances, to supply military-type equipment to countries such as those in the Near and Middle East, the maintenance and integrity of which are considered to be of important interest to the United States.

In view of the national importance of this matter, you may care to discuss it informally with the members of the Foreign Affairs Committee of the Senate who are with you in Paris. You will, of course, desire that a new policy, in case you approve it, should receive the approval of the President before it is put into force.

We have grave doubt that it would be advisable at the present time for the United States to send a military mission to Turkey. We understand that Turkey has not as yet asked for such a mission. We believe that it might be preferable not to endeavor to make a decision with regard to this matter at the present time. In case, at a later date, Turkey should request some kind of American military mission, we could make our decision at that time after taking into consideration the type of mission desired, the world situation and other factors involved.

Insofar as we are aware, no action has been taken so far as the Soviet is concerned, to implement that section of the memorandum contained in our telegram 4122 of August 15 to Paris which reads: "The implementation of this policy * * * will require in the first instance frank discussions with the principal nations involved." We have assumed that you will probably care to talk this over with Molotov at such time, and in such manner, as you may consider appropriate. Although we consider the maintenance of integrity and independence of Iran and Greece also to be extremely important to the United States, we have not undertaken the preparation of a memorandum relating to them similar to that regarding Turkey since the Soviet Union has made no formal demands upon them as it has upon Turkey. It seems to us important, however, that in emphasizing to the Soviet Union our interest in the maintenance of Turkish independence and integrity the impression should not be left with the Soviet Union that we are not also interested in the independence and territorial integrity of Greece and Iran.

I have read this letter to the Secretary of War and to the Under Secretary of Navy and both of them have given it their full approval.

Sincerely yours,

William L. Clayton

190

§ On March 12, 1947, President Truman expressed the determination of the United States to aid Greece and Turkey against aggression, whether overt or ideological, and to extend similar aid to any other threatened European nations. As head of economic affairs in the State Department, Clayton was intimately involved in the formulation of the Truman Doctrine and was consequently called on by the House Committee on Foreign Affairs to explain the economic situation in Greece.

A STATEMENT ON
THE ECONOMIC SITUATION IN GREECE

Washington, D.C.
March 24, 1947

The general political situation in Greece has already been outlined by Mr. Acheson. I should like to explore with you the economic position of the country. . . .[8]

* * *

Greece finds herself today with virtually no gold or dollar resources left, with relatively little reconstruction accomplished, and with an economy which threatens to collapse at the onset of almost any serious adverse development. The shock to confidence from the inflationary experience of recent years was itself enough seriously to disrupt the normal functioning of the economy. This added to the destruction wrought by the war, the political uncertainties facing the nation, and the guerrilla activities imperiling life and property in the interior, has meant virtual paralysis of the normal economic processes by which Greece might otherwise have been able to work out her own salvation.

The assistance heretofore provided by UNRRA and the British has succeeded in preventing actual starvation. It has been far from sufficient to restore Greece to a position where she could become self-supporting. With the imminent cessation of the help provided by

[8] This statement was delivered on March 24, 1947, and printed in *Assistance to Greece and Turkey*, Hearings before the House Committee on Foreign Affairs, 80th Cong., 1st sess. (1947), pp. 63–69.

UNRRA and the British, Greece needs substantial outside assistance if suffering and political turmoil are to be avoided. Such assistance can only come from the United States in the time and in the amount required.

I shall endeavor to outline the program of assistance which is proposed. The Congress has already been advised that with the termination of UNRRA shipments Greece will require minimum relief aid of $50 million if serious malnutrition and further retrogression in the minimum operation of the economy are to be prevented. This sum will be provided under the post-UNRRA Bill if this is approved by the Congress.

Provision of relief aid in this amount will not, however, be sufficient to restore domestic security or provide the minimum reconstruction and stability which are necessary if Greece is again to take her place among the self-supporting democratic nations of the world.

For this purpose it is believed that approximately $300 million will be necessary. Of this approximately half would be devoted to making available to the Greek armed forces the arms, ammunitions, clothing, rations, and equipment necessary to deal effectively with the guerrillas. The political and military reasons for strengthening the Greek Army have been discussed by others, but I should like to emphasize that the establishment of military security is an essential prerequisite to economic stability. The economic difficulties of Greece have been seriously complicated by a general lack of confidence in the future of Greece as an independent state. Establishment of military security will enable the Greek Government and people to concentrate their efforts upon the solution of their economic problems, and renewed hope and confidence will encourage Greek private enterprise to undertake a larger share of the tasks of reconstruction.

The civilian program envisaged will cost approximately $150 million. I would like to indicate very briefly the nature of this program, in particular the import or foreign exchange elements involved.

We have estimated that imported equipment and materials for reconstruction until June 30, 1948 will cost approximately $50 million. The first priority in reconstruction must be given to the restoration of transport and public utilities. Internal transportation in Greece is a serious bottleneck to further recovery. Until the railroad network is fully restored and sufficient rolling stock provided, the present excessive diversion of traffic to trucks will have to be continued with attendant high costs which hamper internal distribution and exports.

Greek roads have deteriorated very seriously and are in such unbelievably bad condition that the life of vehicles is only a fraction of normal and operating costs are excessively high. The two principal Greek ports, Piraeus and Salonica, were very badly damaged and have been restored on only a provisional basis.

In order to make progress toward the restoration of the Greek transport system, it will be necessary to import considerable quantities of rolling-stock, rails, structural steel and bridge building material, road machinery and earth moving equipment, some vehicles and the services of the United States contractors and technicians.

Restoration of damaged and destroyed electric utilities and communications systems must also be given a high priority. Substantial imports of electrical machinery and communications equipment will be required.

Agriculture, which is the basis of the Greek economy, depends heavily upon the various flood control, irrigation and water control facilities. During the war these facilities were neglected by the invaders and the equipment necessary to keep them in good condition was either destroyed or removed. The dams, dikes, canals and ditches have, as a result, deteriorated very seriously, and unless they can be reclaimed very soon, further deterioration and loss of agricultural output is inevitable. For example, the Thessalonica Plains project which drains and irrigates an area of roughly 460 square miles along the Axios River in north central Greece has been virtually without maintenance since the beginning of the war. In order to reclaim this vital project, such pieces of equipment as hydraulic dredges, drag lines, bull dozers and tractors are needed as well as maintenance equipment for these items. Such equipment will have to be imported.

During the war much industrial plant in Greece was idle and the Nazis removed and destroyed considerable industrial equipment. Mines suffered very seriously. Imports of industrial equipment will be required to permit Greek production to return to pre-war levels.

Any visitor to rural Greece is impressed by the wanton destruction of rural dwellings, of which over 100,000 were destroyed and 50,000 badly damaged. The foreign exchange costs of beginning the restoration of this tremendous loss are a small but vital element in the job.

Aside from the problem of basic reconstruction, Greece urgently needs further assistance in the rehabilitation of agriculture. UNRRA has made a start by the importation of some livestock, farm machinery, food processing equipment and the like. This program includes $20 million for this important task.

This $20 million and the $50 million for reconstruction are to cover the cost of foreign goods and services entering directly into these programs. But in order to carry out the reconstruction program it will also be necessary to employ local labor and materials. Greek labor and raw material producers will be paid in drachmas. However, the Greek laborer or raw material producer cannot be expected to make available his services or products unless he can convert the drachma he receives into the goods and services required by himself and his family.

Even with the additional supplies of food and clothing to be provided for abroad under the direct relief program the total supply of goods and services available for purchase will be barely sufficient to permit holders of drachmas to convert them into the necessities of life. Large drachma payments must be made in connection with the proposed reconstruction program, and such increased drachma purchasing power will exert a tremendous pressure upon the limited supply of goods. In such circumstances, each new drachma recipient would bid against his neighbor for available supplies, and the result would be a rapid rise in prices. Wage earners and raw material producers would soon find that their drachma receipts were inadequate to produce the necessities of life, and they would demand increased payment for their labor and products. If the basic shortage of goods were not remedied, increased wages and prices to producers would not enable them to procure the goods they require, but would only lead to more frantic competitive bidding and further price rises. Price controls and rationing are only temporary palliatives under such circumstances, and experience has shown that the effective operation of controls of this nature cannot be expected in Greece under such circumstances.

It is our firm opinion that the reconstruction program in Greece cannot be carried out successfully unless consumers' goods are made available from abroad, roughly equivalent in value to the drachma expenditures in connection therewith. The best available estimate of these expenditures is $80 million. Greece itself is the cheapest source of the labor and of much of the raw materials required for the reconstruction program, and of course such labor and materials should be utilized to the utmost. The precise method of carrying out an integrated program of reconstruction, including the procurement and distribution of the necessary consumers' goods should, I believe, be left for determination by the American Mission, which it is proposed to send to Greece.

To summarize: the $150 million civilian program for Greece consists of the $20 million agricultural rehabilitation program, and a reconstruction program which includes $50 million for foreign exchange costs and $80 million for internal costs.

I should like to emphasize that all the estimates I have given you are necessarily rough approximations, and that it is essential that flexibility be maintained, so that adjustments between various portions of the program can be made in the light of experience and developments which cannot now be anticipated in detail.

The funds made available under this program must, of course, be utilized to best advantage so that our objectives may be achieved efficiently and economically. It will be necessary to send a civilian mission to Greece to administer this Government's interest in the program. We cannot now say what the size of such a mission would be, or how it would be organized; these questions are still under study.

It is clear that we should not make any expenditures for the Greek program until specific plans have been developed, and have been approved by us. The mission in Greece would be in a position to carry a large part of the responsibility for this activity. It is also clear that the expenditure in Greece of funds that may be made available to the Greek Government must be subject to control by our mission there.

Furthermore, it is my considered opinion that in the United States any purchases with these funds should be made through the procurement agencies of this Government, or, if made otherwise, should be subject to careful supervision and strict control.

Finally, we must see to it that competent persons are sent to Greece to ensure the development of controls at key points and to supervise their application. Time is so short, and the expenditures involved so great, that we must be assured that sound policies will be adopted and effectively administered in matters such as the following: fiscal methods; a modern tax structure; strict husbanding and control of the foreign exchange earnings of the Greek people; conservation of remaining gold resources; a restriction on unessential imports; and the expansion of Greece's exports. These measures, no less than the financial advances we are proposing, are necessary to put Greece back on her feet.

I have stressed the economic situation in Greece because it is one of crisis. General economic conditions in Turkey are more favorable than those in Greece. In fact the latest information available indicates that Turkey has sufficient resources to finance the essential requirements of her civilian economy. It also appears that Turkey should in due time be able to procure through existing credit channels part of the additional resources required for a program of general economic development. However, Turkey urgently needs military and other capital equipment which she herself cannot at present procure without seriously impairing her general economic position. The necessity for assisting Turkey in bearing the burdens of her military defense is very real and an immediate beginning should be made. The $100 million recommended for Turkey will be devoted to equipment for the Turkish armed forces and for projects such as the rehabilitation of the Turkish railroad system, which will contribute most directly to the maintenance of security in Turkey.

The bill now before you provides that the President shall determine the terms upon which assistance will be furnished to Greece and Turkey from the appropriations authorized. These terms may be loans, credits, grants or otherwise. In view of the unusual conditions confronting us in this situation, I do not believe that it would be wise or practical to specify now what these terms might be.

Any set of financial relationships, to be sound, must be related to the realities and objectives of the case. I believe that assistance for military purposes, being essential to our own security, and not in itself creating the wherewithal to repay, should be made as a clear grant.

Financial assistance for civilian purposes would appear to fall in a somewhat different category. Repayment could be sought when the direct effect of the financial aid was to create the ability on the part of the receiving country to meet such obligations in foreign exchange. However, I do not believe that we should create financial obligations for which there is no reasonable prospect of repayment.

§ *On April 22, 1947, President Truman appointed Will Clayton the U.S. representative on the Economic Commission for Europe, which had been established by the Economic and Social Council of the United Nations. Clayton's evaluation of the purpose and potential of this new organization follows.*

A Speech on the Economic Commission for Europe

The first meeting of the Economic Commission for Europe has for its purpose the creation of an organization designed to promote the most effective employment of the human and material resources

196

of Europe to the benefit of all.[9] If this objective can be measurably achieved an important step will have been taken on that road to world peace and world prosperity which we all seek. All states represented here bear in varying degrees the scars of war, some visible and some not. All have a common interest in hastening the restoration of economic health in Europe. All can make a contribution to that end; as separate countries are a part of Europe, so Europe is a part of the larger world. It is appropriate therefore that this Commission, within the framework of which its members may join their common efforts, should be an integral part of the United Nations.

In creating this Commission the Economic and Social Council recognized that the problems with which it is expected to deal can be most effectively handled on an European basis. It is the responsibility of the Council to fit securely into the world picture the European phase of economic revival; the organizational relationship between the Commission and the Council insures that this will be done. The United States is vitally concerned in the economic revival of Europe. This is true because we are an occupying power and because we know full well that world peace and prosperity are impossible without European economic revival.

The success of this Commission will be measured by its ability to find prompt solutions to certain vital and urgent problems which stand in the way of European recovery. Fortunately we are not without experience in dealing with some of these problems. The Emergency Economic Committee for Europe, the European Central Inland Transport Organization, and the European Coal Organization have dealt for some time now with the urgent problems in their respective fields which faced post-war Europe. The terms of reference of the Economic Commission for Europe provide that the highly important functions of these organizations shall be taken over by the Commission. The experience of these three organizations goes far to prove that nations can indeed work effectively together for their common good.

The European Coal Organization is an outstanding example. Through common agreement it has brought about an equitable sharing of an inadequate supply of coal among countries, each of which desperately needed more coal than it got. The successful operation of the European Coal Organization has been an added spur to us in

[9] This speech was delivered before the initial meeting of the new Economic Commission for Europe in Geneva, Switzerland, May 2, 1947, and later printed under the title "The Economic Commission for Europe: Toward Beneficial Employment of Human Resources" in Department of State, *Bulletin*, 16 (May 18, 1947): 977–78.

the United States to expand to the utmost our shipments of coal to Europe. What the existing bodies have accomplished in their limited fields can be done in the larger field of this Commission.

The problems of each country seem to it the most pressing, but if experience teaches anything it is that no country can solve its economic problems in isolated economic actions which appear to relieve pressures at home while creating pressure abroad and by opening up a whole Pandora's box of troubles for all of us. It is just as if the whole world had an economic nerve center receiving and giving out for good or bad the economic impulses set in motion by individual action. Anywhere an understanding of the delicate adjustment of the economy of the modern world shows that unilateral action which may harm one's neighbors must in the end result in harm to all. There are no panaceas or easy remedies for the problems with which this Commission will deal. The last war dealt the world a staggering blow, the force of which is only just now beginning to be fully understood. Reconstruction can only be achieved through hard teamwork pulling together, not separately.

The Preparatory Commission on Trade and Employment now meeting here in Geneva is working out a broad pattern of international trade relations designed to bring about an expansion in world economy to the end that all people, everywhere, may enjoy higher living standards. The Economic Commission for Europe is a complementary body to deal with urgent problems arising from the dislocations of war. As Secretary Marshall recently said, "European recovery has proceeded at a slower pace than anticipated." This fact gives a special urgency to the task before us here. Let us get on with the job in hand as quickly as possible.

§ *As a direct result of his involvement in the development of the Truman Doctrine, Clayton composed a memorandum outlining a plan to strengthen European resistance to Communist expansion. "I felt that something akin to the Marshall Plan would have to be developed by our country in order to save Western Europe,"*[10] *he later recalled. This document is the earliest known articulation of the principles underlying the Marshall Plan, though it was never given*

[10] "The Reminiscences of William Lockhart Clayton" (unpublished oral history, Oral History Research Office, Columbia University, 1962), p. 193.

to Secretary Marshall since he had left for Moscow shortly after Clayton returned to Washington. Clayton wrote Dr. Robert Ferrell in 1964 that long before he went to Geneva for the GATT Conference, he "had been thinking very seriously of the situation in Western Europe and the fact that these countries would require financial assistance from the United States in enormous amounts, otherwise some of them would undoubtedly succumb to Communist threats and offers of material help."[11]

MEMORANDUM ON THE CREATION OF A NATIONAL COUNCIL OF DEFENSE

March 5, 1947

I am deeply disturbed by the present world picture, and its implications for our country.[12]

The reins of world leadership are fast slipping from Britain's competent but now very weak hands.

These reins will be picked up either by the United States or by Russia. If by Russia, there will almost certainly be war in the next decade or so, with the odds against us. If by the United States, war can almost certainly be prevented.

The United States must take world leadership and quickly, to avert world disaster.

But the United States will not take world leadership, effectively, unless the people of the United States are shocked into doing so.

To shock them, it is only necessary for the President and the Secretary of State to tell them the truth and the whole truth.

The truth is to be found in the cables which daily arrive at the State Department from all over the world.

In every country in the Eastern Hemisphere and most of the countries of the Western Hemisphere, Russia is boring from within.

This is a new technique with which we have not yet learned how to cope.

We must cope with it and quickly or face the greatest peril of our history.

Several nations whose integrity and independence are vital to

[11] Will Clayton to Robert H. Ferrell, October 28, 1964, L, CP, ACCO.
[12] This memorandum may be found in CP, TL.

our interests and to our security are on the very brink and may be pushed over at any time; others are gravely threatened.

If Greece and then Turkey succumb the whole Middle East will be lost.

France may then capitulate to the Communists.

As France goes, all Western Europe and North Africa will go.

These things must not happen.

They need not happen.

The Secretary of State is leaving now for Moscow.

The odds are heavily against any constructive results there.

The Secretary will probably be back in Washington before May 1st.

Meantime, we have discussed with the Congressional leaders a program to help Greece maintain her independence. This goes only part of the way; it tells only part of the truth.

We must go all out in this world game or we'd better stay at home and devote our brains and energies to preparation for the Third World War.

Assuming an unsatisfactory outcome of the Moscow conference, I think on return of the Secretary of State, a joint statement should be made by the President and the Secretary to the Congress and to the American people.

Such a statement should say:

1. The United States is determined on the preservation of world peace by all honorable means.
2. The United States does not covet the lands or possessions of any other peoples.
3. The preservation of world peace depends first of all upon the preservation of the integrity and independence of sovereign nations.
4. Nations can lose their integrity and independence by attacks either from the outside or the inside.
5. The United Nations is organized to deal with attacks from the outside but not from the inside.
6. The evidence is indisputable that a systematic campaign is now being waged to destroy from within the integrity and independence of many nations.
7. Feeding on hunger, economic misery and frustration, these attacks have already been successful in some of the liberated countries and there is now grave danger that they may be successful in others.
8. The security and interests of the United States and of the world demand that the United States take prompt and effective action to assist certain of these gravely threatened countries.

9. This assistance should take the form not only of financial aid, but of technical and administrative assistance as well. The United States does not wish to interfere in the domestic affairs of any country, but countries to which it extends financial aid must put their internal affairs in proper order so that such aid may be permanently beneficial.

10. Congress is asked to create a Council of National Defense, composed of the President, the Secretary of State, the Secretaries of War and Navy, and the Chairmen of the Foreign Affairs Committee of the House and the Foreign Relations Committee of the Senate.

11. The Congress is further asked to appropriate the sum of Five Billions of Dollars, for use by the Council of National Defense, either as grants or as loans, for the purpose of assisting sovereign countries to preserve their integrity and independence, where such action is considered by said Council to be in the vital interests of the United States.

12. It had been expected that the International Bank for Reconstruction and Development would be able to furnish all requisite financial assistance to war devastated countries, but it is now clear that this institution is not organized to render the kind of assistance which is required in the circumstances herein described. The facilities of the Bank will nevertheless be needed for worthy projects of reconstruction and development.

13. Two objections will be made to the program here proposed: one political and the other economic.

14. It will be said that this will involve us in the affairs of foreign countries and lead us eventually to war. The answer to this is that if we do not actively interest ourselves in the affairs of foreign countries, we will find that such affairs will become so hopeless that the seeds of World War III will inevitably be sown.

15. It will be said that our National Budget will not permit of this large expenditure.

The war cost us over three hundred billions of dollars and the blood of hundreds of thousands of our young men. We are now appropriating around ten billions of dollars annually for the maintenance of our armed services. We are seriously talking of reducing taxes at a time when our people are enjoying the highest standard of living in their history, when our Corporations and farmers enjoy the biggest earnings, after taxes, which they have ever known in peace time, and when our gross National product of goods and services has a greater dollar value than has ever been known in war or peace.

W. L. Clayton

§ *While engaged in negotiations in Geneva, Switzerland, for multi-*
lateral reduction of trade barriers, Clayton was informed that Con-
gress had passed a wool tariff bill which threatened to wreck the
Geneva negotiations. He immediately flew to Washington and per-
suaded President Truman to veto the bill. En route from Europe on
May 19, 1947, Clayton wrote down his thoughts on the European
economic crisis. Upon his arrival, he immediately circulated this
memorandum among his colleagues in the State Department and on
May 27 presented it to Secretary Marshall. As he later wrote his
daughter, this document "was the basis of the Marshall Plan."[13] *A*
substantial portion of Marshall's famous Harvard speech on June 5,
1947, was taken directly from Clayton's memorandum.

MEMORANDUM ON THE EUROPEAN CRISIS

May 27, 1947

1. It is now obvious that we grossly underestimated the destruction to the European economy by the war.[14] We understood the
physical destruction, but we failed to take fully into account the
effects of economic dislocation on production—nationalization of
industries, drastic land reform, severance of long-standing commercial ties, disappearance of private commercial firms through death or
loss of capital, etc., etc.

2. Europe is steadily deteriorating. The political position reflects the economic. One political crisis after another merely denotes
the existence of grave economic distress. Millions of people in the
cities are slowly starving. More consumer's goods and restored confidence in the local currency are absolutely essential if the peasant
is again to supply food in normal quantities to the cities. (French
grain acreage running 20–25 percent under pre-war, collection of
production very unsatisfactory—much of the grain is fed to cattle.

[13] Will Clayton to Ellen Garwood, January 7, 1950, L, CP, TL.
[14] This memorandum, which was entitled "The European Crisis," is in
CP, Rice.

The modern system of division of labor has almost broken down in Europe.)

3. Europe's current annual balance of payments deficit:

UK	2¼	billions
France	1¾	"
Italy	½	"
US—UK Zone Germany	½	"
	$5	billions

—not to mention the smaller countries.

The above represents an absolute minimum standard of living. If it should be lowered, there will be revolution.

Only until the end of this year can England and France meet the above deficits out of their fast dwindling reserves of gold and dollars. Italy can't go that long.

4. Some of the principal items in these deficits:

From the U.S.: Coal, 30 million tons .... $ 600 million
  " " " : Bread grains, 12 million tons ... 1,400 "
  " " " : Shipping services at very high
      rates on imports and exports— xxxxx "

Before the war, Europe was self-sufficient in coal and imported very little bread grains from the United States.

Europe must again become self-sufficient in coal (the U.S. must take over management of Ruhr coal production) and her agricultural production must be restored to normal levels. (Note: No inefficient or forced production through exorbitant tariffs, subsidies, etc., is here contemplated.)

Europe must again be equipped to perform her own shipping services. The United States should sell surplus ships to France, Italy and other maritime nations to restore their merchant marine to at least prewar levels.

5. Without further prompt and substantial aid from the United States, economic, social and political disintegration will overwhelm Europe.

Aside from the awful implication which this would have for the future peace and security of the world, the immediate effects on our domestic economy would be disastrous; markets for our surplus production gone, unemployment, depression, a heavily unbalanced budget on the background of a mountainous war debt.

These things must not happen.

How can they be avoided?

6. Mr. Baruch asks for the appointment of a Commission to study and report on our national assets and liabilities in order to determine our ability to assist Europe.

This is wholly unnecessary.

The facts are well known.

Our resources and our productive capacity are ample to provide all the help necessary.

The problem is to organize our fiscal policy and our own consumption so that sufficient surpluses of the necessary goods are made available out of our enormous production, and so that these surpluses are paid for out of taxation and not by addition to debt.

This problem can be met only if the American people are taken into the complete confidence of the Administration and told all the facts and only if a sound and workable plan is presented.

7. It will be necessary for the President and the Secretary of State to make a strong spiritual appeal to the American people to sacrifice a little themselves, to draw in their own belts just a little in order to save Europe from starvation and chaos (not from the Russians) and, at the same time, to preserve for ourselves and our children the glorious heritage of a free America.

8. Europe must have from us, as a grant, 6 or 7 billion dollars worth of goods a year for three years. With this help, the operations of the International Bank and Fund should enable European reconstruction to get under way at a rapid pace. Our grant could take the form principally of coal, food, cotton, tobacco, shipping services and similar things—all now produced in the United States in surplus, except cotton. The probabilities are that cotton will be surplus in another one or two years. Food shipments should be stepped up despite the enormous total (15 million tons) of bread grains exported from the United States during the present crop year. We are wasting and over-consuming food in the United States to such an extent that a reasonable measure of conservation would make at least another million tons available for export with no harm whatever to the health and efficiency of the American people.

9. This three-year grant to Europe should be based on a European plan which the principal European nations, headed by the UK, France and Italy, should work out. Such a plan should be based on a European economic federation on the order of the Belgium-Netherlands-Luxembourg Customs Union. Europe cannot recover from this war and again become independent if her economy continues to be divided into many small watertight compartments as it is today.

10. Obviously, the above is only the broad outline of a problem which will require much study and preparation before any move can be made.

Canada, Argentina, Brazil, Australia, New Zealand, Union of South Africa could all help with their surplus food and raw materials, but we must avoid getting into another UNRRA. *The United States must run this show.*

W. L. Clayton

§ *Clayton possibly influenced the conception, formation and consummation of the Marshall Plan more than any other single individual. In the following reminiscences he recalls the events and circumstances of the fateful spring and summer of 1947.*

A Statement on the Geneva ITO Conference

One of the hardest things I had to do was in connection with the wool tariff.[15] I was at Geneva when it came up, you know—had been there for weeks negotiating for the reciprocal trade agreements, and when this wool tariff came up I had to fly back to Washington. And you know I got sick.

The day before I was to take the plane I caught a terrible cold. I had to be vaccinated, because there was smallpox in N.Y. and they weren't letting anyone in without a vaccination. When the doctor in Geneva came to scratch my arm, I told him. He examined my chest and found I had a deep bronchial infection. Gave me some medicine but it didn't do much good. We were 30 hrs. on that plane before it got to Washington—and you know that's a stretch that even young men tell me it takes 2 days to recuperate from! Right in the middle

[15] This statement on the International Trade Organization is from an interview with Ellen Clayton Garwood in December 1947.

of the wool tariff I had to go to bed! I had called Dr. Myers and he'd said it was touch and go whether I'd have pneumonia.

It was terrible—I couldn't go before Congress! They passed that wool tariff while I was flat on my back! When I got up I went to see President Truman. Clinton Anderson,[16] you know, the Secretary of Agriculture, was fighting me; he had told the President that if he vetoed the bill it would cost him 8 Western states in the next election. The President was courageous. I said to him, "If you don't veto this tariff, Mr. President, it will cost the U.S.A. a complete loss of standing in the world and it will wreck the Trade Conference and set us back a century." He said he couldn't let that happen. And he vetoed it. And then he gave authority, besides, to cut the wool tariffs 25 percent.

On the way back to Geneva I had to go by London where they were starting negotiations for the Marshall Plan and spend a week there. They'd held up the Conference about a month waiting for me. It took a long time—all this business.

You see the Geneva Conference had two aspects. It was a review conference for the tentative International Trade Charter drawn up previously in London, and at the same time, it was an agreement between the 23 participating nations for mutual tariff cuts. We completed 122 agreements.

But to get back to the wool situation. They'd waited a long time for me so when I reached Geneva I sat right down with the Australian envoys. And my they were tough! That's a hardheaded bunch; nice as they can be, but ornery! They had a member of their cabinet there, a Mr. Dedman[17]—an awfully nice fellow, and I told him quietly the story of what had happened in Washington. The fellow said "A 25 percent reduction!" You see they had wanted a 50 percent. "Why," he said, "we can't even discuss it on that basis!" Then I told him and I gave it to him straight.

"All right," I said, "if that's your attitude. But let me tell you that, by it, you will have wrecked this conference, and don't think I'm not going to say you have. After all our administration has been through, after all the sacrifices it has made politically, if you can't even discuss our proposition, then I wouldn't be surprised if Congress clamped the full tariff back on wool, and I wouldn't blame us and I wouldn't even care. In fact they will probably 'up' the tariff 50 percent. They almost did it anyway!"

[16] Clinton P. Anderson, Secretary of Agriculture (1945–48).
[17] John J. Dedman, Australian Minister for Post-War Reconstruction (1945–49).

Dedman then said he'd fly back to Australia and discuss it with the Cabinet there. He flew back 10,000 miles the next day. After the meeting the boys who were with me from our organization said, "I guess if he were wondering whether that was your last word you didn't leave him in any doubt!"

You see the whole question was so important because the British and all their dominions were holding out on the negotiation until this tariff was settled. We had 23 countries participating, with ½ the trade of the world involved, and negotiations for tariff reductions on ⅔ of the trade of those countries. We *had* to succeed!

Well, about 10 days later I was at the Embassy in Paris, and Dedman sent his card in. When he came in to see me he was a changed man. He's really a fine person. He was as affable and courteous as he could be. He had received permission from the Australian Cabinet to accept the 25 percent reduction!

A STATEMENT ON THE MARSHALL PLAN

The Marshall Plan was like one of those inventions that several people come up with at the same time.[18] (The cotton gin was an exception, but shortly after Eli Whitney a Mr. Morton developed one a great deal better.)

Still I was in a position to get the information that would naturally make me the person to start the Marshall Plan. I was in Geneva—working on the GATT negotiations—and I was working as the head of our delegation on the Committee for ECE (Economic Cooperation for Europe) for two weeks, and all the Europeans came to me. Jean Monnet, for instance, said France had scraped the bottom of the barrel, and had had short crops and was forced to import wheat but couldn't pay for it.

[18] This statement, which is in CP, Rice, was written some time in 1956.

A STATEMENT ON NEGOTIATIONS WITH FRANCE

I had conferences with the French about the Ruhr in summer of 1947.[19] The U.S. established, in conjunction with the British, French and Russians, the level of industry permitted the Ruhr, stipulated the maximum steel production: so many tons—7,500,000, average production not to be over 5,200,000. The U.S. was considering raising that figure and the French objected. Before the war Germany had 20,000,000 tons steel capacity. In my conference with the French we hoped to find a formula for controlling the disposition of the steel products which would satisfy them. I talked to M. Bidault,[20] Minister for Foreign Affairs.

In France I went to see Blum[21] who had come to Washington as head of the French delegation to negotiate a loan to France and for the settlement of economic, financial questions relating to the war and lend-lease, questions relating to the army and all questions of that kind. Blum told us that the French were in accord with the principles of the expansion of world trade and employment which the British had agreed to in 1946. In 1947 at the Geneva conference on reductions in tariffs, the French raised their tariffs. Most tariffs in Latin countries are specific and not ad valorem so that due to inflation those specific duties were no longer protective for prices had gone up so much. France wanted to revise her tariffs to give the same protections as before, wanted to alter the specific rates to ad valorem and put her ad valorem rates on the same basis of protection as her tariff had been before inflation. In French style, however, they did more than that, and that we violently objected to. In this view Blum agreed with us; while he was in Washington I went to see him and found him sympathetic. In our conversations in the subsequent weeks, after much pulling and hauling, we got their tariff in proper shape. I went to see him where he was living on a small farm outside of Paris, in a modest, little cottage. It was summer but a cold day. This cottage had formerly been a stable; it was a rainy day, late in the afternoon, and Blum was in an old dressing gown,

[19] This statement is from an interview with Ellen Clayton Garwood in December 1947.

[20] Georges Bidault, French Minister of Foreign Affairs (1947–48).

[21] Leon Blum, French Ambassador Extraordinary (1946); Prime Minister and Foreign Minister of the French Provisional Government (1946–47).

hard at work in his library. He spoke French so clearly and slowly that I could understand him perfectly. He assured us he was in agreement and that France would cooperate with us in reducing her tariffs; that he would look into the matter. He had no official position at that time; he was head of the Radical Socialists.

The thing that impressed me was the intensity with which the French people—as evidenced by the attitude of their political leaders—regarded the possibility of an attack by Germany again. It was understandable, for in the recollection of some people Germany had attacked 3 times; in the life time of millions others she had attacked twice. It was a phobia with them and it came out in the talks on the Ruhr; mixed in it was the wish to keep Germany down as an economic competitor.

To Herbert Elliston

January 26, 1953

Dear Herbert:

I have your letter asking for information regarding the beginnings of the Marshall Plan and will be glad to give you[22] what I can from memory. I have never kept a diary and keep practically no memoranda.

I went to Geneva in April, 1947, as head of the U.S. delegation to the International Trade Conference. This Conference lasted about five months and during that time the first meeting of the E.C.E. (Economic Commission for Europe) was held in Geneva. I also represented the United States at that meeting.

These two international conferences gave me an opportunity to talk with key men from the Treasury and Foreign Offices of European countries.

I very soon saw that Western Europe was rapidly approaching a great financial, economic and political crisis.

[22] An unsigned carbon copy of this letter to the Editor of the *Washington Post* may be found in CP, ACCO.

This was particularly true of France and Italy where there had been two years of very poor crops and where they were beginning to scrape the bottom of the barrel for dollars with which to pay for essential wheat imports.

I naturally kept the Department of State informed of this situation.

You will recall that the Truman Doctrine which saved Greece and Turkey from communist domination had been adopted in 1946.

About May 20, 1947, I flew back to Washington to try to prevent the passage by Congress of a bill, the intent of which was to raise the tariff on wool about one-third.

On the way to Washington I prepared a memorandum outlining the desperate state of affairs in Italy and France and the urgent necessity of financial assistance to those two countries particularly, to avoid their being taken over from the inside by a communist coup.

This memorandum was typed on my arrival in Washington, was handed to Secretary Marshall and discussed with him, and I believe became the basis of his now-famous Harvard Speech.

We should not overlook in this connection that Dean Acheson made a speech in Mississippi around the latter part of April or early May, 1947,[23] in which he stated that it would probably be necessary for the United States to set up a program of financial assistance to Western Europe of very great proportions. I believe this speech was the first official suggestion of a program which later became known as the Marshall Plan.

You ask about George Kennan's connection with the Marshall Plan. As I recall, a few months prior to my departure for Geneva, George Kennan had been made the chief of a small policy group which was organized within the Department of State. In that position he naturally had much to do with the beginnings of the Marshall Plan and with the preparation of Secretary Marshall's Harvard Speech.

I flew back to Geneva about June 20 with instructions from the Secretary of State to visit London, Paris and Rome and acquaint the heads of governments in those three countries, and any others that I had an opportunity to see, with our thinking regarding the Marshall Plan. Obviously, at that early stage of the enterprise, almost none of the details had been worked out.

[23] Speech before the Delta Council in Cleveland, Mississippi, May 8, 1947.

I spent nearly a week in London during which time Ambassador Douglas[24] and I had numerous conferences with Mr. Attlee[25] and his Cabinet. We drew up an "Aide Memoir" which was initialed by both sides and was thereafter used as a kind of "Bible" on the subject.

Mr. Bevin[26] flew to Paris from these conferences and had a two or three day meeting with Mr. Molotov[27] and his Russians, which as you will recall, resulted in the Russians denouncing the Marshall Plan and later on forcing Czechoslovakia to withdraw their announced intention of taking part in it.

One of the prime conditions which Ambassador Douglas and I laid down was that the European countries coming into the Marshall Plan must set up an organization charged with the duty of working out a plan for submission to the United States and that this organization must be a permanent one with which the United States could deal throughout the life of the Marshall Plan.

It was this condition of permanence which seriously threatened to wreck the whole project.

To understand this you must remember that many countries at that time were almost frightened to death of the Russians, and the Russians were making a great effort to prevent the consummation of the Marshall Plan within the pattern that we had laid down.

You will probably recall that the Russians said that they had no objection to the Marshall Plan if the United States would deal with each country separately, let that country make out its bill with particulars of what it needed, and then let the United States sign a check to cover the total. The Russians made it very clear that what they objected to in the Plan was the idea of the formation of an organization of the European countries, as required by the United States.

The European countries did set up an organization—O.E.E.C. (Office of European Economic Cooperation) and did finally agree to make that organization permanent throughout the life of the Marshall Plan after Douglas and I had told them that it was impossible for us to go forward with the enterprise on any other basis.

Sir Oliver Franks[28] was the first head of the O.E.E.C. and he did a magnificent job.

I want to make it plain that throughout our negotiations with the O.E.E.C., we took the position that it was the job of the O.E.E.C.

[24] Lewis W. Douglas, American Ambassador to Great Britain (1947–50).
[25] Clement Attlee, Prime Minister of England (1945–51).
[26] Ernest Bevin, British Secretary of State for Foreign Affairs (1945–51).
[27] V. M. Molotov, Russian Commissar of Foreign Affairs (1939–49, 1953–56).
[28] Sir Oliver Franks, Provost of Queens College, Oxford (1946–48); British Ambassador to the United States (1948–52).

to work out their own plan of cooperation together with an estimate of the dollar requirements of each country. Naturally the first estimate was much too large and had to be whittled down substantially.

During our (i.e.: Ambassador Douglas, Ambassador Caffery and I) negotiations with the O.E.E.C., a group came over from the State Department headed by George Kennan and they sat in with us and assisted us for several days.

I am afraid the above only gives you sort of a general outline of what you want but if you will ask questions regarding any particular aspects of the matter, I will try to answer them.

Obviously, what I have written herein is not for publication or quotation but is for your own use.

With regards and every good wish to you and my good friend, Eugene Meyer, I remain

Sincerely yours,

W. L. Clayton

AN ARTICLE ON GATT, THE MARSHALL PLAN, AND OECD

My reason for choosing the . . . title [of this article][29] is that these three organizations have many aspects of interdependence in origin and, to some extent, in operation. I am sure I would have had difficulty in writing about any one of them exclusively.

One day in March, 1947, I walked into President Truman's office with a big book under my arm. The book contained lists of thousands of commodities on which hearings had been held (or offered to be held) in order to give interested parties an opportunity of presenting their reasons against a reduction in import duties. The book also indicated the extent to which the Department of State felt reductions in duties could be made in the forthcoming tariff negotiations in Geneva.

[29] "GATT, The Marshall Plan and OECD," *Political Science Quarterly*, 78 (December 1963): 493–503.

The President spent some time in questioning me about different commodities; then he initialed a memorandum approving the purpose and use of the book. This was our authority for the multi-lateral negotiations at Geneva, resulting in an agreement known as the General Agreement on Tariffs and Trade, commonly referred to as GATT. Fifty nations now belong to GATT, and in the fifteen years of its existence, it has greatly contributed to almost doubling international trade to the present total of about $125 billion annually.

When I presented the book to the President for his approval, I said that we had not included wool, as we were hoping to leave wool out of the negotiations at Geneva. I often wonder now how I ever could have thought that this would be possible.

When Mrs. Clayton and I stepped off the Queen Elizabeth at Southampton on our way to Geneva, one of the Secretaries from our Embassy in London met us. One of the first things he handed me was a dispatch from Washington to the effect that a bill relating to the wool tariff had been introduced in Congress, and if this bill became a law, it almost certainly would result in an advance in the tariff on wool.

It soon was quite apparent, after the Geneva Conference opened on April 11, 1947, that the success of our tariff negotiations there depended on our ability to offer a substantial concession in the U.S. tariff on wool. The principal country interested in the export of wool was Australia, and, of course, Britain backed up Australia in this stand with all the power she could exert.

I was fortunate in having Dr. Clair Wilcox, Chief of the Office of International Trade Policy, assisted by Mr. Winthrop Brown, Chief of the Division for Commercial Policy, in active charge, under me, of negotiations.

I spent most of my time, especially at dinner and in the evenings, with representatives of other countries, many of whom I had met at other international conferences—FAO, UNRRA, and the meetings of the governors of the International Bank and International Monetary Fund.

In my meetings with these representatives of other nations, we not only talked about tariff negotiations and the Charter for an International Trade Organization (which was also on the Agenda of the Geneva Conference), but I took this occasion to inquire as to economic, financial, and food conditions in their respective countries. I was surprised and in some cases shocked regarding conditions in the countries of Western Europe, particularly as to the serious food situation which most of them faced.

Crops were short, not only because the growing season had been unusually adverse, but because the whole economic situation was such as to discourage the farmers from putting in a normal acreage of grain.

In most cases, the farmers knew that their surplus grain, if carried to market and sold, would yield only paper money, in which farmers had no confidence. The things that the farmer desperately needed—farming implements, clothing and manufactures of various kinds—were mostly unobtainable, because industry had not got back into full production of such items. Under these circumstances, farmers not only curtailed their acreage but in many cases grazed their cattle on the grain instead of harvesting it. Thus, the division of labor, on which modern peacetime society rested, had almost broken down in these countries.

This made it necessary for the governments of the countries thus affected, particularly France and Italy, to import grain from the United States, Canada, and other countries, and this meant that the gold and dollar reserves of such countries, slender as they were, became dangerously depleted.

This situation weighed heavily on my mind, and I longed for an opportunity to present it personally to Secretary Marshall, and to Under Secretary Acheson. The latter had made a speech on May 8, 1947, at Cleveland, Mississippi, in which he referred to the very serious conditions in Western Europe and said that the United States might have a rescue job to do there.

The opportunity to present this matter to Messrs. Marshall and Acheson came sooner than I expected.

It was agreed that I should return to Washington to see if I could help prevent the passage of the wool bill, to which I have referred. Mr. Acheson and I had acquired some reputation of success with Congress. I have been informed that during the Eisenhower Administration a complaint was made to Sam Rayburn that the State Department could not get anything through Congress. Rayburn replied: "You ought to do like Acheson and Clayton used to do. They would start at opposite ends of the corridors of the House Office Buildings, and those that one could not convince, the other would take on. They made the lives of the Congressmen so miserable that they had to agree to their project!"

So Mrs. Clayton and I boarded an airplane May 18, 1947, for New York. Flying was not so good in those days as now, so we were more than twenty-four hours en route, which did not help a very bad cold, which I had contracted a few days before leaving Geneva. When we arrived in Washington, I had some fever, went to a doctor, and was told that I had a touch of bronchial pneumonia and that I should go to bed at once. I did this, and, meantime, the Congress passed the wool bill. I am quite sure they would have done this anyway, regardless of any efforts I might have been able to make.

On my arrival in Washington, I found the Planning Committee of the Department of State, under the chairmanship of George Kennan, actively considering the Western European situation because of the receipt of cables from our various Embassies and from me calling attention to the seriousness of this situation and the fact that it was deteriorating rapidly.

I had made notes on the plane of a memorandum, which I wanted to hand Secretary Marshall, regarding the economic, political and food situation in Western Europe.

On account of my illness, this memorandum was not completed and handed to Secretary Marshall until May 27, 1947.[30]

* * * * *

This memorandum, plus my several talks with Secretary Marshall, between May 27, 1947, and up to the time he left to make his speech at Harvard on June 5, 1947, merely confirmed the information that many of our Embassies and I had been cabling to the Department of State.

Since the wool bill had been passed by the Congress, our only chance of preventing it from becoming law was to induce President Truman to veto the bill. The Department of State gave me the job of submitting to him the arguments why this should be done, but it was suggested that I should arrange for a certain official, having an opposite point of view, to accompany me and present his reasons why the bill should become a law. This was all arranged, and, in due course, this official and I presented ourselves at President Truman's office and made our arguments. The principal argument of the other official was political. My principal argument for the veto was that if this bill became law, the U.S. Delegation at Geneva might as well pack their bags and come home, because the success of the Geneva Conference depended upon the United States' ability to make some concession in the wool tariff, and the bill that we were talking about undoubtedly would cause an advance in the wool tariff.

The President listened attentively to our arguments but reserved his decision. Several days later, I learned that President Truman had vetoed the bill. I then asked for another appointment with him and told him, as I had before, that unless we were in a position to make

[30] See "Memorandum on the European Crisis," May 27, 1947, p. 201 in this book.

some concession in the wool tariff, the Geneva Conference would be a failure. He indicated that he understood this. I had a little typed memorandum, giving us authority to make a concession in the wool tariff of 25 per cent. I put this memorandum before him, and he did not hesitate to initial it.

This action of the President, following his veto of a bill which would have resulted in increasing the wool tariff, was the greatest act of political courage that I have ever witnessed.

With this, I flew to Geneva, via London and Paris.

Secretary Marshall asked me to talk with the principal Western European governments regarding certain points that we would have to insist upon in connection with our assistance to them.

There were two main points which Secretary Marshall and the Department of State insisted upon:

1. That the recipients of Marshall Plan aid should organize themselves into a committee of cooperation, not only for the life of the Marshall Plan but even after Marshall Plan aid should end.
2. Furthermore, that this committee, composed of recipients of Marshall Plan aid, should work out the measure and mechanics of this aid and present it to the United States as an agreed plan.

Such a committee indeed was informally set up under the chairmanship of Sir Oliver Franks (now Lord Franks).

I arrived in London June 22, 1947, and immediately reported to the United States Ambassador, the Honorable Lewis W. Douglas.

Thereafter, Ambassador Douglas and U.S. Ambassador Caffery in Paris and I worked as a team of three on the Marshall Plan. We attended many meetings in Paris of Sir Oliver Franks' committee, which was called Committee for European Economic Cooperation (CEEC).

On my arrival in London, Ambassador Douglas and I met with the British Cabinet for a discussion of the Marshall Plan matter.

At that time, Mr. Ernest Bevin, British Minister of Foreign Affairs, was preparing for a trip to Paris on about June 27 for a meeting with Mr. Bidault, French Minister of Foreign Affairs, and Mr. Molotov, Russian Minister of Foreign Affairs.

At that time, the road was open for Russia and her satellite countries to be included in the Marshall Plan.

The meeting between Messrs. Bevin, Bidault and Molotov was for the purpose of trying to reach an agreement, which these three would present to all the other recipients of Marshall Plan aid as to the mechanics of setting up the enterprise.

I stayed in London for several days, and we had no difficulty in agreeing with the British regarding the Marshall Plan, all of which was set down in a memorandum which was called an "Aide-Memoire." I do not here quote this memorandum, because I have no copy of it.

Regarding the Paris meeting of Messrs. Bevin, Bidault and Molotov, it should be stated that Poland and Czechoslovakia already had cabled direct to Washington that they wished to be included among Marshall Plan recipients, but Moscow had caused both countries to withdraw this agreement.

At the Paris meeting, the Russians insisted upon each country acting on its own, just making out a list of its requirements, presenting it to the United States, and letting the United States fill the bill.

The Russians would not agree to any kind of a Western European organization or institution having to do with Marshall Plan aid.

After two or three days, it was clear to Molotov and his delegation that the English and the French were determined to agree to Washington's condition in this matter, so Molotov and his group just walked out of the meeting.

I not only had the wise counsel of Ambassadors Douglas and Caffery in dealing with Sir Oliver Franks' committee, but I conferred often with Jean Monnet who came several times to Geneva to see me, and whom I saw often in Paris.

Soon after I was made Assistant Secretary of State for Economic Affairs in December, 1944, I had met Jean Monnet in Washington and, as he represented the Treasury Department of the French Government, had numerous dealings with him.

I have always believed that tariffs and other impediments to international trade were set up for the short-term, special benefit of politically powerful minority groups and were against the national and international interest.

As shown by Paragraph 9 of my memorandum of May 27, 1947, I felt that the Marshall Plan presented an opportunity to introduce the principle of regional free trade in Western Europe.

I discussed this matter frequently with Jean Monnet who convinced me that Western Europe was too weak in 1947 to accept conditions of regional free trade. I recognized then that Monnet was correct in this viewpoint. Europe had to get a good deal more flesh on its bones before setting up a common market.

However, the object which Secretary Marshall and the Department of State had in mind in insisting upon the formation of a Western European Committee of Cooperation was to get these countries working together, so that the effects of Marshall Plan aid would cause Western European countries to follow policies conducive to benefits for the entire section rather than for individual countries.

European countries did not customarily work together in matters of this kind, and representatives of several countries took the position that they could not agree to the continuation, after Marshall Plan aid ceased, of any organization that they might set up.

Ambassadors Douglas and Caffery and I were meeting from day to day with Sir Oliver Franks and his group (a total of sixteen countries), and when the representative of one of these sixteen countries made the statement that European countries were not in the habit of looking over the back fence of their neighbors to see what they were doing, I stated that perhaps we were all pursuing a will-o'-the-wisp and might as well forget about it.

The whole situation got very tense. It was quite clear that representatives of at least three countries were prepared to vote against the idea of the continuation of such an organization after Marshall Plan aid ceased,[31] so the suggestion was made one Thursday or Friday that we should adjourn to the following week in order to give time for the representatives of these three countries to go back home and talk with the heads of their governments. This was done, and when we met again the following week, the representatives of these three countries said that their governments had agreed to the continuation of the organization, even after Marshall Plan aid had ceased.

The committee, informally organized into Committee for European Economic Cooperation under the chairmanship of Sir Oliver Franks was then set up formally, in the Spring of 1948, under the title of Organization for European Economic Cooperation (OEEC). This organization fully justified the faith of Secretary Marshall and his advisors, because it managed to secure the removal of many of the restrictions on imports between European countries. In time, the United States and Canada became associate members of this organization; still later, it was changed to Organization for Economic Cooperation and Development (OECD), which is its present name.

I opened this paper with a reflection upon the interdependence of GATT, the Marshall Plan and OECD. I feel impelled to conclude with another reflection of a different character. It is that without the courageous and resolute political leadership of the kind exhibited by President Truman in the instances I have cited, the needs I describe could well have met with responses unpleasant to contemplate.

---

[31] One of these countries was Norway (Clayton interview with Ellen Clayton Garwood, December 1947).

§ *Bowing to pressure from his wife, Clayton reluctantly submitted his resignation from the State Department even before his authorship of the May 27 Marshall Plan memorandum. He did remain in the Department, however, until October 16, at which time President Truman finally accepted his resignation. Clayton later revealed that upon his return to Washington late in the summer of 1947, Truman had offered him the position of Administrator of the Economic Cooperation Administration. He explained to Alfred Clason that he "was unable to accept it and indeed resigned my position as Under Secretary of State for Economic Affairs to devote more time to Mrs. Clayton."*[32]

To Hon. Harry S Truman

Geneva, Switzerland
May 14, 1947

My dear Mr. President:

As you know I have been trying for some time to leave Government service because Sue[33] is not well and needs my undivided attention for six months or a year in an effort to restore her health.

I have remained because there never seemed to be a very convenient time to leave. The end of the Trade Conference in Geneva about August 1 should, it seems to me, be such a time.

I am returning home Monday, the 19th, for a week or ten days and will, at that time, present a formal letter of resignation to Secretary Marshall to be handed to you.

If desired I will, of course, remain on duty until the Geneva Conference has been concluded, but wish to be relieved entirely by September 1.

It will make Sue happy if you will be good enough to give me a prompt acceptance of my resignation.

[32] Will Clayton to Alfred Clason, November 16, 1953, L, CP, ACCO.
[33] Clayton's wife, Sue Vaughan Clayton. An unsigned carbon copy of this letter may be found in CP, ACCO.

While in Washington on this short trip, I hope I may have an opportunity to see you for a few minutes to express, in person, my deep appreciation of your confidence in me. It has been a pleasure and an honor to serve under you.

Respectfully yours,

Will Clayton

§ *Before his return from Europe on October 2, 1947, Clayton presented his ideas for the final organization of the Marshall Plan in a memorandum dated September 19, 1947.*

Memorandum on the Marshall Plan

September 19, 1947

Before leaving within a few hours I would like to jot down quickly a few notes on some aspects of the Marshall Plan on which it has been difficult for us to determine our policy here:[34]

1. I do not favor asking the Paris Conference to reconvene and I believe it has been decided not to do so. It will be impossible I think to avoid some modifications in the Plan, to conform to views of the Administration and the Congress; in fact I think it is really desirable that this should happen. No matter what is done the Communists are sure to charge that it is a United States imperialist plan. I don't think we should let this worry us.

2. I think $16 billion is the maximum amount of aid we should consider to meet balance of payments deficit of the 16 countries plus Western Germany for the 4 year period 1948–1951. Another $2 billion might be considered as a loan to bolster the monetary reserves of these countries.

[34] This memorandum is in CP, TL.

The $16 billion could be divided:

1948—6½ billion
1949—5   billion
1950—3   billion
1951—1½ billion
Total 16 billion

These figures are from my general knowledge of the situation and without very much reference to the general report.

For example I think we know that the following should represent maximum balance of payments deficits of the different countries for 1948:

U.K.	2,500,000,000
France	1,300,000,000
Italy	850,000,000
Western Germany	1,150,000,000
All other Countries	700,000,000
	$6,500,000,000

Of course some of them would like to have more but the above will be sufficient to enable them to continue to eat and work unless prices advance materially. If we compare this with the balance of payments deficits of these same countries in 1946 we will find that it considerably exceeds those figures.

We can also get a check against the above figure of 16 billion by taking the figures in the general report:

Grand total balance of payments deficit with
Western Hemisphere .... 22.44 billions
less capital goods .... 3.13   "
nets .... 19.31   "
Less balance of payments surplus which the
16 countries expect to have with soft currency countries .... 2.81   "
nets 16.50

We can still deduct from this at least 750 millions for the ship-building program (we should sell or charter our own ships to them) and another 750 millions for various types of capital goods still in the program.

3. In my opinion the bulk of this money can never be repaid and we would only be fooling ourselves if we took notes and included

them in our assets. The U.K., France, Italy, and Germany can never repay, particularly when we consider the dollar obligations which these countries already have outstanding and which they must hereafter incur with the International Bank and other credit agencies for purposes of reconstruction, development and modernization. All the sums advanced to these countries should therefore be in the form of grants. Some of the other countries can repay and will doubtless wish to do so.

4. The above amounts contemplate of course procurement of materials in short supply outside of the United States. We should take the position immediately that we will ask the Congress to do this, otherwise in my opinion the program will be a failure. The United States cannot furnish all the food and other raw materials required and such supplies cannot be obtained in other countries unless we put up the bulk of the money.

We can probably get some help in the program from Canada, Brazil and Argentina. I understand Canada expects to have a surplus of exports over imports with these countries of about 850 millions annually. If we could pay out dollars for half this amount she might be able to furnish the remaining one-half on grant. Argentina ought to put up 100 millions annually of food and raw materials and Brazil 50 millions. Cuba might furnish 50 millions worth of sugar annually. Venezuela might do something. I doubt if any other Latin American country would be able to do much.

5. I think the local currency counterpart of our aid should be deposited with trustees (perhaps the International Bank) in each country under very definite conditions as to use. In no case should any of these funds go into the budget. Such funds can probably be used to best advantage in paying the local expenditures (wages, materials, etc.) in reconstruction and development projects by the terms of the trust instrument. It should be so drawn as to make it possible to prevent any such capital expenditures from unduly competing for labor and materials with the production of food, coal and goods for export.

Administration.

I believe we must be reconciled to the setting up of an independent agency for the administration of the program. Of course State, Treasury, Commerce and Agriculture should be represented on this agency. Furthermore, the questions of foreign policy, negotiation of agreements with foreign countries, and all relations with foreign countries in connection with their commitments should be left exclusively in the Department of State.

I suggest the Department of State have a representative making his headquarters in Geneva to visit and keep in touch with our missions in the capitals of the 16 countries to check up constantly on the performance of these countries of their commitments to be set out in the bilateral agreements with them which of course will include their mutual undertakings in the proposed mutilateral agreement. It will probably be necessary to have one or two well selected men attached to our missions in the principal capitals—London, Paris, Rome—handling this aspect of the matter with the heads of the missions. Obviously the representative at Geneva should work only through our established missions.

This Geneva representative would pretty well correspond to the Harriman Mission in London in connection with Lend-Lease during the war and it would be very desirable if he had the status of an ambassador at large. There would be little or no danger that the right kind of man would in any way trespass upon the responsibilities or functions of the heads of mission in the various countries.

§ *In the following documents, Clayton differentiates between Western Europe and Latin America with regard to the applicability of the Marshall Plan.*

TO NORMAN ARMOUR

Washington, D.C.
December 2, 1947

I understand there is considerable talk of a Marshall Plan for Latin America to be proposed and discussed at the forthcoming Bogota Conference.[35]

[35] This memorandum to Norman Armour, retired U.S. diplomat and former Ambassador to Chile, Argentina, and Spain, may be found in CP, ACCO.

A few evenings ago the Chiefs of the Brazilian, Chilean and Colombian Delegations to the Havana Conference had dinner with Clair Wilcox,[36] Harry Hawkins,[37] Ambassador Nufer[38] and me.

We spent most of our time discussing the Charter. Later in the evening, however, the Colombian said to me: "Mr. Clayton, there is a good deal of talk now about a Marshall Plan for Latin America. What is your position on that?"

I replied that the Marshall Plan was not at all applicable to the Latin American situation for the following reasons:

1. The purpose of the Marshall Plan is to enable Western Europe to continue to eat and work until they can get back into production.

2. Accordingly, we have insisted that all capital items, except agricultural equipment and a certain amount of mining equipment be eliminated from the list of requirements of Western Europe under the Marshall Plan and this has been done. We have explained that the European countries must look to the International Bank and private sources for such credits as may be necessary for reconstruction and development.

3. Some Latin American countries have balance of payments problems but they are manageable problems because they do not arise from the necessary heavy importations of food and raw materials as is the case with Western Europe. What Latin America needs is capital goods—equipment, machinery, tools, engineering services, et cetera, for the development of their resources and for industrialization. The Export-Import Bank has made some sizeable loans to Latin America for this purpose, as witness the case of the Brazilian Steel Mill, the Chilean Steel Mill and other development loans. Their main dependence must, however, be the International Bank for which Congress has already provided capital. We could not think of asking Congress to duplicate this by grants for development purposes.

I explained that the International Bank was just getting started and that I understood there was considerable dissatisfaction by Latin American Countries because no loan has as yet been made for development purposes to any Latin American country. I pointed out that the Bank was proceeding cautiously in view of the extreme instability in Europe but in my opinion if the Marshall Plan should be

---

[36] Economist who served as Vice-Chairman of U.S. delegations to London, Geneva, and Havana for consideration of the International Trade Organization Charter.

[37] Economic Counselor for the American Embassy in London (1944–48).

[38] Albert Nufer, former economic affairs counselor in Havana Embassy, Ambassador to El Salvador (1947–51).

adopted, as I believed it would be, this would put a firm economic foundation under Europe and would give courage to the International Bank to go ahead. I further explained that I had brought up this subject with Jack McCloy[39] at the London meeting of the Bank and had pointed out to him that it would be necessary to make a start with Latin America soon, and that I intended to have another talk with him on the same subject in the next few days.

Finally I would like to say that I believe we should do everything we can to make it clear to our Latin American friends that the Marshall Plan is wholly inapplicable to the Latin American situation and that we cannot consider extending it to that area.

W. L. Clayton

A SPEECH ON THE MARSHALL PLAN

In discussing the European Recovery Program, commonly known as the Marshall Plan, one enters a highly competitive field.[40]

Newspapers, magazines, the radio, the Congressional Record, all are full of the Marshall Plan.

The very excess of presentation and argument has served to confuse some of the issues.

Many thoughtful citizens are wondering what course the United States should follow in this matter.

At first, there was scepticism regarding Europe's need for so much help; and there was doubt as to our ability to provide it without serious injury to our own economy.

These questions have been thoroughly studied in the last few months. Committees of distinguished and competent citizens have examined both questions with the greatest care.

The reports of these Committees, together with other available evidence should be convincing that Europe does require this aid and

[39] President of the World Bank (1947–49).

[40] This speech was delivered before the Committee for the Marshall Plan for European Recovery in New York City, December 18, 1947. CP, Rice.

that the United States is able to furnish it without serious injury to itself. Most unbiased persons are now satisfied on both these points.

It hardly seems necessary to further labor this aspect of the matter. Suffice it to say that Europe's desperate need arises from the fact that two world wars struck a more shattering blow to her highly industrialized economy than any one realized until recently. And our ability to help arises from the fact that, to play our part in winning World War II, we expanded our own economy to almost double the pre-war volume. The real question is whether we will keep all these goods for ourselves or use a very small portion of our vast production to help Western Europe stand on its feet until it can stand alone. An annual average of 2 to 2½ percent of our gross national product for 4 years should do the job. We can supply this and continue to live better than we did before the war. Adequate protection against inflationary impacts can be had through the imposition of limited controls and the adoption of wise fiscal policies.

There are still two vital questions which have not been so much discussed and to which answers do not as readily come as they do to the two questions we have just mentioned. Nevertheless satisfactory and conclusive answers are there if we will but dig for them.

These questions are:

Will the Marshall Plan work? And, is it in our interest?

These are pertinent and proper questions, deserving thoughtful and considerate attention.

We are a practical people and if the Plan won't work we want none of it.

The Marshall Plan is not a relief program; it is a recovery program for Western Europe. Hence our interests rather than our humanitarian instincts should be mainly considered, although the problem is certainly not lacking in humanitarian aspects.

The purpose of the Marshall Plan is to help these people help themselves to restore and strengthen their economy to the point where Western Europe can stand on its own feet by 1952 without special outside assistance.

All of you know why we are dealing with Western Europe instead of Europe as a whole.

That decision was made in Europe and not in the United States.

It has been reinforced by recent events in London.

Now, will the Marshall Plan work?

Europe is a very sick Continent. Facts and figures to prove this, or the why of it are unnecessary. All informed and intelligent persons know that it is so and why.

Production is still lagging; in some countries confidence in money has been destroyed; the area to a great extent is still separated into small, tight economic compartments just as if the world had stood still these past hundred years.

Restoration of confidence in money is almost the number one MUST.

One hears people say: Of course I am willing to help but not until Europe goes back to work.

My observation during five months in Europe this year convinced me that Europeans are still just as hard working and serious as we are in the United States. They will always work if they have something to work with and if they can get paid for their work.

If you or I were a farmer or a factory worker in Europe, we might hesitate to exchange our labor for paper money which would not buy the things we needed because of shortages. We might wonder what the future buying power of the paper money would be or whether the things we needed could be had, and would probably end up by not working quite so hard, or by diverting our labor into something we could consume ourselves.

And still restoration of production in Europe has made remarkable progress, everything considered.

Coal and food are the principal laggards.

In recent weeks there has been a significant increase in coal output in England and the Ruhr, which proves that it can be done.

The Paris Conference for European Recovery organized itself into a Committee of European Economic Cooperation.

The report of this Committee presents an economic recovery program for Western Europe based on these major points:

A strong production effort by each of the participating countries, with stated goals for food, coal, steel and other essentials,

Creation of internal financial stability,

Lowering of trade barriers between the participating countries and with the rest of the world,

Development in partnership of common resources.

The participating countries are dependent on heavy imports of food and raw materials. Normally these were paid for by exports, mostly manufactured goods, by services or by income from investments abroad. The war dealt this system a heavy blow, and despite post war progress this complicated economic machine still limps along. Without adequate outside help it will soon break down.

In Secretary Marshall's Harvard speech, he said: "The truth of the matter is that Europe's requirements for the next three or four years of foreign food and other essential products—principally from America—are so much greater than her present ability to pay that she must have substantial additional help, or face economic, social and political deterioration of a very grave character."

To put it very simply, the Marshall Plan proposes to make it possible for Western Europe to continue to eat and work until she can get her economic machine going again.

We are not planning to send only food and coal. There will be no recovery in Europe if there are no raw materials for the factories, even though the people do not starve or freeze. People out of work, walking the streets, with factories closed, cannot reconstruct their shattered economies.

Europe can recover under the Marshall Plan if the following steps are taken:

The European recipient countries should make definite commitments to carry out the programs already formulated, particularly the following:

Restore production to, and in some cases above, pre-war levels, with stated annual goals,

Make money sound again,

Lower trade barriers,

Execute a multilateral agreement with mutual commitments on the above. Provide for a continuing organization to periodically check performance against such commitments, and to publish the results of such checking. The only sanction such organization need hold is the powerful one of public opinion.

The United States should make bilateral agreements with the recipient countries, tying in the multilateral agreement just referred to, as a part of same. This bilateral agreement should clearly set forth all the conditions under which aid is given, relating principally to production, sound money and lowering of trade barriers. Periodic checks should be made of performance under the agreement. We will hold in our hands at all times, the powerful sanction of discontinuance of aid if, contrary to our expectation, any country fails to live up to its agreement.

We must not only render adequate material assistance, but we must hold out a helping hand in other ways; we must give spiritual and moral help and encouragement; we must make technical and administrative assistance available; we must understand Europe's problems and help solve them. Europe does not want our sympathy, but she does crave understanding and a helping hand.

The United States Government should keep a small, highly competent, carefully selected organization in Europe, working through our Embassies, for the purpose of carefully following European progress under the Marshall Plan, checking performance against commitments and extending a helping hand in every proper way.

If these steps are followed by Europe and the United States, the Marshall Plan can and should work.

It is freely admitted that our participation in the European Recovery Program is not without risk, but our decision must be made in the light of the alternatives.

And this brings us to the question, Is the Marshall Plan in our National Interest?

This question has two aspects, economic and political. They are so closely related that they may be considered together.

The heart of the foreign policy of the United States centers in the determination to preserve peace in the world by every reasonable and honorable means.

The Marshall Plan and our Trade Agreements program, the latter now linked with the proposed International Trade Organization of the United Nations are the economic keystones of our foreign policy. The Marshall Plan is to deal with the emergency needs of one part of the world. The I.T.O. will be concerned with the long term trade and economic problems of the entire world.

The United States does not covet the territory or possessions of any country. At the height of our financial, industrial and military power we set the Philippines free and sent a Commission to participate in the act of lowering the American flag and raising the flag of the new Philippine Republic. If this is Yankee imperialism or dollar diplomacy, let those who shout that silly charge make the most of it.

People all over the world desperately want peace; but all Governments do not follow the paths of peace.

Historically, one of the most fruitful breeders of war has been the destruction of the independence of small countries by some international bully.

Throughout Europe today there is deep fear. Many of you have seen it at close range. Country after country is struggling desperately to maintain its independence and integrity.

If an enemy were pounding at their gates, we would understand perfectly well what is going on.

But that's the old fashioned way. The new technique is to bore from within in the hope that this will not particularly disturb the rest of the world and will not bring in powerful allies to help.

The whole world sees the intended victim writhing in the grasp of a great power bent upon subjection and control, but because armies are not on the march and bombers on the wing, most of us cross to the other side of the street and go about our business.

Western Europe is made up of our kind of people. Many of our forefathers came from there. Those people hate Communism but if they must resist it under conditions of economic frustration, cold and hunger, they will lose the fight.

The Communists are waging a desperate battle to prevent the adoption of the Marshall Plan.

If it is adopted, they will wage a desperate battle to prevent its success.

If we should say that we will not supply the necessary help without which there can be no European recovery within the foreseeable future, it is almost certain that every country in Continental Europe would lose the battle to maintain its integrity and independence.

The Iron Curtain would then move Westward at least to the English Channel.

Consider what this would mean to us in economic terms alone. A blackout of the European market would compel radical readjustments in our entire economic structure—changes which could hardly be made under our democratic free enterprise system.

The picture is still more frightening in terms of peace.

A Communist-dominated Europe, with an active campaign to bring Latin America under the same wing, will not contribute to the peace of the world.

One hears the view expressed that we're already too late. This is a defeatist attitude with which we should have little patience. It is alien to our character and experience.

This is what Hitler hoped we would believe in 1940 and 1941.

It is what the Communists hope today that we will believe.

If we had listened to these same voices in the dark days of 40 and 41, Hitler and his gangsters would now be sitting astride a good part of the world.

If we act now with courage and intelligence, to assist in the efforts of the countries of Western Europe to restore their economies, the independence and integrity of these countries can still be preserved.

That is in our National interest and is the surest road to peace. It is the road which I believe we're going to follow.

V

THE CONTINUING FIGHT

FOR FREE TRADE

§ *As far as Will Clayton was concerned, the Marshall Plan would not have a lasting effect on the European economy. The surest way to promote permanent prosperity for that economy was through the liberalization of trade policies, a goal toward which the Geneva Agreement on Tariffs and Trade and the proposed charter for an International Trade Organization were giant strides. In the following documents, Clayton discusses the fruitful results of the Geneva International Trade Conference, attended by twenty-three nations between April 11 and October 30, 1947.*

A Speech on the ITO Charter

It is a pleasure to have this opportunity to tell my friends in America something about the new charter for world trade.[1] This charter, as you know, was completed by a committee of 17 nations in Geneva last month and will be considered by 50 or 60 nations at a world conference that will meet in Habana in November. In the meantime, the countries at Geneva are continuing to work out a definite agreement to lower barriers to trade among themselves. This agreement will cover more countries, more products, and more trade than any previous agreement in the history of the world, and its completion should go far toward getting the Habana conference off to a good start.

When the United States made its first proposals for a charter setting up an international trade organization, it faced a world in which the normal patterns of trade had been disrupted by the war.

[1] This speech, which was entitled "Geneva Draft of ITO Sets a Practical Pattern for World Trade," was delivered over the facilities of the Columbia Broadcasting System, September 10, 1947, and later printed in Department of State, *Bulletin*, 17 (September 21, 1947): 592–94.

Production was cut down, business was dislocated, and the economic and political future was filled with uncertainty. In such a situation we might have decided to postpone our proposals until things got back to normal, but we knew if we did so that nations might set up a whole series of new restrictions that the world might never succeed in breaking down; so we went ahead, and I think that the results already achieved at Geneva have demonstrated that we chose the wiser course.

The question is often asked whether the present financial difficulties of some of the countries in Europe and the plans they are drawing up in response to the proposal made by Secretary Marshall do not mean that our trade program has lost its importance for the time being. The answer is emphatically no. The plans now being drawn up relate to the emergency needs of one part of the world. The trade program has to do with the long-run needs of the whole world. The two are interdependent. Neither can be wholly successful without the other. Both are part of a common policy. If we cannot ease the burdens of Europe in this emergency, our chances of reducing the barriers to trade will not be good. But the reverse of this statement is just as true. If we cannot reduce the barriers to world trade and thus make possible a great expansion in the production, distribution, and consumption of goods throughout the world, there is little hope that any aid we may extend under the Marshall proposal will accomplish its purpose or be more than a stopgap measure.

As the United States approached the problem of postwar trade policy there were three courses it might have pursued. First, it might have concluded that the rest of the world was so committed to restrictionism that the attempt to tear down the barriers to trade was hopeless. It might have washed its hands of the whole job and tried to live to itself. But we must remember that we are part of an interdependent world. Prosperity and peace for us depend on prosperity and peace for everybody else. Economic isolation is clearly impossible. Second, the United States might have sought to lay down a simple set of idealistic principles to govern world trade and tried to persuade the other nations of the world to accept it. But trade is a complicated business and the times in which we live are full of difficulty. Other nations have their own problems and their own policies. No simple set of rules could be accepted. No rigid set of rules would work. If we are to be realistic we must be practical, and if we are to be practical I am afraid that we must deal with details. If we are to have a world trade charter it must be a charter that will fit the facts Third and last, we could have sought a realistic document, one that would meet the practical problems of the real world. Such a charter would set forth fundamental principles on which all nations could agree, but it would also make such detailed provisions as might be required to meet emergencies and to fit diverse national economies into a common pattern of world trade. This is the only kind of a charter that would actually work. It is the only kind that would provide us with a real alternative to anarchy and chaos in the commerce of the world. It is the kind of a charter that the United States has always sought and it is the kind that was adopted in Geneva last month. This charter sets up an international trade organization to support and strengthen the International Bank for Reconstruction and Development and the International Monetary Fund, but it does more than that. For the first time in history it asks all nations to commit themselves in a single document to a policy of nondiscrimination in their customs charges and requirements and in their internal taxation and regulation.

Under such a policy each country will impose the same duties and requirements at its customs houses to the goods that come from every other country, and it will impose the same internal taxes and regulations on its own goods that it imposes on goods that come from abroad. The charter asks the members of the new trade organization to do away with all other forms of discrimination. It asks them to reduce tariffs and other barriers to trade and it lays down detailed rules to insure that the freedom that is gained by reducing visible tariffs shall not be lost by building up invisible tariffs.

It also lays down rules under which import and export quotas (the most serious of all forms of trade restrictions) can be limited, controlled, and eventually abandoned.

The charter makes the first attempt in history to apply uniform principles of fair dealing to the international trade of private enterprise and public enterprise.

It makes the first attempt through intergovernmental action to eliminate the abuses arising from the operations of international monopolies and cartels.

It spells out for the first time a code of principles to govern the formation and operation of intergovernmental commodity agreements.

It marks the first recognition in an international instrument of the interdependence of national programs for the stabilization of production and international programs for the liberation of trade.

It recognizes the interdependence of international private investment and the economic development of backward areas and emphasizes the importance of such development to the well-being of all the peoples of the world.

Back of these general purposes and principles there are many details, and the delegates at Geneva have been spending most of their time on these details. It will be remembered in this connection that our Government took the earlier draft of the charter to the American people in public hearings in seven cities in February and March of this year and asked them for their criticisms and suggestions. Almost all of the points which were raised at these hearings were incorporated in amendments which were introduced by the American Delegation at Geneva, and I am now glad to report that we were successful in obtaining all of these changes in the final draft. The present charter should therefore be closer than the preceding versions to the desires of business, agriculture, and labor in the United States.

There are four criticisms that have been made by people who have examined the charter, and I should like to say a word in conclusion about each of them.

First, it is said that the charter is idealistic. In one sense this is true. In another sense it is not. The charter is idealistic in that it establishes objectives toward which all countries can agree to work. It draws on the experience of the past, but it does not direct itself to the problems of the past. It sets up goals for the future, but it does not limit itself to provisions than can only work in normal times. It is concerned with the actual problems of the work-a-day world, and in this sense its idealism is tempered with a realism that is clearly practical.

Second, it is said that the charter contains a great many exceptions, and this is true. But these exceptions are carefully defined. Many of them are temporary; all of them are limited in extent; and no nation will be able to use any of them unless it satisfies the conditions upon which all nations have agreed. If it were not for the exceptions, the charter would not be practical, and it is because it is practical that it can be expected to work.

Third, it is said that the charter is a compromise. So it is, and so is almost every law that was ever passed by Congress or by the legislature of any state. So is every treaty between any two powers. So are the Charter of the United Nations and the constitutions of every international agency that has been established since the war. Compromise is a virtue, not a defect. It means that the charter will not be imposed by force, that it will not be rejected because it is one-sided but that it can be voluntarily accepted because it meets the needs of every country in the world.

And finally, it is said that the charter is long and complicated, and this is true. It contains nine chapters, one hundred articles, and several thousand words. It is probably shorter than some acts of Congress; it is certainly simpler than the income tax law; but it is still long and complicated. It is complicated because it is realistic and practical, but the multitude of technical detail in the document serves only to emphasize the solid basis of agreement that has been achieved.

The important thing that we should recognize is this: the conference now drawing to a close in Geneva is a landmark in the history of international economic relations. It has covered the longest period in diplomatic history of intensive collaboration on a single document. This committee of 17 nations started its work in London in October and November last year, carried it forward in New York in January and February, and completed it in Geneva by working continuously from April to the end of August. It has demonstrated that nations, when they have the will to do so, can work together peacefully and productively for common ends.

This conference, moreover, has covered a wider range of problems than has ever been tackled by any other economic conference in the history of international affairs. It has produced and written into single document not one agreement but six—one on trade policy, one on employment, one on economic development and international private investment, one on cartels, one on commodity arrangements, and the constitution of a new United Nations agency in the field of international trade. The successful completion of any one of these agreements would have been an occasion for congratulation. The completion of all six of them in the troubled times in which we live is little short of a miracle.

The work on the world trade charter is not yet done; it goes to the conference at Havana in November; it goes to parliaments and to Congress in the United States next year. In the meantime, I hope that the American people will study it, analyze it, criticize it, and decide that they will give it their support.

A Statement on the Geneva Agreement on Tariffs and Trade

The year just past was marked by one of the most significant and far reaching events that has ever taken place in the history of international trade.[2] This was the signature by the representatives of 23 countries at Geneva, Switzerland, on November 18th, of the General Agreement on Tariffs and Trade. The agreement represents the most comprehensive action ever undertaken for the reduction of barriers to trade. The signatory countries carried on three quarters of the world's trade before the war, and the agreement covers two-thirds of the trade among these countries. It included more than 45,000 individual items on which duty reductions, bindings of low rates, or other significant concessions have been made.

The principal significance of the agreement is that it is the first major step to be taken by important nations acting together to reverse the trend toward trade restriction and economic isolation which has persisted since the First World War. For the United States it represents the substantial attainment of a goal toward which this Government has been working for more than 12 years under the Trade Agreements Act of 1934.

The Trade Agreements Act has been the economic cornerstone of United States foreign policy ever since 1934. Its enactment was a recognition of the fact that trade, in order to move at all, must move in both directions, and that United States tariff duties and trade barriers of other countries were unduly restricting our imports and exports and therefore were harming our own and the world's economy. Under the Act pre-war agreements were concluded by bilateral negotiation with 28 countries involving the mutual reduction of excessive trade barriers. The agreements helped to expand United States foreign trade, to increase employment, and to foster friendly relations between the United States and other countries.

While the method of negotiating trade agreements bilaterally with individual countries accomplished outstanding results, there was

[2] This statement, which was entitled "The Geneva Agreement on Tariffs and Trade," was written some time in 1948. A copy may be found in CP, ACCO.

a strong need for a more comprehensive course of action under present conditions. The world has been growing smaller at an extremely rapid rate, while the necessary arrangements for the conduct of trade and exchange have become increasingly complex. The economies of the nations of the world are interlocking, and trade and financial problems usually have implications and repercussions for many countries. Furthermore, World War II left the world economic and financial situation in a chaotic condition. The industrial plants and agricultural resources of many of the nations most important in the United States foreign trade were devastated. Their economies were converted wholesale to war purposes. Their capital structures were seriously damaged, their manpower was reduced, and their assets abroad were depleted or liquidated. All these factors impaired the ability of the nations to resume their pre-war export trade and to earn exchange to pay for their very greatly increased import requirements. Consequently, there has been a tremendous growth of arbitrary and discriminatory controls over international economic transactions, particularly quota and licensing controls over imports, and foreign exchange control over international payments.

This is a general situation calling for general treatment. No single country can deal with it by itself. Some countries which have tried to avoid raising new trade barriers have found uncontrolled trade leading to the exhaustion of their supplies of convertible currencies while they acquired non-convertible currencies which they could not spend. Also, each country is hampered by its uncertainty as to the policies of other countries. No European country, for example, can plan very far ahead because it does not know what its neighbors will do.

It appeared, therefore, that the post-war economic situation required action on a many-nation basis, and the post-war economic program of the United States was based on this premise. The many-nation trade program had its inception in November 1945, when the United States published its *Proposals for the Expansion of World Trade and Employment* which suggested the establishment of an International Trade Organization and the adoption of a Charter or code of principles under which international commerce could expand multilaterally and on a non-discriminatory basis with the fewest possible restrictions and with resulting increases in employment and production and higher living standards throughout the world. The Geneva meeting, which opened April 10, 1947, and closed on November 17, accomplished the writing of a semi-final draft of the Charter which will govern a large part of the economic relations of member nations, as well as conclusion of the General Agreement on Tariffs and Trade.

The General Agreement consists of (1) schedules of tariff concessions, and (2) general provisions dealing with such matters as quotas, internal controls, customs regulations, state trading and subsidies. Each country applying the agreement undertakes to grant to the other parties to the agreement the reductions or bindings of tariff treatment specified in the schedules of tariff concessions and to observe the rules laid down in the general provisions in its commercial relations with them. The general provisions are not limited to the items in the schedules, but cover the whole of the trade between the parties to the agreement. They therefore establish for the first time a generally accepted international code of fair treatment in commercial relations.

The tariff concessions made by the United States were formulated within the limits and according to the procedure specified by the Trade-Agreements Act and Executive Order No. 9832 of February 25, 1947. As required by the latter, the General Agreement provides that if, through unforeseen developments, a particular tariff reduction should increase imports so sharply as to cause or threaten serious injury to domestic producers, the country granting the concessions may withdraw or modify it in whole or in part. If a concession is so modified or withdrawn, other interested countries may then withdraw or substantially modify equivalent concessions.

The concessions obtained by the United States from the other countries with respect to products of which the United States was their principal supplier had a total value (in terms of 1939 trade) of $1,192,364,000. In addition to these concessions, the United States is interested in concessions granted by the other countries on a substantial range of other products of which the United States is only a secondary supplier. The value of United States trade in such products is estimated at more than $200,000,000.

One of the most important features of the General Agreement is its treatment of tariff preferences. Preferences affecting a significant part of United States trade with countries in the British Commonwealth have been substantially reduced and preferences on a considerable list of products which the United States exports to the various countries of the Commonwealth have been eliminated entirely. In addition, it was agreed that no new preferences may be created, and no existing preferences may be increased whether or not on products listed in the schedules of the Agreement.

The negotiation of this Agreement is therefore impressive and encouraging. Unfortunately, however, no claim can be made that the

commitments and professions made in it will produce a trade mil-
lenium this year or next. The prevailing economic difficulties mentioned above continue to require many countries of the world to
maintain the network of licenses, quotas, exchange controls and
bilateral clearing and barter agreements which are interfering with
trade everywhere. In fact, these devices are being renewed and multiplied, instead of disappearing, and in the General Agreement (as
well as in the draft Charter for an International Trade Organization)
it has been necessary to include exceptions which will permit restrictionism and discrimination to continue. The most important of these
exceptions are temporary, and they are surrounded by careful safe-
guards. But they offer no assurance that the conditions that govern
world trade will shortly be set to rights. Indeed, before these conditions get better it is even possible they may take a turn for the worse.

The underlying basis for the striking contrast between desirable
principles as evidenced in the General Agreement and actual practice
is the basic imbalance of the world's trade. On the one hand, there
is an extraordinary demand for America's goods. On the other hand
there is the inability of other nations to produce and ship to us in
payment the goods we are ready and willing to receive. The consequence is a drain on foreign reserves of gold and dollars that would
spell bankruptcy if it were not limited by import controls and other
restrictions.

What is the solution to this problem? The first and most obvious
step is the promotion of reconstruction and recovery in Western
Europe. As these countries get back on their feet, as production is
resumed and goods once more become available in relatively large
supply, the need for restrictionism and bilateralism and discrimination
will disappear. The second step is the application in full force of the
provisions of the General Agreement, the proposed Charter for an
International Trade Organization, and the International Monetary
Fund Agreement. For it is only by subjecting them to international
control that we can really be assured that these practices, even if
rendered unnecessary, will not in fact continue to impede world trade.

This will be a slow process. It is not to be expected, for instance,
that the General Agreement will immediately result in an overall increase in United States exports. Such an increase would but exaggerate the already serious dollar-shortage problem. It is not to be
anticipated, either, that the agreement will immediately bring into the
United States a volume of imports so large that the existing imbalance
in the world's trade will be rectified. The agreement should help, but
our trade can hardly be brought into better balance until foreign
production is restored.

The significance of the Geneva agreement is to be found, then, not in an immediate shift in exports or imports, but in its long-run influence on the policies of the principal trading nations of the world. Current practice is determined by the disturbed conditions of economies disrupted by war, the reconstruction of which is only beginning. It is of incalculable importance that under these conditions the world's trading nations have accepted sound principles to govern international commerce as they work their way back to stability, prosperity and peace. Only the general acceptance of these principles now holds forth the hope that at the end of the transitional reconstruction period it will be feasible to break down the restrictions and reverse the trend toward economic isolation which the war and its aftermath have fostered.

To Hon. Alben W. Barkley

Washington, D.C.
April 21, 1948

My dear Senator Barkley:

I have reference to our recent conversation in which we discussed the signature by Czechoslovakia of the Protocol of Provisional Application of the General Agreement on Tariffs and Trade, and the implications of this action for the United States in the light of the events surrounding the governmental changes of last February in Czechoslovakia.[3] This matter has been given the most careful study both within the Department of State and in meetings of the President's Cabinet.

The President today has decided to issue a proclamation putting into effect the provisions of the General Agreement on Tariffs and Trade with respect to Czechoslovakia, thereby implementing an obligation entered into by this Government more than five months

---

[3] An unsigned carbon copy of this letter may be found in CP, ACCO.

ago, on October 30, 1947, when the General Agreement was concluded at Geneva, and prior to the Communist coup of February, 1948. Since Czechoslovakia has now placed the General Agreement in effect with respect to the United States and the other contracting parties, this country as well as the other contracting parties is obligated to apply the agreement to Czechoslovakia. This Government's attitude towards the events of last February in Czechoslovakia has not changed from that indicated in the joint statement of February 26, 1948 by the Secretary of State of this Government and by the Foreign Ministers of the Governments of the United Kingdom and France. These events, however, do not directly affect the legal status of the reciprocal obligations under the General Agreement.

The General Agreement is a comprehensive trade agreement among twenty-three countries. It is part of a world wide program, sponsored by the United Nations and actively participated in by the United States, designed to reduce trade barriers and to restore international trade to an orderly and stable basis. It is clearly to the interest of such a program to include the fullest possible participation by any countries which are willing to undertake the necessary obligations.

Concern has been expressed by a number of persons that making effective the General Agreement as between the United States and Czechoslovakia will give undue assistance, without receiving adequate reciprocal advantage in return, to a country subject to the influence of the Soviet Union, while depriving the American economy of the goods which are necessary to maintain our defensive strength. I would like to emphasize in particular that should Czechoslovakia or any other contracting party fail to fulfill the obligations of the Agreement or adopt any policy which impairs or nullifies the tariff concessions, the application by the United States to that country of such obligations or concessions under the Agreement as may be appropriate in the circumstances may be suspended. In addition, if, as a result of unforeseen circumstances, any of the concessions extended in the Agreement should result in such increased imports from Czechoslovakia as to cause or threaten serious injury to domestic producers in this country, the United States is free to withdraw or modify the concessions to the extent necessary to prevent or remedy the injury.

In addition to this safeguard with respect to imports, the United States also exercises export controls to protect the American economy generally, to promote the objectives of foreign policy, and to safeguard national security. Since March 1, 1948, no shipments to European destinations, including Czechoslovakia, can be made without appropriate license. These export controls prevent shipment of goods contrary to the national interests of the United States.

There is enclosed a statement being issued to the press today which contains some of the considerations discussed in this letter and outlines the pertinent facts relating to the reciprocal concessions included in the General Agreement on the part of the United States and Czechoslovakia. It should be noted that the entry into force of these concessions granted by the United States on products of special interest to Czechoslovakia, will also benefit certain other countries which signed the General Agreement in Geneva and which are participating in the European recovery program.

> Sincerely yours,
> W. L. Clayton
> *Advisor to the Secretary of State*

§ *Clayton expressed the following thoughts on Russia's post-war boundaries in Eastern Europe.*

To Lamar Fleming, Jr.

> Washington, D.C.
> May 18, 1948

Dear Lamar:

I must apologize for the delay in acknowledging your letter of March 19th[4] with the memorandum from Mr. Simmons.[5] The truth

[4] Lamar Fleming to Will Clayton, March 19, 1948, LS, CP, ACCO. An unsigned carbon copy of Clayton's reply may be found in CP, ACCO.

[5] E. P. Simmons, President of Sanger Brothers department stores of Dallas, Texas. In the memorandum Simmons states, "When the war was over we had the army, the navy, and the air force, in other words, we had the power to establish the lines of Europe where they should be established. Why did we not do this? Why did we completely dismantle the greatest military force ever assembled in the World and leave Russia sitting right in the middle of Europe with a powerful army which she had not disbanded and which she showed no intention to disband and thereby place ourselves solely at her mercy to decide what should be done in Europe?" E. P. Simmons, undated memorandum, CP, ACCO.

of the matter is, in my flying around from one place to another, principally Havana, this letter got misplaced and did not have attention.

Mr. Simmons complains that we withdrew our armies from Europe instead of leaving them there for the purpose of "establishing the lines of Europe where they should be established."

Mr. Simmons apparently has forgotten the demands of the American people at that time to "bring the boys home." In spite of everything that was done we couldn't get them home fast enough.

There was a general feeling then that the Russians would behave. I think the people of the country believed this more than it was believed in the Department of State.

The U.N. had just been established and people reposed great hope and faith in its ability to work things out.

Any government which assumed that Russia did not intend to play ball and acting on that assumption tried to keep a U.S. Army in Europe big enough to make them play ball instead of trying to work these differences out through U.N. would in my opinion have been impeached in Congress.

Sincerely yours,
William L. Clayton

To John Kenneth Galbraith

Washington, D.C.
October 21, 1948

Dear Ken:

Briefly, my idea on the matter we discussed in New York last Friday is as follows:[6]

1. Until Russia retires to her pre-War boundaries, there will probably be no real peace in the world in the foreseeable future.

[6] An unsigned carbon copy of this letter to John Kenneth Galbraith, economist, author, member of board of editors of *Fortune* magazine, may be found in CP, ACCO.

2. Russia will retire to her pre-War boundaries only if she should be vanquished in another world war or if the forces of democracy should be sufficiently organized to cause her to lose the cold war.

Both sides will be careful to avoid any act which might precipitate World War III. The continuing struggle then presents itself as a gigantic cold war between the Russian World and the Western World.

3. To win any kind of war with Russia, the West must be much more closely knit than at present. Western Europe must federate or unionize, politically, economically and militarily.

4. In these circumstances, the United States faces enormous responsibilities as leader of the Western World in its struggle for preservation of its freedom. Spiritual, military and economic leadership must be available as required. Civilian and military goods must be furnished as needed, on practically a lend-lease basis. If war must come, our European allies should be prepared to stop and hold the Russian armies short of the Atlantic and the Mediterranean until we can go to their assistance.

5. The United States itself must rearm and prepare.

6. What is the spiritual, economic and social capacity of the United States to meet the great responsibilities which this leadership will impose on us? Are our people prepared to make the necessary adjustments and sacrifices? What are these adjustments and sacrifices?

* * *

Obviously, this is only a brief outline of the proposed study.

Sincerely yours,
William L. Clayton

§ *The Havana Conference convened on November 21, 1948, to negotiate a charter for the proposed International Trade Organization which had been discussed earlier by the participants at the Geneva Conference. When the Havana meeting adjourned on March 24, 1948, fifty-three of the fifty-six nations present had signed the completed Charter. However, as Clayton later wrote to his son-in-law, "we met so much objection on the part of large corporations in the U.S. on certain aspects of the charter that the Administration never did put it before Congress as they realized it would be de-*

feated."[7] *The failure of the United States to adopt the Charter was the greatest disappointment of Clayton's government career. Nevertheless, so long as there was a chance for its adoption, he continued to seek support for it.*

A Speech on the Havana Conference

"Why and How We Came to Find Ourselves at the Havana Conference" is a good story, but it will take us over a long and difficult road.[8]

The story needs to be told because it will help to a better understanding of the Havana charter.

No doubt the inspiration for that great enterprise lay in the general realization that the nations of the world made a tragic mess of their international economic relationships following the first world war and in a determination that this same road should not be traveled again.

It is only necessary to mention such matters as reparations, the handling of the war debts, the raising to fantastic heights of tariffs and other trade barriers, the practice of bilateral and barter trading, and the bitter retaliations and discriminations which flowed from these actions.

The first significant declaration of a determination to prevent a recurrence of these tragic mistakes was contained in the Atlantic Charter in August 1941. The victorious German Army was then far inside Russia, having long since swept western Europe. There were no illusions in the United States regarding the peril with which we would be faced if Germany should win the war.

Under these dramatic circumstances President Roosevelt and Prime Minister Churchill met upon the Atlantic and signed a pledge which became known as the Atlantic Charter. The Atlantic Charter announced, among other things, that the two Governments: ". . . will

---

[7] Will Clayton to St. John Garwood, February 23, 1960, L, CP, ACCO.

[8] This speech, which was entitled "Why and How We Came To Find Ourselves at the Havana Conference," was delivered before the Economic Institute of the Chamber of Commerce of the United States, Washington, D.C., June 15, 1948, and later printed in Department of State, *Bulletin*, 18 (June 27, 1948): 825–927.

endeavor, with due respect for their existing obligations, to further the enjoyment by all States, great or small, victor or vanquished, of access, on equal terms, to the trade and to the raw materials of the world. . . ."

By 1943 thirty-four other nations had subscribed to the principles of the Atlantic Charter.

Four months after the publication of the Atlantic Charter the Japanese attack on Pearl Harbor brought the United States into the war.

Within a short time thereafter we concluded the first of a series of master lend-lease agreements with our European Allies.

Article VII of this agreement committed the signatory Governments to the principle of "the expansion, by appropriate international and domestic measures, of production, employment, and the exchange and consumption of goods, which are the material foundations of the liberty and welfare of all peoples; . . . the elimination of all forms of discriminatory treatment in international commerce; and . . . the reduction of tariffs and other trade barriers."

The United States Government lost no time, even in the agonizing years of the war, in taking energetic action to mobilize the thinking in other governments and to prepare measures to carry out these declarations.

In November 1943, a distinguished British delegation led by Lord Keynes came to Washington by invitation to discuss with us the shaping of a world economic program. A broad range of economic subjects including trade and finance were discussed at that time. Similar discussions were held in January 1944 with the Canadian Government. Following these talks, we began work in Washington to shape up a program of action. For this purpose, an interdepartmental committee was formed, headed originally by Mr. Myron Taylor[9] and later by Mr. Dean Acheson as Chairman of the Executive Committee on Economic Foreign Policy, established by the President. As Assistant Secretary of Commerce, I took part in the deliberations of this Committee and later, as Assistant Secretary of State for Economic Affairs, succeeded Mr. Acheson as Chairman of the Committee.

The international trade policies formulated by this group were presented in a document called *Proposals for the Expansion of World Trade and Employment*. Before publication in December 1945, these proposals were discussed with the British Government and were

[9] Myron Taylor, member of the Postwar Planning Committee and vice-chairman of the Advisory Council on Postwar Foreign Policy, Department of State (1944).

mutually agreed to. Subsequently, in the early months of 1946, other governments expressed their approval of the principles contained in the U.S. proposals.

Having achieved a wide measure of agreement on basic economic principles, the United States then drafted a charter to give effect to these principles. This document was known as *Suggested Charter for an International Trade Organization.* It was circulated to all United Nations governments for their consideration.

Meanwhile, the United Nations had been organized in February 1946, the Economic and Social Council called a preliminary meeting of 18 countries to prepare for a conference on trade and employment. This meeting was held in London from October 15 to November 30, 1946. The draft charter suggested by the United States was used as the basis of discussion.

The text of the draft resulting from the London meeting was put into better shape by a drafting committee convened at Lake Success in January and February 1947. This became known as the "New York draft" and served as the basis for the Second Preparatory Conference convened in Geneva in April 1947. Prior thereto, however, this Government diligently endeavored to acquaint the American public and the Congress with the project in hand. Conferences were held with numerous business groups including the United States Chamber of Commerce. A representative group selected from departments of the Government held informal public hearings in seven major cities of the United States to receive "grass roots" opinions about the proposed ITO. The Senate Committee on Finance conducted a detailed inquiry, the record of which covers several thick volumes.

This "referendum" of public and congressional opinion was extremely valuable. Over 100 specific suggestions were received for revising or extending the charter. The entire record was carefully studied to pick out every meritorious suggestion for use in the Geneva negotiations. Both the Geneva draft and the present Havana Charter bear the imprint of these suggestions.

As you probably know, there were 19 countries represented at Geneva, and negotiations there lasted some five months. They were complicated and prolonged by the fact that these same countries were also negotiating a General Agreement on Tariffs and Trade which required bargaining on thousands of specific items. In addition, agreement on general undertakings had to be reached to give value to the tariff reductions on these items. This enormous and very difficult task was successfully concluded and now stands as a landmark in international trade relations.

The charter negotiations at Geneva were concluded late in August 1947. On November 21, 1947, the World Conference on Trade and Employment convened at Havana to perfect the final draft of the charter. Representatives of 56 countries attended the Conference. This meant that two thirds of the countries at Havana had not participated in the preliminary conferences at London and Geneva. The charter was finally initialed by representatives of 54 countries.

* * *

In retrospect it seems almost inconceivable that representatives of 54 nations, great and small, developed and undeveloped, with divergent interests, and speaking many different languages, could agree on a constitution of principles to govern their international economic relationships.

The drafters of the American Constitution didn't have an easy time reaching agreement on that document, but just suppose they had neglected to forbid the States of this Union to erect tariff barriers. In that case, today, 160 years later, we would certainly have a flourishing crop of protectionist measures dividing the United States into 48 economic principalities.

For example, I am quite sure that my State of Texas would have prohibitive tariffs, among other things, on shoes, woolen and cotton goods. Since Texas is the greatest producer of the raw materials for these articles, it is too much to expect that loyal Texans would have overlooked the great advantages to be obtained in the employment of Texas capital and Texas labor for the conversion of Texas raw materials into finished products for Texas citizens. The fact that other areas might do the work better and cheaper, leaving Texas capital and labor to devote itself to more profitable undertakings, would, of course, have nothing to do with the matter.

And suppose some President of the United States, realizing that this situation had seriously interfered with the sound development of the country, had invited the governors of the 48 States to meet with him in Washington to try to come to agreement on remedial action.

How long do you think it would take these 48 governors, all speaking the same language and living under the same political system, to reach effective agreement, if indeed any agreement could ever be reached?

One needs only to draw this kind of parallel to the Havana conference to illustrate the enormous complexity and difficulty of the task undertaken there.

Indeed we were told again and again that it could not be done. The program was too ambitious. It would involve too many commitments. Circumstances and systems were too diverse. Fair dealing in international trade was old-fashioned and impractical anyway. The disorganization caused by the war was too great. The problem of reconstruction was too pressing. Nations were too much preoccupied with immediate difficulties. They would not look to the future. The future in any case was too uncertain. It could not be done.

But it was done.

The charter is complex and difficult. It is long and detailed and technical. It is far from perfect; indeed, it falls short of what we fought for. But behind its many chapters and its scores of articles, there lies a simple truth. The world will be a better place to live in if nations, instead of taking unilateral action with little regard to the interests of others, will adopt and follow common principles and enter into consultation through an international organization when interests come into conflict.

And this, throughout the entire range of trade relationships, is what the signatories of the charter agree to do. Each will surrender some part of its freedom to take action that might prove harmful to others and thus each will gain the assurance that others will not take action harmful to it.

This may well prove to be the greatest step in history toward order and justice in economic relations among the members of the world community and toward a great expansion in the production, distribution, and consumption of goods throughout the world.

The International Trade Organization will deal with questions that nations have always held to be of the greatest importance. It will seek solutions for problems that have been a perennial source of irritation and ill will. It will serve as a center where the peoples of the world with their diversity of economic interests can meet on common ground.

If the United States should ratify the Havana Charter, many other nations will promptly ratify it.

If the United States should fail to ratify the charter, there will be no International Trade Organization. Such an eventuality would be a tragedy; it is unthinkable.

It has often been said and correctly that the United States is the giant of the economic world. But it is not so generally recognized at home as it is abroad that we are looked upon as leaders in the world in the movement to reestablish the principles of nondiscriminatory, multilateral trade; that we are regarded as the exponents of liberalism in international economic relations; that we are recognized as proponents of policies designed to bring about a great expansion in the production, distribution, and consumption of goods throughout the world, to the end that people everywhere may have more to eat, more to wear, and better homes in which to live.

Peoples and governments, generally, understand that the purpose of all this is to lay a firm foundation for world peace and world prosperity.

It would be difficult to exaggerate the weight of the responsibilities which this position of leadership places upon us.

The policy itself is one which expresses the enlightened self-interest of the United States. The productive capacity of the United States in the industrial field equals that of the rest of the world combined. We must import from all over the world all kinds of raw materials to feed our huge productive machine. In metals and minerals, we are self-sufficient only in coal and one or two other items. Our fast-growing and prosperous population requires a great variety of goods. Much of our industrial and basic agricultural activity operates so efficiently that vast surpluses are produced at reasonable cost. These surpluses must find markets abroad. We have much to gain and nothing to lose from a great expansion in the interchange of goods and services around the world, a result which can only come from a return to multilateral nondiscriminatory trade.

If the United States should fail to ratify the charter, that action would not only be contrary to our best interests but would be a shock to the whole world. It would be a surrender of our leadership in international economic affairs; it would be more than that; it would be regarded as a repudiation of much that has been accomplished under that leadership.

If we deliberately vacate our rightful place in this field, does anyone believe that there is another nation in the world today prepared to step into our shoes?

What, then, would the consequence of such action be?

It is certain that every country in the world would feel that it was again on its own, that it was compelled to rely on unilateral action, in short that it had no other recourse except to return to the practices of the international economic jungle—everyone for himself and the devil catch the hindmost.

Bilateralism, import quotas, export quotas, exchange controls, cartels, subsidies, discriminations, retaliations—all the devices known to man for limiting the international exchange of goods and services—would again become standard procedure throughout the world.

Do we want to see a return to that kind of world? Is that in our interest? We must realize that the United States could not long remain an island of free enterprise in a sea of state-controlled international trade. The United States would be forced into the international trading practices of the rest of the world.

But that is not all.

We would find it extremely difficult to carry on international trade in isolation from domestic trade.

There are two roads we can take here.

One road leads in the direction of free enterprise and the preservation of democratic principles.

The other road leads in direction of Socialism and state trading.

We must soon choose which road we will take.

The Twentieth Century Fund recently issued a report recommending strongly a broad anti-cartel policy by the United States and declaring that support by the United States of the International Trade Organization is essential to such a policy.

The report further states that if the United States refuses the ITO charter, the result will be not a better agreement but a looser one or perhaps no agreement at all.

There are only two questions we have to ask ourselves in trying to decide what we will do about the ITO charter; and those two questions are:

1. Would the United States and the world be better off if there were no ITO, leaving each country to act on its own as heretofore?

2. If the present charter is rejected, would we be able later on to obtain agreement on a better charter?

In my opinion the answer to both questions is NO.

254

To W. H. Harrison[10]

March 11, 1949

Dear Bill:

It was good of you to take the time to write me regarding your views on the Havana Charter.[11]

I recognize, as well as anyone I think, the weaknesses and imperfections of the Charter. For example I am worried about the International Investments provisions. Knowing the difficulties in the way of getting any worthwhile commitments on this subject, the U.S. Delegation had not intended to attempt anything in this field, but did place it on the agenda on the urgent insistence of the National Foreign Trade Council and other organizations.

I would favor lifting the whole question bodily out of the Charter rather than take what we have there and I believe this deletion could be effected without any serious difficulty.

I cannot recognize, as a practical matter, the validity of your arguments against Charter provisions relating to cartels. I think this is one of the best provisions in the Charter. The Twentieth Century Fund agrees on this and has issued a very informative volume on the subject.

The exceptions referred in your criticism of the provisions relating to "imports, exports and exchange" and "protection" are almost altogether temporary, at least in so far as any serious application of such exceptions is concerned.

We are dealing with a very sick world and it would be impossible to get binding commitments on these subjects without exceptions to cover present conditions and situations.

I have carefully read your comments under the heading "Economic Aid" but I don't think there is anything serious here either.

I have also carefully considered your stated objection to the

[10] President of the International Telephone and Telegraph Corporation of New York. An unsigned carbon copy of this letter may be found in CP, ACCO.

[11] W. H. Harrison to Will Clayton, March 7, 1949, LS, CP, ACCO. Harrison expresses fear that the Havana Charter "will tend to increase nationalism at the expense of the free flow of goods and services." He then enumerates specific objections to which Clayton replies.

Charter under the heading "Restrictions" and I feel here that you fail to take into account the fact that the continuance of certain controls and restrictions is inevitable under present conditions and nothing that the Charter might say could change this situation.

Let me sum up my view this way: All of the bad practices which exceptions to the Charter recognize are practices now being indulged in right around the world and they will continue to be indulged in until conditions alter to the point where they can be abandoned.

No matter what we do, countries which have serious balance of payments problems are going to practice controls of different kinds in order to protect their meager store of foreign monies. I am sure you will agree with me that they *should* continue to control the expenditures and commitments of their citizens abroad so long as there is a definite limit on the amount of foreign money that they can make available for meeting such commitments.

Suppose the situation were reversed in the United States and we had need to import much more than we could export. In those circumstances we in the United States would do exactly what foreign countries are doing.

The Charter recognizes the temporary necessity of certain restrictive and undesirable practices but it surrounds such practices with controls and conditions which keep them within reasonable bounds and it provides the discontinuance of these practices as soon as the conditions which brought them about have changed.

We have to look at the Charter in terms of alternatives.

If we reject the Charter there will be no restraint on the unbridled practice of all kinds of nationalistic devices. I have spent the last few years in almost daily contact with representatives of foreign governments around the world and I firmly believe unless we can bring these governments into some kind of international trade organization with definite objectives and principles where we can sit around the table face to face and discuss these problems, the world will soon become a kind of economic jungle with every fellow for himself and the devil take the hindmost.

Frankly, Bill, I think you had better take another careful look at this question and view it in the large instead of a too meticulous regard for imperfections.

The International Telephone and Telegraph Company ought to be for this enterprise!

With very kindest regards, I remain,

Sincerely yours,
W. L. Clayton

§ *In the late forties the American people displayed a fascination with the concept of international federation. In 1946 the people of Massachusetts voted nine to one in favor of strengthening the United Nations to provide a modified form of world government. In a similar referendum in Connecticut in 1948, the vote was favorable by a twelve-to-one margin.*[12] *Two organizations were formed during this period to mobilize support for political internationalism. The United World Federalists favored operating through the United Nations and including all nations; the Atlantic Union group, on the other hand, favored a regional federation in the Atlantic area, composed of the United States, Canada, and the nations of Western Europe. Will Clayton's case for Atlantic Union follows.*

MEMORANDUM ON UNITED WORLD FEDERALISTS' POLICY

January 17, 1949

Mr. Clark[13] believes that a "sound and complete policy" has now been found by UWF with respect to the transformation of the United Nations into an effective Federation and the settlement of the main issues between the Soviet Union and the West.

The solution, he thinks, is one big negotiation with Russia on both these interdependent matters.

This negotiation "might extend over several years since the obstacles are great and the utmost patience will be required." (Having had some rather extensive negotiating experience with Russia, I can keenly appreciate the force of this statement.)

"It has been a necessary thing to make it plain to Russia that her further expansion would be promptly opposed."

Presumably, therefore, the negotiation would proceed on the basis that the vast Central European territory into which Russia has

[12] Chester Bowles, "World Government—'Yes, But . . . ,'" *Harper's Magazine*, March 1949, p. 17.

[13] Vice President of United World Federalists. A copy of this memorandum, entitled "Comment on Mr. Grenville Clark's Memorandum of December 1st, 1948," may be found in CP, ACCO.

already forcibly expanded since the end of the war is now hers without further question.

It is not clear as to what the situation would be if other States, now free and independent, should fall into the Russian orbit by the usual methods, during the "several years" which the negotiations would require.

I do not advocate going to war with Russia for the restoration of the integrity and independence of Czechoslovakia, and other States which she has forcibly subdued to her will.

But I am opposed to any plan of negotiation with Russia which tacitly recognized her right to keep her heel on the necks of the millions of people of these Central European States forcibly brought under her dominion since the end of the war.

Any negotiation which recognizes such right, or ignores the question, cannot possibly bring peace to the world, even though agreement were reached on every other point of difference.

There will be no peace in the world until Russia returns to her prewar boundaries.

The obvious question is: How can this be accomplished short of war?

Possibly it may never be accomplished but I believe that it can be; but not under the present policies and procedures of the democracies.

Regardless of the Marshall Plan or similar plan, Western Europe cannot in the foreseeable future return to a position of financial independence with a decent standard of living for its people so long as it continues to function as eighteen or twenty separate and independent economic compartments as it does now.

As a practical matter, the United States does not possess sufficient reserves of strength to carry Western Europe on its back, for long, as it is doing now.

The only solution, it seems to me, is Union or Federation of the remaining free States of Europe. And I am inclined to favor the inclusion in such a union of the United States and Canada.

Such a Union would present to Russia an aggregation of political, economic and military power so great the further Russian expansion westward would be impossible, and the probabilities are that the natural pull from the West on Russian Satellite States lying in between would be so much greater than the pull from the East that most, if not all, of these States would in time successfully reassert their independence.

Everything possible should be done to increase trade, travel and cultural intercourse and exchanges between the West and the East.

On the question of trade alone, Russia will have enormous difficulties in holding the Satellite States in her sphere of influence. The Western and Eastern economies are complimentary which is not at all true of the Russian and Satellite economies.

The goods and services which the Satellite countries require are for the most part the identical goods and services of which the Russians are themselves buyers; and the goods which the Satellite countries wish to sell are for the most part the same sort of goods which the Russians wish to sell.

There is thus no natural economic basis for inclusion or retention of the Satellite countries in the Russian sphere of influence.

If we go on as we are or if we negotiate as Mr. Clark suggests "for several years," we will wake up one day and find Russia in possession of the atom bomb and then we will face a different situation.

Anyone having any doubt as to the ultimate aims of Stalin ought to read the article by "Historicus" in the January issue of "Foreign Affairs."[14]

W. L. Clayton

To John S. Knight

July 30, 1949

Dear Mr. Knight:

I have carefully read the editorial over your signature in your July 23rd issue entitled "Plan for Atlantic Union Lacks a Sound Blueprint."[15]

My own idea of the proper reply to the various questions which you raise follows:

(1) You suggest that adoption of Senator Taft's[16] one paragraph declaration that "we should make it clear to the USSR that if

---

[14] "Stalin on Revolution," *Foreign Affairs*, 27 (January 1949): 175–214.

[15] An unsigned carbon copy of this letter to the editor and publisher of the Chicago *Daily News* may be found in CP, ACCO.

[16] Senator Robert A. Taft of Ohio (1939–53).

it attacks Western Europe it will be at war with us" is a surer guarantee that there will be no such attack than the formation of an Atlantic Union (Western Europe, the United States and Canada) which you say "requires a constitutional amendment, ratification by thirty six states and years of delay."

Aside from certain constitutional questions concerning the validity of the proposed Taft declaration, other serious objections occur.

Can the United States produce evidence of warlike intentions toward Western Europe on the part of the USSR, which such a declaration would imply?

I seriously doubt that there is any such evidence, or, indeed, any such intentions.

The danger is not so much that Soviet Russia will precipitate an armed attack on Western Europe as it is that economic deterioration in Western Europe, temporarily arrested by the Marshall Plan, will eventually give victory to the Soviets in the cold war.

In that event the Communists would occupy all of Europe.

And then indeed Soviet Russia would find herself at war with the United States. Isolated politically and economically, we would be the attacker fighting for our very existence.

But, meantime, the general fear of war immobilizes the capital, brains and initiative of much of the free enterprise system of the world and throws the burden of European recovery on Governments. And Governments operating as separate sovereignties in tiny economic compartments just can't do the job.

(2) You indicate that reestablishment of confidence in the integrity of European currencies, with private enterprise encouraged to operate freely in Europe, which it is claimed would result from the adoption of the Atlantic Union Plan, could probably come only from throwing our gold reserves into the depleted international "kitty" and from using our money to encourage European socialism and a perpetuation of authoritarian controls over business and private lives.

Although I do not admit the necessity of any such step, may I say if a portion of the gold now stored at Fort Knox should be needed in a sound and permanent plan to stabilize and make convertible the currencies of the world, restore world trade, raise the standard of living and remove the threat of communism and war, the United States could make such gold available with great profit to itself.

The United States is now spending each and every year more than the equivalent of all the gold that it possesses in an effort to ward off communism and war.

Originally, much of this very gold belonged to these same countries of Western Europe, where it served as a support to their currencies. It flowed to our shores because we refused to accept goods for goods. Much of the mess we now find ourselves in stems from this very fact. Under the Atlantic Union no such mistake could be made again, because the Nations composing the Union, like the 48 States of the U.S.A., would presumably have no customs houses between them.

(3) You say that the military aspects of Atlantic Union would undoubtedly be less costly to Europe but vastly more expensive for us.

The total military costs of Atlantic Union would undoubtedly be less than the aggregate of such costs to the separate states at this time. It is unnecessary to argue this point. The United States would, of course, have to bear its proper share but this would unquestionably be much less than the 20 billion dollars plus which we are now putting out in one way or another to prevent another world war.

(4) You question whether Atlantic Union would arrest the spread of communism. You express the view that communism flourishes wherever a nation has lost its national pride, the capacity for self-help, and its moral integrity.

You seem to question the belief of the sponsors of the Atlantic Union that communism feeds on frustration, hopelessness and economic misery.

I think both views are correct, but may I point out that as a general thing the loss of national pride, the capacity for self-help, and moral integrity are generally associated, in a nation, with conditions of economic misery and frustration.

You seem to fear if no passports are required in a federated union, the United States, instead of repelling communism as we have done to date "would soon become a happy hunting ground for the crack-pots of the world."

Our record in repelling communism arises not so much from our ability to keep out the crack-pots (since this species is indigenous to our country, imports are unnecessary), but is due rather to the creation of an economic climate highly inhospitable to the spread of communism.

It is believed that Atlantic Union would in time create such a climate throughout its entire area.

(5) You are of the opinion that Atlantic Union might bring a higher standard of living in the other nations but a lower standard for Americans, because it would involve a "distribution of America's wealth and resources." You say "when the economic pie is cut into

more pieces for the 'have-not' nations America's portion is sure to be smaller."

Nobody contemplates cutting the economic pie into more pieces. It is merely intended to add more pie through an intense re-activation of the forces of free enterprise.

(6) You question whether Atlantic Union will strengthen the United Nations. And you speak of "an Atlantic Union gun against Russia's head."

The idea of Atlantic Union cannot possibly contemplate holding a gun against anybody's head. On the contrary, it expects that the guns which now menace the peace of the world will be lowered with the return of decent living conditions for the millions of people of Western Europe who do not have enough to eat, or enough to wear, and who go cold in winter.

* * *

Undoubtedly there are great difficulties in the way of the formation of an Atlantic Union of the Democracies.

You are familiar with the history of the formation of our own Union of the thirteen colonies.

You know how difficult that was.

At times the difficulties appeared so great that the effort seemed doomed to failure.

Admitting all of the difficulties in the formation of an Atlantic Union, is it not the only way out of the mess into which the world is fast heading?

Can you suggest a better way?

The Kremlin has divided the world in two—the communist world and the free world.

The policy of the communist world is aggressive and expanding.

If the world goes on for another ten years as it has done for the last five years, 1960 will find the United States politically and economically isolated.

How long then could we continue as a free enterprise, democratic nation?

The end of the Marshall Plan (even if continued until the summer of 1952 and there is no certainty of that) will find Western Europe annually 2½ to 3 billion dollars in the red with the rest of the world.

Without outside help, the only practical way this situation can be met is through a substantial lowering in the standard of living of Western Europe—a standard already too low.

Do you not believe with me that the probabilities are that communism would then march to the English Channel?

If Atlantic Union is not the answer, what is the answer?

Atlantic Union would break down the tiny economic compartments in which Western Europe now operates, and which keep her tools of production inefficient, unable to compete in the markets of the world; it would solve the dollar problem; it would dispel the fear of war; it would release and vitalize the labor, genius and capital of men everywhere; it would give a great new hope to the world that at last we are on the right track.

All that we have done the last few years has been leading up to Federal Union of the free.

Must we fight another world war to realize that our freedom can be preserved only through Union of the free? If so the realization may come too late.

Sincerely yours,
W. L. Clayton

§ *Government agricultural policy continued to be a sore point with Clayton during his post-governmental years. Yet even this subject, in his mind, was part of the larger problem of economic nationalism. The following attack on federal farm policies ends with a plea for freer trade.*

A STATEMENT ON GOVERNMENT AGRICULTURAL POLICY

January 27, 1954

The U.S. Farm program, founded on moral and economic fallacies, is dragging American agriculture down a road which can lead only to ruin.[17]

The whole false structure was near collapse more than a decade ago, but was saved by World War II, the Marshall Plan, and Korea.

[17] A copy of this statement, which was entitled "Our Bankrupt Farm Program," may be found in CP, Rice.

Under the Farm program, the richest country in the world sabotages the processes of nature; subsidizes the creation of artificial scarcities in food and fibre, diverting them from consumption into Government warehouses; pays farmers not to produce and has even paid them to destroy that which they had produced.

The principal crops concerned are wheat, cotton and tobacco. These are world crops—not American crops. Their prices are made in world trading.

At heavy cost, our Government has exerted some influence on these prices. To the farmer, the most serious aspect of this cost is the surrender from time to time of important portions of his export markets.

Just a few years more of this and the American farmer will find that the Government has subsidized him out of practically all his foreign outlets—outlets which normally take one-half his cotton, forty percent of his tobacco and one-third of his wheat. Total U.S. exports have been running at record levels but cotton and wheat exports are less than one-half their normal volume. Tobacco has fared better but is now slipping badly. Our "umbrella" is bringing other suppliers rapidly into the world market. South Africa has substantially captured the important British market in tobacco.

Meantime, our Government has in storage, out of the channels of trade, more than five billion dollars worth of farm products. This figure is growing rapidly and will probably reach the statutory limit of 6.75 billion dollars in another six months. Will Congress raise this limit, along with the limit on the National debt? Will the Government provide more storage capacity? If not, Government support at ninety percent of parity will be ineffective, in some cases, because of lack of storage room.

What will our farmers do with the millions of acres of crop land normally producing for export?

What other crops can they plant without creating grave new problems of so-called "surpluses?"

They can let this land revert to pastures for the production of meat, an activity not yet controlled by the Government. Many of them have already done this with well-known results—among them a march of cattlemen on Washington.

The truth of the matter is that agriculture cannot go on much longer half free and half Government controlled. Either some way must be found to deal with this problem short of Government controls or the Government will take complete control.

If the Government takes complete control, we will then be far off the straight and narrow path of spiritual and material greatness and will be headed down the broad highway to socialism and decay.

There are other aspects of this matter, the momentous implications of which will be recognized by thoughtful students.

The U.S. Farm program, and its forebear, the U.S. protective tariff, are jeopardizing our leadership of the Free World.

Until 1929, American farmers bought in a protected market and sold in a free market.

While industry and the stock market boomed during the decade following the first World War, there was a steady decline in farm prices, following the precipitous break in 1920. This was an issue in the Presidential election of 1928. Promptly after Mr. Hoover's inauguration in March, 1929, he redeemed his campaign pledge by calling a Special Session of Congress to deal with the Farm question.

Having become politically conscious, the farmer, in effect, said to the protectionists: "Give us protection, or we will destroy yours." The result was the passage of the Federal Farm bill, the creation of the Federal Farm Board, with half a billion dollars of Government money to "stabilize" farm prices, and the enactment of the Smoot–Hawley tariff bill.

The half billion dollars was promptly lost, principally in trying to "stabilize" cotton at sixteen cents; cotton went to five cents per pound.

The Roosevelt administration took over in 1933, and promptly passed the Agricultural Adjustment Act, which continued the Farm Board principle of price "stabilization," but with practically unlimited funds, and with authority to curtail production and to "quota" or embargo imports of those agricultural products receiving Government "support."

Hence, our present Farm program is essentially a government price-fixing device, plus production and import controls.

No such program can square with our responsibilities of world leadership.

The Nations of the Free World are held together by a common purpose to preserve their freedoms and to seek world peace; they are held apart largely by economic difficulties and differences.

These economic factors have been present in varying degree since World War I, but, until now, were neutralized through vast grants in aid by the United States.

Apparently, our policy of gifts, except for war goods, is now coming to an end, as it should; and, in doing so, the economic difficulties and differences in the Free World are coming to the surface.

In practically all the necessities of modern life, the industrial revolution has made every country in the world a deficit producer in some things and a surplus producer in others. No country is self-sufficient. Every country in the world must cover its deficits by trading its surpluses for the surpluses of other countries.

Nobody denies this condition of interdependence but man's heritage of communal pride, prejudice and unenlightened selfishness keeps his political and economic concepts deeply rooted in tribal traditions, forebear of that blood-soaked fetish known as National Sovereignty.

We in the United States mix political internationalism with economic nationalism and forget that problems which were purely domestic yesterday may today vitally concern the welfare of hundreds of millions of people in other parts of the modern world.

Western Europe is an important deficit area in food and fibre and in most of the raw materials to feed her factories. These things must be imported from all parts of the world. They must be paid for. In the long run, this payment can only be made by exporting her surplus of manufactured goods.

But political and economic developments and readjustments, following two world wars, have multiplied the barriers which Western Europe now finds in the way of her exports.

Aided by vast grants from the United States, Western Europe's productive machine is now more efficient and productive than before the war. Her people are very intelligent and very proud; they are tired living off the bounty of Uncle Sam; they want to trade and earn their way.

But productivity is a barren thing unless there are markets for the produce.

Formerly the markets of Eastern Europe and China were natural and substantial outlets for the manufactures of Western Europe, but they may not now be availed of without incurring the severe displeasure of the United States; the Colonial Empires of Southeast Asia, formerly important markets, are now in a ferment; most other countries are trying to industrialize by the protectionist principle. The big United States market is still protected by tariffs and quotas and other devices to discourage imports.

Meantime, our surpluses of food and fibre are very important to the economy and the standard of living of Western Europe and of all the world; generally these surpluses are available only at prices fixed by our Government.

As long as there are in the world hundreds of millions of people who go to bed hungry and cold every night, there is not really a surplus pound of cotton or a surplus bushel of wheat. As leader of the

Free World, it is our job to seek ways to increase the buying power of these people instead of indulging in schemes which reduce it and thus add to their misery.

We should not be surprised when the foreigners who are harmed by our actions resent it.

And they resent it doubly because of the impediments we have placed in the way of the sale of their goods to us, the only sound means they have of paying for their purchases from us.

These impediments take the form, not only of tariffs, but of quotas, embargoes, the "Buy American" law, and customs regulations designed to discourage imports.

No wonder the Russians say to our allies in NATO: "You see! The United States not only won't let you trade with the East—they won't even let you trade with the West!"

Until adoption of the present Farm program, our entire economy was nurtured in the freest kind of domestic competition. Under it, there have been many economic casualties, of course, but out of it all, free enterprise has substantially survived, and our economy has grown to be the strongest in all the world.

The whole world is avidly seeking dollars with which to buy our goods. This is the most convincing proof that, for the great bulk of our production, the only fear we need have is that the rest of the world won't be able to earn enough dollars to buy our surpluses.

Our present Government price-fixing Farm program, with its import quotas and embargoes, should be eased out and finally discarded.

Goods are produced to be consumed, not to be withdrawn from the channels of trade, at enormous cost and waste.

Government subsidy of any segment of our economy is unsound policy; but the farmers have an argument when they point to the protective tariff; however, they have used the argument poorly. A transitory, pseudo-protection, such as they have got, is self-defeating.

What the American farmer needs is a free market at home in which to live and operate; and cleared channels of trade to all the world in which to sell his surpluses.

Foreigners to whom we have been giving the dollars with which to buy these surpluses for many years will certainly not—indeed cannot—continue buying them unless we now give them the opportunity to earn the necessary dollars by the sale of their goods to us.

With dollars scarce, the first dollar commodity the foreigner will cut off his list will be farm products. This is already happening. He can buy such things in many different countries and pay for them with goods of his own production.

What will we then do about the vast surpluses which our farmers normally produce annually?

What will become of the labor which the production, processing, transporting, and merchandizing of these surpluses normally employs?

There is perhaps one sound basis for a program of modest Government economic assistance to agriculture.

Our greatest national resource is our soil. It is the responsibility of organized society to see that the productive quality of this soil is preserved for future generations. Government may, therefore, properly make payments to farmers for following its recommendations regarding rotation, diversification, fertilization, prevention of soil erosion, etc., *provided* such program is not prostituted into a disguised crop control device.

American farmers are the most efficient in the world.

If we unshackle them, returning to the free-enterprise, free-market system to which we owe our greatness; if we re-open foreign markets to them, the unsubsidized American farmer can hold his own against the world.

Our gross production of goods and services now exceeds an annual rate of three hundred fifty billion dollars. An increase in our imports of one percent of this sum, or three and one-half billion dollars, and abandonment of Government price fixing and controls would solve the American Farm problem. These increased imports would enable our foreign customers to earn the dollars with which to continue to buy our surpluses of farm products and other goods; they would contribute to the variety and enrichment of life in our country, while stimulating our producers to greater efficiency.

But they would do much more than that.

The adoption by the United States of a policy leading eventually to free trade would hearten the world; it would cause other countries to follow our example; it would release and stimulate productive facilities the world over, it would raise the standard of living throughout the world; it would unify the free nations of the world as nothing else could; it would go far toward ending the threat of Communism to world peace.

If, on the other hand, we persist in our present policy of economic nationalism, it is almost certain that Western Europe and Japan will be driven into the economic and probably the political arms of the Communist Empire. On that day we will have lost the

Cold War and the United States will be isolated in an unfriendly world, waiting in its garrison for World War III to begin.

If it should be urged that the adoption of a free trade policy is for us politically impossible, the answer is that nothing is politically impossible in the United States if it is vital to the national interest, and if it has adequate leadership.

Congress is composed of members representing Districts and States. A great share of their attention is devoted to the affairs and interests of their constituents; but their paramount duty is to the Nation, and this is the duty which prevails when real statesmanship is inspired.

The President of the United States, on the other hand, is elected to serve *All the People*. Those Presidents who will go down in history as great men are the ones who fought the battles of all the people, even against Congress itself.

President Eisenhower is the only man in the United States with the necessary prestige and confidence of the people to arouse them and Congress to action in this vital matter.

Once the people are aroused, Congress will not fail to obey their will.

§ *The esteem in which Clayton's views were held in matters of foreign economic policy even after he left the government is illustrated by a letter from Representative Hale Boggs asking Clayton and Christian Herter to contribute a statement on free world foreign economic policy to the Joint Economic Committee. The two, according to Boggs, represented "the best experience and highest intelligence the Nation has to offer."[18] The consequent statement transmitted to the committee on October 23, 1961, was written primarily by Clayton, but represents the thinking of both men. The text follows.*

A STATEMENT ON FOREIGN ECONOMIC POLICY

Twenty-seven years ago, with enactment of the Trade Agreements Act, the United States committed itself to a liberal foreign economic policy.[19] That basic commitment has been renewed in eleven extensions of the act, but with restrictive amendments. Next year it must be renewed again. But "renewal" is a deceptive word if it suggests that what has been done eleven times in the past quarter century will suffice another time. It will not.

The time has come for the United States to take a giant step.

Two developments since the end of World War II pose the inescapable challenge and the one hope of answering it. The challenge is the cold war, in which the Soviet Union aims to divide the free industrial nations and at the same time win the underdeveloped countries of the world to communism.

The answer lies in the second development, the European Common Market. The nations of the free world must work together, as the Common Market "six" are doing already. In our experience we have found no international issues more divisive than economic issues. We assume that there will be no hot war. We are thinking in terms of winning the cold one.

[18] Hale Boggs to Will Clayton, June 5, LS, CP, ACCO.
[19] This statement, which was made October 23, 1961, was printed in *A New Look at Foreign Economic Policy*, A Report to the Subcommittee on Foreign Economic Policy of the Joint Economic Committee of the Congress, 87th Cong., 1st sess. (1961).

Here is the situation:

There are 3 billion people in the world. About one-third live under Communist rule. One-sixth live in the major free industrial lands. The rest, who are one-half of the total, live in the poorer, less developed countries—the uncommitted or, as we prefer to call them, the "contested."

The 1 billion under communism live in a huge and relatively self-contained land mass with enormous natural resources. All of their foreign trade and most of their domestic trade is conducted by the state. Their governments are totalitarian.

The one-half billion in the major industrial countries—the West plus Japan and Australia—live under stable popular governments. They possess preponderant economic power in the world community. This is a point of critical importance for the purpose we have under consideration. Eighteen percent of the world's population commands two-thirds of its industrial capacity. It is our firm conviction that the way in which this preponderant power is used will be a major factor in determining the issues and the outcome of the cold war.

The 1½ billion people of the contested areas occupy one-half of the land surface of the earth, principally in the Tropics and farther south. They have vast natural resources of their own, but many of their people are hungry. Hunger and political instability go hand in hand.

The Communists are concentrating their subversive efforts principally on these poorer, underdeveloped countries. Soviet political and military pressures against these countries have been continuous since the end of World War II. In the 1950's the economic dimension was added.

Khrushchev[20] fixed the terms of the cold war, in its economic aspect, in his declaration to the Twentieth Party Congress in 1956:

* * * from the fact that we advocate peaceful competition with capitalism one should under no circumstances conclude that the struggle against the bourgeois ideology and against the remnants of capitalism will be relaxed by our people; our task consists in a continuous attack on the bourgeois ideology and the unmasking of its antisocial and reactionary character.

The declaration of Soviet economic hostilities against the non-Soviet world has been made. The immediate objective in this war is the control of the contested countries, more than three score and ten in number. The ultimate objective is the control of the world. The

[20] Nikita Khrushchev, Premier of the Soviet Union (1958–64).

struggle will be relentless, irreconcilable, merciless. The West need expect no quarter from the enemy. If Western determination is less than the Soviet bloc's, eventual Soviet triumph is assured.

In all of the contested countries, particularly those just now emerging from colonialism, the Russians have organized groups of native Communists who preach to the people, over and over again, that the best and quickest way to raise their level of living is by the Communist system. And who can say that people who have always been slaves to hunger will not put food before freedom?

In forming policies to meet the situation described, three significant facts of current life must be kept in mind:

1. *The increasing interdependence of nations.* Domestic economic policy can no longer be made without regard to possible external effects, nor can existing external conditions be ignored when domestic policy is being shaped. This country has known for years that it is not an isolated political system. It must realize that that is no less true of the body economic.

This is particularly the case for the United States because it possesses preponderant economic power in the Western community. If the United States domestic policy is damaging to Western unity, the West is diminished in the cold war. The same may be said of the domestic policy of any of the principal allies.

It is ironic that the United States should continue to erect barriers against the nations whose raw materials it, in fact, must have. Despite its domestic resources it must import many of the raw materials essential to its industry. So far as we know the only major mineral the United States has in exportable surplus is coal. The Automobile Manufacturers Association lists 38 imports necessary to the production of motor vehicles. The telephone companies list 20 imports from many lands—in Asia, Africa, and South America—which are essential to their industry.

The domestic agricultural policy of the United States is the base of its import quota system. If it continues to support farm prices above world levels, obviously it will continue to have a restrictive quota system.

On a broader scale, the lesson of unbalanced international payments is there for all to see. Few even dreamed so recently as 5 years ago that there would be talk of American costs, interest rates, and taxes in the same breath with gold and "hot money."

2. *The new role for technology.* We are impressed by a statement of Dr. Guy Suits, of the General Electric Laboratories:

Growth (in science and technology) has been so rapid that 90 percent of all the scientists who ever lived must be alive today. Science and technological change had almost no impact on the outcome of World War I, while it was a major factor in World War II * * * Lord Keynes didn't recognize technological innovation as a factor in the economy 20 years ago, yet today it assumes major proportions.

Technological change has been a determining factor in the conflicts of the past two decades. It would be folly to suppose that it will be a smaller force in the future.

We have been impressed also by a statement of Gerard Piel, publisher of the *Scientific American*, in his brief paper, *Consumers of Abundance*. Dr. Piel observed, and we feel correctly, that "the advance of technology has begun to outstrip our capacity for social invention." He noted particularly that in the past several years "despite a steady rise in gross national product, unemployment has been rising."

In effect, while abundance has been definitely achieved in the West by the advance of technology, Western institutions are no longer able to keep abreast of the rapid change. In many sectors of Western opinion, automation has taken on the aspect of a serious menace, although it is an indispensable factor in military security, competitive parity in the world economy, and the ultimate relief of Western man from the stultifying effects of repetitive labor.

3. *The population eruption.* A score or more of the countries in the contested areas are now growing at a Malthusian rate; i.e., their populations are doubling every 25 years. In this connection, we would like to quote from the preface to Prof. Philip M. Hauser's distinguished volume, *Population Perspectives:*

The revolutionary changes in population size, composition and distribution during the modern era, and especially during the course of this century, have precipitated problems which are among the most serious confronting the contemporary world.

The United States has been aware of the effects of population change right at home. The rapid migration of the rural population to the cities in the wake of an irresistible technological advance in agriculture has had grave effects on the urban areas. "Exploding cities" are a matter of concern. The situation may become much worse as the increasing younger generations disperse into the suburbs.

The explosion of cities in the United States comes at a time when Japan, in contrast, has achieved a historic measure of population restraint. An authoritative view of the effects of this unprecedented development must await careful and extended inquiry, but there is no escape from the conclusion that it has had very favorable effects on economic developments in Japan.

Our main concern in the population explosion is with the contested countries. These populations are growing at a rate double that of the Western community, but they possess only a negligible fraction of the economic resources of the West. In these circumstances of unprecedented proliferation, the daily struggle for food and space among populations already undernourished cannot fail to become more bitter. This is our concern.

Overt social conflict is a commonplace affair in the Malthusian world. It is a kind of conflict upon which the agents of world communism feed and upon which the fate of unstable governments often rests. In the contested countries of the world, the average income of hundreds of millions of people is about $100 per year, as against about $2,500 in the United States. Most of these people have gained their political freedom since the end of World War II. While they intend to retain that freedom, they are even more determined to raise their level of living, with more to eat, more to wear, and better houses in which to live.

The gap between the developed and the less developed countries hits close to home in the case of Latin America. Frank Tannenbaum, professor of Latin American history at Columbia University, says in a recent article entitled *The United States and Latin America—The Sins of the Fathers:*

> Stated simply, the task we face in Latin America can be put in a single question. What can the United States do to help bridge the gap that lies between a $2,500 average annual income in North America and the $200 average income in Latin America? * * * The difference in income is so wide that, until it is narrowed, we cannot expect the people of those countries to identify themselves with our aspirations, projects, or policies.

Let us look at some of the things that the United States has done which have the effect of curtailing the markets for Latin American products, thus reducing their income and widening the gap between the rich and poor countries. At the behest of politically powerful minority groups in this country the Government has instituted import quotas on lead, zinc, and petroleum. For many years there have been import quotas on sugar and other agricultural commodities. There is an export subsidy on the export of our cotton. All of these things are produced in Latin America.

So long as there is great disparity in living standards between the industrial and the contested countries, today's rapidly shrinking world will not be a peaceful place in which to live. The economic gap between the two groups of countries is now widening. The gap must be narrowed. Otherwise, permanent world peace is an illusion.

The gap can be narrowed while raising the living standards of both groups.

But time is running out.

Almost precisely 99 years ago, on December 1, 1862, Abraham Lincoln said in a message to Congress:

> The dogmas of the quiet past are inadequate to the stormy present. The occasion is piled high with difficulty, and we must rise with the occasion * * * we must think anew and act anew. We must disenthrall ourselves and then we shall save our country.

The Trade Agreements Act as it stands today is hopelessly inadequate to meet conditions as they are and as we can see them developing.

The last renewal of the act, in 1958, was hailed for its long term. Four years is the longest that any renewal has run. But it was less meaningful than it appeared to be. The negotiating authority vested in the President was small, and when the American negotiators prepared to do the actual negotiating at this year's session of the General Agreement on Tariffs and Trade in Geneva, they found themselves hamstrung by the law's protective clauses.

At this juncture we see only one course to consider as the Reciprocal Trade Agreements Act presents itself for action next year.

If the act were allowed to expire, this would be a clear victory for protectionism. The symbol of our liberalism would be gone. The President's negotiating authority would be gone. But the protectionist clauses of the act would remain, for they are permanent law.

The challenges of the times demand a substantial broadening and reshaping of the act for another term of several years. This approach recognizes the limitations of the act as now written, and recognizes that the United States needs an enormously stronger hand than it has if it is to meet the competitive challenge that is built into the Common Market. But we hope that this would not mean a postponement of reckoning with the greater question we must face.

We believe that the United States must form a trade partnership with the European Common Market and take the leadership in further expanding a free world economic community.

As a minimum step in that direction, the Trade Agreements Act must give the President authority to negotiate tariff reduction across the board in place of his present authority to negotiate item by item. Our allies in Europe are no longer dealing in item-by-item terms, and we must adapt our negotiating authority accordingly.

It is frequently suggested that there be a Federal program to aid industries and workers, and even whole communities, injured by competing imports, to help them adjust to new ways of economic activity. We believe that the dislocations of labor or capital as a result of increased imports can be adjusted better by the affected parties than by the Government, but we would support a public program for extreme cases.

We note that the government-aid adjustment program of the Common Market itself has had relatively little use. Actually, in this country it is hard to find an industry whose troubles can be traced to imports alone, and we suspect that too liberal an adjustment assistance program would be more of a temptation to inertia than a stimulus to innovation.

More than any broadening or reshaping of the existing law, however, we believe that the most hopeful vehicle for strengthening the West and thus for defeating Khrushchev in the cold war is to be found in the example of the Common Market. The object of a common market is to enlarge the number of consumers within a free trade area. The United States was formed into a common market when the Thirteen Colonies were welded into one nation by adoption of the Constitution.

For many years Europe has dreamed of a United States of Europe. Now they have made a beginning. Unfortunately only six countries joined in the initial effort. Seven others formed instead the European Free Trade Association, thus creating a rival organization and a serious breach in a vital area.

The recent decision of Britain and other Western European countries to open negotiations for joining the Common Market "Six" gives promise that one of the elements of Western disunity soon will be eliminated. So long as Western Europe is divided by the "Six" and the "Seven" there is not only a lack of economic unity, there is great danger that this will lead to grave political differences. The New York *Times* has referred to Britain's announcement as a turning point in history. Indeed it is. The Common Market ushers in an age of new competition, new ideas, and new initiative.

But the happy prospect of healing Western European differences still leaves the two sides of the Atlantic with a gap in economic policies that is getting wider, not narrower, all the time. On the one hand, Western Europe, for centuries divided into many separate economic and political compartments, is attempting now the elimination of her internal trade barriers and their customs houses so that her 325 million people and their goods can move freely from one country to another. On the other hand, the United States is in reverse. It takes too frequent refuge in protectionist devices. But even if this country stood still it would be drifting backwards because it would not be keeping pace with Europe's determined move forward.

At the close of World War II the United States embarked upon a policy designed to bring about a great expansion in the world economy. There resulted the GATT and later the Marshall Plan, with the Organization for European Economic Cooperation to implement it. OEEC, now the larger Organization for Economic Cooperation and Development, was organized at the request of the United States by countries recipient of Marshall Plan aid. It is perhaps not too much to say that it was the father of the Common Market. (It is interesting now to recall that the American proposal for an OEEC caused the Russians to walk out of the first international Marshall Plan meeting in 1947, and to force Poland and Czechoslovakia to withdraw their tentative acceptance of Marshall Plan aid. The Soviet Union realized then that such a group might one day become an effective roadblock to Communist ambitions.)

If the United States is to continue to meet its responsibilities of Western leadership in preserving the freedom of the Western World, it must again, as in 1947, put the national and international interest ahead of the short-term special interest of its politically powerful minority groups. It cannot be repeated too often that communism is waging war against the West—relentlessly, craftily, cunningly. The West will lose this war unless it can maintain Western unity and can keep the contested countries independent and out of the Communist bloc.

If the Communists are able to win and organize most of the contested countries, communism will dominate the world. The West has NATO, but it is limited largely to a military alliance. There will probably be no shooting in Khrushchev's war. The Communists have a cheaper, shrewder way. They plan to take us alive, with all our assets intact. If they can encircle us, our grandchildren will live under communism, as Khrushchev has said. Western unity is essential to Western survival.

The 20 OECD countries—18 Western European countries plus the United States and Canada—comprise one-half billion of the most highly industrialized peoples in the world. Acting in unity, there is almost nothing that they could not do. Unfortunately, they are not so acting. Except for the Marshall Plan, the Communists have held the initiative and the West the defensive in this worldwide struggle. Defensive postures win few wars.

If the United States fails to associate itself with the Common Market movement there will be constant economic friction between Western Europe and the United States and its allies in the Pacific. A unified Western Europe, with its highly developed industrial and technological complex and its disciplined workers, would comprise the most efficient workshop in the world.

Heretofore, the United States, with the largest home market in the Western World, has been able to offset high wages (three times the Common Market average) by the mass production of goods, thus keeping costs on levels competitive with those of other industrial nations. The European Common Market already has a home market, in terms of population, almost as large as that of the United States. If all, or nearly all, the Western European countries join the market, as we expect they will, it will then have a much larger home market than the United States, and the implications of that are only too clear.

The Common Market is justifying the most optimistic expectations of its friends. Official reports show that, since 1958, trade among the "Six" has risen by approximately 50 percent—a growth far greater than shown by any other industrial nation. Businessmen of the "Six," many of whom originally opposed this plan for eliminating tariffs, quotas, and other protective barriers, are now in the forefront of pressures for speeding up the transition. As the provisions of the market went into effect there were marked increases in sales of Volkswagen automobiles in France and Renaults in Germany. Also, the number of mergers and corporate alliances across national boundaries has increased rapidly.

By far the biggest, most reliable and profitable markets for United States exports are in the industrialized countries of the free world. When competition has forced all or practically all such countries to join the Common Market, the only way this country can hope to hold its export markets is by associating itself with the Common Market movement. And the United States must hold and add to its export markets, to pay for essential imports and to permit continuation of its heavy commitments abroad.

The longer the United States waits, the more difficult it will be to align its trade policies to match the Common Market's own actions. By the end of this very year, the "Six" will have reduced their tariffs to each other by 40 to 50 percent.

Thus we recommend that the United States open negotiations, as soon as practicable, for a trade partnership with the European Common Market, at the same time stressing the absolute necessity of enlarging the area.

It should not be difficult to show the contested countries that their best interests demand that they associate themselves in this historic process. Among those countries, including the 42 that have

278

gained their freedom since the end of World War II, less than 10 have populations of more than 25 million and many have less than 10 million. There is talk about industrializing these little entities, though we believe that their first interest demands farm rather than factory production. Granted that industrial effort will be made, it will be a net loss if such countries only set up little industries to serve local populations and bind in their inefficiency permanently by tariff quota protection.

One way to ease the adjustment for the contested countries, and to meet our principal objective of raising their living standards, would be to grant unilaterally to groups of contested countries, as distinguished from individual countries, the right to free trade on their exports of raw materials to industrial countries. Another way would be by reduction in import tariffs by the contested countries at the rate of 5 percent per annum in consideration of the industrial countries reducing their duties at the rate of 10 percent per annum.

Without restrictive tariffs or other impediments to the movement of goods across national frontiers, production would be rationalized on the basis of comparative advantage, just as it has been in the 50 States of the U.S.A.

Under such conditions there would, in our opinion, take place the greatest expansion in productive facilities, including those of the United States, that the world has ever known. The facilities would be located in the most advantageous areas, based on labor, skills, climate, availability of raw materials, transportation, and markets. Most of them would be built by private capital. Many would be built in the contested countries because of favorable operating conditions and because, no matter where located, the whole trading area with its 2 billion people would be a potential market, without barriers.

In this way, sound development of the contested countries would take place. Their standards of living would rise. The economic gap between the richer and the poorer would be narrowed. Communism as a threat to world peace would recede.

We are fully conscious of the domestic American political difficulties inherent in the policy we recommend, but we believe nonetheless that at this juncture in our history we must face the issues realistically.

Christian A. Herter.

William L. Clayton.

§ In his post-governmental years Clayton assumed a new role as elder statesman and administration critic. The remaining letters in this volume reflect Clayton's attitudes toward American foreign policy and his attempts to influence that policy.

*   *   *

§ On May 18, 1948, Clayton wrote to Lamar Fleming, Jr.: "It seems to me that the greatest present danger is in the Middle East. I have believed for a long time that the situation is more vulnerable there than anywhere else."[21] His fear that the Middle East would succumb to communist influence was even greater by 1957.

MEMORANDUM ON THE MIDDLE EAST RESOLUTION

Houston, Texas
January 14, 1957

As I understand it, the Administration's purpose is to keep Russia from taking over the Middle East as she has taken over Eastern Europe.[22]

I am in complete accord with this.

But I seriously doubt if the passage of the Administration's resolution would do any such thing.

In effect, that resolution says to Moscow: "If you break into the Middle East house you had better not enter by the front door because if you do and the owner yells loud enough, we will help him throw you out; but if you enter by the back door and take over, with the connivance of some little Stalin of the area, there is nothing we can do about it."

Most of us will need only one guess as to which route the Russians will choose. They generally use backdoor methods, anyway, because they have found them less costly and less risky.

By the 19th Century standards, the so-called power vacuum in the Middle East would be occupied by some great and ambitious world power.

[21] Will Clayton to Lamar Fleming, May 18, 1948, L, CP, ACCO.
[22] A copy of this memorandum may be found in CP, ACCO.

By 20th Century standards, this vacuum should be occupied by the sovereign states of the Middle East themselves.

As I understand the intent of our policy, it is that the right of these states to so act for themselves shall not be abridged. Let us make this clear to the whole world in language which all can understand.

If Russia should take over in the Middle East, it would give her the power to dictate conditions to Western Europe which would almost certainly alienate that area from the United States and leave us effectively isolated.

Democratic government in the modern world cannot long exist in isolation.

I have suggested a declaration in this language: "The United States regards as vital to her interests the preservation of the independence and integrity of the States of the Middle East, and if necessary her armed forces will be used to that end."

It is said that this would violate the charter of the United Nations. I am no expert on this subject, but I did observe the impotency of the United Nations in regard to Hungary and the inhuman but effective action of the Russian Empire with respect to that poor country.

Of course, substantial economic and technical assistance should be extended to the Middle East but it seems to me best to cover this separately. This subject may take more time because it will probably provoke more argument. Mr. Acheson has suggested that other free nations should join us in an economic assistance program, and his suggestion is certainly worthy of serious consideration.

Mr. Acheson has also referred to several Middle East problems which demand solution, among them the Suez Canal and the Israeli–Arab controversy.

It seems to me all these matters can be best handled if we first make clear our policy in the political and military fields. This is the heart of the whole matter and there should be no great delay in acting on the necessary declaration. Subsidiary questions can then be given attention.

If six months ago we had taken a firm stand on the Middle East as here suggested, it is extremely unlikely that Israel, England or France would ever have thrown their armed forces against Egypt.

Will Clayton

To Hon. J. William Fulbright

Houston, Texas
February 5, 1957

Dear Bill:

Looking over an old file, I ran across a copy of a letter I wrote you on March 2, 1956, and your reply, about the Middle East situation. I suggest you have your secretary show these to you.[23]

I enclose copy of a memorandum I sent Sam Rayburn[24] recently on this subject, also photostatic copy of an article by Joe Alsop[25] from Moscow.

I am glad you keep a hot fire under Dulles.[26] It seems to me one of the chief functions of diplomacy is to foresee adverse developments and endeavor to prevent them, or at any rate to be prepared for them.

Measured by this, I think Dulles has been one of our poorest Secretaries of State.

We have to judge men by their works.

The situation in the Middle East is tragic and may turn out for us a disaster.

The Free World alliance is falling apart and, so far as an outsider can tell, little is being done to hold it together.

Sincerely yours,
W. L. Clayton

[23] An unsigned carbon copy of this letter to the U.S. Senator from Arkansas (1945———), may be found in CP, ACCO.

[24] Speaker of the House Sam Rayburn, U.S. Representative from Texas (1913–61).

[25] Author of a syndicated column, "Matter of Fact," with his brother Stewart (1945–58).

[26] John Foster Dulles, Secretary of State (1953–59).

§ Although China was not an area with which Clayton was concerned in the State Department, he followed developments there with great interest in later years. During the fifties, he made the following statements about U.S.-China relations.

To Ellen Garwood

Houston, Texas
February 15, 1955

Dear Ellen:

Thanks for your sweet letter of the thirteenth.[27]

I read the article on Formosa which you sent me.[28] I think it is good.

I enclose a copy of The New Republic of February 7. There are three articles in it which I think you will be interested in—the one on Formosa[29] and the articles by Lowenthal[30] and Forrest.[31] The latter two articles look prophetic now in view of what happened so soon after they were published.

I am very unhappy about Formosa. I think we have got ourselves in almost an impossible situation. If we had not made the treaty with Chiang[32] and if it had not already been ratified by the Senate, I would strongly favor dumping the Formosa problem in the lap of the United Nations. Attlee[33] and the Labor Party in England are saying, "We don't want to die for Formosa," and I must say that it is the way I feel too.

[27] Ellen Garwood to Will Clayton, February 13, 1955, LS, CP, ACCO. An unsigned carbon copy of this letter may be found in CP, ACCO.

[28] Unidentified article on Formosa.

[29] "Formosa: The Chance for Peace," *Saturday Review of Literature,* February 7, 1955, pp. 6–8.

[30] Richard Lowenthal, "The Day of Conflict Will Come," *ibid.,* pp. 9–12.

[31] William Forrest, "Malenkov's Challenger," *ibid.,* pp. 12–13.

[32] Chiang Kai-Shek, President of the Chinese Nationalist Government (1943——).

[33] Clement Attlee, former British Prime Minister (1945–51) and a leading spokesman for the Labour Party.

It even looks as if we might help Chiang defend Quemoy and Matsu. We have absolutely no business doing that. There is no question but what those islands belong to China and despite the fact that we are doing everything in our power to preserve the fiction that Chiang is the government of China, everybody knows that it is a fiction.

We got off on the wrong foot in 1949. We should have recognized that the communists had China and that they are the government of China, whether we liked it or not. Of course, we don't like it but that couldn't alter the facts. I recognize that we had some responsibilities toward Chiang and his troops on Formosa but we could have made a deal, I am sure, at that time whereby the U.N. could have taken responsibility for Chiang and his troops. But this is all beside the point now. We are committed and that's that. The fact of our commitment plus the recent turnover in the Russian Government undoubtedly greatly increases the danger of war in the next two years.

* * *

Affectionately yours,
W. L. Clayton

To Hon. J. William Fulbright

Houston, Texas
February 12, 1959

Dear Bill,

I have asked myself the question: Looking at the world picture as it is, what is the next step for the West to take?[34]

I enclose a short memorandum which suggests a "giant step," to use the words of the "Sputnik" editorial in Life Magazine.[35]

[34] An unsigned carbon copy of this letter and the following memorandum may be found in CP, ACCO.

[35] "A Proposal for a Giant Step," *Life*, November 18, 1957, p. 53.

Of course, the State Department will hold up its hands in horror at the idea of sitting down in the same room with representatives of China when we have refused to recognize China. I would sit down and negotiate with the Devil himself if I thought it might contribute to world peace. The whole question is just that and not a question of punctilio of procedure based on outworn precedents of olden times.

If, as I fear, we refuse to take this "giant step," than I would propose that immediately and unilaterally we greatly liberalize our position on East-West trade. We shouldn't sell arms to the Communists, but we are wrong to prohibit other trade. This step alone would strengthen the unity of the free world. Our partners are all chafing under the restraints that we have imposed on them.

Sincerely yours,
W. L. Clayton

Enclosure

MEMORANDUM ON U.S.-CHINA RELATIONS

Houston, Texas
February 12, 1959

If we ever had diplomatic initiative vis-a-vis Russia, we surrendered it so long ago that it has been forgotten. We just sit now while the Russians make one proposition after another, to all of which we must say "no."

We act as if it were all a bad dream and will go away if we just give it time.

This may do for some international situations but not for the kind with which we are now faced.

Surely we have enough ingenuity and daring to make some move which will place the initiative in our hands.

There are today two especially dangerous situations between the Communists on one side and the West on the other. One is the

Formosan-Chinese situation; the other is the Berlin dispute. Some day both must be liquidated.

The Western nations may not see eye-to-eye on method, but all have the same interest to find acceptable and peaceable solutions.

On the other hand, there is reason to doubt the genuineness of Russia's interest regarding the Far Eastern imbroglio; and reason to doubt China's genuine interest in the Berlin situation.

Barring a shooting war in the next ten or fifteen years, the threat to world peace at that time will almost surely come from China, not Russia. Russia probably recognizes this and fears it. There is intrinsically little between the two countries of mutual interest and much which could lead to mutual jealousy and distrust.

The West must find some way to take advantage of this.

The Congress of Vienna was called to deal with problems growing out of war.

Why not call the Congress of Geneva to deal with problems that threaten to result in war?

It could last as long as we were willing to listen and to keep talking; would give us an opportunity to exploit whatever differences may exist between Russia and China; and would put them on the defensive.

Principal participants: United States, Britain, France, West Germany, Russia, China.

We would hold some powerful cards in such a conference, but they would be of no use unless we were prepared to play them if the stakes were high enough—I refer especially to recognition of China, her admission to the United Nations, and East-West trade.

Such a conference would need to agree on conditions of German reunification, and on the status of Formosa. It has been suggested that the latter could be a protectorate of the United Nations for five years, and then vote on the question whether she should become a part of China, or have independent status.

§ *Fidel Castro's seizure of power in Cuba was extremely alarming to Clayton, a man who had dealt with Latin American countries for years in the cotton business. The immediacy of communism and the threat it posed to Latin America caused him to suggest, in 1964, policies which would strengthen economic relations with the United States' southern neighbors. Earlier, in 1962, he had called for more drastic action.*

To Hon. J. William Fulbright

September 19, 1962

Dear Bill:

I have been thinking deeply about our situation in Latin America, and the following is my conclusion:[36]

No one familiar with Latin American economy and psychology can doubt that the Latin American countries are dangerously drifting for lack of definite leadership on the part of the United States.

This drifting could easily lead to socialism and then communism in several important Latin American countries.

The impact of any such development on the outcome of the cold war would be decisive and tragic.

The Monroe Doctrine would be destroyed.

The Communists would win the cold war.

What should the United States do to prevent this Communist victory?

When Castro[37] publicly announced that he was a Communist, he gave notice that the Monroe Doctrine had been flagrantly violated.

Within twenty-four hours thereafter, the United States should have blockaded Cuba or taken other drastic action to end the Communist government set up by Castro and thus end the violation of the Monroe Doctrine.

Not having taken this action at that time, the United States should take it now, with or without Latin American participation.

Failing any such action, the United States might as well channel all its strength in preparation for World War III.

Sincerely yours,
W. L. Clayton

[36] An unsigned carbon copy of this letter may be found in CP, TL.
[37] Fidel Castro, Premier of Cuba (1959——).

A STATEMENT ON LATIN AMERICA

Looking at the world political and economic situation, I am convinced that Latin America is the most pressing problem now facing the United States.[38]

Perhaps we can live with one Cuba, if we must, but we could not live with half a dozen Cubas.

What can we do to assure the freedom and independence of all countries of Latin America and our prestige and influence in them?

I do not think the Alliance for Progress, by itself, is the answer.

I believe the answer is to be found in opening up our markets to the products of these countries and assisting them to open up the markets of the rest of the free world to their exports.

Latin American countries themselves have shown us the way.

Already a common market has been set up by five Central American countries and a free trade area has also been started by seven of the principal Latin American countries: Mexico, Brazil, Uruguay, Argentina, Chile, Peru and Colombia. Later, Paraguay and Ecuador joined this free trade area, making a total of nine countries.

On the other hand, the U.S. has substantially closed its markets to Latin American sugar, petroleum, lead and zinc, to name the principal items affected.

The quota system for sugar was first adopted by us in 1934 and was revised in 1937, 1948 and 1962.

In 1934 we consumed about 6½ million tons of sugar. Today we consume annually about 10 million tons of sugar.

In 1934 the domestic quota for sugar was about 1,800,000 tons. In 1937 it was about 2 million tons and in 1948 2,300,000 tons, whereas in 1962 it was over 3½ million tons (all figures include both beet and cane sugar).

There is perhaps no lobby in Washington more active and effective than the sugar lobby.

But for the quota system, or a very high tariff on imports, we would produce little sugar in the United States. We can generally buy it from Latin American and other countries much cheaper than

[38] This statement was delivered before the Subcommittee on Inter-American Relationships of the Joint Economic Committee, January 16, 1964; a copy may be found in CP, ACCO.

we can produce it. The dollars we would pay for it would be promptly returned to us in payment for goods that we can produce cheaper or better than the sugar countries.

The substantial closing of our markets to foreign sugar, petroleum, zinc, lead and other commodities has been done in the short-term, special interest of politically powerful minority groups and against the national and international interest.

Moreover, the United States has established heavy export subsidies on cotton, which is also one of the principal exports of several Latin American countries.

During the Hoover Administration, when the United States had occasion to complain of a foreign country for "dumping" a commodity in the United States, we defined dumping as the sale of a commodity in the country of destination at a lower price than in the country of origin.

The United States Government is selling cotton for export at 24 cents, whereas for domestic use the Government price is 32½ cents.

Thus, we are dumping our surplus cotton in the world markets. This causes deep and bitter resentment on the part of our Latin American and other foreign cotton-growing competitors.

On December 19, 1963, Senator Javits[39] of New York made an outstanding speech in the United States Senate on Latin America. Senator Humphrey[40] of Minnesota, immediately following Senator Javits, said this of Senator Javits' speech:

"I wish to associate myself with the text and substance of the Senator's speech. I believe it is one of the truly great speeches made on this whole subject matter. The Senator is to be commended."

In the speech referred to, Senator Javits said:

"It is essential that the U.S. revise its trade policies toward Latin America and put its full support behind the formation of a Hemispheric Common Market."

This is not only sound doctrine; it is imperative doctrine. It will pinch the toes of a few U.S. producers, but it is decidedly and definitely in the national interest.

This is the age of the common market or free trade area. General de Gaulle[41] cannot change the course of history; he can delay it, and that is what he is doing.

In the four years that the European Common Market has been operating, intra-market trade has increased 100 per cent and total

[39] Jacob K. Javits, U.S. Senator from New York (1957——).
[40] Hubert H. Humphrey, U.S. Senator from Minnesota (1949–64).
[41] General Charles de Gaulle, President of the Fifth Republic of France (1959–69).

trade has increased more than 50 per cent. The European Common Market is now the greatest trading unit in the world.

Rightly, Senator Javits strongly supports the formation of a Western Hemisphere Common Market or Free Trade Area.

But both the United States and Canada contain highly efficient, giant industries with which the small industries of Latin America, each geared to the buying power of the country in which it is situated, could hardly compete.

I suggest that a Western Hemisphere Free Trade Area should be established, as a beginning, on the following limited bases:

1. The United States, Canada and Latin American countries would reduce their tariffs on imports of raw materials originating in other Western Hemisphere countries at the rate of ten per cent per annum for ten years, until such tariffs are at zero. Where import quotas are employed on such trade, such quotas are to be modified annually, so that at the end of ten years they will have completely disappeared.

This second step must be taken if the Latin American area is ever to be developed industrially. In ten years' time, a common market or free trade area of 200 to 300 million people (larger even than the United States Common Market) will be created, justifying the establishment of highly efficient, giant industries in Latin America.

3. It is expected that the Western Hemisphere Free Trade Area will further multilateralize the above plan by negotiating arrangements with other free trade areas, or common markets.

4. At the end of ten years, the foreign ministers of Western Hemisphere countries will meet to discuss their future problems in respect of trade and to advise their respective governments on the course that should be pursued for the future.

A Western Hemisphere Free Trade Area on the above basis would accomplish the following:

a. Raw materials originating in the Western Hemisphere would circulate freely throughout the whole of the Western Hemisphere.

b. All goods—raw materials and industrial products—originating in Latin America would circulate freely throughout Latin America, now with over 200 million people and growing in population faster than any other area of the world. This provision would be similar in an economic sense to the adoption of the United States Constitution which welded the thirteen colonies into one nation, under an edict that there should never be any tariffs, quotas or other government-made impediments to trade between the colonies, or states.

Who is to say that the end result of this economic policy for Latin America would not be similar to that achieved in the United States?

In the January 1961 issue of FOREIGN AFFAIRS, there is an excellent article by Alfred C. Neal, President of the Committee for Economic Development, entitled "New Economic Policies for the West." I quote one paragraph from this article:

> It is too little recognized, especially by the new political leaders, that modern industrial development is heavily dependent upon what economists call 'economies of scale' and 'external economies.' The first of these pertains to the size, and therefore potential output, of a plant. Most of the commonplace goods associated with a high standard of living (and high productivity) cannot be made in small plants and workshops. The reasonably eonomic size of a flat-rolled steel-products mill is about a million tons per year; for a bar mill, about half that. Similarly, petroleum refineries, automobile tire and synthetic rubber plants, automobile and tractor plants, all require large outputs to achieve reasonably low cost. The low income of underdeveloped countries and their low level of development make almost all of them too small a market to support such plants. Without forming large customs unions among themselves, their development will be limited for a very long time to agriculture and the extractive industries, to the earlier stages of processing of their products for export markets, and to a few small-scale local industries (bricks, slaughtering) whose products enjoy the protection of high transport costs or perishability. This is precisely the kind of economy that their political leaders wish to escape from. Politically as well as economically, it is important that we help them to find avenues of escape that lead somewhere other than to the Soviet Union.

This avenue of escape is a road that leads to markets for Latin American products and, at the same time, leads to a Latin American Free Trade Area.

There is no other way of which I am aware to lay the foundation for the industrialization of the Latin American economy.

§ *Clayton anticipated the concern of many of his fellow Americans about U.S. involvement in Southeast Asia. On February 25, 1965, he made the following prophetic statement in a letter to R. F. Moody, President of Compañia Hulera Euzkadi of Mexico.*[42]

[42] An unsigned carbon copy of this letter may be found in CP, ACCO.

To R. F. Moody

February 25, 1965

Dear Mr. Moody:

Thanks so much for your note of February 15, with enclosures, which I carefully went over at home last night.[43]

I think one of the reasons that we don't do as much in the "propaganda" field as the Communists is that we are too busy doing constructive things which in the end justify our theory of life. I freely admit that we can go too far in the direction that I have indicated and that we must give some attention to actions and charges that the Communists make against the free-enterprise system. I freely admit that I do not know where to draw the line.

Take, for instance, South Vietnam. I feel that as long as the people of this area felt that they must resist the Communists in the latter's effort to deny their freedom, it was their "war" and all we could do was to give them military advice and financial aid. But when it got to the point where the South Vietnamese took the position that it is an American "war" and they want to make what they can out of it, then I think we are in a very anomalous position and riding for a fall.

We just can't defend our way of life all over the world, and I doubt very much, even if we should have the power to do this, that it would succeed.

I have recently read the leading editorial on South Vietnam in the "Saturday Review of Literature."[44] It is a shocking description of the South Vietnamese enterprise in which we are engaged.

With regards and every good wish, I remain

Sincerely yours,
W. L. Clayton

[43] R. F. Moody to Will Clayton, February 15, 1965, LS, CP, ACCO.
[44] "Vietnam and the American Conscience," *Saturday Review of Literature*, February 27, 1965, pp. 22–23.

INDEX

Acheson, Dean: and Committee on Economic Foreign Policy, 248; and Congress, 213; Delta speech of, 209, 213; and Greece, 190; influence of, in State Department, 9; on May 19 memo, 13; memo for, 150; and Middle East, 280; *Present at the Creation*, 9n; testimony of, 186; and UNRRA Council, 140
Africa, 52
Agricultural Adjustment Act, 34, 264
Agricultural Marketing Act, 24, 31
Agricultural policies, government, 5, 21–36, 48–54, 262–68
Alsop, Joseph, 281
American Cotton Company, 2–3
American Liberty League, 5–6, 17, 32–33
Anderson, Benjamin M., Jr., 22
Anderson, Clinton, 205
Anderson, Frank, 3
Anderson, Monroe, 3
Anderson, Clayton and Company: Clayton's connection with, 107–8; competition of, with cotton cooperatives, 33; founding of, 3; and free trade, 6; opens foreign offices, 3; policy of, toward Germany, 45–47; profits from New Deal policies, 5
Anglo-American Financial Agreement. *See* British Loan
Arutyunyan, Amazasp A., 10, 139
Asia, 52
Atlantic Charter, 75, 91, 247–48
Atlantic Union, 16–17, 256, 258–62
Atomic bomb, 127–29
Attlee, Clement, 210, 282

Balance of payments, 202, 220
Barkley, Alben W., 2, 47, 242–44
Baruch, Bernard: asks for study, 203; and Baruch-Hancock report, 82;

and Clayton, 7, 161–63, 179–80; and War Industries Board, 3
Baruch-Hancock report, 82
Berlin crisis, 285
Bevin, Ernest, 210, 215–16
Bidault, Georges, 207, 215–16
Blum, Leon, 51, 207–8
Board of Economic Warfare (BEW), 7, 62–68
Boggs, Hale, 269
Bohlen, Charles, 9n, 14
Brand, Robert, 11, 145
Bretton Woods Conference, agreements of: compliance with, 149; critics of, 147; and establishment of International Monetary Fund and International Bank for Reconstruction and Development, 100–101, 115, 116, 119, 132–34, 159; ratification of, 169
Bridgman, G. Temple, 67–68, 80
British Loan (Anglo-American Financial Agreement), 11–15, 146–63, 169, 174, 179–80
Brown, Winthrop, 212
Bryan, William Jennings, 2
Byrnes, James F.: ask Clayton to serve as deputy, 8; Clayton calls, 10; letter to, 85–86, 185–89; memo to, 150–52; at Paris Peace Conference, 168; at Potsdam, 128; on Surplus War Property Administration, 79–80

Caffery, Jefferson, 14, 211, 215–17
Capitalism, 36–43
Cartels, 106–7, 134
Castro, Fidel, 285–86
Catto, Thomas, 146
Century Group, 45
Chalkley, Sir Owen, 45
Chapultepec Conference (Inter-Amer-

294

ican Conference on War and Peace), 9, 15, 111–21
Chiang Kai-Shek, 282–83
Churchill, Winston, 136, 139, 247
Clark, Grenville, 256
Clason, Alfred, 218
Clayton, Ben, 3
Clayton, Fletcher Burdine, 2
Clayton, James Monroe, 2
Clayton, Sue Vaughan, 2, 7, 80, 218
Clayton, William Lockhart: on aid to Russia, 109–11; to Alben Barkley, 242–44; on American economic nationalism, 43–44; on American intervention in World War II, 44–45; on American Liberty League, 32–33; on Atlantic Union, 258–62; becomes Assistant Secretary of Commerce, 59; becomes Deputy Federal Loan Administrator, 59; to Bernard Baruch, 161–63, 179–80; on BEW-RFC controversy, 66–67; biographical information on, 1–17; on British Loan, 152–63; business interests of, 107–8; on capitalism, 36–43; on cartels, 106–7, 134; and Chapultepec Conference, 111–21; on China policy, 282–85; on Communist expansion in Europe, 198–200; conversation of, with Milo Perkins, 62–63; on cotton cooperatives, 33–36; on Czechoslovakia and GATT, 242–44; on East-West trade, 284–85; and Economic Commission for Europe, 195–97; on economic origins of war, 87; on economic requirements of peace, 81–84; on economic situation in Greece and Turkey, 190–95; on effect of World War II on trade, 48–54; to Ellen Garwood, 282–83; on European crisis (1947), 201–4; favors uninterrupted trade with Japan, 47; on Fidel Castro, 285–86; on foreign economic policy, 129–36, 168–71, 269–78; on Franklin D. Roosevelt, 66–67; to Fred Vinson, 147–49; on GATT, 211–17, 238–44; on Geneva Conference, 204–6; on government agricultural policies, 21–36, 48–54, 262–68; on government tariff policies, 21–32; on Greece, Turkey, and Iran, 185–89; on Havana Conference and Charter, 246–55; to Herbert Elliston, 208–11; on international trade and domestic employment, 96–101; on International Trade Organization Charter, 233–37, 246–55; to James F. Byrnes, 85–86, 150–52, 185–89; on John Foster Dulles, 281; on John Maynard Keynes, 145–46; to John S. Knight, 258–62; to J. William Fulbright, 281, 286; to Kenneth McKellar, 164–67; to Lamar Fleming, Jr., 244–45, 279–80; on Latin America, 111–21, 222–24, 285–90; on Marshall Plan, 197–229; on Middle East, 279–81; on national council of defense, 198–200; on negotiations with France, 207–8; to Norman Armour, 222–24; on nuclear weapons, 127–29; on OECD, 211–17; on overseas shipping, 60–61; on Paris Peace Conference, 168–71; and philosophy of free trade, 21; political position of, 64; position with Economic Cooperation Administration, offered to, 218; on post-UNRRA relief, 181–84; on post-war aid to Great Britain, 145–52; on post-war economic policy and planning, 92–95; on post-war problems, 71–79; on Potsdam, 136–39; on preclusive strategic purchases, 66–70; qualifications of, for State Department, 105–8; and Reciprocal Trade Agreements Act, 122–27; on relations with Latin America, 48–56, 111–21; on relations with Russia, 198–200; on reparations, 136–39; resigns as Surplus War Property Administrator, 84–86; resigns from Reconstruction Finance Corporation, 64–65; returns to Democratic party, 33; to R. F. Moody, 291; to Robert Ferrell, 198; role of, in Reconstruction Finance Corporation, 59; on Russia's post-war boundaries, 244–46; on South American dollar balances, 61–62; on Southeast Asia, 290–91; on Soviet policies, 185–89; on Soviet Union and UNRRA, 142–43; speech by, for Roosevelt's reelection, 87–91; on Stalin, 139; statement by, on his company's policy toward Germany, 45–47; on surpluses, 71–79, 81–84; on Surplus Property Act of 1944, 84–86, 87; on Surplus War Property Administration, 79–80; on synthetic rubber, 59–60; on Truman Doctrine,

190–95; on United World Federalists' policy, 256–58; on UNRRA, 140–45, 164–67, 172–76; on Vietnam, 290–91; on war debts, 26–32; and War Industries Board, 179; on Western Hemisphere free trade area, 289–90; to W. H. Harrison, 254–55; on world trade, 74–77
Collado, Emilio, 11
Committee for Economic Development (CED), 71–73, 76, 78–79, 96–101
Committee for European Economic Cooperation (CEEC), 14
Common Market, 269, 274–78
Cooperatives, 33–36
Cotton, 21–32, 48–54, 263–68, 288
Cotton Distribution Committee, 3, 179
Coughlan, Robert, 87
Council of Foreign Ministers (CFM), 151, 170–71, 176, 179
Council of National Defense, 198–200
Creekmore, E. F., 36
Crowley, Leo, 62, 65

Dalton, Hugh, 151–52
Dardanelles, 188
Davis, John W., 5
Dedman, John J., 205–6
Defense Supplies Corporation, 63, 65, 66, 112
de Gaulle, Charles, 288
Dewey, Thomas E., 88–91
Dirksen Amendment, 164–67
Douglas, Lewis, 14, 210–11, 215–17
Dulles, John Foster, 281

Eady, Wilfrid, 150
Economic Commission for Europe (ECE), 195–97, 206, 208
Economic Cooperation Administration (ECA), 218
Eisenhower, Dwight D., 268
Elliot, William Y., 67
Emergency Economic Committee for Europe, 196
European Central Inland Transport Organization, 196
European Coal Organization, 196–97
European customs union, 14
European Free Trade Association, 275
Export-Import Bank: capital of, increased, 113, 115, 169; Clayton as Vice-President of, 7; Clayton resigns from, 65; financing of exports

by, 133; and Latin America, 9, 55–56, 223; reconstruction loans by, 159, 174, 175

Federal Farm Board, 24, 29–30, 264
Federal Loan Administration, 7
Ferrell, Robert, 198
Fleming, Lamar, Jr., 7, 16, 244–45, 279–80
Foreign economic policy, 129–36, 168–71, 269–78
Formosa, 282–85
Forrest, William, 282
Franks, Oliver, 210, 215–17
Fulbright, J. William, 281, 286

Galbraith, John Kenneth, 245–46
Garwood, Ellen Clayton, 66, 127–28, 282–83
General Agreement on Tariffs and Trade (GATT): and Czechoslovakia, 242–44; at Geneva, 198, 201, 204–6, 208–9, 211–17, 218; negotiation of, 13, 249–50, 276; as prelude to International Trade Organization, 233–37; restrictions on, 274; statement on, 238–42; as step in progression toward worldwide free trade, 15
Germany, 45–47, 66–70
Goebbels, Joseph P., 88
Gold monopoly, U.S., 28–29
Great Britain, 10, 145–63, 179–80
Greece, 185–89, 190–95, 199

Halifax, Lord, 11
Hamilton, John D. M., 89
Hancock, John M., 82
Harriman, Averell, 110
Harriman mission, 222
Harrod, Roy, 10
Harvard Business School, 36
Harvard speech, 201, 209, 214, 226–27
Hauser, Philip M., 272
Havana conference, 246–53
Hawkins, Harry, 223
Herter, Christian, 269–78
Hewlett, Richard, 127–29
Hill, Jerome, 2
Hilldring, John, 188
"Historicus," 258
Hitler, Adolf, 51
Hoffman, Paul, 76
Hoover, Calvin, 78–79, 96–101
Hoover, Herbert, 264, 288

Hull, Cordell: on Madagascar incident, 69; philosophy of, 106, 107; and Reciprocal Trade Agreements program, 6–7, 89, 91, 123, 134–35; relations of, with Roosevelt, 67; on tariff, 99
Humphrey, Hubert, 288

Inter-American Conference on War and Peace. *See* Chapultepec Conference
Interim Committee (on atomic weapons), 127–29
International Bank for Reconstruction and Development (IBRD): and enemy states, 171; and European reconstruction, 203; and International Trade Organization, 235; and Latin America, 223–24; limitations of, 200; president's request for approval of, 115; role of, 132–33, 159, 174–75; as trustee for aid funds, 221; U.S. contribution to, 174
International Monetary Fund (IMF): and enemy states, 171; and European reconstruction, 203; and International Trade Organization, 235; and liberal trade, 241; limitations of, 100–101; role of, 115, 116, 132–33, 174–75; U.S. contribution to, 174
International Trade and Employment Conference, 13
International Trade Organization (ITO): charter for, 212, 233–237, 249, 254–55; desirability of, 251–53; establishment of, 239, 246–53; and liberalization of trade policies, 233; negotiation of, 15–16; and Reciprocal Trade Agreements, 228; as step in progression toward worldwide free trade, 15
Iran, 185–89

Javits, Jacob, 288–89
Jones, Jesse: dispute of, with Henry Wallace, 62, 67; as head of Reconstruction Finance Corporation, 7, 59; letters from Clayton to, 61–62, 64–65, 79–80

Kennan, George F., 9n, 14, 209, 211, 214
Keynes, John Maynard: and British loan, 11; discussions with, 145–46, 248; on individualism, 40; and lend-lease, 150–51; and technological innovation, 272
Khrushchev, Nikita, 270, 276
Kindleberger, Charles, 14
Klagsbrunn, Hans, 80

Labor, 50
LaGuardia, Fiorello, 166
Latin America: American policy toward, 273–74; Export-Import Bank aid to, 55–56; and Marshall Plan, 222–24; relations with, 285–90; trade with, 52–53
Legge, Alexander, 24
Lehman, Herbert, 144
Lend-lease: disposal of inventories of, 169; extension of, 108–11; financing inventories of, 174; and Great Britain, 150–51, 153–54; Harriman mission for, 222; termination of, 10, 11; and trade, 75, 91
Life magazine, 87, 283
London Preparatory Conference (for International Trade Organization), 249
Lowenthal, Richard, 282

McCabe, Thomas, 80
McCloy, Jack, 224
Maisky, Ivan, 138
Marshall, George C.: and conditions for Marshall Plan, 215–17; on European recovery, 197; and Harvard speech, 14, 201, 209, 214, 226–27; leaves for Moscow, 13, 198, 199; memo to, 201–4, 209, 213–14; proposal by, 234
Marshall Plan (European Recovery Program): and American agriculture, 262; Clayton's role in, 13, 197–229; discussions concerning, 14–15; end of, 261; and European economy, 233; and expansion of world economy, 276; inadequacy of, 257; negotiations for, 14–15
Mead Committee, 186
Metals Reserve Company, 63, 66, 112
Meyer, Eugene, 211
Ministry of Economic Warfare, and suspicion that Clayton's firm was trading with Germany, 45–47
Molotov, V. M., 139, 210, 215–16
Monnet, Jean, 110, 206, 216
Monroe Doctrine, 49, 52, 286
Morgenthau, Henry, 108–11
Mutual Aid Agreement of 1942, 12

Nation, 8
National Association of Manufacturers, 87
National Farmers Union, 8
National Farm Institute, 153
Neal, Alfred C., 290
New Republic, 8
New York Cotton Exchange, 4–5
Nichols, J. C., 64
Nitze, Paul, 16
North Atlantic Treaty Organization (NATO), 276
Nufer, Albert, 223

Office of Inter-American Affairs, 7
Office of War Mobilization, 8, 79
Organization for Economic Cooperation and Development (OECD), 14, 211, 217, 276
Organization for European Economic Cooperation (OEEC), 210, 215, 217, 226, 276
Orr, Sir John, 146

Padilla, Ezequiel, 120
Pan-American Union, 55*n*
Paris Peace Conference, 168
Patton, James, 8
Perkins, Milo, 62–63
Petain, Marshall Henri, 68
Piel, Gerard, 272
PM, 8
Potsdam Conference, 9–10, 128–29, 136–39, 141
Preclusive buying, 7, 66–70
Preferences, elimination of, 11–13, 149–52, 155, 240
Preparatory Commission on Trade and Employment (Geneva, 1947), 197
Procurement of raw materials, 67–70, 112–13
"Proposals for Consideration by an International Conference on Trade and Employment," 11–12
"Proposals for the Expansion of World Trade," 156, 239, 248–49

Rayburn, Sam, 213, 281
Reciprocal Trade Agreements (RTA): advocacy of, 6–7, 122–27; authority of, 169; as commitment to liberal economic policy, 269; as cornerstone of foreign policy, 228, 238; enunciated by Cordell Hull, 6; inadequacy of, 274; lessons of, 94–95;
as reason for Clayton's return to Democratic party, 33; role of, 134, 240; as step in progression toward worldwide free trade, 15
Reconstruction Finance Corporation (RFC), 7, 8, 59, 62–68
Relief after UNRRA, 181–84, 195–97
Reparations, 10
Reston, James, 172
Robbins, Lionel, 145
Rockefeller, Nelson, 7, 105
Roosevelt, Franklin D.: agricultural policies of, 5, 264; and aid to Russia, 108–9; and Atlantic Charter, 247; calls Mrs. Clayton, 7, 80; role of, in BEW-RFC dispute, 62, 66–67; support of, by Clayton in 1936 election, 6
Rubber, synthetic, 59–60
Rubber Development Corporation, 65
Rubber Reserve Company, 63, 66, 112
Russia: aid to, 108–11; American relations with, 256–62; capitalism in, 38–40; and Cold War, 269–78; and Marshall Plan, 210, 216; and Middle East, 279–80; policies of, in Near and Middle East, 185–89; and post-war boundaries, 244–46; at Potsdam, 10

Sengier (head of Belgian "Minerva"), 67–68
Shipping, 60–61
Shouse, Jouett, 32
Simmons, E. P., 244–45
Smith, "Cotton Ed," 4–5
Smoot-Hawley Tariff, 101, 264
Snyder, Carl, 37–38
Southern Delivery, 4–5
Staff Committee (State Department), on sale of surplus military equipment, 185–89
Stalin, Joseph, 10, 136, 139, 258
State-War-Navy Coordinating Committee, 186
Sterling Area, 148, 155–56
Stettinius, Edward, 8, 109–11, 121
Stimson, Henry, 127
Suits, Guy, 271–72
Summers, Hatton, 12
Surpluses: capacity for production of, 159; dumping of, 288; and European crisis, 202; importance of, 265; markets for, needed, 71–79, 81–84, 92–95, 131
Surplus Property Act of 1944, 84–86, 87
Surplus War Property Administration:

298

Clayton resigns from, 17, 84–86; Clayton's role in, 7–8; establishment of, 79–82; organization of, 79–80; role of, 81–84

Taft, Robert A., 258–59
Tannenbaum, Frank, 273
Tariffs: as cause of cotton farmers' problems, 21–26, 26–32; as detrimental to South, 2, 5; difficulty of reducing, 250; France raises, 207; reduction of, 205–6, 211–12, 235, 240; revision of, 87–91, 92–95, 99, 150–51; and standard of living, 135; on wool, 201, 204–6, 209, 212
Taxation, 42–43, 50, 200, 203
Taylor, Myron, 248
Texas Cotton Products Company, 2
Tower, John, 128
Trade: with Communists, 284–85; destruction of barriers to, 87–91, 150–51; effect of, on employment, 96–101; with Great Britain, 153–61; increase of, through Reciprocal Trade Agreements, 121–27; with Latin America, 287–90; and World War II, 48–56
Trade, bilateral (barter): and British, 162; harmful effects of, 53, 155, 241, 247; Republican platform on, 90
Trade, free: advocacy of, 6–7, 9, 14–15; as cure for depression, 21; revolt against, 44
Trade, liberal: and British Loan, 147–49; desirability of, 262–68, 269–78, 287–90; and European economy, 181; through GATT, 238–42; and permanent prosperity, 233–37, 266–68; role of UNRRA in, 140–45
Trade, multilateral, 53, 160, 162–63
Trade, post-war: and American economy, 92–95; and American international relations, 48–56, 129–36; and Great Britain, 149; with Latin America, 113–20; liberalization of, 71, 81–84
Truman, Harry S: appoints Clayton to UNRRA Council, 10, 140; and atomic bomb, 127, 129; and British Loan, 152; courage of, 215, 217; on Czechoslovakia and GATT, 242–44; letter to, 218–19; at Potsdam, 128, 136; proclaims Truman Doctrine, 190; on relief for Europe and China, 181–84; and wool tariff, 205, 211–15

Truman Doctrine, 13, 185, 190, 197
Turkey, 185–89, 194–95
Twentieth Century Fund, 253, 254

Ukraine, 143
United Nations Economic and Social Council (UNESCO), 195–97
United Nations Food and Agriculture Organization (FAO), 71, 146, 171
United Nations Investment Bank, 95
United Nations Organization: admission of enemy to, 171; faith in, 245; limits of, 199, 280; and multilateral trade, 162–63; San Francisco conference of, 124; strengthening of, 256
United Nations Relief and Rehabilitation Administration (UNRRA): advocacy of, by Clayton, 10, 140–45; American contribution to, 169; Clayton's statement on temporary nature of, 172–76; council meeting of, 151; and European economy, 181–84; funds of, 115; and Greece, 190–92; relief after, 181–84, 195–97; and Soviet Union, 164–67
United States Chamber of Commerce, 87, 249
United States Commercial Company, 7, 65
United World Federalists, 256–58

Versailles Treaty, 168–70
Vietnam, South, 291
Vinson, Fred, 11, 147–49
Vyshinsky, Andrey Y., 138–39

Wallace, Henry A.: and agriculture, 34; and Board of Economic Warfare, 7; dispute of, with Jesse Jones, 62, 66–67; on European dictators, 43–44; letter to, 55–56
War Damage Corporation, 7, 65
War debts, 26–32, 158
War Industries Board, 3, 179
Washington Post, 7–8, 172–76
Western Hemisphere Free Trade Area, 289–90
White Russia, 142
Wilcox, Clair, 212, 223
Wilson, Carroll, 73
Wilson, Woodrow, 6
Winant, John, 152
Wolcott, Leon O., 43
Wood, R. E., 12, 152
Wood, Tyler, 10
Wool, 201, 204–6

Yalta Conference, 136–38

THE JOHNS HOPKINS PRESS
Designed by Victoria Dudley
Composed in Times Roman text and display
by Monotype Composition Company
Printed on 60-lb. P & S, R, and
Bound in Bancroft Arrestox, A-44000
By The Maple Press, Inc.

Also by Joseph Heywood

Fiction

Taxi Dancer (1985)
The Berkut (1987)
The Domino Conspiracy (1992)
The Snowfly (2000)

Woods Cop Mysteries

Ice Hunter (2001)
Blue Wolf in Green Fire (2002)
Chasing a Blond Moon (2003)

Non-Fiction

Covered Waters: Tempests of a Nomadic Trouter (2003)

RUNNING DARK

A WOODS COP MYSTERY

JOSEPH HEYWOOD

RUNNING DARK

A WOODS COP MYSTERY

THE LYONS PRESS

GUILFORD, CONNECTICUT

AN IMPRINT OF THE GLOBE PEQUOT PRESS

The Lyons Press is an imprint of The Globe Pequot Press

10 9 8 7 6 5 4 3 2

Printed in the United States of America

ISBN 1-59228-617-8

Library of Congress Cataloging-in-Publication Data

Heywood, Joseph.
    Running dark : a woods cop mystery / Joseph Heywod.
       p. cm.
   ISBN 1-59228-617-8 (trade cloth)
   1. Game wardens—Fiction. 2. Upper Penisnula (Mich.)—Fiction. I.
Title.
PS3558.E92R86 2005
813'.54—dc22

                    2005006035

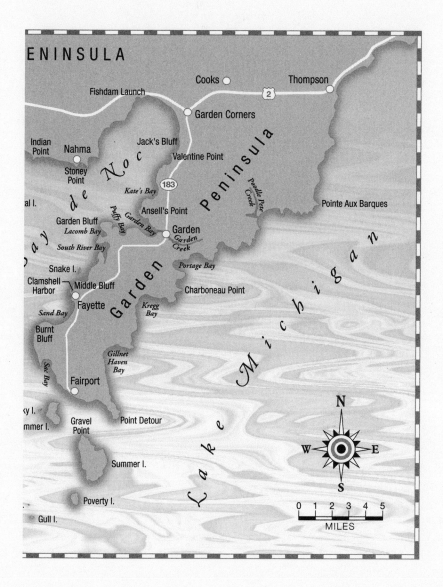

ENINSULA

Cooks

Thompson

Fishdam Launch

2

Garden Corners

Indian
Point

Nahma

Jack's Bluff

Valentine Point

Noc

Peninsula

Stoney
Point

*Paudle Pexe
Creek*

al I.

183

Kate's Bay

Pointe Aux Barques

Ansell's Point

Garden Bluff

Puffy Bay

Garden Bay

de

Garden
*Garden
Creek*

Lacomb Bay

bay

South River Bay

Garden

Snake I.

Portage Bay

Clamshell
Harbor

Middle Bluff

Charboneau Point

Fayette

*Kregg
Bay*

Sand Bay

Lake

Michigan

Burnt
Bluff

Sac Bay

*Gillnet
Haven
Bay*

Fairport

ky I.

Gravel
Point

Point Detour

mmer I.

Summer I.

Poverty I.

Gull I.

N

W   E

S

0   1   2   3   4   5
MILES

PART I

THE UPPER PECULIAR

· 1 ·

NEWBERRY, NOVEMBER 11, 1974

"Dey're dirtier den dirt."

Eldon "Shuck" Gorley was in the Newberry DNR office for the last official time—to turn in his badge and state-owned equipment. Grady Service, within three days of going out on his own as a conservation officer, was guzzling black coffee and studying a report from Lansing while he waited for a meeting with the district law supervisor. Gorley, carrying a severely dented thermos, sat down across from Service and poked through a box of donuts that someone had left on the table. "Be da first deer season I ha'n't worked in twenty-seven years," the retiring officer said in his raspy voice. He was unshaven, had wavy white hair, leathery skin, and bushy salt-and-pepper eyebrows. "Your first in da Upper Peculiar," he added, looking at Service.

Service chuckled. The Upper Peninsula surely was peculiar, especially for conservation officers. Gorley was not a gregarious man and had just spoken more words than Service had heard from him since he'd arrived from training downstate. Gorley's nickname came from his ability to "out-stupid stupids" with a well-honed and effective "aw shucks" routine.

"Treat each season like a gift, eh," Gorley said. "We only get so many."

"I will," Service said, not sure what the older man wanted. Gorley rarely talked or showed emotion, but was respected as an aggressive and thoughtful officer.

"You get da chance," Gorley continued, "youse might wanta be sittin' up on da Gutpile Ridge Grade Road night 'fore da opener. Dose Ketola brothers, dey like ta slow-roll da clear-cuts out dat way. I dogged 'em da past twenty years and always come up empty, but dey're dirtier den dirt, and dey'll be out dere, bet on dat. Dey buy old twenty-twos, use 'em once, and chuck 'em. You get 'em, trow da book at 'em for me, eh?"

"The Ketola brothers," Service said.

Gorley nodded and grinned. "Dirtier 'n dirt, an' I made sure da whole town knows I'm retirin' 'fore da opener and a green-butt rookie's takin' my place. Good huntin'."

Service shook the man's hand. He had a powerful grip and clear blue eyes. Gorley placed his thermos in front of Service. "Little beat-up, like me, but I won't be needin' 'er anymore." The name SHUCK was etched crudely on the metal thermos. Gorley paused and added, "I knew yer old man. He was a warden's warden, and if he hadn't loved his hooch . . ."

Gorley didn't finish the sentence. Grady Service's father had served in World War II in the Marine Corps and had joined the DNR when he returned. He had been drunk when he'd stepped in front of a truck at night and was killed. Service had been sixteen years old, and though father and son had never been close, the loss hit the boy hard, causing him to withdraw into himself and trust few people. Service likewise had served as a marine—in Vietnam—and now he was in the U.P. as a conservation officer, history repeating itself. He had sworn he would not be like his father, but so far he was following the old man step for step and he found it unsettling. At six foot four and two hundred and twenty pounds, he didn't look much like his old man—and he certainly didn't want to be like him—yet this was the only job he had ever wanted.

"We all got stren'ts an' weaknesses," Gorley said. "Back when your old man and me got dese jobs, dey wanted toughs. Chances of gettin' convictions in da courts was so low, was our job ta rough up da poachers and put da fear of da DNR inta dem. Back den we used our saps first, talked later. But now da law's changed and we have ta use our brains a lot more den our fists, and dis is how she ought to be. You can't enforce da law by out-gooning da jerks. I heard you got stone dukes just like your old man, but you been ta college. Use dat noggin. Dat's all I gotta say."

They nodded at each other as Gorley left the room, one finishing a long, difficult career, the other just starting out.

There had been a hardness and an edge to Shuck Gorley's voice that reminded him of his father and all the men who had served with him, the old-timers now known as horseblankets because of the knee-length heavy wool coats they had worn back then. He had inherited his old man's stained and frayed coat. His father had always worn outer clothes two or three sizes too large to allow him to pack layers underneath in cold weather. It had always hung on his father like a loose sack, but it fit Grady Service almost perfectly, and he liked wearing it, though he wasn't sure why. *Stop thinking about the old man*, he cautioned himself. *This is your career*, your *future*. When he finished his cup of coffee he said aloud, "Ketola brothers," and shifted his attention to his first solo patrol.

Service was rooting through file cabinets when Sergeant "Sugar Sam" Surrey, the area law supervisor, came looking for him.

Surrey had so far proven to be a helpful and supportive supervisor. Service was to ride two more days with him and then be on his own.

"Little early in the career to be trollin' files," Surrey said, grinning.

"I was looking at the file on the Ketola brothers."

Surrey chuckled. "Shuck never could get those boys and it's stuck in his craw his whole career. Think a green-butt rookie like you can do what he couldn't?"

"Just getting to know the territory," Service answered, putting the folder back in the cabinet drawer. There had not been much to learn. The file was filled with reports and notes from Gorley, mostly speculative and accusatory; the reality was that he had never been able to catch the brothers doing anything illegal. Service wrote down their address and made a note to check his county plat book later.

· 2 ·

GUTPILE RIDGE, NOVEMBER 14–15, 1974

"Shouldn't youse be oot in da woods?"

It was the night before rifle season for whitetail, and Grady Service's first solo patrol as a conservation officer. He sat in his Plymouth Fury 444, engine off so he could hear. All the lights were off, inside and outside. He got out and stood beside the vehicle, smoking and cupping the butt in his hand to hide the glowing ember, half listening, parked beside a massive jack pine blowdown at the edge of a clear-cut adjacent to the Gutpile Ridge Grade Road. The area had been logged over two years before and now bristled with new growth and sprouts of plants, rough grasses, and trees. In some ways it reminded Service of areas that had been carpet-bombed in Vietnam. At night deer would drift into the area from adjacent cedar and tamarack swamps, and poachers would slow-roll the logging roads and rutted two-tracks looking for animals to freeze with their spotlights so they could shoot them.

Many COs insisted poachers seldom worked after 1 A.M. or so, especially the night before the state's firearms opener, but Service had tried to put himself in a poacher's mindset and decided the best time to be out would be only a few hours before the season officially opened at first light—a time when most hunters, and presumably lawmen, would be fast asleep. Service knew that at night the animals would be deep into their feeding routine and presumably more interested in food than danger as they got ready to drift back to their day cover.

It had been colder for the last ten days, in the low teens at night, with daytime highs barely above freezing, and tonight, finally, it was snowing. Feeling the small icy flakes on his face, he was glad he had gotten the Fury tucked away before the snow started. His tracks would soon be hidden from anyone cruising the logging road.

Just after 3:30 A.M. he heard a vehicle trying to negotiate the frozen two-track. He could hear it sliding and bumping around on frozen grooves so deep and solid they could rip steering out of the driver's control.

There were not a lot of deer near his position. The real concentration was a half-mile south, further into the clear-cut. He knew that poachers would look for large herds and pick off animals closest to their vehicles. Typically they would use their headlights or a handheld spotlight to mesmerize an animal and knock it down with a single shot. Some would gut the animal and haul it out immediately; others would gut it and leave it where it fell, coming back later to pick it up. With this snow and cold, Service figured they would leave this one. In summer and early fall, the weather was too warm and would quickly cause the meat to spoil, but it was well below freezing tonight and spoilage would not be an issue.

It was a poacher's dream: black night, no moon, no stars, just soft waves of wet snowflakes fluttering gently in the darkness. Snow cover would mute sound and make tracking easier.

When the vehicle appeared, only its parking lights were lit, and they seemed to have been half taped to further reduce light.

Even with poor visibility he could see that it was a pickup, and as soon as it passed, he got into the Fury, started his engine, and pulled out to follow, closing steadily until he was seventy-five feet behind it. Some officers would run without lights only if they had a sneak light to help them see the way. Such devices were cannibalized from military-surplus jeeps and jury-rigged to DNR patrol units. Service preferred to run with no light of any kind. Even as a boy he had been comfortable in complete darkness, and now he was driving in darkness so intense it might be the devil's belly. But darkness was not his foe; it was his ally and his edge. As a boy his old man had never let him use a flashlight. At night he was expected to get comfortable with the black and use his eyes. The old man's bizarre rules had always pissed him off and frustrated him, but when he got to Vietnam, his ability to deal with darkness had not only made him a better marine than most who were with him—it had probably saved his life. Now on his first patrol, he felt in total harmony with the blackness that surrounded him.

As the truck moved into the area where there were herds of deer milling around, Service maintained his interval and kept his window down so he could hear. Snow swirled through the window onto his sleeve and neck, but he felt no cold—only anticipation for what the people ahead of him might do. Training done, he was finally alone, hunting poachers.

After fifteen minutes the truck stopped. Service did the same, immediately turning off his motor. A light flashed over the roof of the truck into the field to the east, and Service got a glimpse of a deer in the light, followed by a tiny muzzle flash and the snap of a small-caliber rifle. The light then went out and it was dark again. *Driver's the shooter,* Service told himself, *passenger the spotter.*

Service watched the men get out of the truck and ease their doors shut without latching them. He got out when the men disappeared into the stump-filled field and quickly moved over to the pickup, carefully staying in the truck's tracks to obscure his boot prints. He saw a rifle on the front seat and backed away, using his hat to brush away any sign of his boots, memorized the license plate number, and returned to the Fury, wishing he had parked further back in case they decided to check behind them with flashlights.

A few minutes later, the men got into the truck without checking their rear and pulled away. Service started his engine and followed. When the pickup got out to Broken Heart Road, the driver of the vehicle switched on his headlights and aimed west on the hardtop. Service followed, his Fury still dark, hanging back more than he'd done on the two-track in case another vehicle came along from either direction to light him up.

No vehicle came and the truck made its way steadily, never exceeding the speed limit. The vehicle left the hardtop several times to take short jaunts down snow-covered dirt roads and once pulled over to the shoulder, turned off its lights, and sat for more than four minutes before moving on. Service made a mental note of a couple of visual landmarks and the mileage on his odometer, and continued to follow.

Eventually they turned down an improved gravel road and from that, cut up a short two-track driveway, where they stopped at a large pole barn. Service watched one of the men get out and open the door. The vehicle disappeared inside, the door closed, and it was dark again.

It took less than ten minutes to find a rifle where the men had briefly parked to discard it. Service checked the weapon to make sure it was unloaded and smelled the barrel. It had been fired. He assumed it had been wiped clean, but made sure to handle it with his gloves just in case.

Rifle in possession, he returned to the clear-cut, parked a quarter-mile from the area where he had seen them shoot the deer, and trudged a half-mile through fresh wet snow, weaving his way around stumps and debris until he found faint footprints with his penlight. The tracks led to a deer, still warm. A steaming pile of viscera lay nearby.

Service knelt beside the carcass, where he made two tiny incisions in the deer's hide to conceal his markers, and carved a small mark on the hoof of the right foreleg. It was an eight-point buck, not a monster by any measure, but a nice deer with a tight basket rack, probably a two-year-old animal.

When he got back to the Fury he used his penlight to check his plat book. The truck he had followed had turned into a forty-acre parcel owned by Stanley and Leo Ketola. Gorley had called this one, he thought, then corrected himself. No, the old CO had set it up—for him. He could have made the arrest when the men shot at the deer, but something held him back—his first patrol, maybe—or something else he couldn't quite peg. Maybe it was the desire to have his first arrest be unassailable in court. In training he had heard over and over that officers needed to think through what they were doing or risk spending a lot of time in court in front of juries that often sided more with the scumbags than a sense of justice. When you were tied up in court, you couldn't cover your territory. He had decided early on to do his best to make his cases ironclad.

Having located the kill and the rifle, he returned to the house where the truck had disappeared into the pole barn, made his way through an aspen stand to a woodpile that had obviously not seen recent use, and tucked the rifle between some logs in the stack.

He spent the rest of the early morning patrolling back roads, noting where tent camps were located and where tracks led down entry roads to hunting camps. Just before first light he was in Brown's Hotel in Newberry ordering scrambled eggs and Swedish pancakes, the waitress giving him a questioning look.

"Shouldn't youse be oot in da woods?"

"Plenty of time," he said, nursing his coffee. He assumed the poachers would get to the carcass barely after first light, tag it to make it look legal, and keep hunting until later. If they were as good as Shuck Gorley claimed, he assumed they would find the quarters he had inserted in the belly incisions, and the external hoof marking.

"Youse're da new game warden," the waitress said, bringing his breakfast.

"Grady Service," he said.

"Nikki-Jo Jokola," she said. "Youse want coffee for da t'ermos?"

"Thanks," he said, handing it to her.

When he tried to pay for the coffee, she refused and held up her hands. "Shuck, he found my twins when dey got lost one time. Dose two scamps wandered down to da river and were gone all night, but Shuck, he found 'em, made sure dey was safe, and chewed dere butts out." She smiled at the memory. "You take care of folks da way he did and we'll call 'er even, eh."

After his leisurely breakfast, Service drove over to the Luce County sheriff's office and made arrangements for backup. He had a handheld radio in his Fury, the sort COs called "brick" radios. He would call the deputies when and if he needed them, presumably later in the morning.

Shuck Gorley looked befuddled when he stepped out onto the porch of his house in his green long johns. "What're you doing here?" the retired officer asked Grady Service.

"Using my head. You want to take a ride with me?"

Gorley considered the invitation. "I'm sure not goin' hunting openin' day wit' so many downstate sound-shooters skulkin' around out dere," he said.

"Okay with your wife?"

"She give up on me an' life a long time ago," Gorley said matter-of-factly. "Let me get some duds on."

At 8 A.M. Service dropped the retired officer a half-mile short of the Ketola property, and drove past the entrance to the driveway, hiding his truck in some trees further down the gravel road that passed in front of the property.

As it often did when the sun began to rise, the air temperature seemed to drop. Service took his thermos and cut through gnarled jack pines to the house, found a scrub oak tree to lean against and began his wait, shifting from one foot to the other to keep the cold from creeping up his legs. He was less than thirty feet from the pole barn.

The pickup truck pulled in just before ten. Two men got out, each with an open beer in hand. They looked to be in their late sixties or early seventies.

"I guess we had da luck," the passenger said.

"No talkin'," the driver shot back.

The exchange suggested the driver took the lead in things, and that the man knew his business. Professional poachers never talked in public about what they did. Keeping their mouths shut was what made them successful. His old man used to say that big egos were what got lawbreakers caught. The ideal poacher would be a tongueless mute.

Service waited for them to go to the back of the truck to pull the deer out of the bed before he made his move. The passenger had a hold on the back legs of the animal. Service grabbed the man's arm, making him spin and stagger backward.

"DNR!" Service said. "Conservation officer." When he stepped toward the pole barn door, the driver bumped him with his shoulder, but Service deftly kicked the heel of the man's support foot and he collapsed. Service grabbed the deer by the antlers, wrenched it away from them, and said, "On your knees. *Now!*"

"*Holy Je-Moley!* What's da bloody deal!" the driver shouted with alarm. Service looked at the tag affixed to the antler. The animal was legally tagged.

Service glanced in the truck, saw two rifle cases, took them out, unzipped the cases, and made sure they were unloaded. One was a Model 94 Winchester .30–30, the other a pump-action Remington with a short barrel, probably a .30–06. Both were empty; only the .30–30 smelled like it had been fired recently.

Service saw right away that the mark on the right forehoof had been shaved away. The two men knelt impassively in the snow as the conservation officer poked around until he found the first of the two slits he had made in the deer's skin earlier that morning. He inserted his finger. The first quarter he'd put inside was gone; same with the second quarter in the second incision.

"Lose somepin'?" one of the men asked.

"You got names?" Service said.

"Stanley Ketola," the driver said. "My brudder Leo," he added with a nod.

Service asked in a nonthreatening voice, "Where's the twenty-two, Stanley?"

The brothers looked at each other. "We don't got no twenty-two," Stanley said. "Right, Leo?"

"Ketolas don't hunt deer wit' no plinker," Leo added with an affirming nod.

Service said, "I was behind you fellas last night, followed you, saw you shoot the deer, followed you back here, witnessed the whole deal, start to finish."

Stanley Ketola grunted. "Me and Leo never liked no DNR fairy tales."

Service examined the carcass. The .22 wound was separate from a larger hole. "You two stay right where you are," Service said. He walked back to his watch spot, got his thermos and set it down so both men could see the inscription on it, and filled his cup. He saw them exchange glances.

Service took a swig of coffee and let out a sigh. "You boys been around and you know how this goes, right?"

"Yeah," Stanley said. "Da easy way or da hard way. Dat's a fairy tale, too, *bub*."

Leo grinned and nodded at his brother.

"How about we look in the pole barn?" Service said. "That okay with you fellas?"

"You got a warrant?" Leo asked.

"Do I need one?"

Leo blinked and Stanley glared at his brother. "Dat buck dere's legal. Guess you'll be movin' on, eh?" Stanley said. "You don't got reasonable suspension to be pokin' around da property."

Service sighed: reasonable suspension? "Tell you what," he said. "Anything I find in the barn I won't hold against you unless I can *prove* this buck is illegal."

Neither man showed any emotion, but both obviously were trying to analyze the unorthodox challenge.

"What's da deal?" Stanley asked warily.

"You shot this deer just after three-thirty this morning and you both just drove in here with open containers of alcohol," Service said, fingering the tag on the antler. "But we'll forget the open containers, just to show you fellas I'm not tryin' to be chickenshit here."

"We got dat buck dis mornin'," Stanley said emphatically. Service felt certain that Stanley had been driving last night and that he had done the shooting, but Leo had tagged the animal. He had no idea why.

"We?" Service said.

Leo laughed. "Brudders, we always say we, eh?"

The two men were stone-faced.

"So you fellas are telling me you both shot this buck before first light, right, one of you with a twenty-two, the other with a bigger caliber? Is that your story?"

"Holy moley, we din't say dat," Stanley said.

"You shot the deer," he told Stanley. "This morning."

Leo stammered, "Hey, dat's *my* buck. I shot 'im dis mornin', maybe seven-t'irty. Da buck's legal and no bloody way youse can prove udderwise, eh?"

Service said, "I'll take that as a yes."

"Yes to *what*?" Stanley said, his voice rising slightly. "We din't agree to nuttin'."

"What I hear you saying is that you got dirt in the barn and dirt out here," Service said.

"Dis is baloney," Stanley said, his eyes showing stress. "Youse're loony."

"Look, guys. I know you've been at this a long time," Service said. "You're professionals and I'm a professional. I say I've got you cold, you say I don't. How about we show our cards?"

The two men looked at each other and stared at him. "We want our lawyer," Stanley said.

"What do you need a lawyer for? You got a legal deer, right?"

Leo said, "Get off'n da property."

Service said, "I thought you guys were pros, but all I see is a joke."

Stanley bristled. "We don't gotta put up wit' dis crap from no rookie woods cop."

Service knelt and dramatically poked his finger into the second hole in the deer hide and wiggled it around, probing deeply.

The men watched his hand.

"You lookin' for change?" Leo asked, laughing out loud.

"Shut yer pasty hole, Leo," the other Ketola snapped.

Service eased out a tiny swatch of blood-soaked red cloth and held it up. "The human mind is predictable, boys," he said. "People always think in series of threes—in this case, marked hoof, two quarters in the hide—and you fellas were feeling pretty good about finding three markers and eliminating all the evidence." Service waggled the red patch. "This is number four. I put it there last night—ahead of the second quarter."

The two men studied each other. Stanley said, "Dat s'posed to prove somepin'?"

Shuck Gorley suddenly walked around the back of the pickup with the .22 rifle in hand, yelled, "Catch!" and flipped the rifle at Leo, who caught it awkwardly.

Service looked at the men. "Nice grab," Service said. "Let's summarize where we are: I saw you shine and shoot. I followed you here, I went back and fetched the twenty-two from where I saw you ditch it, I marked your deer, and now the twenty-two has your fingerprints on it, Leo. I think Stanley shot the animal, but since you claim it, you get the brunt of the charges."

Leo Ketola dropped the rifle on the ground.

Service used his brick radio to call the county and within ten minutes they pulled up the driveway. The sullen brothers stared off into the distance while they waited. Service poured coffee for Shuck Gorley.

"Carcass, rifle, lies—now we have a reason to go into the pole barn," Service chanted, walking past the kneeling brothers.

There were twelve deer suspended from stainless steel hooks in a cooler in back, and parts of birds and a couple hundred pounds of lake trout and walleye fillets in a commercial freezer.

"You fellas been busy," Service said to the brothers as the Luce County deputies put them in their patrol cars.

Stanley Ketola looked out at Gorley and grinned. "Well, you never got us, eh Shuck."

Service wiggled the thermos in front of the older brother. "Who do you think sent me out there to wait for you two, and who do you think spread it all over town that he wouldn't be working anymore? He knew you boys would be cocky with a rookie on the job."

The patrol cars backed down the driveway with their prisoners and headed for Newberry.

Shuck Gorley stuck out his hand and grinned. "Thanks for including me."

"This was yours all the way," Grady Service said. "You called in the order. I just made the pickup."

Gorley stared at him. "I think you got a heap more brains than your old man had," he said. "You stay safe out here."

Service continued his patrol until nearly 10 P.M. that night, and when he got home his wife Bathsheba was already in bed. He looked for leftovers in the fridge and found none, showered, and crawled into bed beside her.

"You decided to come home," his wife said coolly with her back to him. When he put his hand on her hip, she pulled away.

"I had a lot to do." He briefly explained the arrest of the brothers and how Gorley had been after them for years and always came up short.

"Like little boys," she said. "They cheat, you try to catch them, and for what—a bunch of stupid animals? Good God, Grady, is this any way for a grown man to live?"

She could not have found more destructive words.

PART II

WAR IN THE GARDEN

3

GARDEN PATROL, NOVEMBER 20, 1975

The hunters had suddenly become the hunted.

Grady Service had no idea what was happening. Sergeant Holloman had called the trailer at 2:30 A.M. and told him to report to Sergeant Blake Garwood at the Fishdam boat launch at noon.

Grady Service was less than eight months into his responsibility for the Mosquito Wilderness Tract, the same area his CO father had patrolled before him. His wife, Bathsheba, was gone, having abruptly departed six months ago for Nevada to file for divorce. She had lasted less than a year trying to adapt to life as a CO's spouse before throwing in the towel. Service felt that some of it was his fault, but he was still angry, and sometimes he even missed her when he crawled into bed alone at night. But since his transfer from the Newberry district to the Mosquito Wilderness he had focused all his energy on his new responsibilities, and thoughts of Bathsheba were fewer.

He protested because it was the second week of his second deer season as a CO—and first in his new territory—and he didn't want to leave the Mosquito Wilderness unprotected.

"Just meet Garwood at the launch," was Holloman's clipped response. "And don't be late."

"It's not my territory," Service argued.

"As I recall, our patches say *Michigan* Department of Natural Resources," Holloman said. "Which means we go where we're needed. Blake's partner came down with the flu; he needs help and you're it. This takes priority over deer hunters in the Mosquito."

Service didn't try to argue about his lack of knowledge and dislike of boats. He knew from some of the other officers that the Fishdam River launch site was used for patrols down Big Bay de Noc along the Garden Peninsula. During his time in Newberry he had participated in some Lake Superior marine patrols during salmon and steelhead runs, but he had never done a patrol in northern Lake Michigan, and from what other officers had said, duty in the Garden could range from deadly boring to just plain deadly. He didn't relish either alternative.

The Garden Peninsula was a twenty-one-mile-long, shark-tooth-shaped, cove-pocked neck of land between Escanaba and Manistique. It was part of what geologists called the Niagaran Escarpment, limestone, dolomite, and shale-gypsum formations that snaked south from the Garden across a string of rocky, barren islands that eventually led like a geological arrow to Wisconsin's Door Peninsula. When the first whites arrived in the area they found Noquet and Menominee Indians using the area's rich soils for gardens, giving the area its name, which persisted to this day.

The western extremities of the peninsula were largely untillable, with limestone sometimes found within inches of the surface, and though some people still farmed the center and east of the peninsula, few except the occasional fruit grower and small dairyman could earn any semblance of a living. The primary economic focus of the peninsula had been and remained one thing: fish. Since the establishment of Fayette State Park, locals were happy to take dollars from tourists, even though tourists were a nuisance and sportfishermen not particularly welcome. Fish in the Garden were about money, not recreation.

Fayette had risen during the Civil War, when the North needed iron for its armies. The smelting operation had closed in 1891, leaving intact ruins and a ghost town that had been turned into a campground, state park, and historic site. Fayette, Service thought, was like the rest of the Garden Peninsula. When there was no more money to be made, the village had been abandoned.

Fewer than a thousand people lived on the peninsula, which had two villages, Garden and Fairport. The DNR had reason to know both of them well. Fairport had been a commercial fishing center since 1880, and nearly all of its residents still fished—a few of them legally, a lot more of them illegally. In 1969 DNR fish biologists had finished studies of Lake Michigan yellow perch, whitefish, walleyes, and lake trout, and decided that heavy pressure on fish stocks had to be reduced. Commercial licenses that lapsed would no longer be renewed. Unlike the past, if you didn't fish every year, you couldn't just jump back in and start up another year because it looked like there were big runs and money to be made. You had to keep fishing every year in order to keep your license, and if you let it lapse for a single season, you couldn't renew. And no new licenses would be issued until biologists judged the fish populations could handle it. "Order Seventeen" became an instant bone of contention.

Garden fishermen immediately donned sweatshirts that said DNR = DAMN NEAR RUSSIAN, and rebelled. Since 1969 there had been repeated confrontations between the DNR and the fishermen who were harvesting illegally. Locals had used long guns and pistols to take potshots at officers, mostly to scare them away; they also had rained rocks on them, vandalized and stolen their vehicles, assaulted and threatened them with knives and scissors and clubs, sometimes with large groups surrounding one or two uniformed game wardens. So far there had been no serious injuries, but everyone knew that the clock was ticking as long as the dispute continued.

After a confrontation a few months back, the Delta County prosecutor had declared to the state that he would no longer allow county deputies to assist conservation officers until such time that the state beefed up its force, its equipment, and its training. The U.P.'s law boss had simultaneously reduced the frequency of CO patrols down the peninsula for nearly two months, a decision that had many officers angry and ashamed, and had Gardenites crowing with delight.

Service had never been called in to assist in the Garden, but the decision to cut back the DNR presence there had rankled him because he saw it as just the sort of gutless decision imposed by some spineless bureaucrat in Lansing. It never occurred to him that Lansing might not have had anything to do with the curtailment.

Blake Garwood was a tall, stooped man with black hair and a full mustache that drooped over the corners of his mouth. The marine safety sergeant's duties involved regular lake patrols, and Service had met him only once, and then just to be introduced.

The sergeant arrived fifteen minutes after Service, but earlier than their meeting time.

"Lend a hand," Garwood said, tossing an orange life jacket to Service. The two men moved boxes of gear from the trunk of the patrol car to the dark green eighteen-foot Glastron on the trailer. Some of the boxes held various lengths of nylon rope and some homemade welded grapples. Empty green plastic fish bins were already lashed securely into the boat. Loading done, Garwood backed the trailer down the ramp until its wheels were in the water. The two men unlashed the craft, pushed it off the trailer, and Service held a line to the boat while the sergeant parked the vehicle and trailer against the trees at the landing. They both pushed the boat away from shore and hopped aboard. Service looked at his watch. It was noon, straight up.

The sky was gunmetal gray, but there was no snow and visibility was good.

"Your partner's sick?" Service asked.

Garwood was fiddling with a battery cable. "Garden flu," the sergeant said glumly. "It can hit anyone at any time."

The outboard motor gurgled and rumbled as they worked their way out of the sinewy river mouth, curving left, passing jutting boulders as they moved toward the open water of Big Bay de Noc.

"Your first time out here?" the sergeant asked, yelling over the straining motor as he tightened his life preserver.

Service nodded. The boat was bouncing and bucking against three-foot swells.

"You got green gills?" Garwood asked.

Service shook his head. He had never been seasick, but he also knew that motion sickness, like flu, could strike at any moment. Garwood patted the bench seat behind the console where he sat, indicating that Service should join him.

"We got shit for power. Putting the weight back here will help us get onto a plane," he yelled as he pushed up the throttle. The boat's nose rose up and the motor howled and groaned as the boat drove through the surface resistance and began to skip over the water, dislodging a fine spray that soaked both of them. Service used his hand to brace himself on the console as the boat raced along, slapping the waves beneath them.

"We're running south toward Round Island," the sergeant shouted. "We got a tip last night from a tourist that some rat fishermen out of Fairport and Garden are working whitefish spawners. No way to tell if this will amount to anything, but we have to check it out. Keep your eyes open and do what I tell you."

Service nodded, uncased his binoculars, and began scanning ahead.

Twenty-five minutes later Round Island appeared over the bow, and Garwood was pointing with his binoculars. Service saw a white boat with a horizontal red stripe and a huge outboard motor. Two men seemed to be scrambling to pull in nets.

The sergeant shoved the throttle forward and Service glanced at the instruments, which showed 32 mph, the tachometer at 5,000 rpm, and near its red line. "This is all we have!" Garwood yelped.

Service saw the striped white boat's motor come to life, its nose lift, and bubbles erupt from the stern. One of the two crewmen was dumping something out of white boxes over the back.

"How many boxes?" Garwood asked.

"Four," Service called out. "So far."

Despite having speed and the angle coming in, the white boat began to steadily pull away from them. As they passed the area where the boxes had been dumped, Service caught a glimpse of fish floating in the water. "Whitefish, I think," he yelled as they raced past them, knowing they could have been anything.

The sergeant nodded, picked up the ship-to-shore radio microphone, and requested ground units be dispatched to Fairport. Service had no idea why Garwood thought the boat was headed to Fairport instead of Garden, but he kept his mouth shut and let the sergeant do his job.

"ETA, thirty minutes," Garwood said, concluding his transmission. "Marine Patrol One clear."

At 12:40 P.M. Service saw the two-hundred-foot-high multicolored limestone cliffs of Burn't Bluff looming ahead. The white boat continued to steadily pull away.

"This bloody equipment—" the sergeant griped, not finishing his thought. Service saw him pushing the throttle so hard that it looked like he'd risk breaking it off if it would have produced more power.

Service saw another boat appear in front of them and run parallel to the white boat, keeping up with it. Both boats were two hundred and fifty yards ahead, but he could see that the second craft's motor was a huge red Evinrude.

As the two boats rounded Burn't Bluff heading southeast, the two craft separated, the new arrival veering northeast toward Sac Bay and the white boat cutting due west toward open water. After four or five minutes the white boat angled sharply back to the southeast and accelerated, raising a gaudy roostertail.

"Fairport for sure," the marine safety sergeant called out.

Just before 1 P.M. Service saw through his binoculars what looked to be a pier on the west end of the village. Beyond it were at least two more, one of which led to a commercial fish house, the other cluttered with moored commercial fishing tugs. The piers looked crude, made of nothing more than large black boulders held together by aged gray railroad ties, laid horizontally. As they passed three hundred yards offshore, Service saw four vehicles pull up to the westernmost pier and discharge eight people. Two men from a lime-green pickup with a white camper cap brandished rifles.

"Guns," he reported to Garwood, who didn't alter course.

Service heard the report of a rifle followed almost immediately by a splash not five feet from their port side. A second shot was not as close, but in the same general midship area, and Service hunched slightly as the bullet ricocheted off the water and zipped over their heads.

Garwood didn't flinch.

The white boat stopped at the pier cluttered with larger cigar-shaped commercial fish tugs, but nobody got off, and as the Glastron closed the gap, the back of the white boat erupted in froth and bubbles as it took off racing west. Garwood cut his wheel to get in behind the white boat and shorten the distance between them, playing the angle. As they zoomed back past the western pier in pursuit, the white boat cut sharply to starboard and reversed direction back to the east.

"They're trying to suck us in!" the sergeant yelled as they headed back for the tug dock. Garwood didn't alter course.

Service heard another shot and saw a water spout twenty feet directly in front of them. A second shot stitched the water twenty feet to their port side, and Service shouted, "More shots fired!"

Garwood was immediately on the radio, profanely wanting to know where their "goddamn land units" were, but the radio was silent.

They were beginning to close on the tug dock when the white boat turned sharply, its bow coming up out of the water, pivoted, steadied, and came roaring directly back at them. Service immediately saw somebody on the bow with a rifle. Four shots sounded in close order, but Service didn't see where the rounds hit because the Glastron swerved sharply as Garwood began to zigzag in evasive maneuvers. The hunters had suddenly become the hunted.

"Drop line!" Garwood screamed. "Throw the line!" he said, gesticulating at an equipment box. Service grabbed handfuls of nylon coils and began flinging them over the stern.

"Cocksuckers!" Garwood cursed, aiming the Glastron for shoals between Summer and Little Summer islands. Once into the shallows, he retarded the throttle to idle and cut the wheel hard, causing the boat to yaw sideways in a lazy circle. "Line?" Serviced asked as the motor idled.

"To foul their props," the sergeant replied. "Sometimes it works."

The white boat immediately turned back toward Fairport and Garwood slammed the throttle forward and renewed pursuit.

As they passed the north tip of Summer Island, Service saw a small aluminum boat near shore. It had a large blue motor and two men in red hunting clothes, both with rifles aimed at the DNR boat. He tapped the sergeant's shoulder and pointed. "More long guns."

"This is how Custer felt!" Garwood said with a distressed laugh as he pushed the throttle to red line, and veered northwest to keep out of rifle range.

In the process of avoiding the potential ambush they lost sight of the white boat, but as they approached the Fairport fish house dock they saw a CO patrol car parked near it and three more DNR vehicles quickly roll in behind it, spilling their passengers. Garwood roared toward the end of the dock and cut the throttle. As they drifted past, a stocky blond man with a scoped, high-powered rifle jumped on board, unslung a second rifle, and thrust it at Service.

"How many shots fired?" the man asked.

Service thought for a moment. "Eight—four we saw hit the water."

"Damage?"

Garwood shook his head. "Service threw line."

"You get their prop?"

Garwood shook his head again. "Did the white boat pull in?"

The new man said no. Garwood headed west, and they began to poke into every bay and inlet north of Fairport toward Garden. During the search the new man introduced himself as Len Stone. He wore the three stripes of a sergeant on his jacket sleeve.

Later Garwood picked up the mike and radioed Fayette State Park.

"This is Marine Patrol One. We're low on fuel; can we top off with you?"

"Affirmative," came the reply from the park, which was between Fairport and Garden.

As they motored into Snail Shell Harbor, the small bay in front of the park, the radio crackled. "This is Air Four, Blake. I've got a white boat in a slip in Fairport."

"We'll head down that way as soon as refueling is complete," Garwood radioed. "Thanks, Pranger."

Service asked, "Is that Joe Flap?"

Garwood nodded.

Joe Flap had been a contemporary of his father's. Flap had been a DNR pilot, but when the department came under budget constraints, he had become a CO; when budgets were healthy again, he resumed flying for the DNR. The pilot had flown combat in Korea with the marines and for the U.S. Forest Service out west after that. He had come to Michigan after a stint of bush flying in Alaska and northwest Canada, and had crashed so many times he was nicknamed Pranger. Service had always assumed that Flap would leave Michigan and head back west or to Alaska. He was surprised to hear his voice.

Heading south, the radio came to life again. It was one of the shore units. "Where are you right now, Marine Patrol One?"

"Sac Bay headed southeast," the marine safety sergeant reported.

"Hold your position. We've got a Troop unit with us and we'll go down to the docks and check out Air Four's report."

"Marine Patrol One is clear," Garwood said, cutting the throttle to idle and allowing the boat to wallow into the rocky confines of the small bay. There was no sign of the boat with the Evinrude motor that had ducked into the bay during the earlier pursuit of the white craft.

Thirty minutes later they got word that the boat in the slip did not have a red stripe and that all seemed quiet in Fairport.

"Okay," Garwood said to Stone and Service, "let's pack it in for today."

It took two hours to get back to the Fishdam River launch, and while they pulled the boat, a mud-spattered blue pickup did a donut in the lot and sped away too quickly to get a license plate. Service saw only that the driver was a dark-haired male and his passenger, a woman with long, unkempt blond hair.

As they prepared to leave, the same vehicle came by twice on US 2, the last time racing east toward the Garden Peninsula.

Garwood walked with Service to his patrol unit. "This was a good tip, and if our equipment was equal to theirs we could have had them," he said wistfully.

"Is this a normal patrol down here?" Service asked.

The sergeant shrugged. "What's normal? If we don't change our tactics or upgrade our equipment soon, we're gonna keep sucking hind tit with these rats."

Stone said with a hiss, "Dis is so much *bullshit*," and drove off with Garwood.

Service drove around the perimeter of the Mosquito Wilderness on the way to his 1953 Airstream trailer, thinking about the frustration of the day's mission and the intensity he'd seen in Garwood and Stone. He didn't really think much about getting shot at, because he had been in that position before and this time the firepower was limited. He got into his bunk just after 10 P.M. and rolled around, trying to get comfortable. His last thought before falling asleep was that he needed to build a damn cabin and stop living like a damn gypsy.

4

ESCANABA, DECEMBER 15, 1975

". . . Only a fool pokes a stick into a hornet's nest."

The small conference room in the Escanaba DNR office was smothered in attitude, expressed mainly in body language. There were twenty conservation officers jammed into the room, all of them from the two law enforcement districts that spanned the north shore of Lake Michigan. The room was as quiet as the aftermath of a fatal accident, in part because the officers were only a couple of weeks out of the fifteen-day-long firearms deer season and nearly worn out from long days and nights, dealing with every imaginable human behavior. Service felt a mixture of gloom and anger in the air. He found a seat behind the other officers and sat quietly. Several of the men nodded to acknowledge his presence, but nothing was said. Even the usually ebullient Colton Homes looked glum. Homes was in his early thirties, a six-foot Sumo with chipmunk cheeks, a military haircut, a perpetual smile that implied that he was up to something, and black horn-rim glasses that made him look like a hungry owl.

They waited ten minutes before two unsmiling lieutenants and Captain Cosmo Metrovich sashayed into the room. Metrovich was the Upper Peninsula's regional law enforcement supervisor; his officers called him the law boss, and in the U.P. he was the penultimate authority for game wardens. Service had been in the U.P. nearly a year and a half, and whenever Metrovich's name came up, even over beers, nothing was said about the man, good or bad. Maybe the silence was because he was new to the force, Service thought, but in the Marine Corps, and even in the Michigan State Police, gossip and carping about supervision was a refined art. He had expected much the same from COs, but so far had not seen it and wondered what this signified. His company commander in Vietnam had always insisted a bitching grunt was a happy grunt.

"All right, men," Metrovich began. "I've asked both districts here today to review the strategy for the Garden Peninsula."

Sergeant Lennox Stone from Menominee thrust his hand in the air and waved it like a tomahawk.

Service's only exposure to Stone had been the one bizarre and frustrating marine patrol on Big Bay de Noc, and that day Stone had not bothered with small talk. All Service knew was that Stone, like himself, was a native Yooper, and that he was reputed to have started with the DNR when he was fourteen, sitting in fire towers, and later working as a state hunter, trapping, poisoning, shooting, and removing problem animals before taking a game warden's position. Stone, in his mid-forties, was short and barrel-chested with piercing blue eyes and a shock of blond hair overrun with cowlicks.

"Far as we know," Stone said, "dere ain't no strategy down dere to da Garden."

Service saw Homes and a couple of other officers nod in agreement, and based on his one-time experience down there, he had to agree that unlike the marines, where every action was thought out in advance, it was difficult to see any strategy in effect in the Garden.

The captain showed a tight-lipped grin. "It's good to have a man willing to speak up," Metrovich said. "We're a team, and I expect all of you men to speak your minds," he added.

"Maybe da boys is full-up saying how dey feel and gettin' ignored," Stone said, putting his hand just under his chin. "Dose outlaws down to da Garden do as dey damn well please, Cap'n."

"Not everyone in the Garden Peninsula is an outlaw," Metrovich said, sharply correcting his sergeant.

Stone ignored the rebuke. "We know da ones in da cemeteries sure ain't—at least no more, Cap'n—but all da rest of dem we got our doubts about, eh?"

More nodding heads and a few smiles.

"You cannot paint all residents with the same brush," the captain said.

"Like to paint 'em wit' tar and feathers is what," Stone mumbled.

The captain slapped the table. "*This* is the problem!" he said forcefully. "You men have to look at the big picture . . . and at history. These people have lived off fish for generations, and we have to expect—and try to *understand*—that it will take time for them to adjust to the new rules and regulations."

Stone didn't back down. "Cap'n, dat buncha rats has never followed rules or laws, and even if you don't wanta see it, dey've declared war on us. We got good officers don't want to go down dere because dey know dey won't get no support. Even county and Troops don't go down dere unless dey got to. Dis Order Seventeen's got no teeth."

Service saw that Captain Metrovich looked uneasy and heard a shift in his voice. "All right, while it's accurate that Order Seventeen does not carry criminal penalties, I will remind all of us that there are license revocation procedures clearly outlined, and these *will* be adhered to, understood?" the captain said. "Due process, gentlemen, due process."

Stone grimaced. "No offense, but you call dat strategy, Cap'n, to act like gentlemen wit' a buncha rats?"

The supercilious Metrovich glared at the sergeant. "We do not have to become the animals we hunt," the captain said haughtily. "This is not the good old days when game wardens did their talking with their fists."

Stone said, "Wit' all due respect, Cap'n, whatever it is we're doin', it ain't workin'. Maybe it's time to go back to da old ways, or give da boys somepin' different."

Service saw that even Lieutenant Dean Attalienti nodded at this. The other lieutenant, Cooper Edey, showed no reaction. Edey was responsible for the district that contained the Garden Peninsula, but he was retiring soon, seldom showed emotion, pretty much went along with what Metrovich wanted in order to get along with him, and, Service had heard, never went on risky patrols with his men. Technically, Edey was his boss, and so far, with the single exception of his one unscheduled Garden run, Edey and his sergeant had left him alone in the Mosquito, which suited Service just fine.

"The strategy," Metrovich said, "is stated thusly: Only a fool pokes a stick into a hornet's nest."

Stone huffed audibly. "Dis ting's about money, Cap'n, and I say if it's about money, den we need to make some dents in dere bloody wallets."

Attalienti stepped up beside the captain. "What have you got in mind, Len?"

"Order Seventeen is administrative wit' no criminal penalties, and only if da bad guys repeatedly violate da rule, can we start proceedin's to revoke dere licenses. But all dis takes a long time, and meanwhile da bastards keep dere stuff and dey're out dere still takin' fish and makin' good money. Dose rats down dere tell da newspapers dey take fish to keep off welfare, which is a buncha hooey, eh. Dose rats got fifty-t'ousand-dollar houses, got new trucks, got new snow machines, and dey got new boats wid two-hunnert-horse motors dat leave us suckin' wind. Seventeen says where and when dey can fish and what dey can fish for, so I say we see anyting even suggests dey're violatin', we move in, seize dere nets, take dere boats, grab dere motors, secure dere snowmobiles, seize *anyting* dey need to fish and impound da whole stinkin' bloody lot and immediately start condemnation proceedings."

Captain Metrovich was shaking his head, trying to reason with Stone. "Proceedings take a long time, and what you're suggesting surely would be reversed by the courts. It would undoubtedly be characterized as illegal seizure—and harassment."

"Maybe," Stone said, "but we all know dat dose courts don't move so fast, an' every day we got dere gear, dose assholes down dere to da Garden won't be takin' fish. We don't need no criminal penalties in Order Seventeen. All we gotta do is grab dere stuff an' trow it all inta da courts and make da rats hire lawyers ta get it back."

The room began to buzz and Captain Metrovich had to hold up his hands to reassert control. "We *have* a policy," he repeated. "We will make our patrols and enforce the laws we have and, if there are violations of Order Seventeen, we will follow the extant process. Am I being clear?"

Even Stone took this declaration stoically.

"One final item," Metrovich said. "Chief Nill is stepping down, and I have been asked to deploy to Lansing for six months to serve as acting chief. In my absence Lt. Attalienti will be acting captain."

"Why's the chief steppin' down?" Colt Homes asked.

"He has a health problem," Metrovich said, not expanding.

None of the men congratulated Metrovich on his assignment and none of them stuck around to talk. They got up en masse and quickly left the building.

Service was walking to his vehicle to head for home when Attalienti pulled him aside. "You know where the Beer Barrel is?"

"The bar in Rock?"

"Be there tonight at seven-thirty. Wear civvies and drive your personal vehicle. Park behind the house with the barber pole out front, hoof it over to the bar, and don't be late."

"I'm supposed to work tonight," Service protested, his mind already back in the Mosquito Wilderness on things he needed to do there.

"This *will* be work," the new acting captain said, walking away.

Now what the hell was going on? Service wondered. Since he'd gotten into the Garden mess, nothing made sense, and he was beginning to feel frustrations that reminded him of those he thought he had left behind in Vietnam.

5

ROCK, DECEMBER 15, 1975

"I'd rather get stung in the face than in the ass."

Service found it mildly ironic that he couldn't remember the last time he'd seen a train run the railroad tracks that paralleled Rock. It was a town settled by railroad workers and known as Malton Spur and Maple Ridge before being named Rock by a long-forgotten postmaster. The area was well named: Glaciers had left a deep layer of drift rock that had to be turned over before any planting could be done, and as far as Service knew, the only reliable crop remained rocks and some small, hard potatoes and stunted sugar beets, equally hard. Rock was a town without flair, and it was appropriate that the Beer Barrel was a two-fisted drinker's bar that made no pretense of being anything other than what it was.

Service was dressed in jeans, a red plaid wool shirt, and a black down vest. He parked his black ten-year-old Ford pickup behind a white shotgun house with an ancient and faded barber pole out front, and walked a hundred yards over an icy gravel parking lot to the bar. The interior was dark, the floor and furniture nicked, and he and the acting captain appeared to be the only ones there. Attalienti led him upstairs to a small office, opened a small door in the floor beside an old oak desk, and said, "Sit here and keep quiet. Your job is to listen." Service nodded and sat down, wondering if the acting captain had all his marbles.

The meeting in the room below didn't start for another hour, and over that time a dozen officers filtered in to be greeted by Attalienti and Sergeants Garwood and Stone.

Service's viewpoint was directly above tables pushed together in the main bar. Attalienti sat among the men, Stone and Garwood on either side of him. "I called you here because I think Len is right about this Garden money angle," Attalienti began. "I think our lawyers in Lansing may get their assholes tight, but the Garden deal *is* about money, so we're gonna put some bodies on this and poke the stick into the hornet's nest." The acting captain paused to let the words sink in, and added, "I'd rather get stung in the face than in the ass."

Service saw all the men grin.

Attalienti continued, "You men are here because you're going to be the core team, even if you're in different districts. I don't mean to disparage anyone, but we have some officers who're not crazy about patrolling the Garden. You men may not be crazy about it either, but knowing what I know about each of you, I think you'll go. You've been hand-picked for this."

Service saw more nodding and sensed an unspoken swell of determination in the room below.

"Edey has decided to retire in January. As acting captain, I will appoint Len Stone to be acting lieutenant in Edey's stead. Len will spearhead this effort," Attalienti said.

Eddie Moody, a new officer from Manistique, leaned forward. "Do we put the hammer on the rats right away?"

"No," Attalienti said. "The big push will start in April after the ice goes out and the walleye and perch spawns begin. Between now and then we will conduct routine road and snowmobile patrols."

Colt Homes spoke up. "How is dat different?"

"Nobody goes solo into the Garden," Attalienti said. "No exceptions."

Stone spoke up. "We never go down dere wit' fewer den two vehicles and four men. I'll always be one of da four. We'll conduct no patrols without having county and Troop resources on standby. Between now and April we'll go down dere, varying our days an' times. Dey've been outnumbering us down dere, but we're gonna try to rectify dat, and when April comes we'll start going in with *real* force."

"You'll be on *every* patrol?" Moody asked Stone.

The blond sergeant said, "Can't let you boys have all da fun, can I?"

This lightened the mood in the room, and for more than an hour, Service listened and made notes while the officers and supervisors talked about rendezvous points, communications and backup procedures, and other technical matters.

After the men were gone, Attalienti walked with Service to his truck.

"You hear okay?"

Service nodded.

"That seem like work enough for you?"

"Yessir," Service said.

"You're probably wondering why I had you stashed upstairs, and I'll answer that. You were a recon marine in Vietnam, and I know you keep your cool and use your brain. Garwood said you didn't flinch during your patrol with him, and Shuck Gorley made a special point of calling me to talk about you—and I can tell you, Shuck is *real* picky about endorsing people. When I was an officer working with him, it took five years for him to decide I could be trusted. I have a job I'd like for you to do, but if you accept, what you're doing will be strictly between us, understood?"

Service nodded.

Attalienti continued. "I understand how Len Stone feels, but Metrovich also has a valid point: Not everybody who lives on the Garden is a rat. Our main focus there has been the major commercial operations out of Garden and Fairport, the ones with the tugs, paid crews, and wholesale fish houses, but they already feel our presence. The guys I want to put the heat on now are the rat fishermen, the greedy little bastards with fast boats who flaunt the law and do whatever they please. We're gonna put a dent in them."

"But?" Service said.

"You can't dent something you can't identify. I've been contacted by a Garden resident who's fed up with behavior down there and wants to help us. Frankly, I don't know if this is legit, a provocation, or hooey. But if it's real, it means I need to send somebody into the Garden alone to work with the contact."

"How do we beat the crow line?" The Garden was famous for its early warning system—a series of homes with lookouts who immediately used their telephones to report the appearance of any marked police vehicle on Garden Road, the main route down the peninsula.

"That will be your problem to solve," the acting captain said.

"Me?"

"I want you to go down there. Chances of one of the rats recognizing you is minimal, and you haven't been involved in this mess long enough to be affected by the confusion and lack of direction. If you volunteer, you'll report to me directly until you can authenticate the veracity of the volunteer informant. If you develop doubts—and I mean the *slightest* tickle in your gut—we're gonna drop this. But if you think it feels right, I want you to go undercover to observe and gather information. You will be there strictly for surveillance. You will *not* be enforcing laws. Your job will be to stay invisible until you can gather what we need and get the hell out. *Capisce?*"

"What about the Mosquito?"

"Others will cover your area for you, and you're going to be out at a time when there won't be much going on anyway. Are you in?"

Service said, "Who's my contact?"

"It's good you volunteered," Attalienti said with a grin. "You were asked for by name." He had a twinkle in his eye. "The contact is a prominent personality in the Garden and is concerned about maintaining confidentiality. They'll come to you."

"When?"

"Soon, I'd think," the acting captain said. "Come see me afterwards."

Service asked, "How will Lansing react to this?"

Attalienti grinned, "Hell of a lot easier to ask for forgiveness than permission. I want to know who the rats are, who leads them, how they stage operations, their land-side tactics, meeting and gathering places— everything you can learn that will help us to understand who and what we're dealing with. Observe and learn—do not act. Understood?"

Service nodded, but he wasn't really paying attention. Why had he been asked for by name, and why the hell did this feel more and more like Vietnam?

· 6 ·

SLIPPERY CREEK, DECEMBER 17, 1975

. . . he wondered if having one leg halved discomfort, or doubled it . . .

It had been two days since the meeting in Rock, two days of routine patrols in the Mosquito. Conservation Officer Grady Service arrived home at Slippery Creek the way he had departed the night before—running dark, no interior lights, no headlights. It had begun to snow the previous afternoon, and overnight the storm had left six fluffy inches on the ground.

There were tracks leading up his road, and next to the trailer he saw a small dark pickup still sweating snow off its metal skin. The tracks told him it had arrived not long before him.

He parked behind the truck and approached it cautiously. He had spent last night's patrol alone, and the sudden appearance of another human being always put him on alert.

The driver's window slid down. "Officer Service?" He nodded. "We need to talk." The voice came from a face cocooned in a parka hood pulled tight around a gaunt face.

He nodded, opened the cabin door, and left it open as he shed his own parka and boots.

"Sorry to barge in on you like this," the voice said from the doorway.

"Coffee?" he asked, glancing over and seeing that she had no left leg and a metal crutch attached to her left wrist.

"Could use it," the woman said, closing the door. She took off her parka and unzipped her knee-high boot, which folded over. It had a feminine contour and a low heel.

"Fixings or black?" Service asked over his shoulder.

"Natural," she said.

The woman sat silently while Service began to boil coffee. His father had always boiled coffee and though it was too strong for most people, it was what Service preferred.

"Am I interrupting something?" she asked when he turned back to the table with cups and saucers that didn't match.

"No." He was used to being called on at all hours.

He brought the pot to the table, filled two cups, and sat down. His feet felt cold from a night in boots and snow, and he wondered if having one leg halved discomfort, or doubled it, from winter cold.

She grinned slyly. "One leg is like half a glass of water. Am I half empty or half full?"

"What can I do for you?" he asked, cursing himself for fixating on the one leg. *Dope*, he told himself.

She sipped the strong coffee and showed no reaction. "Your Captain Attalienti said I could talk to you, so the real question is what can I do for you people—not vice versa. I'm Cecilia Lasurm," she said with a formal air. She had a low, gravelly voice, jet-black hair cut short, a long neck poking out of a thick black turtleneck, no makeup or jewelry. Her eyes were huge and engaging, a faded blue color with green streaks.

"I teach in the Garden," she said. "Born there, went to school up to Northern, and came back to live and teach."

"Garden or Fairport?" Service asked.

"This shows how little you people know," she said. "I live in between," she said, "but the only *school* is north of Garden and it's called Big Bay de Noc. The Garden, Cooks, and Nahma school districts consolidated years ago."

"I'm sure the officers who are down there regularly know this," he said.

"Granted," she said, "but there are a number of obvious things they don't see or understand. I'm not a particularly subtle woman," his guest announced. "The Garden is controlled by a bunch of thugs and punks. Most people there don't want it that way, but if you go against them, your barn burns, your tires get cut, and windows start breaking."

Service understood. The lawless had always harassed the law-abiding into deaf- and dumbness in some reaches of the U.P.

"I've spent nearly a year trying to find the right man, asking around, talking to people, trying to find the most competent game warden I could. Word is you're new and cut no slack for scofflaws. I don't need a knuckle-dragger. I want a thinker," she added.

"There are a lot more experienced people than me," he said. "The Garden isn't my turf."

"I want you, and Attalienti says you're my contact. I also know that the DNR brings men in from all over the U.P. to handle jobs in the Garden. Right now your officers are not there as often as they used to be, and the local jerks think they've driven you out. I came to trade."

Service leaned forward.

Lasurm continued. "There's only one main road in and out, and the outlaws have lookouts and a CB-radio and telephone system for passing the word when the law comes down Garden Road. They probably have the back way covered too, but that road's narrow and too easy to cut off and trap a lawman, so you're forced to use the western route to go south, or come in by water; either way, you can't exactly sneak in. What you people lack is information—a scorecard, who does what to whom. I can give you that."

"How?"

"I teach at the elementary school, and I am also the district's so-called visiting teacher—which means I go to houses to take lessons to shut-in kids. I have the kids and relatives of all the troublemakers in my classroom, and have for the past few years. Some of those kids are in high school or just out. When you have a job like mine, you hear and see things others don't. For example, I can tell when the fish runs start and the rats go to work because their kids help unload fish, and the spines of the walleyes and perch puncture their hands. I see it every year. It's like being a priest."

"A priest can't break the confidence of the confessional."

"Don't be literal. I said *like* a priest." She frowned. "If somebody doesn't start talking and teaching you people what in blazes is going on, we're going to be at war for a long time, and sooner or later one of those potshots is going to hit somebody and all hell will break loose."

Interesting, Service thought. "What do you get out of this?" he asked.

For the next hour she explained, and though he didn't agree with some of her assumptions and theories, he realized that if she knew as much as she claimed, she could be the key that would finally open the Garden Peninsula to the law. All she wanted in return for her coop-eration was that the Garden normalize for a few years so the kids now in elementary school could grow up in an environment where locals were not always pitted against all outsiders—DNR, trolls, sportfisher-men—anyone "not from the Garden." Her intensity was palpable. "You realize if they catch you down there alone, they might kill you," she concluded.

She had given him enough tidbits to convince him she was worth the risk. "I can't promise anything," he said, knowing the go, no-go deci-sion was his.

"You just take the offer where you have to and when you're ready, put an ad in the Manistique classifieds." She handed him a piece of paper that read MATTHEW 7:7.

"You run this and a date, time, and place, and I'll be there to talk," she said.

"Matthew seven-seven?" he asked.

"Ask, and it shall be given you; seek, and ye shall find; knock, and it shall be opened unto you."

"I thought you weren't subtle."

Cecilia Lasurm smiled.

7

MARQUETTE, DECEMBER 19, 1975

" . . . you're well suited for this secret squirrel stuff."

Attalienti had moved to Cosmo Metrovich's office in the Marquette DNR building adjacent to Marquette Prison, which had been built before the turn of the century and housed some of the state's most dangerous criminals. The architecture of the regional office featured a strange roof with hooked ends that resembled the beaks of birds of prey. Officers referred to the regional office as The Roof.

It was almost closing time and Fern LeBlanc, Metrovich's long-legged secretary, gave Service the once-over before ushering him to the captain's office, which looked out toward Lake Superior a few hundred yards away.

Service closed the door and stood in front of the captain's desk at parade rest.

"Relax," Attalienti said. "Coffee?"

"Had my daily ten-cup ration," Service said, sitting down.

"Make your contact?"

"Yessir," Service said, quickly relating the specifics of the visit from Cecilia Lasurm.

The acting captain listened impassively, his hands on the blotter in front of him, and when Service had finished, asked, "What do you think?"

"I think we've never had an opportunity like this before and maybe we won't have another one."

"How do you want to proceed?"

"I spend time with her, pick her brain, and look over the area."

"How will you beat the crow line?"

"I don't know yet," Service said, "but to maintain secrecy once I have a plan, I don't think I should reveal it, even to you."

Attalienti grinned. "I think maybe you're well suited for this secret squirrel stuff."

"I want to take two weeks, longer if needed."

The acting captain looked surprised. "Two weeks is a heckuva long time to arrange coverage for your area."

"This is either worth doing right or not doing at all. We have time now, and you said we won't start the real operation until April. If I'm going down there, I don't want to waste my time."

"If you can take the pulse of that place, you won't be wasting your time, but operating alone carries inherent risks."

"Understood," Service said.

"Not just the risks to you, but to the woman as well. You have to get in and out of there without footprints. We can't implicate her."

"She wants to do this, and so do I. My gut says it's the right thing to do."

"Do you always trust your gut, Grady?"

"Yessir."

"Good," Attalienti said. "All I ask is that you let me know the timing so I can arrange coverage. We're going to say you are on leave for a family emergency."

"Thank you." He didn't bother to point out that he had no family.

"When you take out the ad in the Manistique paper, use an intermediary to place it."

"Sir?"

"Let's not underestimate that Garden crowd. At times it seems like they have our playbook."

"I didn't think we had one," Service said.

"We don't, but we're trying to develop one, and this is the sort of paranoia those assholes can create. The best way to cover a trail is to not have one in the first place," the acting captain said.

8

SLIPPERY CREEK, DECEMBER 24, 1975

Naked Skydivers Go Down Faster.

G rady Service pulled into the clearing where his Airstream was tucked away and saw a red pickup that was both vaguely familiar and out of place. He used his radio to report out of service, and sat wondering what this was about. He took out his notebook and leafed through the pages.

On the opening day of deer season Service had found a red Ford pickup parked in the lower Mosquito River area. That night he had monitored the truck until after dark, waiting for the hunter to come out. When it got to be an hour after shooting hours, he began to wonder if the truck had been dropped off and the hunter gone elsewhere with friends. It had snowed steadily since midday, and there were no tracks into the dense line of naked tamaracks that served as a natural windbreak for the massive cedar swamp beyond.

He had called in the license number for warrants and wants and come up empty. The license number in his notebook matched the plate on the truck now parked near his trailer. His notes showed that the truck was registered to a Brigid Mehegen of Harvey, which was just south of Marquette. She had been born in 1947, which made her twenty-eight. That night he had just about decided to drive on when he saw a flashlight bobbing through the trees. He walked over to the truck, keeping the cab between the approaching light and him, and waited.

There were audible grunts interspersed with muted curses, and when he stepped out to identify himself, a woman chirped, "You got a broken back?" She had a rifle slung over her shoulder and looked tired.

"Pardon?"

"I hauled a damn buck all the way to the tamaracks. Least you could do is offer to help."

"Let's go," he said.

The deer was just inside the tree line. Service illuminated it with his penlight. It was a huge, black ten-point animal. The tag was correctly affixed to an antler.

"Swamp buck," he said.

"Here," she said, working the lever to show him the rifle was unloaded, and handing him a beat-up Winchester 94. She pulled off her hat and ran her hand through medium-length brown hair. "I thought I hit 'im pretty good, but it took me till mid-afternoon to find the sonuvagun. He swam the river and crawled under a blowdown. Funny how wounded deer head for water," she added. "You think people have the same inclination?"

Service didn't know and didn't care. Mid-afternoon: How far back had she been? The river was more than a mile from where they stood. "What time did you shoot it?"

"A little after nine this morning. I took an hour to drink half my coffee to give the big bugger time to lay down, but when I went after him all I found was some hair and a little blood and I figured it was damn gutshot. I had a partial trail for about two hundred yards, then nothing. Thank God he went to the river and started bleeding more."

"You crossed the river?"

"Yeah, twice, but it wasn't too bad because the old adrenaline was pumping, eh. Now I'm *freezing*," she said, her teeth chattering.

He was not sure whether to be impressed at her determination or her foolishness. The thermometer was almost down to twenty, under a bitter and stiffening northwest wind. Being wet in such conditions invited exposure and hypothermia. He grabbed the deer's antlers, but she pushed his hand away and dragged the deer to her truck alone. She let him help her heave it into the bed and he let her get in the cab, start the engine, and turn on the heater. She took off her gloves and put her hands over the vents, waiting for the warm air to come.

She handed him her hunting license and driver's license without him having to ask.

"I've been dogging this big boy since July," she said. "My own fault I made a lousy shot, but I wasn't going to lose him to jerks or brush wolves."

Brush wolf was the Yooper term for a coyote. "Been hunting long?" he asked. A woman hunting was unusual. Alone was unprecedented, even in the U.P. where women were famous for going their own way.

"My grandfather started taking me with him when I was ten, and I went on my own as soon as I was sixteen. I've gotten a buck every single year, but this is the best one so far. I used to hunt the high country west of Cliff's Ridge, but the damn ski resort crowd got to be too much to deal with. Bampy used to hunt down this way and he told me where to come." She paused for a second and added, "Sorry I jumped you for not helping. I can get a tad cranky when I get tired and cold."

"It's okay," he said, handing her licenses back to her. Bathsheba had gotten more than cranky when she was cold, and nearly as often when she was warm.

"You're Service," she said, and added, "I'm Brigid Mehegen, a Troop dispatcher out of Negaunee," she said. "It's my job to keep track of new law enforcement personnel in the area."

"Grady," he said.

"Thanks again," she said, closing her door and rolling down her window. "With all the deer you guys confiscate, you probably eat venison year-round," she said with a gleam in her eye. This myth—that they allegedly took home all the illegal game they confiscated—irritated all game wardens.

"Not that often," he said defensively. In fact, all the illegal game that officers confiscated went to families and shut-ins who needed food.

She laughed out loud. "I'm puttin' you on, guy! I know you're all a buncha Boy Scouts."

"That old buck is likely to be tough," he said. Who *was* this woman?

"Not the way I'll cook it," she said. "See you around sometime," she said, putting the truck into gear and driving away.

Three or four times since deer season she had been the on-duty dispatcher when he was on the radio, and she had given him a bump and made wisecracks about the cushy life of game wardens and how he'd better be nice if he wanted Santa Claus to come. He had smiled and shook his head when he heard her on the radio, but didn't think much more about it. He met a lot of peculiar people in the woods, and she was just one of many. The dispatcher was totally unlike his ex-wife who had dispatched their marriage.

He had not seen her in six weeks, but as he got out of his patrol unit, Brigid Mehegen popped out of her truck. She was wearing a red parka and beat-up Sorels.

"I hope you have an oven in that little bitty rig," she greeted him.

"A small one."

"Size doesn't count as long as it gets hot," she said with a wink.

He stood staring at her as she opened the passenger door of her truck. "Help?" she said.

They carried two large cardboard boxes and a smaller one into the trailer. He turned up the heat and helped her take off her coat.

"Beer's in the bed of my truck," she said, taking something in aluminum foil out of a box and putting it on the tiny counter in the area that served as his kitchen and dining room.

There were two six-packs of Strohs long-neckers in a paper bag in the truck bed, and when he came back inside, Mehegen had shed her sweater. She wore a T-shirt that proclaimed NAKED SKYDIVERS GO DOWN FASTER. It was clear she wore nothing underneath.

She took two bottles of Strohs from one of the six-packs and a church key out of one of her cardboard boxes, popped the caps, and handed a beer to Service. She tapped her bottle against his and said, "*Slainte.* I cooked the roast this afternoon; now let me get it warming and boil some water for the potatoes. I brought plastic plates. I figure why waste time doing dishes when we can toss them, right? My environmentalist friends would throw an eco-freaky hissy-fit, but what the hey—what they don't know can't sour their stomachs, right? You like garlic in your mashed spuds?"

He nodded, and she said in a husky voice, "Okay, drink your beer and get outta that monkey suit while I do some woman's work."

Service opened the bathroom door to serve as a wall, shed his uniform, and put on sweatpants, wool socks, slip-on logger boots, and a plaid wool shirt.

Mehegen was sitting down when he stepped back to the other end of the Airstream. She held up her bottle like a pointer. "It's Christmas Eve and neither of us has another to fuss over, but I don't want you jumping to the conclusion that I came here to get laid," she said.

He had no idea how to respond.

"Unless *you* think that's a good idea," she added. "Do you?"

He felt his face reddening and she laughed. "Okay, I can see the Boy Scout game warden's not all that comfortable with a direct female. No sweat. Let's just enjoy this dinner and get to know each other. But no cop-shop talk. I talk to cops all day, every day, and while I appreciate what all you guys do, I get sick of the yammer. Okay by you?"

He found himself dumbly nodding.

She got up when the water boiled and dropped small red potatoes into the pot. Then she took something out of the smallest box and put it on the table.

"You know about *Luciadagen?*"

"Is that like Sadie Hawkins Day?"

She laughed so hard that tears formed in her eyes. "It's a Swedish deal, ya big lug, 'Saint Lucia's Day.' The Swedelanders in the old country used to celebrate it around December thirteenth, and considered it the first day of winter—never mind that they were a good week ahead of the actual solstice. They'd crown a young girl as the *Luciadagen* queen, and the women would start cooking around midnight. In the morning there'd be a feast, and afterwards they'd all go out skiing, maybe the men would shoot their rifles a bit, then they'd all jump in the sauna."

He stared at the glistening concoction on the table. It was shaped like a cat that had been hit by lightning.

"*Lussiketbröd,*" she explained. "It's part of the festival. Saffron dough brushed with egg whites, filled with sugar, cinnamon, chopped nuts, and raisins. Go ahead and knock off a piece," she said with a wink, handing him a small jackknife.

"Isn't this dessert?" he asked.

"Hey guy, it's Christmas Eve and we're celebrating. We don't have to stick to the rules, eh? Time for you to eat some of my cat," she added, lowering her eyes and smirking.

He did as she ordered and tasted the bread, which was light and sweet. "Good," he said.

"My cat tastes good?" she asked as he chewed.

"A little dry," he said.

She laughed and said, "That's the spirit!" She touched his arm. "She gets wetter as the meal goes on."

"Mehegen isn't a Swedish name," he said, awkwardly changing the subject.

"Yoopers, we're all a buncha mongrels, eh? We take what we like from all the cultures around us."

She took several garlic cloves, smashed them with the flat of a knife, took off their skins, snipped off their tops, wrapped them in aluminum foil with a little butter and chopped fresh chives, and put them into a warm oven.

When the potatoes boiled, Service tested them with a fork, drained them in a colander over the small sink, transferred them back to the pot, and mashed them for her. She insisted on adding the salt, pepper, garlic, and butter, and stuck the batch back on the burner.

She took his empty beer bottle, set it aside, and opened another for him. "Your wife left you over to Newberry," Mehegen said, opening another bottle for herself. "She couldn't cut it," she added.

Before he could react, she said, "Hey, I'm *not* snooping. Every cop in the Yoop makes it a point to know everything about every other cop up here."

He didn't bother to point out that she was a dispatcher, not a road officer, and as far as he was concerned, his private life was none of her business. Not that he had much of a private life anymore.

When the roast and potatoes were done to her satisfaction, she sent him out to her truck to fetch two bottles of wine from a warm sack in the backseat.

She let him open both bottles to let them breathe. "Red wine should be room temp, right? I bought that warming sack over to Green Bay. Cost me way too much, but up here with so much bloody cold, how do you carry wine around and drink it properly if you don't keep it warm? Be damned if I'll stoop to screwtop wine."

"Right," he said as she filled two plastic wineglasses with dark red liquid, handing him one as she sat down. "You want to say a prayer?" she asked.

"No, but you can."

"I don't pray," she said. "I plan." She held her glass up and touched it to his. "Dig in."

Service expected the roast to be tough, but it was tender and flavored with slices of onion, garlic, basil, and rosemary. Over dinner and wine she gave him her life's story. Age twenty-eight, divorced twice, not planning to trouble herself with marriage again. No boyfriend at the moment. She was working for the Michigan State Police, taking law enforcement classes at Northern. She had applied for the Troop Academy in Lansing even though the Troops had never hired a woman. She said her post commander assured her that it was being "seriously pursued at the senior command level," and in a couple of years would happen. Meanwhile, she would finish school and, if necessary, take a county job where she could find one.

"You're a skydiver?" he asked, looking at her T-shirt.

She smiled. "I thought you'd never ask." She pulled on her boots, clomped outside to her truck, brought in a diminutive eight-millimeter movie projector, plugged it in, and threaded on a spool of film. "This isn't all that long, but you might get a hoot out of it."

She refilled her wineglass. "Keep your yap zipped till it's done, okay?"

The film was amateurish, with the camera bouncing and jerking all over. Obviously the camera operator had jumped first, and then captured two people plummeting from the side door of a Beechcraft Bonanza. Service watched as the two spread their arms in free flight and flew toward each other. As the camera zoomed tighter he saw that it was a man and woman and they were wearing helmets and boots and nothing else, and when they got to each other, they somehow maneuvered and tried to copulate as they fell toward the ground. "Just like eagles," Mehegen said. "We jumped at twelve thousand. I had the camera."

The camera angle went from a view of the upcoming ground to actually being on the ground, watching the naked couple land and do their parachute landing falls, just as Service had learned to do in the marines.

The two were kissing and laughing and brushing off leaves and ground detritus. Then the camera was focused on a single woman, equally naked and bowing for the camera. It was Mehegen.

The film ran out and clicked as it spun on the spool. "Well?" she said.

"Art film, not a movie," he said.

She giggled. "I know *that* definition. Bare tits and ass make it art." She poured more wine for herself. "My friends had more fun than I did," she said. "That was my third jump and their fiftieth. I thought I'd wet myself waiting to go out the door."

"Did you?"

"No," she said as she took scoops of melted ice cream and put it on slices of *lussiketbröd*.

Service didn't like to drink a lot, especially if there was any chance of a duty call.

"Is there room in that bed of yours for two?" she asked.

He said, "I think it's designed to sleep one."

She laughed. "You know what they say: What sleeps one will lay two."

"New math. I haven't tried that," he said.

She smiled. "Well, that's both a damn shame and fandamntastic news," she said digging into the bread and ice cream with a spoon. She took one small bite, put the spoon down, stood up, and leaned over and kissed him on the forehead before moving down to his lips.

"Christmas Eve," she said. "We can take turns playing Santa."

Service awoke to two gunshots. A naked, sleeping Brigid Mehegen was draped over his shoulder. He pushed her aside and rolled off the bed, grabbed his sweats, went to the other end of the trailer to find his boots, and stumbled around trying to get them on.

Two more shots sounded outside. He grabbed his four-cell flashlight, unsnapped his .357 revolver, pulled it free of the holster on his gunbelt, and stepped onto the porch. His light illuminated a gigantic animal that snorted and startled Service, who slipped on the icy porch and fell hard.

"Turn that bloody light off—you're scarin' the bejeezus outta my reindeer!" a stentorian voice roared.

Prone in the snow, Service rolled onto his side, shone his light toward the voice, and saw two of the biggest horses he had ever seen. They were light-colored and their rear haunches were spackled with even lighter spots. "Those *aren't* reindeer," he said.

The animals appeared to be harnessed to a van. The voice on top said, "I'm Santa Claus, and I decide what reindeer look like."

The van suddenly lit up. It was decorated with Christmas lights outlining the windows, including the windshield. "You done boning my granddaughter?"

Service heard Brigid Mehegen's voice behind him and it was anything but pleased. "Jesus, Perry, what the hell are *you* doing here?"

"Came for my Christmas prezzie," the man shouted at her. "I don't see that a hormonally driven hornycane should change tradition. You know your Bampy likes getting his presents Christmas Eve, and here it is already by-God Christmas morning!"

"Dammit, Perry, act your age and go home! I'll be there tomorrow."

"It's already tomorrow," the man pointed out. "And I'm already here!"

"You don't deserve a present," Mehegen snapped at him.

"I'm your beloved Bampy."

"Where's the gun?" Service demanded as he got to his feet.

"Right here in my holster," the old man said, patting his hip.

"Well, leave it right there."

"I just wanted to get my granddaughter's attention," the man said.

"You're a stubborn, self-centered old man. I never should have told you where I was going," Mehegen said. "Who'd you steal the horses from?"

"They're reindeer," he insisted. "And I didn't steal them. They sort of followed me."

Mehegan stepped beside Service and poked him lightly in the ribs. "They still hang horse thieves, right?"

"Uh, I believe so," he said.

"Hokum," the old man grumbled.

"He's a cop," Mehegen said, touching Service's arm.

"Not a real cop, just a game warden," the man said.

"Horses are animals," she countered. "So are reindeer. That *makes* it his business."

"Why do you always have to go and ruin my surprises?" the old man complained.

"Because you never think anything through," she said, her rage barely contained. "You are going to return those horses right now and hope the owner hasn't called the county."

"There's no reason for that tone of voice," he complained. "I'm your grandfather, father of your beloved mother."

"Not tonight you're not," she said sternly. "And mom was Bitchzilla on her best day. Where do these horses belong, Perry?" One of the animals turned and nudged Mehegen with its nose and she stroked it gently. In a mock whisper she said, "Don't worry, we'll save you from this madman." Turning to her grandfather she demanded to know if his "rig" was running.

"Would run good enough if I turned the key," he said from his rooftop perch.

"Get your scrawny ass down here," she said. In an aside to Service, she added, "Let's unhitch the horses. Do you ride?"

"Not if I can help it," he said.

"You can't help it tonight," she said, looking at her grandfather. "He'll drive and we'll ride behind him. How far?" she asked with a growl as the old man slid off the roof of the van, bounced off the hood, and landed on his behind in the snow.

"I wasn't counting," he grumbled, brushing himself off. They went into the trailer to put on more clothes and socks and get their coats.

The ride took close to an hour, and by the time they approached a farm with open fields several miles from Service's property, dawn was breaking. They were greeted by a cheery voice. "You found my kids, eh? Dey're always runnin' off. Dose two Percherons is smart horses, and no matter how I lock 'em in, dey always find a way out. Dey act up on youse?"

"No," Mehegen replied.

"Dey're s'posed to be workin' animals, but I can't find a job dey like. More like t'ousand-pound puppies."

Service and Mehegen dismounted and the old man whispered to the animals, who stepped toward him, nickering and nuzzling him while he slipped them some sugar cubes. The animals were twice as tall as the man, but obediently did what he asked, bumping him gently with their noses, their tails swishing the early morning air.

"Merry Christmas," the man called as he walked down the road between the animals.

"See, it worked out fine," Mehegen's grandfather muttered as he got out of the van.

"Keys," she demanded, holding out her hand.

"I got a license to drive," he countered.

"Not with me you don't," she said, snatching the keys away from him and ordering him into the back through the sliding side door.

Service got into the passenger seat and Mehegen started the engine. When the Christmas lights came on, she screamed, "How do you turn these fucking things off?"

"Toggle on the left dash," her grandfather said. "Potty mouth."

"Shut up," she commanded, turning the lights off. "How do you like my grandfather?" she asked as they pulled away. Service had no reply.

"Hey, a little respect," Perry said. "Where's my present?"

She didn't answer, and when they got back to Service's trailer she got out, opened her truck door, pulled out a gun case, and thrust it at him. "Merry Christmas. Now get the hell out of here."

"You don't have a nip and a taste of *lussiketbröd* for your Bampy?"

"Git," she said harshly. "I mean it, Perry!"

The old man opened the gun case and gulped. "A new scattergun!"

"Sixteen-gauge, your favorite," she said. "Don't shoot your foot off."

"I had my scattergun stolen," Perry said in Service's direction. "Some Philistines from down below copped it."

"You walked out of the woods and left the damn thing," Mehegen snarled. "You try to blame everything on people from below the bridge."

"Only because they deserve it," he said resolutely.

She handed the old man's keys to him, took Service's hand, and led him to the porch. "We're going back to bed," she said, tugging Service's sleeve.

"*Lussiketbröd?*" the old man said in a pleading, almost pathetic tone.

"Next year—if you're still alive," she said, pulling Service inside and slamming the door. She immediately put her arms around his neck and said, "Memorable Christmas, eh?"

"Is he always like this?" he asked.

She laughed. "He's a pip, and he's got the world convinced he's sane, but I know he's totally nutso." She pulled out a chair. "Sit. Still, you gotta admit, he knows how to capture attention." She added, "This isn't done yet."

Service sat down as Mehegen got out a plastic plate, cut a large piece of the bread, uncapped a beer, and sat down beside him.

Seconds later there was a rapping on the door. "Sugarpie, it's snowing out here."

"Come in," she shouted at the door.

Perry stepped inside carrying his new gun case.

"*That* stays outside," she said.

"A flatlander will steal it," he protested, clutching the case to his chest.

"It's okay," Service said, trying to play peacemaker.

"No it's not," Mehegen insisted. "He's not allowed to have firearms in the house."

"This isn't his house," Service reminded her. "It's mine, and I have firearms in here."

"I left my pistol in the van," Perry offered.

Mehegen threw up her hands and rolled her eyes. "Close the door! You're letting the snow in."

Perry saw the bread and immediately grabbed at it, but Mehegen lightly slapped his hand. "Act civilized," she said. "You remember how, right?"

"Was me taught you manners," he said, sitting down, the gun case propped against his leg. "And I don't like that tone of voice."

The man devoured the bread and cut himself a second helping before grabbing at the beer, which he didn't quite get and knocked over the edge of the table. It hit with a pop, spewing foam across the floor.

Service grabbed a sponge and immediately got on his knees to soak up the beer. "Paper towels," he told Mehegen, who stepped past him just as there was an explosion from the table. Service felt her collapse heavily on top of him.

"Goddamn it, Perry! *Goddamn it!*" she began shrieking as she scrambled off Service.

He looked up to see the end of the gun case tattered and burned, and a hole in the ceiling. Snow was wafting gently through the hole, landing on the bread and table.

Mehegen began to shout at her grandfather, but Service grabbed her arm and began laughing, until all three of them were laughing and unable to speak.

It was late morning before they could get Perry on his way and the roof hole patched.

Work done, they immediately went back to bed. "I warned you not to invite him in with that damn shotgun!" she said.

"Where did he get the ammo?"

"From his van. He's been carrying it ever since he lost the other one. Merry Christmas," she said, kissing him lightly.

They tried to make love, but kept breaking into laughter and finally gave up. Mehegen went to sleep in the crook of Grady Service's arm as he lay there wondering if his ride on the Percheron had permanently removed a layer of his skin.

9

TRENARY, DECEMBER 28, 1975

"I watched da whole sad parade."

It had taken several telephone calls to track down Joe Flap's current address. Apparently the pilot didn't stay put too long in any one place and moved from rental to rental. For the moment he was living in Alger County on a farm northeast of Trenary on Trout Lake Road.

Christmas Eve with Brigid Mehegen and her daffy grandfather had been memorable to say the least, but what stuck in Service's mind most was her T-shirt and homemade movie: NAKED SKYDIVERS GO DOWN FASTER. Late Christmas Day he'd begun trying to track down Joe Flap.

Service grinned when he saw an airplane tail poking out of a barn-turned-hangar. There was a faded yellow windsock on the silo attached to the barn. A flatbed truck with a snowplow was parked next to the two-storied house, half of which was unpainted with exposed pink insulation. The other half was painted aquamarine blue, and not recently by the looks of it.

Another five inches of snow had fallen, and the temperature had dropped nearly to zero for the third consecutive night. Lake surfaces had gone from skiff ice to the real thing, and if it remained cold it wouldn't be long before ice-fishing fanatics would be hauling their shanties onto lakes.

There were fresh footprints from the house to the barn.

Service found Joe Flap sitting on a bar stool. He wore a sleeveless gray sweatshirt streaked with grease, military flight coveralls turned down to the waist, a green John Deere ball cap, and his traditional Errol Flynn pencil 'stache. His old horseblanket coat was hung from a peg and it was as greasy and stained as everything else around the man. Service saw that the engine cowling was open and the pilot had some sort of device with protruding wires held in his lap. Flap was a short, wiry man who shaved his head and had a scar that ran from the center of his skull down to his left eyebrow, a memento of one of his numerous crashes. Service had never known the man's age; he hadn't seen him in years, and now he looked a lot younger than he remembered.

Service plopped a case of Old Milwaukee on a workbench.

The pilot stared at the beer, then at Service. "You got youse a pretty good memory," he said. "Heard you joined da green," the pilot added, "and got da Mosquito, too."

"I haven't been there that long," Service said.

"Long enough ta make some of da dirtballs whine."

Flap got up, opened two cans of beer, and handed one to Service.

"Glad you made it home in one piece," he said with a crooked grin. "Dat Vietnam was one serious clusterfuck."

Service raised a can in salute. "There it is."

They both lit cigarettes.

"You've been flying the Garden," Service said.

"When dey need me."

"Is there an airfield down there?"

"Skis out on da ice," Flap said.

"An inland strip?"

"If dere was, da ratfucks down dere would turn it into a flak trap."

"No place to let down?"

"Couple places, mebbe in an emergency, but only if I was plumb-out-of-IOUs-desperate—and even den I'd have second thoughts." Flap studied him. "You got somepin' in mind?" he asked, arching an eyebrow.

Thoughts too amorphous to share yet, Service reminded himself. "I heard you on the radio last month."

Flap looked at him. "You know," he said, "our people never went to da slip where I spotted dat white boat."

"No?"

"Dis time our guys were willing, but da Troops wit' dem were new and a little shaky, which isn't unusual, eh. Dey made one ceremonial loop and bugged out. I watched da whole sad parade."

"You never said anything on the radio."

Joe Flap shrugged. "What would be da point? If our so-called leadership don't have da balls to get in da dirt wit' da grunts, why should grunts hang out dere *cajones?*"

"You're saying this isn't the first time?"

"Depends on who goes. Get da wrong mix and dey settle for a symbolic drive-through. Problem den is dat all da locals see a bunch of game wardens wit' dere tails between dere legs. Dis sure ain't da same outfit your old man and me signed on wit'."

Service had heard similar lamentations from a couple of people, but he had ignored them. "Do the locals down there monitor your radios?"

"I s'pect so, but I usually run radio-silent an' open my mouth only when I have to. Why?"

"I had that one patrol down there and I didn't much care for what I saw," Service said.

Flap nodded solemnly. "You're not alone, son. Your old man was still alive, he'd get some of da boys together and dey'd go down dere one night wit' saps and brass knuckles."

"Times change," Service said.

"Mebbe," Flap said, "but assholes are forever assholes, and dere was a time not dat long ago when a warden wouldn't back down from anyone. You did, you might as well turn in your badge."

Flap was right, but this tight-jawed attitude had also caused several men to be killed in the line of duty over the nearly ninety years that the state had employed uniformed game wardens. "You think we've backed down?"

"How many shots fired at your patrol dat day—seven, eight?"

"Eight," Service said.

"You return fire, defend yourselves?"

In fact, they had swerved and run when the attacks became direct. Until Stone boarded the boat, they had had only handguns for defense.

"Don't feel bad," Flap said. "Da boys ain't *never* shot back at dose rat-fucks. Da Garden's startin' to put a stink on green uniforms. You just vis-itin', or you got an official reason for droppin' in?"

"I didn't realize you were still flying for the department."

Joe Flap grunted. "I'm fifty-two: Guys my age make a hundred grand wit' da airlines, and all da stews they can screw."

"You regret not joining the airlines?"

Flap sneered. "I ain't no bloody bus driver."

"I always thought you'd head west again," Service said. "Or up to Alaska."

"Used ta say that, an' I almost did. But when dis Garden mess kicked up, I decided ta see 'er through. I ain't much for walkin' away from a scrap."

The two men made small talk for a while and Service asked his fa-ther's old friend about aircraft procedures and capabilities, but kept his other thoughts to himself.

Joe Flap walked him out to his patrol car. "Sorry you had ta join dis sorry outfit," he said. "Your old man—"

Service cut him off. "My old man's dead, Joe. Let's leave him that way. I'm not him—I'm me."

The pilot looked at him quizzically. "I guess we'll see about dat. Bear scat don't never fall far from da bear."

10

SHOW-TITTIES POND,
DECEMBER 31, 1975

"Do they expect you guys to live like this for twenty-five years?"

Once again Brigid Mehegen had shown up unannounced, pounding on Grady Service's trailer door just after dark. He opened up to find her with a bottle of Cold Duck in one hand and a package of meat in reddish-brown butcher paper in the other. "Just so we're clear on this," she said, extending the gifts to him. "Fuck buddies, nothing more."

Service laughed and let her in, put the sparkling wine in a bucket of snow outside the door on the stoop, stashed the package in the fridge, and opened beers for them. "Does Perry have a New Year's Eve act?" he asked. He liked Mehegen, but this was all a bit too fast, and there was an aura around her. She was attractive and engaging, but was she a flake or a free spirit? He wasn't at all sure.

"I told him if he shows up, I will put two in his hat and gut him."

Ten minutes later the telephone rang, and Service groped around for a pen to make notes. "You're sure they're there now?" he said, reaching for his boots as he hung up.

Mehegen handed his gunbelt to him. "Where are we going?"

"We?"

"I came to spend the night with *you*—as in one plus one equals one. You got a problem with women riding along?"

He was in too much of a hurry to argue, and he had to admit it would be nice to spend another night with her.

Walking to the patrol car he explained, "The woman on the phone wouldn't give her name, but she claims two guys up on STP shot two deer with a crossbow last night. They're driving a blue pickup, make unknown. She said their names are Ivan Rhino and Eugene Chomsky."

Mehegen got into the passenger seat and buckled her safety belt. "The caller saw them do it?"

Service said, "One of them's been yapping about it." He looked over at her. "You stay out of the way."

Mehegen saluted with her left hand and smiled. "STP?"

"It's a summer hangout for local teens and occasionally the biker crowd. Most years it barely qualifies as a pond, and it's not named on maps. The name is strictly local."

She laughed. "You talked right around that one."

"Show-Titties Pond," he said.

She laughed even louder. "You take your honeys out there in your day?"

"I was busy with other things," he said. From age twelve through college he had played hockey virtually year-round.

"I can't believe you were celibate," she said.

"I wasn't," he said.

After a few minutes she asked, "Do you know you haven't turned on your lights?"

"Yep."

"Do you always drive around at night without lights?"

"Usually," he said.

"The DNR endorses this?"

"There's no written policy," he said. He had been told during training that there once had been, but department lawyers ordered it rescinded, feeling they could work better from ambiguity than specificity. Officers were never ordered to run dark and many didn't. In the U.P., where there were more two-tracks and logging trails than hardtop roads, the practice tended to be a standard operating procedure.

"I'm surprised the Lansing lawyers allow it."

"Nobody asks."

"And if you plow into somebody?"

"They'll have to ask."

She braced both hands on the dashboard.

He braked suddenly, stopping the vehicle in the road, and took out his plat book and penlight. The caller told him there were two camps owned by flatlanders from the Port Huron area. Service looked up the Floating Rose Township maps, found STP, and saw there was state land all the way around the pond except for the northwest corner, where two twenty-acre parcels showed the owners as August and Angie Agosti. He turned off the penlight, dropped the book on the back floor, and accelerated.

Most back roads had stayed fairly mushy until mid-December when it got cold; now all the two-tracks and gravel roads were snow-covered, pitted and frozen. They would likely stay frozen into late April or early May. He kept both hands on the steering wheel as the ruts yanked violently at his tires.

He knew that a tote road-driveway led north up the west side of the pond to where the private parcel was, but he stopped in a logging area west of the STP entry road, parked the Plymouth, left the motor running, and started to get out.

"Are we going for a walk?" Mehegen asked.

"One of us is."

"Don't pull this," she said.

"You're gonna be a cop, right?"

"That's the plan."

"I've got my brick," he said, showing her the handheld radio. He held up two microphones for his vehicle radios. "You know radios, right? County on one, DNR on the other."

She sighed. "I know."

"I'm gonna walk in and scout the place. When I call, bring the car up to the camps. Can you do that?"

"I guess."

He gripped her upper arm. "This is important: You're my backup. When you come, no gumball flashing and no siren unless I tell you to light it up and play your music. Understand?" He showed her the toggles for the overhead gumball and siren. He didn't mention the stupidity of game wardens having gumball lights. In the woods you needed to be as nondescript as possible, and a big light on your roof made you stand out, even if it wasn't lit. Obviously somebody in Lansing wanted COs to look like the Michigan State Police. Having done both jobs, he could tell the originator of the idea that the only similarities in the jobs were wearing a badge and being armed.

He eased open his door and took out the ruck, which he kept filled with emergency gear. The ruck still smelled new, and he shook his head when he thought about how he came to have it.

He had been in Newberry three weeks before starting official solo duty in the district when his sergeant told him to report to the garage where the district's fire-fighting equipment was stored.

There he found an elongated green panel truck with a DNR emblem on the side. A man was sitting behind a sewing machine in back. The truck was filled with racks of shirts and trousers and coats and hats, and bins of boots. The man had medium-length gray hair, a jowled round face, and thick black-rimmed glasses that made his eyes look bigger than they were. He also wore a green felt cap with a pin sprouting colorful feathers, and a well-tailored and crisply pressed dark green jaeger jacket. His face was flushed, his nose bulbous.

"I am Vilhelm, quartermeister, just like za Wehrmacht," the man said imperiously. "Ve haff only so much time, so you vill now please to stend on line and poot out arms, *ja*." The man stepped forward, pointed to a piece of tape on the floor of the truck, and demonstrated with his arms. "Like zis, *ja*."

Service stepped up and extended his arms.

"*Sehr gut*," the man said extending his measuring tape. "You haff important new job, *ja*." When he finished measuring he wrote down some numbers and said, "You are beak fellow."

The man went back to a rack, rattled some hangers, and brought out a long-sleeved gray DNR uniform shirt for Service. "Try on."

It felt a little snug. The man poked at Service's back with a sliver of chalk. "We tuck here, *unt* here, *ja*." When the man reached for Service's pants, he took a step back and the man's reaction was immediate. "You vill not moof, *ja*." The man measured his waist and inseam. "Off!" he said, tugging at Service's pants and went to another rack, coming back with a pair. "You try."

They were a little tight in the waist. "Okay, *ja*, I let zis out, no problem," he said.

"You were in the German army?" Service asked.

"*Ja wohl.* Ve lose. I am conscripted. How old am I?"

Service thought the man looked to be mid- to late seventies. "I'm not good at guessing ages."

"Zixty. Ve are trapped by Ivan from za East, Americans and Tommies in Vest. I lose leg on za Oder. I am zixteen by one month, *ja*. Za surgeon, he cleans and cauterizes za stump, makes bandage, and ve all retreat. Ve vill not surrender to Ivans. I valk mitt crutch and carry Mauser more zen one hundred kilometers so I can raise my hands to American GIs. Zey put me in hospital, giff me *gut* care, zen I am POW for more zen one year until zey investigate to make sure I am not Nazi. Ven Wehrmacht took me, I was apprentice to tailor in Munich. America welcomes Germans with a trade, unt zey let me come to America."

Service didn't ask how he ended up in Michigan working for the DNR.

"You fought in Vietnam," the man said, staring at Service.

"Yes." How had he known?

"You haff za eyes," the man said, patting his arm. "Velcome home, velcome to DNR. You haff important job, *ja*? Now, you smoke, *unt* I vork."

Service lit up on the back of the truck while the man sewed. After awhile the tailor had him try on the shirt again. It fit perfectly, and the man smiled and nodded. "*Ja, sehr gut!* I come back one year, you need fix, I fix, you need new, I get or make." The man reached into a box and dumped a green rucksack and equipment bag on the ground behind the truck. "I make from GI zurplus canvas tent. Two dollars each. Zey vill last forever. Za uniforms all ready in three days, *ja*?" Service dug out the money and paid.

"Hey, Willie," another CO said, coming up to the truck. "Your Kraut pension come through yet?"

"Zere iss no pension for losers," Wilhelm answered with a pained grin. "Stend on line, arms out, *ja*."

Another officer grabbed Service as he was putting the ruck and bag in his patrol car. "Experience counts with Willie. The older guys get all the good stuff and the best service. If you want an extra good fit, you offer him booze, venison, beer, or fresh fish. That's why Willie comes to this district every year—for venison and wild game, just like back home in Germany."

"Thanks," Service said, feeling for a moment like he was back in the marines, learning to work the system.

Ruck on, he made sure his shotgun was unlocked behind the seat and looked at Mehegen. "All you have to do is this," he said, taking her hand and showing her how to pull the weapon loose. "It's Remington, twelve-gauge, semiautomatic, slug in the boiler, four more slugs behind that."

She got out and felt her way around to his side as he tightened the straps of his ruck. He checked his watch as she slid into his seat. "Give me at least ninety minutes to get back there and snoop around, but when I call, come fast."

"What if I don't hear from you in ninety minutes?"

"Call the county for backup."

He walked into the cedar swamp, angling northeast.

There was no moon. Snow was coming and going in varying intensity, the temperature around thirty and falling. Little snow made it through the canopy filter, most of it piling up overhead. When the sun came out, it would be a frigid rain in the understory.

He moved steadily, not hurrying. The roots of the cedars were a tangle, some of them sticking up nearly a foot, threatening to twist an ankle or break a leg. In cedars, you learned to take your time, even if you had good night vision, which he did.

It took twenty minutes before he saw a tiny halo of light in the distance and guessed it came from the camps. He always carried a compass, but rarely needed it. If he was on course, he should be seeing the lower of the two camps. He slid more to the north to approach the upper camp first. Behind the cabin in the trees he found a trailered boat with an outboard, two Ski-Doo snowmobiles, and a vintage Indian motorcycle, all of the vehicles draped with snow-covered canvas tarps. Indians were antiques and worth a fortune to certain collectors. His old man had once owned one and used it for patrol until he fell off it and broke an arm; his supervision told him to stick to four wheels. Service wondered what happened to the old motorcycle. It had been red, and a beauty.

The cabin was dark and there were no vehicles nearby. He moved behind the cabin and into thick willows for cover. He could see a light on the corner of the other camp, and as he moved south he saw light coming from behind the other cabin. He crouched to make a low profile and advanced steadily, stopping often to listen. When he got to the edge of a clearing, he squatted and watched. There was a sliver of glow in the clearing, and suddenly embers rose into the night and something screamed and metal slammed and he could hear pounding. *What the hell?* His first thought was a burn barrel.

"Hold that fucker down," a voice growled.

"Damn bandit," another voice said.

Service saw two figures near the sliver of fire, and there was just enough light to see the silhouette of the barrel.

Somebody began to pound the metal barrel, bellowing, "There, there, *there!*"

Now what? Service thought.

He could hear something thrashing frantically inside the barrel, but the sounds had faded from screams to moans and hisses. He snapped on his four-cell flashlight.

"Conservation officer!" he announced. "What's going on here?"

"Got Bandit!" a voice said excitedly.

"Shut up, Eugene!"

"*Gumby!*" the other voice said. "Not Eugene. Gumby—not Eugene!" The tone was something between frustrated and pissed.

Service said, "What's in the barrel, guys?"

"Not your business," one of the voices said.

"Bandit," the first voice said. "Got 'im good!"

"Can I see?" Service asked.

"You got a warrant?" one of them challenged.

"Yeah, got weren't?" the other voice chimed in.

"Shut up, Eugene."

"Gumby!" the other voice insisted.

Service looked them over. Two males, one of them six-five with a cherubic face and an extra wide body of muscle and baby fat. The other was shorter, lean and feral in appearance, furtive in movement, with long hair hanging loose and wild.

"Stay right there, boys," Service said. He stepped forward and used the end of his flashlight to slide the lid off the barrel. Sparks exploded into the night and showered him as something leaped out of the barrel and began to run circles in the clearing, falling, getting up, and plunging on through the snow, its fur singed, the snow causing a hiss that blended with the animal's keening.

"Got *Bandit!*" the larger of the two men said. "Got 'im good!"

"Step over here by the barrel," Service said.

"We don't got to," the long-haired one said.

"Got badge?" the bigger one asked.

Service had his radio on a strap. He kept the light on the two men and toggled his radio. "Two-one-thirty, move up, no lights no music." Should he call for county backup? His mind was torn between keeping an eye on the two men and knowing he had to put the animal out of its misery. He glanced in the barrel and saw charred and stinking remains of other animals. The stench pinched his nostrils. *Sickos*, he told himself.

"Okay guys, we're gonna walk around the cabin to the road. Stay in front of me." The larger man walked backward looking back at Service. "Gumby see badge?"

The larger man was Gumby. "Ivan Rhino?" Service asked the other man.

"Gumby," the big man insisted. He looked to be late teens at the oldest.

"Shut up, Eugene," the other man said, ignoring Service.

They had just reached the east side of the cabin when Gumby smacked the other man so hard he went down on his face and immediately scissored Gumby's legs out from under him, dumping him in the snow and pummeling his face.

Service saw vehicle lights coming up the tote road. He stepped over to the two men on the ground and jabbed the smaller one away with his boot.

Gumby immediately clamped onto his leg and started clawing at his holster, shouting, "*Get gun! Get gun!*"

Service bopped him once on the head with the butt of his flashlight and the man collapsed on his side in the snow.

"Fucking retard," the other man grumbled.

Mehegen pulled up in the squad. Service had the smaller man help his partner to his feet and guided them roughly toward the vehicle. "Call the county," he said. "Two prisoners to transport."

"What for?" she asked.

"Make the call," he said with a growl. "There're extra cuffs on the parking brake. Toss them to me." Mehegen did as ordered, stared at him.

"Sit," he told the skinny one. He cuffed the small man's leg to the big man's wrist, took the second set, attached it to the larger man's wrist and the smaller man's wrist. He could hear Mehegen on the radio, knew the county wanted a ten-code beyond a request for transport in order to assign a priority, but he still didn't know exactly what he had. He stepped over to the patrol car and whispered, "Just say yessir to whatever I say, okay?"

"Yessir," she said.

"Okay, Officer Mehegen. You've got the shotgun, right?"

"Yessir."

"If these two don't behave, if they try to get up or cause any trouble, shoot them."

"You can't do that!" the smaller man said.

"Yessir," Mehegen said.

Service went out into the clearing and found the animal. It had collapsed next to a fallen log on the edge. Heat rose into the night air, blended with the stench of burned hair. Service put the light on the animal. The raccoon was still breathing shallowly. He took his backup piece, a .38 snub, out of his pocket and put one round in the animal's head. He used a stick to knock the top off the glowing barrel and wedged two more coon carcasses out of the hot coals and went back to the patrol car.

"County in twenty minutes," Mehegen said.

"Good."

Service undid the cuff from the little man's leg and told both men to get up. He snapped the cuff on the little man's other arm and led them around the patrol car. "In here," he told the smaller man. He opened the passenger seat door, put his hand on the top of the man's head, and pushed down, helping him to get in. The big man remained docile.

"Shoot him if he even sneezes," Service said.

He heard Mehegen say, "Yessir."

He led the larger man to the steps that led onto the porch of the small cabin.

"You're Gumby, right?"

"Yeah, Gumby."

"Your partner's Ivan Rhino, right?"

"Yeah, Ivan."

"Gumby, how about we go inside and look around your place."

"Got weren't?"

"Why would I need a warrant?"

"Ivan said."

"I don't need a warrant if you invite me in. You want me to see your place, right?"

The man thought for a moment. "Okay, yeah."

Service reached for the door, but the boy balked. "What?"

"Him-her inside?"

"Somebody's inside?"

"Him-her?" Gumby said, his head nodding rapidly.

"Did you guys shoot some deer, Gumby?"

"So's him-her can eat 'em," he said, smacking his lips.

"It's good to eat deer," Service said. "You like to eat deer?"

"Him-her does," he said with a nod at the door.

"Your mother?"

"Her."

"Got a name?"

"Cunt."

"The woman's name is Cunt?"

"Ivan says," Eugene said.

"You want to tell her we're coming inside?"

Gumby opened the door a crack. "Comin' in, Cunt!"

"Turn on the lights," Service told the boy.

"Turnin' on light!" Gumby shouted before reaching gingerly inside the door.

"*Retard!*" a muted female voice bellowed from somewhere in the cabin.

Gumby tried to go in, but Service restrained him and eased through the door first, into a messy living area.

"Ma'am, this is the DNR. Please step out here so we can see you."

No answer. "Where are the deer, Gumby?" Service asked the boy.

They walked into a dining area off a small kitchen. There were four deer heads on the floor, several severed legs on a table covered with newspaper, ragged haunches, blood and deer hair all over the floor, piles of guts overflowing buckets, the place an abattoir.

"Deer," the boy announced.

"You use a gun to kill them?"

"Robin Hood," the boy said.

Robin Hood? "A bow and arrow?"

"Yeah, Robin Hood."

"Can we talk to the woman you live with?"

"Her-him? Got weren't?"

"I'm inside now; I don't need one, remember? You invited me in."

"Oh yeah."

"I've been nice, haven't I?"

"Hit Gumby's head."

"Because you tried to grab my gun."

"Yeah," the boy said.

Service toggled his brick radio. "Two-one-thirty, let me know when you see lights from the county boys."

"Ten-four."

"Ma'am?" Service called out.

"She's not here," a female voice called back.

"How are the Agostis?" Service asked the boy.

He shrugged.

"They own this place."

"We found," the boy said, shaking his head.

"What the hell are you doing out there, Eugene?" the woman yelled from a darkened room at the end of the cabin.

"Gumby!" Eugene shouted. "*Not* Eugene!"

He stepped toward the room with Service behind him.

"Turn on the light, ma'am," Service said.

"Him got badge!" Gumby shouted.

"Dummy," the woman shot back with disgust.

"Show Robin Hood," Eugene said, stepping gingerly into the darkness before Service could stop him.

"Get the light on, Gumby."

Service heard movement and what sounded like a scuffle. The boy stepped out of the room, looked back, said, "Her-him *hurt* me!"

He took one step forward and fell on his face. Service saw a knife handle sticking out of the lower right side of the boy's back.

"County's coming," Mehegen announced over the radio.

"Call an ambulance," Service told her.

"Are you okay in there?" she asked.

"*Get* an ambulance!"

Where was the woman? He looked at the boy, knew the wound was serious, but he couldn't do anything to help him until he knew where the woman was. The boy looked like he had gone right, so Service crawled on his knees to the door, reached inside with his left hand, groped for the light switch, flipped on the light, and stayed outside the door to the room.

Two deputies came through the living room, guns drawn. One of them reached for the knife in the boy's back. "Don't touch him," Service said.

"He'll bleed out."

"Let the medics handle it!" Service said forcefully. He had seen knife wounds in Vietnam.

Service peeked in the door. A woman sat on the bed holding a sheet up to her chin. There was an unassembled double-barrel shotgun on the foot of the bed and a crossbow and brass lamp on a side table. "Where are the bolts, ma'am?"

The woman had long stringy blond hair, didn't answer.

"Ma'am, if you're armed and you try something, you are going to be shot dead—do you understand what I am telling you?"

She looked at Service and smiled fecklessly. One of the deputies stood on the other side of the door opening, his revolver drawn.

"Ma'am, please lower the covers."

The woman leered. "You wanna see my titties!"

"No, ma'am."

"Why not? I got *real* nice titties," she said, crestfallen.

"Cunt got *big* ole titties," Gumby mumbled from the floor.

The woman lowered the sheet to reveal pendulous breasts hanging off an emaciated frame.

The deputy pointed his pistol at her. Service stepped gingerly inside and snapped the covers off the bed. There were two crossbow bolts by the woman's left leg.

The deputy handed Service a pair of cuffs. Service handcuffed the woman, got her up, and draped a blanket around her shoulders.

The other deputy was still staring at the knife lodged in Eugene's back.

"You okay, Gumby?" Service asked, trying to soothe the boy.

"Her-him punch," he said.

Service knew what a stabbing felt like initially. "Just once?"

"Two, three times. Her-him don't punch hard. How come hurts?"

Service knelt beside the boy, asked the deputy to help him. They tilted the boy slightly, got his shirt untucked. In addition to the knife stuck in him, there was a stab wound and a slash. The slash wasn't bleeding much. The stab wound was bleeding steadily, but not spurting. Artery intact, he told himself, and steady but not heavy flow from the protruding knife, which looked to be in deep. Was there organ damage? No way to tell. Most vital organs were buried deep inside the body and not easily reached by anything other than cataclysmic force. In Vietnam a chaplain once proclaimed this was by God's design. If so, Service told the man, God must have planned on people wreaking violence on each other, which made humanity's flaw either a screw-up on the part of humankind's creator, or a matter of malevolence, neither of which he thought much about. The chaplain called him a blasphemer. So be it, Service thought: To live you had to deal with life as it came to you, which meant bumping heads with assholes and understanding you were mortal.

Mehegen was suddenly kneeling beside Service, her hand on Eugene Chomsky's face. "Don't move. It's gonna be okay."

The boy stared up at her with wide eyes as she continued to talk softly to him. Mehegen glanced at Service and gave him a look that chilled his blood.

"Where's the fucking medevac!" Service screamed.

Mehegen took his arm and led him out to his Plymouth. The ambulance was coming up the road, bumping and sliding, lights flashing. Service leaned against the grille while Mehegen poked in his pockets until she found his cigarettes. She lit one for each of them.

The ambulance attendants moved quickly, and Service half-listened to them barking orders at each other and the deputies as they brought Eugene out of the cabin, loaded him, and raced away.

"Medevac?" Mehegen asked. "Did Scotty beam us elsewhere?" Service had no idea what she was talking about. "Captain Kirk, Mr. Spock, *Star Trek* . . . on TV?" she prompted.

He shrugged. He didn't own a television. He walked over to the sheriff's cruiser where Ivan Rhino sat glowering in the backseat, and then moved on to the next vehicle where the woman was in custody, the blanket still draped over her.

A deputy interrupted him. "You'd better step back inside," he said.

A second bedroom in the cabin was littered with firearms, fishing rods, a couple of salmon nets, boxes of ammo stacked up, two chain saws, and piles of tools. Service studied the mess, said, "There's a boat on a trailer, a couple of snowmobiles, and an Indian motorcycle under tarps in the wood line behind the next camp."

He went back outside and opened the door of the car where the woman sat. "Ma'am, what's your name?"

The woman turned her head away and he turned to a nearby deputy. "Find any ID?"

"Not yet."

No ID, and where was their truck? How did the caller know the men's names, and identify the truck, but not mention the woman? Was she a late arrival? If so, how did she fit in?

Service told the deputies he would drive up to Marquette later and write up his report. They discussed charges and decided they would start with stolen property, illegal deer, and the raccoons. Once they got more on the stabbing, that would become primary.

Not thirty minutes later another deputy, a sergeant, came up to him. "The boat and motorcycle in the woods match the descriptions of stuff stolen from some lake camps this summer. We've had camp break-ins since last June, more than thirty of them, and probably a bunch not yet reported because the owners are down below and don't know. Just last week an old guy over in Carlshend got the shit beaten out of him and ended up in the hospital—broken arm, jaw, lost some teeth, broken rib. The descriptions he gave us were pretty discombobulated, but we'll put together a lineup and see what he says. You should have waited for backup," the sergeant added.

Service grunted and shrugged. The man was right, but it had been his call to go in alone, and you did what you thought you had to.

He went back into the building with evidence bags and began bagging animal parts. Mehegen worked alongside him. The sergeant and his deputy concentrated on the bedroom where the stabbing had taken place. Service examined each piece of meat and saw that one of them had a hole near the shoulder joint. He took out his pocketknife, dug around in the hole, and, using gentle leverage, pried out a slug.

Mehegen said, "What's that?"

"Slug. Let's check all the meat again."

They eventually located a second slug about the same size as the first one. Service slid both into plastic envelopes and they hauled all the evidence, including the crossbow and bolts, out to the Plymouth. Service also bagged the raccoon carcasses from behind the cabin.

The sergeant and his men were still working when Service and Mehegen began an external search.

Two hours later they were still traipsing around the woods and swamps that abutted the pond and camps. "What the hell are we supposed to be doing?" Mehegen demanded to know.

"Looking for their truck," he said.

"Shouldn't we be looking near a road?"

"My God!" he said, bumping his forehead with the heel of his hand. "I never thought of that."

"Dial down the sarcasm," she said.

"The tip I got told me about a truck. The camp was filled with contraband, and they didn't exactly go to great lengths to hide any of it, so where is their ride?"

"Are you always so suspicious?"

"It's in my wiring."

"My feet hurt," she said. "Can we like . . . you know?"

"Not yet," he said. "I have to get up to Marquette to do the paperwork, and drop evidence at the district office in Escanaba. You want me to drop you back at the Airstream? This will be a rest-of-the-night deal."

"Not a chance," she said. "In for a dime, in for a dollar."

"What exactly does that mean?" he asked.

She shrugged and grinned. "It's a cliché. When I'm tired, clichés pop out. Aren't you tired?"

"Sure," he said.

"Then show it," she said. "It will make me feel better to know I'm not the only one dragging."

Mehegen remained in the patrol car while he put the evidence in the district office locker, and she slept on the drive to Marquette and while he went into the county building, wrote his report, checked on Eugene Chomsky's condition, and talked to deputies. Chomsky had already undergone a transfusion and almost two hours of surgery. The knife had not touched vital organs, but there had been heavy internal bleeding and he had gone into shock. He was listed as critical but stable.

Service asked that Ivan Rhino be brought into an interrogation room. Rhino looked even more cadaverous and disheveled than he had looked at the camp, his eyes sunk in his head, his skin yellow. Service offered the prisoner a cigarette, which he accepted. Service lit it for him.

"What was the deal with the raccoons?"

"Ask the dummy."

"Burning them alive was Chomsky's idea?"

"Everything was his idea," Ivan Rhino said.

Service looked at the man. "Eugene's not going to die," he said. "What about the woman?"

"What woman?" Rhino said, exhaling a cloud of smoke.

"I suppose you don't know anything about a pickup truck?"

"I don't know squat, man, and I don't talk unless there's a lawyer sitting here holding my swinging dick."

Rhino had not asked how Eugene was. If Eugene died, everything would be dumped on his shoulders.

Service left the prisoner and went to find one of the deputies who had been at the camp. He found one huddled with a detective named Kobera, who looked like he'd been jerked out of bed and dropped into the room. The deputy said, "Everything we found out there is on a list from the camp break-ins. There's other stuff too, not on the list, which says they've been busy again."

"Arraignment?" Service asked.

"Gotta get lawyers for them and give the old man a look at Rhino. We'll arraign tomorrow afternoon, late," he said. "Rhino says he has no money for a lawyer."

Service mashed out his cigarette. "The woman talking?"

"Total lockjaw."

"Anything in the system on Chomsky and Rhino?"

"Not yet. We'll give you a bump when we get our shit more together," Kobera said. They exchanged phone numbers.

Mehegen slept until they were ten minutes from his place. She didn't snore, but cooed like a pigeon. When she woke up she asked, "What time is it?"

He had no idea. "The sun's up," he offered.

Back in the trailer he poured a glass of champagne for each of them. They toasted the new year, got undressed, ignored the shower, and crawled into bed. Sometime later she put her head on his shoulder. "Do they expect you guys to live like this for twenty-five years?"

He smiled, but his mind was back in the camp. They had a crossbow, so why the bullets? And how the hell could they interview Gumby? His language was awkward, his thoughts jumped around, and he seemed to have the emotional stability of a child. The boy's jumbling of pronouns left Service wondering if he had missed something. Service thought, the boy seemed to have gotten my gender right when he talked about my badge, so why the other confusion? The case had looked cut and dried last night. It didn't feel that way this morning.

11

GARDEN PATROL, JANUARY 8, 1976

"Dat ain't no confetti!"

Just like last time, Service was alerted in the middle of the night for a Garden patrol, but this time the caller was Acting Captain Attalienti. Despite webs of sleep-induced fugue, he questioned the advisability of showing his face—given the pending recon.

"Don't sweat it," the acting captain said. "Meet Stone at the Fish-dam boat launch. Be there at zero-nine hundred."

"I take it we're not checking nets," Service said. He had heard that snowmobile patrols generally met well before daylight.

"Think of it as a parade," Attalienti said. "No snowmobiles."

Service arrived at 8 A.M. and waited. Colt Homes was first to pull in; he parked next to him and got in. "Heard you pinched some camp raiders," he said.

"I got a tip that a couple of guys whacked some deer with crossbows." He didn't mention the recovered slugs because he still hadn't worked out what had actually happened.

"Don't you *love* dis shit!" Homes chirped. "You never know where it will lead. I heard da value of da recovered goods is around forty grand."

Service hadn't heard this. What he had heard was that the old man who'd been beaten up had positively identified Ivan Rhino in a lineup, and Eugene Chomsky by photograph. Neither man had a record. Rhino was twenty-two, from Peru, Indiana; Chomsky not yet sixteen, from Milwaukee—a juvenile runaway. Rhino had a court-appointed attorney and was not talking. Chomsky was still in the hospital, his condition raised from critical and stable to just stable. He would live.

Because the robbery and break-in charges were far in excess of what the men would get from illegally killing deer, or even for burning raccoons alive, Service had not attended the arraignment. He was glad the Chomsky boy would live. The only lingering question for him was the identity of the woman. So far, she remained in jail, unidentified, and facing charges of attempted murder and felonious assault.

"Here's da kicker," Homes said. "Da broad from dat night hired Odd Hegstrom. Can you believe *dat?*"

"*Ode*, like in poem?"

"No, man. It's spelled O-d-d and pronounced *Ode*. He's an Icelander, Greenlander—somepin' like dat."

Service shrugged; the name meant nothing.

Homes said, "He's a lawyer out of Ironwood. When Order Seventeen come down, da Garden fish house boys hired him ta fight da DNR. He's a very tough operator."

"And he took the woman's case?"

"Everybody's shaking dere heads, but at least she'll have ta identify herself now."

Service immediately wondered if she was a Garden woman, but shoved the thought aside. The potential for other connections was too large to dwell on. Still . . .

Eddie Moody was the next to arrive, then Budge Kangas, a veteran CO from Menominee County, and, finally, acting lieutenant Lennox Stone.

The four men stood in the morning air drinking coffee and smoking as snow continued to fall. Stone handed them dark green ski masks. "We're gonna take a little ride this morning," he explained. "I'll lead, followed by Kangas, Moody, Homes, and Service. Keep a close interval, say, three car lengths."

"What're these for?" Moody asked, holding up a mask.

"Psychological warfare," Stone said with a grin.

"Garden Road?" Homes asked.

"Yep, right down da gut, all da way ta Fairport."

"Why?" Kangas asked.

"We need to test da crow line."

"What's to test? We know it's there."

"We'll talk about it after we're done," Stone said.

They pulled out and headed east precisely at zero-nine hundred. It was five or six miles east to Garden Road. Light snow continued to fall. Garden Road began at a spot called Garden Corners, the main landmark a nondescript gas station called Foxy's Den; the road stretched the length of the peninsula. The patrol drove the speed limit, lined up like spring goslings, and passed through the village without incident. It struck Service as odd (if not ominous) that they had not seen a single northbound or southbound vehicle during the run down to the village, and there had been nobody on the streets when they passed through.

The convoy continued south for eight miles, past Fayette State Park.

The park was the former site of a pig-iron and smelting operation that grew out of the need for iron spawned during the Civil War. In its heyday it had been a stinking hellhole someone had once compared to Cleveland's worst slums. Service had never been into the park and had little interest in seeing the ghostly remains of a town; the U.P. was filled with them, most of them the detritus of companies scarfing up the state's natural resources and moving on.

Their destination was Fairport, a village seven miles below the park, and the terminus of the twenty-one-mile-long peninsula. The snow had stopped as they left Garden, and they were bathed in morning sunshine as a few illuminated flakes swirled off the trees.

They were approaching a sharp turn with a cedar forest on both sides of the road, when Service was startled by something striking his hood and skipping off his windshield, quickly followed by more impacts. Ahead he saw things raining out of the cedars toward the other vehicles, and wondered how Stone would play it.

They went less than a hundred yards when Stone radioed, "Dat ain't no confetti! Hang a one-eighty, boys!"

Service cut sharply to the left, stopped, backed up, jerked his wheels to the right, stopped and shifted to drive, steered sharply left, and headed back to the north. Missiles continued to bounce off the Plymouth, but as soon as he got up the road away from the cedars, the assault stopped. He watched in his rearview mirror as the others turned and began to follow.

Coming into Garden he saw a crowd of twenty or more men on the porch of Roadie's Bar on the east side of the road, and as he got closer, he saw they were wearing black ski masks. They began to heave softball-size rocks and bottles at him. A brick or something as heavy smacked his passenger window with a popping sound and spidered it, but did not break it out.

"Service, you're too far out front," Homes yelped on the radio, and Service executed a quick U-turn in front of the bar. The rock throwers immediately fled, some of them through the front door, others down the sides of the building.

When the other vehicles got closer, he did another U-turn into the lead and they drove out of the village and off the peninsula without seeing another vehicle.

Out on US 2, Stone accelerated and passed Service, settling into the lead position, and led them to the Ogontz boat launch, which was five miles south of US 2 and located on the west shore of Ogontz Bay.

Four other DNR vehicles were already parked in the lot, officers milling around outside.

Dean Attalienti nodded at him as he got out of his squad with his thermos and joined the group.

The acting captain said, "While you men went down Garden Road we went down Harbor Road on the east side. We got eight miles in and got cut off by trees dropped across the road, so we turned around, and a mile back they had dropped more trees. It took us thirty minutes with a chain saw to clear the barricade."

"Dey rain rocks on youse?" Stone asked.

"Just the tree barriers, but now we know that they have enough people for the crow line to cover both sides, and we have to assume some of the middle roads and trails, too. They obviously don't want us down there without knowing about it, and they've put enough resources on it to get what they want. All this business today was to let us know it's their turf."

Service considered telling them that the rock throwers at Roadie's had fled when he'd made his sudden U-turn in front of the bar, but he kept his mouth shut. Mobs acted like mobs as long as they felt in control. The slightest threat to such a group usually shifted psychology to every man for himself.

"We got stoned north of Fairport," Stone said.

"I got hit in Garden when I was in front of you," Service added. By the time the patrol caught up to him, his attackers had disappeared.

"I seen da rocks and stuff on da street," Stone said.

"We need unmarked vehicles," Homes offered.

"Not just unmarked," Attalienti corrected him, "but blenders—vehicles that look like they belong down there—trucks, vans, that sort of thing."

"So what was the point of today?" Moody asked.

"A probe in force," Attalienti said.

"But we turned tail an' ran!" Homes said angrily. "Now dey tink dey've won another round."

"Winning a round isn't winning the fight," the acting captain said. "You men did fine today."

"I'm sick of being a target," Homes groused.

Ninety minutes later, Service was back in the Mosquito looking for snowmobile tracks; the machines were banned from operating in the wilderness tract, but this didn't keep a few idiots from trying it. While he drove around he thought about the excursion onto the Garden, and decided it had not been a total waste of time. Now they knew the crow line covered the entire peninsula, and whoever organized it had enough manpower not only to put together simple assaults, but to drop trees behind the eastern patrol—a clear message that they could cut off and isolate officers whenever they chose.

It was also interesting how the crowd at the tavern had split so quickly. This suggested they didn't want one-on-one confrontations, which meant they were in total group-think down there. Marines were taught to fight alone and in groups, but in all circumstances to keep fighting until ordered otherwise. Attalienti was right: The Garden crowd seemed to have considerable manpower at their disposal, and some sense of tactics. But it was still not much more than a mob, probably held together by beer as much as fidelity to a real cause.

The sniping tactics around the peninsula suggested recklessness and a desire to harass rather than homicidal intent. If they had wanted to kill officers, today would have been the day—but there had been no gunshots, just rocks and projectiles. The Garden people weren't looking so much to kill their rivals as to simply keep them at bay while they took fish illegally and made their money. This wasn't about philosophy or politics—it was about money. And if Cecilia Lasurm could point them to the leaders, there was a chance the DNR could focus pressure and gain some control.

Attalienti was on the phone with him around 8 P.M. "I'm having second thoughts about your recon. It seems to me that the only way to beat the crow line is to go in on foot at night and hope there's no snow to give you away. Have you got a plan in mind?"

"I thought we agreed that whatever I work out will remain with me."

"Yup, you're right; I guess I'm just a little edgy. You'll let me know when you get the timing worked out?"

"That's what we decided."

He liked Attalienti, but he'd begun to wonder if he was one of those managers who had to have his hand in everything, delegating nothing. On the plus side, the acting captain was showing a distinct interest in the welfare of his men.

12

HARVEY, JANUARY 10, 1976

"Are you serious?"

Mehegen's house was a small bungalow with Cherry Creek meandering through the back yard. As soon as Service pulled into the driveway, Perry came out of the house and stood on the front stoop.

"She's not home," the old man announced gruffly. He was wearing a red plaid wool shirt, suspenders, and black pants tucked into knee-high leather logging boots.

"Steal any more reindeer?" Service asked.

Perry said, "How much did it cost to fix your roof?"

"Nothing. The fix we put on it will last." Sooner or later he had to build a permanent cabin on his Slippery Creek property. "I'll just wait for Brigid."

"So you can bone her?" Perry said.

"Jesus," Service said.

The old man grinned and held up his hands. "Don't take it personally. She bones everybody. Got it in her genes, no pun intended."

"You should watch your mouth," Service said.

Perry shot back, "I didn't say anything to you I wouldn't say to her."

"Are you going to invite me in?"

"What the hell for? You're not here to see me."

Service was opening the door of the Plymouth as Mehegen pulled into the driveway and jumped out. "Sorry I'm late," she said breathlessly. She skipped over to Perry and pecked him on the cheek. "You didn't invite him in, offer him coffee or a beer?" she asked, her hands on her hips.

The old man shrugged. "What do I care if he has a beer?"

Mehegen rolled her eyes, waved at Service. "C'mon."

They sat in the kitchen at a small table with a yellowing formica top. She put out two cups and reached for the coffee.

Perry stood in the doorway. "What, nothing for your old granddad?"

"What do I care if you have coffee, old man?" Mehegen said.

Perry swore softly and made a show of stomping upstairs.

"Well," she said, "our New Year's Eve was the most interesting one I've ever had. I'm glad you called me," she added. "I was beginning to think I was going to have to take the reins on this. Should I be encouraged?"

"Where do you get your parachutes?"

"This is about *parachutes*?" she asked incredulously.

"It's a simple question," he said.

"Asked by a cement-head," she said. "I thought this was about a different recreational activity."

He remained silent, waiting for her to get it sorted out in her mind.

"Wildcat Jump Club," she finally said. "All of our purchasing is done through the club, and we store our stuff out at Marquette County Airport. We've got a building out there."

"Is there a way to borrow a chute?"

"What the hell for?"

"Something," he said evasively.

"Open your eyes! This is the season for jumping *into* a bed, not *out* of a goddamn airplane."

"I need to borrow a chute," he repeated.

"For you?"

"No details," he said. "Sorry."

She studied him briefly and sighed. "These days the harnesses are custom-built to fit each jumper; chute size reflects experience and the kind of jump being attempted. You can't just borrow a generic size."

"For discussion purposes, say somebody about my size," he said.

She laughed. "Are you serious?"

"I'd appreciate the favor," he said.

She raised an eyebrow and smiled. "With a quid pro quo, right?"

"As long as you don't ask for details and set me up to talk to your guy."

"When?"

"As quick as you can arrange it."

"People are funny about loaning their gear," she cautioned.

"Just get me someone to talk to."

"You're certainly not your happy-go-lucky self today," she said.

Perry huffed through the foyer and slammed the front door.

"I have to get going," he said.

"You're gonna owe me, pal."

Perry was chipping ice off the edge of the driveway when Service went outside.

"That was fast," the old man said.

"That's why it's called a quickie," Service said, getting into his patrol unit.

13

GARDEN PATROL, JANUARY 21, 1976

"Three patrols and you're bitching like an old-timer."

It was nine degrees Fahrenheit when Service left the Airstream, bound for the old Indian cemetery on the Stonington Peninsula. This time he had two days' advance notice to get ready. He was told to bring along his snowmobile and make sure it was in working condition. He had spent a good portion of yesterday changing plugs and oil, and doing other routine maintenance. It was not quite 6 A.M. when he towed the trailer with the Rupp into the gathering area. A weathered picket fence peeked out of the snow, marking an old grave, he guessed. The group would not assemble for another forty-five minutes, but he hated to be late; he spent the time worrying about how well he had packed for the patrol. Group activity irritated him; he preferred working alone in his own territory.

Last week he'd acquired a second thermos in Rapid River, and today he had both filled with coffee, laced with sugar and cream. He poured a small cup and sat as other vehicles began to pull in and jockey around to park. He stayed in the Plymouth, smoking. It was too damn cold to be out shooting the shit.

Eventually Colt Homes wandered over, rapped lightly on his window, and gestured for him to get out. Service refilled his cup and got out, twisting his head to stretch his neck and back. He had so many layers of clothing on, he felt like an overstuffed sausage: wool long johns, two pairs of knee-high wool socks inside Bean arctic felt liners and military-surplus white Mickey Mouse boots, heavy wool uniform pants, a wool undershirt, his winter-weight uniform shirt, a black wool sweater, and military-surplus gauntlet-style mittens that reached up to his elbows, and all of this under one-piece insulated coveralls that were too tight with everything crammed underneath.

Homes had taken up a spot in the center of the vehicles and was crunching an apple as he waited for the men to gather around him. The others shuffled toward the center, their boots making the Rice Krispie snow crackle and pop in the frigid air. The men all wore the same black coveralls and stomped their feet to keep circulation going.

"She's a fine mornin', boys," Homes proclaimed.

"Cram the bull, Homes, we're freezing our balls off out here," Budge Kangas complained.

"Dere's no wind," Homes countered. "It could be a lot worse."

"It *will* be a lot worse when we get on the sleds," someone pointed out.

"Exactly," Homes said, "and den we'll stop and it will feel warm!"

Service counted seven men, including himself: Homes, Moody, Kangas, Shaw from Mackinac County, and Stevenson and Larry Jakeway, both from Menominee County.

Budge Kangas said, "I'm at a hundred and twelve hours for this pay period. Are those Lansing assholes ever going to kick in overtime? These Garden shindigs are always twelve hours, *minimum*."

"That's what override's for, right?" Eddie Moody asked. Like Service, he was relatively new to the job.

"Override is eighty-nine point two hours," Kangas said. "That's a bit short of one-twelve by my math, and I've got two ex-wives and five kids to support."

"Try using rubbers," Homes quipped, and all the men laughed, even Kangas.

Service thought about the pay situation the men were talking about. Each man was paid for 89.2 hours, every two weeks. Some periods they might work 80 hours, others more than that, and the differential, in the officer's favor, was designed to give them control over their schedules and make up for night calls, holiday work, and other disruptions, not to mention investigations that could eat a lot of an officer's time. You couldn't be effective in the woods with one eye on a clock. So far, Service decided, he was probably working close to ninety hours and he didn't mind. He hadn't joined the DNR for money; he'd made more as a Troop. And he liked being busy.

"Fucking override," Kangas said. "How long is that even gonna last?"

Homes said, "Okay, enough jaw jockeying, let's get down ta business. I'm takin' seven this morning."

"Yer outta your mind, Homes. Gimme four," Moody said.

"Where's Stone?" asked Stevenson, one of the officers from Menominee County.

"In a vehicle. He'll meet up with us at Fayette. Joe Flap's been upstairs watching the rats put in a gang of nets over the past few days."

"How do we know it's rats?" Kangas challenged.

"We don't," Homes said. "It could be tribals, but we won't know dat until we look."

Kangas pressed his point. "It's legal for tribals to net north of Sac Bay after November first."

Homes grinned. "But rats can't, and some of 'em are counterfeiting tribal permits an' some are hiring on wit' da Indians, taking pay or a percent of da haul, and all three of dese practices are illegal. Plus, da tribals have ta be using da proper-size mesh on dere nets—so we've gotta go look, get it?" Then he added, "I've got seven, Eddie's got four. Who's next?"

Shaw, the officer from Mackinac County, whose first name Service couldn't remember, said, "Give me six."

Stevenson chimed in, "Two."

"Jesus," Homes said. "Are you trying ta shit on our patrol?"

"These patrols turn to shit on their own, no matter what we do," Budge Kangas piped up.

Service asked, "What are we doing?"

"Buck each, guessing how many of our machines will start," Homes said.

"I'll pass," Service said. Why would the men bet against themselves and the outcome of the mission?

"You can't pass," Homes said. "We'll give you five."

Bets made, Homes announced it was time to get the vehicles off the trailers and get them cranked up.

Service's snowmobile started up right away and Homes yelped that this was a good omen, because Service was driving the worst pile of shit in the entire Yoop.

Stevenson and Shaw could not start their machines. Service and Moody had both taken turns pulling the starter rope for Shaw, but it was no use. Homes told the two men to reload their sleds and take their patrol units over to a location off US 2, just north of Garden Corners. They were to wait there until the mission was completed, or until they were called in as reserves, in which case they would dump their trailers and race down Garden Road in their trucks.

"How far across?" Service shouted at Homes over the popping of the surging motors.

"Eight miles, more or less, due east. It'll take us about an hour."

"On flat ice?" Service asked. He had limited snowmobile experience. Homes laughed. "Since when is Bay de Noc ice flat?"

Service pulled a black balaclava down over his face, jammed his helmet over it, and pulled his goggles into place. He looked around. None of the helmets or machines were the same. A couple of men had newer model Rupps. There was a Ski-Doo and an elderly Polaris, none of them the top of the line power-wise, but all of them with better suspension than his machine.

The patrol pulled out with Homes immediately gunning his throttle and surging ahead, bouncing and yawing across the ragged ice of Big Bay de Noc. Service was last in line and struggling to maintain a steady speed, even with the others pulling ahead of him. Most of the time he rode standing on the machine, bending down to the handlebars and keeping his eyes glued ahead as he steered around moguls and ice chunks the size of refrigerators, popping tentatively over various pressure ridges created by alternate freezing and thawing. His posture was like riding a horse English-style, letting his knees rather than his back take the pounding from the ice as they surged eastward, their machines screaming and straining, leaving blue plumes of oil fumes hanging in their wakes. The ice ahead of him looked like a boulder-strewn wasteland rendered in white and gray, with hints of dirty blue and pale green.

Homes halted a mile west of Snail Shell Harbor and scanned ahead with his binoculars, waiting for the others to catch up.

"Stone said he'd mark net stakes wit' red patches," he yelled at them over idling engines as he continued to look at the area ahead. "He come out here on foot before first light. Spread out, an' when you find a stake, yell so we can figure out the layout."

Service had no idea what what was going on, but puttered slowly eastward with the other officers.

Moody found the first stake, and by then Homes announced he could see a lifting shack that was eight feet or so long, and two or three feet wide—shaped like a big Popsicle. Inside it the rats would place a space heater to protect the men pulling the nets from beneath the ice while they harvested their take. It took a while for Service to see what Homes was pointing to. The shed had been painted white and pale blue-gray to make it less visible. It was damn effective camouflage, Service noted, not the work of an amateur.

Homes sent Kangas north to try to locate the northernmost stake, and when that was found they reconvened at the first stake where Homes used an ice spud to clear the hole in the ice and hook the net line. The net line was connected to a crude wooden superstructure made of two-by-fours that the fishermen slid under the ice through a series of holes. The nets were attached to the superstructure, with weights to hold them down on the rocky bottom where the fish schooled. Homes probed in the hole with a long pole tipped with a hook until he caught something and pulled it up. The net was green nylon and began to ice as soon as it hit the open air, making it heavier and harder to move and manipulate. A few fish were stuck in the net. Homes took one look and said, "Large mesh. Let's look for net registrations. Dis one is naked," he added.

Kangas said, "The one on the north end said SSM one-twenty-two. It's red."

"Sault Saint Marie tribe," Homes said. "One of dem might be licensed for large mesh—if it's theirs. But are we dealing with tribals, or rats trying to act like tribals?"

Homes used the radio to contact Stone. He explained the situation, and Stone said he would make a call and find out who held license SSM 122.

The men used the time to find the rest of the marker stakes and to clear holes. An hour later Stone called back and said no license number 122 was assigned to the Soo Tribe, and told Homes he and the men should commence pulling the nets.

They eventually located nine nets connected in a series called a gang, and began the process of pulling them, taking turns in the lifting shack. While some men hauled, others removed illegal whitefish from the nets and stacked them on the ice like firewood.

They had been at it for more than three hours and had six of the nine nets piled on the ice. Stone came driving out in an unmarked green Ford pickup just as they were loading the unwieldy nets into a sled to be hauled back to the Stonington by one of the snowmobiles. They immediately transferred the icy, stinky nets and illegal fish into the bed of Stone's truck. Later they would move the nets into the evidence locker in the Escanaba office across from the U.P. State Fairgrounds, and let the legal process work. The fish would be frozen for later distribution to the needy.

"Dis will hurt da rats," Stone said, appraising the day's work. "Each net costs dose bastards eight grand new." Service blinked several times: The value of the gang was more than fifty *thousand* dollars? Suddenly the economic underpinnings of the seizure strategy made sense to him.

Hobby fishermen didn't invest fifty grand in equipment. The rats who told reporters they fished illegally to stay off welfare were bullshitting; this was about money, big money by U.P. standards.

"Surprised we haven't had visitors," Homes said to Stone.

"I expect we will," the acting lieutenant said, staring south toward Burn't Bluff. "Air Four's got his eyes on da Port Bar up near da park. Dere's a heap a machines dere, an' if da rats get liquored up and come lookin' for trouble, Pranger will give us a call." Stone turned to Service. "You want to help Moody in da lift shack?"

Service went inside and found a perspiring, red-faced Moody. "I'll take over," Service said after watching for a minute or so. Moody stepped back and lit a cigar. He crossed his arms and pulled on his elbows to stretch his muscles. "Be nice to have a winch," Moody said wistfully.

Service, who lifted weights and ran every day to stay in condition, soon found his neck, back, and arms burning from the effort of pulling the net, but he eventually got into a rhythm. He was paying attention only to what he was doing when there was a loud crunch and he was bounced off the wall of the shack and dropped hard to one knee, dazed but still clutching the net he had been recovering.

Moody grunted, "Fuck!" and shouldered the door open.

Service heard someone screaming, "Youse Nazi bastards have pulled your last fuckin' nets!" and Moody was yelling something about a truck.

Service tried to get out the door, but someone came crashing in and began punching and clubbing him. Service ducked, slid on wet ice, and sank a leg into the hole in the ice as the man landed on top, flailing at him with a board or a stick, an attack that was more emotion and testosterone than effect. Outside Service heard men shouting and the roar of unmuffled snowmobiles and knew that whatever was happening was larger than his attacker in the shack. He wrestled the man to the side, got a hand free, and jabbed him in the throat with the heel of his hand. The attacker immediately rolled off and started gagging. Service got to his feet, but the man was persistent, and although still gagging audibly, he clawed fruitlessly and furiously at Service's legs, trying to tackle him. Service took a half step, pivoted, and drove a fist into the man's temple, stopping him where he was.

Service shouldered his way through the door looking for Moody, but found the hood of a truck against the shack. All around him snowmobiles were racing around, and men in twos and threes were fighting and wrestling and swearing and grunting, and as he tried to figure it all out, his attacker again came at him from behind and tried to put him in a bear hug. Service pivoted away and smashed the man's collarbone with a short, hard chop. The assailant bellowed in pain and dropped to his knees as Service drove his hand into the man's throat again, and looked up to see another pickup truck coming directly at the lift shack.

He was too tired to think clearly, and before he could decide how to evade, the truck slid sideways and stopped about five feet away from him. Stone, hanging out the driver's window, shouted, "Jump in!"

"My machine!" Service protested.

"Da rats got it!" Stone said. "Get your ass *in!*"

Service got a foot on the back bumper and rolled into the bed of the truck, landing on a pile of slimy, icy green nylon that reeked of fish.

A man with a black ski mask was trying to run toward Stone's truck, a rifle in hand, but the truck began to fishtail and bounce wildly, its tires burning the ice as Stone tried to get purchase and accelerate. As soon as he had a little momentum he headed west, away from shore onto the bay ice.

From the rear of the truck Service watched snowmobiles turning to pursue, but it was hard to stay focused as the truck bounced and slid and yawed over the ice. Service managed to find a strip of metal welded to the side of the bed and took hold, feeling the cold sear his bare hand.

The wind blowing against him was freezing the leg he had dunked to mid-thigh and his face and hands, but he had no choice but to hold on. He managed to wrap some net mesh around his hand to keep his skin from direct contact with metal.

Eventually most of the snowmobiles broke off the chase and turned back to the east. Only a few continued to follow; Service counted four. It took several seconds to realize these were the other officers, and the machine that was missing was his. It also dawned on him that both thermoses, his helmet, goggles, gauntlets, binoculars, and flashlight were still on the Rupp.

As they approached the Stonington, Stone slowed considerably and began a deliberate and careful meandering course to the southwest, paralleling an eight-foot-high pressure ridge built up between the shore and the water's edge. After a while Stone stopped the truck and told Service to get out and walk. As soon as he was over the side Stone gunned the engine and the nose of the truck shot up the pressure ridge like a sounding whale, and crashed down hard on the other side, still on four wheels, but leaving the confiscated fishing nets draped over the cab and tailgate.

Service scrambled over the ice berm, pushed the nets back into the bed, and got into the passenger seat.

"Okay?" Stone asked, driving north and weaving between icy boulders sculpted by wind on the snow-covered barrens.

Service put his hands on the heater. "My stuff's on my machine."

"We'll get you more. You see da boys?"

"They're coming. The rats ran with them for a while."

"Dat's typical. Dey had dere attack. Typically dey chase for a bit, an' den retreat."

The marines had used similar tactics in Vietnam, Service remembered; only when they chased their enemies, they meant to kill them.

The other officers were still a couple of hundred yards out on the ice when Stone found a relatively clear path through the barrier cedars and followed it to the unplowed two-track road that led into the area where the squads and trailers were parked at the cemetery. He left the engine running, and handed Service his thermos. He groped under his seat and pulled out a flat pint of brandy, uncapped it, and set it between them. "Drink."

The officers pulled up on their snowmobiles as Stone got on the radio. He called Air Four several times, got no response, and finally reached Shaw on the radio.

"Where are youse?" Shaw asked.

"Back where you guys started dis morning," Stone said.

"On our way."

"You guys hear what happened out dere?" Stone asked.

"Sort of. Air Four called us and said you needed backup. We ran hard but got only to the parking lot before we got pelted with rocks and bottles."

"Air Four called *you*?"

"He said he couldn't raise any of youse."

"Okay, see you in a few."

Service got out. All the men were wide-eyed. Moody had a nasty cut on his ear. Homes had a cheek that was swelling fast, and Kangas was carrying his left arm like it had been broken.

"What happened?" Service asked.

"Asshole with an ice spud," Kangas said. "Fuckers were on us before we could react."

Service lit a cigarette and watched Homes scoop snow to hold against his face. Air Four had reached backup, but not the group under assault. Had their radios failed? Communications failures had been a way of life and had cost lives in Vietnam.

Stone got out of his truck and handed Service another cup of coffee.

"Who won?" Homes asked with a stupid grin.

"We got six of dere nine nets," Stone said. "Right now dat's da only score we care about, boys. Budge, I'm gonna follow youse over ta da hospital in Escanaba."

"I don't need a babysitter," Kangas complained.

"Dat shoulder needs attention."

Homes grinned. "It was like a joust out dere."

"What that was," Kangas said, "was a clusterfuck."

Moody joined in. "Why didn't somebody warn us we were about to get rammed?"

"She happened too fast," Stone said. "Air Four called Shaw and Stevenson for backup, but Joe couldn't reach us."

"Our equipment is shit," Kangas said. "We can't chase when we need to, and we were damn lucky to get outta there with the rats hot on our asses."

Shaw and Stevenson pulled in and got out. Shaw's windshield was broken out; he had jammed cardboard in the opening to help disrupt the wind flow. Stone walked around the two patrol cars and stopped behind Stevenson's. "You got a bullet hole back here—small caliber. You see da shooter?"

"Never knew anything was fired until now," Stevenson said, looking shaky.

The eight men slowly began to relax and exchange bits and pieces of the action, but Stone cut them off, insisting that Kangas and Moody get to the hospital, and the others pack it in and write their action reports.

Service and Homes were the last to leave. "What forms do I use for lost equipment?" Service asked.

Homes poked around in his Plymouth, but came up empty-handed. "Stop at the office in Escanaba tomorrow and draw what you need. Connie will handle it."

As a marine, Service had been accustomed to debriefings fairly soon after actions; the informality and apparent disorder of this aftermath left him confused and shaking his head. You couldn't learn from mistakes if you didn't catalog and dissect them.

"If we don't get our shit together," Service said, "somebody's gonna get killed."

Homes grinned and patted the larger man on the back. "Three patrols and you're already bitchin' like an old-timer. Do you realize dat's da first time we ever run a truck all da way across da ice from Garden ta Stonington?"

Service looked at the other man's beaming, swelling face. "You'd think an old-timer would learn to duck."

"You'd think," Homes said, as if nothing had happened, and handed Service five one-dollar bills. "Beginner's luck," he carped as he got into his patrol car and pulled away, towing his snowmobile.

The attackers had come in from the west. With air cover and workable communications, the tactic shouldn't have mattered, but commo had failed and the rats had gained tactical surprise. This, more than anything else he had seen, convinced Service the rat leaders knew what they were doing. He also thought about the man with the rifle out on the ice. Once again, if the rats had been intent on killing, they had both surprise and superior numbers today, and yet the only shot fired had been a small caliber into the trunk of a car up in the state park's parking lot. The leaders not only knew what they were doing—they were also exerting powerful discipline over their people. Service was impressed, and felt a cold rage growing inside him. The rats were beginning to look like a formidable enemy.

· 14 ·

ESCANABA, JANUARY 22, 1976

"I mean, none of you guys want that duty, right?"

The adrenaline and scrap of the previous day had more lingering effects than Service had expected, and he was increasingly pissed that the rats had gotten the thermos Shuck Gorley had given him. He pulled into the parking lot of the Escanaba DNR office, cursed the continuing snow, and glanced at the sign across the street, which read U.P. STATE FAIRGROUNDS. He shook his head. The actual state fair was held downstate, but that didn't keep Yoopers from declaring their own state above the bridge.

Connie Leppo was the effervescent dispatcher-secretary for the law enforcement district. She smiled when she looked up and saw him. "Heard youse guys went another round wit' da rats yesterday."

"You hear anything about Moody, Kangas, and Homes?"

"Looks like youse're da only one didn't get a mark out of it."

"Mine are hidden," he said.

She said, "Budge has a slight separation of da shoulder, Eddie took four stitches in his ear, and Colt you couldn't damage if you hit 'im in da head wit' an anvil shot out of a cannon."

"I lost some of my equipment. Homes said I need to fill out some forms."

"I heard," she said, setting a manila folder on the counter. "Just one form, and it's in dere."

"Thanks," he said.

"Len broke two fingers," she said.

"How?"

"On a rat jaw."

"He never said anything." When had Stone been out of his truck?

"He wouldn't," she said with a combination of admiration and disapproval. "He's old-school, like your dad."

What had Shuck told him—that times had changed and brains counted more than clubs? His old man would have gone ballistic yesterday, and Stone may have lost it temporarily during the melee, but he had kept enough presence of mind to get the nets into the truck and get them out of there. Confiscating nets had been the whole point of the patrol.

Service sat at the long table in the conference room and took care of his paperwork, including his handwritten report on the previous day's action. Leppo brought him two cinnamon rolls and coffee. "Mum made da bakery fresh dis morning," she said, "and she's got a little side business. You like 'em and want more, let me know, eh. She needs about twenty-four hours for special orders."

"Thanks," he said, peeling off a chunk of a roll.

She continued, "I'll ship your paperwork up to da regional office." Marquette will take care of getting youse a replacement machine. One thing: It won't be new."

He nodded, said facetiously, "I'm shocked."

She grinned. "I bet. The rest of da stuff you get locally. You pay for it and submit da receipts. Stone will cut a check to reimburse you."

"That sounds simple enough." And inconvenient.

"Except dat you have ta shop at an approved state facility, which means Delta Sporting Goods, or you go up ta Marquette, ta Lindstrom's."

"What about the gauntlets? They're military surplus."

"Da state doesn't buy directly from da feds. All surplus stuff we get from local dealers, but we don't have a good one up here, so za quartermeister, he leafs us za extras," she said, switching to a rough German accent. "*Unt* I haff za key to za zhtorage roomp. Finish your bakery, give a zhout, and I'll open it for you, *ja?*"

He put his report on Leppo's counter and she led him to the storage room and let him pick out a new set of gauntlets. "Da good news is, you can't very well pull snowmobile duty in da Garden if you don't have a machine ta ride, eh?"

"What's good about that?" he asked, looking at her.

"I mean, none of youse guys want dat duty, right?"

As he walked out to his patrol car, a green garbage truck pulled into the lot and a man got out and began carrying trash barrels to dump into the back of the behemoth.

The sign on the truck said BAY DE NOC TRASH HAULING: LOWEST RATES IN THE COUNTY. There was a local telephone number under the company name. The DNR office was almost in the middle of town. Why wasn't the city picking up the state's trash, and why wasn't the state buying surplus equipment directly from the feds? He put both questions out of his mind and headed back to the Mosquito, squinting through his spidered windshield and making a mental note to ask Leppo about the procedure for getting it fixed.

SLIPPERY CREEK, JANUARY 29, 1976

Only one thing was certain: He'd hit a nerve.

Cecilia Lasurm leaned her crutch against the wall inside the door, hopped over to a chair, sat down, took off her gloves and hat, which she dropped on the floor, draped her coat and purse on the back of the chair, lifted her leg, and unzipped her boot. Service had been up to Marquette earlier in the day, after an uneventful morning patrol. He'd returned minutes before she drove up. The last time he had seen her, she had worn black trousers and a black turtleneck. Tonight she wore a knee-length pleated blue wool skirt, her face glowed with makeup, and pearl teardrop earrings dangled from her earlobes. When she lifted her leg to shed the boot, he had been shocked by its length and shape and had looked away, telling himself such feelings were not only unprofessional, but also weird.

"I believe this snow will never stop," she said.

Waves of Alberta clippers had been skidding across the upper Great Lakes, leaving two to four inches a day since the New Year began, and long-range forecasts called for the assault to continue. "There won't be any on the ground in August," he said.

Lasurm didn't react to his lame joke. "We've got a lot more than usual," she said, "but not as much as here."

"Garden, the epicenter of the Yooper Riviera," he said, attempting another joke and wondering why.

Lasurm smiled. "I must admit that the DNR's presence has been reestablished, but you people are still taking a licking down there. The way to break a bully's hold is to erode people's fear of him. You have to expose him to his followers."

"I see," Service said unenthusiastically. Two days ago another patrol, this one attempting to pull nets off Burn't Bluff, had been fired at by a sniper. Homes had been there and called that night to vent. With Metrovich gone to Lansing, and Attalienti and Stone running the show, officers were expecting a change in approach and results. So far they were not seeing either, and he knew that potentially, a lot depended on his recon.

"Coffee?" he asked.

"Thank you," she said. "That four-car stunt a few weeks back," she said. "What was that supposed to accomplish?"

Service filled their cups and sat down. "Our deal is that you have to convince me that you've got something worthwhile."

Lasurm raised an eyebrow. "All business, eh?"

"If I come down there, I'll need to be in the area at least ten days, and maybe two full weeks."

She nodded resolutely. "You'll stay with me."

"Too risky for both of us," he immediately countered.

"You let me assess my own risk," she said. "As I tried to explain before, I'm everywhere and nowhere. People don't really notice me. Besides, are you expecting to check into a no-tell motel, or live rough in the woods? One sighting and that will be that. You're already on their list."

"What list?"

"You people have your list and they have theirs. They make a note of each one of you they see and then try to identify you. They've even sent people up to other counties to check you guys out."

"Where do they get the names and addresses?"

"I don't know, but I know they have your name. You've been down there at least twice, and maybe you were part of the four-car run when you guys all wore masks. That whole deal got their sphincters tight. Why did the DNR come down in four cars and why were they wearing masks?" Lasurm laughed softly. "You shoulda heard them whine about that!"

Stone had told them the masks were for psychological purposes, and apparently they had actually had some effect. This surprised him.

"They got your Rupp, and at first they thought your name was Shuck."

"That was the name on one of my thermoses," he said.

"They were able to determine that Officer Gorley is retired up to Newberry, but eventually they got your name."

"How?"

She shrugged. "I don't know everything."

"Do they know where I live?"

"Don't Yoopers always know where the game warden lives?"

"Then why are we meeting here?" He was flabbergasted.

"Because tonight they're putting down nets," she said, "and they don't have the people or the time to be sitting around watching you and your little trailer. If they weren't busy tonight, I would have cancelled. Next time, we'll select another place. You should assume they know where you live, but that doesn't mean they are watching around the clock. So," she went on, sucking in a deep breath, "you're to have ten days to two weeks with me on the Yooper Riviera. When?"

"I haven't decided yet."

"You need to decide and give me some warning so I can do what I have to do. Do you think you can get in undetected?"

"I'd better," he said.

Lasurm sipped her coffee. "The incident at Burn't Bluff the day before yesterday? One shooter," she said.

"You saw what happened?"

"No, I heard the shots and saw someone, but I couldn't see who. I can only attest to number."

"But that you're sure of."

"Absolutely. Four shots were fired in close order, and then I saw him about fifteen minutes later."

"Where were you?"

"Trying to carry something from my truck to the house."

"You live near Burn't Bluff?"

"Technically I live *on* it, though in reality I'm about three hundred yards east. The shooter came out through my west wood line to meet a vehicle. When they do these things, they usually drop off the miscreants and pick them up afterwards. And no, I did not see the pickup vehicle."

He had wondered about this, but he wanted more information on the list. "You claim they have a list."

"They *have* a list—it's not a claim. And how do they manage it? I don't know. There are sympathizers everywhere. Perhaps some of them even wear green?"

It was unthinkable that a CO would knowingly confirm information for the rats. "You said you would provide us with names," he said.

Lasurm opened her purse and took out a small piece of notebook paper. "The leaders," she said, "in order of importance."

He read the names: Peletier, Groleau, Renard, St. Cyr, Troscair, Gagnon.

"All French," he said, tapping the list, "but Gascoyne and Metcalf aren't here." Gascoyne owned the commercial fish house in Fairport, Metcalf the Garden establishment.

"Gascoyne and Metcalf hired Odd Hegstrom," she said. "Some of the rats, as you and your comrades so colorfully characterize them, work for Gascoyne and Metcalf and have their own fishing interests on the side. The big fellows would like to see the so-called rat operations out of business because they cut into fish stocks, which means their profits, but the same people who compete with them illegally also work for them at times and, in some cases, sell fish to them, which puts the fish houses between a rock and a hard place."

"The fish houses buy from the rats?"

"Sometimes it's cheaper than sending out your own boats and crews, especially those times of year when it's illegal to lay your hands on the fish you need for business. Better to let others risk their boats, nets, and so forth, yes? You people need to understand how interconnected everything is in the Garden, blended by business interests, intermarriage, and money. The word down there is that Hegstrom convinced Gascoyne and Metcalf he could get them ten more years of fishing before the ax falls."

"Based on what—and why ten years?" Service wondered if the state had tried to subpoena the fish houses' financial records, and if not, why not?

"I don't know," she said.

Stone and Attalienti had made similar observations about the Garden, and it was becoming clearer to Service that his two supervisors had more than a rudimentary idea of what was really happening. Still, why had Hegstrom promised ten years, and why had that been a selling point for the fish house operators?

"Peletier is the lead rat," he said, looking at the list and refocusing the conversation.

"When Pete talks, the rest of them listen."

"What does he do for a living?" Service asked.

Lasurm said, "Like most people down there he can do a lot of things, legally and illegally. Officially he's a carpenter."

"Does he lead from the front or the rear?"

"I don't know," she said, "but you can assume if he's not involved on a particular day, he knows about it and has given it his blessing. Most of his people know to keep their mouths shut. As evidence, have you had a single informant other than me?"

"Mouths shut, or else?"

"Your words, not mine," she said. "All of them on the list can trace ancestors back to the original settlers of the peninsula. Most of them came up from Beaver and St. Martin islands. A few came down from Quebec." Lasurm paused for a second and continued. "Pete is married to Ranse Renard's sister. Renard is married to St. Cyr's eldest daughter, and so forth. Interconnected: They're all part of one thing and of a single mind about the DNR and its rules." She made direct eye contact and said quietly, "They *really* don't care for you fellows, and with good reason if you look at it from their perspective."

Lasurm studied him for a moment before continuing. "I wonder if you know your own department's history? In the 1880s fish harvests were down and the state banned fishing with nets for certain species in some locations around Beaver Island. The fishermen objected, and said the state could not tell them what to do," she said. "In 1897 the state sent a game warden out to the island and he ended up shooting at a boat and confiscating a fisherman's gear. The locals hyperbolized this as the Beaver Island War. The result was that some of the fishermen migrated north to the U.P. where they expected they could pretty much do as they pleased," she said, drawing in another breath. "And here we are nearly eighty years later, and the state and the fishermen are doing precisely the same damn thing: Fighting over fish. How's that for irony?"

Could she be right about this? He also wondered why no one had ever written an in-depth history of the department. A marine wore the Corps' history as a second skin. "What about the differences between farmers and fishermen?" She had mentioned this during their first meeting.

"The fruit growers are a separate branch of the farming community. They raise about fifty varieties of apples and do okay. The other farmers—even those claiming to live hand to mouth—as well as some of the rats have started cultivating dope as a side business. They're calling it Garden Green."

"Dope?"

"Marijuana. It's not what you'd call a developed crop yet, but it's under way, and those who use it swear it's among the most potent around. The real legit farmers resent the rats and dope growers because they scare away customers."

Dope? He'd seen some drug use in Vietnam, especially among rear echelon motherfuckers, and it was obviously a problem throughout much of the United States, but here in the U.P.? After a second he decided it made sense. If the rest of the country was rife with drugs, why not here? He reached for the envelope he'd picked up in Marquette, put it on the table in front of Lasurm, and slid out the photograph. He wasn't sure why he was showing it to her, except that if Lasurm was as knowledge- able and connected as she claimed, and the woman in jail was from the Garden, she might provide an ID and help move the case along.

Lasurm stared for a long time and he noticed that she spread out her fingers and placed them on the surface of the photograph—to cover it or draw it closer, he couldn't tell.

When she finally looked up at him she said, "Is this what you people call a mug shot?"

"Yes."

She drew in a deep breath, lifted her hand as if it had suddenly quin- tupled in weight, bent down, picked up her boot, and slid her foot into it. "I have to leave now," she said with a flat voice.

"Do you recognize the person in the photo?" he asked.

"I have to go now," she repeated, hopping to the door and attaching her crutch to her wrist. "It's a long drive."

"She's in the Marquette County Jail charged with attempted homi- cide and felonious assault, and probably some counts of grand theft. Odd Hegstrom is her lawyer."

She ignored this as she walked out the door. Her departure was so abrupt that he wasn't sure what to think. Only one thing was certain: He'd hit a nerve. He immediately began to question the jailed woman's Garden connection and Cecilia Lasurm's motives. She was their sole in- formant so far. Or was she? What if she was working for the other side? He refilled his coffee cup and took off his boots. Even if it was a setup, he knew he had to go to the Garden.

16

GARDEN PATROL (AIR RECON),
JANUARY 31, 1976

" . . . look for shadows on da snow."

J oe Flap tended to the controls of his single-engine Beaver with a dis-
interest that had Grady Service in a cold sweat. They had taken off
from Escanaba at 11 A.M., headed northeast, and looped south to run
down the west coast of the Garden Peninsula. For the first time in
weeks they had seen a cloudless, snowless sunrise, and though a bluebird
sky surrounded them, the flight was anything but smooth. It was vaguely
reminiscent of the *chop-chop-chop* of running a snowmobile across the
ice of Big Bay de Noc.

Joe Flap said, "Toivo-da-Yooper's down Detroit for da Red Wings
game, eh. It bein' Detroit, dere's flatlanders in da row behind 'im, and
dis guy's yackety-yack and says real loud, 'Only two tings come down
Canada: hockey players and hookers.'"

Flap looked to see if Service was listening before continuing. "Toivo,
he turns around real slow, eyeballs da jerk, and says, 'Da wifey's from
Canada.' Da flatlander's eyes get real big an' he says, 'Yeah, what position
does she play?'"

Service let the pilot laugh himself out and said, "Three things come
from Canada."

Flap scrunched up his face. "Eh?"

"They send us snow, too."

The pilot clucked and shook his head. "Was a joke."

Service stared out at the Garden Peninsula as they cruised at 120
miles per hour. There was no wind at ground level, and not much at two
thousand feet—when Flap cared enough to keep the altimeter needle
steady. Service saw fields and farm sections and pastures, snow-covered
roads, woodlots and rolling hills, the whole thing looking idyllic and be-
nign, the picture of serenity from above; he pictured hardy people in their
houses, fires crackling in their fireplaces and wood burners. Blue-gray

plumes of wood smoke wafted from chimneys and corkscrewed straight up until the surrounding air skinned the heat out of the rising air.

"What're we lookin' for?" Flap asked.

"Nothing in particular. Just give me the Joe Flap special look at the Garden."

Flap considered this. "Well, I ain't pranged here," the pilot said, adding, "yet."

They crossed US 2 west of Garden Corners and headed south along the peninsula's jagged western shoreline. Service had a map in his lap and traced their route: the wide half-moon arc of Jack's Bluff and the insinuation of Valentine Point and Kates Bay, which barely jutted in from Big Bay de Noc; Ansels Point; the two-mile-long Garden Bay; Puffy Bay next; then the massif of Garden Bluff, and off to the west in the bay, Round and St.Vital islands. Ahead were South River Bay, Snake Island, and Middle Bluff, which marked the location of Snail Shell Harbor in the lap of Fayette State Park; Sand Bay lay south of the park; the jagged cliffs of Burn't Bluff next, and Sac Bay tucked politely beneath the towering bluff's southern bulge. Then, on down to Fairport with Rocky, Little Summer, and Summer islands off to the south, and farther out, the purple-gray silhouettes of Poverty, Gravelly, Gull, and St. Martin islands.

Service used his binoculars to scan for nets or lift shacks on the ice, but saw nothing.

Joe Flap braced the stick between his knees and flew with both hands on his own binoculars. "Sometimes you don't see da lift shacks if dey got da good camo, so youse look for shadows on da snow. An' look for foot trails packed down where dey move from hole to hole."

He added, "Dere at eleven o'clock, see the shadow?" They were near Ansels Point. Service looked and finally located the structure, which, like the one they had encountered on the patrol, was painted to blend in.

"Can you land anywhere down there?" Service asked.

"Almost," Flap said, nosing the aircraft down.

From two thousand feet the ice had looked smooth and smoky gray-blue. As they descended Service could begin to see the jagged rises, severe moguls, and precipitous pressure ridges that characterized the chaotic surface; by the time they were lined up for a landing, he was sure the ice below would shred the bottom of the plane, but Joe Flap eased the bird down onto the aircraft's skis with an assertive *thump*. He let the plane skid and hop for a moment before slamming the throttle forward, jerking the nose of the aircraft into a steep banking climb with the engines screaming their objection. Service thought he was going to lose his stomach.

The ride on the ice had been bumpy, the sound like an ironing board skimming across a rock garden, but the ride was not nearly as harsh as on a snowmobile or in Stone's truck, there being more give in the aircraft's skis and struts. "We'll run up da eastern shore and cut back across da center," Joe Flap said, banking the plane south and twisting the nose back to the northeast as they began to gain altitude.

The one thing Service had seen on the way down was that the various bluffs along the west coast were close to sheer and at least two hundred feet high. Even with snow, he could see that the multihued limestone outcrops were pocked with holes and small caves, offering good places for shooters to hide themselves to ambush lawmen below.

By contrast the east coast of the Garden Peninsula sprawled before them was more wooded and flatter than the west coast, and punctuated by numerous cedar and tamarack swamps that looked like black tumors from above.

On their next run Service asked Flap to descend to five hundred feet and fly along the road that led from Garden down to Fairport as he studied the terrain where the rock-throwing had taken place. He saw two-tracks and snowmobile trails within a third of a mile of the cedar swales where the attackers had hidden. He made notes on his maps as they flew. There was little talk, and most of the time Joe Flap was watching the ground with his binoculars and not paying attention to anything that might be at their altitude.

After nearly three hours of crisscrossing the peninsula, Flap turned the aircraft west toward Escanaba.

"Do you make night runs down here?" Service asked as they flew along.

"When dey ask," Joe Flap said.

"No, I mean do you make *your own* night runs down here?"

"Sometimes I come up and just look around at night. You can see stuff good if dere's a good moon, or if dey use any light at all. If we had enough people on da ground at night, we might make some good pinches, but dey don't seem ta want ta do dat, and I can't blame 'em. Hard enough to deal wit' rats in daylight, eh."

17

GRAYLING, FEBRUARY 1, 1976

"All this over fish?*"*

He had decided that using Brigid Mehegen to help him get a parachute would not be smart: too close to home, and her grandfather was nosy, eccentric, and unpredictable. Better to get help from someone he knew he could rely on.

Grady Service and Luticious Treebone were about the same height, but Tree was considerably heavier, the difference being a lot more muscle. When the towering black man swaggered through the swinging doors of Spike's Keg o' Nails, all sound stopped—as if all the oxygen had been sucked out of a vacuum jar. The big man smiled, waved a hand regally, and announced, "As you were, people—I ain't Jimmy Hoffa."

The patrons laughed and went back to their conversations.

Treebone took a seat across a small table from his friend. "How come when *you* need something, I always gotta drive up to some whiteboy redneck roadhouse?"

"Lots of Detroit people have places up here," Service said.

"Not of the brother hue," Tree said. "You see why I couldn't be no woods cop. I ain't got the prejudice, but I gotta see my own people, you know?"

"And Kalina hates small-town living."

Treebone rolled his eyes and nodded solemnly. "There is that."

"You bring it?" Service asked.

"In the trunk. I ever leave you hang?"

Luticious Treebone took reliability as a religion. Service had graduated from Northern Michigan where he had been a fair student and a competent hockey player. Tree had played football and baseball at Wayne State and graduated cum laude. They both had volunteered for duty in the Marine Corps, and met at Parris Island boot camp; they both took the same specialized training, and spent a tour in the same long-range recon unit in Vietnam, both of them coming back with numerous decorations and little desire to talk about what they had seen or done. Both had attended the Michigan State Police Academy in Lansing and spent two years as Troop road patrollers before transferring to the DNR. After just one year as a CO in Oscoda County, Treebone took a job with the Detroit Metropolitan Police. They had been friends for more than twenty years, and were closer than most brothers.

"How's Kalina?" Service asked. Kalina was his friend's wife. It had been because of her he'd taken the job in Detroit.

"Wonderin' how the single life's sittin' with you."

"I haven't bought a leisure suit yet."

Treebone howled. "They got that disco shit up there?"

"Hell, we just learned about some guy named Elvis. You gonna ask what I'm up to?"

Treebone shook his head. "I know you're going outside the envelope and I really don't wanna know more than that, man. You believe they give you your daddy's old territory?"

"I'm not spending a whole lot of time there," Service said, and explained to his friend the situation in the Garden Peninsula. He did not talk about his surveillance assignment.

"All this over *fish*?"

"Fish *is* money."

"I hear you, but more money in fish than dope? The brothers hear that, there won't be no fish left in the Detroit River or Lake St. Clair!"

"We got dope too," Service said. "Supposed to be a new thing. You want to see what you can find out about it? Street name is Garden Green."

"I heard of that shit, man, but even if they got supply, a buncha Yoopers not gonna be supplyin' Motown, dig?"

"If it turns out to be nothing, so be it."

"Kalina is dying to know if you're dating anybody special."

"Nothing steady."

Treebone laughed. "I told her you'd be married to your job."

"It's not like that."

"Bullshit. You gonna invite me up there this summer to chase some of those pretty little brook trout you don't tell nobody about?"

"You bet." Trout fishing was a passion that both men shared. When they first met, Treebone had been a confirmed worm-dunker, but had since converted to fly fishing and—when he had time, which wasn't often—was learning to tie his own flies.

"From what you say, it sounds like you boys in green don't have your act together up in the Garden."

"We're trying."

"They sendin' you in to do a snoop, am I right?"

Service said nothing.

"I know you'll think it through before you commit," his friend said quietly. "Just remember—this ain't 'Nam, and you are no longer in the business of capping bad guys. It's our job to catch 'em, gather evidence, and let the courts take it from there. End of speech. Now can we eat?"

They were eating cheeseburgers when a young woman in a ski sweater came over to the table and nervously tapped Treebone on the shoulder. "I'm sorry to interrupt your lunch, but do you play for the Lions?"

"No, ma'am; I just got out of the joint."

The woman scrambled away with a red face.

Service looked at his friend and shook his head. "You just have to stir the pot."

"Just reinforcing the stereotype. A big black man's either an ex-con or a jock."

"And everybody north of Detroit is a redneck."

"No man, north from Detroit to the bridge they're rednecks; *above* the bridge, you motherfuckers are a whole different species—one they don't even have a word for."

Service looked at his friend and saw he was not smiling. "I hope this is not gonna be an armed snoop," Treebone said.

When Service didn't respond, Treebone grimaced.

"Be cool," his friend said as they embraced. "You need somebody to get your back, you call."

18

PREACHER LAKE, FEBRUARY 6, 1976

*"Once people take on a deep notion about
something, you can't change their minds."*

His old man had driven him to the Mimolov swamp when he was thirteen. They had parked on a jack pine plain and walked nearly a mile through muddy swales and cedar tangles until they got to a single ruined building standing on a hummock of high ground. The building's roof had rotted away, but most of the walls of lime- and fieldstone still stood.

The old man sat on the stone sill where a window had once been, lit a cigarette, popped the cork of his pocket flask, took a long pull, and said, "What do you see?"

Service had no idea what the old man wanted; he rarely did.

"Guess what this place was?" the old man asked with slight irritation.

"A church or a school?"

"Church," the old man said. "Good. Now, what do you see?"

"The roof's gone, windows too. Porkies, probably."

"Okay. What else?"

Service saw nothing and leaned against a wall, wishing the old man wouldn't pull this stuff on him. The stone floor was littered with chunks of stone that had broken off under years of freezing and thawing, and there were holes between the fieldstones, but no sign of nests. He looked along the base of the wall. No spiderwebs, no animal droppings, no tracks in the dust, no sign of animals at all. It was normal for animals to move into abandoned structures almost immediately.

"No animals," Service said.

The old man nodded. "Right. A preacher named Proudfit built a church here, all by himself. Back then the loggers were thicker than mosquitoes. He hired a guy to go round to the logging camps to announce services, and one Sunday the loggers came and found Proudfit hanging. Nobody knew if somebody had hung him, or if he'd done himself in, but the church got marked as dark and people stayed away, and over time it came to be a place where scores got settled. Two men had a beef, they came here and fought it out—sometimes to the death, sometimes with spectators—but usually it was just the two men alone with their hatred. Some say hundreds have died here. More likely it wasn't anything close to that, but people were afraid of this place. At one time there were a thousand people living within a mile of here. They called it Preacher Lake. Within six months of Proudfit's hanging, they were all gone, abandoned their shacks and cabins and moved on. The Indians still claim the place has spirits all around it, which is why animals won't come into it—not a bird, not a snake, not an ant."

"There's no lake," he told his father.

"Never was. Just a string of beaver ponds, and they're long gone."

"Do you believe in spirits?" Grady asked his father.

"Makes more sense to me that Proudfit built this place on bad ground—that there's something here animals can't tolerate. 'Course, porkies ate the wood, so not all the animals are afraid of it, right?" The old man dropped a cigarette on the floor and mashed it with the heel of his boot. "Once people take on a deep notion about something, you can't change their minds. Don't matter if what they believe makes sense or not," his father said.

"Do people still come here?"

"Not to kill each other. Your great-grandfather showed me this place, and I've been comin' since I was a tyke. I've never seen another human being except those I brought. You ever need real privacy, this is your place."

Service had never forgotten that day. He had visited the place regularly over the years and had never seen anyone, which he attributed to the area's isolation and inaccessibility rather than fear of evil spirits.

It was the perfect place to meet Cecilia Lasurm.

During his time in Newberry, he had gotten to know the waitress Nikki-Jo Jokola, pals without romantic involvement. When he was ready to place the ad in the Manistique paper, Nikki-Jo took care of it, and they'd put Nikki-Jo's phone number in; when Lasurm called her, Nikki-Jo told her to dress warm and where and when to meet him.

He had selected the site so that she had to negotiate a long, almost perfect oxbow in the road, and he had placed himself so that he could make sure she wasn't being followed. He had arrived three hours before their meeting to wait for her. When she drove by, slipping and sliding, he could see her talking to herself and fighting the steering wheel, but she was alone. He had quickly trotted back to his vehicle to wait for her to reach him.

When she pulled up, he was waiting on his new Rupp, the motor running. Lasurm looked tired and nervous.

"You mighta picked an easier place to get to."

"We don't want easy," he said.

The snow was knee-deep, the surface crusted over. He had a sled behind the snowmobile, which was loaded with gear. He had already broken trail into the old church, stacked firewood, and arranged an area for their arrival.

He started the snowmobile and held out his hand for her to get on behind him.

"You sure this thing will handle it?" she asked.

"You should have seen my old one," he said.

She smiled. "I have."

His mouth hung open. "You know where the Rupp is?"

She nodded. "They think of it as a trophy. They get drunk and urinate on it."

Service cringed. *Rats.* When they got to the remains of the building, he helped her inside, lit a kerosene lantern, and ignited a fire between some rocks on the stone floor. He put a small iron grill over the fire and put on the coffeepot. He had rigged a tarp to make a lean-to inside the ruins, and set it up so that they and the fire would be protected from snow falling through the open roof.

"This seems extreme," she said.

"Coming into the Garden is extreme. I wanted to make sure that you weren't followed and that we'd have complete privacy."

He had balsam boughs stacked on the floor, covered with a canvas tarp. Two sleeping bags were rolled up on the tarp. He didn't expect to spend the night, but winter weather was fickle and it paid to be prepared.

He had trapped two snowshoe hares the day before in the swamp behind the Airstream, and now he put the meat on a metal grate over the fire and began to grill them.

Lasurm watched him go about his tasks, sipped her coffee, and remained silent.

"You're thinking about living rough in the Garden?" she asked.

"There may be a couple of days when I have to," he said. "There's a lot of territory down there and I've got to cover it on foot. I thought about snowshoes or skis, but I don't want tracks. It's easier to cover footprints."

"There are several places down there where you can hole up," she said. "Did you bring maps?"

She used a pencil to mark the places and described them to him. "You're going to work at night?" she asked.

He nodded.

"This place makes me feel uneasy," Lasurm said, looking around the abandoned, decaying structure.

He related the story his father had told him years before, and after he stopped talking, she said, "I feel what the Indians feel, don't you?"

"No," he said, pouring coffee for her.

"You don't know how to read me," she said as he turned the cooking hares with his knife. She held up her leg and wiggled her boot. "I can't say I miss the other one," she said. "It's more of an inconvenience than anything. Life is about managing inconvenience . . . would you agree?"

"I never thought about it."

"I'm not surprised," she said. "I would think that game wardens prefer to swim in either black or white water. For you people, the ambiguity of gray is the real inconvenience."

"It's not that simple," he said.

"I'm sure you find gray very frustrating," she said.

"What is it that brings out your preachy side?" he asked.

She laughed. "You don't need a church to be spiritual."

"Like the Indians?"

"Anywhere was their church, and I'm *not* preachy. I'm simply comfortable in my own beliefs."

"Such as?"

"Lots of things churchgoing Christians would not agree with."

He sensed she was pressing him to ask for more, but he had his own agenda. "You're gonna run a lot of risk with me in the Garden," he said.

"I don't fear risks," she said, "but if you're going to be out nights, you're going to have to be in by certain hours, or stay out all the next day. People in the Garden aren't nosy so much as observant, and what they see, they talk about. They say information can move from one end of the peninsula to the other faster than a lightning bolt. We call it Garden speed."

Where was she going with this?

"For all practical purposes, my house is on Burn't Bluff. I'm two and a half miles from Fayette and the Port Bar, which is a short walk from the state park," she said. "It's four miles south to Fairport and seven miles north from my place to Garden." She drew pencil lines on the map to show him. "If you get caught out, there are several places where you can lay over for the day." Again, she marked the places on the map and described each one to him.

If nothing else, Lasurm was thorough.

"Did you kill people in Vietnam?" she asked.

"Vietnam is in the past," he said. Where was she going now?

"We only left there last year and then with our tails between our legs," she said. "How does the U.S. lose a war to rice growers?"

"We didn't lose," he countered.

"Perhaps not on the battlefield," she said. "But there was no true political commitment or mobilization of national will, and wars are not all won and lost on battlefields. They sent you over there and you fought and you were on your own with not a lot of support from back home."

"You're not really talking about Vietnam," he said, watching her eyes and trying to read the tone in her voice.

"What's Lansing's commitment to the Garden?" she said. "They send you people in to enforce what amounts to an administrative rule and give you no tools. Why? Is Lake Michigan more important than Lake Superior or Lake Huron?"

"What are you driving at?" he asked.

"If you check around the government I think you'll find that each salmon or trout taken in state waters by a sportfisherman represents about eighty dollars to the state economy. That same fish from a commercial license brings the state a buck and a quarter."

"Those numbers are news to me." Astonishing news.

"It's news to a lot of people," she said, "and if the numbers aren't a hundred percent accurate, they certainly reflect the magnitude of the ratio. If you're Lansing, why revitalize commercial fishing? There's a lot more money to be made boosting sportfishing."

He couldn't dispute her logic, and wondered why he'd never heard such data before.

"Sportfishing is more important than commercial fishing for the state economy, and tourism is our second-leading business. The DNR planted Pacific salmon to eat the alewives and cut down on the summer die-offs, which stunk up beaches and put off tourists. I doubt they foresaw the economic windfall," Lasurm said. "Do you know about Jondreau?"

He did. "A L'Anse Chippewa," he said. "We were briefed on the case during training. COs busted him ten years ago for not having proper safety equipment on his boat and he fought the ticket."

She nodded. "It happened in 1965," she said. "The lower court dismissed his case, but he took it to the state supreme court, which found in his favor. This had limited impact in terms of tribal rights, but it helped the tribes see that the courts could be useful. More important is Albert 'Big Abe' LeBlanc," she said. "LeBlanc is a Bay Mills Chippewa. He fished in a closed area during a closed period, and when he was arrested, U.P. Legal Services helped him fight it. You know—UPLS?" she said, lifting an eyebrow.

He shrugged; he'd never heard of it before. LeBlanc had been arrested while he was in the Newberry district, and a lot of the officers had bitched that it could lead to Indians fishing and hunting whenever and wherever they wanted. There had also been a lot of national publicity and heated editorials about the case. Attalienti's secretary was named LeBlanc. Was she tribal, a relative of Big Abe?

"Don't they teach you people *anything* in your training? U.P. Legal Services was created by Odd Hegstrom. What we have now is a federal case, *U.S. versus the State of Michigan,* and in all likelihood the feds will uphold treaty rights as they now interpret them. The LeBlanc case started last year, but there's no way it will come to trial for another two or three years, and it could be ten years before it all gets settled."

"And then?" he asked.

"I don't have a crystal ball," she said, "but what if the state eventually buys out all those people who still had valid commercial licenses for Lakes Michigan and Huron and lets only the Indians have all of Superior's waters and certain parts of the other Great Lakes?"

"That seems like a reach," he said. But the fewer licenses in effect when this happened, the less the state would have to pay out, and there was little doubt that Order Seventeen was aimed at reducing the number of licenses. Everybody in law enforcement had assumed this had been done to revitalize commercial fishing in Lake Michigan, protecting the commercial fishermen from themselves in the short term to improve their long-term interests—but what if they were all missing the real intent?

"Talk to your people and see what they have to say," she said. "It certainly makes for an interesting what-if, eh?"

It did; and ten years fit the time frame Hegstrom was alleged to have given the Garden commercial fishermen. If she was right, Order Seventeen was the preparatory move to boost sportfishing in Lake Michigan and remove white commercial fishermen. If those fishermen had ten years left to make money, they were going to keep violating, and to hell with what Lansing said. After a moment he concluded that if they were going to violate, they'd try to do it in such a way so as to not jeopardize their licenses. This crude analysis also supported Len Stone's contention that the whole Garden situation was driven by money. Lasurm knew one helluva lot, but he couldn't just take her word for it. He needed to probe Lansing and find out what was going on. If he could just figure out how.

When the meat was done, he cut portions and put them on military mess plates and gave Lasurm salt and pepper. They ate quietly.

"There's something about meat grilled outdoors," she said.

After their meal, they talked more about logistics while he was in the Garden, and he told her he was aiming for arrival on February 14, so long as the weather was bad. If not, he'd push it back twenty-four hours, or until a time that it got bad.

"You're coming in bad weather?" she said.

"Anything short of a Big Blue Norther," he said.

"You really *are* an interesting man," she said.

"Last time we met, you walked out when I showed you the mug shot," he said.

"The girl in that photograph is twenty-two. She is my daughter, and she's a junkie."

"She's the real reason you came to us," he said.

"Too bloody late," she said. "For her."

"Who got Hegstrom to take her case?"

"I don't know," she said, "but I can guess. We'll talk more when you come to the Garden."

It was a less than satisfying answer, but he told himself it would have to suffice.

19

LANSING, FEBRUARY 10, 1976

"If the state owns it, Jumping Bill manages it."

Detroit *Free Press* columnist had once written that finding out what went on inside state government in the capital was akin to going to the moon: a helluva challenging journey to a destination without air, water, logic, or significant gravity. Michigan's elected legislators were notorious paradoxically for ferocious independence and blind party loyalty. But even some of the most popular elected officials were often ignorant of the engine that ultimately drove the governmental machine.

One night Service's old man had come home with a friend, both of them soused and stumbling around like the earth was on gimbals. "Son, this is the most powerful man in Lansing."

Service remembered his first impression of Bill Fahey: five feet tall and equally wide, with a thick red nose and diaphanous gray angel hair that seemed to grow in clumps. The little man had grinned and mumbled, "Geez oh Pete, da game warden speaketh truth!"

"Jumping Bill" Fahey held the official title of state properties manager, a job he had held since 1947. "If the state owns it, Jumping Bill manages it," his father explained. "He's the state's landlord."

Service had thought about this some and never quite understood how someone in such a nondescript position could be so powerful; he wrote it off to his father's sense of hyperbole and too much alcohol in both men.

Jumping Bill came around regularly after that, and Service eventually discovered that they had become pals after his old man wrote the man a ticket for shooting a deer ten minutes after shooting hours had ended, and Fahey had paid his ticket without bellyaching. Out of this unusual meeting, a friendship was born. Fahey was originally from Gladstone, and still had a hunting camp north of Rapid River. One time Service had queried the old man about his other friends and discovered that his father had written tickets on every one of them, usually after they had become friends.

One morning Service got out of bed to find his father and Fahey drunk on the kitchen floor, a stringer of gutted and dessicated brook trout between them. Service had washed the trout, rolled them in corn-meal, and fried them. The smell brought the drunks back to life, and when they crawled into chairs, he served them trout for breakfast, setting a bottle of Jack Daniel's between them.

When his father died, the governor had attended the funeral and had heaped praise on the officer who had been drinking on duty and stepped in front of a truck. Service never doubted that Bill Fahey had somehow engineered the governor's appearance, and it was then that he began to suspect that Fahey's power was something more than mere drunk-talk.

When Service graduated from the Michigan State Police Academy, Fahey showed up for the ceremony, red-faced and mumbling, stinking of gin, food stains on his twenty-year-old tie. He'd not seen or talked to Fahey since his father's funeral, and was surprised to see him. He was even more surprised to see Colonel Edgar Browning Proctor, the top Troop in the state, fawn all over the little Yooper, who rarely uttered a complete—much less coherent—sentence.

Fahey pumped his hand, grinning and slurring, "Geez oh Pete."

After the ceremony, Proctor (who was called EBP behind his back—for "extra big prick") had pulled Service aside.

"You're a friend of Fahey's?"

"My dad was."

"Your father?"

"Frank Service."

Proctor had gaped at him. "You're Ironfist Service's son? I didn't know," the state police commander said. "I was post commander in Iron Mountain, and I knew your dad. If you're half the cop your father was, I'm glad we've got you in the Troops."

Fahey told him after the graduation party to look him up if he ever needed anything.

Until now there had been no reason.

Fahey answered his own phone. "Properties, Fahey."

"Mister Fahey, it's Grady Service."

"Geez oh Pete," Fahey said. "How does it feel to ramrod the Mosquito?"

"Good," Service said. Had his father's friend been keeping track of him?

"Geez, you sound good," Fahey said. "What can I do youse for?"

"I'd like to talk to you about something," Service said.

"Not on the phone," Fahey said. "Face-to-face. You comin' down to Lansing soon?"

"Nossir."

"Geez oh Pete, I'd better fix dat, eh? You'll get a call, okay?"

Two hours later Attalienti telephoned. "You're going to Lansing to-morrow," the acting captain said.

"I am?"

"Metrovich just called me. The director has requested you as our li-aison with SPO on a special project."

"SPO?"

"State Properties Office."

The current director of the DNR was John "Jungle Jack" Curry, who had come to Lansing in 1967 from Alaska where he had been the number-two man with Alaska Fish & Game. The Michigan salmon pro-gram was attributed to the director, and officers told Service that even Curry was caught by surprise at the program's success. The salmon had been planted with no firm idea of whether they would survive or not. The program's main goal was to reduce alewife overpopulation. It was also common knowledge that Curry had not shown a lot of concern about the Garden situation.

"Why me?"

"SPO has decided to conduct some kind of real estate and asset audit, and the director wants someone to run interference. Metrovich got the impression that State Property asked for you by name, and, if so, Jungle Jack's not one to buck the flow, so you're going. The request is highly irregular and Cosmo and Curry both have their antennae quiver-ing with suspicion. I'm sure Curry doesn't want some dirt-boot CO deal-ing with another agency, but he's too savvy to cross swords with the property kingpin. You're to meet a man named Fahey at Lou Coomes restaurant in north Lansing at noon tomorrow. Fahey's the director of State Proper-ties. I were you, I'd head down there tonight. The weather from the bridge down to Grayling can get ugly. After your meeting you are to re-port to Curry and Metrovich."

Service started to laugh and stopped when he realized that Fahey's little exercise in muscle might just have earned him a couple of enemies in his own department. "Goddamn Lansing," he said out loud.

The restaurant was not far off US 127 and had a towering neon sign that looked like the gaudy trail of a comet. The restaurant was filled with men in dark suits.

The maître d' eyed Service's uniform and said, "This way, Officer."

She led him to a private dining room where Fahey was already seated, a napkin—already stained—tucked in over his tie. He had a drink in front of him and a large bowl of olives stuck with green and white toothpicks.

"Geez oh Pete!" Fahey greeted him. "You made it."

"You made it happen," Service said.

"Easy enough when you've been around as long as me. In your dad's honor we're gonna have an old-fashioned U.P. lunch—cudighi on Finnish rye, smothered in onions and hot Italian mustard. The cudighi comes from an old Finn up to Lake Linden. People back home are always sendin' me stuff. I get a box of Trenary Toast once a month, but one of my staff members broke a tooth so that gets tossed soon as it arrives."

Fahey handed him an envelope. "This is a memo from me to your director. It apologizes for any inconvenience and explains that the audit is postponed until a later date. 'Course, I don't suggest when, because it's good to keep others on edge. State bureaucrats hate unscheduled audits, so he'll be relieved when he gets this—at least for a while. How about a drink?"

"Just coffee," Service said. "I'm on duty."

"Geez oh Pete, not a chip off the old block—but hey, it's the smart thing to do. You remember that trout breakfast you made for the old man and me?"

Service remembered. He said, "Do you know Acting Chief Metrovich?"

When Fahey transitioned from small talk to business, his fool's mask evaporated. "Acting's all he'll ever be. Cosmo's all shine, no metal. Wouldn't say it's raining until somebody above him says it's so. When Cosmo's six months are up, he'll retire and a man named Grant will get the captain's job. He's new to the DNR, but he's a man with depth. He came to Lansing from the federal government in Washington, D.C. The U.P. needs a captain with the kind of pluck you fellas have."

"The men never talk about Metrovich," Service said.

"People don't talk about air, either. It's just there. Cosmo isn't heavy enough to leave footprints if he walked across a swimming pool filled with Jell-O. Attalienti may make a good captain down the road, but not in the U.P. They're taking a good look at him now. He might do well in one of the southern law zones. Deano's a good man." Fahey didn't say who "they" was.

Fahey had surprisingly incisive insight into the law enforcement division, and Service decided to test it. "Len Stone?"

"Yooper-tough and right out of the old school. He'll get the permanent lieutenant's job and, if he wanted to, he could move downstate for a captain's job—but they'll never get Len out of the U.P. Besides, he can retire in eight or nine years."

A waiter brought their lunches and they tried to eat while three different men "popped in" to pay homage to Fahey. They all had jokes for him, and Fahey had a quick comeback for each of them. The well-spoken and thoughtful man of minutes before immediately backslid to ridge-running bumbler when people came into the room. Their last visitor was a long-legged woman with black hair and green eyes who talked to Fahey but stared the whole while at Service. Fahey introduced her as "Shay-the-Lay," and she laughed and corrected him. "It's Shay da Leigh."

"Never was good wit' names," Fahey said with a chuckle.

"Except when you want to be," she said, excusing herself for interrupting.

"Good girl," Fahey said when she was gone. "And a crack lawyer in the Legislative Services Branch. You're a senator or a rep and you want to draft a bill, you call in LS and they help you to write it and put it in the appropriate capitolese. Shay's the best they've got, great brain and an even greater wild streak. She was raised over to Bessemer. You can trust her."

They finished eating in privacy and Fahey had two more vodka tonics. "So, what was it you wanted to talk about?" his father's pal finally asked.

"The Garden."

Fahey nodded solemnly. "Those boys sure didn't take to Order Seventeen. Still taking potshots at you fellas, I hear."

"Somebody's going to get killed," Service said.

Fahey pondered this as he took a drink. "Smart boys down there. They see the handwriting on the wall."

"Such as the end of commercial fishing in Lake Michigan?"

Fahey raised an eyebrow and cracked a grin. "Just like your old man. I don't know how, but that sonuvagun always knew what was going on," he said. "The fur trappers came first, then the mining companies and the loggers, and now the oil companies are coming in. The fact is that commercial fishermen aren't important enough to have the power to get what they want. See, in Lansing, clout and power count. Companies have pretty much always gotten what they wanted as long as the state got a good cut. Money speaks, eh?"

"There's more money in sportfishing than commercial fishing," Service said.

"Geez oh Pete, this salmon thing's bigger than anybody dreamed, even Curry. The commercial net boys keep at it, they'll kill the salmon. You know what brought down our fish stocks more than any other factor?"

"Lampreys."

"Nylon," Fahey said. "With nylon fishermen no longer had to make their own nets out of linen or know how to repair them, which they did all the time. Nylon's lighter, cheaper, stronger, and requires a lot less up-keep. Capital and costs down, profits up. Nylon changed Great Lakes commercial fishing."

Service decided to push a little. "I heard the Indians might get to keep their nets."

Fahey straightened his shoulders and took another drink. "Well, all that's in the federal court system and there's no way to predict those buggers, but if I were a betting man, I'd bet the Indians will come out of this winners."

"And white commercial fishermen will get bought out?"

"You've got good sources," Fahey said, raising his glass in salute. "The few who've been able to hang on to their licenses would get bought out."

"Do you know Odd Hegstrom?" Service asked.

"Since the old days. Smart fella—and cagey as they come."

"He created U.P. Legal Services."

"Not with a lot of support from the state bar or Lansing. People think Odd's addicted to fighting windmills, but that's malarkey. He just doesn't like to see people pushed around, and when he goes into a fight, he likes to win. Usually he does."

"Political ambition?"

"What does a man need political office for if he's already got power? Odd's not all pro bono. He's got one helluva law practice, and though he's got the tribes pro bono now, I'd expect that down the road they'll become real billable hours and a cash cow. Why the interest in all this?"

"I'm just trying to figure out the Garden."

Fahey laughed. "When you do, let me know. I've never figured those buggers out. The situation there's not all that complicated, eh. People up there know the end's in sight and they're gonna milk it all the way."

"Lansing knows this?"

"Some do, some don't. Most who know don't really give a bloody hoot. The Garden is a skirmish in a small war to get the state to where it wants to be economically. The Garden ain't Gettysburg. Hell, it ain't even the Toledo War!" Michigan and Ohio had taken up arms because both wanted the strip of land that contained Toledo. The compromise gave Toledo to Ohio and the Upper Peninsula to Michigan, and hard feelings still lingered above the bridge. The U.P. had been incorporated into the state's territory without having a say in it, and then its resources had been taken away by mining and logging companies, all with Lansing's blessing.

"And if the Garden gets bloody?"

"Some might like that. Be a good excuse for the governor to call in the National Guard the way it happened during the Detroit riots. The Garden boys know this, so they have to walk a fine line between fighting the inevitable and keeping doing what they want to do to make their dough. They can't let it get out of hand or they've got no chance, eh."

"They've got no chance anyway," Service said.

"They don't know that."

Service was impressed not only with Fahey's knowledge, but also with his crisp and simple explanations of history and political realities.

A waiter brought them a six-inch-square cinnamon roll and put it between them as he poured coffee.

"Coffee's boiled," Fahey said. "Bakery's from L'Anse. Lou has it delivered daily just for Yoopers working in Lansing. You going back this afternoon?"

"If I can."

"Hard to predict those guys, but Curry and Metrovich will be suspicious of why I asked for you. They'll be trying to figure out what the heck I'm up to, and how you fit in. When they ask why, just tell 'em the truth. Your old man and me were pals."

Which meant he should tell a half-truth. If he hadn't asked for information from Fahey, he would not be in this position.

"Anything else?" Fahey asked.

"I always wondered how you got your name."

Fahey laughed with a mouth full of cinnamon roll. "Never mattered to me I was the size of a popcorn fart. I been a competitive little shit my whole life. I played baseball at Michigan Agricultural College—that was State before it got renamed. I wasn't the most talented player on the team, not even close, but I *love* baseball. It's the only game that stops after every play and gives every player the chance to think through all the possibilities for the next play. Baseball's a thinking man's game, and I always managed to stay several jumps ahead of the other guys."

And still did, Service knew. Fahey's unimpressive physical appearance would make him easy to underestimate. "How'd you get your job?"

"The college got me a summer job in properties, and after I graduated I went off to law school."

"Where?"

"Harvard," Fahey said with a little grin, watching for Service's reaction. "I finished law school at age twenty. Pearl Harbor came along and I volunteered for the U.S. Marines and they sent me out to the Pacific. I got discharged in 'forty-five as a sergeant, and came back to Lansing and got into properties part-time while I studied for the state bar. When I passed the bar, they offered me the manager's job and I took it. I don't mind Lansing, and it isn't all that far from home, especially with the bridge. They gave me a bigger title since then."

The Mackinac Bridge had opened in 1957. Before that travelers were forced to cross the straits by ferry, and at certain times the delay could be hours for one of the five boats, and sometimes weather prevented any crossings at all. The bridge had opened a flow of tourists and newcomers that some Yoopers still resented. Like Brigid Mehegen's grandfather, for one.

Service did a quick calculation. Fahey was fifty-seven or fifty-eight now. He looked a lot older. *Harvard?*

Service drove to downtown Lansing, parked in a public lot, and walked over to the Mason Building. He signed in at the central registration desk on the ground floor and sat down to have a smoke while the uniformed receptionist called upstairs. Did they think he stole the green uniform and badge? The message was clear: Stay out unless you belong here.

Jungle Jack himself came down on the elevator to fetch him and escorted him up several floors to his office. He'd seen Curry at graduation but had never talked to him. The director was a tall, gaunt man with long, graying red hair. He wore a houndstooth sport coat instead of a suit and had a smear of blue ink on his left hand.

The director had a corner office that lacked fancy appointments. There were three framed sheepskins on the wall: a PhD and an MS from the University of Minnesota, and a BS from Montana State. There was also a color photograph of Curry, an equally tall, thin woman, and two ectomorphic boys, probably the wife and sons. None of them were smiling. A stuffed gray wolf was on a pedestal in the corner, and on the wall behind the director's cluttered desk, a stuffed four-foot-long Chinook salmon, at least a fifty-pounder by the looks of it.

Curry walked behind his desk and Service stood in front of it, handed him the envelope from Fahey, and watched him rip it open and read.

"Postponed until when?" the director asked, looking up from the memorandum.

"Mr. Fahey didn't say."

"And why a postponement?" Curry pressed.

"He didn't give a reason."

Curry did not invite him to sit. "He asked for you by name."

"He was a friend of my father's," Service explained.

"And a friend of yours? I'm told you Yoopers all stick together."

"First time I've seen him since I graduated from training," Service said.

"But he asked for you. Did you talk about the audit?"

"Nossir, we just made small talk, and he apologized for me having to drive down here for nothing. We had lunch and I came here as directed."

"Bureaucrats," Curry groused. "I'm sorry you had to waste your time," he said, a statement made out of convention not conviction.

"You've got the Mosquito," the director said.

Not a question. "My father had it too."

Curry ignored the reference to his father. "Fahey was the big mover in getting the wilderness designation."

"I didn't know that."

"Not many people down here have actually seen it, but those who have swear it's one of the state's natural jewels."

"It is."

"Might be worth my time to take a tour." This was also convention absent conviction.

"Any time, sir."

The director let the memo flutter to his desktop. "Postponed," he said. "I'd like to know what Jumping Bill is up to. He's a slippery one."

Curry led him down a corridor to Metrovich's office and walked away without another word.

Metrovich waved him in. "Take a seat," the acting chief said. "How'd the meeting go?"

"The audit's been postponed. I delivered a memo to the director from Mr. Fahey."

"Did you read it?"

"Nossir. The director told me what was in it."

"I see," Metrovich said. "You're sure you didn't read it?"

"I saw it was a single page, typewritten."

"Okay then," Metrovich said. "I guess that's it."

Service wasn't sure he'd been dismissed because the acting chief was staring past him. "Shall I go, sir?"

The acting chief did not respond, and Service walked alone out to the elevator. When the door opened, he found himself alone with Shay da Leigh, her hand poised next to the buttons. "Sporting goods or housewares?"

"Lobby," he said.

"Me, too."

The door shushed closed.

"Fahey's one of a kind," she said.

"I'm learning that," he said.

"You know, of course, that a junior conservation officer meeting alone with one of the state's most powerful people has triggered a wave of paranoia in the department."

He smelled flowers and citrus wafting off her. Her skirt swished when she shifted her weight. It had been a long time since he'd heard a woman's skirt make such a sound. "I got that feeling," he said.

"People here fight for face time," she said. "It's an unspoken currency."

He nodded. Why was she talking to him? "You have business with the DNR?" he asked.

"One of my clients," she said.

"You write legislation for the department?"

"Not exactly. The director insists on writing first drafts. I get called in to clean them up. Mostly I edit for clarity and style. Have you seen the ink on Curry's hand?"

Service nodded.

"I doubt he ever washes it," she said. "The ink is his way of showing the department he's a working director, not a paper-pushing figurehead. He's angling for bigger things. I give him a year until he moves on."

The elevator bounced when it stopped. "Let a girl buy you a drink?" she asked. Her skirt whispered when she asked him.

"I have to head north."

"A drink and a talk about the Garden?" she pressed, one eyebrow raised.

"I guess I have time."

"Jumping Bill thought you might," she said. "This meeting isn't serendipity."

20

HASLETT, FEBRUARY 10, 1976

"You cops are all missing the gene for trust."

On the way out of the Mason Building, da Leigh suggested they meet in Haslett at a bar called Pagan's Place, "across from the amusement park."

He parked across the street under a row of leafless elms and changed from his uniform to jeans and a sweater. A sign above him said LAKE LANSING AMUSEMENT PARK: CLOSED UNTIL SUMMER. He glanced at the sign and went inside and saw her on a stool at the bar. Despite the time he'd spent in Lansing as a state cop, he had never gotten familiar with the fastest routes; he'd never cared to, knowing his time in the capital was temporary. By contrast, Bathsheba loved the city, knew the shops and restaurants, and never tired of going out and feeling the whirl and smug superiority of government employees.

Da Leigh sat so that her legs stretched out in front of her.

"I like the way you walk," she said when he sat down. "Self-confident, not quite cocky. Most men can't pull that off."

He ordered a draft beer from the barmaid, but da Leigh amended the request. "Two aquavits," she said. "Linie."

He protested mildly. "I have a long drive tonight."

"It's true," she said. "You people really *are* Boy Scouts."

"It's common sense," he said, "not moral high ground."

She laughed and clucked appreciatively. "So," she said. "The Garden."

He waited for her to take the lead. The aquavits were delivered in tall shot glasses. The woman lifted hers, held it out to him, and clicked his glass, saying "Skoal." She swallowed hers in one gulp, set the glass down, and ordered two more.

He drank as she drank, felt the aquavit explode in his belly like a plume of rolling napalm.

"I write a lot of administrative rules," she said. "And believe it or not, it's an art."

"I'll take your word for it."

"My hand was on Order Seventeen," she said. "Start to finish."

"For whom?"

"Curry was the driver, but the governor's people were aware of it and saw a couple of drafts."

"Why not write it as law?" he asked.

"Too slow. If the legislature gets involved, it becomes a political football, and U.P. legislators have purchase in both houses. Yoopers elect their people over and over; they understand the principles of paleopolitics, and how seniority leads to rewards. An administrative order avoids the morass so that the department can get something into play immediately, and others can start getting used to the idea. It's expedient."

"But the order gets shifted into law later."

"Sometimes, but not always. It's not a given."

"Curry wants to boost sportfishing," he said.

She smiled. "He actually has sympathy for commercial operators, but the state budget is under fire, and the DNR budget is always among the first things attacked. Sportfishing will bring in a lot of revenue and he can't ignore that. He didn't come all the way from Alaska to fail. Are you sympathetic to people in the Garden?"

Two more aquavits were delivered and consumed after another chorus of "Skoal."

"I just want to understand what we're dealing with," he said.

"Curry fancies himself an intellectual, a steward of state treasures. He barely tolerates law enforcement."

"We enforce the law. We don't look for the director's approval."

"He allows questions and input from a select few pets, and he has a wet finger up in the air continuously."

"Order Seventeen is a process. It carries no penalties."

"Licenses can be revoked," she said defensively.

"It's a lugubrious process that requires multiple infractions. I don't understand why we don't subpoena the offenders' financial records," he said.

"People and companies are guaranteed privacy, remember? Due process?"

"It makes our work difficult."

Another round of drinks came and went. Service felt hot and rolled up his sleeves.

"Laws and administrative orders are not written to facilitate ease of enforcement," she said.

"Officers are being shot at," he pointed out.

"I've heard," she said. "You?"

He nodded, and she asked, "What are you people doing about it?"

"About Order Seventeen or being shot at?"

"Do you think I'm the enemy?"

"No comment," he said.

"It was Jumping Bill's idea that I 'bump' into you. Do you think *he's* the enemy?"

"No," but he also understood that Fahey had not survived so long without being a trader and compromiser. "The LeBlanc case is a shadow over everything," he said.

She licked her lips. "You bet. The state has to play this right or the sportfishing plan could get shredded. The feds have deep pockets; we don't. What we really need is a Republican in the White House to tell the states that it's our right and responsibility to manage our own environmental concerns and resources."

"Jerry Ford is a Michigan Man."

"He's been caretaking and cleaning up since Nixon waved bye-bye. It's not clear Jerry can win if he runs on his own. Seriously," she added, "how *are* you handling the Garden?"

"Following the letter of the law and practicing ducking."

She laughed out loud and touched his forearm, the warmth of her fingers searing him.

"You cops are all missing the gene for trust," she said. "Is that part of your selection process?"

"No more than for lawyers," he shot back.

"Touché," she said.

"I like to deal with what I can see." What had Lasurm said—that he wanted a world in black and white? She wasn't far off.

"Rocks and trees and guns," she said. "This thing down here is just as real. We even get shot at."

"Words don't splatter brains," he said.

She paused and looked at him, patted his hand. "You're right. It's not the same, and I wasn't trying to demean the risks you guys run. But this world has multiple realities, each with its own rules. Some of them are not nice."

Her apology took him by surprise. "I didn't mean that as a put-down," he said.

"I deserved it," she said. "I get criticized for being shrill when I think I'm just being direct and passionate. The Pill and the sixties have begun to liberate us in the bedroom, but it's not the same when we have our clothes on. Curry's being pushed to hire women in law enforcement," she said. "The state police are considering it, and the Natural Resources Commission doesn't want the DNR to be second to the Troops. How does that grab you?"

"I don't have a problem with it."

"Will your wife feel the same way?"

"Divorced," he said.

She ordered two more drinks, doubles this time, which they drank down. Service felt the napalm cooking his brain.

"Women don't threaten your view of the world order?"

"No."

"How do you separate long legs and sex appeal from professional competence?"

"Ask her politely."

Da Leigh poked him in the arm, threw her head back, and laughed out loud. "We're getting drunk."

"Getting?"

"You don't like to think?"

"I think about things I can do something about," he said.

"Trees and rocks and guns," she said.

"Sometimes long legs," he added.

She tucked her chin down and looked at him. "How long since the divorce?"

"A while."

"You seeing someone?"

The napalm had coated his brain, its heat making the tissue swell. "A fuck buddy," he said.

She blinked and giggled. "That's a new one," she said.

"Was for me too," he admitted.

"It sounds liberated."

"Or two losers looking for justification."

She shrugged, grinned and held up her shot glass. "Linie: The Swedes make it and send it on a ship around the world before they sell it. Can you imagine going around the world like that?" she asked with a leer.

"We confiscate their gear," he said, trying to get the conversation back to business, "and ask the courts for condemnation proceedings."

She studied him and grinned. "That takes a lot of time, and the courts don't make it easy or automatic."

"But while the court decides, they don't have their gear. No gear, no poaching."

"That's outside the spirit of Order Seventeen."

"It's expedient," he said, playing back her own logic.

"No wonder they're using guns."

"They were using guns *before* we started this."

"You think this is the right thing to do?"

"Doing something is more important than being pushed around right now." Even with the aquavit in him, it was clear after today that conservation officers were risking their lives as part of a larger political strategy: The powers in Lansing did not give a damn whether they stopped the poaching or not.

They each had one more aquavit and when the drinks were gone, da Leigh looked at her watch. "My house is ten minutes from here." She rested her hand on his arm and insisted on paying the bill. "Expense account," she explained. "Don't worry, your name won't appear."

On the sidewalk she threw her arms around him and kissed him for a long time. "You're not a Boy Scout in all things, are you?"

"Nope," he said.

"Thank God," she said.

She kissed him at the front door in the morning. "Jumping Bill's finagling to get you down here the way he did has put you in a tough position," she said.

"He arranged it knowing that," he said.

"Bill doesn't do anything without purpose. Your being here was his game and his decision, but *you* be careful, Boy Scout. Don't go get yourself shot by one of those goddamn Gardenians."

21

NEWBERRY, FEBRUARY 11, 1976

"Sometimes the flaw's so visible it's invisible."

On the way out of Lansing he swung by the Capital City Airport and spent an hour with a meteorologist from the National Weather Service.

Nikki-Jo Jokola smiled and winked when Service sat down in a booth in the bar of Brown's Hotel. "Youse're a bit late for breakfast today," she said. "And we had a nice meat loaf for lunch."

"No thanks." He gave her a piece of paper with information for the next newspaper ad. "For the thirteenth," he said.

"I'll drive down to Manistique tomorrow morning," she said. "Shuck's sick."

"With what?"

"The out-of-da-action blues. If you have time, stop by an' see him."

It took a long time for the retired officer to come to the door, but his hangdog face lit up when he saw Service. "Your replacement's thicker'n lead," Shuck Gorley said. "Name's Parker. He transferred up from Ingham County to 'get inta da action.'"

"I didn't pick him," Service said. He didn't even know him.

"Roars like a lion, brains of a spruce grouse," Gorley said.

Service laughed. The spruce grouse was so low on avian intelligence that it was in danger of consignment to Darwin's dustbin. "This Parker stop in to pick your brains?"

"Dat one couldn't pick a hot dog wit' a fork. He don't need ta talk to me. He knows it all."

"Nikki-Jo's worried about you," Service said.

"Dat woman worries if she don't got worries," Gorley said disgustedly.

"She cares about you."

"Dere ain't a problem. Just dis Parker yayhoo. How's da Garden?"

"Pretty damn confusing."

"*Dat* mess, it don't never change," Gorley said. "Get inside, youse're lettin' my heat out. I got coffee on."

Service followed the man into his kitchen. The house was clean and orderly. "I lost your thermos."

"Your thermos," Gorley corrected him, "not mine. How'd you lose 'er?"

"The Garden," he said, and then he related his Garden patrols, everything he'd seen and experienced and had been thinking. Gorley listened attentively until he was finished.

"Dean told me he might use youse down dere."

"Based on what you told him," Service said.

"We need good officers dere. Da Garden's always been lawless, eh. We always had trouble gettin' guys to serve down dere. An' dat crow line dey got now, dat ain't new, but back when I done patrols down dere, da line wasn't dere first line a' defense."

"It wasn't?"

"Nope. Dey had inside dope, always seemed ta know when we were comin' down dere. We never figured out why or how, but da old captain, Cortney Denu, he made da officers handwrite all dere reports and send 'em direct to him, an' he personally sent 'em on to Lansing. Only he opened 'em—same wit' plans. And when an op was bein' put together, we never met in Escanaba. We met somewhere outside Delta County. Once we started dis, we managed to get in on dem and make a few pinches."

"But now everything is running out of Escanaba again."

"Dat was Cosmo's doin'. Da people down to da Escanaba office whined, said dey was insulted by Cap'n Denu, said it hurt dere feelings; so Cosmo, he put tings back da way dey were when dey weren't workin'."

Service didn't know what to say. A probable security leak had been identified, and now it was being ignored? Did Attalienti know about this?

"We had security problems here too," Gorley went on. "Some years back we had a poacher named Jepson, tall, baby-faced sonuvagun, and we worked like hell tryin' ta nab 'im, but he was always one step ahead. I had west Chippewa County back den, and George Zuchow had eastern Luce, where dis Jepson character lived, and George and I tried like da dickens to nail 'im. After close to a year, I said ta hell wit' it—all da bloody time I spent on dat case was lettin' other stuff go. You can't get 'em all."

Service understood.

"Den I got in a wreck and busted my leg and dey put me on restricted duty. I had to go inta da office every day and help do dispatch and run errands for da lieutenant and junk like dat. Seemed like Zuchow come in every day ta bitch and moan about Jepson and how he'd eluded him again and what he was gonna try next. I mean, every day. 'Course, da whole office started following da war between dose two. And every day about da same time, George showed up, da bakery guy come to da canteen and brought new donuts and took da old stuff away, and I watched him and noticed he sorta hung around, not doin' anyting couldn't be done in one minute. So I went to da LT and I asked who da bakery jamoke was, and he said talk ta da secretaries. Da secretaries said dey t'ought da LT was havin' it brought in for everybody. Next day da bakery guy comes in jabbering with George, and I put my hand on 'is chest and I tell 'im to show me some ID, and he rabbits, but I grab 'im and put 'is nose on da floor and we got out 'is wallet. Da jerk's name is Jepson! He's da brudder of da bloody poacher. Nobody ordered no fresh bakery. Dis guy's been bringing it in on 'is own and listenin' ta what's going on and passing da word on. Dey *bot'* went to jail."

"Sometimes the flaw's so visible it's invisible," Service said.

"Routine can be as good as pokin' your eyes out," Gorley said.

22

MARQUETTE-HARVEY-TRENARY, FEBRUARY 11, 1976

"Even your old man wasn't dis crazy."

Attalienti leaned back in his chair and listened to what Service had to say about security in the Escanaba office.

"That happened years ago; it was thoroughly investigated, and written off to coincidence," the acting captain said. "What was the Lansing thing about?"

Service guessed Attalienti suffered the same paranoia that existed downstate, local supervision being an extension of Lansing. He considered telling him everything, but held back. "I don't know. I showed up for the meeting and Fahey said the audit was postponed, and he apologized for making me drive all that way."

"You talked to the director and Cosmo?"

"I told them exactly what I told you."

"Why did Fahey ask for you?"

"He was a friend of my father's."

"I don't think I buy that," Attalienti said.

"We had a lunch in honor of my old man and talked."

"Cosmo's in a twitter. He's called me three times and says Curry's all over him. Both of them are certain there's more to the meeting with Fahey than your just being the son of his friend."

Service had to take a deep breath so that he could say quietly, "I had lunch. The audit's postponed. Fahey gave me a memo for Curry and I delivered the memo to the director. I met with Metrovich—end of story."

"Careers can get destroyed by people who dabble in politics," Attalienti said.

"I'm *not* dabbling in anything," Service said forcefully to the acting captain. "*You* sent me down there," he added.

Attalienti stared at him. "Okay, sorry. They're just rattling my cage and I had to rattle yours. Don't sweat it."

"There's nothing to sweat," Service said. "I'm going into the Garden the night of the fourteenth," he added.

"Why then?"

"The weather window's what I want."

Attalienti looked at him like he was unbalanced. "They're predicting a blizzard."

"Exactly," Service said.

"I don't like this at all," the acting captain said, frowning.

"You said it was my call."

"But in a blizzard?"

He called Brigid Mehegen at home and asked if he could drop by.

There was no sign of Perry. "Got Valentine plans for us?" she asked coyly.

"I'm not going to be around," he said.

"What does that mean, 'not around'?" she asked.

"Family emergency."

"Where?" she said, her voice demanding and suspicious.

"Far away," he said.

She gave him an annoyed look. "I arranged that meeting you wanted. My guy said reluctantly he'd talk to the 'whuffo.'"

"Whuffo?" Service said.

"Jumper talk for straight-legs," she said. "You know: Whuffo you want to jump out of a perfectly good airplane?"

"Thanks," he said, "but I thought about what you said. Borrowing wasn't the smartest idea."

He could see her weighing his words, measuring him. "Is there anything I can do to help with your family emergency?" she asked.

"Thanks, but it's something I have to take care of on my own," he said.

"I was hoping we could get some time together," she said.

"Rain check?" he said.

"It's snowing, in case you haven't noticed. Have you heard the weather forecast?"

"Been too busy," he lied. "Where's your grandfather?"

"Snowshoe hunting with a couple of his pals," she said disgustedly. "What is it about old men and hunting?" she asked. "Do you want something to eat?"

"I had a big lunch," he said.

"The bedroom's available," she said, "or did you have a big one of those too?"

He laughed, but didn't answer.

She hugged him politely before he left, and gave him a searing look that let him know she knew he was bullshitting her.

So much for the fuck-buddy concept, he thought as he backed out of her driveway.

Joe Flap was waiting at his house near Trenary.

"I want you to fly me to the Garden the night of the fourteenth," Service said.

"Have you seen da weather forecast?"

"It's what I want."

"Fly you ta da Garden for what?" the pilot asked.

Service lifted his hand, opened his fingers, and made a downward fluttering motion toward a tabletop. The pilot shut his eyes and said, "Oh shit."

"Yes or no?"

"Even your old man wasn't dis crazy," Joe Flap said. "I'm in."

The pilot got two beers from the fridge and the two men sat down at the table and spread maps out and began discussing what Service had in mind. At one point, Flap asked, "How youse gonna gauge da wind?"

"I'm not. You're the pilot."

Joe Flap looked at the map and shook his head. "You got balls, kid. But da jury's out on your brains."

23

MARQUETTE, FEBRUARY 14, 1976

"She'll pop up like a butterfly in a hurricane."

The noise inside the single-engine DHC-2 Beaver was nearly unbearable, but Service wore a headset with an interphone connection, and he tried to ignore the ear-shattering roar as he checked his gear for the umpteenth time.

Joe Flap had taxied into position for a northeast takeoff into a heavy wind that made the aircraft shake as they sat waiting for clearance. Six inches of fresh snow had fallen in Marquette during the day, with up to another twenty inches being called for tonight. The snowfall in the Garden was less, as it normally was, but even down there forecasts called for ten to twelve inches over the next twenty-four hours. Service was pleased. The worse the weather, he reasoned, the fewer the people who would be out.

Service knew his pilot was less than pleased about his plan, but he had committed to helping; now he sat in uncharacteristic silence, fiddling with the choke, leaning the mixture of the engine and constantly exercising the ailerons to make sure they weren't icing up.

"Can we get off in this wind?" Service asked over the intercom.

"She'll pop up like a butterfly in a hurricane," the pilot said. "I filed VFR, and Minneapolis Center is pissed and Green Bay is pissed and da tower people here are in a snit, and da snowplow drivers are bent outta shape, but VFR is my bloody call, not a buncha scope-dopes and ground-pounders, eh." VFR meant Visual Flight Rules, the term for a pilot operating independent of ground-based radar control. "I can see my prop, eh? Dat makes 'er visual."

"Can you get back?" Service asked.

"I piss more gas den it takes ta get youse down to da Garden. I got a good eight hundred miles range. If dey close da field here, I'll take 'er downstate to Traverse City or even Grand Rapids. You don't gotta worry about Joe Flap. Youse keep your mind on youse," the pilot concluded sharply.

The tower called on the radio. "DNR Air Four, the plows are clear of the runway. You're cleared on to the active, contact Green Bay at . . . " Service listened as Flap wrote the frequency on his leg pad. "Wind, zero four zero at thirty-two knots, gusting to forty. You sure you wanna do this tonight, Air Four?"

"Wind's right in our snoots—tanks for da info, DNR Air Four."

Flap released the brakes, which vibrated and made a clunking sound, and pulled onto the runway facing into the wind. He pushed the throttle up slightly, let the engine rumble, and shoved it further forward. The bulky aircraft began to vibrate more violently and to move slowly forward. Service sat in a seat behind the pilot and looked out a large triangular window on either side. He could not see the sides of the runway, and when he looked forward all he could see was a sea of snow flooding the windscreen. "DNR Air Four is rolling," Joe Flap reported to the tower.

The engine strained and roared and the gear chattered, barked, and vibrated under the strain of moving. Service thought it would take a long time to get airborne, but suddenly the nose came sharply up and they were aloft, bouncing around in uneven air. He looked at the instruments and saw they were climbing at a rate of just over a thousand feet per minute.

Joe Flap was on his radio, "Green Bay, DNR Air Four is airborne, VFR, requesting angels two."

"Roger, DNR, squawk three one four four, you are cleared to two thousand, maintain heading of zero four five. You're all alone up there tonight, Air Four."

"Roger, Green Bay, tanks for da help. Level at two thou, steady on zero four five. Youse have a good night."

Service felt the aircraft turning to the right as the pilot altered course to the southeast for the twenty-five minute flight to the Garden Peninsula.

He used the time to go over their plan again. The highest terrain in the U.P. was seven hundred and forty-six feet. In the marines he had jumped numerous times at six hundred feet above the ground elevation; tonight, for safety, he would step out at seven hundred and fifty feet, which would provide adequate time to deploy his chute and equipment bag. Treebone had used his connections to get the chute from someone at the Air Guard unit at Selfridge Field in Mt. Clemens. Probably Joe Flap would cheat up a little, thinking he was helping, and there was no way to stop the pilot from doing this; if he was a little higher, he'd be in the air a little longer, but not all that much. Flap had argued vehemently for him to jump at two thousand feet, but Service figured there was too much potential for windage and getting too far off his drop zone. He'd rather go out low and get it over with fast. Because there would be no time for a second chance at such a low altitude, he had not bothered with a reserve chute, knowing if he had a problem, he'd end up as brush wolf chow. He had discussed the jump at length with Tree, who agreed that the simpler, the better. Tree didn't lecture him on the advisability of jumping; his friend had stuck to details, making sure he had covered everything he needed to address.

The temperature at Marquette had been minus eighteen at takeoff. Manistique and the Garden were eight or nine degrees warmer, but with the Beaver flying at a hundred miles an hour, the wind would be blasting him when he got outside, and the wind chill would be brutal. The trick was to minimize exposure and get on the ground as quickly as possible.

"Heading into da Garden," Flap said over the interphone.

"How's the wind?"

"Pretty steady at about twenty, right out of da northeast."

"Okay."

The plan was to drop him over farm fields northeast of Cecilia Lasurm's house and let the wind carry him down to a field about a mile north of her place. If Joe put him in the right field and if he got down without breaking a leg, getting to her place should be easy. Not the time to dwell on "ifs," he chastised himself. He needed to focus on those things he could control. Getting him to the drop zone was the pilot's job. Sweat the stuff you can control, he told himself.

Their indicated airspeed was just under one hundred and ten knots. The wind was banging them around from time to time, but the old Beaver, built in 1954, was Joe Flap's favorite, and the pilot quickly recovered from each burble.

Service was dressed heavily. He wore the same long johns and socks he'd worn during the snowmobile patrol, but this time he had no uniform and no badge, and wore insulated sweatpants over his long johns, and a wool sweater and heavy white parka over his snowmobile suit, which he had streaked with white paint. He also had a lightweight white parka with olive-charcoal camo patterns, but this was in his equipment bag, and he would use it as an outer layer after he was on the ground. The top layer would provide no warmth, but it would make him hard to see against against snowy terrain.

Joe Flap announced, "Youse got eight minutes."

Service said, "Removing hatch." He unlatched the door and stowed it against the starboard bulkhead with a strap. Flap said it wouldn't affect his flight profile or comfort to have the door out; he could always crank up his heat to compensate. Service wrestled his gear bag over to the door and checked that the zipper was secure. The bag was white and had two straps so it could be attached to either side of his parachute harness at the waist. Once his chute was open, he would release the equipment bag, which would drop away and ride down ahead of him on a thirty-foot-long lanyard. There was a risk of landing on the bag or having the lanyard get tangled in trees, but he was jumping into an open field and hoped there would be no complications like telephone wires or fences. Don't think about it, he told himself. Focus on what you're doing and keep your head in the game. Basic roulette, he thought, red or black, odd or even, make your bet and watch the wheel spin.

"Disconnecting interphone," he told the pilot.

Service tucked the headset in a bin on the fuselage, pulled on a white wool balaclava and forced his helmet down over the top of it, dropped the face shield into place, and locked it. He looked up at Joe Flap who held up four fingers, meaning four minutes until he jumped. He hooked the equipment bag to both sides of his harness and swung his legs over the edge of the hatch. The aircraft had no internal cabin light except for the glow of flight instruments in front of Flap. The snow was racing sideways, a blur of small white arrows. Service stepped down to the right-wing strut facing aft and wedged his boot into the metal V. The wind was pushing the equipment bag against the back of his legs and making it difficult to stay on his perch, but he clung to the strut with his left glove and put his right hand on the D-ring of the parachute.

He seemed to be suspended in the frigid wind for hours until the engine power was pulled back and gunned, the signal for him to go. He tucked his chin to his chest and stepped aft off the strut, dropping straight down. As soon as he left his perch he pulled the ripcord and heard a sibilant *pfft* as the pilot chute came loose and began deploying the main chute. He relaxed, waiting for the parachute's opening shock, and told himself it was not quite as cold as he had anticipated. Adrenaline kept him focused on the things he had to do rather than on the elements.

When the air settled into the canopy, there was a sudden, violent yank at his crotch and he had the sensation of climbing as his weight settled under the silk. He looked up, saw the canopy above him, and immediately disconnected the equipment bag and lanyard so that the heavy bag would proceed downward ahead of him.

When the bag fully deployed, he felt a sharp tug below him and knew he had done all he could. He reached up both risers of the military chute and pulled with his right hand and pushed with his left to shift his body sideways to the wind, as close to forty-five degrees as he could manage. His mind was empty, his only focus the direction of the wind and relaxing himself for impact.

He had no idea how long he had been dropping, but he guessed the ground was close. He looked straight ahead toward an imaginary horizon, reached up the risers with his gloves, put his feet together, and relaxed his knees for impact. He felt no fear, only an urge to get on the ground as he popped loose the cover of the right riser release.

At the instant he felt contact, he let himself roll to his left side, and when he plowed into deep snow with his body, he released the right riser and the chute collapsed partway, and stopped dragging him. He instinctively rolled onto his belly and up to his knees, freed the second riser, and began yanking the shroud lines and silk canopy toward him. When the canopy was bunched around him, he used the lanyard to pull the equipment bag to him, unzipped it, got out his white camo parka cover, took off the parachute harness, stuffed his helmet, the harness, and parachute into the equipment bag, and finally allowed himself to pause and take a deep breath. Time to assess. First thought: Jesus, this wind is goddamn cold.

How long since he had stepped off the strut? Two minutes? He listened but couldn't hear the Beaver. The wind was growling and screaming, roiling fresh snow into a swirling white wall. You asked for shit weather.

No lights in evidence. Good. If he was on the drop zone there should be a tree line due south of him. First order of business: Get into the trees, relax, have a smoke, and evaluate the terrain and his situation.

He slid the equipment bag straps over his shoulders, cinched them as tight as he could over his bulky clothes, and trudged off into the fluffy, knee-deep snow, the wind coming over his left shoulder, his heart still racing from the suddenness of the jump and the landing. He had no idea how Joe had navigated to the drop zone, but he had. He hoped.

He thought he heard unmuffled engines moving toward him from his right and froze in place. What the hell? He dropped to one knee. The wind velocity had picked up, and the snow was still moving parallel to the ground as falling snow mixed with snow being whipped up from the surface. It also felt like the snow's consistency had changed from fluff to ice pellets, and he had no idea what that presaged for weather. The wind itself was a naked roar overhead, like a locomotive approaching, and somewhere below that sound, he could sense as much as hear engines coming closer. He went prone in the snow, knowing that the white gear bag would look like a snowdrift.

Snowmobiles came from the west, advancing steadily through the soft fresh snow, and passed twenty yards in front of him. He counted four, and wondered what fools would be out in this. People who knew the trails well enough not to worry about running into something, he knew.

When the machines were past, he got up and eased forward to where they had moved from his right to his left. He found the foot-wide track of the machines and stepped gingerly over it, rubbing out his own tracks once he was over. He moved into fresh drifts, knowing his tracks would soon be blown closed. If the locals were out tonight in near-zero visibility, he told himself, they could be out any time, anywhere. Keep *that* in mind while you're here. Planning for the worst was the only reasonable approach, he knew from experience. His old commander in Vietnam always insisted that the plan changed with first contact with the enemy, and he had no doubt that the Garden rats were his enemies as he marched south, wondering where the goddamn tree line was.

Ten minutes later the wind had shifted to directly behind him, and ahead he heard the clatter and rubbing of tree branches being whipped against each other. Soon he was at the edge of the tree line. He paused briefly, stepped inside, and felt around in the dark until he found a blowdown. He brushed away snow piled on the downed tree, used his boots to kick out a space beneath it, and got down into his hidey-hole. He dug into his equipment bag, took out a Snickers bar, and chewed it slowly. Sugar was quick energy, and energy equaled endurance.

He sat beneath the log reviewing preparations he had made with Lasurm. She would provide food and he would eat what she ate; she had started shopping after their last meeting, building up her stocks a little at a time so nobody would notice a change in her shopping habits. Batteries, cigarettes—she had a list of everything he needed. He had given her cash to pay for it. It wasn't clear how or if he would be reimbursed by the state.

Tonight Lasurm would have her outside lights on—one on the house, the other on her garage. She had been turning the two lights on for a while, again to make it look like her normal habit, but he told her if for some reason someone questioned this or got curious, she could turn on the garage light for one minute, at ten minutes after the hour, starting at 9 P.M. and continuing until 2 A.M. If he was not there by then, she should assume he was not coming, and await another ad in the Manistique paper.

Candy bar done, he got out of his hide, hoisted and adjusted his pack straps, and checked his compass. The tree line stretched east about a quarter mile, and he could make his way through the woods inside the cover and follow the elbow to where it bent to the south toward Lasurm's place. Or, he could cut directly through the woods to the next field and look for her lights and head directly for her house.

The wind was still making a racket in the trees, but the snow was not as heavy inside the cover with branches acting as an overhead filter. He chose to cut through on the direct line, and when he got to the outer edge, he stopped and searched south, looking for any sign of light. He found nothing but darkness flensed by blowing snow. He estimated he was about a third of a mile from her place. He checked his watch again. If her outside lights were out, she would not signal for another forty minutes.

If this was the right tree line.

A third of a mile would make a light shine like a beacon, but not in this weather. He needed to find the house, get in close, keep it in view, and wait. He checked his compass and began walking south into the open field, the wind still at his back and the temperature dropping. His brief stop had left him chilled. If he stopped again he would strip off his outer layer and put it on again when he moved. Dangerous to get sweaty in this kind of weather, he lectured himself. Hypothermia could settle in quickly. He moved slowly and deliberately to minimize perspiration, telling himself he would not stop again until he had the house in sight. This is a *truly* stupid idea, parachuting into hostile territory during a blizzard to see a one-legged woman who just wanted peace in the Garden.

PART III

NIGHT GARDENING

24

BURN'T BLUFF, FEBRUARY 14, 1976

The animal's fur was as coarse as a Brillo pad.

The snow paused just before 10 P.M. Service saw the darkened form of a house some two hundred yards ahead of him and walked toward it. It was the same house he had seen during the air recon with Joe Flap, a three-story box with a widow's walk on top, an old farmhouse with no trees close to it. The garage was unattached, thirty or forty feet south of the house. No lights, but he thought he saw the movement of smoke plumes from the chimney. There would be a ninety-degree turn in a county road several hundred feet south of the garage, and another east-west treeline, with Burn't Bluff at the western terminus.

He got next to the house, sniffed wood smoke, which reminded him of how badly he wanted another cigarette. When the garage light flashed on for one minute, and at 2201 went out, he breathed a heavy sigh of relief, circled to the south side of the building, stepped into the storm entry, and pounded twice on the door. If someone other than Lasurm answered, he would tell them he had run his car off the road and ask them to call the Delta County sheriff's department. It could be a hassle, but he would bull his way through, and let the county haul him out, knowing he would have to scrub the mission. *Be there*, he entreated as he waited.

The door opened three steps above him, and Lasurm's big blue eyes peered out into the darkness at him. She held the door open and he stepped up and past her onto a landing. Stairs led up and down from where they stood.

"Up to the kitchen," she said.

He shrugged off his pack and carried it upstairs into a kitchen with twelve-foot-high ceilings. The only light came from a few scented candles, and he smelled smoke from a fireplace.

"The lights," she said, hopping up to the kitchen behind him. She was not using her cane. "Word went around that people should keep their external lights off at night. You'd better get those wet clothes off. There's a fire."

He peeled down to his sweatpants, wool undershirt, and socks, and left his outer clothes in a pile on the kitchen floor.

She poked him in the lower back. "Straight ahead."

The only light in the room was from the fireplace. He felt around for something to sit on and eased into a stuffed chair.

She brought a bottle of Hartley's and two glasses and poured a generous brandy for each of them. "Why did they want the lights out?" he asked.

"People down here don't ask questions," she said.

"When did this happen?"

"A week ago," she said. "Are you thinking they anticipated someone like you might come?"

"Possibly," he said, but he didn't want to jump to conclusions; likewise, he didn't believe in coincidence.

"How *did* you get here?" she asked.

"I fell down a rabbit hole," he said. She didn't need to know the details.

She chuckled audibly in the darkness. "Does that make me the Queen of Hearts or the Mad Hatter?"

"That jury's still out," he said. He had an overpowering sense that he was being watched, but when he looked around he could see only the two of them.

"Hungry?" she asked.

"No thanks."

"Nonsense. I was so nervous all day I couldn't eat. When I saw the paper, I couldn't stop staring at the ad. Now you're here," she concluded, "and I'm starved."

Service followed her into the kitchen, watched her mix vanilla extract and heavy cream into pancake mix. When the pancakes were done she garnished them with orange peel and fresh mint, and he ate a couple and realized he was hungrier than he had admitted, and gobbled down six more.

He was reaching for syrup when he detected movement and heard a low snarl from the living room doorway. He instinctively looked without moving his head and felt his blood run cold.

The dog was the color of wet cement and splotched with black spikes of hair sticking up haphazardly. It had a long, pointed nose, its ears were flat against its head, and its intense yellow eyes were locked on Service. The dog's lip was curled back, showing a mouth full of menacing teeth.

Cecilia Lasurm said, "Miss Tillie, I see you've decided to join us." The animal crawled forward on its belly, keeping its eyes on Service. "She's paying homage to you," Lasurm said.

"It feels more like I'm being measured," he said. For a meal.

"Everything is fine, but please don't move until I tell you to," Lasurm said, adding, "She's never killed anything bigger than her."

He tried to force a smile, but failed. He didn't even nod as Lasurm got up from the table and came around to him, using the table edge for support. "Look at me," she ordered, and when Service turned his head she leaned down and kissed him on the mouth with a soft, lingering wet kiss. When she pulled away she looked down at the animal, which had gotten to its feet and was walking forward, wagging its stump tail. "Reach down with your hand," the woman said.

The hairs on his neck were electrified as he let his arm dangle.

The dog moved her head against his hand, and, summoning all the willpower he could, he rubbed once between her ears and let his arm dangle again. The animal's fur was as coarse as a Brillo pad.

"Miss Tillie is paying her respects," Lasurm said. "I'm afraid she's a bit overprotective."

The dog slunk back into the darkness of the living room.

"I found her on the highway ten years ago. She'd been shot several times with a pellet gun and she was starving, but she let me put her in my truck and take her to a veterinarian. She's been with me ever since. But she doesn't like guests, and all the locals know to stay away. Coffee or tea?"

"What the hell is going on?" he asked.

She said, "I've never allowed a man in here before. I had to find a way to let her know you were okay, so I kissed you."

"You knew that would work." Was her mind all there?

"I didn't know it wouldn't," she said sheepishly.

"It was *my* arm hanging there."

"She didn't bite," Lasurm said. "Dogs make you uncomfortable?"

He nodded, did not want to talk about it. Dogs scared the shit out of him, and he had been petrified of them as long as he could remember—all sizes, all breeds, all temperaments. He would willingly approach a criminal with a gun or endure a close encounter with a sow bear and her cubs, but when he confronted a dog, he was always in danger of falling apart.

"Let's be clear on this: The kiss was strictly for Miss Tillie," Lasurm said. "Am I making sense?"

"No," he said. "Yes." He had no idea. She was an odd woman in all ways, and his stomach knotted as he considered that coming here was a mistake—potentially a big one.

She sat down across from him. "You'll have all day tomorrow to get acquainted with Miss Tillie. She'll alert you if anyone gets within a hundred yards of the house, and if they get to the door she will be there to greet them. All you need to do to settle her and have her back off is to say, 'Gentle.'"

"Gentle," he repeated. "I won't be answering doors."

"Some females like to please," Lasurm said. "Will you go out tomorrow night?"

He nodded. *Some females like to please?* What the hell had he gotten himself into?

"Do you want me to drop you various places? I routinely visit some of my students at night."

"No, I'll do better on my own."

"All right, then, let me show you something." She went into another room and came back in faded, stained Carharts with one leg folded up. She had gotten her crutch and carried a small flashlight.

She led him into the basement where there were two furnaces. One of them was ancient, and she fiddled with something on the side and opened it like a door. "Strictly a facade," she said, switching on her flashlight. "It's level in here, but sometimes it can get a little icy."

He followed her down the dark tunnel, bending over to keep from bumping his head. The tunnel was less than six feet high and a little more than three feet wide. They walked for five minutes before entering a wide area. She found a switch and turned on a light. "My great-great-grandfather built the house in 1890. This was the storehouse. The tunnel allowed my grandmother to get to their supplies when they were snowed in. I've added heat, which vents all the way back to my chimney at the house. If you have to make yourself scarce, you'll be comfortable enough down here."

She left the light on and continued down the tunnel. He glanced at the compass pinned to his jacket and saw they were walking almost directly west. They walked for another fifteen minutes and came to a smaller underground room. There were some steps leading upward and boulders piled against the west wall. She patted one of the boulders. "Behind here there's a natural cave that leads all the way out to the bluff's face," she said. "When I was a kid I played down here all the time, and my mother insisted my father block off the cave to keep me out. Burn't Bluff is a honeycomb," she said.

"Limestone," he said.

She smiled. "Above us there's a small stone structure that looks like a pump house. The door is steel and bolted from the inside, with a padlock on the outside." She handed him a shoelace with a key dangling from it. "That will get you in. When you come back each night, coming in this way will make it easier for you."

"There will be signs where I've opened the door," he pointed out.

"It's winter," she said. "You're going to leave signs wherever you go, but this is set back in the woods and it's nasty, cluttered footing with a lot of windfalls. In summer people sometimes drift through here, but not in winter."

He followed her back to the other room in the tunnel, and she showed him how to work the heat before they trekked back to the house.

She led him through the kitchen to the front of the house, told him to grab his bag, and took him upstairs to a small bedroom. "It's an old house," she said, "but it's warm. We have to share a bathroom, but that shouldn't be a problem."

The room was narrow with a single bed and an old dresser. The floors were wood, with two faded throw rugs.

"You know if they find you here, you could get hurt," she said.

He nodded as she turned on a light and used the rheostat to lower the brightness. The house might be old, but it had been modernized.

"I'll be awake at six-thirty," she said. "I have to be at school by eight-thirty. If you want breakfast, it will be ready at seven-fifteen. If not, you're on your own."

He nodded dumbly, and she paused at the door and looked back. "I invited you here to do something positive," Lasurm said. "I hope you don't disappoint me." Miss Tillie glared at him with her yellow eyes and followed Lasurm.

"Fucking dog," he mumbled, but his mind was already shifting more to the mission than the threat of the animal. The next two weeks threatened to take him into a state of weirdness, but he was sure he was ready for whatever got thrown at him. Lasurm was strange and so was her ugly dog, but if the mission went the way he expected it to, he would not have to see much of either of them over the next two weeks.

25

THE GARDEN PENINSULA:
FIRST RECON, FEBRUARY 15, 1976

He needed not just to out-rat the rats, but to temporarily become one.

The outside door of the fake pump house was jammed by snow and ice, but Service managed to wedge it open with a shoulder. He was glad to be free of the house, despite it being warm and comfortable. Miss Tillie had followed him around all day, growling and snarling and making various sounds, none of which sounded particularly amicable. He had said the word *gentle* to her so many times, it was stuck in his mind like what Germans called an earworm.

When he got up to have breakfast with Lasurm, he had reviewed the list of names she had provided at the last meeting, and sat with her and his plat books making pencil marks by the homes and hangouts of the Garden rats. Before coming to the Garden he had contacted Lansing and gotten the registration numbers for snowmobiles, boats, and wheeled vehicles for the people on the list. If he encountered them during his travels, he would have some notion of whom he might be dealing with.

The weather had improved, but not significantly. The temperature had gotten up to eight during the day, and snow continued to fall, but the sun had not come out to melt and form a thin surface crust on the snow.

Lasurm would not be home for an hour. They agreed last night that she should maintain her regular routine during his time with her. It was 5:30 P.M. when he crawled out of the well house, cinched up the ruck he had carried in his equipment bag, and began his trek northward. He intended to skirt the edge of Burn't Bluff going north and veer inland toward the village of Garden, coming up on it from the south and inland. Lasurm said a lot of the troublemakers hung out at Roadie's Bar at night—the same place where he had been attacked by rock throwers.

The village was ten miles north of her place, and at his normal walking pace he could do ten-minute miles almost endlessly; but there was fifteen inches of fresh snow and deeper drifts, unfamiliar rolling terrain, fences and roads to cross. He would have to make numerous stops to make sure he was not seen. Because of all this, he decided to figure on a conservative rate of thirty minutes per mile. This meant he would need five hours to get to the village and five hours to get back. If he gave himself two hours in the village itself, he could still be comfortably back by zero five thirty, well before morning twilight. If something held him up in the village, there was high ground east of South River Bay, and no well-traveled roads for almost a square mile. Lasurm had shown him where an abandoned sawmill was located, and if he ran out of time and night, this would be his layover destination for the next day.

Knowing how far he had to walk and the pace he wanted to maintain, he wore long johns under his snowmobile suit and carried the rest of his layers in his ruck to put on when he stopped for breaks.

Once clear of Lasurm's tunnel, he crawled and walked northward through the slash for the first mile before aiming northeast to skirt Sand Bay, his mind lost in thought, and relying on his instincts to watch for any potential contact with others. Law enforcement was being used as an instrument in a state plan to eliminate commercial fishing in Lake Michigan in favor of sportfishermen and their wallets. Most of the conservation officers risking their asses in the Garden probably didn't have a clue about what was really going on, and this thought put him in a nasty mood. To counter his temper, he kept repeating the goals of his mission: identify the rat leaders and their followers; determine how and where they stage their operations; observe their landside tactics, where they meet, and how they behave. Overall: observe and learn. Most of all, do not act and do not enforce—observe only. He and Tree had gone on many missions in Vietnam that were similar to this. More often than not they went into the jungle to find and watch the enemy, not to kill them. *This is* not *Vietnam*, he reminded himself as he pushed through the deep snow. *Your Vietnam was eight years ago. Your Vietnam is history—finished.*

South of Fayette he angled through the woods east of the Port Bar and increased his walking speed, the wind hard out of the north. Initially his eyes had been filled with tears from the wind, but now that was finished. His balaclava seemed to protect his face as he walked on, not dwelling on the conditions. His job kept him outside year-round, making the weather largely irrelevant.

Why the hell did he keep thinking about Vietnam? He remembered meeting an air force master sergeant at the NCO club at Danang one night. The KC-135 boom operator had been in the Strategic Air Command during the Cuban missile crisis, and had told him how all of SAC's bomber and tanker crews had been briefed before being put on the highest alert level. They were told that President Kennedy was going to give the Soviets an ultimatum: Get your missiles out, or we'll take them out. Every airman understood that such an attack could lead to a nuclear exchange, but back then, every fighting man understood the stakes and his duty. The boomer couldn't understand how one president could trust fighting men with such a secret, while the troops being killed in Vietnam knew little or nothing about what the national intent was. They were losing the war through attrition and lack of national will.

The mess in the Garden felt too much like Vietnam, Service decided. Lansing was not leveling with the troops on the ground about what their actual objectives were, and as a result, conservation officers were left trying to enforce a toothless law for goals that might be specious at best. Lasurm had explained the economics of sportfishing versus commercial fishing, and Fahey had confirmed this in Lansing, which left him feeling somewhere between anxious and ambivalent.

The rats were waging a guerrilla war—an insurgency for personal economic reasons. Yes, insurgency was the right term, he thought as he walked north. The rats were insurgents, pure and simple, conducting what his old commander Major Teddy Gates called a low-intensity conflict. Gates had taught his marines how to think about—and, more importantly, how to think *like*—the enemy. As a result, they had enjoyed many more successes than failures compared to other American units fighting against NVA troops. Insurgents in Vietnam, he remembered, attacked police in small units, using speed, surprise, and terrain to shock the government and force them to concentrate their troops and expend more resources. The more the government did this, the more impotent it looked.

Nobody was getting killed in the Garden, he knew, but Lasurm made it clear that intimidation of residents surely was taking place. Evidence: In an area with almost one thousand people, you might expect more than one person to step forward and complain, but so far only Lasurm had shown the requisite gumption, which reinforced how effective intimidation was in keeping the locals in line for the rats. Lasurm's actual motivation remained in doubt. She had given him reasons, which sounded good but didn't bite. And how did her daughter fit into this? The woman was in jail, Odd Hegstrom was her lawyer, and

Lasurm denied that her motives grew out of her daughter's situation. Replaying this information, he concluded that the less contact he had with Lasurm, the better for both of them.

The situation here was perplexing. The DNR and police authorities had so far reacted classically: COs no longer conducted solo patrols. Delta County deputies and the Troops made no routine patrols at all, and came into the Garden only when there was a reported emergency or a formal complaint. Even in these circumstances they tended to drag their feet in responding. In essence, the lawless had gained control of the peninsula, and Service had seen firsthand their harassment tactics.

The longer he considered all the angles, the more he was certain that this was a sort of domestic Vietnam; if someone didn't get the insurgents on their heels—and soon—they would continue to increase their confidence, and eventually somebody would get killed. This realization was a real-life Yogism of déjà vu all over again, and the more he thought about it, the angrier he got—not with the sort of white-hot anger that made him want to strike out immediately and blindly, but with the blue rage that Teddy Gates had taught them: To get the enemy off your back, put the bastards on their heels.

His old commanding officer used to say, "Don't get mad: Get even." Gates was an adherent of Sun Tzu, the Chinese general who was the first to codify rules of warfare around 500 B.C., and whose work was unknown in Europe until just prior to the French Revolution. Sun Tzu's lessons were based on having professional soldiers, good leadership, and common sense. As he walked, Service began to think about the lessons Teddy Gates and Sun Tzu had taught.

The closer he got to the town, the more certain he was that while the DNR needed accurate, timely intelligence, it also needed to treat this as the kind of conflict it had become. Their primary target should be the mind of the enemy leader. Lasurm said Pete Peletier was the top rat. If true, who was he, and what was his hold over the others? You couldn't attack the mind of a leader unless you had some idea of who you were dealing with. Don't wallow in doubt, he told himself as he marched on.

Less than a mile from the village Service stopped walking, found cover in a small aspen stand, and lit a cigarette. He got out a small iron grate he carried in his pack, pried the lid off a Sterno can, placed it under the grill, and lit the wick. He poured tea from a thermos borrowed from Lasurm into a cup and set it on the grill over the tiny flame. His plan, he realized, had been no plan at all; it was Attalienti's wish list. The trick had been to get into the Garden undetected, which he had done. Now what? Fulfill the wish list and split? No, he told himself. Not enough. You have to rethink the deal, top to bottom. Initially, he was disgusted by his shortsightedness, but this mood quickly shifted to a certainty that his gut was right: He was here for two weeks, and when it came time to withdraw, he somehow needed to leave confusion and mistrust among the rats about their leader. At the moment he was not sure how to accomplish what he wanted, but he had the germ of some ideas to ruminate on during the hike back to Lasurm's. Reconnaissance of the village would have to wait.

En route he detoured to the Port Bar, which was just outside the south gate of Fayette State Park, and stopped long enough to write down the registration numbers of snowmobiles, and descriptions and license numbers of trucks and automobiles parked around the bar.

As he headed into the final two and a half miles to the house, two things were clear in his mind. First, if Pete Peletier was the actual rat leader, his followers needed to begin to doubt him and wonder if he was representing them, or using them for his own ends. Second, to do the things he needed to do, he needed not just to out-rat the rats, but to temporarily become one.

"You aren't there to act," Attalienti had told him. But Attalienti wasn't here, and his views were based on his place in the DNR's shameful history here. No, Attalienti was wrong; he couldn't enforce the law here, but he could do more than just gather information. The bastards here needed to feel the isolation and uncertainty that the marines had felt in Vietnam.

When Cecilia Lasurm came down for breakfast, coffee was already brewing and Service was making eggs and toast. "Good morning," she greeted him with a quizzical look.

"There's a list of things I need," he said, placing a plate of scrambled eggs in front of her.

She studied the note he had left on the table and looked up at him. "Five vise grips, two screwdrivers, a funnel, eight rolls of duct tape, twenty pounds of sugar in two-pound bags, green spray paint, ten pounds of small potatoes . . . What in the world is going on?"

"You'd best shop in Escanaba," he said, placing two hundred-dollar bills in front of her. "I'm trying to think like a Chinaman," he whispered.

"At large or institutionalized?" she asked, making him laugh.

26

GARDEN PENINSULA, FEBRUARY 21, 1976

"All this turns you on—just like the rats."

For three consecutive nights he had explored the edges of roads and reconnoitered the layout around the houses of the rats on his list. Along the way he found five road-killed deer, cut out their hearts, and impaled them on some sticks he cut. They were frozen so there was no blood trail to worry about. They were now stockpiled inside the door of the pump house.

Tonight he had watched the Port Bar and its cheesy lighthouse facade. Five snowmobiles and two trucks on his list were parked nearby. Through frosted glass he saw people moving around inside. Once a man came out a side door and pissed in the snow, laughing like he had just cinched an Olympic gold medal.

When it was quiet Service poured a pound of sugar into the gas tanks of the snowmobiles. Sugar would take an hour or more to work, but then the machines would die and be unstartable until the owners pulled the carburetors, gas tanks, and fuel lines, and flushed everything. He slithered underneath the truck, used a vise grip to pinch off the fuel line near the gas tank, where it went from metal to rubber, and used duct tape to fasten the vise grip to the chassis. No matter what the driver did, the engine would not start with the line crimped, and the cause could not be discovered until somebody got underneath with a light.

Each night he carefully varied his routes, and tonight when he returned to Lasurm's, they drank coffee in silence. He showered and went to bed, only to be awakened from deep sleep by a heavy weight flopping on the end of the bed. He pulled the pillow off his head and saw Miss Tillie at his feet. She curled her lips when she saw him, and he tried to go back to sleep, telling himself not to move.

"Stop terrorizing the poor man," Cecilia Lasurm chided the dog, which immediately jumped off the bed. Service heard the animal's claws and feet on the wood floors and he rolled over.

"What time is it?" he asked sleepily.

"Noonish," she said. "You've got everybody spooked," she said. "And angry."

When he didn't respond, she added, "I'm on my way to a home visit. I'll be back early."

"Did they notice?" he asked.

"Notice what?"

"That Peletier's truck was left alone."

She shot him a quizzical look and walked out, the rubber tip of her crutch squeaking against the stairs as she descended.

During a dinner of bowtie pasta and meatballs, Lasurm poured red wine for herself and looked at him. "You're addicted to risk," she said. "If there was no risk, you wouldn't be a cop. All this turns you on—just like the rats."

He loaded his fork with pasta and shrugged. She was probably right, but he doubted she truly understood the difference between calculated and spontaneous risk. What he was doing now was calculated, he told himself.

"Is work all you think about?" she asked, dropping her fork onto her plate.

It suddenly felt like he was talking to Bathsheba, and the thought jarred him. He rinsed his plate in the sink, left it, and went into the tunnel to get ready for the night. Jesus, what was *her* problem?

27

THE GARDEN MISSION,
FEBRUARY 24, 1976

"We don't need another damn cowboy here."

H e had visited every known rat's house at least once during his nightly forays. One night, he had sat on Middle Bluff watching the rats pull their nets to collect fish, the nets basically in the same location of those he'd helped to seize, which meant the poachers had already replaced them. Where did that much money come from? He had followed them from the Port Bar as they eased their snow machines through the state park's historic ruins, across Snail Shell Harbor, and out onto the thick ice of Big Bay de Noc.

Snowmobiles provided excellent transportation in winter. Soon after their introduction in the late sixties, sales had unexpectedly soared, and now the houses and trailers of even the poorest U.P. residents sported TV antennas and at least one snowmobile out front. Since the machines ran easier on packed, hard trails than in deep, fresh snow, most drivers opted for the path of least resistance and followed the same routes to their various destinations. What appeared unpredictable before now began to take on a pattern as he penciled the rat routes into his notebook. This was information that could be used against the rats when his mission was done. He had sabotaged vehicles on only three occasions, but figured he had three or four days left, and decided it was time to step up pressure in his self-declared psychological war. As a precaution, he wrapped and taped cloth over his boots to blur the pattern and size of his tracks.

Ranse Renard lived directly across Garden Road from Pete Peletier, both houses about a mile north of Fairport, six miles south of Lasurm's. Tonight he had watched both houses since 10 P.M. Renard had pulled into Peletier's driveway just before midnight, shouting and pounding on Peletier's front door. The door had opened and the two men had disappeared inside.

Renard emerged around 3 A.M., drove across the street to his house, got out, walked to the front door, turned around, and walked back to his truck, muttering under his breath. He took a flashlight out of the truck, got on his back, and wriggled underneath the truck to check his fuel line.

What was the man *thinking*? He'd just driven the truck across the road. Drunk *and* paranoid, Service told himself. He fought back a smile as he waited for Renard to settle inside the house before he approached the man's truck, popped the hood, pried off the distributor cap, jimmied the rotor loose and took it out, replacing the cap. He threw the rotor into the deep snow on the angled roof of the man's house. When Renard tried to start his truck again, he'd probably assume the problem was underneath and crawl under the truck, only to find that the fuel line was unimpaired. Service jammed a small potato deep into the exhaust pipe. *Give the man two problems to deal with,* Service thought as he got ready to leave—only to see a string of snowmobile lights coming south on Garden Road. Six machines pulled into Peletier's driveway. Their drivers dismounted and began shouting, "Pete—Pete!"

Peletier came to the front door and shouted, "Shut up, boys! My kids are sleepin'!"

Service watched him usher them inside, gave them fifteen minutes, crossed the road, quickly dumped sugar into all six machines, and made a fast tactical withdrawal into the woods.

A quarter-mile south of Lasurm's, he was working his way north through a tree line a hundred yards west of Garden Road as a half-dozen trucks came racing south. He wondered if a rat rally was getting under way. It began to snow as he opened the steel door of the pump house and disappeared into Lasurm's tunnel.

He dumped his pack and outer gear in the storeroom and turned toward the tunnel to the house to find Miss Tillie snarling at him. "Gentle," he said softly, "you four-legged pile of shit."

Lasurm was awake and waiting in the kitchen. He looked at his watch. It was not yet 4:30 A.M. "What're you doing awake?"

"Worrying, fretting, stewing—take your pick," she said. "You came down here to make peace, but now you're doing anything but that, and they're suspicious. They think an outsider is out to get them, and they're talking about trying to trap him. They're going to travel only in groups now," she said.

This confirmed what he had seen tonight. "It won't do them any good," he said.

"I would think a little fear would be a healthy thing," she said.

Fear and caution were not synonymous. He refused to defend or explain himself. "I'm gonna need more sugar."

She sighed. "I doubt a truckload of sugar would take the edge off the likes of you."

"I don't have an edge."

She sneered, "Any sharper and you could walk through walls."

"Talk about an edge," he countered.

She got up, snapped her crutch onto her wrist, and pushed the rubber tip against his chest like a sword. "Grady, it's your job to uphold the law. I don't approve of violence. God knows we've had plenty of that down here. I don't mean to tell you how to do your job, but you've gone over the line."

"Stay out of this," he said, immediately regretting it. She had opened her home to him and probably was taking more risk than him. He wasn't in the mood for this claptrap.

"I *can't* stay out of this!" she said sharply. "I'm in the middle of it, and the DNR is coming today," she said.

"Says who?" Why would Attalienti schedule a patrol while he was here? To maintain the appearance of normal DNR operations, he concluded, which made some sense, normalcy and routine the best covers for secrecy.

"Word's out. They always seem to know, don't they?" she said.

"They didn't know about me," he told her.

"They made everybody turn off their lights before you came."

There had to be another reason, he had already decided, there being no real trail to track him or his plan. Until tonight he'd seen no real caution from them—certainly nothing to suggest they were doing anything but operating confidently on their own ground.

He headed for the cellar stairs, Lasurm following close behind. "Where do you think you're going?"

"Out," he said.

"You just came in! You don't have enough night left."

"I'll have to make do," he said.

"You're letting your testosterone lead you! I wanted a smart, tough game warden, tough being secondary," Lasurm hissed at him. "We don't need another damn cowboy here."

He turned around and looked up at her, knowing she was right. He had come to the Garden with a mission, and had gathered the information

Attalienti wanted. Would it help in the future? He didn't know. But his gut had driven him to step over the line and violate the captain's directive against action, and now if COs were coming down today, they might encounter more anger than usual—anger he had created by sabotaging rat equipment. Daylight be damned; he had to go out and support his people any way he could. "Don't forget the sugar," he reminded Lasurm, avoiding her eyes.

28

GARDEN PENINSULA,
FEBRUARY 24, 1976

One thing was for sure: None of them walked alone.

The only on-ice net activity he had seen had been off the state park, and based on this he headed north from Lasurm's, hoping to get into position on Middle Bluff. To keep himself hidden he kept to the woods as much as he could, eventually climbing out to an overlook on the bluff where he saw seven snowmobiles and Stone's green truck and another DNR vehicle on the ice. It was now 8:30 A.M.; it had taken only two hours to get to the bluff from Lasurm's house.

Where were the rats? If this thing was about money, they couldn't afford to lose more nets, could they?

He sat watching his DNR pals until around noon when he saw men with ski masks filtering their way on foot through the woods along a buttonhook peninsula on the south side of Snail Shell Harbor. He saw no snowmobiles, but eventually a truck drove out across the harbor ice and made its way toward the DNR men. He could see through his binoculars that it was Ranse Renard's truck. Why weren't the others with him? Renard drove forward slowly, almost like a man with a white flag. *Where was Peletier?*

As he watched he heard grunting in the snowy woods just north of him. He immediately ducked into the trees to try to locate the source.

A man in a tan-and-white snowmobile suit was working his way down the crest of the bluff toward the cliff. He was carrying an uncased rifle with a scope. *Shit.* He couldn't just sit and watch the man take a shot at the officers. But he didn't want to show himself.

The man reached the lip of the bluff and knelt by a broken birch tree not more than thirty yards away. The winter sun was low and in their faces, the sky gray with hints of pink.

Service took off his pack, got down on his belly, and crawled through the trees behind the man, who had taken out a pint bottle, poured something, took a drink, and held up a sandwich, obviously in no hurry. Service could see lettuce hanging out the sides of the bread. The man took several hits from the bottle while he ate. Nervous, Service told himself, keyed up.

The rifle was standing against a fallen tree, the black barrel silhouetted against the surrounding white. The area was strewn with boulders, including several directly behind the man, most of them sunk into a depression. Service was within five yards, the man slightly above him, and he still hadn't decided what to do.

The man picked up the rifle, worked the bolt, and said, "Shit!" He immediately put down the gun and charged east along the path he had followed across Middle Bluff. Service had no idea what had set the man off, and he didn't care. He waited until he was out of sight, crawled upward through a seam in the rocks, and grabbed the rifle, a Remington bolt-action with a Weaver K4 scope. He retracted the bolt: no shell ejected. He checked the magazine: empty. The man had forgotten ammo! Service used the barrel to helicopter the weapon over the edge and retreated to his position, quickly hiding his tracks as he went.

The man was back in fifteen minutes. Service saw him use binoculars to watch Renard out on the ice. A figure in black was standing next to the truck. Probably Stone. The other officers kept working.

When Renard's truck turned around and headed back toward land, the would-be shooter began cursing and stomping around the rocks, kicking clods of ice and snow.

Service crawled south and saw the men on the opposite peninsula walk out of the woods to meet Renard, who stopped to let several men climb into the bed of the truck before continuing across the frozen harbor. Other men in the woods began to withdraw on foot in twos and threes. Renard had six men in his truck. Was this the core group? If so, what role did the others have—active sympathizers or merely curious observers? One thing was for sure: None of them walked alone. But where was their leader?

The shooter stopped cursing, snatched up his gear, and departed at a clumsy jog. Service trailed him across the bluff to a road, where a dirty pickup truck was snugged nose-first against a snowbank. He used his binoculars to get the license number, wrote it down, and waited for the vehicle to leave. The truck was dirty and slush-covered, but something about it seemed familiar.

He suspected the man would return with help to search for his rifle, which meant Service needed to vacate the area.

There were several possible routes, but he decided on one through the thickest woods to cover himself while daylight remained. When he got close to the Port Bar, he saw there were no vehicles; he hiked farther south another half-mile and found a place under some logs. He scooped out an opening and settled in to wait for darkness. Waiting patiently and alone was what game wardens did best.

While he waited he thought about what he had seen. Even on foot the rats were clinging to each other, and the fact that they came in on foot suggested he had crippled enough machines to make them wary. He had not gotten to all that many machines, which further suggested the rats were not as numerous as the DNR had suspected. He also knew that each time he struck, he was costing them time and money—and each time Peletier went untouched, his followers had to wonder why he was exempt.

Lasurm looked at him warily when he wrote down a telephone number and told her what he wanted her to do. "You want me to call Attalienti and tell him there's a rifle on the rocks at the base of Middle Bluff?"

Service held her coat out to her and nodded. "You have a party line here," he said. "Best use a pay phone."

She slammed the door on her way out. He felt bad about the way he ordered her around, but she was beginning to challenge him, and he didn't need complications right now. Attalienti was going to be pissed that he'd taken the man's rifle—but what was he supposed to have done? Let him shoot, or jump him before he could get off a round? This solution was a compromise that had allowed him to remove the threat and maintain his anonymity. To fight a rat you sometimes had to act like one.

29

GARDEN PENINSULA,
FEBRUARY 26, 1976

"Even Napoleon didn't fight every day."

Service awoke with achy muscles and a windburned face, swung his legs to the floor, and checked his watch: 3 P.M. He rolled back onto the bed and went back to sleep.

Lasurm awoke him two hours later. "Aren't you going out tonight?"

"Did you make the call?" he asked, checking his watch again. What day was this? It was all starting to run together.

She was sitting on the side of the bed and smelled of alcohol. "The sugar is downstairs."

"Did you make the call?" he asked again.

"Do you *ever* lighten up?" she said. "The DNR pulled more nets yesterday. Renard and his people went out to talk to them, but there was no confrontation. He lodged a protest—told them someone is vandalizing fishermen on the peninsula. He thinks it's the DNR, and that he's the victim." Service knew that Renard had talked alone to Stone; his people had not been with him. The report of what he had said was Renard's version.

"Did you make the call?" he repeated.

"Yesterday, from Rapid River," she said. "Attalienti said he'd take care of it."

"That's all he said?"

"It's what you wanted, right?" She held up a glass of wine and took a drink. "Oh, I guess he also asked when you're coming out."

"You *guess*?"

"He asked," she said. "Don't be so damn literal, and stop being surly. I think you're feeling guilty about what you've done here. And you're exhausted. You've slept for nearly twenty-four hours."

"And you said?"

"My God," she said. "Do you *ever* break focus? I said I don't know, but it's soon, right?" She stared at him waiting for a reply.

"Am I cramping your style?" he asked

She took another drink and grimaced. "You haven't even *seen* my style." She saluted him with the glass. "I need another drink."

She drained her glass and went downstairs with Service following. Here we go again, he thought.

The wine bottle on the kitchen table was nearly empty, and she was fumbling with the cork of a new bottle.

"Are you sure you want to do that?" he asked.

She rolled her eyes and continued her efforts. He took it away from her and opened it.

"You going to warn me against the sin of overindulgence?"

"Sermons are your specialty," he shot back.

She wagged a finger at him. "You're a naughty bastard," she said. "Even Napoleon didn't fight every day. Do you think the Great Lombardi thought about football when he was making love to his wife?"

"Maybe *she* did," Service said. Lombardi had died in 1970. Now what the hell was she talking about?

Lasurm dribbled red wine down her chin and laughed out loud. "That's actually funny! Do you think it's a coincidence that the great general and the great coach each had a Marie in his life?" Her eyes were cloudy and she looked pouty. "When you look at me, what do you see?"

He shrugged, knowing there was no right answer.

"Exactly," she said. "Nothing. I'm nothing, the invisible woman."

"I . . . ," he said

"Shut up! Did you not pick up on the fact that I've never allowed another man in this house? Did I not make that clear?" she added. "No, don't answer that either. You pick up on everything that fits what you want to hear."

"You make me sound like an asshole."

"You tell me what it makes you. You came down here to gather information and now you're acting just like them. The end justifies the means, an eye for an eye, all that biblical shit."

"I thought you were a good Christian."

She sneered. "Don't confuse spiritual with religious. What we each believe, even *if* we believe, has nothing whatsoever to do with any of this," she said wagging a finger at him, taking another drink.

"Any of what?" he asked.

"Don't play games," she said. "You're perpetuating the cycle you're supposed to be ending. I asked for you because I wanted to break the cycle here, clear the air, but you can't *break* laws to *uphold* laws. I didn't ask for Attila the Hun," she lamented. "And I did my homework on you, too: Responsible, smart, courageous, energetic, thoughtful, tireless, fair, loyal, but you're just like the rest of them."

All men, all COs, or all men on the Garden? He wasn't sure what she was talking about.

"It's one thing to mess with somebody's mind," she said, "but you can't beat them up."

"I haven't laid a hand on anybody."

She sneered. "Now *that's* a fact—but the word is somebody beat the hell out of Moe Lapalme yesterday and threatened him with his own rifle."

So that was the man's name. Service stared at her. "I took a man's rifle while he was gone getting ammunition and slung it over the bluff. He wasn't there at that moment. Remember, you called Attalienti to tell him where it is? I never touched anyone. If this guy is claiming otherwise, he's lying because he forgot his ammo and left his rifle unattended to go fetch it. He doesn't want to look like a fuckup."

She looked at him for a long minute, evaluating. "There are people who believe what Moe Lapalme says."

"Are you one of them?"

She said, "No, I don't believe most of what Moe says, but he can be very persuasive. He's the kind who could understand being beaten up, but he'd never admit to screwing up. Never. Nothing that goes wrong is ever Moe's fault."

What was she getting at with this Lapalme? His name had not come up in the original list of rats. "I never touched him, Cecilia," Service said. "But the Marquis of Queensbury Rules were for sport, not real life," he said, adding, "One leg." *Why had he said that?*

"Yes, of course; you see one leg or two, black or white, crippled or whole," she said, emptying her glass. "If you were the one with one leg, would you be a different person?"

"I wouldn't be doing this job."

Her blue eyes flared. "Meaning your job defines you?"

"That's not what I said—and what the hell is this conversation supposed to accomplish?"

"You *see!*" she said, "You see? Not everything has to lead to an accomplishment. A conversation is just that—an exchange. It doesn't have to *lead* somewhere, or even *anywhere*. Life is not about keeping score!"

"Naughty or nice, we all go to Heaven?" he said.

"There you go again," she said. "Heaven—a goal, the ultimate destination, only those with the highest scores get admitted—like MIT or something," she added. "That is so much *crap!*" she said with a disparaging laugh.

"Three days," he said wearily. "Three more days and I'll be out of your hair."

She tried to pour another glass of wine for herself, holding the bottle over the glass. Only a few drops came out of the opening. She plopped the bottle on the table and looked him in the eyes. "You haven't even gotten *into* my hair," she whispered. "Get me drunk and don't even take advantage of me. Man and woman this close together for two weeks, and all he does is nothing, sees one leg is all. I'm almost forty, you know . . . "

She was talking to herself now.

" 'Nuther bottle," she said, slurring her words.

"You're way past last call," he said.

She nodded once, pursed her lips, and fumbled to get her crutch on her wrist. "Help me," she said. It was a plea, not an order.

He helped her to her feet, but she began to tilt and he picked her up in his arms. She weighed next to nothing. "Drunk crip," she mumbled. "I won't tell if you won't." She began to giggle as he carried her up the stairs, her crutch hanging off her wrist and banging along.

Service heard the dog behind them, and Lasurm said sharply over his shoulder, "Leave us *alone*, Tillie!" The animal stopped and retreated.

"Know what?" Lasurm asked when he set her on the bed. "I'm a Marie too. Cecilia Marie Lasurm." She had an arm hooked over his shoulder. "You getting me ready to bed?" she asked, and immediately began to giggle and whispered, "Meant ready *for* bed, not *to* bed." He ignored her.

"Undress me," she said.

"You're fine the way you are."

"Even one leg?" she said. She lifted it and wiggled her foot. "It's a nice leg," she said. "Yes?"

"Yes, a great leg. Sleep," he said.

"Really? A *great* leg?"

"Yes, great."

"You're not goin' out tonight?"

"Not tonight."

"Promise?"

"Promise," he said.

"Shame," she said.

"What?" he asked, but her head was on the pillow and she was asleep.

He stood in the shower early the next morning, relishing the needles of hot water on sore muscles. His job frequently took him out of his vehicle, but this was a lot more walking than he was used to, and all of it through snow without benefit of skis or snowshoes. He could feel it every afternoon when he awoke for the next night's patrol.

A sound brought him out of his reverie and he saw the shower curtain sliding back; he immediately pivoted away, but Lasurm reached into the stream of water and touched him. "Scars," she whispered, her hand tracing lines on his chest and arm. She took the palm of his hand and put it under her robe. He felt scars where breasts should have been. "We both understand pain and decisions," she said. "You didn't pull your hand back." She patted his arm and backed away.

He stepped out of the shower, picked up a towel, and walked to her bedroom door. There were no lights. "I'm here," she said softly. "The invisible scars are the ones we feel the most," she added.

He lay down beside her and felt the warmth of her skin against his, and began his recitation. The women he had known seemed to always want to know about his wounds. "Left ab, Vietnam, rocket fragment. Right ab, AK-forty-seven round, also Vietnam, and it hurt like hell. Left forearm, a fifteen-year-old squirrel hunter accidentally potshot me with a twenty-two. Upper right thorax, Vietnam, grenade." The other scar had come when he stepped in front of his grandmother's 410 shotgun. He didn't count that one because it had been his own fault.

Later she lay beside him, whispering, "My grandmother died of breast cancer. Then my aunt and my mother. And my oldest sister. The doctors insisted I shouldn't assume their fate would be mine. One doctor actually told me that if a coin flip comes up heads one hundred times in a row, the odds of heads on the next toss remains fifty-fifty. I listened to what the doctors said and told them to take them off, get rid of them. I was twenty-three. My own doctor refused. I had to go all the way to Houston to find a surgeon who would do it." She nibbled Service's neck and whispered, "We're a lot alike. We loathe passivity. Faced with a problem, we look for solutions, for action."

"You said I'm perpetuating the cycle here."

"You're here because I asked specifically for you," she said. "But what you've done won't stop this thing."

"Not in the short term," he said, remembering Teddy Gates talking about Sun Tzu: Attack the mind of the leader, create doubt, undercut trust.

"Long term doesn't interest me," she said. "In September my doctor diagnosed ovarian cancer. He talked of surgery, radiation, chemotherapy, all of that. But I told him no, just let it be. I've already lost my breasts. They're not taking the rest, and if I die—well, we all die, don't we?"

"You can't just do nothing," he said.

"I would expect that response from you. I'm not doing nothing. Sometimes thinking and watching are doing a lot. I called you and the DNR in to do something about the Garden. If I can't live, I can at least leave a legacy." She rolled over and faced him. "I told my principal I wouldn't be in today. He assumes it's the cancer. I want to spend the day right here."

"I have to go out tonight," he said. "Cecilia."

She smiled. "You'll always have to go out there."

"Tell me about Moe Lapalme," he said.

"We have all day," she said, pulling him toward her. "Say my name again. Please?"

"Cecilia," he whispered.

30

GARDEN PENINSULA,
FEBRUARY 27, 1976

"I've probably worn out my welcome."

The effigy hung from a wire strung across Garden Road where it crossed Garden Creek at the north end of the village common area. The figure was suspended by an oversize noose, draped in a gray uniform shirt, and had a German army helmet on top with DNR painted on the sides of the helmet. A sign on the body said FISH NAZI, the letters in bright red. Service was wedged between a cluster of buildings that overlooked Garden Creek, and he stood in the shadows, irked beyond words. He wanted to cut it down, but knew there wasn't enough time. He had another idea for getting back at the rats. Lasurm was right. He had gone over the line, but he knew he couldn't pull back now. Not yet.

He spent the day making signs and rigging his surprise, and when Lasurm got home from school, she came down to the storeroom looking for him, saw what he was doing, and said, "Creepy."

"It's a going-away gift," he said, admiring his work.

"Going away when?" she asked.

He detected concern in her voice. "Tomorrow night. I want you to drop me east of Garden after dark, and I'll take it from there."

"This is your last night?"

"I've probably worn out my welcome."

"Not with me," she said, putting her hand on his shoulder. "Moe Lapalme is making a lot of noise about why Peletier's equipment never gets touched," she added.

"He's trying to deflect attention," Service said, hoping Attalienti had recovered the rifle.

"That's Moe," she said, "first in line for glory and a no-show when things don't go right."

"You use a certain tone when you say his name," Service said.

"Are you sure you want me to drop you off?" she asked, evading his question.

"I'll be under a tarp in back of your truck," he said.

"And tonight?"

"Things to do. I wouldn't want to leave you with all that sugar. Waste not, want not."

She smiled and shook her head. "There's going to be a meeting tonight at Lapalme's house."

This was interesting. "Guess I'd better put Moe on the itinerary."

"They'll have guards on their vehicles," she said.

"Heavy snow coming in tonight," he told her. "Do you know how hard it is to watch something when you're cold?"

"You seem to do all right," she said.

"I do it every day. Where does Moe live?"

She told him that Lapalme lived in a small house just north of Garden, on a treeless lot packed with the hulks of abandoned trucks and cars.

"Just be careful," she said.

It was a long, exhausting ten miles to Lapalme's house, the snow swirling heavily out of the northeast. He found a hiding place among the derelict vehicles dumped on Lapalme's property and settled in. There were six pickups, two sedans, and several snowmobiles parked in Lapalme's driveway. No noise came from the house. He reconnoitered carefully and located the "guards" seated in lawn chairs in the garage with a small charcoal grill going. He got close enough to see a case of beer next to them. He watched them drinking and knew they were cold, focused on the hot coals and not paying attention.

The license numbers on the vehicles were not those of the ringleaders, except for Renard, but he had no intention of being selective tonight. Whoever was here would be Lapalme's pals, and that made them targets. He worked deliberately, moving from vehicle to vehicle, pouring a full two pounds of sugar into each tank. When he was done, he strung the sugar bags like clothes on a clothesline between two trees in the yard, and made his withdrawal.

One thing his two weeks had taught him: The rats were only modestly organized, and they only appeared to be more together than they were.

Cecilia Lasurm was in his bed when he got back.

"Your last day," she said from under the covers. "I called in sick again."

He undressed, showered, dried himself off, and got into bed next to her.

"Do you think your being here will change the situation?" she asked.

"I don't know."

"You can't even lie for my benefit?"

"Okay, it will change."

She laughed and kissed him tenderly. "You are not walking all the way up to the highway tonight," she said. "I don't think you're gonna have the energy for it."

31

GARDEN PENINSULA,
FEBRUARY 28, 1976

"Don't look like youse broke nothin' important."

It was a Saturday night, and Lasurm had dropped him a mile east of Garden just after dark. From there, he had made his way toward town to a copse of trees along Garden Creek where he sat and watched Roadie's Bar. The parking lot was full, and stayed so until nearly 3 A.M., meaning the owners were probably violating state liquor laws. He made a mental note to pass this along. When the parking lot was finally empty, he crept onto the porch and quickly hung his message. Each frozen deer heart had a cardboard name tacked to it. All the hearts were skewered vertically on a long, thick willow branch. He used a rock to drive one nail into the main post in front of the bar. Above the deer hearts he left a sign that said SOON TO FALL. Peletier's name was not on the list; Renard's and Lapalme's were.

Service went from Roadie's to Lapalme's where he used lock grips to decommission both vehicles in Moe's driveway, dumped sugar in three snowmobiles, and left a note: "Run while you can."

Lasurm met him just north of Lapalme's at 5 A.M., drove him to Big Bay de Noc School, and parked in the faculty lot.

"They'll be watching your trailer," she said.

"I'll place an ad in the paper," he told her. They had already agreed to meet again, and he knew it would not be solely for DNR business. There was no parting kiss. They did not say good-bye. He got out of her truck, hoisted his unwieldy gear bag, and trudged northeast through the fields and woods toward US 2.

Joe Flap's pickup was backed into the drifted-over opening of a two-track, and the white-clad Service slid quietly out of the tree line, tossed his gear into the bed of the truck, and got into the passenger seat.

"Nice you could make it," Service said.

"I'm always where I promise ta be," the pilot said, grinning. "Don't look like youse broke nothin' important."

"Drive," Service said, wanting to put distance between himself and the peninsula he had haunted for two weeks. He'd broken laws. What was more important than that?

"People're wonderin' where youse've been," Flap said, doing a U-turn across US 2 to head west.

As they passed Foxy's Den at Garden Corners, Service saw a garbage truck turning south on Garden Road.

PART IV

FAITH IN LIGHT

· 32 ·

MARQUETTE, MARCH 2, 1976

"You have an outlaw's heart."

M oe Lapalme's rifle was on a small table in Attalienti's office. "It took awhile, but Len managed to find it," the acting captain said. "No prints, and the serial number has been filed off. How'd it get to the bottom of the bluff?"

"Forgetfulness," Service said, piling his notebook and maps on Attalienti's table and explaining how he had found Lapalme setting up to shoot at officers on the ice off Fayette.

The acting captain nodded. "Too bad we don't have a round from the earlier shootings." Meaning, having the rifle was not adequate evidence. "But I guess it's one less long gun for the rats," Attalienti said.

There was something peculiar in the acting captain's demeanor. Wariness, maybe?

Attalienti said, "I have an idea how you got into the Garden, and I'm not happy about it. Joe Flap flew out of Marquette on Valentine's Day night, and the people over there called me to complain about our reckless ways. They assumed it was an official department flight."

Service decided to keep his mouth shut, to neither confirm nor deny.

Attalienti continued. "I told you before you went that the mission was strictly surveillance, no enforcement."

"I didn't do any law enforcement," Service said.

"You took a man's rifle."

"Was I supposed to let him take a shot at our guys?"

"You're clairvoyant? You *knew* he would shoot? We can't punish intent."

"It was clear to me what was going on." What was Attalienti driving at?

"Delta County has been getting a steady stream of complaints from the Garden—vandalism, harassment. That jerk, Ranse Renard, accused *us* of harassment." Attalienti paused and looked at Service. "All the complaints fall during the past two weeks. You wouldn't know anything about that, right?"

Service didn't answer.

"If one of my men turned vigilante, I would be forced to deal harshly with him."

"Do you want my report, sir?" Service asked.

Attalienti nodded, and Service launched into a forty-five-minute verbal recounting of what he had seen, including names and addresses of all the rats, where they met, how they operated, how their trails and meeting places worked. He had delivered everything the captain had asked for—everything but his understanding that Lansing's unspoken goals would undercut anything law enforcement tried in the Garden. "The real force down there is Pete Peletier," Service concluded, "and he's smart enough to keep separated from everything. We'll have one hell of a time nailing him."

The acting captain said gruffly, "Those are the same names as the complainants."

Service put a check mark next to six houses on the plat maps. All the houses were along Garden Road, spread out over five miles. "That's the crow line," Service said. Lasurm had identified these during his first night with her.

Attalienti looked at the map. "Difficult to evade," he said, "strung out that far."

"Have to run dark at night, in unmarkeds by day."

"Running dark on Garden Road is dangerous. It's not some two-track back in the bush."

"They operate at night," Service said. "We have to be out there when they're out there. Maybe the phone company could switch off the lines for a brief period."

"That would work once," Attalienti said sarcastically.

"Or maybe the phones could suffer a spontaneous malfunction."

Attalienti glared at him. "You have an outlaw's heart. We will not break laws to enforce laws."

"I was thinking more along the lines of an act of God," Service lied. "Do you know Sun Tzu?"

"The Chinese restaurant in Ishpeming?"

Before Service could reply, the other man said, "Peletier isn't on the list of complainants?"

Service said, "His recent luck seems to have been better than the rest of them, which probably has them wondering why."

Attalienti shook his head disapprovingly and held up his hands. "Delta County won't respond to the complaints. They've asked the Troops to handle them."

"When?"

"Tomorrow or the next day. I asked them to hold off until I knew you were back and safe."

"I'd like to go with them."

"That's your basic stupid idea. You're going back to the Mosquito and you're going to stay there."

"I thought I was part of the Garden team."

"Not anymore."

"I want to help."

"And I want to keep a good warden employed."

"I'm out?"

"Out of the Garden."

When he had returned to his trailer, Service had been forced to crawl through snowbanks six feet deep. He and Joe Flap had dug out the door so he could get inside to turn on the heat and water. Now as he drove up to the trailer, he saw that the area had been freshly plowed. Len Stone was sitting in a truck with an oversize plow on the front. Service invited him in and the acting lieutenant put a bottle of Jack Daniel's on the table in the kitchen area, peeled off his parka, and sat down.

"I ain't here," Stone said, uncapping the bottle and holding it out to the young officer. "Deano ream your ass?"

"He said I'm off the Garden team."

"Dat's just cap'n talk. He's gotta protect his own ass, eh? But da Garden's mine, and I choose who I want wit' me. You don't gotta say anyting. I figure Joe Flap flew you down dere and you used a parachute, which is about da craziest bloody ting I ever heard," Stone said with a wide grin. "Deano suspects da same, but I don't tink he can make up his mind ta say parachute. He sent me ta talk ta Joe Flap, but Joe, he's one of us. All he said was he wanted ta fly dat night."

Service took a slug of whiskey and passed it back to Stone, who said, "Youse got da rats whinin' like a buncha babies!"

"They already replaced the nets we took," Service said.

"I told youse, dis is about money. You messed wit' dere trucks and snowbugs and dat was good, but you can't be doin' dat stuff no more. You make your report to Deano?"

Service nodded. "He said I have the heart of an outlaw."

Stone laughed and nodded. "Can't be good at dis job if you don't!"

"I want back in," Service said.

Stone held up his hands. "Take 'er easy an' hold da horses. Not right away. For now youse concentrate on keepin' yer nose clean. Bottom line, you stole dat man's rifle, an' I don't want to know what else. If it come out it was youse, dere'd be trouble, and I'm tellin' youse, Lansing would let yer ass swing in the wind. So youse just take care of da Mosquito, and when it's time ta come back, I'll let youse know. Ask me, dis ting is gonna go on for a long time."

Service explained much of what he had seen, and after a couple of hours, Stone put on his coat and stuck out his hand. "I can't say what you done down dere is right, but everybody's been in dis job has had ta make da same kinda decisions. Maybe you wandered off da legal reservation, but I hope youse did it for good reasons, Grady."

When Stone was gone, Grady Service couldn't sleep. What he had done in the Garden was wrong, and so were his reasons. This wasn't Vietnam. It wasn't even a real war. He had sworn to uphold the law, and had stepped over the line for spurious reasons. He vowed that from here on, as long as his career lasted, he would go to the line, but no further. Shuck Gorley was right: An officer's mind was what counted. He had acted like his old man would have acted. Never again: It was time to be himself, not the shadow of his father. His last thought of the night was that he would bust Pete Peletier—no matter how long it took.

MARQUETTE, MARCH 15, 1976

"You fight dirty."

Cecilia Lasurm was waiting for him on the sidewalk in front of the Marquette County Jail. The snowbanks along the street were six feet high and smudged gray from vehicle exhaust. Snow was falling and would soon lighten the dreary gray. Lasurm was wrapped tight in an ankle-length parka. Her call had taken him by surprise.

"I need to talk to you," she had said, and he agreed. March was the dead month for most game wardens, a time between seasons; a time to repair and replace gear, and wait for the snowmelt when the action would start up again and the poachers would be on the big lake after spawners. He was still tired from his sojourn in the Garden, glad for the respite, glad to be home in his Mosquito.

She looked small, with lines etched around her eyes. Her face was red from the cold wind. "Thank you for coming," she greeted him.

"We could've talked elsewhere."

"Trust me," she said, taking his hand and leading him into the building.

They signed in and walked down to an interrogation room. Inside, a white-haired man sat at a table with the girl who had stabbed Gumby.

Lasurm said, "Her father and I never married. She was born when we were both sixteen. He joined the Coast Guard after high school and never came back. I can't blame him. Anise was headstrong from the beginning. When she was sixteen she got mixed up with the wrong people. She always thought of herself as a pathfinder and rebel, but she wasn't. She was easily led. Three years ago she fell in with Moe Lapalme—she was nineteen. I threw her out. She lived with Moe for awhile, drifted on, and took her father's name."

Lapalme had to be twice the girl's age, and Service suddenly saw the blue pickup truck racing by the Fishdam boat access, the girl with the long blond hair, and it all fell into place. "You knew she was back," he said.

"Word goes around the Garden," she said with a shrug.

"All that stuff you told me," he said, "about your reasons."

"I meant it all. My daughter just makes it more personal."

"You might have mentioned this before," he said.

"Would it have changed anything?"

He shook his head. "You called me up here to tell me this?"

"And to talk to Odd Hegstrom."

Service stared into the room. The man was talking to the girl, pushed back in his chair looking passive. "Her attorney," Service said.

"He would like to talk to you," she said, opening the door.

"Are you coming in?" he asked her.

"I can't," Lasurm said as he stepped into the room.

The young woman's hair was clean and untangled, but her eyes remained blank. She looked only a little like her mother.

Hegstrom pulled out a chair. "Thank you for coming, Officer Service. I believe you've met Anise Aucoin."

"Briefly," Service said, not looking at her. "Should there be a DNR lawyer here, or somebody from the prosecutor's office?"

Hegstrom's gaunt cheeks puffed. "What do you think?"

"I don't really know," Service admitted.

"How about if we make this off the record?"

"Is there such a thing?"

"There is with me. Did you actually see my client wield a knife?" Hegstrom asked. "Or any weapon?"

"She was in another room, in the dark. Everything is in my report."

"Yes or no?"

"No, but she was the only other person in the room."

"We're not in court, Officer Service, and you're not an attorney arguing a case. I'm just trying to understand what happened. If you couldn't see inside the room, you can't be certain what transpired. Would you agree?"

"The victim came out, the lights went on, the woman was the only person in there," Service said. What was Hegstrom after?

"Did you look under the bed, in the closets, outside the window? Was there an attic?"

Service said, "No, no, no, and I don't know. You can play this ludicrous game, but a jury won't buy it. There were deputies with me. It's their crime to investigate."

"Persuading a jury is like writing a pop hit," Hegstrom said. "The chords are all the same. You just have to find the most appealing order."

"My job is apprehension. Others handle prosecution."

"Did you read my client her rights?"

This caught him off guard. He assumed the deputies had done this. "I personally didn't Mirandize her."

Hegstrom rubbed his chin. "What was my client's demeanor when you entered the room?"

"She had concealed weapons."

"Bolts are weapons even without the crossbow to propel them?"

"She had just stabbed a man. The crossbow was close by."

"You allege."

"She had bolts by her leg, under the covers. They have sharp points. What're we doing here, counselor?"

"How did my client react when you entered the room?"

"She didn't."

"Did she threaten you in any way?"

"No."

"Are you saying she was unresponsive?"

"No. She asked if I wanted to see her breasts."

The woman smiled, the first sign that she was mentally present.

"What did you think?" Hegstrom asked.

"I didn't. The first priority was to clear the room of weapons."

"Where was the knife?"

"Stuck in the victim's back."

"I see," Hegstrom said thoughtfully. "And where is that weapon now?"

"In evidence with the county."

"You personally secured it?"

"No, the deputies did."

"Has the integrity of the chain of custody been maintained?"

"You'll have to take that up with the county."

"My client's prints were not on the knife. Did you know that? How do you explain that, given the charges against her?"

No prints? Nobody had told him this. Had Detective Kobera tried to call him about this while he was in the Garden? He kept quiet.

Hegstrom continued. "No fingerprints, Officer Service. Again, what was your impression of my client's emotional state when you entered the room?"

"I thought she was out of it."

"Unresponsive?"

"Out of it," Service said. "Jacked up—on a long flight with no ETA."

"Is that a medical diagnosis?"

"It's a professional observation."

"You have no medical or psychiatric training." It was not a question.

"Obviously not. Is this a deposition?"

"Do you see a recorder here? This is off the record, Officer. What we hear you saying is that you never personally witnessed the alleged stabbing, and you did not read Miss Aucoin her rights, or secure the evidence. You also appear to be unaware that no prints were recovered."

"You're oversimplifying everything," Service said.

"Facts *are* simple by definition," Hegstrom countered. "It's the array and interplay of facts, the interpolation and interpretation that render them complex."

"Are we done?"

"I didn't mean to irritate you," the lawyer said.

"I'm not good at mind games," Service said.

Hegstrom tilted his head and smiled. "I would think a game warden would be especially adept at such games. I've never met a police officer who hasn't bent the rules or occasionally broken them to make a case."

Service got to his feet. Was Hegstrom signaling that he knew he had been in the Garden? Had Lasurm told him? He left the room with a sense of dread and immediately began to try to replay the events of the stabbing. Who had removed the knife? Ambulance personnel? More likely it was someone in the emergency room. He hadn't read Aucoin her rights because that fell to the deputies who had actually made the arrest. In the future, he told himself, he would make sure he did this and not depend on others. How could the knife have no prints? Hegstrom had asked if they had checked the window or closet, and whether there was an attic—why was he asking such questions? Most importantly, had Cecilia Lasurm betrayed him for the sake of her daughter?

Hegstrom looked at him. "To paraphrase something, Grady—remember that faith in light is admirable at night."

Lasurm was not in the area of the room when he emerged. He found her out on the sidewalk, looking cold. "You want to let me in on what's going on?" he demanded, barely containing his growing rage.

"My daughter's a junkie," she said.

"That excuses her behavior?" he shot back at her.

"Don't be ridiculous. A substance abuser is responsible under the law."

"Do you doubt she did it?" he challenged.

"It's Hegstrom's job to find out."

"No," he said angrily. "The police determine that. Hegstrom's job is to make sure we've done our jobs fair and square, and that his client gets a fair trial."

"That *client* is my daughter."

"Hegstrom intimated that he knew I was on the Garden."

"I don't think for him," she said. "He didn't hear any such thing from me."

Service stared at her. "How far would you go to save your daughter?"

"I resent that question," she snapped at him.

"Answer me."

"She deserves the best defense, but I would never betray a confidence. I thought you understood that."

"You don't exactly have forever to let this thing run its course."

She bristled and furrowed her brows. "I'm well aware of my circumstances. You fight *dirty*."

"I have a dirty job."

"Which you chose to make dirtier in the Garden," she said with a hiss. "I have no idea what Hegstrom is thinking, or what he said to you, or why. He's got a job to do and, like you, he'll do whatever he thinks he needs to do to win. If this sounds like a sermon, so be it. Anise is an adult, and if she's guilty, she'll pay. If I wanted to set you up, Grady, I could have told Hegstrom about you and let him spring it at trial to destroy your credibility."

"Unless you told him and he's trying to steer my testimony and work a deal to avoid trial."

"I did not tell him, and I did *not* ask Odd Hegstrom to take my daughter's case," she said. "I understand you're angry, but I don't deserve to bear the brunt of your frustration. You tried to spread paranoia in the Garden. Maybe it's getting to you instead."

He sighed in frustration. "I'd better go," he said, wanting to avoid further escalation. He needed time and space to think and try to understand what this was about.

34

TRENARY, MARCH 16, 1976

"Connie, she takes care of mosta dat."

"Joe, did you tell anybody about the flight?"

Joe Flap squinted at him. "Da cap'n called me 'cause da airport people called him an' complained. Dey assumed it was a department flight, and dey said it was stupid and dangerous. Dey're a buncha pussies."

"Did you file a flight plan?"

"Bare bones, basic VFR, out and back."

"The visibility was terrible that night."

"Remember what I said, if I could see my prop it was visual? Dat's da pilot's call."

"Did you list a passenger?"

"Didn't have none ta list, did I?" Flap said, obviously pleased with himself.

"Stone figured it out," Service said.

"Len's a smart guy. He knows youse, he knows me, an' he knew your old man. It don't take an Einstein to add two plus two."

Hegstrom was also smart. How could he know about such a flight, and, if he knew, how could he figure out what it meant?

"You want a beer?" Flap asked.

"No thanks. What does the airport do with flight plans?"

"Dey twix 'em off to Air Traffic Control and send a copy down ta da District."

"The DNR district?"

"Yeah, Escanaba."

"Why?"

"Back a few years, dere was a budget crunch downstate, and Lansing cut pilots, planes, and flight hours. Da district believed da air patrols were cost effective, and asked for flight plans to be used in puttin' together dere arguments wit' da Lansing eyeshades."

"What's in a flight plan that could be useful?"

"Not a damn ting; I told 'em it was stupid, eh, but dey ignored me."

"They still do this?" The value of air patrols had long since been established and had become standard procedure at certain times of the year.

"Far as I know. I told Cosmo and Edey about it, but bot' of dem give me da brush-off."

Service called Len Stone from Flap's house. "Do you get copies of DNR flight plans?"

"I'm not da best inside guy, eh? Connie, she takes care of mosta dat. Why?"

"I'm not sure yet."

35

ESCANABA, MARCH 16, 1976

"I'm a trashy kinda guy."

"Been a while," Connie Leppo greeted him when he walked into the district office. "Your family situation okay?" As the district's dispatcher-secretary, she took it on herself to monitor what was going on among district personnel.

"All taken care of. And I got my equipment replaced. Thanks for asking."

"Youse gonna make da party at Sheila's tomorrow night?"

Party? His expression must have shown his confusion. "Saint Paddy's Day," Leppo said. "Tomorrow?"

If he'd ever known, he had forgotten. "Sheila?"

"Sheila Halloran, a Troop secretary over to Gladstone post. Her boyfriend's Al Eagle, da district fish biologist."

He hadn't met either of them. "I guess I missed the invitation."

She rolled her eyes. "It's posted in da coffee room. Da party's out to Al's camp up da Tacoosh."

The Tacoosh was a fast, rock-bottom river that flowed into Little Bay de Noc near Rapid River.

"Dere's a map on da board too," Leppo added. "You enjoy my mom's bakery?"

Connie talked a lot. "Great," he said, trying to recall what he had done with the baked goods she had given him. "Len said I should talk to you about paperwork."

Leppo grinned. "Da poor man slouches like a prisoner when he's gotta sit behind dat desk."

"What determines which papers get filed or thrown away?" he asked.

"It's called da file retention schedule. Lansing lawyers tell us what we gotta save and for how long. Anyting dey don't classify we can decide what ta do wit'."

"What about DNR flight schedules?"

She looked up at him. "Ah, dose. Dey're local, an' we pitch 'em."

"After somebody looks at them?"

"Nope, I plunk 'em right in da circular file. We got enough paper in dis place, we don't need more, eh. Somebody way back got da bright idea to have 'em sent here, but nobody looks at 'em, so I toss 'em."

"Edey didn't look at them?"

"Nor da guy before him. We get a new boss, I always ask, and dey always say toss it."

"What else gets tossed?"

"Records Lansing says can go. We flag files, and on certain dates each year we clean 'em out or send 'em ta storage. An da wastebaskets, da janitor takes dose to da Dumpster every night."

"Do you cut the paper up or do anything to it before you toss it?"

She looked puzzled. "Sometime we bag 'em and take 'em to da Dumpster. Why would we cut stuff up? It's trash."

"The city picks up our trash?"

"Nope—Bay de Noc Trash Haulers. Dere on contract wit' city an' county. Dis way city an' county can keep down payrolls wit' benefits and all dat. Times're tough, eh."

"How often do they pick it up?"

"Couple times a week."

"On a set schedule?"

"Usually on Tuesdays and Fridays."

"At a specific time?"

"Seems to me I see Gary in da mornings. Sometimes he comes in for a cuppa coffee. What's dis about?"

"Gary?"

"Gary Aho. He's a good guy, eh?"

"I saw a BDN truck over by Garden Corners," he said.

"Probably Gary on da way home. Dey got a big operation, offices in Manistique, Gladstone, Escanaba, Menominee."

"Gary lives near Garden Corners?" He had seen the truck in the early morning.

"Cooks, just north of dere," she said.

Cooks, Lasurm had told him, was part of the consolidated school district that included Garden. This made Aho an area resident. The hair bristled on the back of his neck.

"The drivers take their trucks home?"

"Way I understand it, da drivers lease dere trucks from da company. Da company does sales, negotiates contracts, and handles da bookkeep-

ing an' billing. Drivers have to take care of da trucks and pay for maintenance."

"Sounds like it would be hard for a driver to make any money."

"Gary says he does okay. He's a bachelor, eh."

Service glanced at the calendar. Tomorrow was a pickup day.
"Where does the trash get dumped?"

"County landfill, I tink, but I'm not sure. Can't just dump garbage
anywhere, right?"

"Do we have a copy of the contract?"

"You betcha," the secretary said.

"Can you make a copy for me?"

"If you watch phones while I run da copier."

"Deal."

When she brought him his copy, he asked her another question.
"Gary comes in for coffee?"

"He doesn't come in every time, but he's a regular vendor, and
dey're like part of da family, right? Is everything okay?" Her eyes showed
concern.

"Sure; I'm just trying to understand how we do things here."

She laughed. "Never had an officer worry about da trash before."

"I'm a trashy kinda guy," he said with a wink.

He took the contract and a cup of coffee into the district conference
room and sat down to read. The contract had been renewed by Edey last
July, and would come up for renewal again this summer. It called for two
ten-yard trash bins and one weekly pickup. Service looked into the parking lot. There was only one bin.

He walked out to Leppo's desk. "The contract calls for one pickup a
week," he said.

"Yah, but Gary said da company is shorta bins right now, so dey
brought us one and he makes two pickups a week. I told you he's a good
guy. He takes good care of us, and he says we got da best coffee and bakery on his route."

"Have you watched him make his pickups?"

"Sure. He usually loads, den takes da truck down da alley and stops
dere for ten, fifteen minutes before he pulls on. Not sure if dat's procedure or a timing thing," she said.

Or something more insidious, Service thought as he scribbled a note
in red ink on the copy of the contract, and dropped it into Leppo's waste-
basket when she stepped away from her desk.

36

ESCANABA-FAIRPORT, MARCH 17, 1976

"It's bait."

"You wrote *what* on the contract?" Len Stone asked.

"'Cancel: July seventy-six. Connie, please file.' I used your initials," Service confessed. "It's bait. I also threw in a copy of the weekly schedule for all officers."

Stone grinned. "Youse really want me to go along wit' dis? We could look pretty stupid, eh?"

"We could," Service agreed.

"All dis 'cause youse seen a trash truck over to Garden Corners?"

"Not just that. Aho lives in Cooks. He violated the contract. He's in and out of our office whenever he wants, which makes him invisible. How many times have you done surveillance and come up empty?"

"Goes wit' da territory."

"That's my point," Service said. "Knowing it might yield nothing, you still went."

Stone contemplated this briefly. "How do youse want to play it?"

"We wait in the alley and see what happens. We leave your unmarked on the street. If he doesn't stop in the alley, we jump in the unmarked and follow him."

"All da way ta da dump?"

"If that's how it works out," Service said. "I'll talk to Connie. If he goes into the building, she'll bump us on the radio when he's leaving."

The green truck pulled into the lot at 10:42 A.M. and backed up to the bin. The driver wore green coveralls, jumped down from the cab of his truck, and went into the district office. He came back out fifteen minutes later with a clear plastic bag, dumped it in the bin, and began hydraulically lifting the bin to dump the contents into the metal thorax of the truck.

Connie Leppo called them on the brick radio. "Three one hundred, Elvis has left da building."

Stone smirked. "She tinks dis is a game."

The driver climbed back into his truck.

"He's coming," Service said as the driver backed up. It wasn't Connie's job to detect security problems.

"I got eyes," Stone said. "Hair's too long for Elvis."

"And he's too skinny," Service added as they stepped into the door of the DNR garage that flanked one side of the alley.

The truck stopped in the alley twenty feet beyond them. The driver hopped down, climbed up the side, and dropped out of sight.

"He's carrying a gym bag," Service said.

"I seen," Stone said. "Move."

The two officers waited at the rear of the truck on the side opposite where the man had disappeared. When they heard him beginning to climb out they moved around the truck, and when the man's boots hit the slush, Service clutched his arm. "How's business?"

The startled man froze, but recovered with a sheepish grin. "How's she goin', guys?"

"What's in da bag?" Stone asked.

"Trash," the driver said.

"I thought trash belonged in da truck," Stone said.

"I needed ta sort it out."

"Youse mind if we see what's in da bag?"

The man shrugged, unzipped the bag, and held it open. "*Playboys*," he said.

"From the district office?" Service asked.

The man grimaced. "No, man; I saw 'em earlier, thought I'd fish 'em out before I dumped da load."

"You like da articles?" Stone asked facetiously.

The man looked confused. "No man, da tits."

Service snatched the bag from the man, turned it upside down, and shook it vigorously. The magazines landed with a plop in gray slush, and papers fluttered down behind the magazines. The contract lay faceup, the red note from Service's hand visible. Ink from the marker was smeared pink by moisture.

"Geez, dose musta gotten stuck to da magazines," the driver said too quickly.

"Let's go back to da office," Stone said, holding the man's arm.

"Do we gotta?" the man protested weakly, but he went along with them without further protest.

Connie Leppo shot them a worried look as they escorted the driver past her station into the district conference room. Service stepped back out to her. "Call the trash company, Connie. Ask them how many bins and pickups we're supposed to have, and ask them if they ever run short of bins for customers."

She reached for the phone as Service went into the room. "Coffee, Gary?" he asked the driver.

"You know my name?"

Service shrugged. "You're our regular guy, right?"

"Three years," Aho said. "You guys got da great bakery here."

Service stopped at Leppo's desk, but she was still on the phone. He went into the canteen, filled three mugs with coffee, used a Sears catalog for a tray, and returned to Leppo's station.

She looked up at him. "We're s'pposed ta have two bins," she said. "And one pickup a week. Dey do run short once in awhile, but never for more den twenty-four hours, and never for state agencies. Our contract is too valuable."

"Did you tell them we have only one?"

"I did just what youse asked," Leppo said, looking perplexed.

"Thanks, Connie. Relax."

"Youse comin' to Sheila's party?"

"Probably not."

"Too bad. She'll be a blast," she said.

Sheila or the party? Service wondered as he set a mug in front of the driver. "Black okay?"

"For java, not for broads," Aho tried to joke.

Service made a point to stand beside the man, forcing him to look up. Stone sat across the table. "Gary, why are our papers in your bag?" Service asked.

"I told youse, dey musta gotten stuck to the magazines, eh?"

Stone grinned. "Dat's bullshit, son."

"I don't get dis," Aho said. "It's trash. You're trowin' it out, right?"

"It's trash when it arrives at the dump," Service said. "Under the contract, you are the agent of transfer. It remains our property until it arrives at the dump; then it's theirs."

"Most people don't mind somebody picks up somepin' dey don't want."

"We mind," Stone said coolly.

"What's da big deal?" Aho asked.

"You don't get to take trash for personal use, and if you do, it's theft," Service said. "You're stealing government property." He had no idea if this was legally correct and didn't really care. He wanted to find out what Aho was doing and why.

"Man," Aho said, shaking his head disconsolately.

"What do youse do wit' da papers, son?" Stone asked.

"I told you, da magazines're for me."

"Dat's fine; an' da papers?" Stone pressed.

"I just wanted the *Playboys*."

Service said, "Gary, we called your company. The contract calls for two bins and one weekly pickup."

The man raised his hands in a gesture of peace. "Right, right. We ran short. I did it dis way as a favor ta you guys."

"Don't lie!" Service said sharply. "The company says it has never shorted the state and wouldn't because our contract is too important."

"You musta talked to da new girl at da office," Aho offered.

Service picked up the conference room telephone. "Connie, please get the head man at BDN on the phone." He looked over at Aho, who motioned for him to hang up. Service said, "Thanks, never mind, Connie."

Stone said, "Youse got to level wit' us, son, spit 'er all out. Whatever youse tell us, we're gonna check it out closer'n a fourteen-year-old comin' home from her first date. Youse got no wiggle room."

Gary Aho looked to Service to be in his late twenties. He had long black hair tied back in a ponytail and a wispy goatee. "What's with the papers?" Service asked, hovering over the man.

"It's a favor, okay?"

"A favor?" Stone said.

"For my uncle."

"What's dis uncle's name?" Stone asked.

"Pete Peletier, my mother's big brother."

Service had to swallow a smile. "The Peletier who lives down to Fairport?" Service asked.

"You know Pete?" Aho asked.

"Heard about him," Service said. "You're sayin' you go through our trash and pass it along to your uncle."

"I don't look at nuttin', man. I give it all to him," Aho said. "It ain't for me, eh?"

"What's your uncle do wit' it?" Stone asked.

"I don't know, man. Can I go now?" Aho asked.

"No, Gary," Stone said. "Youse'll give us da whole story or youse're going to jail."

"Jesus," Aho said. "I'll lose my job!"

"Da whole story," Stone reiterated.

"How long have you been doing this?" Service asked.

"Since I took da route."

"What did you do before that?"

"Twisted wrenches over ta Manistique."

"You lease your truck from BDN," Service said. "You must've saved up a bundle for that up front."

"Uncle Pete took care of it."

"He loaned youse da cash?" Stone asked.

"No man, it was a gift."

"In exchange for taking DNR trash," Service said.

"He said it was no big deal," Aho said defensively. "Just trash."

"He was wrong," Stone said.

"When do you take the paperwork to him?" Service asked.

"On da way home."

"To Cooks?"

Aho looked alarmed. "Man, you guys know where I *live*? You been spyin' on me?"

"No, Gary, some people over your way have loose lips. We heard about what you were doing for your uncle."

"I never told nobody, man," Aho said. Aho's expression went from suspicious to morose.

"You deliver the papers to your uncle's house?" Service continued.

"Yeah," Aho said, nodding lethargically.

"Do you call ahead?"

"I just show up and give 'em ta him."

"What time?"

"When I get dere—six, seven?"

"In the morning?" Service asked. He had seen a truck in the morning.

Aho grimaced. "No man, at night. I got a day route."

"Do you pick up trash in the Garden?" Service asked.

"No man. Another guy's got dat route."

He'd seen the other driver, Service told himself. Not Aho.

"You drive da big truck to your uncle's?" Stone asked.

Aho grinned. "No big deal—it's da U.P., eh."

Service understood. Yoopers parked bulldozers, dump trucks, logging rigs, and eighteen-wheelers in the driveways of their homes.

"How about we take a ride?" Service said.

"C'mon, man, you can't do dis ta me. I got my route ta finish."

"Youse prefer a room at da graybar hotel?" Stone asked.

"No," Aho said.

"Okay, den. We'll sit here today and dis afternoon, we take a ride, eh? Da route can wait."

"What do I get out of dis?"

"Maybe you don't get busted," Service said. "But you'll be a material witness and give us a statement. When the case comes to trial, you'll testify."

"Against my uncle? He'll want his money back."

Aho looked wrecked, but Service got the feeling some of this was for show. He couldn't really pinpoint his sense of unease, but it gnawed at him. "One lie and we bust you, Gary."

"Dere ain't no free bakery today," Stone added.

"Dis is so much bullshit," Aho whined.

Service got a pad of legal paper and a couple of pencils and put them in front of the man. "Write," he said.

"Okay I print?"

Stone nodded.

Service and his lieutenant stepped into the lobby. Stone said, "We gotta make sure we grab Peletier wit' da bag before we nail da SOB."

"Minus the one-handers," Service added. "We don't want to give him any outs."

"Da prosecutor may not back us up on dis," Stone said.

"You want to let it drop here?" Service asked.

"No, let's play 'er out, see where she goes."

"I'll ride in the trash truck. You use the unmarked?"

Stone said, "I'll borrow somepin' dey don't know over dere."

It was dark when Aho eased the nose of the big truck into the driveway of Peletier's house just outside Fairport. Service clambered out of the back, dropped down the far side, and moved quickly to the garage. He reeked of trash and he was cold. Aho went directly to the front door and knocked.

Pete Peletier came to the door and looked past Aho at the nose of the big truck. "What's goin' on, Gar?"

Aho held out the bag.

The man ignored it. "What's dat?"

"You know," Aho said, jiggling the bag.

Again, Peletier ignored the offering. "Where's your pickup?"

"I had ta use da big truck tonight," Aho said, still holding out the bag.

"Had to?" Peletier said.

Aho jiggled the bag again and his uncle snapped at him, "Stop shaking dat damn ting. I never seen dat bag in my life. Now get da hell outta here. I got tings ta do!"

Service knew they'd been busted. Peletier was acting like the bag contained plague. He *knew* something was up. No way Peletier could have seen him dismount from the truck. All he could see from the house was the nose of the trash hauler in the driveway. Stone was a mile back, waiting for a radio call. *Shit!* Peletier had asked Aho where his pickup was. Son of a bitch: Aho had snookered them. He normally came in his personal truck, not the trash hauler. The big truck had tipped off his uncle. *Bastards,* Service thought as he stepped out beside Aho and said, "DNR."

Peletier looked amused. "Dis like *Hawaii Five-O?*" the man asked. "Youse lost, Officer?" He pointed southwest. "Last I heard, da Big Island and Dano were dat way."

"Gary Aho, you are under arrest for theft of government papers." Service recited the man's rights and asked him to put his right hand behind his back, where he cuffed it.

Aho said, "You said it would be okay. This is a fuck job!"

Peletier said sharply, "Put a cork in it, Gary."

"You promised," Aho whined at Service as he cuffed the man's hands behind his back and held the cuffs to control him.

"Nazis," Peletier said with a growl.

Service picked up the bag with his right hand. "I'll be back for you, Pete," he said to the man.

"You got nothing, asshole," Peletier said. "*Nothing.*"

Service lifted Aho's cuffed hands. "We've got him, and there are always fingerprints," he added, holding the bag out.

Peletier didn't look particularly upset, but he shook a finger at his nephew. "Youse keep dat big mouth shut until da lawyer comes ta see youse."

"He's already made a statement," Service said as he engaged the radio and called Stone in to pick them up.

Service heard the door slam as he shoved Aho into the front passenger seat and got in behind him. "Hit it. I think we're gonna have company."

As Service would have done, Stone immediately shut off all lights, inside and out, and fishtailed onto Garden Road as he accelerated. It was several miles before an oncoming vehicle lit them up and swerved as it passed, the driver obviously startled. Running without lights was a good way to stay hidden, if you didn't hit anything.

"You guys are nuts!" Aho said, holding his cuffed hands in front of his face.

Service used the brick to call the Manistique Troop dispatcher and asked for assistance and an escort from the nearest unit. A state police officer immediately responded that he was westbound on US 2, a mile east of Garden Corners.

Service radioed, "Unit Eight Six, we're running dark, heading north in an unmarked. Light it up and start your music. We'll flash lights twice when we have you in sight."

Stone slowed for the ninety-degree turn just south of the village and accelerated straight through town. Service saw vehicle lights coming to life in Roadie's parking lot as they flashed by.

"Eight Six, we're clear of Garden. What's our speed?" Service asked Stone.

"Eighty," the lieutenant said matter-of-factly.

"Eight Six, we're northbound at eighty mike-paul-henry, running dark."

"Eight Six is southbound on Garden Road, all lit up."

Service did a quick mental calculation. "Intersect, four minutes max," he radioed. "Probable pursuit."

"Roger, Eight Six will swing in behind and follow you up to US Two."

Another state police vehicle reported on the radio that he was also headed for Garden Corners, ETA in one minute from the west on US 2.

"Do we stop an' circle da wagons?" Stone asked, concentrating on the road.

"We'll let the state transport the prisoner," Service said as he spotted an oncoming emergency vehicle's flashing lights.

Stone flashed his headlights twice and the trooper wheeled a tight one-eighty and fell in behind them.

Moments later they skidded into the gas station at Garden Corners. A state police cruiser was already there, emergency lights blinking.

A half-dozen trucks and vans roared up behind their escort and men tumbled out and immediately began to throw rocks.

Service jerked Aho out of the sedan, pushed him into the backseat of the waiting cruiser, and told the trooper to take the prisoner to Escanaba. The officer didn't question him.

Stone had his revolver out of his holster and was pointing it at the rock throwers, who had left their headlights on, flooding the COs and using the lights as a blinding shield. "Next one gets a round!" Stone shouted.

"Nail the Nazi fucker!" somebody shrieked.

"Next one!" Stone roared.

Service knew it was a bluff. They were trained and expected to shoot at a specific target, not wildly and blindly, and rocks at this range did not equate to lethal force.

The men swore and called them names and began to slam doors. The trucks backed out quickly and raced south on Garden Road, honking their horns.

Stone holstered his revolver and patted the shoulder of the first trooper who had come to their assistance. "Youse ever want to transfer, youse let me know," he told the Troop, who started laughing out loud.

En route to Escanaba, Service said, "Peletier knew something was up. He played dumb over the bag. Arriving in the big truck was a prearranged signal." He knew it had been his fault for not anticipating this.

After a lull, Stone said, "Ya know, sometimes I seen dat trash hauler parked at a house down by Garden. I shoulda said somepin'."

"He probably swaps the big truck for his pickup," Service said, disgusted by his failure to nail the secretive rat leader. So close—and it was his fault they'd missed.

Stone looked over at him. "Buck up, boy. Youse stopped da leak been right dere in front of us for years. Youse figured it out. None a' us did. Dat alone is one helluva day of police work."

"I'll drop the bag at the Troop lab in Ishpeming tomorrow," Service told his lieutenant. "Peletier's prints will be on the bag."

"Don't waste da time," Stone said. "His lawyer will claim he give da bag to his nephew as a gift and why wouldn't his prints be on it, eh? An' he won't know nuttin' about no papers. We could try for a search warrant for Pete's house, but dere won't be shit to find by den." Stone looked over at him. "We're in dis for da long haul. We plugged da leak. We'll take dat for now."

Service lit a cigarette.

Stone said, "You got an extra one?"

"You smoke?"

"Tonight I do."

37

BIG BAY DE NOC PATROL, MAY 6–7, 1976

The only sharks out here were in boats.

T he average date for ice-out on Big Bay de Noc was April 20, but not this year, when it was eight days late because of the hard winter and late spring. Service had not been back to the Garden since the confrontation with Peletier and Aho two months before. Aho, after his arrest, initially had been fired from his company, but was re-hired when the prosecutor withdrew the charges, saying he didn't think a jury would find Aho guilty. This made it not worth the cost to the county, especially after Lansing also passed on taking the lead in the case. Service was unhappy about the developments, but Stone once again pointed out that they had stopped the leak, and told him it was time for him to come back into the Garden fray.

Stone and Attalienti had been busy in the Garden since ice-out in the bay. Stone and a marine patrol had gotten lucky two days after ice-out when they forced two rat boats onto boulders and ice berms on the shore of Ansels Point. The rats had abandoned their craft and scrambled into the woods. Within an hour the owner of the two boats called the state police to report them stolen. Stone towed the boats back to Escanaba, started condemnation proceedings in district court, and had his men clean up the craft and put them in working order, including blue flashers on six-foot-high metal posts and yelper sirens. Finally, the DNR had a couple of boats that could keep up with the rats, and Stone planned to use them until the court said otherwise.

This morning the fifty-foot PB-4 was to come across the bay to Burn't Bluff from Escanaba and grapple for nets southward. Service and Homes had put in at Thompson Creek, on the northeast extreme of the Garden Peninsula, and were running south checking out some of the shoals and bays along the east coast. Homes told him sometimes the perch spawned on the east side, but most of the action was on the west. Because soft ice preceded ice-out and made it impossible to run their ice-netting operations, and because ice-out was late, the rats were almost into the legal fishing dates. This meant they had lost money because of the weather conditions and that, out of desperation to take fish before legal fishing began, they could be anywhere.

Service and Homes were in one of the captured boats, a sixteen-footer with a two-hundred-horsepower Mercury outboard. Homes had renamed the boat *Little Rat*. The other confiscated craft was a twenty-footer, also with a two-hundred-horse motor; it would launch today from the Fishdam site as *Fat Rat*.

Service and Homes were to patrol south past Point Detour, continue past Summer Island, and move north through the cut between Poverty and Little Summer. *Fat Rat* was coming south from the Fishdam, and the two DNR Glastrons would be coming over from Ogontz. The PB-4 would come east from Escanaba.

They would all rendezvous mid-afternoon off Sac Bay, where Stone planned to grapple for nets. Attalienti and three other patrol cars were on the peninsula to provide land cover. Service had to admit that this patrol seemed more organized, with more resources and force committed than he had seen previously. A state trooper was parked at the Port Bar acting as a visible deterrent, and Service guessed that the information he had brought out was being used by Attalienti in planning Garden operations. Joe Flap would be overhead all afternoon and into the early evening.

Homes piloted the *Little Rat* like A.J. Foyt, putting the stripped-down sixteen-footer on the plane and running it wide open, throwing up a ten-foot roostertail as they raced southward, the hull slamming against the waves. Service had never been particularly comfortable in boats, and thought about telling Homes they were wasting fuel as a way of slowing him down, but they had two extra tanks of fuel on board. He clutched his seat, let the spray sting his face, kept his mouth shut, and endured.

They ran around the south shore of Summer Island and turned north. Homes finally slowed down to creep their way through the shoals that stuck up in places like a broken atoll. When they reached Sac Bay, they found the PB-4 thirty yards off the ice-packed shore. Someone was in the fourteen-foot aluminum deck boat, close to shore, throwing the grapple rope and dragging it across the bottom, hoping to snag illegal nets—either those that had sunk when the ice went out, or new ones they had just set by boat.

Homes eased the *Little Rat* alongside the PB-4, pulled the throttle to idle, and had Service toss out the sea anchor. There was a slight breeze and a small chop. Stone leaned over the rail of the PB-4. "Dere's a heap a' perch up to Ansels Point," he told them as they bobbed beside the mother ship.

"Nets in the water there?" Homes asked.

"Haven't checked," Stone said. "Buncha fish on gravel next ta shore down here, so dey'll be against shore all da way up to da Chicken Farm. Da rats know our schedule 'cause I been keepin' us pretty regular since we took dose two boats. Dey got somebody on shore watchin' us right now, and dey know how long our shifts been runnin'. Pretty soon dere gonna come out wit' dere short nets and see what dey can grab. Youse boys run up between Stoney Point and Ansels and anchor up. We'll give youse a bump on da radio when we start for home, but we'll anchor between Round Island and Chippewa Point and see what happens. Da rats only got a week till dey can net legally, and da dirty ones will want to get into da fish before dat." Stone looked down at Service from the larger boat and winked. "Since Feb-u-ary da rats been real nervous. Somepin' musta shook 'em up good."

"Bingo!" the man in the deck boat yelled. "Not marked," he added, as he began to pull the net hand over hand toward his boat. Stone flung his grapple into the water and began hauling to see if there were nets closer to the big boat. Service saw Ed Moody working the front of the PB-4, and waved as Homes ordered the sea anchor up. When Service hauled it into the boat, they blasted off northward.

They were anchored about halfway between Stoney and Ansels Points, bobbing in three-foot chop, the wind picking up from the north. The sky was overcast, no moon, no stars. The PB-4 had reported leaving its station, and since then, the radio had been silent.

Service and Homes ate ham and cheese sandwiches and drank coffee as they waited. It seemed to Service that as a conservation officer, he was always waiting.

"Who was working with Moody and Stone?" Service asked.

"Name's Moomaw, from downstate. Len's runnin' guys up here from all over, givin' 'em a week ta ten days in da Garden and shipping 'em home. Da more guys we give experience up here, da more support we'll have around da state. You fucking anybody dese days?"

"Just your wife," Service said.

Homes laughed out loud. "She's more fun den my mum, eh!"

"What's a short net?" Service asked.

"Hundred, two hundred feet with small mesh. Easier ta trow and re-cover den da longer gangs, best for shallow water work. We're gonna sit here and wait. Eleven or so, we'll start putt-putting toward Ansels, see what we can see. Want a candy bar?" Homes held it out. "Keep da energy up out here, eh."

Service chewed mechanically, not paying attention to the taste or the sugar.

"Da rats will run dark," Homes said, "but sometimes dey need to flip on dere flashlights ta handle dere nets. We'll look for dat, an' if we see anyting, we'll charge dere sorry asses."

"Without lights?"

"Just like on land. We want ta surprise da bastards."

"What about support?" Service wanted to know.

"Da rats will try to run ta Garden, I'm thinking. Attalienti and da boys will be land-side, strung out along da coast. Got three trucks ready to head south to where we need 'em, and Troops on standby in da wings. Attalienti says he has a pretty good idea where ta find and intercept da rats. How he knows, I don't know, and I ain't askin'. Our job is ta cut da rats off from Garden and hope dey run north. If dey do, dis time we got da boats dat can keep up; dis time, we got darkness and speed on our side. *Fat Rat* will wait out near Ogontz, and the PB-4 and the Glastrons will be south of us, so we'll have plenty of backup, just not close. Don't worry," Homes said.

"What's the Chicken Farm?" Service asked. Attalienti was definitely using his information, and it was filtering down to the officers.

"Dis Twenty Questions? It's a shoal north of Kates Bay. My wife any good?" he added with a chuckle.

"Below average," Service said.

"Man," Homes said, and guffawed. "You *have* been wit' her!"

The wind continued to rise, and with it came increased wave action. By ten the waves were regularly at five feet, some higher, and their anchor had come loose. They had drifted before Homes started the engine and began burrowing slowly over the peaks, the motor gurgling and chortling like an emphysemic gasping for air.

Service sat just in front of Homes with his binoculars sweeping the horizon ahead of them. It was almost too rough to see. A couple of times he had to grab hold to avoid being bucked out of the boat. Going overboard, he decided, could be lethal if help wasn't close by.

It was almost eleven when Homes tapped him on the shoulder. "We're about a mile out." Service felt Homes's binoculars over his right shoulder.

The engine shut off suddenly.

"What?" Service asked.

"North wind reduces wave action along da shore. Let's try ta listen for a while."

Service thought he heard something.

"What is it?" Homes asked.

"Sounded like metal against metal."

"Where?"

Service pointed a little left of their bow.

"Dat's Ansels," Homes said. A minute went by. "Okay, I heard it too. Dey tink dey're safe, making so much noise. Dey tink we all went home . . . dis will be *fun!*"

Fun wasn't the word Service had in mind, but Homes seemed to relish any action that entailed risk.

"Scalded dog!" Homes said before Service could ask what was next. "I'm gonna run full out. You keep your glasses ahead. When we have visual, I'll turn on da lights and da yelper."

The engine went from a growl to a high-pitched whine, the nose popped up, they bounced over a few waves, and began skimming the tops like a skipped rock, wave tops continuing to hammer the metal hull. Service checked his flashlight to make sure it was tethered to his life preserver. Likewise, he had attached a lanyard from his PFD to the trigger guard of his revolver. He wished there was more light and less wind.

Service tried to concentrate on the view through his binoculars, but the ride was too rough, the spray blasting from the bow. Even so, he thought he detected a blink of a light.

"There," he called to Homes, "a light."

Homes leaned forward. "Where?"

"Ten o'clock."

"Yes," Homes shouted. "I see the motherfuckers!"

The blue light began to rotate and the yelper began its eerie warble as they raced toward the target.

"Hundred yards," Homes yelled at Service. "I'm gonna put us alongside. You jump over an' shut dere motor off!"

The other craft was less than fifty yards away when Service saw light-colored froth erupt behind it.

Homes yelled, "Dey're runnin'!" Service thought he sounded almost happy about the prospect.

"Make sure you get dere bloody motor shut off!" Homes repeated as the quarry began to flee, holding the interval between them. Service knew his job was critical, that both men would board to make the arrest and prevent evidence from being cast over the sides.

Homes seemed to find more power, and as the distance closed, the other boat immediately began a series of abrupt right and left turns. No matter what they tried, Homes stayed with them. He seemed to anticipate each maneuver and they were closing steadily. Service saw piles of shore ice passing precariously close, and hoped Homes was paying attention.

Amazingly, the other boat seemed to gain some space with a double left turn when Homes was cutting right, and when they turned back, the other boat was moving away. Homes soon had them closing, and instead of north, the other boat was running due west into the main bay.

Service felt a sense of foreboding. Homes made it seem like the rats would throw up their hands, or if forced to run, try for the north. So far they hadn't done anything Homes had predicted. Not a good sign, he told himself, but Homes had gained on the other craft and was almost beside it now.

"Ready?" Homes called out.

Service moved forward to the bow in a low crouch, braced himself, put a foot on the gunwale and waited, his heart pounding. Stepping out of an airplane was a lot easier than this shit.

The distance between the two craft decreased steadily, and whenever the quarry tried to turn, Homes was ahead of their moves and drawing ever closer—like he had radar, or a sixth sense. Finally, they were within six feet, and Homes cut sharply into the other craft and grazed it gently. Service saw a man in dark oilers standing there, and aiming at the figure, he launched himself over the side into the other boat.

As his feet hit the deck, something struck him on the forehead, and he found himself on his knees. He tried to get up, propping a leg against a gunwale, but another blow came, this time to the back of his head. He had the sudden impression of time suspended, and of levitating before smacking the water face-first, and skipping before sinking and bobbing quickly back to the surface, gasping for air like he was at death's door, so focused on the cold and getting air that he had no idea where the boats had gone.

Fucked was the first word that came into his mind. Then, calm down, assess the problem, focus on what you have, not on what you don't have. He had his light and his pistol. Marine flares? No flares! Why didn't they issue marine flares? *Focus on what you've got*, his mind repeated. Thoughts coming in clusters, no order. Water temperature: What was the water temperature? He had taken a reading near Sac Bay. Thirty-eight there, or forty-eight? No, take the worst case. Warmer out here? No, assume same. Worst case. *Don't fight*, his mind said. Don't struggle. You're in the water and you can't change that. Conserve heat. You're in good shape, adapted to the cold, perhaps more this year than at any other time in your life. Big bodies cool slower than small bodies. Fifteen to thirty minutes before the lights go out, he told himself. *Stay alive.*

He pulled himself into a cannonball position, which lifted his head up enough so he could see, but the waves immediately pushed his face under and he had to go through the contortion again, trying to make his body as tight as he could to reduce exertion and keep heat in. Slow down, relax; don't swim—float! He eventually learned to take a breath before the waves dumped him, even to look around. No sound of the boats, no lights. All alone. *Fucking rats!* he thought. He needed to see a light, any light. Why the hell were game wardens boarding boats like pirates? This was the sort of shit frustration caused.

No idea how much time had passed. Too much? No, still alive. Too cold to be dead yet. He had heard an instructor in winter survival training say, "You're not dead until you're warm and dead." Where the hell was Homes? Body cold, but no shivering yet. That's good. Glass half full. He had wool under nylon, under an insulated jumpsuit. Thank God for wool. Not great for swimming, but he wasn't swimming tonight, just floating, trying to take one breath at a time, and not going anywhere except where the wind wanted him to go. *Don't think*, he warned himself, *Stay calm—no matter what.* Taste in his mouth: Salt. Blood? Forget it. The only sharks out here were in boats.

At some point he heard a sound, or imagined it. He uncurled his body and fumbled to get his finger into the trigger guard of the revolver, which was attached to his preserver by a lanyard. Stay calm, control breathing. Okay, finger set. He closed his eyes, tried to substitute hearing for sight. The crests of the waves seemed higher than five feet now. Eyes closed. There, yes. Sound for sure. A motor running hard. He lifted his arm as high as he could, fired a round, found himself temporarily blinded by the intensity of the muzzle flash. Had anyone ever calculated the candlepower of that? *Stay in the fucking game*, his old man's voice, the familiar refrain no matter what was happening. More sound. He lifted his arm, fired two rounds in succession; he ignored the muzzle flashes this time, his ears ringing. He hoped the rounds would land on some rat's head. Then: Wait, don't fire again too soon. How many shots left? Not counting, not paying attention. *Dummy!* No, wrong attitude. Okay, no problem. Not like he was going to reload out here. He laughed out loud, closed his eyes. Yes, a motor drawing toward him; he lifted his arm, fired another round, got dunked by a huge wave, came up coughing and choking on water. Christ, his lungs were going to fill with ice. How many rounds left? Never mind. Save it until nothing left. Under the water again, choking more, he bobbed to the surface and said out loud, "This ain't good."

A female voice: "If I was Florence Nightingale I'd strip and get under da blankets wit' youse."

"Is this a topless beach?" he asked, no idea why. He felt pressure near his rectum. "What's that?"

"We need your body temperature."

"Ninety-eight point six is normal," he said.

"You're not normal," the voice said.

"That smarts."

"Truth always does," the voice said. "Haven't lost the sense of humor, eh?"

"Damn," he said, flinching at the feel of the thermometer.

"I used Vaseline," the voice said.

"It feels like a baseball bat."

"I didn't feel a thing," the nurse said. "Everything's a little constricted," she said. "Ninety-four point eight. It's coming up."

"It?" he asked.

"You're not *that* warm yet," she quipped.

"That's not what the mermaid said."

"Mermaid?"

"Can modern science measure the buoyancy of breasts?" he asked.

"Say again?"

"Never mind. You wouldn't understand." Neither did he. His mouth was launching words unvetted by his mind. He felt heat on his forehead and neck.

"Drink," the voice said. "Tea and sugar."

"No candy," he said. "Bad luck."

"Tea," she said, trying to reassure him. "Tepid, not hot."

He sipped and spit it out.

"Too hot?" she sounded concerned.

"My lips don't work so good."

"Try again?" she asked softly.

"Okay."

This time he got it down. "Where am I?"

"Hospital," the voice said. "Escanaba."

"Where's Homes?"

"Right here, partner."

"I'm sorry about your wife."

Homes laughed. "She isn't."

"Rats?"

"I finally got control of da assholes, called for emergency help, turned da boat around, an' come looking for youse. Len had an ambulance waiting for us at Ogontz, and da county was dere to transport da prisoners. Da *Little Rat* drifted away and got lost. The Glastrons went ta search for it."

Service said, "Another drink?"

The nurse said, "You want to try to hold the cup?"

"Okay."

She helped prop him up against his pillow and put the cup in his hands.

"You're not so blue anymore."

"That's good, right?"

"That's very good."

"Did I pass out?"

"I don't know," Homes said, "but you looked *dead*, man. We got you on da deck and you started babbling some weird shit about mermaids wit' big tits."

"Can we talk about this later?" Service said, turning away from Homes.

The man in the white lab coat was short with a prominent nose, a perpetual smile, and dark hair combed back. "You Otter?"

"Service, not Otter."

"Sorry, your guys called you Otter. Cop humor, I guess. You'd think I'd learn. I'm a doctor."

Service let his eyes scan the room. Light was seeping through the shades.

"Warm enough?" the doctor asked.

"Head hurts."

"It should. I put six stitches in your forehead, eleven in back."

"Tasted salt."

"From the cuts. You're either damn lucky or Superman."

"Sir?"

"You've got a concussion, not a mild one, and you could use a neurologist, but we don't have one in town. I'm an internist. Your brain's internal, right, so that makes it my territory. You feel dizzy, nauseous?"

"Just sore, thirsty."

"We've got you on an IV for fluids. Body temp's normal now. You were in the water almost an hour. Most people wouldn't have lasted nearly that long. I'm not sure why you did."

"How long have I been here?"

The man looked at his watch. "About twelve hours. We're gonna keep you tonight, release you tomorrow if everything goes okay."

"Can I get up, walk around?"

"Later, maybe. There's a buzzer by your right hand. Use it if you need anything or feel dizzy. By the way, I'm Vince Vilardo."

"Grady."

"Not Otter."

"Not Otter—Grady Service," Service repeated. "Did we get the rats?"

"Rats?" the doctor named Vince said. "Don't worry about that. Right now you're gonna go to sleep."

"How can you know that?"

Vince smiled and held up a syringe. "I'm your doctor."

38

ESCANABA, MAY 9, 1976

"You really ought to clean up the place. It gives the Garden a bad name."

Service peered into the room where Moe Lapalme sat with two black eyes and a bandage across his nose. Learning that it had been Lapalme in the boat had not been surprising. Moe might not be one of the leaders in the Garden, but he was in the thick of it. During his two-week recon he had not encountered Lapalme until he saw him with a rifle at Middle Bluff. Where had he been before that?

Colt Homes stood next to Service. "He's da one."

"Never know it by me," Service said. "All I saw were dark oilers. Too dark and too fast to see a face. Did he look like that when I left the boat?"

"It was kinda close quarters," Homes said sheepishly. "I went over right behind you and jumped da driver. Dere was some wrestling, and when I got 'em settled down, you were gone, and I about shit my pants. Neither of da bastards wanted ta turn da boat around."

Homes explained that he had threatened to shoot both men if they didn't calm down and do what he ordered. The scuffle in the boat had taken them way off course, and by the time Homes got the situation under control, he had no idea where Service was. Only the sound and muzzle flashes of his revolver had enabled them to find him and fish him out. "By den," Homes said, "I was wondering if we had a funeral on our hands. Lapalme thought da whole thing was kinda funny."

"Not now, I'd guess."

"It was close," Homes said seriously. "*Too* bloody close."

"We get their nets?"

"Yesterday morning. Unmarked, but in da area where you dropped the buoy. Found da *Little Rat* south of da Stonington. Joe Flap spotted it from above."

"Lapalme, of course, knows nothing about the nets."

"Never seen 'em before. Dey was just out for a boat ride when we come roarin' up on 'em and scared 'em, which was why dey bolted."

"Blood tests?"

"Both blotto and change," Homes said.

Meaning they had been over the blood alcohol level for legally oper-ating a vehicle—on land or water. "At least we have that."

"An' some blood on Lapalme's oilers. He denies touching you."

"Probably the truth. It felt like a club, not fists."

"Three-pound fish bat to be precise," Homes said. "Your blood type was on da bat and it matched da type on da oilers. Neither Lapalme, nor da other guy, have your blood type. 'Course, dey say it was a pal who cut himself earlier. Dey've been arraigned for attempted murder, assaulting police officers, resisting arrest, fleeing, fishing in a closed zone during a closed period, driving while intoxicated, and more charges are going ta be added. We got dere boat, dere's no registration, and da VIN is missing."

"Does Murray think he has a case?" Murray was Delta County's prosecuting attorney.

"He says it will come down to da jury."

"Same old story." Juries were notorious for siding with poachers and lawbreakers in the U.P. "Did Lapalme lawyer up?"

"Young worm outta Negaunee named Tavolacci. We've bumped heads wit' him in several counties. He's one of da first lawyers da bad guys call."

"Is he good enough to get them off?"

"Can't rule it out, but if Murray and his people get dere shit to-gether, Tavolacci will plead it out. Dat okay by you?"

"No," Service said, "but it would take two rats out of the pack. I'd like to talk to Lapalme, alone."

"Bad idea."

"Colt."

"Okay, okay. We'd better let Tavolacci know. He'll go ballistic if he ain't at da party."

"It's not about the other night."

Homes cocked his head. "You want a tape recorder?"

"Yes, but if it's okay with you, I'll hang on to the tape." Homes shrugged and handed the device to him.

"You know," Service said, pausing near the door to the room, "I never saw his face. I was in the water almoast immediately." He didn't tell Homes he had previously seen Lapalme in the Garden.

"Don't worry," Homes said. "I told you I jumped da other guy."

"Who is he?"

"Duperow."

"Regular rat?" This was a new name to Service.

"Fringe type—sort of an apprentice," Homes said with a grin.

"He wasn't on the fringe the other night."

"As he is now so painfully aware," Homes said. "If he decides ta get his own lawyer, he'll turn on Moe. You sure you don't want me ta sit in wit' you?"

"Thanks, I'll be fine."

"Da yak-shack's all yours."

"Yak-shack?"

Homes pointed, enunciated, "Interview room."

Lapalme sat across the table from Service.

"I guess we both had a rough night," Service said.

"I never touched you, man."

"You know me?"

"Seen you around."

"Really?" Service said. "Where?"

"How I'm supposed to remember. Your face looks familiar."

"How do you know I'm the one who got thrown out of the boat?"

Lapalme stared at him. "Because I helped fish your waterlogged ass out of the lake."

"Thanks," Service said. "I appreciate that."

Lapalme shrugged.

"Looks like you had some problems," Service said, nodding at the man's injuries.

"That fucking Homes," Lapalme said. "I tried to help Dupe and he beat the shit outta me."

"Homes jumped Duperow?"

Lapalme stared at the wall. "I want my lawyer."

"This isn't about the other night, Moe."

"No?"

"You know Anise Aucoin?"

Lapalme sneered. "That psycho bitch. What did she tell you?"

Service delayed answering, let silence eat at Lapalme's attempt at nonchalance. "What do you think she told me?"

"I—no! I want my lawyer."

"You've seen her since she got back," Service said, a statement rather than a question.

"I dropped that scag years ago, man."

"I don't believe you."

"What're you trying to pull, man?"

Service lit a cigarette and offered the pack to Lapalme. "I'm sure I saw you and her in your truck a couple of months back."

Lapalme leaned away from the table. "She told you that?"

"You're not listening, Moe. I said I *saw* you up on US Two by the Fishdam."

"You'da seen me that day, you'da come visiting," Lapalme said.

"Blue pickup, home just north of Garden. It looks like a junkyard, Moe. You really ought to clean up the place. It gives the Garden a bad name."

"What is this shit, man!"

"You were with her."

"Like I give a shit what you think."

"You like venison, Moe?"

Lapalme got up from the table and knocked over his chair. "You're as crazy as that cunt. I want my fucking lawyer!"

Homes was waiting outside the room. "What was all dat about?"

"Keeping my head in the game."

"You need ta call it a day, pal. Your concussion's showing."

"You're probably right." In fact, he had a headache that seemed to be getting worse rather than better. But he was sure now it had been Lapalme driving the truck with Aucoin as his passenger. Lapalme had slipped up and said "that day," as much as admitting he had made the drive-by at the Fishdam. He needed to talk to Lasurm's daughter, and he needed to talk to her without Hegstrom running interference. But before that, he knew he needed to go back to Show-Titties Pond. Hegstrom had asked some questions he couldn't answer, and before he went off on a tangent he wanted to know what Hegstrom thought he knew.

39

SLIPPERY CREEK, MAY 9–10, 1976

"You're a lout, Service!"

On the way back from the jail, Service stopped at the district office. Connie Leppo gave him a look. "Len said you're s'pposed ta be off for a few days."

"I'm working on it," he said on his way to the evidence locker, where he had left the two slugs recovered from the deer parts at the pond. It took thirty minutes to find the plastic bag with the slugs, and he cursed himself for not having a better memory.

On the drive home he found the afternoon light almost blinding; he put on his sunglasses, which helped, but his eyes continued to tear up and he felt a headache starting.

He had just walked into the Airstream when the trailer door burst open behind him.

"There you are, you scoundrel!"

Brigid Mehegen's diminutive grandfather stood in the doorway, his face flushed, brandishing a shotgun. He wore a pith helmet with a Civil Defense logo on the front. "You broke my grandbaby's heart!"

Service slapped the barrel of the shotgun aside and wrenched it away from the man. "Get out of my house." The ache in his head was sharper.

"This ain't no house. I gotta hurt you bad. It's the code."

Mehegen came in behind her grandfather, spun him around, and got in his face. "The same code says I fight my own fights," she growled.

"I'm upholding your honor," her grandfather said. "Not that you got all that much left."

Mehegen turned him around and ushered him out the door, slamming it behind him.

She looked at the cut on Service's head.

"Are you two a traveling tag team?" he asked.

"That's right: Make funny, Mr. Macho. Every cop in the U.P. is talking about your swim—*Otter*." She sat down at the table. "Don't mind that old man. The fact is, neither of you understand the concept of a fuck-buddy." She paused to let her words sink in. "There can't be any sex when the fuck-buddy disappears for a mysterious and undefined family emergency, *and* doesn't bother to call when he gets back to town. You're a lout, Service!"

Lout . . . scoundrel? He was being skewered with nineteenth-century vocabulary.

"I came here tonight to officially dissolve our fuck-buddyship," Mehegen said. "Do you care to offer a defense?"

"I forgot?" he said. His head was pounding now; he was cold again, and beginning to feel nauseous.

"That's it! You *forgot*? That does wonders for my ego!"

He waved his hand at her, felt the gorge rising in his throat.

"You're . . . *dismissing* me?"

"Unless you want—" He vomited on the floor and her boots and grabbed the edge of the table to maintain his balance.

"I'm getting help!" Mehegen said, her eyes wide.

He grabbed her wrist. "No."

She peeled his hand away and went outside. Moments later her grandfather came through the door. "He's a doctor," Mehegen announced.

"What kind?" Service mumbled.

"It matters, you puking all over?" the grandfather replied. "I was an OB/GYN before I retired."

Service vomited again and started to fall. His guests caught him and helped him back to the toilet.

He awoke in bed, his head still hurting, but the pain somewhat diminished. Mehegen's grandfather was standing by the bed.

"Feeling better?"

"I think I'm done throwing up."

"You got nothing left to expel but organs," the old man said. "You really let loose."

"You're actually a doctor?"

"Until liability and malpractice insurance got so bad it drove me out."

"High?"

"Probably more than you'll ever make in a year, but it wasn't just the money. I got tired of being sued, and my insurance company kept wanting to settle; and of course, my premiums kept going up," he explained. "I wasn't a bad doctor, or a perfect one. My problem was that I was the only OB/GYN for sixty miles, and I was outnumbered by lawyers. One day I just said to hell with it and moved up here. You've had a pretty good concussion. Did a neurologist look at you?"

"There wasn't one."

"That's the U.P. for you. When did you get the whacks on the head?"

"Two nights ago, more or less."

The retired doctor nodded ponderously. "Symptoms coming on this late aren't good. You need to get back to your doctor. He tell you it could take weeks for the symptoms to clear?"

Service tried to shake his head, but couldn't. "No." Actually, he had ignored what the doctor, Vince Vilardo, had told him. Ignored or forgotten. The way he had felt, either was possible.

Mehegen came into the room, kissed her grandfather's cheek, and after he was gone, sat on the end of the bed. "Cops are making a joke out of what you went through," she said. "I don't see the humor in it, and I'm spending the night right here."

Service started to protest but she held up her hand. "Tonight we'll focus on the buddy part. People with concussions are supposed to be watched," she said. "Why'd they let you out anyway?"

"Work," he said.

She rolled her eyes, growled "*Cops*," and went to the front of the trailer, leaving him alone, but he followed her. "That night when you babysat Ivan Rhino, did he say anything when you were alone with him?"

She looked at him. "Not really."

"Nothing at all?"

"I can't believe you want to talk about *that*! He said two words: 'Right on.'"

"When was this?"

"You were inside with the deputies."

"Right on?"

"I thought his synapses were misfiring."

Maybe not, Service thought.

40

LITTLE LAKE, MAY 11, 1976

"He can smell a fart in a tornado."

Service stopped at the Escanaba district office, and Leppo immediately began to yip, "Outta here! Youse're s'pposed to be resting."

He opened the evidence locker and started searching for the slugs he had stored there. He gave up after an hour. He knew he'd put them there. Hadn't he?

Connie Leppo said, "I thought youse got what you needed from the evidence locker the other day?"

He had been here? Leppo held up an evidence custody form. It listed two rifle slugs, caliber unknown. He had signed for them May 9. *Shit*, he thought.

"Okay to use the phone?" he asked. Connie Leppo rolled her eyes and left her desk. He called the Marquette County sheriff's office and got the names of the two deputies who had responded to his call that night at STP. He left before Leppo could come back and scold him for being there. He sat in his Plymouth trying to recall picking up the evidence. He couldn't.

The deputies were Harry Wayne and Maurice Shelby. He called Wayne from a pay phone and asked if they could meet. Wayne agreed, and said he'd call Shelby.

It was fifty-three degrees, the snowpack melting quickly, leaving the side roads slippery with mud and slush on top and a substrate of holdover ice that had been packed down by vehicles over the long winter. He knew the warm-up wouldn't last. It would take heavy spring rains to really take the snow, and even then turquoise-blue ice patches would persist in the dark nooks of cedar roots until well into July. Fifties today, it could be below twenty tomorrow, but spring and summer were coming on.

The two deputies were waiting at Harry Wayne's small log house on Little Lake. There were patches of snow and ice stacked up on the south shore, opposite the cabin. The two men were in their late twenties, and both had been on the job for three years.

Wayne invited him in and offered him coffee. "She got a little wet down to the bay, eh?"

Service nodded. The deputy's comment was a way of acknowledging that a brother cop had gone over the edge and inexplicably come back. It wouldn't be mentioned again in his presence unless he brought it up, a subtle recognition that each officer who survived a close call needed to work out the aftermath in his own time and in his own way.

He got right to the point. "You guys up for a visit to STP?"

"Why?" Shelby asked immediately. "Any DNR violations were secondary to the felonies."

"I'm not questioning that," he said, "and I'm not trying to butt in. I just want to take a walk-through for a little peace of mind. It got pretty confusing that night."

The men looked at each other, and Wayne said, "What the hell."

"How's Eugene?" Service asked.

"They moved him from the hospital to lockup. They have him segregated."

"Because of a threat?"

"Because he's as simple as a brick. Even his lawyer's having a hard time understanding him."

"Did Hegstrom take him on?"

"Nope, just the girl. Chomsky and Rhino have their own court-appointeds. Rhino refused to share."

Service expected the camp road to be drifted over with snow and was surprised to see it freshly plowed.

There was a black New Yorker parked next to the camp building where the stabbing took place. Service pulled in behind the Chrysler and waited for the deputies to arrive. The Chrysler was sparkling by U.P. spring standards, almost no salt scabs or sand buildups on the bumpers.

The deputies picked their way through the mud to his patrol car. "When did the county release this place as a crime site?"

"Mid-April?" Shelby asked Wayne, who nodded in agreement. "Would have been earlier, but Hegstrom wanted to keep it roped off."

Why would Hegstrom want that? Service wondered.

Service knocked on the door and, after a long delay, an elderly man opened the door a crack and peered out. "I thought the police were done with this place."

"Mr. Agosti?" Service said.

"Who else would it be, more hoodlums?"

"I'm Conservation Officer Service," he said, turning to the other men. "Deputies Wayne and Shelby. We're sorry if we've interrupted you."

The man said, "What is it this time?"

"I beg your pardon," Service said. The old man was unexpectedly gruff.

"I wanted to come up in January before Angie and I left for Florida, but the detective said no. So I asked him to call me when the place was released and we headed on down to Florida. You think he'd have the courtesy to call? Not a chance. I had to call long-distance to find out. Angie and I worked hard for what we've got. We saved. We don't throw money around."

Talk about a non sequitur soliloquy, Service thought. No money to throw around? The man owned two camps on a nice piece of property, drove a nearly new automobile, and he and the wife spent at least part of the winter in Florida. "Did you build these places?" Service asked. There had been no camps in the area years ago when he'd been here.

"With my own two hands," the old man said.

"Can we come in?" Service asked.

"Why?" Agosti challenged. "So you can trash the camp again?"

Service glanced at Wayne, who arched an eyebrow. "Is this a bad time? Did we catch you on the way out?" Service asked.

"Just don't have time is all," Agosti said. "Come back tomorrow. I got things to do, and Angie's still in Florida."

"Did you drive up from Florida?" Deputy Wayne asked.

"Four days," the old man said, holding up three fingers. "Rain all the way."

Service looked back and saw Shelby peering into the vehicle and trying a door handle.

"What's all the stuff in the car?" Shelby yelled out as he walked toward the cabin.

"Stuff the wife wants," the old man said.

"For Florida?" Shelby asked.

"That's right, for Florida," the man said.

"Cross-country skis for Florida?" Shelby asked.

"'Course not; those I got to drop to my granddaughter in Chicago."

Deputy Shelby said, "Can you show us some ID, Mr. Agosti?"

"You guys come trash my camps and now *I'm* the criminal?"

The old man's reactions from the start had not been normal, Service told himself.

"Your car's locked," Shelby said.

"What, I'm supposed to leave it open? A body can't be too careful."

"Identification, sir?"

The old man opened the door slightly and patted at his trousers. "Guess I left it in the other room," he said and started to close the door, but Harry Wayne stuck his boot in to block it. Service heard the old man go scuttling away, moving with amazing alacrity.

They pushed the door open and went inside. "Some look-see this is," Shelby said. "Mr. Agosti?" he called out.

No answer.

Service wandered into the kitchen. It had not been cleaned up. As soon as it warmed up, the dried blood would attract flies and other insects. What was the old man doing here?

Shelby called out again. "Mr. Agosti?"

Wayne looked at Service. "He's gone."

"No way," Service said.

"Beam me up, Scotty?" Shelby said with a grin.

"He's here," Service said. "He was out of sight ten seconds max. He's not Houdini."

"Neither was Houdini," Shelby said.

"What?"

"Houdini's real name was Erik Weisz."

"Get serious," Service said, rolling his eyes.

"I *am* serious, that was his name," Shelby insisted.

"Let's open the Chrysler," Wayne said.

"You got a key?" Service wanted to know.

The deputies laughed.

"Illegal search," Service said.

Wayne said, "He couldn't or wouldn't identify himself. He's got to be a hundred and forty years old, and he's got cross-country skis and an uncased rifle in the backseat of his vehicle. Leave this to us, woods cop."

"You never said anything about a rifle," Service said.

"Up here everybody has a rifle."

"Uncased?"

"That too."

Service looked at Harry Wayne for support, but got none.

"There's a *Milwaukee Journal* on the front seat," Shelby said.

"You can buy them at Benny's in Gladstone," Service said. "Daily. Sometimes I even buy one."

"Game wardens can read?" Shelby asked.

"No jokes, guys. Something stinks here."

"We should call Sniffer," Harry Wayne said to Shelby.

"Who?" Service wanted to know.

Harry Wayne said, "Kharlamov. He's our new guy. He moved up from Pontiac. He was a tunnel rat in Vietnam. He can smell a fart in a tornado."

"He claims," Shelby added.

"We'll give him a test," Wayne said.

The banter of the two deputies was beginning to annoy him. "Call him," Service said, sitting down at the dining room table and rubbing his head. It was beginning to ache again. *Where the hell had the old man disappeared to?*

He was dozing when he sensed someone nearby, and awoke to find a craggy-faced man with a shaved head. "You're Service?" the stranger whispered. "Marines, right?"

Service nodded.

The man said, "I heard. I'm Alex Kharlamov, Highlands, K-nine and tunnels."

Kharlamov was short with powerful shoulders and a thick neck. "Where're the guys?"

"I told them to stay outside. They talk too much. Laurel and Hardy told me what happened," Kharlamov said. "There's got to be a hidey-hole."

Service was impressed with the new man's presence. He spoke so softly, his words barely above a whisper. "Did you search?" the new deputy asked.

"Not really."

"Good," the man said. "Ten seconds was the lag time?"

"About."

Kharlamov sat down Indian-style on the floor. "You fish for trout?"

"When I get the chance." Which had not been often enough.

Kharlamov smiled. "I came up here for the trout. Fewer, smaller fish mean fewer people. I like to fish alone."

"You've come to the right place," Service said.

"Could afford it, I'd be a hermit," the man said. "You fish hatches or attractors?"

"Whatever it takes."

"Me, I'm a hatch man. It's like surveillance. Sometimes conditions seem right and the bugs don't show. The key is to be in the right place at the right time, and to wait. Most people aren't patient enough." Kharlamov looked over at Service. "We're gonna have a hatch here."

"You get that from tea leaves or chicken guts?" Service asked.

Kharlamov smiled. "There's a vent grate in the roof overhang. Is there a basement?"

"Not that we could see. Foundation's poured, but it looks like a slab. The furnace is in a closet off the kitchen."

"Crawl space in the ceiling," Kharlamov said, "too shallow for an attic, and the grate's too large for the overhang. When you're sight-fishing, what do you look for?"

"Shadows first, parts of a fish next—never the whole thing."

The deputy grunted softly, slid a metal flask out of his jacket pocket, and held it out to Service. "Pepper vodka?"

Service took the flask. It was inscribed with the words STANDARD BET in an ornate script. He took a drink and handed it back. "Special meaning?"

"Not anymore," Kharlamov said. "You're the one took the swim in the big water?"

"Yeah."

Service got up and watched Wayne and Shelby start their vehicles and drive away. He had no idea where Kharlamov had parked. Only the Chrysler remained by the cabin.

No more words were spoken for more than two hours. Kharlamov sat with his hand flat against the drywall, his eyes staring into a void.

Just over two hours after the other deputies drove away, Kharlamov raised his hand and showed one finger, then two, nodding to make sure Service had seen.

Service was behind the deputy, who had edged to the door of the bedroom where the stabbing had taken place. Service saw the barrel of a revolver poke into view and just as quickly, Kharlamov had the weapon in hand and the old man pinned by the throat against the wall, his face turning red and eyes bulging.

Another figure came darting into the room, not looking left or right. Service shouted, "Police—*freeze!*" but the figure kept going through the front door. He followed to find Deputy Shelby on top of a struggling figure in the snow and mud. The deputies had dumped the vehicle and come back on foot to wait outside.

They checked the two for identification. The old man had no wallet. The other prisoner was a young girl, twelve or thirteen, and she stared at them with hatred, refusing to talk. Shelby read them their rights, cuffed them, and put them in the back of Kharlamov's patrol car, which Harry Wayne brought up to the cabin.

Wayne stayed in the vehicle with the prisoners and radioed his sergeant.

Service went back into the cabin and found Kharlamov in the bedroom the two had bolted from. The floor in the closet was propped open. The deputy handed him a flashlight and motioned for him to climb down.

There was a sturdy ladder down to a landing and another ladder going straight up. Three wooden steps led down into a cellar, which was cold. Service shone the light around, saw rifles and clothes and chain saws and tools. "Looks like Laurel and Hardy missed the jackpot last time they were here," Kharlamov said, a simple statement, no sarcasm.

Service found it difficult to focus his thoughts, and when he finally managed to corral them, they were not on the mysterious goods, but on the trapdoor into the bedroom, Hegstrom's questions, and Gumby's blathering about "him-her."

MARQUETTE, MAY 13, 1976

"If not the girl, who?"

Joe Flap agreed to let Service have his place in Trenary for the night, and a quick telephone call to Nikki-Jo Jokola secured her agreement to place another ad in the Manistique paper. He promised Nikki-Jo this would be the last one.

Acting captain Dean Attalienti looked frazzled as Service stood in his doorway, waiting to be waved in. "You are supposed to be recuperating," Attalienti said.

"I am."

"We had another incident last night—three shots fired at the PB-4 off Garden. One of the rounds went through the cabin and missed Len by a couple of feet. He got out of rifle range, and two of our patrol units went through the village and came up empty-handed. This thing just keeps going on and on," the acting captain lamented. "What do *you* want?"

"The rifle from Middle Bluff."

"For what?"

"Ballistic tests." *If* he could find the missing slugs.

Attalienti looked exasperated. "It was never fired at us."

That day. "Different case, sir."

The regional law boss said, "Don't patronize me. It's in the evidence locker. Sign a chain-of-custody form and leave it with Fern. You're resting, right?"

"Yessir."

He still had not located the slugs, but he delivered the rifle to the state police lab in Negaunee. The intake tech stared at him. "What're we supposed to compare?"

"I'm working on that," Service said, feeling like a fool.

Service got to the Marquette County Jail around 12:30 P.M.

Eugene Chomsky's lawyer had a new briefcase and a stiffness that suggested she was either new on the job, or not happy about this assignment.

She didn't smile when Marquette County Detective Kobera and Service walked into the interview room.

"Emily Linton," Kobera said. "Grady Service, DNR."

Service looked at a grinning Eugene Chomsky. "Hey, Grady!"

"Hey, Gumby."

"Hey, Grady," the boy repeated.

"My client has nothing to say," Linton said officiously.

"Relax, Counselor. This won't hurt your client," Service said.

"Sidebar outside the room," Linton said.

"We're not in a courtroom," Kobera told her. "Chill out, Emily."

Chomsky stared at Service. "Where badge?"

"On my uniform," Service said.

"Like badge," Chomsky said.

Service glanced at Kobera. "Do you think we could get a badge for Gumby?"

"You bet," the detective said, leaving the room.

"How are you feeling, Gumby?"

"Okay."

"Have you seen Ivan?"

"Got my own place," the boy said proudly.

"This is ludicrous," Emily Linton said. "The boy can't comprehend *any* of this."

"*Grady*," Chomsky told her, pointing at Service. "Grady nice."

Service ignored her. "Can you help me with something, Gumby?"

"Okay."

"Stand up."

"Eugene, remain where you are," Linton ordered. To Service: "What do you think you're doing?"

"Not *Eugene*," the boy said. "Gumby." He stood up. His lawyer looked at the ceiling in exasperation.

Kobera came back into the room and stood next to Linton.

Service positioned the boy near the end of the table on the side opposite the door into the room. "You like to play pretend, Gumby?"

The boy grinned. "Uh-huh."

"Can we pretend the table is a bed and you're at the door of the bedroom? You remember that night, right? Remember, you stepped inside to turn on the lights?"

"No," the boy said with a tight jaw.

"You don't remember?"

"Door there," the boy said, pointing at the other side of the room.

Service smiled. "Right you are." The boy remembered. He looked at Kobera as he walked the boy to the other end of the room. "The table's the pretend bed, okay?"

"Okay."

"You went into the bedroom to turn on the light."

"Uh-huh."

"Okay, this is just pretend. I want you to step into the room like you did that night, okay?"

The boy sucked in a deep breath. "Okay," he said, stepping forward and turning to the right.

"Where's the light switch, Gumby?"

The boy put his arm out. "Pretend?"

"Right, pretend. Show me where it is."

"There," the boy said, pointing to his right.

"Good," Service said. "That's good. Now I want you to pretend to turn on the light and say 'ouch' when you get pretend-stabbed."

"I won't stand for this," Linton said, trying to rise.

Kobera kept her pinned in her seat with his hand on her shoulder.

"Pretend, right?" the boy asked Service, concern on his face.

"Pretend. Nobody will hurt you. Turn on the light."

The boy took a half-step right, reached out with his right hand, made a small downward motion, turned to his left and said, "Ouch." There was no emotion in his voice.

Service sat on the table and asked Kobera to stand to the boy's right. Service pushed himself back on the table. "This is about where she was," he said. "Kneel," he told the detective.

Kobera nodded, got down on his knees, and made a couple of swipes with his arm, like he was stabbing at someone.

"Good," Service said. "Let's do it again, and let Jimmy pretend too."

"Jimmy," the boy said. "Okay. Him there," he added, looking down at Kobera.

"Detective Kobera is helping us. He wants to play pretend."

"Not him-her, him-*Cap'n*," Chomsky said.

"Jimmy won't hurt you." Service held out his hand and Kobera tossed the badge to him. Service pinned it on the boy's shirt and the boy stared down at it, beaming with pride. *Him-Cap'n?* They were close to something, he could feel it. But what? The boy had something firmly in his mind, but how could he get it out of him?

"Badge."

"Gumby?"

"Yeah."

"Pretend one more time?"

"Okay."

They went through it again, and his lawyer declared, "That's enough, Eugene!"

Chomsky glared at her and said defiantly, "*Gumby!*" He tapped his chest. "Badge."

Linton's head dropped.

"Thanks, Gumby. You did great," Kobera said.

Service patted the boy's massive shoulders. "You see where we are?" he asked Kobera.

"If this reenactment is even halfway close, there's no way Anise Aucoin stabbed him."

"Do I get an explanation?" Linton asked.

"When we have one, Counselor," Detective Kobera said.

"Badge mine?" Gumby interrupted.

"Yes, you earned it," Kobera told the boy. "Thanks."

"Let's talk to the surgeon who patched him up," Service said when they were outside the room.

"I've got all the medical reports."

"I want to hear the words come out of his mouth."

The surgeon met them in the doctor's lounge and immediately lit a cigarette. There was dried blood on his scrubs and his hair was greasy. "Jimmy," the doctor said.

Kobera said, "Dr. Guild, Grady Service of the DNR."

"It's Fred," the doctor said, shaking hands. "What can I do you guys for?"

The man had a powerful grip. Service reminded him of the case.

"I remember," the surgeon said. "It's all in the medical records."

"I just wanted to hear it from you."

"Sure. The stab wounds were upward and from the boy's right."

"Based on?"

"My eyes and ten years in Detroit Receiving Emergency. They like blades down there almost as much as guns."

"Why didn't the blade hit something vital?" Service asked.

"The third wound was more parallel than the other two. It was still slightly upward, but basically parallel. Up a little bit more and the kid would have had serious problems."

"Parallel to the floor?" Service asked.

"Or the ceiling—take your pick."

Service got down on his knees and feigned two quick thrusts into Kobera's buttocks; then he extended slightly upward and struck again.

Dr. Guild said, "I think that looks pretty close to what happened. The third blow was meant to go deep. The assailant probably lifted a little to get additional leverage."

They thanked the surgeon and walked outside. "You got somebody in mind?" Kobera asked.

"You agree it couldn't have been Aucoin?"

"Theoretically. The assailant was in the closet. If not the girl, who?"

"I'm working on that," he said.

"You going to tell Hegstrom?" Kobera asked.

"In time," Service said. *Where the hell had he put the damn rifle slugs?*

42

TRENARY, MAY 16, 1976

"Who's the 'Cap'n'?"

Joe Flap had vacated his house for the night to visit a friend in Ishpeming.

Cecilia Lasurm arrived around 8 P.M. and stood in the dining room, shaking her rain hat like a wet dog. "U.P. weather," she said.

"It rains everywhere," he reminded her.

"Not in the Gobi Desert," she said, tilting her head back to kiss him. "I was beginning to think our time had passed," she said, hugging him gently, and after they lingered in the embrace, she turned away and sat down at the dining room table. "You pushed it too close out there on the lake," she said.

"Thanks to Moe," he said.

"Word is he never touched you."

"Not with his hands. He tried to give me the last rites with a weighted priest."

Lasurm's eyes were locked on him. "That's Moe. I've been visiting Anise," she added. "I do most of the talking. Near as I can tell, she's been on junk since she left."

"How're you?" he asked.

"My diagnosis is the kind that doesn't change. I'm coping."

"Anise didn't stab the boy that night," he said. "I think I have proof."

"Actual evidence?" Her eyes were intense.

"The detective on the case buys it," he told her.

"She refuses to talk about it," Lasurm said. "Odd had a psychologist talk to her. He thinks she was too high to remember any of it."

Service remembered the blank look on the girl's face that night. "Maybe she will now."

"Have you told Odd?" Lasurm asked.

"Not yet. We know Eugene didn't stab himself. We know Ivan Rhino was in custody in the patrol car at the time, and we're pretty sure Anise didn't do it. All we know for certain is that the boy got stabbed."

"You're not boosting my confidence," she said. "Nobody else was there."

"Who's the 'Cap'n'?" he asked. Gumby and Ivan Rhino had been involved with Anise Aucoin, who was a Garden woman, and Gumby was now talking about "him-Cap'n." It was a stretch, Service knew, but maybe there was another Garden link—and who would know better than Cecilia?

Lasurm lowered her eyes. "The army ranger captain or the fishing boat captain?"

"There's two of them?" *Shit*, he thought.

"Just one. For a while he claimed he served as a ranger in Vietnam, but I knew he was a cook with a habit and he never made it to Vietnam. They booted him out on a general discharge."

"A step above dishonorable," the said.

"I suppose," she said. "When he got into fishing with the rats, he insisted whoever worked with him address him as captain. It's Moe," she said. "Moe is the Cap'n."

"Moe Lapalme?" Service said.

"Moe Lapalme," she echoed. "What's Moe got to do with this?"

"Everything," Service said. If he could find the damn slugs and get a match.

43

MOSQUITO WILDERNESS, MAY 17, 1976

"Aren't we a little young for brain farts?"

It was cold again, in the mid-forties and raining, and Service spent the day looking for trout fishermen, but few were out. Most native trout-chasers preferred live bait or spinners, and wouldn't get serious about their fishing until after July 4 when the rivers would be down and clear again.

John Voelker, the former state supreme court judge turned writer, was a legend in the fly-fishing community, but locals thought of him as eccentric and still clung to their old ways. Too bad for them. Just after noon there was a two-hour hatch of dark Hendricksons over a riffle in the Mosquito, and just downstream in a long run the surface was alive with feeding fish catching emergers and cripples. On the walk back to his vehicle he saw a sow bear and three cubs. She woofed and sent them up a tree before loping away. He knew she would be close and watching him, but it just proved that not every mother bear turned psycho when people came near her cubs.

He was still taking heavy doses of ibuprofen, and the headaches were finally more or less under control. The bug hatch had gotten him in the mood to fish, but the fly rod he usually kept in the trunk of the Plymouth Fury wasn't there. His memory was just not working. This morning he could not find his boots, and was forced to wear the old pair that pinched his feet. He already felt a blister building on one of his heels, and told himself it was his own damn fault.

There were two worm-dunkers working Lilah Creek just north of the wilderness. Service watched them while Hendricksons came off, the men oblivious to the hatch and rising fish. Once people got locked into a method, they were blind to other possibilities. Everyone had blind spots. He wondered how many he had.

Service knocked off at five. The fishermen could have the rivers tonight. His feet hurt, and the missing slugs were still eating at him.

Mehegen's truck was parked by the Airstream and she was sitting on his stoop. She wore boots, tight jeans, a hooded gray sweatshirt, and a faded Detroit Tigers ball cap.

"Hey sailor, buy a girl a beer?" Her grin disappeared as he approached. "You don't look well at all."

"I'm better," he said.

"Than what?"

He opened the door and let her in. "Couple of beers in the fridge," he told her. He sat down and took off his old boots and peeled down one sock. There was a puffy redness the size of a dime on his heel, a blister for sure.

"Grady?" Mehegen said. She was holding the fridge door open, looking inside. "What's this all about?"

She pulled out his boots and held them up. She was smiling.

"Is there also an evidence bag in there?" he asked, joking.

She leaned over, looked around, and pulled out a plastic bag. It dangled from her hand. "Aren't we a little young for brain farts?"

44

BOAT-EATER SHOALS, MAY 19, 1976

"You ready ta get your feet wet again?"

Sergeant Blake Garwood was silent as he steered the twenty-foot *Fat Rat* out of Gladstone, across from Squaw Point marine navigation light, and headed south toward Little Bay de Noc. Grady Service adjusted the straps on his life preserver and grimaced in the icy mist. Yesterday he had taken the slugs up to the state police lab in Negaunee, and met with Detective Kobera to share his thinking—that Moe Lapalme had been in the room with Anise Aucoin and was the one who stabbed Gumby. If the slugs from the poached deer in the cabin matched Lapalme's rifle, they had a good shot at tying Moe to Aucoin and Ivan Rhino, and the prosecutor could use this information to work a deal with Rhino—in return for evidence against Lapalme. He was headed out onto the big lake again for another marine patrol, but his mind was behind him, on land, when Garwood interrupted his thinking. "Coast Guard reports a trawler on Boat-Eater Shoals," the sergeant said.

"Long way from the Garden," Service said. "For rats." From what he had seen, the rats tended to cling to the waters off the Garden Peninsula. The Boat-Eater Shoals were a few miles off the Stonington Peninsula and just northeast of Minneapolis Shoals. As usual, Stone had called the night before and asked him to go with Garwood.

"You ready ta get your feet wet again?" Stone had asked.

"Not literally," Service told his LT.

"Blake's solid," Stone added.

"Good," Service told the man. He was still having headaches, but they were lessening in their severity, and work was work. You couldn't do the work only when you felt okay.

He had thought it would be a routine patrol until the Coasties called in to give them a heads-up. The icy drizzle and a growing wind didn't help.

"Doubt it's rats," Garwood said. "We've had some reports of un-licensed Wisconsin boats working our waters. They probably figure we're so busy over to the Garden that they can slip in and pick up a couple of bonus loads. Should be easier than a rat patrol," he added. "You okay with this?"

Service nodded.

Garwood throttled back to idle a couple of miles from the shoals and let the boat drift, pushed by a steady north wind. "We won't be able to turn a trawler if we have to chase," the sergeant said. "And they won't be able to out-fast us if we catch them pulling nets, so we're just gonna take 'er easy, work our way in slowly, and look for their lights."

"Then what?" Service asked, thinking about the botched assault on Moe Lapalme's boat.

"Depends on what we see," Garwood said with a shrug.

Why was this stuff so unplanned, so off-the-cuff? The department needed more people for marine patrols, and more and better boats to do the job. At least tonight they had the rat boat to give them some speed. What hurt most was a strong sense that Lansing didn't really care: In time, commercial fishermen would be bought out, and only tribals and sportfishermen would remain. All this effort and risk was for nothing but principle. But at least he had found the slugs. That was a definite plus for today.

"Lights to port," Garwood said. It was a few minutes before mid-night, and the drizzle had turned into a blustery rain with variable winds going from soft breezes to powerful gusts.

Garwood had his binoculars up. "Barely moving, but their stern is lit. I think we got lucky. They're lifting nets. We can board her."

Service cringed at the words, asked, "Numbers?"

"Boat that size, three, maybe four total crew. We'll try to come in quiet, run dark and silent, tie up to them, and go aboard."

This sounded better than a high-speed chase and the Errol Flynn ap-proach. "What's the layout?"

"Forty-footer. They bring nets up along the transom and over the starboard gunwale. Power and controls are forward. I'll angle us in and slide over. You go first and make straight for the helmsman forward. I'll take the crew aft."

"And if they cut their nets and run?"

"Not likely—nets cost too much. Remember, they're all about the money."

Service had his doubts, but Garwood was in charge, and not all keyed up like Colt Homes had been the other time.

As they drifted in, their sounds were masked by the sound of winches in the trawler, which was shaped like a double-decker baguette. When their nose rubbed the wooden planks of the larger boat, Service went over the gunwale into the opening. Two men on the opposite side were peeling fish from green nylon netting. Two other men were standing forward at the controls.

The eyes of the two men ahead of him widened and one of them shouted, "Oh shit!" Before Service could announce himself, Blake Garwood came vaulting across, bumped him, and stumbled forward into the two men working the net. Service watched as Blake suddenly lifted up and went sprawling over the gunwale of the other side—and was gone. The two men with the nets stood up and looked at him and at the men up front, and nobody seemed to know what had happened or what to do.

"Drop nets!" bellowed one of the men up front as he slammed the twin throttles forward and the boat surged. The two aft crewmen started doing something to the nets.

"Michigan Department of Natural Resources!" Service screamed. "DNR! Stop the fucking boat!"

"Don't stop, boys!" the man at the throttles shouted over the roaring engines.

Service went forward, pulled out his revolver, and ordered, "Stop!" He fired two rounds through the roof. The captain immediately pulled the throttles back and the boat lurched as it lost momentum and gave way to the waves coming onto the bow.

Jesus, Service thought, *Where was Blake?* They had to get him. Fast. The men stared at him and he stared back. No sound. Shit—the jerk had cut the engines off completely. "Start her up again," Service ordered, the revolver still in hand. "You'd better hope my sergeant is all right, or you are in deep fucking shit."

"We never touched him," one of the men in back said.

"You got spotlights?" Service asked.

"Somewhere," the captain said. He was small with a ratty white beard tinged red in the low cabin light. "Find them and get this thing turned around. Take her slow and easy." He could picture the stinking tub running over Garwood.

Ten minutes later a green flare shot up into the night sky and fizzled.

Service saw the origin and had the captain steer toward it. Since firing the shots, the crew had been cooperative. They soon spotted Blake Garwood and hauled him in, placing a blanket over his shoulders.

"Nobody touched me," the sergeant said sheepishly. "I slipped on something, caught my foot, and went over the side. I heard shots."

"I needed to get their attention," Service said.

"You two scared the bejeezus outta us," the captain said. "We come for fish, not to hurt nobody."

"Why'd you run?" Service asked.

"Reflex," the captain said, avoiding eye contact.

Garwood had managed to secure the *Fat Rat* to the trawler before making his dramatic entrance—and exit. Now they headed north to Escanaba, towing the smaller boat. The captain was not happy, but resigned himself to having his trawler impounded until he could post a bond and get a lawyer to work out the return. He made coffee for Garwood, and Service sat smoking and studying the layout. There was a door in the center of the deck. "What's that?"

"We call it the kiddie hole," the captain said. "Guy owned the boat before me used to take his kids out and pull up on shallow shoals and open that door and let his kids dip smelt with nets."

As they approached Escanaba, Service said to his sergeant, "You had marine flares."

"No shit," Garwood said. "I had nightmares since you took your swim, and figured I'd add a little insurance. I bought 'em myself. I got two years until retirement," he added. "Then I'm moving to the mountains in Tennessee and I don't ever want to see another bloody boat."

45

ESCANABA, MAY 26, 1976

"You're dead when I get out."

Serverino "Sandy" Tavolacci was standing outside the Delta County Jail chewing a cigar stump. He was short and wide and built like a wrestler. It was fifty degrees and overcast, but he wore dark sunglasses and a black trench coat with the collar turned up. His hair was brushed straight back and glistened. Tavolacci, Service had learned, was becoming the mouthpiece of choice for major poachers in the central and western Upper Peninsula.

Gar Murray, Delta County's prosecuting attorney, was standing with the defense lawyer. Last year Murray had written a controversial letter to Lansing, declaring that the Garden situation was on the verge of being out of control, and if Director Curry didn't improve support for DNR officers charged with patrolling the peninsula, Murray would publicly disclaim any responsibility for the death or injury to an officer on patrol in the Garden. Further, he would ask the state attorney general to release him from the obligation of enforcing commercial fish laws in any prosecution stemming from a death or injury to DNR personnel. Murray's letter had created a minor furor in Lansing, with lesser lights calling it an act of cowardice; but Len Stone told Service that Murray had written the letter as a friend and supporter of law enforcement. Murray had been trying to force Lansing to do a better job of supporting the same people they were putting at risk. Good goal, lousy tactic.

Service had never met either man.

Murray had hair the color of a female cardinal and eyes that made him look like a predator on a constant lookout for food. Service introduced himself to both men, but Tavolacci immediately turned away and went inside. Service noticed he walked with mincing steps, like something was jammed up his behind.

"Gar Murray," the red-haired man said, shaking Service's hand. "Don't mind Sandy. He's just an asshole."

"By birth or training?" Service shot back.

Murray laughed. "That's pretty good. You feel that way about all lawyers?"

"Only the ones not on my side."

"A true professional," Murray said, clapping him on the back and holding the door open for him. "Shall we?"

Tavolacci was already in the interview room with Moe Lapalme. Both of them looked agitated. "What da deuce is goin' on, eh?" The lawyer asked when Service and Murray walked into the room.

Murray put his briefcase on the table. "Save the Finnglish today, Sandy."

"Let's expedite. I've got other meetings on my docket," the defense attorney said, no trace of Yooperese in his language or pronunciation.

Detective Kobera was twenty minutes late. Lapalme and Tavolacci carried on an extended hushed conversation while they waited, and Service and Murray stepped outside the room.

Kobera arrived, breathing hard, and handed a large envelope to Murray. "Sorry I'm late," he said.

Service looked at the detective. "We get a match?"

"Damn straight," Kobera said. "You want to do the honors?"

"I'm just a game warden."

Murray looked like his mind was elsewhere, but he said, "Sandy's gonna scream for the evidence. Fuck him," Murray added. "I'll mail it to him."

"I'm gonna read Lapalme the charges and his rights," Kobera said.

"We'll arraign in two hours," Murray said. "I've already talked to the judge."

The three men filed into the room. Lapalme looked cocky. Tavolacci looked wary.

Kobera charged Lapalme with attempted murder, grand theft, breaking and entering, conspiracy to commit theft, and fifty-eight other counts involving stolen goods.

Tavolacci said nothing.

Formalities done, the three men got up and walked to the door, where Service stopped and made eye contact with Lapalme. "Nice seein' you, Cap'n."

Lapalme tried to come up out of his chair, but Tavolacci held him down.

"You're dead when I get out," Lapalme said with a low growl.

Kobera looked at Murray. "Threatening an officer of the law?"

"I'll add it," the prosecuting attorney said.

Service said to Lapalme, "I'll be waiting for you."

· 46 ·

GARDEN PENINSULA,
FEBRUARY 14, 1977

"When you least expect it, when you think you're safe, I'll be there."

The parking lot of Bay de Noc High School was jammed with vehicles. Service waited to arrive until fifteen minutes after the scheduled start of the memorial ceremony, and double-parked as near to the entrance as he could get.

A couple of teenage boys saw him get out of his truck and began to follow him.

He walked into the gymnasium and stopped. The casket was at the end of an aisle created by two banks of metal folding chairs. There was a portable lectern in front of the casket where a priest was reading. When the man looked up and saw Service, he stopped and stared.

Grady Service wore his class-A green uniform, his wheel hat tucked under his left arm. He marched forward, looking neither right nor left. He could smell wet wool and ripe bodies packed too close together, but there was no sound and the air felt heavy.

The priest moved aside as Service stepped to the lectern.

Pete Peletier was sitting near the front, on the right side of the aisle. Service locked his eyes on to Peletier's and began. "My name is Grady Service and I am here to say good-bye to my friend, Cecilia Lasurm."

He felt sweat under his arms and began to question his judgment, but continued. "Cecilia was everybody's friend, and the teacher of many of you. That's why you're here—to honor her memory and the contributions she made to all of our lives. Cecilia believed that the actions of a few selfish people should not be allowed to destroy the reputations of all the good people who surround them." He paused to let his words settle in. There was still no sound.

"Cecilia learned a year ago that she was dying," he said. "When she got the diagnosis, she evaluated her situation and decided she would die on her own terms. She refused pain medication, and she kept doing her job: teaching the children of this school, and coming to your homes to help those children who couldn't get here." Another pause. "Cecilia believed that no matter the obstacle, you should keep doing what you think is right. She hated the conflict between people like me and some of you. Her only dream was that we would settle it so that children here could grow up without cringing every time they saw a police car. I came today to say good-bye to my friend, and to tell you that I know many of you share her dream. Will it happen? I don't know. It's in your hands, not mine. And not theirs."

Service looked at Peletier and said, "Pete." All the heads in the gym turned to look at Peletier. "Pete, thank you for the courtesy of inviting me here today. As you and I have discussed many times, we have more in common than we have differences."

The crowd began to murmur as Service did a crisp about-face, walked to the head of the open casket, leaned down, and kissed Cecilia Lasurm on the lips. He straightened up, put on his hat, saluted her, turned sharply, and marched out of the gymnasium in silence.

Peletier caught him by the elbow halfway to his truck and tried to spin him around.

The rat leader's face was flushed. "You cocksucker—I never invited you. It was *you*," Peletier stammered. "You tried to turn 'em against me. You think getting Moe will change anything? We'll never change, do you understand? Never."

Service looked at the man. "I understand, Pete. I'm counting on that—and that's why I'll be back. When you least expect it, when you think you're safe, I'll be there. You and I aren't done."

Service got into his Plymouth and started to pull away as a dozen young men came running toward him, their arms cocked to throw things, but Peletier held up his hands and they immediately dropped their missiles. The last thing he saw was a red-faced Peletier extending his middle finger.

That night he heard that Cecilia Lasurm's house had been torched and destroyed.

PART V

COLD VENGEANCE

47

MARQUETTE-GLADSTONE,
APRIL 22, 2004

"Red rats."

S ervice hated shopping, especially in sprawling chain stores, but Nantz wanted to stop at Kmart in Marquette. She was trying to secure a shopping cart by shouldering her way through shoppers mingling just inside the entrance, when a huge man lumbered out of the crowd, wrapped Grady Service in a bear hug, and lifted his feet off the ground, swinging him around. "Grady, Grady!"

"Put me down, Gumby!"

"Eugene," the man said calmly. "Eugene." He gently lowered Service, opened one side of his blue vest, said, "Badge," and beamed proudly before trundling off to greet another customer.

As usual, Nantz shopped with the focus of a programmed android.

En route to Gladstone she said, "Are you going to tell me what was up with that back there?"

"That what?"

"Don't play thick, Service. The man who lifted you like you were made of Styrofoam."

Service grinned. "Eugene Chomsky."

When no more was said, Nantz said, "Dinner on the twenty-fifth with Vince and Rose, Lorelei and Whit." Vince Vilardo, the doctor who had treated him after his near-death experience in Big Bay de Noc; they had been friends ever since.

Lorelei Timms was the state's new governor, and Whit was her longtime husband. Through a series of serendipitous events, Lorelei Timms had taken a shine to Service, and now the governor and Maridly were fast friends.

"Walter and Karylanne will be there," Nantz added.

This brightened him. Walter was his son, a son he'd known nothing about until last summer. His ex-wife, Bathsheba, had been pregnant when they'd separated and never bothered to tell him. She had died in an aircraft in Pennsylvania during the 9/11 disaster and only afterward did Service learn he was a father, a role he was still trying to adapt to. He and Walter had been through some rough early going as they tested each other, but things were settling down and he liked the boy and enjoyed his company. Karylanne was his Canadian girlfriend, and Nantz was convinced she was "the one." Walter was not yet seventeen and in his third semester at Michigan Tech University in Houghton and was taking spring and summer classes so he could lighten the load for next fall and winter, when he would have a full athletic scholarship and officially join the varsity hockey team he now skated with on an unofficial basis.

"That's good," he said. He was looking forward to watching his son play college hockey.

"You'll be nice to Lorelei," she said in a tone that wasn't a request.

"I'm always nice to the governor."

"Just don't be so damn blunt. Remember, she actually *listens* to you."

"And you don't?"

"When there's something worth hearing."

He put away the groceries while Nantz poured oil into the deep fryer. Yesterday Simon del Olmo, the young CO in Crystal Falls, had dropped by with a box of fresh smelt he had bought from the retail fish house in Stephenson.

"Be fun to go smelting," Nantz said as she began to roll the tiny fish in flour.

"They don't much run up the rivers anymore," he said.

She rolled her eyes. "They gotta have sex *somewhere*, Service. We all do." She held up one of the six-inch-long silvery fish by the tail. "Sex makes more of these."

"They spawn on reefs off creek mouths now," he said.

"You're making that up," she said skeptically.

"One of the fish biologists told me. It's supposed to be a secret."

Nantz rolled her eyes. "Be good to see Walter," Nantz said. "He hasn't been home in weeks."

"I'm going back to the Garden tomorrow," he said. "Fish runs are starting." Because of personnel shortages, he was doubling his duties as a detective with routine game warden patrols.

As a conservation officer for more than twenty years he had spent most of his time policing the Mosquito Wilderness area, where he was like a neighborhood beat cop. Since his promotion to detective his job had changed and instead of patrolling, he took tips directly from both informants and other officers and plunged into cases, covering most of the Upper Peninsula. But the state was short on money and DNR law enforcement was short on people and since January, sergeants and detectives had been doing double duty—their own work, plus covering regular patrols. Part of him was glad to again be doing the job he had done for so long.

"How long has it been?" she asked.

"My last time there was in seventy-six." He omitted Cecilia Lasurm's memorial service the following year.

"You've never said much about the Garden. And who *is* Eugene Chomsky?"

He opened an inexpensive bottle of Malbec, and started taking the smelt out of the oil with tongs while Nantz put new ones in.

"I swear," she said. "Getting you to open up is like pulling teeth. Eugene Chomsky? He treated you like a long-lost brother."

Service kissed her and stepped back. "This is a really long story."

"You know what the Chinese say," she said.

"A journey of a thousand miles starts with a single step?"

"I was thinking a good fuck starts with a single stroke."

"Are you always horny?"

"Right now I'm curious. Talk, Service. No talk, no sex—*capisce?*"

Grady Service talked all night and Maridly Nantz listened, seldom interrupting.

It was after midnight before he finished. He got up from the table to stretch and make more coffee.

"When COs talk about the Garden, they always cringe," she said. "They didn't tell us any of this down at the academy."

"Because it's mostly ancient history," he said. Nantz had been in the DNR academy the year before. She was scheduled to enter the academy again this year—if it was held, which right now seemed iffy because of the state budgetary crisis brought on by the policies of former governor Samuel "Clearcut" Bozian.

"How much longer did it go on after you were out of it?" she asked.

"In May of eighty-three some of our guys got shot at off Ansels Point, and in December of that year, two of our guys tried to bring some illegal nets ashore at Fairport and got jumped by a mob of forty to fifty people, most of them wearing ski masks. It was about two in the afternoon. They were driving up the pressure ridge on shore when the mob came out of nowhere. Rocks got thrown, punches exchanged. Our guys had to pull their weapons to back off the crowd.

"They immediately called the Manistique Troop post for reinforcements, and they sent down three squads with six guys. The mob turned on them, destroyed one of their radios, slashed a tire. They also wrecked one of our snowmobiles and stole the other one, the one with the sled loaded with nets. We never saw the machine, the sled, or the nets again. The Troops took our guys in and tried to retreat, but the rats had cut trees down to block them, and they had to run out through the snow to get around and out. It was a classic ambush. The rats waited until our guys were nearly ashore before they attacked, and after the Troops arrived, they tried to cut them off. Two arrests were made a couple of days later."

"That was seven years after you were involved," she said.

"Hegstrom told them he could buy them ten years, and he pretty much did. The state began buyouts in seventy-nine. Stone and Attalienti had a good plan, but marginal support and no understanding of the realities on the ground from Lansing. We were pretty much on our own, and everybody knew it—especially the rats."

"The conflict went on," she said.

"It did. State money eventually went to those few commercial fishermen who managed to meet the requirements of Order Seventeen. Some of them got almost sixty grand to hand over their nets and give up fishing. Most got a lot less."

"Sixty grand was a lot of money back then."

"The Garden was always about money," he said with a nod, "not a way of life or resisting authority on principle. About six weeks after the so-called Garden Riot, the director decided to attend a public meeting with Garden people. He went up there with an NRC commissioner. The director wasn't a bad guy, but he had less than six months on the job, and went without telling anyone in the U.P. what he was doing. A crowd of two hundred verbally ripped him a new asshole and put him on the defensive, and he told the people that his officers had been overzealous and maybe too hard-nosed, and that some personnel changes might have to be made. He claimed later that all he wanted to do was defuse the situation. Apparently he was thoroughly briefed and backgrounded by the chief, but being told about it and seeing it are two different things. The meeting was news all over the state: 'DNR Director Criticizes Game Wardens,' that sort of headline. Our guys went apeshit, and we damn near had a revolt. The director grudgingly drove back up to Escanaba and spent an entire day with law enforcement and fisheries personnel.

Naturally, he limited it to the district, not understanding that our people from all over the state had done time up here."

"You were at the meeting?" she asked.

"I asked him to give us one specific example of when we had been too hard-nosed, and he had to admit he couldn't. I think he thought he was doing the right thing, meeting with people in the Garden, but it was a major faux pas. The meeting was like Vietnam all over again, the troops getting trashed for the failings of civilian leadership. The director tried to make nice, but nobody wanted to listen."

"Did he take action?"

Service shook his head. "He didn't dare. He had promised the Garden people a plan, but he never delivered it. Our guys knew what had to be done and they kept doing it. Our big mistake was not being hard-nosed enough," he added. "Without the discipline and training of our guys, people could have gotten killed."

Then he told her what he had done, omitting nothing, including his intimacy with Cecilia Lasurm.

"*You* broke the law?" she asked.

"I'm not proud of it, but Attalienti and Stone protected me. If we totaled up damage on both sides, it would have been a push," he said.

"You're rationalizing," she said.

"I should have been fired," he admitted. "It took until seventy-nine to get some court rulings to uphold our right to seize under Order Seventeen. After that the courts began to routinely condemn seized equipment."

"What did you accomplish?"

"I got a better idea of how they operated and who was involved, but all I did was put them on their heels for a bit. They were breaking laws before I got there and they kept doing it after I left, but more locals finally began to come forward; we used a lot of undercovers, and we began to squeeze them hard."

"The court rulings were a major development," she said.

"Yes and no," he said. "Remember what I said about sportfishermen and state policy? After that infamous meeting with the director, a lot of people turned their anger on the Indians, and they started getting what we had been getting from the rats. When violence turned that way, the whole deal got classified as civil rights violations. The feds tried to move in and clean it up, but they didn't handle it as well as we had. Once the Indian issue arose, the violence wasn't just in the U.P. Some of the nastiest stuff took place down around Traverse City and Ludington, but the battles there were sportfishing groups against Indian commercial netters. It wasn't as nasty or sustained as the Garden had been, but because it happened below the bridge, it got a lot more media attention."

"Only the players changed," Nantz said.

"All but us," he said. "About a year after the Garden meeting, a U.S. district court judge signed a consent form for a negotiated settlement among the tribes, who were fighting each other in addition to the sportfishermen. The order closed all gill netting below the forty-fifth parallel, and gave the tribes exclusive rights to northern Lakes Michigan and Huron, and eastern Superior. The problem is that the Indians are human, and just like the rats, they wanted more. Both Bay de Nocs remained closed at the same times and for the same methods as before, so the tribals began to become rats."

"Red rats," she said.

"Yeah," he said with a smile, "and some of the old white rats worked for or with them."

Nantz studied him. "This is what you have to go back to?"

"In some ways it's even more frustrating now. Every tribal member is entitled to take a hundred pounds of fish a day on a subsistence card the tribe issues. Who eats a hundred pounds of fish a year, much less a day? Lake Michigan fish are filled with PCBs and other crap, but the tribals get their take, and our people check their cards and find them taking spawning perch along with walleyes in areas open to them—and there isn't a damn thing we can do to stop it. When we find them in violation, we write citations and send the tickets to the tribal courts for disposition. Meanwhile, the fish they take finds its way down to Chicago and as far away as New York City. We can apprehend and cite, but the tribal courts decide the penalties."

"The tribal courts don't cooperate?"

"Some do and some don't. Some of the magistrates think their brothers are entitled to all the fish in the lake in payment for injustices done two centuries ago. Some magistrates also believe that tribal members have a right to do whatever they want to do outdoors, and the state has no say in it."

He stopped talking and drank some coffee.

Nantz said, "Did Moe Lapalme come after you?"

"Moe spent four years inside, got paroled, broke parole his first week, and disappeared. He got killed in a fight with a commercial fisherman in Cordova, Alaska, in 1990."

"What about the rat leaders?"

"A couple of them branched out into growing dope—Garden Green—and went to prison in the eighties. There's still dope down there, but we have drug teams on top of it most of the time. A couple of the rat leaders moved out of state and got into trouble in other states. A couple are still down there, acting like exalted senior citizens."

"Cecilia Lasurm," Nantz said. "You knew I was going to ask about her."

"She died in 1977," Service said.

"Cancer?"

"Car wreck," he said.

"You didn't say accident."

"She was in a world of hurt and refusing pain meds, and I think she didn't want to go on."

"Where did she die?"

"She obliterated a telephone pole at the bottom of the M-Twenty-Eight hill south of Munising."

Nantz said, "And?"

"The Troops calculated her speed at over a hundred."

"Were there skid marks?"

He nodded. "Enough to allow them to conclude she had tried to stop."

"You don't think she did."

"I think she wanted her daughter to get her insurance. The brake marks were there to prove she didn't want to die." He didn't tell Nantz that Cecilia had talked to him about this a month before she died. She had sworn him to secrecy forever.

"She was decisive to the end," Nantz said.

"The insurance company fought it, but in the end they paid."

"Her daughter got the money?"

Service nodded. "She was sentenced to time in a rehab center and they cleaned her up, but it didn't take. She moved to Minneapolis, blew through the money, overdosed in St. Paul, and died."

"Did you love Cecilia?" Nantz asked quietly.

He didn't answer right away. "No," he said finally. "I admired her courage."

"Do you really think it takes courage to kill yourself?"

"It takes a kind of courage to make the decision. The act is simple once you're committed. It comes down to facing what's best for you and the people you care about."

"That's bullshit," she said. "Suicide is the ultimate selfish act. What happened to Brigid Mehegen?"

"She's a Troop lieutenant now, in Berrien Springs or somewhere down in the southwest corner of the state. Are you jealous?" he asked.

"Are you jealous of all the men I slept with before you?"

"Not until you put it that way," he said.

She smiled with self-satisfaction. "Can we go back to Eugene?"

"Criminal charges were dropped. He's mentally retarded."

"He burned animals alive," Nantz countered.

"Put a ten-year-old's emotions with Ivan Rhino and that's what you can get. Eugene's actually very kind and, in the right company, he does fine. Attalienti hired him to do odd jobs out of the regional office and paid for it out of his own pocket. When Captain Grant came in, he put Eugene on the payroll so he'd have health benefits, and he found a place for him to live near his place on the Dead River."

"When Kmart came to town, Eugene applied for and got the greeter's job all on his own, full-time, with benefits."

"What was that deal with the vest?" she asked.

"When he first started at Kmart, he spotted a shoplifter, flashed the badge we'd given him, challenged him, and ended up throwing the guy through a plate-glass window. He takes his job seriously. The guy was a Cat dealer, high as a hawk in a thermal. The cops came, found a portable lab in the guy's car, and busted him. The guy tried to sue the store from prison, but the case got thrown out. Eugene got to keep his job, but he has to wear his badge inside the vest and show it only to law officers."

"I'm surprised the corporation didn't fire him."

"Every cop in the county went to bat for him. The store manager got the message."

"About that fuck-buddy of yours," she said, but he covered her mouth and hugged her close, and she settled in and let it go.

"She married a Troop lieutenant. They've got two kids," he whispered.

WILSEY BAY CREEK, APRIL 23, 2004

" . . . Far out, dude."

H
e and Nantz had exercised before sunrise, and then had breakfast. She was talking about this and that, but he wasn't paying
close attention. His mind was on the day's work.

Ice-out had been late again this spring, but northerns were moving
up the streams to marshy areas to spawn, and walleyes had been congregated in the mouths of rivers and creeks for more than a week. They
would soon surge upstream looking for spawning gravel where they
would remain for several days. While congregated for spawning, the fish
were extremely vulnerable to poaching.

This afternoon he had scouted the upper Tacoosh and found
walleyes collected in some rapids. He drove from the Tacoosh to the
Whitefish, hid his truck in some trees, and hiked a third of a mile west to
the river. There were even more fish here than in the Tacoosh, but the
Whitefish's cedar floodplain was still pocked with runoff, and he had to
island-hop his way in and out. Scouting finished, he climbed up a small
rise on all fours and sat down in the grass to have a cigarette. The team
wouldn't meet until four. He had lots of time to sit and enjoy the solace
and the sounds of the swollen river below him.

A doe wandered into the open from some aspens to his right. He made
a *whoosh* sound to see her react. Her head snapped toward him, ears alert,
but immediately looked back the other way. Something over there interested her more than him. She finally turned and bolted away, her flag high.

He leaned over to lower his profile in the grass and watched. After a
few minutes he saw the silhouettes of two men moving through the
cedars. Now and then one of them splashed in one of the pools. He took
out his binoculars and zeroed in on the movement. Too dark to make
out real detail, but one of the men had a stick on his right side. Spear? In
the middle of the afternoon? This would be too easy! He crawled a little
closer to the lip of the hill. Poachers didn't linger long when they were
spearing and netting in rivers. They'd get in, get their fish, and get out.

Fifteen minutes later he heard the men coming back. A game trail led along the bottom of the hill, following the contour. He let them reach the trail, stood up, and slid down. "DNR!"

The men froze. A small brown-and-white mongrel with floppy ears lowered its head and began barking.

"Quiet, Oliver," one of the men told the dog.

"How's it going, guys?" Service asked.

"Lookin' for steelhead," one of the men said. Both men were carrying unassembled spinning rods. One man had a net over his shoulder. It was too small for steelhead.

"No steelies here," Service said. "You've got to go upriver about a mile. There's good spawning gravel up that way."

"We drove down from Marquette," the man said. "Runs up there are lousy so far this spring."

"Our first time for steelhead," the other man said. "There's all kinds of big bass in the river down there." The man looked over his shoulder.

They were walleyes, not bass, but he didn't correct them. "You guys weren't in there long."

"No steelhead. You saw us?"

He did not tell them he'd mistaken their rods for spears.

"How far upstream did you say?" the man asked again. "For the steelies?"

Service told them how to drive up to it. "Too far to hike."

The little dog kept jumping against his leg and licking him, his tail wagging.

He poured coffee when he got back to the truck. Fishing rods as spears? This was not the way to start a patrol, and he wondered if he was starting to lose his edge.

He knew both rivers would provide good hunting for the next few nights, but when he got to the team meeting at the new Escanaba district office near the Mead Plant, Eddie "Gutpile" Moody and Grant Ebony reported to the others that they had pinched three tribal spearing crews at Wilsey Bay Creek last night at the bottom of the Stonington Peninsula. Tonight Moody and Ebony were headed south of Escanaba to Chigger Creek and the Cedar River, but they thought someone should hit Wilsey again, certain that poachers would not expect the DNR two nights in a row in the same location.

"You can make book the word's out today that we were there last night," Ebony concluded. "They won't be expecting more company."

Candace McCants was down from the Mosquito, which was her turf now. Another six officers had come in from the western counties where there were no fish runs.

"I'll take Wilsey," McCants said. "Grady, you want to partner up?"

He agreed, and they sat with Moody and Ebony getting briefed on Wilsey Bay. Service wasn't paying attention, knowing the Korean-born McCants would absorb what they needed. He was feeling some anxiety about going to the Stonington instead of the Garden, but duty was duty, and there was always tomorrow night. He had not thought much about Cecilia Lasurm in years, or even the Garden, for that matter, but last night's talk with Nantz had conjured a flood of memories—of how pensive some of the officers were before patrols, of Homes cowboying across the ice, his swim and rescue, Garwood's swim and the Wisconsin poachers, rocks pounding the sides of their vehicles during land runs, the wild ride with Stone in his truck, the lifting shed being crunched by the rat truck—all of it. Stone, Homes, and Garwood were retired now, Homes just three years ago, and like Stone, still living in the U.P. Garwood had moved to the hills of Tennessee, just as he'd said he would.

Attalienti had been a good captain, but when Cosmo Metrovich finished his run as acting chief, Metrovich had retired, and Attalienti had been sent south to be captain of the southern law zone. Another captain had been assigned in his place, and when he retired, was replaced by Captain Ware Grant. Only during the past couple of years had he gotten close to Captain Grant, who for the past two years had faced some health issues. Sooner or later Grant had to retire, and Service knew eventually he would also have to face the same decision. He had put in way more time than he needed to retire with full benefits right now, but he had recently been promoted to detective—and though the promotion initially had been unwanted and unsettling, he was getting accustomed to the job and finding it a challenge. Even his paranoia about giving up the Mosquito Wilderness had abated. McCants had taken it over from him, and he had total confidence in her ability.

A horseblanket named Surdy had once told him to keep doing the job as long as he was physically able and it was still interesting and fun, which meant he didn't have to think too hard about retiring anytime soon.

"You're creeping me out tonight," McCants said as they walked out to her truck through the rain.

"Just tonight?"

She jabbed him in the ribs with an elbow.

It had rained all day and was supposed to last another twenty-four hours. There were flood warnings for the western counties. He checked the digital thermometer in her truck: thirty-eight. The water wouldn't be much better, and he was glad he was dressed for it: nylon-wool underwear, a second layer of wool, wool socks and uniform pants, wool shirt, bulletproof vest, parka, insulated rain bibs, 400 mg Thinsulate boots. He'd be wet, but he wouldn't freeze. When he first began his career, he had barely noticed the cold. Now he fretted continuously about dressing properly. Age, he thought grimly.

"They'll be out tonight," McCants said as they pulled into the Shell station in Gladstone. She began filling their tank on a state credit card. "The weather sucks. Why do the assholes think we don't work in crappy weather or off the beaten path?"

He left her and went inside and bought a half-dozen candy bars, two large bags of Fritos, and filled their thermoses with hot coffee. They'd need caffeine, carbs, and sugar in this weather.

"You know Wilsey?" she asked as they passed through Rapid River.

"Not really," he said. "You?"

"Never been there before. Did you hear what Grant and Gutpile said about the culvert?"

He had not paid attention. "A *culvert*?" He hated culverts because they pinched down streams, and when the melt was on, pushed the waters up. "We could have used a daytime recon down there," he complained. "I checked the upper Tacoosh and Whitefish this afternoon. There were herds of eyes in both."

"You want to hit one of them instead?" she asked.

"No, they're expecting us to cover Wilsey."

She said, "Five Thirteen south to K-Twenty-four and east till we cross the creek." She grinned. "It sounds like the route to the Emerald City."

"Yeah—follow the yellow mud road."

"Grant said they hid their truck west of the creek. He said there were some northerns up, but not a lot. With this weather they might be in or they might not. Let's cross the creek and see if they're in. If not, we can double back to Squaw Creek."

Squaw Creek was eight miles north of Wilsey Bay, and they would cross it on their way south.

"Pike come up the Squaw?" he asked.

"Mostly eyes."

"Sounds like a plan," he said.

"I've got a thermal imager," she said. "You bring your generation-three?"

"We have a thermal imager now?"

"I borrowed it from a Troop. It's a video unit, but it'll do the job for us—especially in this soup."

The department issued a certain number of infrared binoculars to each district, but they were second-generation and depended on ambient light. Service had bought a set of generation-threes from the Cabela's catalog. His featured an internal light source, which made them effective in total darkness.

"Aren't we the techies," McCants said with a laugh. "There's a small issue down here. Tribals can spear below the annual average waterline, but not above it."

Service looked at her. "What brain surgeon came up with that?"

She shrugged. "Does it matter?"

"Hell yes, it matters. We've got heavy runoff. How the hell do we determine the average annual waterline or floodplain in these conditions?"

"Don't get bent out of shape. Grant said they checked it out yesterday afternoon. The line's about fifty yards below the culvert. He stuck a six-foot pole in the bank to mark the limit."

"How big's the culvert?"

"Five- or six-foot diameter," she said.

"Average annual waterline," he complained. "This is bullshit."

McCants chuckled. "You'd hate it if this job was cut and dried."

"I must be a happy man."

"You are; just cranky."

When they turned east on K-24, McCants turned off all their lights to run dark. The culvert ran under a steep earthen berm and the road crossed over the top. McCants stopped on the berm and Service flashed the external spotlight down into the water.

"It's cooking like Niagara," he said, "and all stirred up. I can't see shit down there."

"I'll find a place to turn around. We'll stash the truck west of the creek and walk down to take a closer look."

They drove east nearly a half-mile before McCants found a driveway into a camp built back in a ragged line of cedar trees. As she turned left into the driveway, Service glanced back down the road over her shoulder. "Lights on the road behind us," he said.

"Damn," McCants said, cutting the truck past the cabin and nosing it close to the building's north wall.

Service quickly walked to the southeast corner of the building, looked west, and saw that the lights were still coming. "They stopped for a sec and then came on," he said. "At the crick, maybe."

"They use a light?" she asked as they went back to the north side of the building and stood between the wall and her truck.

"Couldn't tell," he said. Visibility was terrible.

The lights turned into the camp driveway thirty feet from where they stood, stopped, backed up, and went back to the west.

"Did they see our tire tracks?" she asked as they jogged out into the road to watch what the vehicle did.

The vehicle's brake lights blinked, a couple of small spotlights came on, and then the vehicle moved on.

"They're definitely looking," McCants said. "Let's saddle up. We might as well work from here."

They fetched their packs, flashlights, thermoses, and equipment, and began to jog down the south side of the muddy road, Service following behind her. "I can't believe they didn't see our tracks," McCants said over her shoulder.

He answered, "Like the boys said, they aren't expecting the DNR two nights in a row."

"I don't see the lights anymore," McCants reported.

The rain was suddenly heavier, and it was so dark that Service could barely see her even though she was no more than six feet ahead.

"Grant said there are some boulders and hummocks of hard ground in the marsh grass south of the road," she said.

"You get the tickets tonight," he said as they picked their way along through the rocks in knee-deep water. The marsh grass came up to his thighs, and several times he barked his leg against rocks he didn't see.

"You just don't want the paperwork," McCants said. "Still no lights," she added. "Maybe they decided to move on."

"How close are we to the creek?" Service asked.

"About a hundred yards. Can't you see it?"

He couldn't, but despite the sound of the downpour, he thought he could make out the the roar of water boiling out of the culvert.

McCants picked her way along like she had X-ray vision, and eventually stopped. "Light," was all she said. They were still in knee-deep water. "There," she said, "two o'clock. Let's set up here," she added.

Service bent over and groped around, felt a hump of firm ground. He got on his side on the east side of the cover, slid off his pack, and got out his night scope.

"See it?" she asked.

"The rubber eyepiece fell off this damn thing," he grumbled. It did that a lot.

"Two flashlights moving just left of us," she said. "They have them pointed at the ground. Branching off now, one to our left, one to our right, headed upstream toward the culvert."

"Are they in the water?" His night vision used to be exceptional. No longer.

"I can't tell," she said.

Neither could he. How could she see at all? She was curled up an arm's length away and he couldn't see her through the wall of rain.

She clicked on the thermal imager, which threw out backlight, and lowered the device to just behind the top of the rock.

"They just took a fish," she said. "Look."

He scootched over to her and saw red, yellow, and green outlines of two people. One held the light, the other held a slender black straight line in front. "The dark line's a spear?" he asked. He'd already misread one silhouette today. Suddenly the man made a downward thrust and stumbled around.

"I think he just nailed another one," he said, releasing the device and sliding to his right to escape the glare. Now he was completely blind. "Goddamn thing blasted my night vision," he said. "How far from the road are we, and are they above the marker?"

"The road's just over to our right, and I think they're well above the marker," she said as the rain pounded them, making a steady *whooshing* sound. "I think the other guy just got a fish. The lights are converging."

He saw nothing.

"Move on them?" she asked.

"Let them take another," he said, his eyes beginning to readjust, but not fast enough.

"Got another," she said. "They're together and one of the lights is flickering. I think the battery's going bad. Let's leave the gear and move!" she whispered as she got up and bolted ahead into the rain and black.

He followed, but stopped after a few steps. Where the hell was she? He could hear the rush of the creek ahead. Had she veered left from their hide or gone straight ahead? Probably the latter: Candi always went right to the heart of things, taking all problems head-on.

He felt stupid standing still and began to ease forward. Had she cut through the creek or gone over the berm road? He had no idea. He stopped and listened to see if he could hear her boots, but there was only the rain and creek pouring through the culvert. She probably kicked it in gear, trying to intercept the poachers before they got to their vehicle. *You don't have to run*, he told himself. Let her young legs do the hard work. *Where the hell was the road?* He stopped again, moved his eyes while keeping his head still, trying to get his rods and cones working. No good. He had angled right from the hide, right? Not sure. *Shit.* The creek was ahead. He could hear it. Slow down, you can't catch up now. She's too damn fast. Move deliberately, be ready to help when she yells. He chuckled involuntarily. She had bolted like a deer. *You used to do that*, he told himself. Get the lead out and stop walking like Sandy Tavolacci, he admonished himself. He took one stride confidently and the ground felt solid and smooth. *Okay, go!* He took another stride.

There was a moment when he imagined he was flying, until gravity took hold, his right thigh struck something hard and sharp, and he was underwater and pulling instinctively with his arms to surface. He came up gasping, his chest heaving from the shock of the cold and the surprise. *Jesus Christ!* The current was spinning him counterclockwise. He tried to do a couple of breaststrokes against it, but immediately knew it was too strong, the force too concentrated near the culvert opening. The culvert! *Fuck!* He looked, saw the opening, black and gaping, and realized he was going to go down headfirst. Desperately he kicked and stroked and managed to turn his body around, and then he was inside, on his back, racing boots first down the black tube, rocks and debris banging the back of his head and back. Ahead he saw a gray circle, light at the end of the tunnel. He almost laughed. You are in the fucking water, you clumsy fucking moron!

The water shot him out of the tube like a bullet and the outfall swallowed him as he smacked his right thigh against another large rock, the impact turning him clockwise onto his stomach. He tried to swim up and get onto his back, and looked up to catch a glimpse of a light shining at him before momentum and current swept him downstream into the night.

He tried to swim with the current, and as he did, he accelerated, making his body ride higher so that a couple of kicks and backstrokes enabled him to get on his back, his feet facing Lake Michigan. He considered yelling out, but decided to keep quiet. He had no idea where Candi was, or if she had approached the suspects yet. *Don't fuck it up for her*, he told himself. It's bad enough to stumble into the river, asshole. Don't fuck up the patrol.

Think, he told himself. How far out to the big lake? Two hundred, three hundred yards? The creek was up and fast, but no way it can carry you that far.

Could it? Put out your arms, Christ on the cross going down the river. Wait for obstacles. When you feel something, catch it with your arm, kick your legs, scissor out of the main current into a side eddy.

He missed the first four or five rocks, but managed to stay relaxed and focused, closing his eyes to concentrate on feeling rather than sight. Ow! *Damn!* A large rock bashed the end of his elbow and he missed grabbing hold as he recoiled from the pain. Okay, you survived the big lake. This pissant creek isn't going to win this thing. Get your head in the game. He missed two more rocks before he caught a third one with his left arm, and violently twisted his body left and kicked his right leg over and felt himself drop out of the main current into smoother water. He was still moving downstream, but with less speed. He put both arms down and felt for the bottom and found only cobble, some of the rocks sharp. He jammed his gloved fingers between the rocks like a rock climber and started pulling himself to the left, toward shore.

His face was in pea gravel and sand, his lower body still in water. Hypothermia, he told himself. Replay evolution, crawl out of the slime, get to your feet, *move it*. Motion is life, rest is death.

He got his knees beneath him, put one foot out, used his fist as a prop on the gravel, and pushed up. Hell of a ride, he thought, not wanting to think about all the things that might have happened, all of them negative. Move, don't stand, stop gawking.

A flashlight was shining about seventy-five yards to the north and above him. Was the rain letting up? He could see the berm and the creamy gray froth of water being expelled from the culvert.

"Ca-di?"

"Up here," she called down to him.

He stumbled forward, his clothes heavy with water. He was cold. He got to the bottom of the steep berm and started to scramble up but lost his grip, hit his face in the mud, and slid down. He immediately started back up and kept scrambling until he was facedown on the road.

"We've got them," McCants said. "They went east toward the dead end. They have to come back this way."

"I-wa-in-wa-tah," he said, thinking he sounded like Eugene.

"I know," she said, "we have them."

"Don-un-stan," he said. Why couldn't he talk normally?

"Grady?" Concern in her voice.

"Wen-true-cul-ver," he said, trying to enunciate.

"Oh Jesus!" she said. "Are you okay?"

He felt her hands on him. "Okay," he said. "Okay."

"Are you hurt?"

"Cold," he said, his teeth chattering.

"Here they come," she said.

He looked up, saw headlights approaching, reached for his flashlight. Not there. The lanyard had ripped off during his swim.

McCants lit up the vehicle, a Japanese model. "DNR," she said, letting her light sweep inside. He saw three people, two up front, one in back.

"Dee-en-ah," Service parrotted, knowing it came out convoluted. He tried to take a step but tripped on something, bent down, and clawed at it with both hands. A broom? He worked to lift it.

McCants said, "Their spear. They must've dumped it."

She ordered the driver out of the vehicle. His face was pale under her light beam, his eyes wide with fear as he stared at Service. Why wasn't the man squinting?

"Get the truck, Grady."

"Okay."

Safer to keep moving. Her extra keys were in the thigh pocket of his bibs. He stopped, took off his waterlogged gloves, dropped them on the ground, and groped with numb fingers in the pocket. He heard the keys jingle, clawed them out, and held them in both hands, manipulating them until he got a key between the first two fingers of his right hand. He picked up the gloves, stuffed them in the left thigh bib pocket, and began walking down the middle of the road, not caring about prints now, his boots squishing with each step. Face and hands frozen and numb, feet warming up—*A good sign*, he told himself. Visibility not good but better, his legs stiff, clothes heavy. He squinted into the rain and tried to move steadily if not quickly.

Finally at the truck, the fucking thing parked almost flush against the cabin wall. Jesus, Candi! Go through the passenger side. No, computer and commo console are in middle. Too easy to get hung up.

Squeeze through here, think skinny. He held the key in his right hand, groped an inside pocket for his lighter, found one of the four he carried. Lighter in left hand, he tried it, but got only a raspy sound. *Shit.* Again, go slow. This time it ignited briefly and went out, but he saw the lock. Okay, again. You can do this. Candi's alone with three poachers. Got to get back to her. He fumbled to get the key against the lock with his right hand, tried the lighter again, and got only a brief flame and light, but it was enough. He pushed the key in, turned it right, and felt the lock give way with a soft *pop*.

He hit his chin trying to squeeze into the driver's seat, but finally made it. He got the engine started, put it in gear, touched the gas. No movement. What now? Think it through. He sat still. She had turned left. Wheels still that way? Yes. He straightened them out, tried the gas. Still stuck. Okay, reverse. Tried that, moved a little, felt another thump. What the hell? Okay, back to drive, cut wheel slightly right, accelerator. This time the truck surged forward. He turned on his headlights. *Shit.* There was a windrow of small trees in front of him. Tired of obstacles and blockages, he floored the accelerator, crashed over and through the trees, bounced wildly into a rock field and fishtailed, cutting the wheel hard left and back to the right when he saw the muddy road.

McCants had the driver outside the car. Service pulled up behind them, lit them with his headlights, and got out. The man stared at him as he grasped his arm and ushered him around the truck and pushed him into the passenger seat. He stood outside, shuffling his feet and shivering while McCants interviewed the three people, one at a time, the poachers in the passenger seat, Service standing outside in the rain, shivering.

Tickets written and all three released, McCants searched the creek bank and recovered four dead pike while Service stumbled back into the marsh grass and retrieved their packs.

"Open beers in the car," she said as they headed west to leave the Stonington.

"You write them?"

"All three are nineteen. They were really polite," she said.

"Turn on the goddamn heater!" he grumbled.

"It's on full," she said, stopping the truck, digging her thermos out of her pack and filling the cup with coffee for him. "They swear their tribal magistrate told them anything below the culvert is fair."

"Which magistrate?"

"Etta, in Manistique."

"She wouldn't tell them that," Service said.

"Well, the rule is confusing."

"Out of our hands," he said. "If she told them that, she'll dump the tickets. If not, she'll nail them. You write MIP?"

"No. You could barely talk when you came up on the berm," she said. "Are you sure you're okay?"

"Fine. Some bumps, cold."

She began to laugh.

"What?"

"After you went for the truck, the driver asked me if you had been hiding in the culvert."

"You said?"

"Yeah, he's got a special suit! He said, 'Far out, dude . . .'"

They both laughed. McCants said, "Every poacher in the U.P. is gonna be checking culverts from this night forward. How does it feel to create a legend?"

"Bite me," he said.

"You're lucky the culvert wasn't blocked with debris," she said. "Why didn't you yell for help?"

"I didn't want to mess up your tickets."

"*Jesus*, Grady! There will be other tickets! Been me, you'da heard me twenty miles away. I want to be like you when I grow up, Grady Service."

"I stumbled into the fucking river," he said. "How many of you have done that?'

"But you had on your special suit," she said.

He laughed, but he was also thinking that the poachers had seen him come tumbling out of the culvert, and if he had been in serious trouble, or injured, he would have drowned or died of exposure because they had fled. It was a sobering thought.

49

GLADSTONE, APRIL 24, 2004

"You want me to make some finger Jell-O too?"

He got as far as the living room, his joints aching, dropped his wet clothes in a pile, and curled up on the couch under a fleece blanket. Cat immediately jumped onto his hip and kneaded the blanket to make a nest. Usually her claws dug in and he batted her away, but tonight he was too tired and numb to care, much less feel. He had found the animal years before in a bag of kittens that somebody had drowned. Why this one had survived was beyond him, but it had turned into a feline misanthrope, which made her an animal he could relate to.

Later Newf came down and slobbered in his face. "Leave me alone!" he growled at the 130-pound female Canary Island mastiff. A former girlfriend, a veterinarian, had given the animal to him, and Newf's presence over the past couple of years had finally begun to erode his fear of dogs. He shoved the animal's massive back away, and she plopped on the floor beside the couch and began to snore.

"You reek!" Nantz said, brushing her fingers over his forehead.

Service opened his eyes, felt stiffness and pain.

"Wanna start the day off right?" Nantz asked.

"Oh God," he said, covering his face with his arm.

She cupped her hand behind her ear. "Grady Service refusing sex? Did I hear right?"

"Help me up," he said, extending his hand.

"Honey!" she said when the blanket dropped away from him. "Your thighs!"

He stared down at reddish-blue bruises the size of silver dollars.

"Your face," she added.

"Windburn," he said, trying his legs.

"It looks like you toweled off with sandpaper."

He touched his jaw. No feeling. He hobbled on up to the shower and stood a long time, letting the hot water cascade off him. He didn't want to think about last night.

He started to brush his teeth and stopped when he felt the top two teeth move. What the hell? He leaned toward the mirror, opened his mouth, and probed with his fingers. The slightest pressure pushed the teeth back to almost ninety degrees. He jiggled each of them and felt that they were barely connected, that it wasn't so much the teeth as the gums that had given way. "Just fucking great," he said. His mouth wasn't sore, and there was no mark. When had the teeth come loose?

Nantz was in the kitchen. He got coffee and sat down.

"We need to call Vince," she said.

"We're not calling anyone," he spat back at her.

She tilted her head, put small bowls on the table in front of each of their places, and went back to pour orange juice.

He looked down at the bowl, a poached egg atop a slice of Brie, both on a thick slice of sweet onion and tomato. The egg had been peppered, and a dollop of Tabasco sauce lay on the membrane over the yolk. He broke open the egg with the tine of his fork, put some in his mouth, heard the loose teeth click and move, and put down the fork.

"What's wrong?" Nantz asked. "You love this breakfast."

He sighed, opened his mouth, and wiggled the teeth.

It took a moment for her to understand. "I'm calling Owie," she said. Owen Joe was their dentist, but everyone called him Owie.

"No," he said with such force she didn't try to argue.

He was too sore and stiff to run, ride the stationary bike, or lift weights, but he sat with Nantz while she went through her workout, and felt his tongue involuntarily poking at the loose teeth.

"The Garden last night?" she asked as she dried sweat off her face and shoulders with a towel.

"Stonington," he said. "With Candi." He offered no further information.

"You can't work tonight. You can hardly move."

"Leave it alone, Mar. I'm going." He had been waiting for this night for a long, long time.

He warmed canned chicken soup for lunch. Neither hot nor cold liquids seemed to affect the loose teeth. At least he could have his coffee.

"*Canned* soup?" Nantz asked disapprovingly. "You want me to make some finger Jell-O too?"

"Can you load it with carbs?" he asked.

"You need a dentist *and* a shrink," she said.

He packed his gear bag and ruck after lunch and took a one-hour nap. He got dressed and was ready to leave at 3 P.M.

Nantz walked out to the patrol truck with him and handed him his thermos of coffee. "You're going to the Garden," she said. It wasn't a question. "Remember, we have dinner with Lori tomorrow night."

"You had to remind me," he groused. He put the vehicle into reverse and backed up. He saw Nantz standing by the driveway staring at him, hands on her hips, a sure sign that she was unhappy.

50

GARDEN PATROL, APRIL 24–25, 2004

"Buy us a beer, Pete?"

McCants approached him before the group meeting. "Partners tonight?"

He shook his head, and when it was his turn to talk during the meeting, he said, "Garden Creek," and eyebrows bobbed all over the room.

Sergeant Phil Callow said, "You know policy. No solos to the Garden." Callow had been promoted to sergeant in January from the Newberry district. His old friend, Lisette McKower, now the lieutenant in Newberry, told him that Callow was a good man, and would make a good sergeant once he lost some of his anal ways over regulations. She pleaded with Service to give him time.

"I'm not your report," Service said. "This one is my call." Could the others hear his teeth clicking when he talked?

McCants frowned across the table at him.

"Garden Creek?" the sergeant said.

"Eyes," Service said.

"Yeah," Gutpile Moody, the longtime Schoolcraft County officer chimed in, nodding his head. The other COs all nodded in support.

"I don't like this solo deal," Callow said, not wanting to give in so easily to what could be interpreted as a one-man mutiny.

"I've got my eight-hundred if I need help," Service said. U.P. conservation officers had gotten the 800-megahertz radio system less than a year before; game wardens below the bridge had gotten it a year earlier, and state police throughout the state had been on the system for nearly three years. The state police had intended that it remain their dedicated system, but a state congressman from the U.P., his son a CO, had fought to get the DNR on the same system, and had succeeded. The 800 allowed someone on the system to talk to and monitor any other officer in the state.

"Think I'll take a run down to Poodle Pete," Moody said.

"I don't know that one," Callow said.

"Poodle Pete Creek," Moody said. "It's four miles east of Garden."

"Walleyes?" Callow asked.

"Eyes," Moody said, nodding.

"Okay," the sergeant said, finally relenting. "At least somebody will be close to the Lone Ranger."

Moody stood beside Service after the meeting and Service asked, "Walleyes in Poodle Pete?"

Moody shrugged. "Sounded good to me," he said. "For all I know it's barren, but if I look tonight, then we'll know, right?"

McCants joined them. "I'll be with Gut tonight. You want to borrow my floaties?"

"Bite me," Service said.

"Garden Creek—for real?" she asked.

"For real," he said.

"Eyes?"

"Would I bullshit you?" They were for real. After Lasurm's memorial service, three Garden citizens had contacted him and told him they supported Lasurm. One of them was a teacher. They had been providing information since late 1977, and some of it he passed on to the department. But his special interest was Pete Peletier, and over the years he had discovered that Pete had a weakness. The buildings over Garden Creek had stumped him until the night when he and Blake Garwood caught the Wisconsin trawler and he saw the "kiddie hole." It had taken some time to confirm his suspicions, but eventually he had.

The informant who had tracked Peletier closest was gone to Green Bay for a few days. She had left her garage unlocked for him. It was two blocks from the village center, and thirty feet from Garden Creek.

Service ran dark more than twelve miles toward town before going off-road three miles north of the village and eventually working his way to the town's edge from the east and into the woman's garage.

Peletier no longer led rat fishermen on the Peninsula. Some of the old rats had lasted to collect state payoffs, and now most of them were gone. But the fish still spawned every April in huge numbers, and there was money yet to be made. The new rats were younger, many of them coming from other areas of the U.P. to poach the Garden's rich spawning grounds. Locals still partook, but not in the numbers they had years before. Peletier had been the rat leader and the smartest of the group, staying out of the limelight, but he had never stopped poaching. Only his tactics had changed.

Service had considered making the grab years before, but by then he was no longer part of the core Garden team, and at the time, the equipment was not up to what he needed. Only in recent years had equipment for COs dramatically improved. Service got his exposure suit out of his bag and slid into it. The suit afforded both insulation and flotation, and was designed for prolonged exposure to extreme cold. Such suits and shorter float coats were now standard wear for lake patrols. The only drawback was color: electric orange. He got around this by wearing black coveralls over the suit. He waited in the garage until midnight before moving stealthily down to Garden Creek, sliding into the water, and letting the current carry him downstream feet first. He had taken 800 milligrams of ibuprofen with some peanut butter crackers an hour before, careful to chew on the sides of his mouth. Though he was still stiff from last night, some of the pain from his body had relented. Like most officers he used a lot of ibuprofen. If ever there was a blue-collar magic drug, this was it.

Years before he had stood in the opening between buildings north of Roadie's and gotten angry over the effigy suspended over Garden Road. The effigy had rotted away over the years, though a fragment of rope still dangled from the overhead wire as a reminder. As the creek carried him beneath the first set of buildings, he put up his gloved hand and used the heel of his hand to retard his speed and progress until he was almost into the gap; from there he propelled himself over to the rocks. It was no more than three feet from the floor above him to the surface of the creek. It was entirely black behind the buildings. Light from the street filtered through openings in the structures, but illuminated nothing underneath.

He moved into the rocks, took off his pack, got out his thermos while he waited, and watched beneath the buildings thirty feet to the north of him. The creek passed under them and then swung southwest under Garden Road. According to his informant, Peletier, having been dropped off by one of his grandchildren, would already be inside. The rat leader had purchased the building in 1990 under the name of one of his children, and had installed a sign in front that indicated it was a cabinet shop. No such work went on inside, and the informant said it was not unusual for Peletier to take a hundred pounds of walleyes each night until the spawning run was complete. He gave away most of the fish to friends, his poaching not intended to feed himself or generate cash, but to simply keep doing what he had always done, and to spit in the eye of the DNR. It was the strangest poaching setup he had ever seen, and typical of Peletier's penchant for secrecy.

Service used his infrareds to scan the black water. The internal beam made dozens of white goggle eyes litter the green scope. The fish were packed into the stream. He checked his watch, stashed his pack and scope deeper in the rocks, and slid back into the water to let the current sweep him down to the next set of ancient wooden buildings. As he slid under the floor he got hold of a joist and stopped. He stabilized himself, squatting on the cobble bottom, felt around for the seams in the floor above him, and pushed back against a greasy black post to wait.

The door opened about thirty minutes after he got into position. There was only the slightest glow of light from above, and unless someone had been looking for it they would never have seen it. A long-handled net splashed into the water and swept around before being pulled upward. Even in the low light Service saw the flash of a fish in the net and heard it flopping on the floor above him.

The netting continued for more than an hour. After each round the fish tended to scatter away from the activity and the trapdoor closed, only to open again and resume when the fish had calmed. Service counted twenty-two fish. He could hear them on the wooden floor above, their muted flopping, the sound of many people brushing the heels of their hands over the tight skin of a kettle drum.

The next time the net came down, Service grabbed it with both hands, drove it upward into the hole, and followed it. Popping through the opening, he heard someone grunt and fall heavily to the floor.

Service emerged through the trapdoor, turned on his flashlight, and lit the man.

"Hey! What da hell!" Peletier shouted.

"I bet you thought I'd forgotten, Pete."

"Youse!"

"Buy us a beer, Pete?"

"My arm," the old man said.

"Are you okay?"

"Youse nearly give me a heart attack."

Service said, "Don't worry, Pete. If your arm doesn't work, I'll grab your wallet for you."

"Dis is trespass," Peletier protested.

"Stop whining, Pete," Service said, holding out his hand to help the man up. "Let's get that beer."

He cuffed his prisoner, gathered the fish in a burlap bag the poacher had brought, took the man's wallet out of his pocket, led him onto the street, and locked the building for him. "You've got some nice fish here," Service said, dragging the bag along. He guessed more than a hundred pounds, which at ten dollars a pound meant a fine of court costs plus more than a thousand dollars.

They went between the buildings and Service reached underneath and pulled out his pack before walking toward Roadie's two hundred yards away. He called Moody on the 800. "You guys wanna grab a beer?"

"For real?" Moody radioed back.

"Roadie's."

"Rolling," Moody said.

The patrol truck arrived with its blue lights flashing before Service and Peletier reached the tavern.

McCants looked at the bag of fish and said, "That's a real mess."

"Pete's," Service said, urging him up the stairs.

The blue lights had brought bar patrons to the front windows, but as the officers walked through the door, they retreated. Service headed directly for the bar where he put the sack of flopping fish on top, pulled out a stool for Peletier, climbed up on one next to him, and unlocked his cuffs.

"Four beers," Service told the bartender, who had a Rasputinish beard and eyes to match.

"Youse missed last call," the man said.

"You'll make an exception tonight," Service said, looking around. There were about a dozen people standing back in the shadows. "In fact, put a round up for everybody in the house."

The bartender hesitated.

Peletier nodded, "Do it, Al."

A roly-poly waitress helped the bartender set bottles on the bar top.

Service got out his ticket book, handed Peletier's wallet to him, and said, "Take out your license, please."

Service began writing and stopped. "You got a fishing license, right, Pete? You know you need a new one after March first."

Peletier shook his head. When the tickets were finished, Service tore off his copies and put the originals on the bar. "No license, fishing during the closed season, using illegal methods, and taking during the closed season. You don't have to appear at the court, Pete. You can call them and find out how much the fine is and mail it in. You have ten days to contact the court; otherwise, a warrant will be issued for your arrest."

Service turned to look at the others who were standing back from the bar. "Put a beer in your hand," he said.

The people moved slowly to the bar and lined up. Service removed Peletier's handcuffs.

Service lifted his bottle. "To the DNR."

Nobody drank, and Service chuckled. "Yeah, I can see how that would stick in your craws. C'mon boys, drink up and relax. No need to check for sugar in your gas tanks or pinched fuel lines tonight." Service looked at Peletier. "Long time coming, Pete, and it doesn't begin to make up for all you did, but something is better than nothing." Service paused. "The state pays me to do this job, but tonight I'd pay the state."

Peletier shook his head, rolled his eyes, and smiled. "Yeah, youse got me good, eh. But it took a long time."

Service picked up the bag of fish and headed for the door, flanked by Moody and McCants.

They dropped Service at the garage where his truck was hidden. "Sugar in gas tanks?" McCants asked.

"History," Service said, feeling as good as he had felt in a long time.

"You are unfuckingbelievable," McCants said.

Service looked her in the eye and grinned.

FORD RIVER, APRIL 25, 2004

"Every legend deserves a monument."

In preparation for retirement, Vince and Rose Vilardo had built a small log home on an oxbow in the Ford River. The house sat on a lump of high ground with river on three sides. Huge cedar trees leaned out over the water, in danger of falling in. As usual Service and Nantz were running late because of her. It didn't help their punctuality that the governor's personal security team had frisked them and put them through a metal detector before allowing them to walk up the muddy two-track driveway to the house. Along the way Service saw several black-clad state police officers positioned in the cedars along the river's edge—the governor's security detail.

Vince met them at the door with two glasses of Amarone.

The governor and her husband, Whit, were in the den, which had a picture window overlooking the dark river. Nantz and Lorelei Timms embraced as Service shook hands with Whit.

Service said, "So much security. Only three months as governor and she's already got people so yanked they want to whack her?" Service joked to the governor's husband.

"Looks like somebody already tried to get you," the governor shot back. "Where's Walter?"

"En route," Maridly said. "Allegedly."

"Late," Service said. "Karylanne is almost as bad as Mar. Have you figured out how to balance the state checkbook yet?"

Timms smiled. "If I eliminated everything in the state except health care, we still couldn't make up the deficit."

Service held up his glass. "Sam Bozian."

Governor Timms laughed. "He didn't do it all by himself, Grady."

Service was surprised when Odd Hegstrom walked into the room, leaning on a cane. He had to be in his mid-eighties now, and except for a limp, he had not changed much since the last time Service had seen him.

292 · JOSEPH HEYWOOD

Rose brought Hegstrom a small glass of tomato juice and introduced him to Maridly. When she turned to Service, Hegstrom said, "Grady and I know each other." The distinguished-looking attorney looked over at him and added, "I hear you're still in the heart of the fray."

"I'm going to name Odd to take the remainder of Jeremy Vigo's term," Timms said. Vigo was a longtime member of the Natural Resources Commission, a hay farmer from Chippewa County. Commission members were appointed by the governor and as a group steered policy and other matters for the Department of Natural Resources. Vigo, who had died just before Christmas, had been a well-known champion of tribal causes, a position which often made him unpopular around the state.

Hegstrom seemed to guess what Service was thinking. "Contrary to popular belief," he said, "my firm has never had the tribes as clients for their casino interests. My involvement was strictly personal and pro bono to help with the feds and the treaty issues. I told Lori I'd take Jeremy's term to represent all constituencies, not a narrow few. We both know how legends grow once they start," Hegstrom concluded.

Legends. Service cringed at the word.

Hegstrom plucked a folded fifty-dollar bill out of his sport coat pocket and held it out with an unwavering hand. "Pete Peletier bet me in 1976 he would never be cited by the DNR. This morning he called me and told me about the tickets. He said his fifty was in the mail, so I thought you should have this now." Service did not reach for the money. "Pete can be obstinate, but he's also a man of his word, and I see, so too are you. Please take it."

"I don't want the jerk's money," Service said.

"It's not his, it's mine," Hegstrom said.

"Wiggle words," Service said.

Hegstrom bowed slightly. "Some professional habits are ingrained."

"It was your bet, Counselor, not mine. Besides, isn't there a statute of limitations on bets?"

Hegstrom smiled. "We're both gamblers, Detective, and I never thanked you for what you did for Anise Aucoin," he said, adding, "I was at Cecilia's memorial. That took courage on your part. It was audacious to put Pete on the spot like that. After that, mistrust spread like a virus, and a lot of the residents down there admired your being there — knowing it was a tremendous risk to you. I think things started to open up for your folks after that."

Service had never seen it that way, and changed the subject. "You knew Anise Aucoin was innocent and you knew Lapalme was involved. You asked me some questions that day in the interview room."

"Cecilia said you were aggressive and a man of integrity. I simply planted seeds and you took it from there."

"When it finally sank in," Service corrected him.

"Never discount luck in any undertaking," Hegstrom said, and when Service continued to ignore the money, he slid it back in his pocket and smiled. When Service sat down at the table, there was a dented metal thermos in front of him, crudely stenciled with the word SHUCK. Hegstrom looked at it deadpan, but Service knew it had been Hegstrom who had repatriated the thermos, probably from one of his Garden clients—perhaps even Peletier.

Vince had grilled a pork roast on a bed of apples and onions. The perfume rolling off the plate left Service salivating and wondering. The loose teeth had rattled in his mouth all day, and he wondered if he dared bite into it. The pork would be soft enough, probably, but the baked potatoes would have to be skinned. This tooth thing was a pain in the ass.

He was trying to decide what to do about the food when Walter and Karylanne rolled in. Vince said, "We were just sitting down, so sit. It's gettin' cold, eh?"

Walter was seventeen now but looked older. His time at Tech had already matured him, and Service approved of what he saw. Karylanne and Maridly both talked so fast their words thickened into verbal pudding.

"Hey, Pop," Walter said, eyeing his father's untouched food. "If you're not going to eat that, I can help you out."

Service pushed back from the table, folded his napkin by his plate, and glared at his son. "Touch it and you will become permanently left-handed."

He went to the bathroom, pulled some tissue paper out of a box, opened his mouth, and yanked the teeth one at a time. Both made a grinding, ripping sound, but came out. He rinsed his mouth with water until there was no more blood. He wrapped the teeth in tissue, stuffed them in his pocket, returned to the table, and attacked his dinner.

When he looked up he found everyone staring at him. "*What?*" he said.

Odd Hegstrom tapped his glass with his spoon and said, "Every legend deserves a monument."

Vince Vilardo hit a light switch and a grove of paper birches between the house and river flooded with light. Service stared at dozens of shiny yellow things dangling from the branches.

"Are those *floaties?*" Karylanne asked, giggling.

Service tried to act annoyed but ended up laughing as hard as the rest of them, and leaned over to Nantz and whispered, "McCants dies."

Maridly Nantz squeezed his arm and rested her head against his shoulder.

Grady Service felt content as he half-listened to table banter, but his mouth hurt and he still ached from his encounter in the culvert. The reality was that his body was failing him, no matter how hard he worked to stay in shape. How long could he keep doing this? He worried about Nantz and his son, but these were regular worries. Something deeper inside him was gnawing, a sense of dread growing, that despite all he had seen and gone through over the years, something even worse lay ahead.

AUTHOR'S NOTE

This book is not intended to be a history, but as a work of fiction I hope it captures the rancor, frustration, and nastiness inherent in the events of what I have chosen to call the Garden War, which began in the late 1960s and stretched on into the 1980s.

As wars go, it was relatively bloodless, and no one died. But the violence, tensions, and conflict were real and intense, and if the reputation of the Garden Peninsula and its residents continues to be one of lawlessness, it is the fault of a few, who willfully and repeatedly break laws. In talking to people it is clear that what went on was a form of domestic insurgency, and it was waged against conservation and other police officers who did not make the rules but were merely trying to enforce them.

To step out of the shadows of bullies and thugs takes a special kind of courage, but some courageous citizens of the Garden eventually did so.

In some ways I can understand the anger and frustrations of legitimate commercial fishermen who were threatened by politics and science, neither force in their favor, and both aimed at putting them out of business.

But I hold no sympathy for the rats.

The poaching of spawning fish continues in Big Bay de Noc and surrounding waters, and the illicit sale of illegally taken fish floods markets each spring and drives down prices set by legitimate businesspeople. Fish stolen from the citizens of Wisconsin and Michigan still find their way to Chicago and New York City fish markets.

Poaching is theft, driven by greed, and reveals a dark side of the human character. No race has exclusivity in this dirty business, and until it ends, game wardens and conservation officers will be out there to stop it—in conditions that defy description—with the support and understanding of their leadership in Lansing, and sometimes, when necessary, without it.

Conservation officers, unlike poachers, are rarely motivated by money. They work because they believe in and love what they do. Officers do not always agree with the rules and regulations they are asked to enforce, but enforce them they do.

I owe debts of gratitude to veterans of the Garden War who so selflessly and patiently gave of their time, sharing stories, memories, impressions, and yellowing clippings. Most of all, I thank the erudite late chief,

Rick Asher, whose untimely death in 2003 touched us all. Others who tried their best to educate me include: Lieutenant John Wormwood (retired), Sergeant Ralph Bennett (retired), Officer Dave Vant Hof (retired), Lieutenant Tom Courchaine, Sergeant Darryl Shann, and officers Grant Emery (who introduced me to running dark, and took me on my first Garden patrol on an eighteen-degree "spring" night), and Steve Burton (who taught me the ins and outs of Wilsey Bay Creek).

I would also like to thank the DNR's media spokesperson, Brad Wurfel, who was helpful in countless ways (and whom I had the great pleasure of watching hook more than fifty king salmon with a fly rod in just one October day on the Muskegon River).

Others who have helped me gain a better understanding of the life and challenges of Michigan's Woods Cops include: Sergeant Tim Robson, Sergeant Mike Webster (retired), and officers Bobbi Bashore, John Huspen, Phil Wolbrink (retired), John Wenzel, Paul Higashi, Dave Painter, Ryan Aho, and Sergeant Gene Coulson (retired).

Any errors in the story are mine alone, a reflection of my failures as a student, not those of my teachers.

I sometimes worry that my stories of criminals and scofflaws in the Upper Peninsula will leave readers with the impression that the people who live in that harsh environment are all lawless and antisocial. They aren't. The majority of Yoopers are independent of spirit, passionate with opinions, adventurous, tough, loyal, and caring, and I am privileged to have so many as friends and fishing partners.

The mother of an old friend—a lifelong Yooper from St. Ignace— has taken exception to my calling the U.P. a wilderness. I told her I would happily refer to it differently if she would provide an alternate description. So far she hasn't produced, so I continue to say it is a wilderness that's easy to love, and I am glad we have it.

If nothing else, I hope these stories make people interested enough to take a look at the Upper Peninsula of Michigan and appreciate how lucky we are that its geography and people are a part of our state and culture.

I also thank my kids for putting up with my continual meanderings, and my agent Betsy Nolan and editor Lilly Golden for making me better than I am.

Joseph Heywood
Portage, Michigan
November 9, 2004